FREE MARKETS, FINANCE, ETHICS, and LAW

Larry Alan Bear
New York University

Rita Maldonado-Bear
New York University

Prentice Hall, Upper Saddle River, New Jersey 07458

Library of Congress Cataloging-in-Publication Data

Bear, Larry Alan
   Free markets, finance, ethics, and law / **Larry Alan Bear** and
Rita Maldonado-Bear.
   p.   cm.
   Includes bibliographical references and index.
   ISBN 0-13-457896-1
   1. Free enterprise—Moral and ethical aspects.   2. Economics—
Moral and ethical aspects.   3. Finance—Law and legislation.
I. Maldonado-Bear, Rita M.   II. Title.
HB95.M34   1994
174' .4—dc20   93-18901

Acquisitions Editor: *Leah Jewell*
Editorial/production supervision and interior design: *Edie Riker*
Cover design: *Violet Lake Design*
Prepress buyer: *Trudi Pisciotti*
Manufacturing buyer: *Patrice Fraccio*
Editorial assistant: *Eileen Deguzman*

Printed in the United States of America

10 9 8 7 6 5 4 3

ISBN   0-13-457896-1

Prentice-Hall International (UK) Limited,London
Prentice-Hall of Australia Pty. Limited, Sydney
Prentice-Hall Canada Inc., Toronto
Prentice-Hall Hispanoamericana, S.A., Mexico
Prentice-Hall of India Private Limited, New Delhi
Prentice-Hall of Japan, Inc., Tokyo
Pearson Education Asia Pte. Ltd., Singapore
Editora Prentice-Hall do Brasil, Ltda., Rio de Janeiro

CONTENTS

8 REGULATING FINANCIAL MARKETS: INVESTMENT BANKING, SECURITIES MARKETS AND MONEY MANAGEMENT *313*

9 CORPORATE POWER AND SOCIAL RESPONSIBILITY AND THE ISSUE OF ANTITRUST *389*

TABLE OF CASES

Principal Cases Are Those in Bold Face

TABLE OF ADMINISTRATIVE ORDERS

PREFACE

This book is addressed primarily to graduate and undergraduate business students for whom it might be used either as the basis of a single course, or as an adjunct to any of several courses in finance and economics, generally. We believe, moreover, that much of the material it contains should prove relevant and useful to law students and to most market-engaged professionals as well.

The book was undertaken on the assumption that both *The Market* and *The Law,* as fundamental institutions in American society, are more interrelated, in more important ways, than each of the audiences named above generally realizes. It was undertaken as well on the further assumption that the salutary, or destructive, effects of their coming together are very keenly felt, indeed, by the entire body politic. Herein, we examine the *where* and *why,* the *how,* and the *specific results,* of a cooperative market/law mix (or a crippling market/law crash), in such areas as health care, the environment, product liability, bankruptcy, legal and financial agency, and in the financial market area specifically, commercial and investment banking, securities markets, and money management.

The goal of this book is to further the development of analytical skills that will assist the reader to focus clearly upon key ethical, legal, and public policy perspectives inherent in these major free-market problem areas. And it aims, as well, at encouraging the reader to contribute to the formation of creative, just, and productive solutions to these problems as he or she prepares for, and engages in, a fully satisfying professional career.

We are quick to admit that, in structure at least, this is a rather odd book. Its materials are interdisciplinary. At one particular juncture or another, and often conjointly, they emphasize economic, financial, legal, sociopolitical, philosophical, and natural science matters. We have tried to make our presentation a well-integrated, exciting, and even entertaining one. Given that some chapters contain charts and graphs, others legal cases, and others solely narrative, we have taken special pains to provide the reader with sufficient coping guides to allow the intellectual journey to be undertaken along a straight, clear path, rather than in a labyrinth.

We deal with the several market areas mentioned above, and the interdisciplinary issues therein presented, by reviewing the structure and function of the specific market or system under examination; by determining in a real-world context whether there are weaknesses or failures in, or resulting from, its operations that justify concern on the part of students, business persons, lawyers, judges, legislators, politicians, professors, the media, and the public; and by considering interdisciplinary, outside-the-market, particularly legal, responses aimed at assisting the market to promote constructively the health of the overall economy.

The presence of market weaknesses or failures and, certainly, the formulation of responses to them must give rise to the expression of personal values on the part of students of, and participants in, the process.

There is simply no way to relate to such matters as access to health care services; the effect of free market operations on the environment; tort law reform; market competition engaged in from behind the Chapter 11 shield; S & L failures; insider trading; and pension plan activity—to name but a few areas covered in this book—without relating to such concepts as "right" and "wrong" and "personal responsibility."

Therein lies the "Ethics" in the title of this work.

In this regard, we would make two points immediately. First, this book is in no way intended to develop in the reader formal philosophical skills. Second, we are fully aware that students, market managers, lawyers, judges, and legislators are not continuously involved, in their everyday labors, with complex ethical issues demanding resolution. For that reason, much of the material in this book is devoted to the examination of various market, legal and political structures, and practice, apart from moral mazes.

Having noted all that, we are nevertheless convinced that no student or practitioner can carefully and adequately discharge his or her duties satisfactorily, that is, promote personal growth and the healthy growth of the institution within which he serves, and the society within which she lives, without *perceiving* ethical issues, *weighing* competing or conflicting claims, and *resolving* often difficult ethics-related dilemmas.

We begin, in Chapter 1, with an examination of the argument that the entire area of ethics, in or outside of business (and law), is just so much blah, blah, blah—which is to say the argument that all ethical issues and answers are, in the end, unscientific, unprovable, and an overall waste of time. But before proceeding to that chapter and, further on, to our examination of some market imperfections, let us make our central bias clear.

We take our free-market, democratic capitalism as a given. We regard it as inherently moral and potentially the most productive economic system ever devised to further the general social welfare. However, given its enormous power to bring about change, we are convinced that ethical behavior is essential to its effective functioning. In fact, we would argue that, lacking ethical behavior, the free enterprise system could come apart. Therefore, this book very often raises this question: What ethical conflicts in the system must be recognized and analyzed, and which ethical questions raised and moral choices made by market participants in order to fulfill democratic capitalism's long- term socioeconomic potential?

Further, we do not hesitate to take clear positions from time to time. The alternative is to lead the reader, directly or indirectly, to the assumption that the personal adoption of any specific ethical position is unjustifiable as long as any competing or conflicting position exists and some person somewhere is available to advance it. That assumption is a debilitating intellectual virus that ought not to be further spread abroad.

However, we are fully aware that men and women of outstanding character can differ responsibly on complex issues. Our major concern with regard to making ethical judgments is certainly not that we should persuade our reader to think as we do—only that we should persuade our reader to think.

We wish to acknowledge the following reviewers: Joel L. Fleishman, Duke University; Lawrence S. Ritter, New York University; and Charles E.M. Johnson, Financial Management Counsel.

Finally, we wish to express our debt to our late colleague, Professor Robert Lindsay. Bob Lindsay pioneered the Legal and Social Context of Business Tier at the Stern School of Business of New York University. As such, he initiated construction of the firm foundation upon which our work has been built. We shall forever be grateful to him.

1

A Framework
for Ethical
Decision Making

I. ETHICS INDEED! WHY BOTHER?[1]

The first thing we want to do is define some basic terms. Borrowing from the most entertaining and lucid exposition we know concerning the history of Western humankind and ethics,[2] we offer the following:

We shall use the word "ethics," or "ethical principles," to refer to statements that humans make about what their conduct (actions), or the conduct of others, *ought to be*, which is to say, expressions of opinion as to how persons *ought to* behave.

Assuming *conduct* to refer to what we do, and *ethics* to refer to an appraisal of the value of our actions (what we ought to do), then the word "moral" refers to the entire human situation involved in the existence of both conduct (the *is*) and ethics (the *ought*); that is, *morality* refers to the relation between conduct and ethics.

---

[1] We bothered to read a good deal of material in the course of putting this chapter together. Because so many major sources were utilized in the preparation of Chapter 1, we placed the list of references at the *end* of the chapter. However, we have otherwise chosen, in terms of the reference structure of this entire book, to place sources on the same page where the citation is made. We find it easier, where an inclination to read the footnote exists, to go to it on the page immediately, rather than to have to search somewhere else to find it. On the other hand, footnotes can be disregarded with equal ease wherever authors place them. Later references in this chapter can be traced back to this list of references at the end of the chapter. Any other singular reference will be cited in full on the page that the footnote appears.

[2] See *Brinton*, pp. 4-9, 16. We shall refer to the Paragon House paperback edition of 1990 regarding pagination, since the acclaimed original edition we cite in footnotes could be difficult to obtain.

Please note that we do not argue that these definitions are written in stone. They are simply written in our book and are meant to define what *we* are talking about, here and now.

It follows, for us, the *good*, as an evaluation of human conduct, or as an ethical standard, can be taken to mean morally desirable; the *bad* to mean morally undesirable.

Now for the really hard part. Assuming that experts in philosophy[3] would accept, *arguendo*, our simplistic definitions, those same experts (along with everyone else) could now challenge us with the following issues:

1. "Ought" has no real meaning, so neither does ethical discussion. To be morally responsible for relating *ought* to *conduct*, a person must be able to exercise free will; that is, to be able to choose to do otherwise than he or she actually did. This is impossible because God created the world and all within it in minute detail, and God is in absolute control. We *must do* as God wills. All is determined. *Che sarà sarà*, whatever will be will be.

2. Even if we reject some absolute form of determinism, the real problem remains: There is no such thing as objective morality. There is only opinion. Ethical constructs are never true or false. Therefore ethics have no place in real-world discussions, as, for example, in matters of corporate profit and loss.

3. Even if ethical issues may once have been thought relevant to the existing world, our present world reality precludes their usefulness. In a *Relativity, Quantum Theory*, world, humanity is finally in possession of true conceptual clarity as a result of progressive modern science. There is no need to diddle around with pseudo-problems in moral philosophy.

4. No matter how one deals with items 1, 2, and 3 above, the bottom line is this: *How* people ought to conduct themselves in the best of all possible worlds is one thing; *why* they should actually conduct themselves in accordance with consequent ethical standards is quite another. In the real world of the fiercely competitive marketplace, and in the face of competing real-world obligations, analysis grounded in some sort of moral philosophy is certainly not very useful (efficient).

---

[3] We subscribe enthusiastically to the great physicist Niels Bohr's definition of an "expert," as quoted by his friend Werner Heisenberg: "Most people will tell you that an expert is someone who knows a great deal about his subject. To this I would object that no one can ever know very much about any subject. . . . An expert is someone who knows some of the worst mistakes that can be made in his subject, and how to avoid them."

In dealing now with items 1-3, we hope to arrive at a reasonably productive point of departure for our voyage into the world of workable ethical frameworks (item 4). Join us on this initial trip. We promise to try to keep it reality based.

A. Free Will and Determinism

Are judgments about human conduct (about ought to's) precluded by some determinist theory? That is, by some theory that maintains human beings cannot be morally responsible for their acts, for they cannot actually act otherwise than they do?

St. Augustine believed that human freedom was lost with the advent of Original Sin and could only be recovered by grace. But he also believed that free will belonged to humans by nature and could never be lost. Free will without freedom is a difficult concept to grasp. Theological concerns on this issue dominated discussion for a very long time, occupying such admirable thinkers as St. Thomas Aquinas and Duns Scotus.

Unfortunately, something far less than a thorough discussion of free will will have to suffice here, but we would begin our cursory examination with the British philosopher Thomas Hobbes. He concluded that free will and determinism could, in fact, co-exist because "free will" did not imply freedom of "the will" from causal determination, but rather, the freedom of the human being from compulsion.[4]

John Stuart Mill, despite his adoption of the determinist position,[5] believed in legal punishment for persons committing unlawful acts because punishment (like medicine forced upon the sick) was to the miscreant's benefit, acting upon his consciousness (to deter), and because punishment of criminals secures the just rights of others. And Philippa Foot, writing in *The Philosophical Review*, in 1957, went so far as to state that

> the idea that free will can be reconciled with the strictest determinism is now very widely accepted. To say that a man acted freely is. . . to say that he was not constrained, or that he could have done otherwise if he had chosen. . . and since these things could be true even if his action was determined it seems that there could be room for free will even within a universe completely subject to causal laws. Hume put forward a view of this kind in contrasting the "liberty of spontaneity. . . which is opposed to violence". . . with the

---

[4] Debate between Hobbes and Bishop Bramhall in "The Questions Concerning Liberty, Necessity and Chance," in Morganbesser and Walsh, *Free Will*, p. 41.

[5] J.S. Mill, *An Examination of Sir William Hamilton's Philosophy*, reprinted in Morganbesser and Walsh, p. 57.

> non-existent "liberty of indifference. . . which means negation of necessity and causes."[6]

The law assumes the existence of free will in humans, and requires its exercise as a precondition to punishment. A criminal defendant is required to possess *mens rea*, or criminal intent, in order to be legally sanctioned (punished). He or she must be able to understand the nature and meaning of the act complained of, and be able to conform to the requirements of law.

> What is crucial is that those whom we punish should have, when they acted, the normal capacities, physical and mental, for doing what the law requires and abstaining from what it forbids, and a fair opportunity to exercise those capacities.[7]

We will return later to broader law/morality issues, and we encourage the reader to pursue more thoroughly, on his or her own, an examination of the conditions for moral responsibility. However, we offer now, the following concluding comment (ours):

> When we discuss ethics, morality, and the goodness or badness of a human action, whether it be the sale of 10 kilos of heroin to a dealer in a darkened warehouse or the sale of millions of dollars of junk bonds to an already ailing S&L in a lighted office, this can be forcefully argued: That there is general agreement in society that moral judgments about such behavior are not precluded by any acceptable determinist theory.

B. Goodness and Badness (Right and Wrong) as Subjective, and Impossible to Correlate with Any Objective Moral Principles

Philosophy has been wrestling for thousands of years with questions concerning ethics and the possibility or impossibility of an objective morality.

Some 5,000 years ago, ethics "textbooks," in the form of precepts and directed to males of the Egyptian ruling class, were actually available. While much of the advice was practical—"to get along, go along"—broadly based ideals of conduct were also recommended; for example, rulers should treat their subjects justly and judge impartially between them. Still, there

---

[6] In Morganbesser and Walsh, p. 71.

[7] H.L.A. Hart's "Negligence, Mens Rea and Criminal Responsibility," in Morganbesser and Walsh, p. 161.

was no attempt to define any underlying principles of conduct that could make up a broadly acceptable, systematic understanding of ethics.[8]

The Indian Vedas (Knowledge), going as far back as 1500 B.C., cover ten books and more than 1,000 hymns. They are preoccupied, as Hinduism has always been, with religious fervor whose purpose is to assist humans in achieving union with God. The ultimate reality is the principle of *Ritam*, from which our Western notion of "right" is derived. The Vedas link truth and right—a belief in a right moral order built into the universe. These ancient Vedas may actually be (in terms of their addressing the issue of how people *ought* to live) the first philosophical ethics. In detailed application, the Vedas

> were based on four ideals, or proper goals, of life: prosperity, the satisfaction of desires, moral duty, and spiritual perfection—i.e., liberation from a finite existence. From these ends follow certain virtues: honesty, rectitude, charity, non-violence, modesty and purity of heart. To be condemned, on the other hand, are falsehood, egoism, cruelty, adultery, theft, and injury to living things. . .[9].

Of course, in the centuries following, Vedic principles underwent change. *The* (Indian) *Upanishads* (800-400 B.C.) accepted the caste system as part of the proper universal order, and Jainism adopted the nonviolence principle as the basis for all morality (e.g., to lie to another person is to injure that other person—to do violence to him or her).

The point here is not that Vedic philosophical ethics are universal. They were challenged by Buddhism (which began in India in the mid-sixth century, though it took root in China), and they are of less import than the Chinese philosophies of Lao-tse (604-531 B.C.) and Confucius (550-479 B.C.). But Confucius in particular aimed at the focal issue of morality—how one *should* live (*ought* to live) in order to become a humane, thoughtful person, motivated by the desire to do good (a superior person). The Confucian system of moral and social order, based on history,

> is contained in the one word *li*, which has such a broad meaning that it is untranslatable. In the narrowest sense, it means "rituals," "propriety" and just good manners; in an historical sense it means the rationalized system of feudal order; in a philosophic sense it means an ideal social order with "everything in its place"; and in a personal sense it means faith. . . a valid, unified body of beliefs implicitly accepted, concerning God and nature and one's

---

[8] Peter Singer, p. 495.

[9] Ibid, p. 495. See also, Yutang, ed., "Hymns from the Rigveda," pp. 11-30.

place in the universe. . . . Among the Chinese scholars, Confucianism is known as the "religion of *li*," the nearest translation of which would be "religion of moral order."[10]

None of the above proves anything about the truth and eternal validity of a unified body of ethical beliefs. It does, however, show that concerns in the East about systems of moral, as well as social order, have been made manifest for at least 3,500 years, and quite clearly says something important about humankind's need for, and acceptance of, internalizable moral principles.

That same need is also apparent in Western religious and philosophical history. It is clearly present in Socrates (470-399 B.C.) who believed that the unexamined life was not worth living, but that one's right to teach others a method of inquiry that would threaten conventional beliefs was worth dying for. Socrates argued that virtue could be known and that the good person is one who knows of what virtue consists, who is capable of knowing what is good, and of doing it.

Plato (427-347 B.C.), through whose dialogues we know of Socrates's views and methods, took on the fifth-century Sophists such as Protagoras and Thrasymachus, who believed that good and evil were related solely to time, place, and culture (i.e., they were "ethical relativists").[11] Plato argued that right and wrong *have* an objective basis.[12] Indeed,

> there is a true right and wrong, which is a universal principle for all times. We do not make values or truth; we find them; they do not alter with races, places or fortune. Thus there are two worlds; the world of absolute beauty, and the world of opinion, with its conventions and delusions. This is the root of the dualism in Plato's philosophy. . . .[13]

Some philosophers subscribe to the idea that all Western philosophy consists of footnotes to Plato. Certainly Plato challenges us, as his master Socrates did, to realize that *understanding* is progressive, is a constant search to uncover truth and beauty that is comprehensible but is not necessarily comprehended; is complex and persuades us to doubt; and encourages in us a perpetual desire to search out, and to discover. Under-

---

[10] Yutang, ed., pp. 811-12

[11] See D.H. Monroe, "Relativism in Ethics," in *Dictionary of the History of Ideas*, Vol. 4. (New York: Scribner's, 1973), pp. 70-74.

[12] Plato, *The Republic*, (in Benjamin Jowett, ed. *The Dialogues of Plato*, Vol. 1 (New York: Random House, 1937).

[13] Ibid., p. IX (the Raphael Demos introduction).

standing is, hopefully, what humankind is all about, whether engaged in ethical debate, or in perfecting real-time technological processes for world financial transactions, or in sending spaceships to the moon.

Neither Socrates nor Plato, nor Aristotle, the Stoics, Machiavelli, Hobbes, Hume, Bentham the Utilitarian nor Adam Smith (and we shall return to the latter two) "proved" the ultimate truth of any unified and comprehensible ethical system applicable to every area of life. Nor did the Stoics or succeeding ethical relativists ever "prove" that if moral beliefs seem to differ in different cultures, morality is therefore not objective.

Ethical relativists must be very careful about defining *fundamental* moral beliefs. Take the business of eating one's fellow humans, for example. Assuming for the sake of argument that full fledged cannibalistic societies have existed,[14] and that the overwhelming majority of societies find the practice immoral, does that demonstrate a real difference in fundamental human beliefs? Surely it is conceivable that cannibals who eat the dead bodies of strangers and/or enemies could be disgusted and outraged at the idea of burning the dead bodies of one's parents, mates, or siblings into ashes, and then imprisoning those ashes in a small container forever, whether above or below the ground. A pertinent question might be: Do *all* cultures maintain a whole series of oughts (and ought nots) concerning the proper disposition of dead bodies in their society?

The argument that cannibals kill men, women, and children in order to eat them, while we cremate loved ones only after they are legitimately dead, doesn't seem to us to be relevant to the issue. Those same cannibals could be shocked and dismayed by a culture that kills men, women, and children of another culture in order to seize their lands and treasure, even though the people within the culture doing the killing may eat butchered animal flesh only once or twice a week, and human flesh not at all.

Again, the issue is not so much the specific societal response to murder, as much as whether careful sets of ethical norms regarding murder within and without the tribe are developed, and some corresponding moral order enforced, in *every* single society; which is to say, whether in all societies there are not fundamental questions of "good" and "bad" arising out of matters of universal human concern.

None of which is to suggest that if we found ourselves somehow in cannibal land we should set aside our own "oughts" and partake of a missionary stew. On the other hand, if we were confronted by the aggressive command "Eat or be eaten" we would surely have to face up to the

---

[14] Not everyone believes they did. See W. Arens, The Man-Eating Myth (New York: Oxford University Press, 1979).

issue of balancing competing ethical interests. This is a matter we will pursue further on in connection with establishing ethical frameworks.

One cannot discuss the issue of objectivity and subjectivity in ethics without taking some note of Immanuel Kant (1724-1804). A worldly philosopher who spent 71 of his 80 years in one single German city (Konigsberg) Kant wrote three famous critiques: *Critique of Pure Reason* (1781, 1787), *Critique of Practical Reason* (1788), and *Critique of Judgment* (1790). Another of his extraordinary works was his *Fundamental Principles of the Metaphysics of Morals* (1785).

In terms of his work in the area of ethics, the crux of Kant's argument is that there *is* a common moral consciousness, and doing one's duty is at the heart of it: that in *every* society, moral worth consists of doing one's duty for its own sake, not necessarily for personal enrichment. Kant spends some time defining "duty" and we cannot; however, his moral consciousness and duty can be related to what he terms "a supreme practical principle." This principle

> turns the concept of what is necessarily an end *in itself* into an *objective* principle of the will which can serve as a general practical law. The basis of this principle is that *rational nature exists as an end in itself.* Man necessarily conceives his own existence as being this rational nature, to the extent that it is a *subjective* principle of human actions. But every other rational being regards its existence similarly. . . so at the same time it is an objective principle from which, as a supreme practical ground, all laws of the will must need be deductible. Accordingly, the practical imperative will be as follows: *Act so as to treat man, in your own person as well as in that of anyone else, always as an end, never merely as a means. . .* whoever transgresses the rights of man intends to use the person of others merely as a means. . . (and this is a conflict with the principle of duty. . . . [15]

Note that Kant has proceeded from his supreme practical principle to a "practical" imperative. This brings us to the famous Kantian supreme, formal principle of ethics, his one "categorical" imperative:

> Act only on a maxim by which you can will that it, at the same time, should become a universal law.[16]

---

[15] Italics are Kant's. From *Fundamental Principles of the Metaphysics of Morals, sect. 2;* reprinted in Beardsley, ed., pp. 474-75.

[16] Ibid., p. 473. The Frederick translation of Kant, in Beardsley, uses the words "general law." Other translators, e.g., Hastie, use the words "universal law."

So one should not will oneself (act) to discharge toxic waste into public waters, since if it were a universal law (that all people should will the same) all public waters would soon be polluted. Nor should one be a liar in one's business dealings, since if all were to be so, trust would disappear and doing business would be impossible. This Kantian ethical principle is, of course, a sort of philosophical Golden Rule ("Do unto others,"etc., "Love thy neighbor as thyself," etc.). Sigmund Freud took a dim view of these imperatives. He wrote that

> in commanding. . . with such severity. . . [they] trouble too little about the happiness of the ego, and. . . fail to take into account sufficiently the difficulties in the way of obedience. . . . The fact remains that anyone who follows such preaching in the present state of civilization only puts himself at a disadvantage beside all those who set it at naught.[17]

Freud's criticism proceeds, in large measure, from his desire to portray psychoanalysis as a natural science (like mathematics) that can do the work of moral philosophy as well. Philosophy, he argues, is *not* a "science" and thus does not deal with reality. We shall discuss the relation of ethics and the natural sciences in short order, and we disagree here with Dr. Freud.

However, one more reference is in order to the view that all ethical viewpoints are partial, inadequate, and false. We have all heard the clever rejoinder "Oh yes? And how do you really *know* that?" made to anyone who argues for a particular ethical principle, or who dares to call any painted canvas hanging on some wall, somewhere, "bad." It is almost as though there could be only one basis for any tenable moral or critical position, and you can't "prove" that yours is the one. No one could, since one cannot get beyond subjectivity and prove that his or her particular position contains *the* singular truth.

Of course, one problem with this skeptical position is that one must insist that *it* is the truth, a clearly indefensible argument. The ultimate result here is that there is *no* truth, and no objective good or bad, so we are therefore all free to do as we wish in this best of all possible and irresponsible worlds. A Cambridge philosopher recently wrote:

> The skeptic is right to insist, like the non-skeptic, that in critical and moral views, the whole of everything is never told. But critical

---

[17] Sigmund Freud. *Civilization and Its Discontents* (Riviere trans.; in Vol. 54, *Great Books of the Western World*, 2d ed., 1990) pp. 800-801.

or moral objectiveness is not a claim to know everything; it is merely a claim about the logical status of such questions. Of course the best view of the Taj Mahal, if there is one, is still only one view among many; of course the best view of *Hamlet* still leaves things out.[18]

As does, we might mention, the best view of the rightness or wrongness of hospitals that pay a bounty to physicians for each patient placed in their beds as a form of progressive health care marketing.

Summarizing the last several pages,[19] we would emphasize here that we have not attempted to prove that there are in existence universally valid, objective moral principles that demand ethical debate. We have attempted to prove that for at least 3,500 years, all civilizations, cultures, and societies have felt, collectively, that moral codes, the fitting together of "oughts" and conduct, have been essential to the life and to the progress of their bodies politic.

Many overarching ethical issues have been woven into the fabric of *all* societies over a multitude of generations: religious worship and the relationship between God and humans; governmental structures and the relationship between humans and the state; and economic systems and the relationships between personal and public growth and enrichment. And these are not an exhaustive list of the "proofs" that the need for ethical constructs and moral debate has been, and still is, universal.

In our time, in fact, the need is greater than it has ever been. More than any generation before us in recorded history, we are inundated with data, with information, but data and information alone are not *knowledge*. Ethical principles debated in the context of our technology-focused, data-filled world are crucial to our healthy growth as human beings—indeed, to our very survival. This is because ethical debate produces

the kind of knowledge which gives unity and system to the body of the sciences. . . the kind of [knowledge] which results from a critical ·examination of the grounds of our convictions, prejudices and beliefs.[20]

---

[18] G. Watson, "The Fuss about Ideology," *The Wilson Quarterly*, (Winter 1992).

[19] We have not discussed ethics and law here because we prefer to do so in the material to follow relating to this issue.

[20] Bertrand Russell, *The Problems of Philosophy*, in Vol. 55, *Great Books of the Western World*, (2d ed. 1990), p. 291.

We are fast approaching a time when almost anything, including complex genetic cloning, may be technologically available. But we are far, far behind in our progress toward establishing basic, critical knowledge in the area of why (or which) tasks should be undertaken by a society in the first place. The awesome gulf between the "conduct" and the "ought" needs a host of solid, traversable moral bridges—in all areas of human endeavor including, for one example, worldwide financial intermediation.

And such knowledge, such ethical debate, is not rendered any less important or invalidated by any defensible argument that it is useless or irrelevant due to a lack of irrefutable proof of objectivity or universality.

Yet might it not be asked that important as such knowledge might be, how can one obtain it from a discipline that provides few, if any, *definitive* answers? Doesn't "science" always provide them? And is not scientific data "truth," and the only "truth" we may dare actually to act upon?

Let us now examine the claim that advanced science and technology are the only reliable paths to truth, progress, and prosperity in our time. Could not a good Objectivitist (or Positivist) argue that Buddha, Confucius, Moses, Jesus, Mohammed, Aristotle, Plato, Kant, and the entire venerable theological/philosophical tribe were actually ignorant, after all, of the world of quantum theory, and of the reality of elementary particles?

C. Science as Truth, and Moral Philosophy as an Inefficient Pastime

A philosopher once asked:

> What is the use of philosophy. . . if, unlike science, it cannot be applied to the mastery of physical nature and the production of utilities, whether bridges or bombs? What, finally, at the end of its long history, does philosophy come to if, in such marked contrast to the continuously accelerated progress of the sciences, it cannot claim any single advance on which all philosophers are agreed, but instead must admit that most of its problems seem to be perennially debated, now as in every preceding century?[21]

Hardly anyone is surprised by the fact that philosophy (including moral philosophy and ethics) is required to grapple with uncertainty. The quotation above, then, is unsurprising. But let us consider this brief piece

---

[21] Mortimer Adler, "Philosophy" (Introduction), in Vol. 2, *Great Books of the Western World*, 2nd ed., 1990, p. 274.

from a brilliant American physicist, a winner of a Nobel Prize for his work in quantum electrodynamics.[22]

> There was a time when the newspapers said that only twelve men understood the theory of relativity. I do not believe there ever was such a time. There might have been a time when only one man did, because he was the only guy who caught on before he wrote his paper. But after people read the paper a lot of people understood the theory of relativity... certainly more than twelve. On the other hand I think I can safely say that nobody understands quantum mechanics.[23]

The thinking reader will, of course, quickly point out that "not understanding" quantum mechanics is not the same thing as "not understanding" moral philosophy. Quantum theory, after all, has produced a mathematics capable of accounting not only for atomic phenonema, but even for subatomic elementary particles that make up the atomic nucleus. The elementary particles to which we refer are that much smaller in comparison to the tiny atom, than the atom is to us. A physics and mathematics able to predict the behavior of matter at that level of existence is true physical science. Indeed, it is quantum theory and resultant mathematics upon which almost all of the developed world's current "high" technology is based, ranging from nuclear power plants to the wonders of electronics.

And yet, quantum theory and *quantum mechanics*[24] are truly *not* understandable, at least in terms of classical physics. Albert Einstein, who understood almost everything, disagreed with the theory and felt it to be defective in several ways. Robert Feynman, quoted above, was not joking when he said, in effect, that no one understands fully the nature of all this subatomic matter. How could one? Elementary particles are, themselves, merely a form of transitory truth. Just as the world was once flat, the atom was, for ever so long, *the* elementary particle. Then the atom's nucleus and electrons were the sum total of elementary particles—the ultimate constituents of matter. And now there are smaller (elementary) groupings of muons, mesons, and leptons, etc., that comprise the atomic nucleus. The

---

[22] The theory that explains the interactions between electromagnetic radiation (photons) and certain charged elementary particles such as electrons and positrons.

[23] Richard Feynman, *The Character of Physical Law* (Cambridge, MA: MIT Press, 1965), p. 129. Feynman published these lines in the very year he won the Nobel Prize for his work in an area of quantum mechanics.

[24] Mathematical physics dealing with interactions of atomic and subatomic matter and radiation in observable quantities. The word *quantum*, by the way, derives from the concept that all forms of energy are released in bundles called "quanta."

A Framework for Ethical Decision Making   13

bottom line is clear: Today's elementary particles may be "elementary" only because, currently, we just don't know what's going on in a world that has proven to be far more magical and mysterious than anyone ever dreamed.[25]

We would examine the nature of the quantum phenomenon because we believe that the more one begins to comprehend this "scientific reality," the more one begins to comprehend the existence in it of the very same magic and mystery as exist in moral philosophy and its offspring, ethical debate.

Let's begin with a simpler concept, namely, the theory of relativity (relatively speaking, of course):

> The mysteries of relativity fade... when one firmly recognizes that clocks do not measure some preexisting thing called "time," but that our concept of time is simply a convenient way to abstract the common behavior of all those objects we call clocks. . . . [I]t is remarkably liberating to realize that time in itself does not exist except as an abstraction to free us from having always to talk about this clock or that.   The discovery that there is no time—only clocks—has deep and surprising consequences for many very simple things we tend to take for granted because of our almost instinctual conviction that time has a reality that transcends the behavior of clocks.   Once one accepts this discovery and learns to recognize the many ways in which the erroneous belief in *absolute* time infects our thinking and our language, the mysteries of *relativity* vanish.
>
> The mysteries of quantum theory are not so readily dispelled. . . .[26]

The quantum world is rendered magical and mysterious by one overriding consideration: Particles at the quantum level are physically disturbed and disrupted by the very act of determining where they are and at what speed they are actually moving.

Because we are in the electronic age, let us look at an electron (the negatively charged part of an atom that is orbiting the positively charged nucleus). Looking at an electron is not an easy thing to do. This (currently) elementary particle is 1,836 times *smaller* than a proton, which is, itself,

---

[25] A reasonable and understandable book on the subject of elementary particles and the like is Ginestra Amaldis's *The Nature of Matter* (Chicago: University of Chicago Press, 1982). Since this work appeared in the original Italian in 1961, "quantum-wise" a good while ago, one would need to catch up some after reading it. It is solid, basic material, however, as is the late Heinz Pagel's *Cosmic Code* (New York: (Simon & Schuster, 1982) in terms of a lay reader's introduction to the quantum world.

[26] H.D. Mermin, p. 4. We have learned (and borrowed) much from this wise and witty work and recommend it highly as a brief introduction to the quantum world.

of subatomic size! To locate an electron, you must bombard it with photons (minute energy packets of electromagnetic radiation).[27] But when you bombard it, you disturb it. The bottom line seems to be this: Using great care, one is able to locate the position of an electron precisely. Moreover, using great care, one is able to measure the velocity (speed) of an electron precisely. But the very act of measuring *one* of these two properties of the electron precisely makes it impossible to measure, precisely, the other property. You measure one property, you render the other uncertain.[28]

Look now at the problem if we transfer it from the microlevel of life to the macrolevel (ours).[29]

A police helicopter is perfectly able to determine that a speeding motorist's car is (1) going 75 miles per hour, (2) on Route 95, at approximately the exit 15 turnoff. If the microlevel (quantum) difficulties were the same where we live (at the macrolevel), then, if the helicopter determined that the car was going at exactly 85 miles per hour, it could not provide the car's location at all! But if it did precisely locate the car on Route 95 at the number 15 exit, the best it could probably say about the speed of the car is that it is somewhere between 55-95 miles per hour.

The atomic-world problem has another serious aspect to it that our macro world doesn't. It could be that up here we could eventually invent a device that might correlate the disparate elements. At the macrolevel, scientists agree, no improvement is possible.

Well, then, is it really possible to say that there *is* such a thing as an electron that possesses *at one and the same time* the dual properties of position *and* velocity? There are two possible answers here:

1. Yes. It exists. We just can't prove it.
2. No. If we can't prove it, it does not exist. (Here we really have a problem! Rather like Alice in Wonderland watching the Cheshire cat disappear bit by bit and thinking, "Well? I've often seen a cat without a grin, but a grin without a cat! It's the most curious thing I ever saw in all my life!")

Quantum physicists deny the actual existence of a dual-property electron because they cannot prove it exists. It has even been advanced (because its existence *cannot* be proved) that scientific observations do not *measure* location (space) or velocity (time) with regard to electrons: They

---

[27] Photons may be the carriers of the electromagnetic field. Then again, maybe they aren't.
[28] This phenomenon was encapsulated by the physicist Werner Heisenberg into the "Heisenberg Uncertainty Principle." Einstein died loathing it.
[29] The example that follows is taken from Mermin, p. 8.

produce them.[30] All of which has led the staid journal *Scientific American* to state that

> the doctrine that the world is made up of objects whose existence is independent of human consciousness turns out to be in conflict with quantum mechanics and with facts established by experiment.[31]

Does that mean that the quantum theory answer to the question, "If a tree falls in a forest and no one is there, does it make a noise when it lands?" is, properly, "What tree?"

The magazine's statement is, in fact, a bit much and puts us on a path no quantum scientist feels it even relevant to travel; however, that didn't stop Albert Einstein from inquiring of a friend: Do you really believe that the moon exists only when you look at it?[32]

Still, as long as quantum theory and its resultant mathematical abstractions provide real-world results, who cares whether something does or does not exist if we can't "prove" its properties. Why not simply accept the fact that "the world behaves in a manner that is exceedingly strange, deeply mysterious and profoundly puzzling," and let it go at that?[33]

Most physicists do, and some still object mightily to any discussion of metaphysical implications to be drawn from (objectionable) words like "mysterious and profoundly puzzling." Yet quantum theory *has* given rise to a curious paradox: It has demonstrated its marvelous capacity to produce heretofore undreamed of technical accomplishment—for example, the electronic revolution. But by the same token it has demonstrated that science is limited in scope and simply cannot comprehend the true nature of the world.

The scientific discipline is surely different from the philosophical discipline because rigorous, systematic empirical testing is a constant. Nevertheless, the result is that the most important "truths" of each discipline are tentative now, and may be so forever in terms of any demonstration of their ultimate "reality."

Perhaps so, it might be argued, but natural science, in the meantime, has produced automobiles, jet airplanes, and computers. What solid, demonstrable achievements have ever come from any moral philosophy?

---

[30] Ibid. (citing Pascal Jordan.)

[31] *Scientific American* (November 1979), p. 158.

[32] Abraham Pais, Previews of Modern Physics (October 1979), p. 907.

[33] Mermin, p. 14. Although it may be shocking to say so, even mathematics may be "strange, deeply mysterious and profoundly puzzling." It has been suggested by the English astronomer John Barrow that even though mathematics seems to "work" it is fundamentally flawed, perhaps internally contradictory: a chilling concept for every living scientist! See Barrow's book, *Pi in the Sky* (New York: Oxford University Press, 1992).

Democracy is one answer; government as the guardian of the magic value: *human freedom*. It was not any miracle of natural science that sent unarmed eastern Europeans and Chinese students into twentieth-century streets to face technologically superior tanks. It was an internalized ethical construct: I am a human being with my own dignity, and I have a right to be free.

Not that moral progress goes on unimpeded. There *was* Adolf Hitler. On the other (scientific) hand, there is also the hydrogen bomb.

How do truly outstanding modern scientists actually feel about the utility of ethical and moral concerns?

We feel strongly that there are serious lessons, in their feelings, for students and practitioners of the *economic science*, and surely for readers about to embark on a study of free markets, finance, ethics, and law.

We might begin with Albert Einstein. The scientific way of looking at things, he wrote to his good friend, the German physicist Max Born,

> always answers only the question "why?" but never the question "To What End?" No utility principle and no natural selection will make us get over that. However, if someone asks "To what purpose should we help one another, make life easier for each other, make beautiful music or have inspired thoughts?" he would have to be told: "If you don't feel it, no one can explain it to you." Without this primary feeling we are nothing and had better not live at all.[34]

Mathematician Jacob Bronowski argued that science would always need a coherent set of fundamental ethical values in order to survive, and that modern science, and art, poetry and music sprang from the same source: Renaissance humanism, which promoted the shared simple sense of pleasure in one's own gifts.[35]

It must be noted, with regard to the issue of science needing ethical values to survive, that a recent spate of cases involving falsification and plagiarism in connection with "scientific" research data has raised serious, troubling moral issues in this final decade of the twentieth century. Dr. Walter Gilbert, a Nobel Laureate in biology and a professor at Harvard, fashioned a scientific seminar focusing on standards of behavior, and the United States National Academy of Sciences, in 1992, began examining ethical standards at research institutions.[36] There ought to be that sense

---

[34] Einstein letter to Max Born of September 1, 1919, from *The Born-Einstein Letters* (New York: Walker & Co., 1971), reprinted in Timothy Ferris, ed., p. 809). The year 1919 was when Einstein's prediction of the general theory of relativity was verified. Two years later he received the Nobel Prize for physics.

[35] G. Jacob Bronowski, *Magic, Science and Civilization* (New York: Columbia University Press, 1978), and *Science and Human Values* (New York: Harper & Row, rev. ed., 1965).

of urgency when one realizes that in many key societal areas such as, for example, genetic experimentation, a society must be able to feel comfortable with the ethics of scientific practitioners.

The Danish physicist Niels Bohr, a Nobel Laureate, was a recognized, major contributor to the development of quantum physics, and a good friend, and disciple, of Einstein. They disagreed mightily on the validity of quantum theory. It is said that when Einstein's famous criticism of indeterminacy ("God does not play dice with the universe") was brought to Bohr's attention, Bohr replied, "Nor is it our business to prescribe to God how He should run the world." Bohr argued that science could not, and would never, determine *how* nature is, but could only say some things *about* nature. Therefore, science, he believed, was partial and incomplete, and that only multiple (and always individually limited) points of view, *both inside and outside of science*, could give any real idea of the richness of the world.[37]

Bohr's attitude toward moral philosophy may be seen through the eyes of his friend and colleague, Werner Heisenberg, creator of the Uncertainty Principle, and 1932 Nobel Laureate in physics for his work in formulating quantum mechanics in terms of matrices. Bohr, Heisenberg, and Wolfgang Pauli, an Austrian-born U.S. citizen who received the Nobel Prize in physics in 1945 for his earlier discovery of the Pauli Exclusion Principle[38] were actually very close, socially as well as professionally. Pauli became famous at the age of 20 (1920), when he wrote a 200-page article for an encyclopedia on the (then new) theory of relativity. The three geniuses were together in Denmark, in 1952, at a scientific meeting. As old friends who had participated over many years in the twentieth-century scientific revolution, they walked together, in Copenhagen, along the Langelinie, a beautiful harbor area that houses Hans Christian Anderson's Little Mermaid on a small rock just off the beach. Because Heisenberg recorded some of what transpired when these three giants reminisced, we are privileged to be able to hear some Nobel Laureate insights into the area of ethical philosophy.

Bohr: Some time ago, I addressed [a meeting] on the interpretations of quantum theory. After my lecture, no one raised any objections or asked any embarrassing questions, but I must say, this fact proved a terrible disappointment to

---

[36] P.J. Hilts, "A Question of Ethics," *The New York Times*, August 8, 1992.

[37] This is Bohr's "Complementarity Theory." Cf. "Causality and Complementarity" from Bohr's *Atomic Physics and Human Knowledge*, reprinted in Ferris, ed., pp. 801-807. For a remarkable picture of this extraordinary man, see Abraham Pais, *Niels Bohr's Times: In Physics, Philosophy and Polity* (New York: Oxford/Clarendon, 1991).

[38] The principle that, in an atom, no two electrons can have the same energy.

me. For those who are not shocked when they first come across quantum theory cannot possibly have understood it. Probably I spoke so badly that no one knew what I was talking about.

Pauli: The fault need not necessarily have been yours. . . [their reaction] is part and parcel of the positivist creed. . . [they] have gathered that quantum mechanics describes atomic phenonenom correctly. . . . What else we have had to add—complementarity, interference of probabilities, uncertainty relations, separation of subject and object, etcetera—strikes them as. . . mere relapses into prescientific thought, bits of idle chatter. . . . Perhaps this attitude is logically defensible, but if it is, I for one can no longer tell what we mean when we say we have understood nature.

Bohr: Positivists. . . think that many of the questions posed and discussed by conventional philosophers have no meaning at all, that they are pseudo-problems and. . . best ignored. Positivist insistence on conceptual clarity is, of course, something I fully endorse, but their prohibition of any discussion of the wider issues, simply because we lack clear-cut enough concepts in this realm, does not seem very useful to me—this same ban would prevent our understanding of quantum theory.

Heisenberg: Positivists are extraordinarily prickly about all problems having what they call a prescientific character. I remember a book by Philipp Frank on causality in which he dismisses a whole series of problems. . . on the ground that they are relics of the old metaphysics,[39] vestiges from the period of prescientific . . . thought. . . . To him, "metaphysics" is a synonym for loose thinking, and hence a term of abuse.

Bohr: This sort of restriction doesn't seem very useful to me either. You know Schiller's poem "The Sentences of Confucius," which contains these memorable lines: "The full mind is alone the clear, and truth dwells in the deeps." The full mind, in our case is. . . an abundance of concepts by means of which we can speak about our problems and about phenonema in general . . . Philipp Frank . . . gave a

---

[39] Usually defined as speculative inquiry concerning philosophical matters lying outside the range of verifiable facts.

lecture [at the meeting I spoke to you about addressing] . . .
He gave a lecture [there] in which he used the term "metaphysics" simply as a swearword or, at best, as a euphemism for unscientific thought . . . . I [pointed] out that I
could see no reason why the prefix "meta". . . was
anethma in physics. . . . [It] merely suggests we are asking further questions; i.e., questions bearing on the fundamental concepts of a particular discipline, and why ever
should we not be able to ask such questions in physics? . . . .
[W]hat matters most to me is that we do not simply talk
"the deeps in which truth dwells" out of existence. That
would mean taking a very superficial view.

Later, in Bohr's absence, Pauli asks Heisenberg whether the
latter's "criterion of truth," like Bohr's, "differs radically" from the positivists who dismiss "unscientific" thought.

Heisenberg: I should consider it utterly absurd. . . were I to close my
mind to the problems and ideas of earlier philosophers
simply because they cannot be expressed in a more precise language . . . . I have no principled objections to the
re-examination of old questions, much as I have no objec-
tion to using the language of any of the old religions. . . .
[They] speak in images and parables. . . but I believe in
the final analysis [they] try to express the same context,
the same relations, and all of these hinge around questions about values. . . . Where must we seek for the truth?
. . . Niels has quoted Schiller's "Truth dwells in the
deeps." Are there such deeps and is there any truth?
And may these deeps perhaps hold the meaning of life
and death?

Heisenberg, staring out at a ship in the harbor, falls into a personal
reverie, ending with the conclusion:

The positivists [argue] that the world must be. . . divided into that
which we can say clearly and the rest, which we had better pass
over in silence. But can anyone perceive of a more pointless
philosophy, seeing that what we can say clearly amounts to next
to nothing?

Heisenberg is then jolted out of his reverie by Pauli, who asks him:
"Do you believe in a personal God?"

Heisenberg: [I would ask that question differently. It is] can you or any-one else reach the central order of things and events, where existence seems beyond doubt, as directly as you can reach the "soul" of another human being? . . . If you put your question like that, I would say yes.

Pauli: You think you can become aware of the central order with the same intensity as of the soul of another person?

Heisenberg: Perhaps.

Pauli: Why did you use the word "soul" and not simply speak of another person?

Heisenberg: . . . Because the word "soul" refers to the central order, to the inner core of a being whose outer manifestations may. . . pass our understanding. If the magnetic force that has guided this [inner] compass—and what else was its source but the central order?—should ever become ex-tinguished, terrible things may happen to mankind, far more terrible even than concentration camps and atom bombs. . . . [I]f we may no longer speak or even think about the wider connections, we are without a compass and hence in danger of losing our way.

It is difficult to conceive of a more reflective, real-world discussion of ethical philosophy than the one that took place on the banks of the Langelinie with three of the most brilliant Nobel physicists of the twentieth century.[40]

And, one might add, done in the very shadow of their scientific inspiration, namely the ethical philosopher-physicist Albert Einstein.[41]

---

[40] We have taken these conversations, which are contained in Physics and Beyond: Encounters and Conversations (New York: Harper & Row, 1971), from the excerpt "Positivism, Metaphysics and Religion," in Ferris, ed., pp. 821-27.

[41] For an Einstein masterpiece on the limits of science (and scientists) in the area of ethical and theological issues, see Albert Einstein, *Out of My Later Years* (New York: Carol Publishing Group, 1956) esp. the material on science and religion. See also here, Ferris, ed., pp. 828-35. One trembles to think of Einstein's response to the claim of some computer specialists that artificial intelligence (AI) is just a few electronic blinks away; i.e., machines that will do anything the human mind can do. The AI argument is that minds, after all, are no more than computers made of meat, and all that's needed to establish AI the equal of Heisenberg, Bohr, Einstein, or John Smith or Mary Jones is simply to iron out complexities in the algorithmic (mechanical/computational) behavior of electronic equipment! Anyone who takes this sort of scientific "truth" as a given should read the devastating critique of this "scientific" claim by world-famous mathematician and cosmologist Roger Penrose in his book *The Emperor's New Mind: Concerning Computers, Minds and Laws of Physics* (New York: Oxford University Press, 1989).

If Bohr, Heisenberg, and Pauli were co-developers of the quantum theory, it is fair to say that they built it up on the basic work of two twentieth-century scientists: *Albert Einstein*, whose insights, paradoxically, led to the theory whose full implications he died contesting, and *Max Planck*, the brilliant theoretical physicist who actually laid down the very foundations of specific quantum theory. Planck received the Nobel Prize in physics in 1918. A German of conscience, Planck appealed to Hitler to cease his racial policies; Planck's youngest son was executed by the Nazis in 1945 for his role in an attempt to assassinate Hitler. Planck published numerous scientific papers in his lifetime. Five of them, written in his later years (1927-1947), were published as one work, in book form, in 1949, under the title *Scientific Autobiography and Other Papers*.[42] In the final paper in the book, "Religion and Natural Science," Planck examines the question of whether religious faith and its ethical content must be denied existence in the face of the reality ("truths") of natural science. Planck denies the exclusivity of the natural science he himself fathered, arguing instead that religion and natural science are compatible, each focusing upon the different nature of tasks at hand; and that, as human beings, we cannot make do with only pure rational cognition, or only philosophical/religious beliefs—that the two "mutually supplement and condition each other." Planck concludes his fifth essay by noting that:

> the proper attitude to questions in ethics can no more be gained from a purely rational cognition than can a general *Weltanschauung*[43] ever replace specific knowledge and ability. But the two roads do not diverge; they run parallel to each other, and they intersect at an endlessly removed common goal.
>
> There is no better way to comprehend this properly than to continue one's efforts to obtain a progressively more profound insight into the nature and problems of the natural sciences, on the one hand, and of religious faith on the other. It will then appear with ever increasing clarity that even though the methods are different—for science operates predominantly with the intellect, religion predominantly with sentiment—the significance of the work and the direction of progress are nonetheless absolutely identical.
>
> Religion and natural science are fighting a joint battle in an incessant, never ending crusade against skepticism, against dogmatism, against disbelief and against superstition, and the rally-

---

[42] Frank Gaynor's translation appears in Vol. 56, *Great Books* (2d ed. 1990), pp. 73-117.

[43] Worldview, or philosophy of life.

ing cry in this crusade has always been, and always will be: "On to God." [44]

We do not advocate that what we have written in this section *proves* the necessity for a personal affirmation of the existence of a Supreme Presence, or that one *must* agree with the specific views of all, or any, of these giants of twentieth-century science. What we do insist upon, however, is that anyone who would make the argument that serious consideration of ethical issues in our time is precluded by the scientific method is at a severe intellectual disadvantage.

One major question remaining to be discussed in this section is whether there is anything in the "science" of *Economics*, or in the system of *Law*, that requires us to relinquish the Einstein-Planck-Bohr-Heisenberg-Pauli belief that human life and action must be guided and interpreted, in part, by ethical-moral considerations.

1. An Ethical Exemption for the "Dismal Science"?[45]

Economists have more or less transmuted *utilitarian* philosophy into "scientific" doctrine. The utilitarian philosophers—Hutcheson, Paley, Bentham, Mill, and Sidgwick—did not focus on metaethics (on the subjectivity or objectivity of ethics), but rather on normative ethics (how people should behave). Francis Hutcheson, in the early eighteenth-century, first stated that "that action is best which procures the greatest happiness for the greatest numbers. . . ." Reverend William Paley argued that God wills the happiness of his creatures, so whatever increases happiness is right; whatever decreases it is wrong.[46]

---

[44] The italics are Max Planck's. See *Great Books, note 43, supra,* p. 117. See also, for the scientist's affirmation of the fact that there are valid, essential moral and philosophical issues beyond the reach of science, Erwin Schrodinger, *What Is Life?* (1944), in Vol. 56, *Great Books,* (2d ed.,1990), pp. 461-504, esp. pp. 503-504, and C.H. Waddington, *The Nature of Life,* ibid., pp. 690-747, esp. pp. 741-42. Nobel physicist Schrodinger laid a foundation for quantum wave mechanics and was a philosopher as well as a physicist. Waddington was a famous embryologist and geneticist with many books to his credit, including editorship of a four-volume work on theoretical biology. In *The Nature of Life* (at p. 741 as cited above) he states that "the authority which is required to make possible the socio-genetic method of transmitting information and the authority which is involved in the development of the ideas of ethical good and bad are two aspects of one and the same type of mental functioning." See also, for an interesting modern concept, A. Zee, *Fearful Symmetry* (New York: Macmillan, 1986), esp. chap. 26, "The Mind of the Creator," pp. 278-84. Professor Zee's book is subtitled *The Search for Beauty in Modern Physics.*

[45] A fine, brief review of many issues surrounding the question of whether economics is a natural or a social science is contained in D. Bell (1980), pp. 196-213.

[46] A good brief, but learned, background on utilitarian philosophy may be found in Peter Singer, pp. 504-506.

Jeremy Bentham (1748-1832) came later. He set up a very detailed English philosophical utilitarian system. Bentham argued that we must accept the postulate that human beings act under the influence of the pleasure-pain principle, and that the utilitarian principle therefore is that right equals pleasure and wrong equals pain. Thus, whatever increases the net surplus of pleasure over pain is right, and whatever decreases it is wrong. And how is "increase" (or decrease) measured? By beginning with the action contemplated and proceeding to a measurement (weighing) of all those who will have a net increase of pleasure from the act, and all those who will have net increase of pain (a decrease of pleasure) from it. In this measurement, *each person* in the universe affected by the action is to be counted equally; that is, there is to be no quantitative difference between a poor man's and a rich man's pleasure.

And how is the *quality*, rather than the quantity, of pleasure and pain to be measured? It isn't. Referring to a game in vogue in England at the time (pushpin), Bentham remarked that "the quantity of pleasure being equal, pushpin is as good as poetry." This caused a good many other Englishmen to characterize utilitarianism as "a philosophy fit for pigs."[47]

Such criticism bothered John Stuart Mill (1806-1873). A subscribing utilitarian, he argued that utility maximization was not the guiding principle of that philosophy. What was, was the adoption of a guiding principle for every action, much like Kant's categorical imperative; for example, "I choose not to lie in order to make a profit from another." Such principles are, for Mill, Utilitarian since, when followed, they produce a surplus of pleasure over pain.

It was Henry Sidgwick (1838-1900) who, having set forth a more detailed exposition of utilitarianism than had been developed by Bentham or Mill, finally admitted defeat on this ultimate issue: Even if we postulate that my personal good (happiness) is to be accorded no more weight than the good of any other, how does one deal with the reality of my ego? Which is to say, the individual ego that replies: "What do I care about postulates? I act on behalf of Number One."

The ideal way to deal with this dilemma, from the point of view of economic science, is to declare that self-interest (ego), exercised in the mass (the sum of all self-interested behavior), will provide more pleasure (good) than pain (bad). All by itself, that proposition is not science, of course. It is absurd. What has to be added is that humans are rational creatures, and the behavior economists speak of is *rational* behavior. Exercised egoistically (selfishly) in the mass, rational self-interested behavior produces the greatest good for the greatest number. Whether that rational,

---

[47] Ibid., p. 505.

self-interested behavior concept is the basis for a new "science" is, at the very least, arguable.

Of course, in more specific economic terms, where the philosophical concept of "pleasure" appears impractical, its cousin, *utility*, takes over and becomes linked with the concept of *value*. That word is full of complexities, and we need not grapple with them here. We refer you to Adam Smith if you wish to pursue the problems of defining *value* from the very beginning.[48] Suffice it to say here that, from the focus of economic theory, on the satisfaction of consumer wants, to the specifics of such constituent theories as marginal utility, decreasing marginal utility, indifference analysis (and curves), cost-benefit analysis and Pareto (economic) optimality[49]—each passing from an imprecise, inefficient, morality-based utilitarian philosophy to an efficient, mathematics based "science"—gave birth to utilitarianism's economic godchild: *Homo economicus*—economic man.

We will not argue against the proposition that the concept of *Homo economicus* can contribute valuable insights (and *good*) to society. We are convinced that it can, it has, and it will continue to, without doubt. The proposition we wish to pursue is this: Does this economic construct actually militate against—or even, perhaps, forbid—the incorporation of moral philosophy into the nucleus of elements essential to the healthy growth and progress of the economic discipline, and of the society in which that discipline is imbedded?

It is not difficult to make the case that economics is not a natural science; that is, in terms of strictly objective, quantitative hypotheses, as is organic chemistry, cellular biology, or quantum mechanics. A natural scientist who would confine herself to doing specific predictive work in the field of nuclear fusion, based in part on the hypothesis that all nuclei are not perfectly spherical, would be considered quite rational. Aage Bohr, Niels Bohr's son, won a Nobel Prize in physics in 1975 for demonstrating scientifically the truth of the imperfect spherical shape proposition. But an economist who would confine himself to doing specific predictive work in the field of interest rates, and the rate of inflation and the Dow-Jones average, utilizing any economic theory at all, and whatever mathematics he wished, would be considered irrational—at least if his income rose or fell on the basis of his predictive accuracy.

But the truly fundamental difference between the natural sciences and economics is that the former's activities deal with nature and natural phenomena, the latter's with social processes. And it is extraordinarily

---

[48] *The Wealth of Nations* (1776, New York: Modern Library Edition, 1937, Book I, chap. 4). On Utilitarianism and economics generally, see C. Welch and R.D. Collison Block, *The New Palgrave Dictionary of Economics*, Vol. 4 (New York: The Stockton Press, 1987) pp. 770-78.
[49] Pareto optimality refers to that point where it is impossible to improve anyone's welfare without damaging someone else's.

difficult to understand how the moral equation in human society can be so important to so many scientists dealing with natural phenonema and, at the same time, be so unimportant to so many economists whose "science" exists solely as an interface with that very same society!

The "scientific" argument here would seem to be that human behavior, in our economic world, has nothing to do with morality, only rational utility. Maximizing behavior is predicated on the following construct: *economic man,* who seems to be comprised of equal parts of permanent, consistent preferences; free choice of available alternatives, all of which he understands fully; and a true computer-like ability to calculate in every case which alternatives are best for him. And when that theoretical construct staggers under the weight of reality, other improved theoretical constructs follow, such as "bounded" rationality, or even "x-efficiency" based on effort, which actually seems to argue that *non*-maximization should be the standard assumption in economic theory.[50]

Economist Thomas Shelling argues that the assumption that the sum total of contracting individuals acting in their own rational best interests leads to the best results for society is faulty.[51] What is good for me and you now (for instance, discharging sulfuric acid fumes from our factories into the air, because that is cheaper for us now than investing heavily in a costly scrubber) does not compute for the greater good when subscribed to now, en masse. Later, perhaps, we might see what is in our best interests differently, but if that insight comes long term, it will carry an insupportable price.

There are two ways to deal with you and me under such a circumstance. One is to have government intervene by passing a law; the other, says economist Shelling, is to have

> Our morals. . . substitute for markets and regulations in getting us. . . to do from conscience the things that in the long run we might elect to do only if assured of reciprocation.[52]

We will return to this ethical theme often as we deal with concrete problems in specific competitive markets in later chapters.

But for now we would content ourselves with this observation:[53] That as this book goes to press, Bill Clinton has become, in 1993, the new

---

[50] Harvey Libenstein, *Beyond Economic Man: A New Foundation for Economics,* cited by D. Bell (1980), pp. 211-12.

[51] In *Micromotives and Macrobehavior* (1978), cited and discussed by D. Bell (1980), pp. 212-13.

[52] Ibid., p. 213.

[53] Taking our point of departure from Steven Rhoades, *The Economists View of the World* (New York: Cambridge University Press, 1985), esp. chap. 12.

President of the United States, and only the second democrat to accomplish this feat in the last 24 years. We do not have to be political scientists to recognize the fact that, in order to gain the office, Clinton and his running mate were required to change substantially the content of their party's publicly perceived former economic philosophy. The Clinton-Gore ticket emphasized free-market competition, and investment to encourage economic growth and new job creation, as well as the need to temper demand and encourage supply, and even to put in place such measures as a lower capital gains tax. These are economist/economic theory-inspired ideas, now recognized as realities, and they bode well for the common good.

However, the accepted utility of pro-economic growth policies that pay heed to basic, competitive free-market principles is *not* proof in any way of the following proposition advanced by some economists that

> the economic approach is a comprehensive one that is applicable to all human behavior. . . [all] large or minor decisions, emotional or mechanical ends, rich or poor persons. . . patients or therapists, teachers or students.[54]

The inescapable conclusion to be reached from that extraordinary position is that the science of economics has no need to make (ethical) value judgments, because the *science* of (economic) value incorporates all we know on earth and all we need to know about the moving forces in human existence.

Such a judgment about humankind is, itself, an ethical value judgment, of course. And far too many economists, in and out of academia, subscribe to it and thus move our American business students in the direction of the technical and the insular, into a "tight little intellectual box from which there is no escape."[55]

We do not wish to be seen as advancing the notion that all economists, as a group, reject the salutary role of ethics in individual or group social behavior—either as economic or as social beings. In fact, we wish to leave you with two sterling examples of economists who believe moral values to be a part of *all* that is valuable in an economic world:

> The chief thing which the common-sense individual actually wants is not satisfaction for the wants which he has, but more and *better* wants. The things which he strives to get in the most immediate sense are far more what he thinks he ought to want than what his

---

[54] Gary Becker, *The Economic Approach to Human Behavior* (Chicago: University of Chicago Press, 1976), p. 8); cited in D. Bell (1980), p. 210.

[55] Rhoades, note 54, *supra*, p. 177, and citing Kenneth Boulding.

untutored preferences prompt. This feeling for what one *should* want, in contrast with actual desire, is stronger in the unthinking than in those sophisticated by education. It is the latter who argues himself into the "intolerant" (economic) attitude of *de gustibus non disputandum.*[56]

This famous economist and teacher Frank Knight, commenting on the effects of advertising and salesmanship on people's tastes, notes further that

> Ethically, the creation of right want is more important than want satisfaction. . . . Our general moral teaching would indicate that it is easier to corrupt human nature than to improve it, and observation of the taste-forming tendencies of modern marketing methods tends perhaps to confirm the view and to substantiate a negative verdict on individualistic activity of this sort.

Professor Knight adds that one of the adverse effects of salesmanship and economic rivalry is their tendency to lessen the appreciation for what he terms "free goods" and to undercut the

> fairly established consensus that happiness depends more on spiritual resourcefulness, and a joyous appreciation of the costless things of life, especially affection for one's fellow creatures, then it does on material satisfaction.[57]

The issue here is hardly *the extent* to which Professor Knight would incorporate moral philosophy into economic theory. Rather, it is the fact that he cannot eliminate such elements as ethics, right wants, and spiritual resourcefulness from the total concept of the human being, even though he or she exists in an economic world.

And then there is the following economist-professor commenting on a hypothetical person called upon to make a choice between holding on to some relatively small thing of his own, and thereby causing a great loss of life to many other people, or giving up that small thing, and thereby saving them.

---

[56] "There is no disputing about tastes." (We have seen the Latin phrase before as *de gustibus non est disputandum.*)

[57] From Rhoades, note 54, *supra*, p. 176, citing Frank Knight's *The Ethics of Competition* (London: Allen & Unwin, 1935), pp. 22-23, 52n, 71.

To prevent, therefore, this paltry misfortune to himself, would a man of humanity be willing to sacrifice the lives of. . . his brethren, provided he had never seen them? Human nature startles with the thought, and the world, in its greatest depravity and corruption, never produced such a villain as could be capable of entertaining it. But what makes this difference? When our passive feelings are almost always so sordid and so selfish, how comes it that our active principles should often be so generous and so noble? . . . It is not the soft power of humanity, it is not that feeble spark of benevolence which Nature has lighted up in the human heart that is thus capable of counteracting the strongest impulses of self-love. It is a stronger power. . . which asserts itself. . . . It is reason, principle, conscience, the inhabitant of the breast, the man within, the quiet judge and arbiter of our conduct. . . . It is a stronger love, a more powerful affection. . . the love of what is honorable and noble, of the grandeur, and dignity, and superiority of our own characters.

One individual must never prefer himself so much even to any other individual, as to hurt or injure that other, in order to benefit himself, though the benefit to the one should be much greater than the hurt to the other. . . the man within immediately calls to him. . . that he is no better than his neighbor, and that by. . . unjust preference he renders himself the proper object of contempt and indignation (and he deserves punishment) for having. . . violated one of those sacred rules, on the tolerable observation of which depend the whole security and peace of human society.

The economics professor who authored these lines, in the late eighteenth century, was, of course, Adam Smith.[58] And the puzzling question raised by the quoted material is obvious: How could the creator of the concept of "the invisible hand," of the unintended but useful outcomes of selfish behavior (of *The Wealth of Nations*) also have written a book on such "moral sentiments"?

For one thing, there is some evidence that Adam Smith's changes in the sixth and final edition of the book from which our extended quote came, are evidence of his "uneasy awareness that the blandishments of a commercial society might prove too strong for the attainment of [the] high standard of virtue" to which he personally subscribed.[59] For another, it is important to point out that *explaining actions* by the use of overarching

---

[58] Adam Smith, *The Theory of Moral Sentiments* (6th [final] ed., 1790), pt. 3, chap. 3.

[59] See Heilbroner (and Malone), *The Essential Adam Smith* (New York: W.W. Norton, 1986), p. 61.

theoretical constructs is one thing: *taking personal responsibility for them* as a sentient, ethical human being is quite another. And for Adam Smith and for all of us, those two areas, we would argue, are inextricably linked, never to be uncoupled by economic "science" theory. We shall come back to this subject again.[60]

2. Ethics, Morality, and Law

Lawyers and unethical behavior seem to have been connected in the public mind ever since the first day a lawyer won a case and left a loser on the other side of the argument.

But *The Law* itself, as a working reality, seems always to have been more admired than censured. Perhaps this is because, in a democratic society at least, the law represents not only *Order*, but also *Justice*.

Justice is a concept we all feel is basic to any acceptable *Rule of Law*. But few of us can define that concept satisfactorily.

Defining "Justice" matters. It matters because any effort to deal with ethics at the interface of law, economics, and human behavior must get past the often-asked question: Doesn't conformity to law provide all the *practical* answers we need? If one did not break the law then what, concerning the behavior, is left to debate—at least outside Sunday church services?

"Justice," it has been argued, is simple enough to define. *Equality under law* is what justice is all about. Being treated equally by the law, and before its courts, is what makes law "just." And if laws are just, and one obeys them, what else is worth debating (assuming one has a practical purpose in mind)?

"Justice," it has also been argued, is very difficult to define. Justice is much more than simply rules promulgated by authority (the state; e.g., or the Sovereign)—and this is so whether such rules (laws) pass some "equality" test or not; that is, are applied the same way to everybody. Justice, in fact, is a natural principle of fairness and right, holding for all humanity at all times, everywhere. True justice is derived from *Natural Law* (law derived from Nature/God) not from the laws of society.[61]

---

[60] In any event, it is shocking that so few students of economics and economic theory are actually familiar with this first of Adam Smith's two greatest books. Adam Smith was an amalgam of *both* of his two major works and, arguably, would be so today, even were he to be working in Chicago. We cannot leave this area of economics without citing Donald M. McCloskey's *The Rhetoric of Economics* (Madison: University of Wisconsin Press, 1985). It is a serious book that readers will enjoy whether they agree with McCloskey or not.

[61] The definition of "natural law" has been the subject of jurisprudential.wars as well as of bloody skirmishes elsewhere. We plead unfitness for full combat, and submit that our definition inside the parentheses supplies a tolerably broad working definition.

Non-lawyer Sigmund Freud made the justice-morality distinction thus:

> The first requisite of culture is. . . justice—that is, the assurance that a law once made will not be broken in favor of any individual. This implies nothing about the ethical value of any laws.[62]

Does any *practical* person, who wants more than anything to *get things done* take time to diddle around with the second definition of justice we set forth—that is, with such unearthly details as "natural law" and its related ethical constructs?

We know one who did. His name was Thomas Jefferson. He was the man most responsible for writing the following:

> When in the course of human events, it becomes necessary for one people to dissolve the political bonds which have connected them with another, and to assume among the powers of the earth, the separate and equal station to which the Laws of Nature and of Nature's God entitles them, a decent respect to the opinions of mankind requires that they should declare the causes which impel them to the separation.
>
> We hold these truths to be self-evident, that all men are created equal, that they are endowed by their Creator with certain unalienable rights, that among these are Life, Liberty, and the pursuit of Happiness—That to secure these rights, Governments are instituted among Men, deriving their just powers from the consent of the governed. . . .[63]

The Founding Fathers who signed the Declaration of Independence in July 1776 relied on Natural Law for more than their entitlement to revolution. They stated further that natural law, the law of Nature's God, endowed them with certain unalienable "rights"—and went on to name their three important ones.

What is the real nature, and *effect* on, say, liberty and economic transactions, of these and other "rights"?

The nature of rights, particularly individual human rights, insofar as general origins and meaning (apart from practical *effect*) are concerned, is a truly complex matter. To explore that matter thoroughly, we would have to write a treatise on the origins and *authority* of natural law and the connection between it and the development of rights, followed, of course,

---

[62] Note 17, *supra*, p. 780.
[63] Lines 1-13, Declaration of Independence.

by a proper historical analysis. Such treatises and analyses do exist, and some are well worth reading. But we must content ourselves here with doing two things: providing some follow-up sources a thoughtful reader with time can pursue,[64] and relating these to *rights* and to *justice* in a brief but practical way, focused on how these concepts can tell us something useful about:

1. Why ethics debate and decision are not rendered irrelevant or immaterial with regard to particular human conduct simply because that conduct did not actually violate a law, or laws, in a specific society.
2. The relationship of rights to ethics and law and, in particular, to economic transactions.

"Rights" will play a continuous role throughout this book and in a very specific way, related particularly to economic activity. At the end of this chapter we set out an original case focused on the tension between individual *rights* and economic *efficiency* that is present in our society. Our case is intended to serve as a bridge between this ethical theory focus and the myriad of specific economic/social/legal concerns to be found in Chapters Two through Nine.

For now, we return to items 1 and 2 above.

Americans (and hundreds of millions of their fellow humans throughout the world) take their "rights" very seriously. But at the time that the American and then the French Declarations of Rights were promulgated,[65] continental "liberals" such as Edmund Burke and utilitarian Jeremy Bentham in England were outraged. They found the very idea of human rights flowing from some sort of "natural law" to be preposterous. Bentham believed rights came only from "real" law or not at all. From "natural" law came only "imaginary" rights. "Natural rights" Bentham felt, were "nonsense." In fact, he said, the concept of rights not actually provided by the specifics of "real" law was "nonsense upon stilts." The

---

[64] A place to begin looking at justice is *Great Books*, 2d ed., Vol. 1—"The Syntopicon" (Encyclopedia Britannica, 1990). An introductory essay is at pp. 662-69, and several pages of references follow. Many legal philosophers have dealt with the issue. H.L.A. Hart (1961)—see note 1, *supra*, at chap. 7, "Justice and Morality," and Carl Joachim Friedrich, *A Philosophy of Law in Legal Perspective*, (Chicago: University of Chicago Press, 1958) esp. chap. 30, "Justice, Equality and the Common Man," are easy reading. Giorgio DelVecchio, *Justice: An Historical and Philosophical Essay* (New York: Philosophical Library, 1953) is not. On the issue of "rights" one would certainly want to be familiar with the *British Bill of Rights* of 1689; the *American Bill of Rights* of 1791; and the *French Declaration of the Rights of Man and of the Citizens* of 1789. A fine book is Ronald Dworkin, *Taking Rights Seriously* (Cambridge: Harvard University Press, 1979).

[65] Note 64, *supra*.

concerns of Bentham, Burke, and others in the eighteenth century were, of course, political as much as they were philosophical. If people believed they really did possess individual "natural" rights, and acted upon them, they could prove troublesome to established governments, and certainly were proving to be so at the time.[66]

Now "natural law," which provides humans with "rights," and the "real" laws of society are not mutually exclusive. In fact, it is when they are actually spanned by ethical constructs that they cause upheavals in society.

In July 1846, Henry David Thoreau, a New England American roughing it (somewhat) in a cabin by a pond, refused to pay his poll taxes. He spent a night in jail for this (before being bailed out), and he was very angry. He went back to Walden Pond and wrote an essay whose influence reached far beyond Concord, Massachusetts. It was entitled "Civil Disobedience."

The theme of that essay, in brief, was that while civil (society's) law *is* real law, there is also a higher law that ethical persons must obey. Of course, such individuals must pay the price of their subsequent moral behavior (refusing to obey the law); for example, they must be ready to go to jail.

But *when* does one invoke the higher law? When the civil law is unjust. In fact, Thoreau wrote: "Under a government which imprisons men unjustly, the true place for a just man is in prison."[67]

There was an Indian lawyer familiar with the writings of Thoreau whose name was Gandhi. Sixty years after the publication of "Civil Disobedience," Gandhi developed a technique for redressing social and legal wrongs, by challenging them with nonviolent methods. Gandhi did not deny the validity of "real" law nor the sanctions imposed for breaking it. His methods invited, rather than inflicted, suffering. His method was called *satyagraha*, or *devotion to truth*.

An American who was familiar with the writings of Thoreau and the methods of Gandhi spearheaded a movement to enforce civil rights through civil disobedience and nonviolent processes. Writing in 1963:

> Nonviolent direct action seeks to create such a crisis and foster such a tension that a community which has constantly refused to negotiate is forced to confront the issue. It seeks so to dramatize the issue that it can no longer be ignored. . . . We know

---

[66] The severed heads of the victims of the French Revolution were responsible, in large measure, for Burke's and Bentham's attitudes.

[67] "Civil Disobedience," published May 1849.

through painful experience that freedom is never voluntarily given by the oppressor; it must be demanded by the oppressed.[68]

Martin Luther King, Jr. did not question the validity of segregationist "laws," only their morality in terms of their effect upon an entire racial group. He agreed, of course, with fellow American Thoreau, that jail was the only true, just place in the face of real injustice. The quotation above is from a letter written by him while behind bars.

The prosecutors of German war criminals at the Nuremberg trials of 1945-1946 had to face the existence of "real" German law, which the defendants could claim they were obeying when committing some of the crimes for which they were being tried. "Crimes against humanity" (exterminations, deportations and genocide), one of the major charges they faced, were held to be of a higher order than the laws of the German state. Theirs were termed crimes subject to "international law," but their kinship to natural law is certainly clear.[69]

While we have emphasized the concept of "justice" here in our examination of law and morality, we are well aware of the fact that

principles of justice do not exhaust the idea of morality, and not all criticism of law on moral grounds is made in the name of justice.[70]

Indeed, where justice is interpreted as impartial judgment applied sternly (and equally) to all, the very application of the law raises troubling moral issues.

An interesting example may be found in the *Halakhah,* the totality of Jewish law, which is made up of a written code compiled in the second century A.D. (the Mishnah), written commentary on it (the Gemara), and the biblical law, as revealed to Moses, coming from the first five books of the Old Testament (the *Torah*).[71] The Mishnah and Gemara, together, make up the *Talmud.*

An injunction in the Torah "Thou shalt not favor the cause of a poor man" prohibits the perversion of impartial (truthful) judgment, even for the sake of mercy applied to the poor—for example in a cause involving money, where "justice" demands a finding for the rich man. However, the

---

[68] From Rev. Martin Luther King's "Letter from Birmingham Jail," 1963.

[69] For a fine book not only on the trials themselves but on the issue of the international validity of sanctions applied everywhere in the world to war crimes against humanity, see Telford Taylor, *The Anatomy of the Nuremberg Trials* (New York: Knopf, 1992).

[70] H.L.A. Hart (1961), p. 163.

[71] See Coggins and Houlden, eds., *A Dictionary of Biblical Interpretation* (W.P. Weitzman's "Talmud"; London: SCM Press, 1990) pp. 667-71; and G. Wigoder, ed., *The Encyclopedia of Judaism* (New York: Macmillan, 1989), pp. 684-86.

Torah also exhorts the judge in such a case, when doing "justice," to recompense the poor man from his own pocket, according to the rule of leniency (*li-fnim mi-shurat ha-din*). Literally translated the rule means, *inside the line of the law.*

The interesting thing about the range of ethical Halakhah is that, unlike the written law, which is binding on everyone, the inside law—the moral injunctions—are valid for those who, themselves, desire to reach beyond Halakhah to that inner circle: "inside the law." The Talmudic definition of one who conducts himself so as to be inside the law is *hassid.* An example would be a man who can afford a financial loss not taking money from one who cannot afford it, in a court of law, despite his legal right to "justice."

Additionally, where a person is not, in a given case, under any legal responsibility to perform by Halakhah he may be "culpable according to divine law." In fact,

> The laws of damages contain so many moral injunctions that one of the sages said that he who wanted to behave piously could do so merely by observing the rules laid down [in them].[72]

Islamic law, *Shari'a*, is actually a divinely ordained path of conduct that guides Muslims in this world, but with the goal of earning divine favor in the world to come. The Shari'a goes beyond what Westerners think of as legal relationships (e.g., contracts) to the very relationship of humans, God, and one's conscience. Clearly, then, Shari'a is deeply concerned with ethical standards, as much as with law, dealing quite specifically with civil rights and duties and the like. In this sense, justice, morality, and law are indivisible. Moreover, all law, in the sense of its emanating from God, is "natural law."[73]

Humans can and do disagree on exact definitions for justice, rights and natural law, as well as the connections among them and their interface with systems of societal law. But it cannot be denied, at least since the eighteenth century, that some basic human rights do exist, whether or not they are contained in written "real" law.[74] We can agree on this without

---

[72] Adin Steinsaltz, *The Essential Talmud* (New York: Basic Books, 1976), p. 201. The reader should look at Chap. 24, "Ethics and Halakhah."

[73] Some excellent references to Islamic law and interpretation may be found in Albert Hourani's *A History of the Arab Peoples* (Cambridge, Mass: Belknap Press, 1991) pp. 113-15, and in chap. 10, "The Culture of the 'Ulama'." See also J. Jomier, *How to Understand Islam* (New York: Crossword Publishing, 1989), esp. pp. 49ff.

[74] We believe it would be hard to find a conservative strict constructionist, with regard to the U.S. Constitution, who would deny the "right" of the Soviet peoples to disband their nation and set up independent republics free of communist domination, despite the fact that *that* "right" could hardly be found explicitly detailed in written U.S.S.R. law.

having to agree on a common definition of natural law. Nor do we have to agree on a specific hierarchy of rights, or on the exact weight each must carry in any case of conflicting or competing claims.

But we believe we must agree on two practical propositions relating to ethics, morality, and law. The first is that an integral part of every legal system is a societal acceptance of the fact that civil law, promulgated by government authority is, on its face, entitled to general obedience. Without the individual's voluntary subjection to the rule of law, there can be no *order*. Lacking order, there is no true freedom at all, only license for some and despair for everyone else.

But the second proposition is that such voluntary acceptance can never mean that civil law is not open to challenge by men and women convinced that some laws are wrong—that is, in their negative effect on the basic rights they hold as human beings—and that they are entitled to make ethical judgments about such laws, and to take moral actions to challenge them. The actions taken are, of course, themselves subject to moral analysis, judgment, and legal sanction.[75]

That obeying or disobeying civil law, by itself, fully defines ethical or unethical behavior is simply not an acceptable postulate. That it is not an acceptable postulate has been demonstrated, in our time, in places as disparate as Moscow, Prague, Tiananmen Square and Selma, Alabama.

Still, might it not be argued that ethical tenets that are acceptable in the face of political or racial oppression are not really applicable in situations involving economic behavior in a competitive free market society? That here, what is "legal" does define what is "morally acceptable"?

That is an argument that is dangerous to the health of capitalist free markets, because there *are* market-affecting consequences arising out of business-related behavior *not* directly contrary to law. These consequences often arise out of the responses to such behavior by people called legislators. And there are others, of their creation, called regulators, whose strong responses to (e.g., certain "legal" banking and securities market behaviors) may be neither efficient nor effective. But such responses (and their consequences) are real, and what they represent is philosophy in action. And competitive free markets are clearly affected (in specific ways that will be examined in detail throughout this book) despite the business behaviors having been of far less import than the extermination of tens of millions of people by genocidal maniacs.

None of which tells us, with any specificity, how to deal both humanly and efficiently with ethical economic-law issues, which may not

---

[75] This raises the issue of violence, of course, and the place of blood and death in protest against "bad" law. We will discuss weighing competing moral values later, but suffice it to say here and now that the taking of human life weighs very heavily against the taker on any scale of competing values under almost any circumstances.

be very easy to see, and harder still to weigh when they indeed are there—and are conflicting!

Let us proceed now in that direction.[76]

II. ETHICAL DISCOVERY AND JUDGMENT: A FRAMEWORK FOR MORAL ANALYSIS

Accepting both the justification and the need for ethical debate and decision making in a democratic, competitive, free-market economy/society, we are faced with two key issues requiring some kind of resolution:

1. How does a market participant/decision-maker determine which ethical "oughts" are involved in any given circumstance?

2. If, as is the usual case when ethical concerns are involved, there are competing values or rights at issue, how does the decision-maker weigh them properly in order to come to the "right" conclusion?

A. Determining Ethical "Oughts"

The obvious and truly not flippant answer to (1) is: "By looking for them, carefully." One cannot expect to encounter formally, or to engage in thought about, ethical values, unless one *wants* to be aware of ethical values and *wants* to incorporate them into one's decision making.

Thus, there are four reasons we can think of why a decision-maker might bypass the ethical issues involved in a given situation. The first three are key because they relate to the kind of attitude essential for the search:

- Because the person harbors a conscious, or perhaps only partly conscious, disrespect for "ethics" specifically because of its inapplicability (nonutility) to market manager (or professional advisor) decision making; that is, ethics is blah-blah-blah.

- Because one is anxious about one's capacity to deal with ethical issues one might find if one did look; that is, the person lacks "ethicist" training.

- Because one feels that conformity to "social ethics" (the ones out there), given the individual's position in *his or her* corporate culture, could be professionally fatal.

---

[76] We leave this area with this final brief admonition, delivered more than 300 years ago: "Let not the law of the country be the non ultra of thy honesty; nor think that always good enough which the law will make good: (Sir Thomas Browne, 1686).

- Because she and he simply have no basic point of departure for identifying "ethical" issues; that is, they might be willing but don't really know where to begin.

The first reason we hope we have covered, although we shall certainly return again in this book to the theme of ethical decision making and "efficiency."

The second and third reasons (lack of ethicist training and an antagonistic corporate culture) require brief comment at this point.

Ethicist training, by which we mean formal training of some sort in both theoretical and applied philosophical ethics, is no pre-condition to the possession of honesty, fairness, human concern, and a personal commitment to being decent—the major tools for toiling in the ethical trade. Formal ethicist training *is* a very fine thing, and useful, too; however, pleading the lack of it to a charge of lying, unfairness, callousness, or indecency entitles you to the same consideration you might expect from a court on the plea: "Not guilty by reason of ignorance of the law."[77]

Concern about potential conflict between general societal/religious ethics and "the individual corporate ethic" is, unfortunately, too often based on reality. A degree of personal responsibility for the company's immediate bottom line, and the requirement to conform to "team behavior" values (one very high value; for example, is to make sure one's boss always looks good and that neither one of you has to take the fall when things go wrong).[78]

Keeping one's job, or protecting one's bonus, or raise, or position in the executive pecking order (or one's position as outside legal counsel or accounting firm), are mighty considerations, without a doubt, but that doesn't in any way change what we would call a fundamental formula. By which we mean that ethical decision making always involves *recognizing* the ethical issues existent in any given situation and *weighing* them when competing values exist, so as to come to the "right" conclusion.

One might answer: "Good construct. But in the real world, where rent, clothing, shelter, and the needs of one's loved ones (and, maybe, power and *real* wealth) exist from day to day, one value stands out so tall (and heavy) that all the rest is (hot) air."

We could respond to this by putting forward the Adam Smith of the *Theory of Moral Sentiments*, and say that taking personal responsibility for one's actions as a human being (responding to "the inhabitant of the

---

[77] Besides, you *do* have this book.

[78] A worthwhile examination of this very important area involving the pull of the corporate ethic is Robert Jackall, *Moral Mazes: The World of Corporate Managers* (New York: Oxford University Press, 1988). See also J.A. Waters, "Catch 20.5: Corporate Morality as an Organizational Phenomenon," *Organizational Dynamics*, (Spring 1978) pp. 3-19.

breast, the man within") is what will eventually make or break one in the real world. But rather than leave it at that, let's take a look at a hypothetical situation.

> Your immediate boss is Senior V.P. for Production. Your company's chief product is chemical widgets. Fumes are given off in the manufacturing process and are very strong in one area where 175 employees work. Masks are an impediment to the process to be used, and several alternative exhaust systems have helped some, but have not eliminated the problem of the fumes (which are not acrid or even terribly unpleasant in the area). The only way to lower substantially the level of pollution is to shut down the manufacturing process temporarily and go to the very heavy expense of installing entirely new equipment.
>
> Your boss has received a report from the medical department. It diagnoses 7 of the 175 employees in the affected area as having symptoms (coughing, difficulty with deep breathing, chest pain, etc.) of a lung disease that "quite possibly" could be related to the fumes. The disease is progressive and eventually totally disabling. It does not necessarily result in death.
>
> Your boss's orders are: Be sure there is *no* temporary shutdown of the manufacturing process; that the company, which is now barely operating in the black, will *not* be put to the expense of installing a new system; that the doctor should be advised "to stop throwing around all these 'possibles' and just treat these folks medically, or give them time off or whatever else he has to do: Keep this under control and let's get on with our business!"
>
> Translation: If anything goes wrong here, you're on the street with a fistful of résumés.
>
> Now, in the *real* world, do you examine carefully *everything* that is actually involved here? Or do you say, "My job weighs so heavily here that all the rest is irrelevant—or, at least, not relevant enough to outweigh it on any reality scale"?
>
> Add this assumption: In your home state, knowingly exposing workers to toxic substances is a criminal offense and carries up to five years of jail time.
>
> Add this other assumption: This lung disease *does* kill. Death, in fact, is inevitable. The felony charge would be, at least, manslaughter.
>
> Wait: Change the assumptions.

In your home state, knowingly exposing workers to toxic substances is *not* an indictable offense. OSHA and state civil penalties (company fines) are the full extent of possible punishment. Moreover, your statistical folks can provide you with a cost-benefit analysis proving that it would be cheaper (more efficient) to pay these men and women to cough their way through retirement (or even to pay their survivors) than it would be to shut down operations and install an entirely new system.

Besides, you can now assume that this lung disease *doesn't* cause death. It only cripples. . . .

We expect that if you have read the preceding materials carefully, you have gone through some changes in your head and maybe some confusion; as you would in "real life."

But this much should be perfectly clear: With "real world" value considerations there are no exceptions to this rule. One should always begin with the assumption that no one value is absolute. And further, that *however* you decide the tough questions, you *are* making ethical judgments all the time. You *do* have to take responsibility for those judgments. And finally, that responsibility follows you out past the company door and beyond the company's property.

Let's turn now to our fourth reason for bypassing ethical issues: There is no established point of departure one can see for beginning a search for ethical issues.

Let us begin with this unarguable proposition: There is no such point of departure that has ever reached the exalted status of "Proven to be proper" or, put another way, "Indisputably efficacious."

Theoretical constructs abound. We begin with the oft-stated proposition, which we join in advocating, that the first step in constructing a basis for determining which values are at issue in any given area under consideration is to determine *just whose interests are at stake* in terms of the action to be taken.

The extant popular theory is one that holds that managers do not have a sole, overriding duty to consider only shareholders in their decision-making process. They should consider, as well, the interests and concerns of the firm's "stakeholders." Stakeholders are generally defined as being a basic six in number: Management, employees, owners, suppliers, customers, and the local community.[79] The basis for the theory lies in the Kantian proposition we have already examined and which the philosopher

---

[79] See, for example, Evans and Freeman, "A Stakeholder Theory of the Modern Corporation: Kantian Capitalism," in Beauchamp and Bowie, eds., *Ethical Theory in Business*, 3d ed. (Englewood Cliffs, N.J.: Prentice Hall, 1988), pp 97-106.

referred to as his "supreme practical principle": Always treat people as ends, not means.

> Each of these stakeholder groups has a right not to be treated as a means to some end, and therefore must participate in determining the future direction of the firm in which they have a stake.[80]

"Stakeholders" have "rights"! Like every single "theory of the firm," this one presents some problems. One is that the demonstrable authority for accepting it is the philosopher Kant. A substantial fellow, certainly, but not without his detractors. So, the stakeholder theory is only philosophy, not scientific proof?

We know enough to be careful of that complaint, don't we? Let's delve into it deeper, later.

It has also been suggested that the stakeholder concept is unable, in and of itself, to deal with *competing* stakeholder interests; that is, to manage making trade-offs.[81] We believe that to be true. But another thing bothers us about the word "stakeholder."

It has come to assume the status of a term of art—that is, to denote very specific and particular groups in a very specific relationship to the corporation. Any corporation. As such, the term is too limiting as well as being quantitatively nonspecific. Are the big six stakeholder groups definitive for the corporation's outside legal counsel (or inside, for that matter)? For the corporation's accounting firm? Even if we limit the view of stakeholder to the corporate manager there are problems. Consider the savings and loan (S&L) company executive: Is he or she morally obligated to consider *you* a stakeholder if you live in another state but your taxes are, or could be, used to pay for deposit insurance—and deposit insurance deficits? We develop a "stewardship" concept in Chapter 7 that we think leads to the answer: yes. Then why not expand the well-used word "stakeholder" to include "all of society" or "the world"? Because then it becomes as unsubstantial as a cloud, which we all know is a very hard thing to build on.

We do *not* object to the fact that the specific notion of considering groups beyond shareholders rests on some *moral* basis. *All* theories about who managers are ultimately responsible to, rest on a moral basis—even the one that holds that the total responsibility of managers is to make shareholders as rich as possible, as quickly as possible without actually

---

[80] Ibid., p. 79.

[81] Thomas Donaldson, *The Ethics of International Business* (New York: Oxford University Press, 1989), pp. 44-47.

breaking the law. And this is true even though it comes with the argument that the law, particularly regarding fiduciaries, *requires* this of managers.

We argue in Chapter 5 that the law, including the law of fiduciary duties, demands no such thing, and we have court cases to back that up.

The manager-duty-to-shareholders-only theory is superior to a theory maintaining a manager-duty-to-all-homeless persons-within-10 blocks-of-corporate headquarters only—if it *is* superior—only because it carries weightier values in any sensible ethical trade-off game. We might well agree that it does, but we object mightily to any argument that the duty-to-shareholders-only concept deserves to prevail as a provable postulate of economic (or any other) "science."

That is utter nonsense, and leads us to our principal point here:

> Managerial (and legal counsel and accounting firm) decisions ought to (and we use the word "ought" deliberately) take into account *all relevant interests at stake in the decision-making process.* That is the point of departure for the decision-maker searching for the relevant ethical value issues involved in his or her problem area.

While we attempt, in several chapters of this book, to show that a legal obligation (duty)[82] to consider constituencies beyond stockholders does exist in some free-market areas, we are aware that our "principal point" is based on a moral concept. We have attempted to establish an ethical basis for that concept. We will apply it to very specific situations later in this text, and we certainly argue that our moral point of departure is as worthy of consideration as anyone else's despite the fact that we refuse to cloak it in some pseudo-scientific mantle.

To summarize here, and to clarify continuing concerns:
Assuming that one's *attitude* is a good one; that is,

- that one accepts the relevance of ethical issues to market decision making;
- that one need not be a trained ethicist to act on this acceptance;
- that idiosyncratic corporate values viewed against broader values are not absolute and must be weighed carefully against these "outside" values;

and, subsequently, that there *are parameters* within which to locate and identify pertinent ethical issues, that is,

---

[82] We shall get substantive later on "legal duty." Don't let the words stop you now.

- all relevant interests of all identifiable parties that are to be affected by this decision,

look at the problems remaining:

- We have not relieved decision-making stress. If there is no specific 6-, or 2-, or 15-member group of "stakeholders" on a chart that can be consulted in every case regardless of the issue, how then does one narrow the field within the given broad parameters?
- Within the given parameters could be one-ton interests, and others with all the substance of an elementary particle. Isn't this a weighty matter that still requires some discussion?

First (and we still feel the same), one narrows the field by looking for the relevant parties and interests, carefully. And with this distinct advantage, one really *wants* to do that.

As for stress: The stress involved in maintaining ethical awareness, and acting upon that awareness, is much akin to the stress involved in maintaining freedom and democracy, and acting as a free, democratic individual and nation. One falters, one wonders, one doubts—and mistakes are often made. But those of us living in freedom and democracy in this final decade of the twentieth century know that many who are not are willing to die for the opportunity. There are different forms of stress. Some have glory in them. Maintaining ethical awareness and acting upon that awareness is stressful. And there is no philosopher's stone upon which is written the formula for identifying values and weighing them to determine conclusively, in every case, what is right and what is wrong.

But there *is* glory in the struggle itself—what the Greeks referred to as the *agon*: the human struggle, the trial, the danger, the desire for honor and esteem—even the tragedy (*agonia*) of success and failure. Maintaining and acting on one's ethical awareness is part of the agon that ought to be kept in mind by those

who are likely to have inclinations toward a misleadingly innocent economic interpretation of human conduct. . . . [It] may help redress the balance toward recognition of the great part ritual combat, fully integrated with religious and moral sentiments, has played in our Western past, and still plays in our Western present. . . .[83]

---

[83] C. Brinton, note 1, *supra,* pp. 27-28.

Even in the absence of a philosopher's stone, weighing competing interests is a subject in need of some discussion.

B. Weighing Competing Values

Let us assume that you are a manager at Widget Company. Your product is made with the chemical *almium*. It's an expensive product. Workers who assemble it are very highly paid. Your work force used to be some 92 percent male, and it is now only 84 percent male. Women workers are as skilled as male workers at producing the product. While research into *almium* is still going on, it appears reasonably clear that the chemical negatively affects the reproductive systems of women. It is capable of producing sterility, and of harming fetuses as well. You are responsible for deciding whether to formulate a policy that would bar females from working at Widget Company (except perhaps as secretaries or cleaning women, outside of almium-affected areas).

You are aware that Title VII of the Civil Rights Act of 1964, and the Pregnancy Discrimination Act of 1978, prohibit sex discrimination in employment in all cases except those where sex is a bone fide occupational qualification (BFOQ); for example, where specific job related skills and aptitudes require men only. But you are also aware of the fact that women workers, even if warned in writing of the dangers to their reproductive systems (as your female workers have been), might sue you later for harm, as might their children born damaged, and as might some husbands/fathers. Your lawyers have informed you that you have, as arguments against the two laws mentioned, considerations of industrial safety; the general duty of business to protect the safety of third parties; and a legitimate concern about incurring substantial legal costs.

To ban female workers or not to ban them—that is the policy question. What values would be involved (weighed/traded off) in your decision? Your lawyers have said: "You have a reasonable case. You go ahead and ban them; we'll be delighted to defend the class action lawsuit alleging discrimination that's certain to come." Does that mean that the only value you weigh is: Which decision is likely to win or lose, and what will the costs be to your shareholders?

Add these facts (given to you by your wife):

- almium researchers now claim that the chemical might negatively affect male sperm
- in the last 10 years, more than 100,000 women have been excluded from high-paying jobs in America on the ground of exposure to potentially harmful chemicals

- female-dominated industries like dry cleaning, electronics, and dental labs also involve dangerous toxic chemicals potentially harmful to fetuses. But here, employers have generally *not* put in place exclusionary fetal-protection policies. These jobs are relatively low paying, certainly as compared to making almium-based widgets. Exclusionary policies due to toxic threat are rare in *any* low-wage, female-dominated industry (and your wife provides you with an article by J. Carlton, in the December 4, 1992, edition of the *Wall Street Journal* to prove her point: "Study of Computer Chip Plants Finds Worker Miscarriage Risk."

Of course you've always known that the interests of female workers were involved here as well as your shareholders'. But do you weigh them differently *now*? Are you a strong right-to-life advocate? A strong supporter of choice in abortion? In either case, would your decision here be influenced by such a fact? There really are two considerations here, aren't there?

The first is not *how* do you weigh values, but rather just *which* values are you weighing?

By the way, if you *were* to issue a no-women-workers-allowed policy, you'd cost your company a lot of money. The U.S. Supreme Court has already decided, 9-0, that in such a case your policy would be discriminatory and a violation of your female workers' rights. And interestingly enough, in coming to that decision (or decisions—there were three separate written opinions) the High Court felt that women workers in America, *in general*, had relevant interests at stake here. And the justices weighed them, at least indirectly, in coming to their decision.[84]

You might want to ponder just what your company's "costs" would be resulting from your overruled policy decision. Would a broader consideration of all the values involved in your decision (e.g., work force loyalty and commitment) have made some of these cost possibilities plainer?

To move ahead: If we adopted utilitarian principles in a case such as this, what result would that give us? Can we use such principles to help us weigh competing values?

Which of the alternative workplace policies—the alternative economic arrangements—would have maximized happiness, would have accomplished the greatest good summed over all the members of society? Would the decision to bar female workers be so much more productive of happiness over all (e.g., of husbands, of fetuses, the joys of normal birth, whatever) that it would outweigh the benefits to be obtained from their working (money, need, pride, whatever). Does "overall" mean *all* of the

---

[84] *UAW v. Johnson Controls, Inc.*, 111 S. Ct. 1196 (1991). An excellent analysis of this case may be found in Vol. 105. No. 1, *Harvard Law Review* (1991), pp. 379-90.

United States? Does "their" working mean *all* women workers in the state or nation?

It is, in fact, unlikely that proponents of one or another theory of economic distribution really argue for the adoption of a formula to be applied to all actual real-world situations. Rather, these formulations are meant to contribute to meaningful moral, political, and social thought, are meant to provide concepts that sharpen our view of the world, and provide us *not* with formulas, but with *principles for action.*

Put another way, here is a really important use for these constructs, utilitarian or otherwise, for *all important* theories of economic distribution: They can help us to understand in any given case just *which particular values* are being placed upon the scale for weighing.

To illustrate, let us look at two Harvard colleagues' competing value systems in an area we might best categorize as "economic justice."

The first is Robert Nozick, an economic *libertarian.* Professor Nozick begins, as any "liberal" like, say, Thomas Jefferson might do, from the premise that we all have certain basic "rights." And for Nozick they are moral rights, such as Jefferson's "life" and "liberty." But there's more of John Locke (1632-1704) in Nozick than there was in Jefferson. For Locke and Nozick share "property" as a third basic moral right, not the pursuit of happiness.

Nozick's argument, which deserves a fuller examination than we can provide here, is that rights are to be looked at more as constraints than as allowances. They cannot normally be infringed upon for any reason whatsoever. At base, he argues, our natural rights must be totally free from *any* coercion by anyone else. They are part of our individual uniqueness. Nozick is deeply concerned that what one possesses must have been come by without having morally infringed upon anyone else's rights; however, if, for example, *property* has been come by properly, then such possessions have the status of a moral right and cannot be taken from someone for any reason whatsoever. Therefore, *any* involuntary transfer of one's property (e.g., by government) is morally wrong, is *unjust.* Redistribution of wealth is *unjust* as a transgression of individual liberty, no matter the reason for the transfer.

For Nozick, liberty, overall, is the highest good.[85]

And so liberty is for John Rawls of Harvard as well. But Rawls's conclusions drawn from that same ethical proposition are very different!

In Rawls's famous work, *A Theory of Justice,*[86] he begins by postulating a unique state of nature. In Rawls's scenario, everyone in the initial, natural society has a general wisdom (for example, understands

---

[85] The classic work is Nozick's *Anarchy, State and Utopia* (New York: Basic Books, 1974).
[86] John Rawls, note 1, *supra.*

the laws of physics, the principles of supply and demand) however, everyone has particular ignorance. All are in fact behind a "veil of ignorance" in that they are not able to distinguish themselves from anyone else socially, sexually, or in any other way in terms of an ordinary criterion or by any socioeconomic or racial or any other characteristic.

While this sounds like a strange hypothesis, it is in fact a very clever design to put us into Rawls' "original position." Here the bargaining problems that come up in everyday life, arising out of "the contingencies of social class and fortune," don't affect the choice of principles the bargainers are about to choose, the principles that will determine the basic structure of society.[87]

Rawls's bargainers, in their state of nature, would come up with an ideal "set of principles for choosing between the social arrangements which determine the division [of benefits in society], and for underwriting a consensus as to the proper distributive shares."[88]

The principles of Rawls's *distributive justice* that result from this situation are anti-utilitarian. Like Adams Smith's argument that self-benefit at another's expense is unjust "though the benefit to the one should be much greater than the hurt to the other,"[89] Rawls argues that

> the liberties of equal citizenship are taken for granted and the rights served by justice are not subject to political bargaining nor to the calculus of social interests.[90]

Utilizing his particular state-of-nature point of departure, Rawls comes up with two fundamental principles, the second having two parts. First, each person has an equal right to the most extensive scheme of equal basic liberties compatible with a similar system of liberty for all. Second (since there are and always will be some form of social and economic inequality), inequalities may be allowed to exist only if they are (1) to the greatest benefit of those least advantaged and (2) are attached to offices and positions open to all under conditions of fair and equal opportunity.

For Rawls, then, the dynamic of getting, keeping, and giving is *not* utilitarian and certainly not libertarian! He would require transfers of wealth when inequalities and concentrations of wealth reach the limit of "fairness."

Let's examine this case now:

---

[87] See also J. Rawls, "Distributive Justice," in Laslett and Runaman, eds., *Philosophy, Politics & Society* (New York: Blackwell/Oxford/Barnes & Noble, 1967).

[88] Ibid., p. 76.

[89] Note 59, *supra.*

[90] Rawls, note 88, *supra*, p. 77.

Mr. Smith, in 1985, purchased 1,000 acres of land in a warm, southern state for $1,000 per acre, in a perfectly legitimate transaction. He has been waiting for the opportunity to improve and build on the land and has undertaken to develop a specific business plan involving filling in the land and building condominiums. He anticipates a profit of at least $1,000,000 over his original investment. Before he actually begins developmental work, he is informed by the state that his entire property has been designated a "wetland," essential to the state's ecologic system relative to groundwater purity, animal and plant development, and the like. He is told that

1. He cannot develop the land.
2. The state will not buy it. He keeps ownership and possession, of course, but just cannot develop it commercially.

Is the state's law "right" or "wrong" in terms of ethical values?

There is no question about what Nozick's position would be. Smith's land is not just property. It is a distinct moral value. It should not be subjected to any constraints whatsoever, under any circumstances.

Rawls would have much less trouble than his colleague. And utilitarians would be in a dither trying to figure out the benefits of condominiums versus the deprivations of this particular commercialization (and what time line do we calculate the greater good on, and which side benefits, say, from a utilitarian view that calculates on the long term?).

How do *you* feel this case ought to be decided?

1. Tough luck for Smith. All things considered, he *is* left with his land. Now it's restricted use, that's all. He has to bow to a very important public interest.
2. The state should pay Smith $1,000,000 and own his land.
3. The state should pay Smith $1,000,000 plus his reasonably anticipated profit calculated at present value (based upon his completed plan).

Now: *Who are the parties in interest* in terms of *each* of these three solutions? Are they the same parties in each case? For example, do *all* citizens (and animals) affected by wetlands commercialization figure in, group by group, in each of the three solutions?

Just *which values* are at issue?

Is it relevant that if the law were to favor decision 2, and surely 3, the U.S. Treasury might be out billions of dollars as the result of its own environmental laws, which affect lots of U.S. private property in similar ways? Are the feds then a party at interest? If so, what value is at stake (and "feds," of course, equals "taxpayers," equals *you*!).

Are we involved, in any event, with an ethical issue, or issues, or is this just a nonmoral value, strictly money-value issue?

It's a moral value issue, of course, and the U.S. Supreme Court isn't done with it yet. We'll discuss this further in Chapter 4.

Thus far, we have not provided you with the answer in any of the cases presented in this chapter to the question of which values, exactly, are at issue. Nor have we provided you with definitive "right" answers to the main issues set forth.

Now would be a good time to reveal to you the answer contained on the philosopher's stone: the formula for determining right from wrong in any given situation.

But we don't know what that formula could be. Neither does anyone else.

We are able, however, to reach the following conclusions relevant to weighing competing ethical values and to reaching helpful, meaningful decisions.

1. There *are* firm theoretical constructs available to help one recognize, and even assign weights to, competing ethical values. We have looked at philosophers from Buddha to Plato and Aristotle to Kant, Heisenberg, Bohr, Rawls, and others. One thing that we have seen, even in the economically sublime Adam Smith, is that much of what free-market supporters have accepted as empirical fact is, in fact, *based on moral constructs*. That does *not* render the constructs any less worthy of belief. It merely demonstrates that, in any given case, the constructs *are* theoretical (i.e., scientifically not proven) but utterly weighable on any scale of important values. Which leads into a second conclusion.

2. In actual practice, it pays to assume that there are no *absolute* values. Once recognized for what they are, they merit weighing, albeit that some values are clearly far heavier than others. Americans, for example, are properly protective of their right to "free" speech. But free speech is not an absolute value. No one in America has a right to yell "fire" in a crowded theater when there is no fire, or otherwise use words in such circumstances, and of such a nature, as to constitute "a clear and present danger" that such words will bring about such evil as the government has a right to prevent.[91] Does this mean that in "a clear and present danger" case, the right to free speech disappears? Not at all. It merely means that it is outweighed by more important (weightier under the circumstances) value considerations.

---

[91] Per Justice O.W. Holmes in the famous *Schenck* case, 249 U.S. 47 (1919).

3. In the end, weighing competing values and reaching decisions are subjective processes, and no one can relieve you of personal responsibility.

What we want this book to do is to nourish your subjectivity with value data, and with insights into thinking about value data to the degree that yours will be the subjectivity of a truly aware and thoughtful person.

We will have many more occasions to sharpen our weighing powers.

In Chapter 2 we shall encounter cost and access to health care issues that will lead us to weigh free market versus government health care considerations. In Chapter 3 we will look, among other things, at product liability damage issues that will lead us to weigh our common-law court system against strict government intervention in the product harm area. In Chapter 5 we will direct our attention to the issue of value weighting toward the goal of determining the very nature of the manager/company fiduciary relationship. And these are just a few examples of finding and weighing values; others will be confronted in the area of S&L's, commercial and investment banker duties (and to whom), junk bond and Chapter 11 bankruptcy dealings, and pension investing, which, in the United States, is a trillion (plus) dollar business.

Join us now in a brief exercise in value weighting that we believe will have to be engaged in by heads of state and international governing bodies—under the most excruciating circumstances—well into the twenty-first century.

As the year 1992 drew to a close, communism, while presenting lingering dangers at least on a national basis, was no longer a direct threat to international peace. But in its place a dreadfully destabilizing element appeared on the world scene: the inability of sovereign nations to sustain themselves as members of the international community.[92]

We saw the examples of Somalia, the former Yugoslavia (Bosnia and Serbia), the Sudan and Liberia, shaky regimes in parts of Central America, and Haiti in the Caribbean. Throughout the world, starvation and other forms of suffering and death gave evidence of spreading instability, violence, even anarchy, all demanding an utterly awesome weighing of competing values and a response by stable, industrialized nations—and particularly by the United States of America.

One question, with regard to terrible mass starvation in Somalia and to "ethnic cleansing" genocide in Bosnia, is: Is intervention into the internal affairs of another nation warranted?

---

[92] Cf. E. Sciolino, "Getting in Is the Easy Part of the Mission." *The New York Times*, December 6, 1992, citing in part Helman and Ratner in the December 1992 issue of *Foreign Policy*.

Do note that, in the last several decades at least, freedom from foreign intervention in one nation's internal affairs has been a powerful, generally accepted "right" (value).

Weight here is obviously shifting.

As this book goes to press, the United States with a bit of help from some other nations, is intervening in Somalia in order to guarantee humanitarian food distribution to hundreds of thousands of Somalis starving in a country ruled by thugs with weapons, engaged in genocidal, personal power struggles. By entering into this anarchic situation, what foreign policy has been thus established? Is there now to be a new American "doctrine" (as, for example, the Monroe Doctrine), to be enacted over the next several decades regarding this new world phenomenon: the national state engaged in some fashion in the destruction of its own population?

We are fearful lest any such doctrine be set in stone. If it were to be, the best interests of the United States and of the world would be imperiled. If any "doctrine" of any kind must be called upon in all cases, we would suggest the following one:

> The United States of America, on an international level, is committed to consider and to weigh the interests of all parties involved in our decision making on the issue of intervention, and to weighing competing interests with due regard to the rights and needs of all people and groups affected, but with our initial focus being on our own citizens.

There is no other way to decide, in 1993, what to do about anarchy and starvation in Somalia and, in succeeding years, about genocide in the former Yugoslavia, or mass starvation, anarchy, violent destructive civil war, or aggression, by some other "sovereign" nation.

Of course, the interests of its own citizens will always be paramount in the mind of any potential intervenor government, but these interests will have to be considered, on a case by case basis, in conjunction with the interests of those affected by the decision. The international community must certainly be aided by existing laws, treaties, organizations, and processes, but the reality is that decisions to intervene or not to intervene in the internal situation in another nation will, ultimately, be ethical-value weighted, and the ultimate decision will be moral as well as political.

Some may have the luxury of denying that, but the president of the United States, the chancellor of Germany, the premier of France, and the prime ministers of many countries cannot afford to be among them. The real-world importance of the morality of nations is assuming obvious and awesome proportions in our time.

The decision by the United States to intervene in Somalia, one would assume, was based on weighing such ethical concerns as these:

- The suffering and starvation of hundreds of thousands, if not millions, of human beings who, not incidentally, are black Africans, a group whose worth as human beings has been consistently devalued (by the leadership in Africa, as well as the rest of the world).

- The cost to American citizens in both lives and economic resources. The needs of our own people, many of whom lack proper health care, housing, jobs and decent education, many of whom are themselves objects of violence—these needs are of substantial ethical import and have a moral claim on the nation's political and economic resources.

- The chances for operational success in the undertaking. And "operational success" requires distinct objective and time lines to be considered—and alternatives as well. If the objective is to assure distribution of food supplies for as long as necessary to ensure the end of mass starvation, that is one thing. Assuming the authority of—or setting up—a functioning government has massive implications. One thing, however, is certain: Using the utmost care in determining the risks of failure is an ethical imperative in terms of what "failure" would mean to many human beings.

- The role others *must* play if operational success is to be attained. A conclusion here apart from Somalia might well be that if, for example, the European Community (EC) must undertake responsibility for something other than its own immediate economic development and will not, distinct consequences follow to everyone from such EC value choices, including Bosnians and Serbians.

Our list above may be insufficient, misdirected, or both. No matter, this is not a book on foreign policy, and value lists can be made by many others. However, at the risk of redundancy, we raised the international issue to illustrate the relevance—at an obviously different level—of these three points previously discussed:

1. That in the (managerial) decision-making process, the universe of parties at interest, in terms of their being affected by the decision, must be determined broadly.
2. That those interests must be given a place on the value scale and weighed with utmost care.

3. That no single value is absolute and may be sacrificed, in any *one* particular case, through the recognition that no single value utterly forecloses consideration of some other under specific conditions (for example, the duty of a manager may not, under all conceivable circumstances, be solely to enrich shareholders now, in the greatest degree possible, as long as no laws are actually broken in the process).

This is not the same thing, by the way, as saying that there is no value in categorical imperatives. It is only to argue that they are *points of departure* one should consider seriously. They are not, in and of themselves, *decisions*.

We are going to proceed now to a larger case we have devised, which should help serve as a linkage between the ethical theory portion of this book, and the world of free-market operations we intend to highlight. Our *Case of the Irradiated Veterans* presents directly, for the first but not the last time in this book, a confrontation between individual rights and economic efficiency.

However, before we get into this hypothetical case, allow us to address what must be your intense frustration with not having been provided with either formulas or specific answers related to the various conundrums we have presented. We shall let the great American philosopher and educator John Dewey speak on our behalf:

> . . . it is not the business of moral theory to provide a ready-made solution to large moral perplexities. . . . The solution has to be reached by action based on personal choice. . . [but] theory can enlighten and guide choice and action by. . . bringing to light what is entailed when we choose one alternative rather than another. . . . [T]he function of theory is not to furnish a substitute for personal reflective choice but to be an instrument for rendering deliberation more effective and hence choice more intelligent.[93]

III. THE IRRADIATED VETERANS CASE

Case data: In 1864, the United States government pension plan system for Union Army soldiers allowed veterans to employ attorneys to represent them in their claims for disability benefits before the appropriate admin-

---

[93] John Dewey (1859-1952), *Ethics* (New York: Henry Holt & Co., rev. ed., 1932). Reprinted in J. Ratner, ed., *Intelligence in the Modern World: John Dewey's Philosophy* (New York: Modern Library, 1939), pp. 762-63).

istrative body (i.e., on such issues as whether they truly were disabled and/or whether a given disability was actually related to their military service). However, the Act of Congress (the *statute* or *law*) allowing for this legal representation limited the amount lawyers could charge a veteran for their services. Legal fees were limited to $10 per case, paid by the veteran.

This law has not been changed at any time. It is still the law!

Presently, only some 2 percent of veterans who are disability claimants have legal representation. Assistance provided to some others comes in the form of unpaid, non-legally trained veterans' organization advisors.

The benefits that flow to a veteran and to his family, if he or she can prove that a given disability is service connected rather than nonservice connected, are enormous. Disability payments for life, priority treatment in already overcrowded VA hospitals, and possible death benefits to the surviving spouse and children are some examples. These services and benefits do, of course, cost the government (us) a good deal of money—many billions of dollars.

Please assume that last year a group of individual claimants (veterans), and veterans' organizations, came together as the National Radiation Victims Association (NRVA). The NRVA seeks service-connected disability benefits from the Department of Veterans Affairs (DVA) for serious injuries to them allegedly caused by service-related exposure to nuclear radiation. NRVA argues that providing service connection here requires them to relate to a series of complex issues and proofs (such as medico-legal causal relationships) that can only be presented adequately by trained legal advocates able to marshal evidence and to engage in relevant litigation processes (such as direct and cross examination of expert medical and other witnesses). They cite an undisputed statement by the DVA itself that "the $10 fee limitation effectively precludes attorney representation before us."

NRVA has already brought suit against the DVA in U.S. district court to enjoin (stop) the DVA from enforcing the $10 legal fee cap. That court has issued a temporary injunction preventing the DVA from enforcing that cap. The DVA appeal has now reached the United States Supreme Court.

Putting aside some complex jurisdictional issues better left to law professors to litigate intellectually, there surely are some substantive issues amenable to an economic, legal, policy, and ethics focus by us:

The Basic Argument for the DVA: The United States Congress passed, and has never seen fit to change, the $10 law that is at issue here. The Supreme Court is obliged to attach great weight to the enormous government interest that is at stake. That interest is in operating and maintaining an effective cost-efficient system for handling disputed claims. The DVA operates more than 500 hospitals, outpatient clinics, and nursing homes at a cost of billions of dollars, and monthly payments already being made to veterans with service-connected disabilities costs billions more. Eliminating the fee cap would mean opening the flood gates to such lengthy procedures as are already overwhelming the civil courts, and to higher and higher costs of all kinds and in many areas. The $10 law at issue here is an expression of the majority will of the people (through Congress) and no nonelected judicial body (court) should be allowed to interfere with it. This 1864 law is still valid and must be enforced.

The Basic Argument for the NRVA: This case must rest upon a consideration of individual rights, not systemic, economic efficiencies. We veterans are being deprived, in effect, of our basic First Amendment constitutional right to petition the government for redress. The right to employ counsel, at one's own expense, is a right of every citizen. To deny us that right to counsel is to deny us due process within the meaning of the Fifth Amendment. There is no dispute about the fact that the $10 cap has extinguished our right to have a lawyer represent us. The real issue here is whether the Supreme Court will affirm the right for us, or whether the court will assign the case a purely material value and balance things out solely on some economic scale of costs and benefits. Surely, an 1864 law never contemplated such a complex legal system as exists in America today, where the full participation of lawyers, doctors, scientists and others is necessary if we are to search out truthful answers to complex questions involving; for example, nuclear radiation. Time has rendered this 1864 law obsolete. It should be held to be unconstitutional.

Assume now that both Mr. Chief Justice Rehquist's law clerk, and Mr. Justice Blackmun's law clerk, have sought advice from you, as a member of the National Court of Interdisciplinary Advisors, and that they expect you to tell them in detail what you think the result should be here—and why.

1. You might want to begin your economic analysis of this situation by asking what specific markets seem to be involved here, defining a market by the good or service being exchanged for money, or the promise of money.

2. Is there factual information you would like to have that you do not have now? If so, why do you feel you need it (e.g., on total DVA annual costs)?

3. What "rights" do you feel are involved in this case? Should it be proper for judges to rely upon the "economics" of a given situation being litigated when coming to an opinion? Or should they rely only upon "law" or legal "rights" of some sort (or of various sorts)?

Are there "rights" so important that money and markets are totally irrelevant to their existence (and enforcement)? Can "economic" costs be so great that "rights" would have to give way in the face of financial and/or market ruin? How should the boundary line be drawn, in any case, between the domain of "rights" and the domain of "efficient markets" and dollars? Is *that* an ethical issue?

4. One specific question raised in this case, which is related to current general debate on the role of law in American society, is this: If the "cap" law ($10.00) was not in violation of a citizen's constitutional right in 1864, how can it be today? The First and Fifth Amendments have not been changed, nor has "the intent of the Founding Fathers," since they've been dead a very long time.

5. Whatever your opinion in this case might be (i.e., your "answer"), do you consider that opinion to be *legally* correct, or *morally* correct, or both? Do you believe now, in *any* case, that the result can be legally correct and at the same time morally deficient? Could legality be the automatic determinant of what is ethical for you this far into the game?

This case is based upon a real one decided by the United States Supreme Court. Justices were able to avoid an actual decision on the constitutional issues since they were only facing the injunction question; however, they discussed all issues heatedly, and, as heatedly, disagreed.

There is another important issue here: Under our American system, do these veterans have any recourse outside the courtroom to what they perceive as "justice"? Does not the answer to that question depend on the fact that we Americans do live under a tripartite, checks and balances system that involves three distinct branches of government? For those of you puzzled about this issue, be of good cheer: We'll highlight it for you in Chapter 6 where we discuss Regulation.

Finally, if you feel at a disadvantage for not being a constitutional scholar, be advised of the opinion of a brilliant constitutional lawyer (stated in print) that, in fact, "laymen often know more constitutional law than they think they do, and lawyers often know less."[94]

References

Crane Brinton, *A History of Western Morals* (New York: Harcourt Brace, 1959).

Edmund Cahn, *The Moral Decision: Right and Wrong in American Law* (Indiana University Press, 1956).

---

[94] Charles P. Curtis, *Lions Under the Throne* (Boston: Houghton Mifflin, 1947).

Benjamin Cardozo, *The Nature of the Judicial Process* (New Haven Conn.: Yale University Press, 1921).

Ronald Dworkin, *Law's Empire* (Cambridge, Mass.: Belknap-Harvard University Press, 1986).

H.L.A. Hart, *The Concept of Law* (Oxford, England: Oxford University Press, 1961).

Robert Heilbroner, *An Inquiry into the Human Prospect* (New York: W.W. Norton, paperback, 1980).

Louis Lombardi, *Moral Analysis: Foundation Guides and Applications* (Albany, N.Y.: SUNY Press, 1988).

George W. Paton, *Jurisprudence* (Oxford, England: Oxford University Press, 1964).

Roscoe Pound, *An Introduction to the Philosophy of Law* (New Haven, Conn.: Yale University Press, 1922).

John Rawls, *A Theory of Justice* (Cambridge, Mass.: Harvard/Oxford, 1971).

Monroe Beardsley, ed., *The European Philosophers From Descartes to Nietzche* (New York: Modern Library, 1960).

Edwin Burtt, ed., *The English Philosophers From Bacon to Mill* (New York: Modern Library, 1939).

Timothy Ferris, ed., *The World Treasury of Physics, Astronomy and Mathematics* (Boston: Little, Brown, 1991).

Great Books, Volume 56 (2d edition, 1990): *20th Century Natural Science*.

Morganbesser and Walsh, eds., *Free Will* (Englewood Cliffs, N.J.: Prentice Hall/Spectrum, 1962).

Lin Yutang, ed., *The Wisdom of China and India* (New York: Modern Library, 1955).

Each of the following articles is contained in one or another of the annual volumes of *The Great Ideas Today* (Britannica Great Books), so that the following citations are to the relevant year of publication: Daniel Bell, "The Social Sciences Since World War II, Part Two" (1980); Otto Bird, "Ethics in a Permissive Society: The Controversy Regarding the Objectivity of Moral Values" (1981); N. David Mermin, "Spooky Actions at a Distance: Mysteries of the Quantum Theory" (1988).

See the outstanding article, "Ethics" by Peter Singer, contained in the *Encyclopedia Britannica* (15th edition, 1991, Vol. 18), pp.492-521.

2

Diagnosing and Treating Market Inadequacies

COMING UP IN THIS CHAPTER

We will begin each succeeding chapter in this book with a brief preview of its particular focus along with some comment on the specific materials it contains. We realize that there will be both intrachapter and interchapter shifts in disciplinary emphasis within the text—from the economic to the legal to the political to the ethical, and back again—and we want you to have some guideposts for this interdisciplinary journey.

We will end each succeeding chapter with a brief focus on ethical issues related to the chapter materials.

Please keep in mind that whether you are focusing on law cases, or economic/financial materials, or pursuing issues of right and wrong—or all three seemingly at once!—the goal is always the same: to further the development of analytical skills that will help you to focus clearly upon the key ethical, legal, and public-policy perspectives inherent in major free market problem areas. Another goal is to encourage you to contribute to the formation of creative, fair, and productive solutions to these problems as you prepare for, and engage in, a fully satisfying professional career.

This chapter begins by examining briefly the broad issue of *market failure*, in terms of causes and effects. It is the reality of market failure that gives rise, in great measure, to outside-the-market interference. The law, whether it comes in the form of case decisions or legislation or both, is very often a direct response to perceived market failures.

What we should like to do here is provide sufficient insight into the market-failure phenomenon as will enable us to deal with three major issues related to the efficient functioning of the specific free market areas being examined:

1. How does one determine that a market failure has in fact occurred?
2. Are outside-the-market forces needed to deal with the specific problems presented?
3. What steps should such forces (usually law) take in order to help correct the failure and not simply make matters worse?

The second part of this chapter moves us into our first specific free market area: The United States health care system.

The "health care market" is, of course, an amalgam of many individual markets such as health care providers, medicine, equipment markets, and so forth (as outlined more fully later in the chapter). We begin with this particular market because health care and health costs are of such immediate and ongoing concern to every single American—as well as to every citizen of every nation throughout the world. And because the health care market, with all of its components, is such a curious and clearly unsatisfactory amalgam of economic competition, legal rules and regulations, and political wheeling and dealing—and consequent ethical concerns relating to awesome life and death issues—it is important to discuss it here.

We utilize narrative materials only here, and for two reasons: The first is that case law is not essential to a reasonably clear understanding of the basic free market/law/ethics issues raised and, secondly, we intend to present you with a rather more full and formal introduction to law and the legal system in Chapter 3.

I. THE MARKETS PERSPECTIVE

A "free" market is usually defined as one utterly undisturbed by government intervention, one where the forces of supply and demand are allowed to operate in total freedom.

No such market exists in this world, of course, even in the presence of government-sanctioned "deregulation."

What does exist, of course, are economic systems that, when compared, demonstrate clearly that some markets are less free (and less successful) than others.

Most individuals in the free enterprise system seem willing to accept this reality, albeit grudgingly and with a keen sense of government regulator malfeasance in the matter.

The "efficient" markets doctrine appears to be quite another story and goes far beyond narrow share-price and exchange-rate considerations. By and large, business persons appear to be convinced that the cleansing disciplines of the marketplace are, fundamentally, infallible, whether or not they subscribe specifically to the doctrine of the "invisible hand."

Broadly speaking, within the free enterprise system, efficient markets are thought of as fully competitive markets able to achieve an equilibrium allocation of resources that is Pareto optimal. Which is to say (following Italian economist and sociologist Wilfred Pareto, 1848-1923) that efficient markets do allocate resources and output in such a way that no reallocation can make anyone better off without making at least one other person worse off. Which is also to say that, if the Federal Reserve or some other suspect operator or operation (usually government) doesn't otherwise foul things up, markets will indeed be efficient and will prove the Doctor Pangloss doctrine correct: Whatever is, is right, in this best of all possible worlds.

In the case of free enterprise/efficient markets, the Doctor Pangloss doctrine is undoubtedly far closer to the truth than the Chicken Little theorem; however, neither deserves to be relied upon by anyone truly concerned about dealing constructively with our free enterprise system's actual market failures.[1]

The demonstrable truth is that, often enough, to be labeled significant, allocations achieved by free enterprise and free markets do not turn out to be "efficient": that is, our generally highly successful economic system indeed suffers from *market failures*.

The first of the two major issues to be faced is: What causes market failures? The second is, given market failures, How do we go about utilizing *nonmarket* components rationally and effectively to correct them—rather than making things even worse?

These issues are indeed practical ones, because if present and future business managers are to function in our society creatively and productively, they must learn to recognize, understand, assimilate, and deal responsibly with the key *nonmarket components* deeply affecting their market world. Two of these components are Law and Politics, and a third is Community Concern deep enough to lead to action enlisting each of the first two components.

Let us turn first to the causes of market failure.

It does not denigrate the enormous successes of our economic system to point out some of its more obvious failures. Many involve the social costs of production, such as environmental degradation. Others involve a growing disparity in the distribution of income and concomitant social and political suffering and strife. Then there are the anticompetitive, unfair advantage, and the misallocative effects of monopolistic practices.

---

[1] This is true despite the fact that in the case of non-free-enterprise, centralized, government-controlled, "planned" economies, the Chicken Little theorem seems to hold up. All of Eastern Europe, and the former Soviet Union itself, made this clear as the last decade of the twentieth century began!

Finally, it might be pointed out that we still operate a financial system that evidences, in some respects, disturbing volatility and instability.

One might state a complexity simply by saying that market failures result from a hole in the First Fundamental Theorem; that is, when (1) there are not enough markets and/or (2) when all consumers and producers do not behave competitively and/or (3) when equilibrium does not exist.[2]

However, it would seem more apt in this brief introduction to the issue of market failure to summarize major causes of failure in a less theoretical, formalized way, a way that emphasizes certain inadequacies inherent in particular market structures.[3]

Using this approach, we might think of four major areas of concern within markets: instability, maldistribution of income wealth and power, misallocation of resources, and moral hazard.

Instability concerns are closely related to two distinct phenomena: *lag time* and *perverse reactions*.

Lag time refers to the process whereby parties within the market system (e.g., producers) either miss or misinterpret what other people in the system (e.g., consumers) have already decided to do or to refrain from doing. The lag time required to bring market participants back in sync (e.g., a production-purchase equilibrium) will have evidenced market failure in terms of uncertainty, extra costs, and various types of participant hardship. Perverse reaction is in fact a "wrong direction" response to a market action; for example, a price rise normally expected to reduce overall demand and the quantity of goods offered for sale, depending on consumer reaction, could result in a longer than expected upward move in prices. In such a case, with the upward move feeding on itself, the ultimate downswing could be a real plunge. Such swings could be market disruptive and costly. Such volatility-producing mechanisms can be thought of as basic to a decentralized free market system, and instability might in some cases have to be resolved by the use of non market mechanisms.

Maldistribution of income does not refer to the fact that some people possess more money and goods than others. In a capitalist, free market society, entrepreneurship, creativity, and commitment to excellence are, and ought to be, the *sine qua non* of both personal and national growth and enrichment. However, when income, wealth and power are perceived by the body politic as being concentrated in far too few hands,

---

[2] See J. O. Ledyard (citing Arrow and Debreu) in *The New Palgrave Dictionary of Economics*, Vol. 3 (New York: The Stockton Press, 1987), pp. 326-28.

[3] The following discussion relies heavily on the approach of our colleague Robert Lindsey in his "Market Inadequacies and the Non-Market Context of Business Decisions" (Mimeo, N.Y.U. Graduate School of Business Administration, 1982). See also the interesting review of Robert Kuttner's *The End of Laissez-Faire* (New York: Knopf, 1991) by P. Krugman in *International Economic Insights* (July/August 1991), pp. 28-29.

either individual or corporate, steps will be taken to correct the perceived imbalance. The market itself cannot undo the concentrations produced; thus nonmarket interventions will be called into play.

Misallocation of resources is a broad term encompassing four distinct phenomena: *monopolies, public goods, externalities* and *informational deficiencies.*[4]

There are two kinds of *monopolies*, the "natural" monopoly created by market forces, and the monopoly gained through predatory actions (i.e., actions unrelated to the fact that technology may be such that the cheapest way in the long run to produce a given good is for only one firm to produce it). In either case, the monopolist, in the absence of any nonmarket intervention, may well set prices above marginal cost, causing fewer goods to be produced and consumed and, in general, failing to promote maximum allocative efficiency (i.e., producing a market failure).

There are also two kinds of *public goods*, the "pure" and the "mixed." The two characteristics of a pure public good (e.g., national defence) are: (1) the consumption of benefits by any one individual does not depend upon, or affect, the consumption of that same good by another individual (nonrival consumption), and (2) once provided, the good is beyond the producer's ability to deny anyone the right to consume it (nonexclusivity).[5]

Certainly, most public goods are not so pure. The second kind are referred to as "mixed," that is, one or the other of the two characteristics is absent. National park facilities are an example of rival consumption, as summertime visitors to, say, Yellowstone Park in the presence of congestion can testify. However, apart from the prohibition of offensive and disruptive behavior, nonexcludability does prevail.

The market cannot even attempt to provide the pure public good. And any attempt to provide the mixed public good would result in market failure, either because the good, in the end, will not be produced at all, or will be produced in suboptimal quantities. The answer, then, to the provision of these goods is nonmarket government action.

Externalities are phenomena indicative of market failure, which are best perceived when private and societal marginal costs and benefits diverge. While there are beneficial externalities incident to some market actions, the more common problem is the costly one where, for example, manufacturers spew toxic chemicals into lakes, streams, or the air. These

---

[4] These categories are laid out succinctly and well in Linda N. Edwards and Franklin R. Edwards, "Differential State Regulation of Consumer Credit Markets: Normative and Positive Theories of Statutory Interest Rate Ceilings" (Mimeo, 1978).

[5] Two brief articles by Paul Samuelson, both in *Review of Economics and Statistics*, serve as the fountainhead for modern thinking on public goods: "The Pure Theory of Public Expenditure" (November 1954), pp. 387-89; and "Diagrammatic Exposition of a Theory of Public Expenditure" (November 1955), pp. 350-56.

externalities in the strictest sense exist because there are really no markets at all for pure water and clean air, to use the same examples. And there is no way for the producer and consumer of toxic poisons to negotiate a truly mutually beneficial trade. In the end, it is the government that attends to market failure here, reducing transaction costs, and providing coercion—though it must be kept in mind that the type and extent of proper nonmarket intervention is hardly a settled matter.

Many market failures can be related either to *imperfect* or *costly information*, or both. It has been pointed out that information possesses, in some form, one or both of the dual characteristics of public goods set forth earlier. The government may therefore, in certain cases, have to assume the responsibility of collecting, evaluating, or dispensing it. Government may also undertake to regulate the quality of producers and the flow of information between buyers and sellers—for example, by requiring professional and corporate licensing and certification procedures as well as by "truth in advertising" standards.[6] Government may intervene with severe sanctions to correct a perceived market failure, even at the cost of short-term efficiency—for example, in the case of certain uses of insider information where the market failure is perceived as causing a crisis of confidence in the operations of the market itself.

The subject of insider information gives rise to the fourth major area of concern within markets, namely the *moral hazard* issue. Narrowly and technically defined, this term is held to relate to "the effect of certain types of insurance systems in causing a divergence between the private marginal cost of some action and the marginal social cost of that action, thus resulting in an allocation of resources which is not optimal."[7]

In truth, however, beyond insurance factors alone, we are in the presence here of human behavior that, from the legal or the ethical point of view—or both—causes market failures in the form of everything from unjust personal enrichment to massive public costs and the destruction of public trust. We will be examining the pervasive influence of "moral hazard" in various types of market problems through this book.

We conclude this brief foray into the market failure area by emphasizing the fact that it is dangerous to insist upon a too strict adherence to the efficient markets paradigm. This can lead to that lack of overall perspective which has caused some laypersons to characterize economists as those professionals who know the cost of everything, and the value of nothing.

And surely, *both* costs and values must be kept firmly in mind as we pursue answers to a major issue set forth in the preview section of the

---

[6] Edwards and Edwards, note 4, *supra*.

[7] D. W. Pierce, ed., *The MIT Dictionary of Modern Economics*, 3d ed. (Cambridge, Mass: M.I.T. Press, 1986), p. 287.

chapter: Given market failures, how do we go about utilizing nonmarket components rationally and effectively to correct them—rather than making things even worse?

II. THE INVISIBLE HAND AND HEALTH CARE

A. Is There a "Right" To Health Care?

Balancing economic efficiency concerns with the demands of sociopolitical rights is a constant source of tension in a capitalist democracy. Nowhere is that tension more apparent or more productive of confusion than in that group of markets we refer to collectively as "the health care system." In regard to these markets, the word "free" presents some truly troublesome issues.

A basic economic concern in the area is whether *health* is in fact like any other commodity. In a 1987 article in *The American Economic Review*, the authors of the article stated: "Our answer to this question is an unwavering 'yes' and 'no'." The authors examined health in relation to standard economic frames of reference: wealth, time preference, risk aversion, efficient transfers, and utility. However, they also took pains to point out the importance of the "symbolic aspects of health," stating that "many of the most fundamental beliefs of our society are wrapped up in the valuation of lives and health."[8]

One of the most thoughtful and outspoken of all health economists, Professor Uwe Reinhardt, has urged that

> Although the prism of standard neoclassical economics can highlight a good many of the relationships among actors in the health care sector, our profession's valiant attempts to force all of the health care process onto the Procrustean bed of that theory actually runs the risk of professional malpractice. *Normative* health economics, in particular, is so fraught with potential abuse... that one must wonder whether economists as social *scientists* ought to engage in it at all. If they do, they should forever be mindful of society's concern over distributional equity, which does set health care apart from most other commodities. "Greater efficiency" in abstraction from that concern is simply an oxymoron.[9]

---

[8] Fuchs and Zeckhauser, "Valuing Health: A Priceless Commodity," *The American Economic Review* (May 1987).

[9] U. E. Reinhardt, "Economists in Health Care: Saviors or Elephants in a Porcelain Shop?" *The American Economic Review* (May 1989).

One must ask at the outset whether there is an enforceable, clearly articulated "right" of people to professional health care in America. The answer, practically speaking, would seem to be that if there is, it is legally undefined, and surely subject to limits.

The right to some basic set of health care services is not to be found, explicitly, in the Constitution. But then neither was the right of *all* American children to attend nonsegregated public schools which the Supreme Court articulated in *Brown v. Board of Education* in 1954.[10] (This despite the seeming denial of the existence of that right by a different Supreme Court in 1896.)[11] Of course, the *Brown* case involved state actions taken to deny black children the right to attend white schools, and those actions were properly held to violate the Fourteenth Amendment. In the case of health care the question more likely would be whether *not* taking action to provide basic health care to every citizen (however *basic* might be defined) is a violation of the Fifth (due process) Amendment.[12]

It could be argued that the right of all established citizens of the United States to their continued survival (*life*) is to be found in the Declaration of Independence, and is likewise a fundamental right guaranteed by the Constitution.[13] If so, one would have a "right" to health care at the very least calculated to keep one alive and fit to exercise one's liberty and to allow for the pursuit (if not the attainment) of happiness.

Apart from the Constitution, it has been argued quite forcefully that there is a common-law right to "equal services," that is, a right of equal access to "basic services"—such as drinking water, for example—and further, that this right extends to all citizens, and is beyond the reach of the market.[14] Health care would certainly seem to be such a basic service.

Clearly, government has already conferred upon some of the citizenry certain specific health *benefits* (e.g., through the Medicare-Medicaid laws). However, such laws have left unresolved many basic health care concerns such as access, extent of service, and quality of care.

In sum, while Americans, on the whole , seem to believe that there is (or ought to be) some "right" to decent medical care, both the nature and the extent of that right are most assuredly fuzzy. The late Arthur Okun, a highly respected economist, once wrote that that right "has been kept fuzzy because it...could be very expensive. A formal and clear commitment that individuals could count on would increase the number that called for help."[15]

---

[10] *Brown* v. *Board of Education*, 347 U.S. 483 (1954).

[11] *Plessy* v. *Ferguson*, 163 U.S. 537 (1896).

[12] Cf. *Bolling* v. *Sharpe*, 347 U.S. 497 (1954).

[13] Cf. Justice Bradley's dissent in *The Slaughterhouse Cases*, 83 U.S. (16 Wall) 36 (1873).

[14] Haar and Fessler, *The Wrong Side of the Tracks* (New York: Simon and Schuster, 1986).

[15] Arthur M. Okun, *Equality and Efficiency: The Big Trade Off* (Washington D.C.: The Brookings Institution, 1975), p. 18. See also N. J. Aaron, "The Right to Health Care Has Its

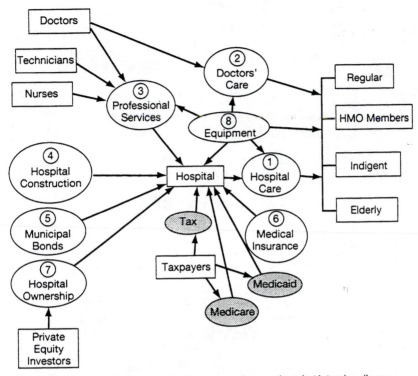

FIGURE 2.1 Some major health care markets and market interplay. (Larry Bear, Rita Maldonado-Bear, and Robert Lindsay, 1991).

In the remainder of this chapter, we will examine some economic, political, and legal aspects of our health care markets in the hope of at least understanding those public-policy choices any democratic citizenry is morally bound to make.

B. Major Markets and an Initial Look at Costs

The health care market is really a composite of many submarkets interacting in a sometimes complex manner. Figure 2-1 is an illustration of some of the major submarkets of participants and their interactions.

Figure 2-2 shows the level of health care costs in the United States and how these costs are financed. It also presents a staggering estimate of where U.S. health care costs could be when the twenty-first century dawns.

Limits," *The Wall Street Journal*, September 17, 1992.

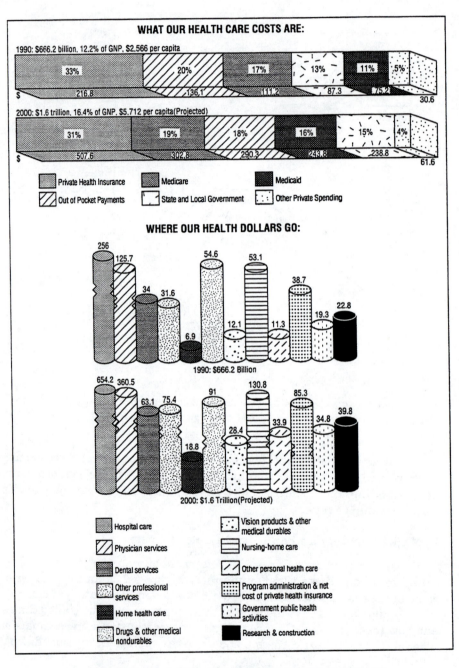

FIGURE 2.2 What our health care costs and where our health dollars go. (Rashi Fein, M.D., "Prescription for Change," *Modern Maturity* (August, September, 1992), pp. 33, 35.)

Medicare and Medicaid, whose costs seem to be soaring beyond the reach of the law of gravity, may be defined briefly as follows.

Medicare mainly covers the elderly, although some nonelderly disabled persons are included as well. There are two parts to the system. These include hospital insurance (HI) for patient care, which is financed by the Social Security Trust Fund and supplementary medical insurance (SMI), whose funds are made up of 75 percent U.S. Treasury general funds (tax dollars) and 25 percent Social Security recipient contributions (automatic deductions from monthly retirement checks).

Medicaid mainly covers low-income people, children and mothers on welfare, and some disabled. The individual states operate Medicaid, rather than the federal government, and the states share the costs on a 57 percent (federal) to 43 percent (state and local) basis. Straight tax dollars are used to support the program, and though formulas are complicated, it is clear that, as a group, the 50 states put up some $32 billion annually. The portion of state budgets dedicated to Medicaid had surpassed 10 percent as of 1990, to which must be added other health (e.g., hospital and clinic) costs.

It would seem safe to predict that escalating Medicare/Medicaid expenditures are such as to cast doubt on the long-term survivability of the federal government's smoke and mirrors game, whereby Social Security surpluses are juggled to make the national debt look less onerous. In their 1988 report, the trustees of the Social Security System, utilizing four different future gross national product/consumer price index scenarios, concluded that the Medicare HI fund, after the year 2000, is expected, at best, to be financially precarious. At worst, it is expected to run deep deficits. In such a case if the Congress authorizes one trust fund to borrow from another—as it has in the past—the national debt sleight-of-handers will have to move to the back of the line. It should be noted here as well that, by the end of the present century, the federal tax/Social Security recipient-funded Medicare SMI future is equally clouded. The same 1988 Trustee's Report noted that

> Growth rates have been so rapid that outlays of the program have doubled in the last five years. For the same time period, the program grew 40 percent faster than the economy as a whole. This growth rate shows no sign of abating despite recent efforts to control the costs of the program.[16]

---

[16] Cited in J.M. Auerbach, "No Social Security Bonanza for the Federal Deficit," *The Wall Street Journal*, August 9, 1988. And there is the added drain on the Social Security system of disability insurance payments to the disabled, which are running at some $31 billion annually. See C.L. Weaver, "Disability Insurance's Crippling Costs," *The Wall Street Journal*, June 23, 1992.

Concern about soaring Medicare/Medicaid costs is compounded by this fact: Despite the billion dollar outlays, both the availability and quality-of-care aspects of our overall health care system still leave much to be desired for a great many of our fellow citizens.[17]

C. Viewing Three Key Markets

1. Hospitals: Profits, Losses, and Quality Care

There are some 6,000 profit and not-for-profit hospitals in the United States. Actually, a good many of the not-for-profits, which are tax exempt charitable trusts, have always been business oriented to a substantial degree and have often earned profits. Legitimate question can surely be raised as to whether such hospitals have been meeting their social obligations, that is, providing adequate services for the poor who cannot afford to pay full, or any, costs.[18] For-profits generally claim that they are in a different category and should not be held to the standard of a voluntary charitable trust. To a degree, they are legally correct, but in this matter of the "commodity" health care, there ought to be a very clear difference between embracing a lower standard of care than one's competitors, and refusing to embrace any acceptable standard at all.

This is not to say that, as a group, for-profit hospitals in fact claim an exemption from service provision to the indigent and/or to the under- and uninsured. The fact is, however, that both profit and not-for-profit hospitals in America have not, on the whole, had a sterling record in this regard.

While most Americans may not be aware of it, there is a 1986 federal law against refusing help to sick patients coming into any hospital, and against transferring them out to public hospitals, *for solely economic reasons.*[19] The law also prohibits admitting patients and then discharging them before they are "stabilized." Stabilization, it would appear, has a vastly different meaning when applied to nonpaying, rather than paying, patients.

---

[17] This is true inside as well as outside Medicare/Medicaid. Even for the very poorest Americans, qualifying for Medicaid benefits is based as much on a family's location as it is on a family's need. In New York, a family of three is eligible for Medicaid ("medically needy") with a monthly income below $725. In Georgia, the monthly income must be below $308. See E. Kolbert, "New York's Medicaid Costs Surge, But Health Care for the Poor Lags," *The New York Times*, April 14, 1991.

[18] Rosemary Stevens's *In Sickness and in Wealth: American Hospitals in the Twentieth Century* (New York: Basic Books, 1989) is a report on hospitals that is well worth reading.

[19] The law bars the rejection or "inappropriate transfer" of any patient seeking emergency care. Hospitals and doctors violating the law face suspension or exclusion from the Medicare program, civil penalties of up to $50,000 per incident, and civil lawsuits. See A.D. Marcus, "Law on Treating Poor Patients Faces Key Tests," *The Wall Street Journal*, May 2, 1991.

In Chicago [indigent] patients considered to be "stable" and thus transferrable included a gunshot victim bleeding profusely from the brain and a man who had fallen from a third story window.[20]

Part of the problem is lax enforcement and, as a result, states themselves are beginning to put antidumping laws into effect.

However, a major part of the problem of hospital care for the indigent surely is that many providers are in serious financial straits continuously. Others have to be fearful that if they were to obey the law fully—or be forced to—they would soon bankrupt themselves.

Moreover, as states, the federal government, and private insurance companies move toward more stringent price and quality controls, it will be ever more difficult for hospitals to recover the costs of indigent care by passing them along *indirectly* to paying customers. Finally, Medicaid limits are not being applied only to billings: Limits are also being applied to potentially billable patients. As the nation approached the decade of the 1990s, more than 60 percent of all *poor* Americans did not qualify for the Medicaid program.[21]

All in all, the decade of the 1980s saw a rise of some 125 percent in hospital losses resulting from care provided to indigent patients: from $2.8 billion in 1980 to $7 billion in 1986, adjusted for inflation. And these losses were felt the most in small community hospitals in the nation's inner cities where the need for services has always been, and will continue to be, the most desperate.[22]

State government and local government hospital and clinic costs (see Figure 2-2) are particularly susceptible to upward pressures in an era where both the abuse of drugs and the rapid spread of sexually transmitted diseases such as AIDS combine to put even more pressure on an already overstressed system. Figure 2-3 is illustrative of one major type of inner-city drug abuse problem that results in escalating health system costs: drug-abusing, mainly noninsured, mothers giving birth to low birthweight babies, each of whom requires highly specialized, very costly, pediatric in-hospital care merely to survive. Thus, this figure is illustrative of maternal costs mainly for the uninsured. Recent data from a study by

---

[20] C. Ansberry, "Dumping the Poor: Despite Federal Law, Hospitals Still Reject Sick Who Can't Pay," *The Wall Street Journal*, November 29, 1988. See also D. Himmelstein and others, "Patient Transfers: Medical Practice as Social Triage," *American Journal of Public Health* (May 1984).

[21] C. Ansberry, "Dumping the Poor."

[22] I. Wilkerson's "Small Inner City Hospitals in U.S. Face Threat of Financial Failure," *The Wall Street Journal*, August 21, 1988, includes the financial data cited. See also H. Stout, "Public Hospitals Are Overloaded, Survey Shows," *The Wall Street Journal*, January 30, 1991.

Deborah Chollet of the Center for Risk Management and Insurance Research at Georgia State University indicates that U.S. companies and their employees pay out more than $5.5 billion each year to care for babies born prematurely or with other complications to *insured* mothers! In severe cases, medical costs for the infant alone were $70,000 as against the normal newborn's $1,250.[23]

Beyond costs alone, the health care system faces serious hospital quality-of-product concerns. The American Hospital Association and several other medical groups combined many years ago to form a Joint Commission on the Accreditation of Health Care Organizations—including one on hospitals (JCAH). Accreditation from JCAH results, for one thing in automatic federal eligibility for the receipt of Medicare money. The work of the JCAH is in many ways valuable. However, it has come under very strong criticism for accrediting some hospitals of very poor quality. This may be due partly to the fact that it has based accreditation on certain prescribed standards rather than actual performance in the provision of health care.[24]

It is beyond doubt that the best hospitals in the United States provide medical services—and research and training—that are the envy of the world. But it would be less than honest to omit the fact that the decade of the 1990s dawned with a study by the Harvard School of Public Health, based on extensive review of patient records in 51 private, non-profit, and government hospitals, that raises serious concerns. The study concluded that over 90,000 people in hospitals in New York State in 1984 were injured in connection with the care they received, and that 7,000 of them actually died as the result of in-hospital negligence. The chief scientist on the study said that its findings broadly reflected the situation in hospitals throughout the United States. And the New York State Commissioner of Health is quoted as commenting: "One cannot help but conclude that the current [hospital] system is failing. Without major reform, the system will continue to fail."[25]

One question clearly presents itself here from an economics/policy perspective: Does the answer to hospital care market cost and quality problems lie in the self-correcting mechanisms of a purely competitive free market process?

---

[23] See report in R. Winslow, "Infant Health Problems Cost Business Billions," *The Wall Street Journal*, May 1, 1992.

[24] An interesting article cataloguing concerns about JCAH is W. Bogdanich, "Prized by Hospitals, Accreditation Hides Perils Patients Face," *The Wall Street Journal*, October 12, 1988.

[25] Study results and quotes from R. Winslow, "Malpractice Study Finds 7,000 Died in New York in 1984 Due to Negligence," *The Wall Street Journal*, March 1, 1990. See also *Health Care: Initiatives in Hospital Risk Management*, (Washington, D.C.: General Accounting Office, July 1989).

TABLE 1 Maternal Drug Usage Reported on Birth Certificates New York City, 1980–1988 *(Rate per 1,000 Live Births)*.

	Any Mention on Confidential Medical Section of Birth Certificate of		
	Cocaine	Heroin	Methadone
1980	1.0	2.3	4.0
1981	1.0	2.4	3.3
1982	1.7	2.7	3.5
1983	2.4	2.6	3.6
1984	4.3	2.5	3.5
1985	5.3	2.4	3.5
1986	11.2	3.0	3.4
1987	15.1	3.3	3.1
1988*	21.1	4.3	4.4

*Provisional

TABLE 2 Maternal Drug Usage and Low Birthweight New York City Birth Certificates. 1985–1987

Drug Exposure During Pregnancy	Percent of Infants with Birthweight Below 2500 Grams	Relative Risk
All drug-exposed births	34.0	3.8
Single agents		
Cocaine only	37.2	4.1
Heroin only	37.4	4.2
Methadone only	31.9	3.6
Marijuana only	14.5	1.6
Multiple agents		
Cocaine and heroin	38.6	4.3
Methadone and heroin	36.8	4.1
Cocaine and methadone	40.3	4.5
All births	9.0	1.0

*Reference group: all births

FIGURE 2.3 Drug Abuse as Related to Infant Birth Problems in New York City. (City Health Information, New York City Department of Health, September 1, 1989.)

To begin with, one might inquire into the relative efficiencies of for-profit versus not-for-profit hospitals. Debate in this area has been acrimonious, with contrary studies clearly demonstrating that each is more efficient than the other. However, a large 1989 study, based on data from 4.2 million Medicare patient admissions at 3,100 hospitals does seem to indicate strongly that for-profit hospitals do rank below not-for-profit hospitals in quality of patient care.[26]

---

[26] The study was published in the *New England Journal of Medicine* in December 1989 and is cited in R. Winslow, "Care May Lag at Hospitals Run for Profit" *The Wall Street Journal*, December 21, 1989.

What is not clear, in any event, is what is meant, precisely, by hospital "efficiency." Is it profit (or loss) per patient regardless of overall health care results? Is greater or lesser access to the hospital's services for a broad population to be part of the efficiency equation?

It does not render the economist's task any less complex to consider the fact that data, published in the *New England Journal of Medicine*, tends to demonstrate a positive correlation between increased government stringency in regulating hospital costs and higher in-patient mortality rates.[27] This does not argue against attempts to control costs; rather, it argues for a continuing focus at one and the same time on maintaining high standards of care.

Then, too, there would seem to be obvious dangers in allowing free hospital competition. One is a likely increase in hospital construction, and the necessity for maintaining market share would surely require redundant purchases of the very latest technology (e.g., magnetic resonance imaging machines at a million dollars or so apiece). And given the financial fragility of so many participant institutions, the possibility of competition leading to a large number of failures and/or mergers raises the specter of dangerous concentrations of power in the hospital market. That result would surely bring about troublesome cost, quality, and distributional equity problems.

Having raised several key issues in this first market area to give a beginning flavor to this complex health care brew, let us now consider policy—and ethical—issues raised by a second key health provider, physicians.

2. Doctors: Efficiency and Freedom

Directly rendered physician services account for some 20 percent of America's $600 billion annual health care bill. However, physicians as determiners of, and referrers to, a wide range of other *service* and *product markets* (i.e., hospital and pharmaceutical) must be understood as having a clear and substantial relationship to far more than $125 billion in health care expenditures.

For this reason alone (although there are certainly others) it is important to understand the role of the physician in our basically fee-for-service health care system, which, unlike many others in the world, is focused rather strongly on physician autonomy and patient freedom of choice.

This tradition of free choice of doctors is one of the strongest bases upon which is built the argument against a national health care plan for all Americans. Even under a private care system, however, it is important

---

[27] Study by S.M. Shortell and Dr. E.S.X. Hughes, cited in W.L. Wall, "Study Correlates Mortality Rates and State Rules," *The Wall Street Journal*, April 28, 1988.

to remember that as between this "seller" and this "consumer," "free choice" has its limitations. Patients do not generally have free choice when it comes to deciding upon their recommended course of treatment, their hospital, or their medication. Some patients might request a second opinion if surgery is ordered; others might be influenced by the particular hospital affiliation of the doctor; even more might request that the doctor allow the pharmacist to fill a prescription with a less expensive generic drug. But the reality of free choice for most patients is that it terminates for the most part once the initial choice of physician is made.

There is little doubt but that doctors (and other service providers such as hospitals) hold obvious informational advantages over patients owing to the highly specialized nature of their services and the uniquely dependent position of those individuals receiving such services. The issue raised by the existence of this patient informational deficiency is central to the resolution of most public-policy debates about "efficient" health care resource allocation: How much of our health care cost, quality, and availability problems arise not out of strict citizen health care need, but rather out of doctor (and perhaps other provider) -induced demand?

If demand, to any appreciable extent, *is* induced, regulatory controls would appear to be a rational policy focus. If, on the other hand, our system is populated by patients who are perfectly capable of enforcing discipline on professional providers, then free market competition and choice would appear to be as supportable with respect to health care as it is with automobiles.

On this central issue economists seem, once more, to disagree. One has even gone so far as to say that economists will *never* be able to resolve the demand creation/information imperfection question,[28] while another has pointed out that

> Pure belief has been able to triumph over data so far, because even highly sophisticated econometric methods ultimately cannot divine what proportion of observed utilization was simply *accepted* by sick patients (or their anxious relatives) and what proportion the latter would have *demanded* of their own free will had they been as well informed as their physicians.[29]

There is disturbing evidence of induced demand available— enough to trigger the belief that free market provider entrepreneurship here can lead to distortions rather than efficiency. Even more: that the

---

[28] M.V. Pauly, "Is Medical Care Different? Old Questions, New Answers," *Journal of Health Politics, Policy and Law* (Summer 1988).

[29] U.E. Reinhardt, note 9, *supra*, at p. 339.

distortions (read "market failure") are closely related to the problem of moral hazard.

> [The rising number of physicians coincides with climbing gross incomes] supporting the widely held belief that doctors, rather then consumers, control demand and compensate for any income shortfall by performing and billing for more services.[30]

Additionally, there was a noticeable rise in the latter part of the 1980s in the incidence of "kickback" prosecutions against doctors (and hospitals). The charge: "selling" patients. In such cases, the doctor books patients into specific hospitals based in part or in whole on the availability of a per patient bounty paid by the hospital to the referring physician. The practice is likely related to the fact that hospital occupancy rates have been dropping, and that physician income is also under pressure owing to the effect of cost-containment measures, some of which will be discussed later in this chapter.

It can be argued that if the hospital provides an adequate (even if not the best available) service, and if the patient happened, truly, to require hospitalization *somewhere* anyway, that all we are involved with here is a competitive health care marketing mechanism. One obvious problem is that what ultimately is being sold here is not an ordinary product in the stream of commerce. Another is that it requires a too broad leap of faith to accept the proposition that all the bounty money changing hands is totally unrelated to consumer informational (and emotional) deficiencies, and is nothing more than the by-product of disinterested diagnosis. On the contrary, reasonable people could surely conclude that both cost (who ultimately pays the kickback amount?) and quality of care are negatively affected by this practice. As well might be one other ingredient necessary to the smooth functioning of any free market system: trust. How many physician producers, one wonders, make all bounty information fully available to consumers?

There has also been a noticeable rise, during the same period of time, in what for lack of a better phrase could be termed "physician joint ventures." Here, doctors join together to form businesses in such areas as diagnostic laboratories, medical equipment leasing services, and radiology centers where diagnostic imaging is a particularly favored specialty. The

---

[30] From a report by the Institute of Health Policy Studies at the University of California, San Francisco; cited in R. Winslow, "Raising Supply of Doctors May Be Bad Medicine for Health Costs," *The Wall Street Journal*, May 8, 1991, See also Wessel and Bogdanich, "Closed Market: Laws of Economics Often Don't Apply in Health Care Field," *The Wall Street Journal*, January 22, 1992, and L. Laster, "Physicians, Heal Thyselves," *The Washington Post National Weekly Edition*, September 21-27, 1992.

participating physicians are generally not specialists in the specific product area. Rather, they are investors merely, but with the added advantage of being able to supply their own customers for the product.

It might be argued that this particular competitive endeavor is not actually illegal. Generally speaking, that would probably be true. And it could be argued that the profit motive in no way interferes with professional judgments about *which* patients truly require *what* services *when* and, certainly, *where*—and, of course, at what cost. Generally speaking, that would be harder to prove. Figure 2-4 appears to raise questions about the cost and necessity, if not the quality, of services provided by a group of doctor-owned laboratories in the state of Michigan.

No less an authority than the editor of the New England Journal of Medicine has said of many of these physician-owned ventures, which account for billions of dollars annually in health care services, that such

> arrangements are wrong because they produce a terrible conflict of interest for a doctor. They give doctors powerful incentives to bend their professional judgments.[31]

None of the above is meant to suggest that the hallmark of most American doctors is rapaciousness and that they see their patients merely as objects for creative entrepreneurship.

Actually, to argue that American doctors are not, on the whole, well trained, highly skilled, and committed to their Hippocratic Oath would be to fly in the face of demonstrable fact. However, in the minority though they may be, many doctors are making the case that unchecked entrepreneurship in the health care market is not consistent with cost and quality efficiency—particularly because the consumer is informationally deficient and participating with an extraordinarily high degree of faith and trust.

One must consider the argument that it is not free competition principles that have distorted health care markets. Rather, it may be that government interference has done so, and that if doctors, hospitals, insurance companies, and others were left to their own devices, without the need to work around stifling regulations, creativity and competition would result in a supply side approach to health care services that would demonstrate great efficiency. One must also consider, in the face of real-world

---

[31] Dr. Arnold Relman, quoted in Waldholz and Bogdanich, "Doctor Owned Labs Earn Lavish Profits in a Captive Market," *The Wall Street Journal*, March 1, 1989. See also Pear and Eckholm, "When Healers Are Entrepreneurs: A Debate Over Costs and Ethics," *The New York Times*, June 2, 1991. As 1992 drew to a close, the *New England Journal of Medicine* stepped up its attacks. See M. Waldholz, "Doctor Practice of Self-Referrals Draws Harsh Criticism from Medical Journals," *The Wall Street Journal*, November 19, 1992.

	Physician owned Labs	Independent Labs
Average Payment	$44.82	$25.48
Avg. no. of tests per patient	6.23	3.76
Range of payments	$21.33–$123.18	$7.15–$30.33
Range of tests per patient	3.42–20.72	1.67–4.68

The Wall Street Journal, March 1, 1989, p. A6.

FIGURE 2.4 Higher Prices and Use By Doctor-Owned Labs. The following is a 1983 study by Michigan Blue Cross and Blue Shield comparing price and usage of 20 doctor-owned labs versus 20 independent labs.

evidence, that this argument is, at best, disingenuous, and that it does not clearly face up to the issue of equitable health care *distribution*. Nothing inherent in the notion of unfettered competition seems to argue in favor of its capacity to promote sufficiently broad consumer *access efficiency*.

And yet, *free choice*, whatever may be its shortcomings in the health care context, is an overall value so (properly) imbedded in the American psyche that, to some extent, it ought to be a consideration in all policy-making discussion in the field.

Processes are available to help ameliorate the problem of consumer informational deficiency, and certainly every effort to make information available to consumers on such matters as doctor and hospital quality of care, costs, and even differential treatment outcomes are to be welcomed. However, for the majority of consumers, such processes as *patient outcomes research* have their obvious limits. It is hard to believe, for example, that we might reach the day when data on carotid endarterectomy will be sufficient to allow the average patient-consumer, concerned about a possible stroke, to override his or her medical specialist on the decision to have or not have an operation that some one study has determined provides benefits only 33 percent to 66 percent of the time, and then only in varying degrees. All this according to data, of course, that might be open to question (e.g., what was the skill level of the participating surgeons?). In any event, rapid progress in technology may make yesterday's information obsolete. Let us briefly examine that health care market.

3. High Tech: The Cost of Modern Miracles

Health care cost priorities are thrown into major focus by American technological genius. Diagnostic imaging (such as magnetic resonance), cardiovascular procedures, and products such as implantable defibrillators and cardiac catheterization, lithotripsy for breaking up calcium deposits, intravascular ultrasound probes, bone growth devices in orthopedics, new implants to restore hearing, and implantable drug infusion pumps are but a handful of examples on an ever-expanding list of our nation's health care miracles. They can provide a heightened quality of life and, in some cases, even save lives that would otherwise be lost. But they also cost government, private insurers, and individuals, billions of dollars directly both in direct hardware and service billings and in related, expanded treatment. Coronary bypass surgery, for example, which adds more than a billion dollars annually to America's national health care bill, became a common treatment procedure because machines were created that could take over from the heart under repair, namely its essential blood-pumping duties.

Several issues come clearly to mind in any consideration of the role of high tech in health care, and particularly, in market efficiency: Are many very expensive diagnostic tests and procedures, for example, done by doctors simply because they are available, even though a thorough physical examination and medical history could provide an adequate diagnosis? Are many other tests performed solely to put in place a technical defense against a possible malpractice suit in the future? Or to satisfy some marketing (or ego) requirement that a particular hospital be as modern and as up to date as all others in the vicinity, despite regional technology redundancy? Or simply out of the necessity to recover costs expended for all that equipment in the first place? Or mainly because the (well-insured) patient insists on being afforded the latest in sophisticated procedures, whether medically indicated or not?

At the very least, a legitimate policy issue is raised with regard to prioritization: How do we weigh the positive value of having miraculous health care technology made available now to those who can afford it, against having *basic* health care made available to those who now have none at all? Medicare, in the fiscal year ending September 30, 1989, paid out over $157 million for just four new high tech cardiovascular procedures used on enrollees—at a time when more than 60 percent of all *poor* Americans were not eligible for Medicaid and received no medical services of any kind.[32]

This leads directly to a consideration of the problem of lack of fair access to America's health care market.

---

[32] C. Ansberry, note 20, *supra*. See also R. Pear, "Medicare to Weigh Cost as a Factor in Reimbursement: Cites 'Explosion' of Expensive Technologies in Move," *The New York Times*, April 21, 1991. Dr. William Schwartz points out that there is a new kind of pacemaker available that virtually eliminates sudden death from disorganized heart rhythms. The cost is approximately $50,000 per patient. There are some 100,000 patients who could employ one. That's $5 billion. Who gets and who pays? See Schwartz's "The Hard Choices in Health Care," *The New York Times*, July 19, 1992.

D. Facing Formidable Issues

1. The Poor and the Uninsured

In 1983, the number of Americans lacking any kind of health insurance was somewhere between 21 million to 27 million.[33] By 1985, that number had increased to 36 million.[34] The majority of these were either full- or part-time employed persons and members of their families. Not surprisingly, race and ethnicity influence the probability of being uninsured. Mexican-Americans and blacks lead the list with 35 percent and 22 percent, respectively, of the total uninsured population—figures well in excess of their percentage of the general population.[35]

Among the factors contributing to the large increase in the uninsured over the brief 1983 to 1985 period were the decrease in the number of people covered by medical insurance sponsored by their employers in concert with their unions; the growth of employment in areas where insurance coverage has traditionally not been good, such as construction and the retail trades; and increases in insurance costs that have outpaced income growth.[36] Then, of course, there are always those people whose state of health and very need for care, in fact, disqualifies them. Actually, the very strict underwriting standards of insurance companies go far toward preventing small businesses in America from providing coverage to small groups of employees, even if there is money available to do so.[37]

It is not just the uninsured and their families who suffer for lack of health care coverage. The resulting burden of having to provide some kind of service to so many who lack anything else falls upon local government hospitals and clinics, and upon taxpayers. This guarantees not only a low quality of service but also a permanent political and public health system crisis.

Despite general knowledge of this crisis, however, the news release issued by the American Cancer Society—which follows in excerpted form—

---

[33] R. Blendon and others, "Health Insurance for the Unemployed and Underinsured," *National Journal*, May 28, 1983.

[34] *Health Insurance: A Profile of the Uninsured in Ohio and the Nation*, (Washington, D.C.: General Accounting Office) August 1988. See also A.R. Gold, "The Struggle to Make Do Without Health Insurance," *The New York Times*, July 30, 1989. The Center for National Health Program Studies at Harvard Medical School projected the final figure in 1991 to be 39 million. See *The Record* [Bergen County, N.J.] February 2, 1992, p. HC-3.

[35] "Who Doesn't Have Medical Insurance?" *The Record* [Bergen County, N.J.], p. A-10, June 6, 1991, citing The Department of Health and Human Services and the Pepper Commission.

[36] G.A.O., note 34, *supra* at p. 3. Data pertaining to the uninsured relates mainly to persons under 65 since the 65 and over population, by and large, is covered to some degree by Medicare.

[37] "Health Insurance: Availability and Adequacy for Small Business," Statement of M.V. Nadel, U.S. General Accounting Office, before the Subcommittee on Health and the Environment of the House Committee on Energy and Commerce, October 16, 1989.

came as a distinct shock to a nation wanting to believe that *basic* health care, at least, was available to everyone under our system (see Figure 2-5).

The National Center for Health Statistics stated in a late 1990 report that while white life expectancy in the United States since 1984 had increased by 0.3 years (to 75.6 years), black life expectancy had decreased by 0.2 years (to 69.2 years). While the study stated that some premature black deaths could be attributable to behavior, such behavior was "often a function of hopelessness, a disenfranchisement from the community . . . related to ethnicity and poverty."[38]

2. Business Costs and Competitiveness

One of the major elements in our health care system is the coverage business firms provide for their workers. In the United States, they account for most of the $120 billion spent annually on nongovernment health insurance. The average employee health coverage cost to those companies that do insure their workers has been estimated to be $3,200 yearly.[39] It has been alleged, on behalf of business, that costs of health care benefits substantially reduce corporate profits and competitiveness in the world. One could argue that measured against the total company wage and benefits package (including pension contributions, Social Security, and the like), and taking into account the element of productivity, it seems a bit strained to lay the less than sanguine state of American corporate competitiveness and profit at the feet of health care costs. Nevertheless, it is surely true that these costs are not insignificant either to management or to labor, the latter looking upon health care coverage as a key contractual benefit.

And it should also be pointed out that company health care costs are not limited to *current* workers. Health benefits are also extended, in many cases, to retirees—more than 8 million of them by recent count, at a cost of roughly $9 billion annually. And these costs are expected to grow to $22 billion (in 1989 dollars) by the year 2008. Further, the present value

[38] Dr. Reed V. Tuckson, cited in C.C. Douglas, "In Black America, Life Grows Shorter," *The New York Times*, December 2, 1990. For a related issue of great import to all the uninsured poor, see R. Winslow, "Death in Hospitals Hits the Uninsured More Than the Insured," *The Wall Street Journal*, January 16, 1991. Finally, there is the editorial printed in America's most powerful medical journal: "Mainstream Private Medicine Has Turned It's Back on the Poor," *Journal of the American Medical Association*, May 15, 1991.

[39] S.M. Butler, "Coming to Terms on Health Care," *The New York Times* (Forum) January 28, 1990; F.W. Swoboda, "The Mercury Rises for Health Care Costs," *The Washington Post National Weekly Edition*, February 4-10, 1991. Preliminary data appear to show that this amount rose to $3,605 annually in 1991, up 12 percent from 1990—which was better than the 1989-1990 rise of 17.1 percent! R. Winslow, "Firms Restrain Rate of Growth of Health Costs," *The Wall Street Journal*, January 21, 1992.

FOR IMMEDIATE RELEASE:
AMERICAN CANCER SOCIETY
ISSUES REPORT TO NATION ON PROBLEMS
OF CANCER AMONG THE POOR;
CHALLENGES COUNTRY TO RESPOND

WASHINGTON, D.C., JULY 17, 1989 — The American Cancer Society today issued a compelling "Report to the Nation" which found that poor Americans are forced to accept substandard health care services and endure assaults on their personal dignity when seeking treatment for cancer. The report, which describes the nature and extent of problems poor people face when seeking cancer education, prevention and detection of services in America, was released to key health policymakers at a special briefing.

The ACS "Report to the Nation" was the culmination of a series of fact-finding hearings the Society held in collaboration with the National Cancer Institute (NCI) and the Centers for Disease Control (CDC) in May and June. At these hearings, nearly 70 disadvantaged prople and 100 professionals who serve disadvantaged populations presented testimony concerning their personal experiences. More than 70 other individuals submitted written testimony at the hearings.

The report found that the five most critical issues related to cancer and the poor were:

1. Poor people endure greater pain and suffering from cancer than other Americans.

2. Poor people and their families must make extraordinary personal sacrifices to obtain and pay for care.

3. Poor people face substantial obstacles in obtaining and using health insurance and often don't seek care if they can't pay for it.

4. Cancer education is insensitive and irrelevant to many poor people.

5. Fatalism about cancer is prevalent among the poor and prevents them from seeking care.

"Based on the findings of this report, we need to declare a new kind of war on cancer—a guerilla war—that will tear down the economic and cultural barriers to early and adequate cancer prevention, diagnosis and treatment, and dramatically increase cancer survival rates for all Americans," said ACS President Dr. Harold Freeman.

The Society estimates that 178,000 people with cancer—who might be saved through early diagnosis and treatment—will die this year alone. According to the Society, poor people's survival rate of cancer is 10 to 15 percent lower than other Americans.

Freeman said the society was releasing the report to health policymakers, advocacy groups, professional societies, social service agencies and other organizations as a national call to action and would strive to take the lead in making a solution to the problem a national priority. According to him, the challenges raised by the report findings must be addressed by government and private organizations at the federal, state and local levels.

He also urged individual Americans not to view poverty as a problem of others: "The circle of poverty is not a closed circle. There are middle class people today who will become poor tomorrow. Let us see our own reflections in the faces of the poor."

ACS Chairman of the Board Kathleen Horsch announced at the briefing the Society's commitment to a three-year demonstration project, designed to help develop and promote unique and effective ways to address the cancer education, prevention and detection needs of the poor. Starting in October, the Society has authorized $1.8 million in grants for three selective communities to develop and test new program models that can be duplicated in other communities.

Horsch also outlined the Society's plans to get the report in the hands of people who can influence the care poor people receive and educate them about the nature and scope of the problem. The Assistant Secretary of the U.S. Department of Health and Human Services James Mason attended the briefing; President Bush, Congressional leaders, Health and Human Services Secretary Louis Sullivan and key members of the White House domestic staff will also be receiving copies of the report.

The hearings were held in seven regional cities with the collaboration of federal and state governments and members of the private sector. A panel composed of ACS volunteers, representatives from NCI and CDC, and state or local policymakers questioned the testifiers.

The American Cancer Society is the national voluntary health organization dedicated to eliminating cancer as a major health problem by preventing cancer, saving lives from cancer and diminishing suffering from cancer through research, education and service.

of *accrued* total benefits, as mentioned above, appears to be in the vicinity of $227 billion as America enters the decade of the 1990s.[40]

Concern about rising costs for coverage have persuaded many companies to try innovative approaches to cost containment. One is labeled "managed care" and it is a form of bulk purchase discounting. In managed care, a "preferred provider organization," often an insurance company, puts together a consortium of individual and institutional health care deliverers (e.g., doctors and hospitals) and they provide their services at competitively low fees so as to obtain exclusive access to the company's large consumer pool. The Allied Signal Corporation managed-care program, for example, was said to cover 48,000 of 76,000 employees as of year end 1989.[41]

---

[40] *Employee Benefits: Company Action to Limit Retiree Health Costs* (Washington, D.C.: General Accounting Office, February 1989). It is also important to note here that the Financial Accounting Standards Board (FASB) issued a new rule on postretirement health benefits in December 1990: Beginning in 1993, companies must accrue, or set up a reserve for, future medical retirees, rather than use the current practice of deducting outlays from profits in the year in which they are paid. It is estimated that if this had been done in 1990, the typical 10,000-employee company would have had its profit reduced by $21.5 million. See Berton and Brennan, "New Medical Benefits Accounting Rule Seen Wounding Profits, Hurting Shares," *The Wall Street Journal*, April 22, 1992.

Alternative approaches affecting employee health care choices, breadth of coverage, and participatory costs, together with moves by management to restrict retiree coverage, will clearly provide the basis for business-labor conflict well into the next century.

3. Fee Setting, HMOs and Triage as Possible Mechanisms for Change

Many mechanisms aimed in one way or another at restricting individual physician and hospital fees have been attempted at federal, state, and local levels. One of these is "utilization review." As with for-profit companies, usually begun by physicians, these firms generally review anticipated procedures such as hospitalization and surgery, and bargain on behalf of the payor with the proposed provider, on both necessity and price.

Medicare cost containment legislation passed at the conclusion of the 1989 congressional session imposed a national fee scale on 7,000 different types of physician services as of October 1991. Moreover, this new approach seeks to reward personal care more than technology-based service through what is called a "relative value scale." This scale measures how much personnel time, effort, physical labor, and overhead go into providing the service billed—a clearly stated preference for person-to-person care over high tech care. Exactly what forms this major overhaul of Medicare reimbursement methodology will take, and exactly what results they might achieve, will require some time to determine.[42]

One of the major systems employed in the service of cost containment is the Health Maintenance Organization (HMO). HMOs are fully prepaid, total health care entities offering medical, psychological, and, often, even social services through a consortium of professionals grouped together as a unit. Hospitalization, if deemed necessary, is covered as well by the HMO group. There is, in effect, no "free choice" of physician in this system, since the HMO provider panel has been self-selected by the professional group itself. Some companies do offer its employees a choice

---

[41] F.Swoboda, "A Surgical Strike Against Corporate Health Care Costs," *The Washington Post National Weekly Edition*, February 10-17, 1990. Managed care also refers to services confined to decisions about what care patients are and are not entitled to, and the cost of provided care. Investigating the propriety of allowing patients to receive particular services is reasonable enough; however, there is a conflict of interest possibility inherent in managed-care fees earned for saving money by denying full access to necessary care for all patients. See N. Cooper, "Health Care Networks' Attempt to Cut Costs Are Trimming Patients' Options," *The Wall Street Journal*, July 29, 1992.

[42] Fee scales are set out in Part II, Department of Health and Human Services, HCFA, 42 CFR, Parts 405, 413 and 415, November 25, 1991 (Washington, D.C.: Government Printing Office). Trouble seems to be brewing here already. See R. Pear, "Despite 1991 Law, Many on Medicare Are Overcharged," *The Wall Street Journal*, March 1, 1992.

between enrolling in a selected HMO or coverage in a standard insurance plan. However, coverage in the latter often does not provide the employee with the breadth of services offered by the HMO, and employees might even be required to contribute something to their own coverage if they opt to have free choice of provider.

Since HMOs are paid flat fees in advance for a given employee group's coverage, one would expect them to be more judicious in their approach to patient services than the fee-for-service provider. Perceived initially with enthusiasm as a cost controlling service delivery mechanism, HMOs entered the decade of the 1990s with close to 35 million enrollees nationwide and, unfortunately, a somewhat tarnished image.[43] They have been accused of deliberately seeking out subscribers who will be low-service utilizers, and even of constructing barriers to service provision (e.g., increasing waiting times) in order to encourage high-utilization consumers to drop out and find some other place to go.[44] And their costs are rising just as are the costs of conventional insurance plans.

In so far as HMOs were perceived to be *the* answer to quality service provision at permanent low cost, they were set up to disappoint. Still, many do offer good care in a convenient form, and at a cost below that of many conventional plans. On the one hand, there is reason to assume that they will continue to be an acceptable way to deal with health care provision. There is no reason to believe, on the other hand, that they are the solution to the problem of rising health care costs and the problem of equitable access.

One of the methods for holding costs in check is based upon a wartime casualty care process. In the face of severe shortage of medical personnel and supplies, the wounded would be placed in one of three groups: those who would most likely die even if given services; those whose prognosis was doubtful even if given services; and those whose prognosis was good if given services. Medical personnel would then provide services (and supplies) to the last group, then to the middle group if possible. Those in the first group were left alone to die. That overall process was called *triage*.

Triage is a word that has been used in connection with American health care cost inflation. Another is "rationing" and a third is "limiting supply"—the outcome in each case being restricted access to services for some group in the society. Suggestions publicly advocated include setting

---

[43] Shellenbarger, "As HMO Premiums Sour, Employers Save on the Plans and Check Out Alternatives," *The Wall Street Journal*, February 27, 1989.

[44] See W.H. Anderson, "HMOs Incentives: A Prescription for Failure," *The Wall Street Journal*, January 2, 1987. See also John E. Ware and others, *Health Outcomes for Adults in Prepaid and Fee-for-Service Systems of Care: Results from the Health Insurance Experiment* (The Rand Corporation, October 1987).

up a national age limit, perhaps 80 or 85, beyond which, like the severely wounded in wartime, the individual would no longer qualify to receive professional life-saving measures.

The question of health care resource limits is a serious one indeed. Still, an actual age limitation might give pause to those Americans who like to think of their nation as a rich and powerful democracy in which all citizens receive basic, life-preserving benefits—especially those Americans who may have already reached the age of 79.

In any event, triage in America has gone beyond the boundaries of suggestion. In some states, young patients whose families are enrolled in Medicaid have been allowed to die because the plan will not pay for certain expensive procedures (e.g., $100,000 bone morrow transplants). This situation is not the result of callousness. The decision, made in the face of limited state and federal resources available for the Medicaid program, has been to utilize existing funds to lower threshold eligibility limits. In that way, many thousands more citizens of the state qualify to receive basic medical care while a far smaller number die for lack of access to very expensive life-saving procedures.[45]

In one state whose strict eligibility requirements allow only a third of the poverty-income-level population access to the Medicare program, the deputy commissioner of health care services is quoted as saying:

> What it is, is triage. You've only got so much money, you can only do certain things. [Another state] may cover a lot more people, but their services aren't as broad as ours. We have chosen the people that we can cover, and we cover them very well, though we're not extravagant.[46]

Forced to view choices in such a harsh and painful way,[47] policy-makers cannot avoid considering a substantial overhaul of the total health care market.

4. Must the Free Market in Health Care Be Abolished?

---

[45] Several states and/or regions within states are focusing on cost controls and universal coverage. Oregon is attempting to provide Medicaid coverage for *all* Medicaid-eligible persons, but with service limitations. The federal government in 1992 refused to allow the Oregon Plan to go forward. See V. Brownworth, "Oregon Health Plan Is the Best Model," *The Philadelphia Inquirer*, October 23, 1992.

[46] Quoted in T. Egan, "Rebuffed by Oregon, Patients Take Their Life or Death Case to the Public," *The New York Times*, May 1, 1988.

[47] Long-term "catastrophic" health care for the aged may be approaching the level of triage. In 1940, the elderly made up 6.8 percent of the population. By the year 2030 it is projected that 20 percent of all Americans will be 65 or older. Long-range policy proposals focused on this reality are surely needed. See D.R. Rice, "Health and Long-Term Care for the Aged," *The American Economic Review* (May 1989).

The ultimate issue for policymakers to confront, given both cost and access problems, is whether "the free market" is incapable of providing solutions in the area of health care and whether such a capability does reside in a non-free-market alternative (e.g., a government sponsored, government-controlled national health care plan) made available at a bearable cost to every single citizen.

In the United States, the "free market" in health care is at least partially a myth. Government and private funding and control mix in complex, often irrational ways, whereas, in Canada, which has a national health system with all funds in government control, doctors are not employees of the state, and citizens can choose their own physicians! There are, however, clear and substantial differences between the American and Canadian health care systems. Each Canadian province produces a formal schedule of benefits each year, which sets the fees that doctors can charge within that province for every conceivable form of service, both surgical and nonsurgical. It also sets the amount available for hospitals. Of course, the basic source of government revenue for the national health plan is taxes.

Funds for physicians are given by government to the medical associations in the provinces. Then the various medical specialties have to fight it out for their particular piece of the total government health care pie. While Canadian doctors cannot, by law, exceed the set fees, and while they do make less than their U.S. counterparts, they are still in the top 1 percent of all Canadian professional workers, and their malpractice premiums are exceedingly low.[48]

As Figure 2-6 demonstrates, Canadian health care costs are lower than those in the United States. However, it would be a mistake to assume that there are no problems with the total government health care plan. Health care costs continue to rise in Canada, too, and given annual budgetary limits, there are often extensive delays in obtaining elective surgery, there are often long waits for hospital beds, and there is limited access to some high-cost, high-technology procedures even though the plan is supposed to be all-encompassing for everyone. In America, full insurance coverage entitles a person to utilize *all* available technology, more of which is available in the United States than is available in Canada.

---

[48] An interesting article on the Canadian system is by M. Specter, "Searching for the Best Medical Care Money Can't Buy: Canada Controls Costs But at a Price," *The Washington Post National Weekly Edition*, December 25-31, 1989. The most recent highly detailed and clear exposition of the Canadian system is to be found in: *Canadian Health Insurance: Lessons for the United States* (Washington, D.C.: General Accounting Office Report, June 1991). An excellent publication covering major European health care systems operated by governments (British, German, and Swedish particularly) and cost and access comparisons with the United States is *Health Care Systems in Transition: The Search for Efficiency* (OECD Policy Studies, No. 7, Paris, 1990).

Figure 2-7 presents a bird's eye view of per capita health care expenditures in 23 nations of the world. U. S. expenditures are at the top with $2,354 followed by Canada with $1,683.

American doctors point with justifiable pride to technical and entrepreneurial initiatives that have developed new and better methods for prolonging and saving lives—methods other nations can now use as well. National health care proponents counter with the criticism that such accomplishments do not make up for the poor services that exist in so many places, and do not respond to the shocking reality that tens of millions of Americans live beyond the reach of any truly decent and basic health care.

In the face of escalating costs, even corporate America has come to consider a government national health care plan seriously. At the same time, there are those in Congress who advocate basic-benefits health care coverage of all employees by all businesses regardless of size, with all unemployed and uninsured citizens to receive similar coverage from their states.[49]

It would seem clear that no national health plan structure can be a panacea for our nation's health care ills. In the face of rising wages for nurses, technicians, and all other health care personnel, of rising costs for equipment and supplies, and of swelling elderly populations, no nation can put the lid on costs by merely instituting new structures for controlling delivery processes and curbing particular fees. This is not an argument against instituting sensible cost controls. It is an argument against avoiding a decision on policy issues of much more serious import.

Any student attempting now to put together the complex ethical, economic, and sociopolitical aspects of health care ought to ponder the following basic considerations as points of departure for argument and decision.

Will any health care system left totally in the custody of the freely competitive economic marketplace end up producing social and economic crisis? If not, why not? And if so (i.e., if there would be market failures) the question then is how do we go about utilizing non-market components *rationally* and *effectively* to correct them?

Has one primary market failure been that a *decent minimum standard* of health care has not been made available to every single citizen? If so, must such a standard be defined at the national level? If yes, then once defined should the decent minimum standard portion of the total

---

[49] M. Tolchin, "Sudden Support for National Health Care," *The New York Times*, September 24, 1989. See also M.V. Nadel, note 29, *supra*. Certainly, national health care or no, our society's message bearers—the media—have clearly announced the presence of a deep national concern through such headlines as "Voters, Sick of the Current Health Care System, Want Federal Government to Prescribe Remedy," *The Wall Street Journal*, June 28, 1991, "Demands to Fix U.S. Health Care Reach a Crescendo," *The New York Times*, May 19, 1991, "Health Care Reform Focus of Early Activity," *U.S. Mayor*, January 21, 1991, and "Nation Urged to Overhaul Health Care: AMA Journal Sounds Alarm," *Washington Post News Service*, May 14, 1991.

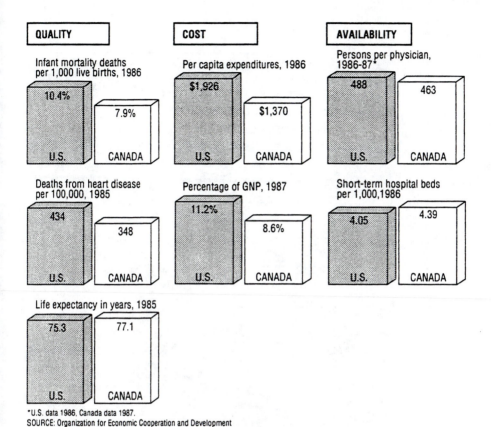

QUALITY

Infant mortality deaths per 1,000 live births, 1986
- U.S.: 10.4%
- CANADA: 7.9%

Deaths from heart disease per 100,000, 1985
- U.S.: 434
- CANADA: 348

Life expectancy in years, 1985
- U.S.: 75.3
- CANADA: 77.1

COST

Per capita expenditures, 1986
- U.S.: $1,926
- CANADA: $1,370

Percentage of GNP, 1987
- U.S.: 11.2%
- CANADA: 8.6%

AVAILABILITY

Persons per physician, 1986-87*
- U.S.: 488
- CANADA: 463

Short-term hospital beds per 1,000, 1986
- U.S.: 4.05
- CANADA: 4.39

*U.S. data 1986. Canada data 1987.
SOURCE: Organization for Economic Cooperation and Development

FIGURE 2.6 Health Care in the U.S. versus Canada. (*Washington Post National Weekly Edition*, December 25-31, 1989, p. 31.)

market be accepted as a mixed public good, beyond the producer's ability to deny the right to consume it? In a free and democratic society, is this a matter of choice, or an ethical necessity?[50]

Can a public-policy decision regarding the definition of a decent minimum standard of health care be left to health professionals? Or would it be wrong, and morally self-defeating, for a democratic society to do so, on the basis that to do so would be to require physicians to dishonor their Hippocratic Oath? Must not all doctors be expected to use every means at their disposal to minister to every patient? If limits must be set regarding

---

[50] In early December 1992, the Health Insurance Association of America (HIAA), in the face of President Clinton's promise of universal health care coverage, made an enormous turn. The HIAA, which has 270 members insuring 72 million people, called for a new federal law requiring coverage for *all* Americans: *basic* coverage, that is, to be defined *by* the government. See R. Pear, "Leading Health Insurers Into a New Age," *The New York Times*, December 6, 1992.

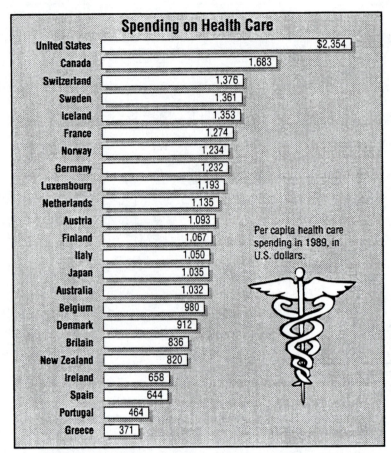

FIGURE 2.7   Comparative National Health Care Expenditures. (The New York Times, June 9, 1991, p. 16.)

these means, is it not for the body politic to do so at the outset, and not the healer?

Does not any society that chooses to make a decent minimum standard of health care available to every citizen thereby set itself up for other hard choices, such as determining the source or sources of funds to support such a mixed public good? Moreover, does that same society determine next how much of that society's remaining national, individual, and corporate resources are to be made available for the total health care market? And what form should entrepreneurial profit-seeking best take in the context of limited growth, free markets—assuming such, in a health care context, not to be an oxymoron.

Could the society avoid some problems by encouraging education-for-wellness on a broad scale? Perhaps by setting funds aside for prevention and wellness programs? How could economists measure effectively the practical costs and benefits that could be expected to result from such a priority decision? Should the society consider diverting specific sources of tax funds to such programs (e.g., tobacco and alcohol excise taxes)?

Finally, and perhaps most important, consider this: Since a decent minimum standard of medical care does not guarantee the best available care to everyone under all circumstances, whatever the technology involved, how best can the society introduce a substantial measure of human concern, *and hope*, and even choice, into the ugly reality of triage?

We would suggest that merely one example of facing up to that issue might be found in confronting the dreadful problem of in-hospital care for low-birthweight children. The short-term costs of applying all available high technology (and personnel) resources to keeping the premature children of drug-addicted and AIDs-infected mothers alive can run as high as $100,000 or more per child. Figure 2-3 provided a beginning look at the drug-addicted mother/low-birthweight problem. When low-birthweight babies born to non-addicted, non-AIDs mothers who simply have not had any exposure to basic prenatal care information and assistance are included, the short-term health care system costs of merely keeping these babies alive on a national scale are absolutely staggering. Longer-term costs, in terms of child abuse and neglect, foster care, learning disabilities, continuing physical ills, and consequent social disruption, are added on eventually to the health care and other systems.[51] Funding applied to sensitive, full-range prenatal care *made available to all* both separately and in conjunction with drug prevention and treatment programs—*and with a concentration on effective marketing process*—should be far more productive for mother, child and society than in-hospital low birth-weight care, and far less expensive.

In the presence of substantial, total access prenatal care programming—which does not now exist—society might then want to consider what financial limits to place on the availability of in-hospital, low-birthweight care.

This chapter has dealt with unique and complex phenomena, but the materials do present an instructive example of how free markets, finance, ethics, and public policy are interrelated, and how they must be blended constructively if our democratic society and its producers and consumers are to grow and prosper, in good health, together.[52]

---

[51] See for example, M.L. Norris, "The Class of Crack's Innocent Victims: The First Wave of Drug-Disabled Children Jolts Ill-prepared Schools," *The Washington Post National Weekly Edition*, July 8-14, 1991, and P. Van Tassel, "Schools Trying to Cope with Crack Babies," *The New York Times*, January 5, 1992.

[52] Two thought-provoking pieces in the area of health care markets, cost efficiency, and ethical considerations are to be found in *U.S. Health Care Spending: Trends, Contributing Factors and Proposals for Reform* (Washington, D.C.: General Accounting Office Report, June 1991; S.M. Smythe, "Crafting a Future for the Health Care of America's Children: A

IN LIEU OF THE PHILOSOPHER'S STONE

We might want to think about parties at interest and value weighing with regard to issues like these:

1. From 1985 to 1991 overall consumer prices grew by 21 percent, but prescription drug prices jumped 66 percent, on average. The top 20 sellers jumped 79 percent.[53] Are drug prices unfair, unconscionable, unethical? Exactly whose interests should be weighed here? Shareholders? The public? Prescription buyers? *Everyone* because of health care costs to the economy? And *which* public interest should you weigh? Cost of product *to* consumers? Development of new products *for* consumers? Who pays for development? Would you weigh the "ethics" of cost differently if you knew that high-tech pharmaceuticals originate in some substantial measure out of government (taxpayer)-subsidized research in universities and government agencies such as the National Institutes of Health? Is there market failure here? If so, just what outside-the-market forces should be brought to bear to correct things?

2. Should employers who self-insure for their employees' health care be allowed to change their announced benefits structure any time they please? Example: Employers are told that AIDS care is covered. John and Mary are diagnosed with AIDS. Their employer tells them that as of now, AIDS coverage is limited to $500 per person. Is *that* ethical? If you aren't sympathetic to AIDS, what about cancer? If an employer can cut down (or drop) coverage on one disease, he or she can do it on anything. If the employer can't reduce coverage, what then? How about this: 8.5 million retirees are covered by their former employers. Can *their* benefits be cut back by unilateral decision at any time? (Just when they need them the most?) Do not try to be a lawyer here. As an economist, what data would you need to weigh competing interests properly?

3. Nursing-home expense can cost from $30,000 to $75,000 per year. Medicaid does pay for *long-term care*, but only if a person has minimal assets of his or her own. Your parents come to you and say: "We're getting old, and we don't want your $250,000 inheritance to get wiped out when we require long-term care. We want to do some Medicaid estate planning. We want to shelter all our assets so that Medicaid officials can't touch them. There *are* legal ways. It's only bending the rules, not breaking them. Help us find a lawyer who can get this done. Now don't you be concerned."

Process of Confronting the Tradeoffs," Montgomery Dorsey Symposium, July 25, 1991.
[53] *The Wall Street Journal*, September 11, 1992, p. B13.

Are you concerned? About whom? Which interests do you really think should be weighed here in order to have some ethical decisions made about "Medicaid estate planning"? By the way, you should be aware of this fact: In your parents' home state, as of now, 40 percent of all families below the poverty line do not qualify for any Medicaid family coverage. It is family coverage versus long-term care and just not enough money to go around.

Based on the material contained in Chapter 2, how do the above three issues tie into your perceptions about where responsibility lies in each of them?

3

The Legal System, Product Liability, and the Creative Use of Bankruptcy

COMING UP IN THIS CHAPTER

This chapter is divided into three parts, all of them connected sequentially.

The first section is a brief summary covering the constitutional basis of American law; the structure of the federal and state court systems; where to find "the law"; how to read a court case decision; and a brief characterization of civil law compared to criminal law.

Is it really possible to give the nonlaw student or nonlawyer professional a concise summary of all of the above? In a lawyerlike way we say, "Well, that depends." It depends upon the purpose the summary is meant to serve. In our case, the summary is brief because the purpose is simple: It is meant merely *to introduce* the reader to the overall system. Specific constitutional law, substantive dealings with specific court decisions, and close examination of various aspects of civil and criminal law (as related to free, competitive markets) come later in this book.

Please look at this brief introduction as an ongoing process. Though concise, it is carefully packaged. Familiarize yourself with such matters as *the common law, stare decisis*, and *dicta*. They will stand you in good stead later on. As for the how-to-read-a-case portion, we would like to emphasize two things: First, you should pay close attention to the processes suggested. They will make the reading of later cases go more easily. Second, the *Virginia* Supreme Court case we have chosen to illustrate the process is deceptively simple. Its structure and language are easy to follow. In substance, however, it is quite complex. It presents ethical (and other) issues that go to the heart of the ongoing American debate about how Supreme Court justices do—and should—decide constitutional rights cases. In this sense, it is a close relative to the abortion cases that keep so many Americans on edge.

The second section of this chapter involves us, for the first time, with the direct relationship between common law court decisions and free market operations. You will be required to read four court cases in the field of *product liability*. The first three cases do not relate to current product liability areas. They are older cases, and they are here because they represent quite well the development, over a critical period of 57 years, of the *basic* law of product liability in the United States, particularly in the area of *warranty* and *strict liability*. The fourth case, *Grimshaw* v. *Ford Motor*, adds the specific dimension of intentional corporate misbehavior and raises clear ethical issues. You should be able to apply your how-to-read-a-case process to each of these four cases.

The third and final section of the chapter carries product liability to its ultimate level, the area of *mass torts*. This is where one product (though not necessarily one manufacturer or supplier) causes extensive harm to many people, (e.g., in the case of asbestos).Since you will already have read four law cases, we cover the final section through narrative, assuming that key words like *lawsuits, cases*, and *damages* now have more meaning for you. We close with a narrative perusal of the Chapter 11 bankruptcy area that began, in its very modern manifestation, with a mass tort damage avoidance-filing. The dilemma is whether or not Chapter 11 (the law) gives some undeserving parties a very swift sword with which to wound those who must face legitimate (and supposedly efficient) market discipline.

I. AN OVERVIEW OF LAW
AND THE LEGAL SYSTEM

A. An Introduction

Individually, Americans often complain that their laws are intrusive, expensive, inefficient, unwise, unfair, and unworkable. Collectively, Americans are fond of saying that we are a nation governed overall by laws, not individuals, that we live by the Rule of Law. And in so saying, we proudly distinguish ourselves from those other nations where individual and collective destinies are subject to capricious and often despotic human rule.

Over the next several chapters of this book, we will examine, in the context of free markets and the free enterprise system, the specific form and content of various American laws ranging from those governing a manufacturer's liability for product harm, to those involving competition and antitrust. And along the way we will indeed relate to such issues as fairness and efficiency.

But here we must begin with the broader picture. Whatever our concern about individual laws, it is surely true that we are entitled to take pride in our overall adherence to the law, an adherence that has resulted, for one thing, in national political stability—a major factor in attracting foreign investment into our free enterprise system.

We do not intend to pursue the overall question of what law is (or ought to be) in America in a basically philosophical manner. There are many outstanding texts that do that, and we refer the student to them enthusiastically.[1] However, there is no way to begin any discussion of law in America other than at the beginning, and the beginning is the Constitution of the United States. And the Constitution is nothing if not a philosophy by which its citizens are to be governed, at least as long as they intend to constitute a Republic.

The American *written* Constitution is not extraordinary simply because it was the first of its kind to govern an entire nation, nor because it has given rise to many other such written constitutions around the world. It is extraordinary because it actually works. And it has worked continuously since ratification was completed on July 2, 1788.

The American Constitution had a very difficult gestation. It had 13 parents (states), after all, many of whom were adherents of federal constitutional "birth control." The problem was not that many colonists and colonial leaders feared citizens having too many rights. On the contrary, they feared giving too many such rights away to a suspect centralized power.

Massachusetts, in convention in 1788, barely voted to ratify the federal constitution, 187-168, and then only after the Federalists agreed to fight for nine amendments. Rhode Island rejected the constitution on March 24, 1788, in a popular referendum, 2,708 to 237. Also in 1788, the New Hampshire Convention ratified 57-47 only after proposing 12 amendments. And Virginian opposition, led by Patrick Henry, lost out to James Madison's federal constitutionalists 89-79 only after Madison agreed to recommend a Bill of Rights to be added to the Constitution, composed of 20 new articles, plus 20 other changes.

In light of the tumultuous events of 1788, one might well wonder why judicial determination of the elusive intent of the Founding Fathers—particularly with regard to the scope of individual rights and liberties—is generally limited to an examination of what might have been in the minds of the *men* attending the Constitutional Convention in 1787!

---

[1] A basic book is H.L.A. Hart's *The Concept of Law* (Oxford, England: Oxford University Press, 1961). An excellent recent work is Ronald Dworkin's *Law's Empire* (Cambridge, Mass.: Belknap/Harvard University Press, 1986). Other materials are cited in Chapter 1, note 1.

In any event, Congress responded to state convention concerns for basic change by submitting a dozen amendments to the Constitution, to the states, on September 25, 1789. Only ten were accepted, these being referred to collectively as the Bill of Rights. The Bill of Rights was formally ratified and made part of the Constitution on December 15, 1791.[2]

It should be clear that the citizens of the original 13 states took the role of law in their lives very seriously, particularly the role of *national* law, by which all the states were to abide. The fundamental issue was not to have or not have a constitution. There already were *state* constitutions in existence. The fundamental issue was whether to accept a federal constitution that would give control over their lives and their states to a powerful, centralized authority.

And this issue was fundamental precisely because implicit in the fierce and democratic struggle of the people over the ultimate structure and function of a federal constitution was the agreement that *if such a constitution were to be ratified the people would consider themselves bound by it utterly*. That implicit agreement to be bound by the Constitution has been renewed by all succeeding generations—with but one brief, and horrible, period of conflict (the Civil War) in the nineteenth century, which resulted in correction of the original Constitution's most serious defect—its concession to slavery. And it is at least in part the eighteenth-century democratic struggle of free citizens, out of which the final document was forged, that has given the American written Constitution the long life that has made it unique in the entire world. And it is that which has formed the basis for an American society in which law plays such a powerful and pervasive role.

Law in America is not really about disputes, although specific dispute resolution is surely a means to its ultimate end. There are structures mandated by the Constitution because institutions and order must exist if there is to be any hope of continued liberty. But law in America is not about structures either. Law is about what the Constitution is about: the values by which free men and women have chosen to live their lives.

We can and do argue vociferously in this country about just what these values should be and how they might best be put into practice—and enforced. The struggle in this, the third century of the constitutional system, to give contemporary, and thus lasting, meaning to the Constitution itself is the basis of citizen concern with what the nine justices on the U.S. Supreme Court do. We will look hard at what the justices have done,

---

[2] Three of the original 13 states did not formally ratify the Bill of Rights until 1939: Massachusetts, Georgia, and Connecticut.

and at their value judgments, in each of the subject areas to be covered in this book.[3]

But as powerful as the institution may be, the story of the law and how it serves to implement values is not a story told by the Supreme Court alone. In the dynamic interplay of law with markets, the free enterprise system, and politics, there is much more to "the legal system." There is a larger, non-Supreme Court federal judiciary, state courts and constitutions, a Congress, state and local legislatures, and administrative agencies.

We shall attempt to place each of these into substantive areas of this book in order to illustrate the role of law in the economic system. And we will examine the consequent interplay of both the legal and economic systems with that population of some quarter billion souls referred to collectively as, "We the People." For now, however, we turn to the structure of the American legal system.

B. Looking at the System

1. The Federal Structure

First there are the courts. The courts of first resort—where all plaintiff/defendant *civil*, or U.S. attorney/defendant *criminal*, cases begin—are called United States district courts. These are, in fact, federal trial courts. The number of U.S. district courts existing in each state depends upon state size. There are many more such courts in New York than there are in Rhode Island.

Appeals from the result of a trial in a district court go to the United States court of appeals—the federal appellate court. There are 11 Federal Judicial Districts in the United States (just as there are federal districts for many different U.S. endeavors; e.g., for central banking there are 12 Federal Reserve Districts). Anyone appealing a jury decision or a judge's ruling in a U.S. district court is entitled to be heard in a federal appellate court, which is the circuit court of appeals for that district.

One major question is: What cases go into a federal court, rather than a state court? Criminal cases are easy: One can be tried in a federal court whenever one violates a federal law. Some acts violate both state and federal laws (e.g., illegal drug dealing), and technically a defendant could be tried in the courts of either entity. Usually, however, federal

---

[3] There are those who would argue that Supreme Court justices do not make value judgments, that they defer to Congress, the President, and the states to honor the will of the majority, and merely unearth the intent of "the Founding Fathers." Unfortunately, a majority of the present Supreme Court professes to believe this. At the very least, such beliefs are suspect. Value-free constitutional law is an oxymoron, and a particularly offensive one at that. See E. Chemerinsky, "The Vanishing Constitution," *Harvard Law Review* (November 1989).

authorities stick to basic federal crimes (e.g., securities violations under federal statutes) and leave street crime, generally, to local law enforcement. However, jurisdictional disputes are not unknown.

There are special rules, however, governing the kind of civil cases the federal courts will hear. Basically, there are two ways to get a dispute into U.S. district court: diversity of citizenship, and federal question resolution.

Diversity refers to (individual or corporate) plaintiffs who are from one state, and defendants who are from another. The original intent behind diversity was to allow an out-of-stater to go into a federal court because the state court might be tempted to favor its own citizens over interlopers. Diversity *jurisdiction* (i.e., giving U.S. courts authority over a case) has fallen into disfavor owing to the enormous glut of business at the federal courthouse door. In fiscal year 1988, for example, some 239,000 civil cases were filed in U.S. district courts, and 28 percent were based on diversity jurisdiction.[4] That constitutes a lot of cases, and serious questions have been raised about whether interstate bias is serious enough to warrant all the work. As of May 18, 1989, the monetary minimum value of a case at issue must be $50,000 to qualify for diversity jurisdiction—not terribly difficult when one considers that attorney fees are included.

Federal questions to be resolved in a U.S. district court are not limited to constitutional issues—though these are surely one way to get in. Environmental, securities, antitrust and similar federal laws are some examples of other clear federal issue raisers.

There are also special courts for handling large volumes of special claims, the key ones being the tax courts and the Court of Claims. The latter entertains, mainly, claims against the federal government founded on acts of Congress and certain regulations.

Finally, there is the issue of when one's case is entitled to be heard in the U.S. Supreme Court. The general answer to the question of what cases *must* the Supreme Court hear (*mandatory* jurisdiction) is: *hardly any*. By and large the Supreme Court has enormous discretion with regard to the cases it will hear in the course of any given year (or "term" as lawyers call the period during which the Court hears lawyers argue their cases). When justices of the Supreme Court decide to allow a case to be argued before them, the usual form of their agreement to hear a case is called "granting *certiorari*"—which literally means they agree to allow themselves to be more fully informed.

A new law that took effect in June 1988 basically eliminated all the cases the Supreme Court *had* to hear other than certain (very few) appeals from state appellate courts, some criminal case appeals by the

---

[4] W. Feinberg, "Is Diversity Jurisdiction an Idea Whose Time Has Passed?" *New York State Bar Journal* (July 1989), p. 15.

federal government, a few appeals in some antitrust and Interstate Commerce Commission cases, and appeals from special three-judge federal appeals court decisions striking down state laws as unconstitutional.

What cases might Supreme Court justices decide they want to hear? Perhaps cases where U.S. courts of appeals in different districts have decided the same issues differently; perhaps cases involving issues that appear to be of great immediate significance (e.g., abortion and affirmative action); and cases where they seem to feel that legal/constitutional clarity demands particular elucidation.[5]

2. The State Structure

State court systems are quite similar to the federal system, consisting basically of the lower courts (i.e., courts of primary jurisdiction) and then intermediate appellate courts, and finally the high court of the state.

There are various lower state courts. Most states have district courts or their equivalent where lesser criminal cases, and low monetary value civil cases, are heard. Many even have special small claims courts for (economically) minor dispute resolution. More serious criminal and civil cases go to higher trial courts (e.g., "superior" courts in Massachusetts), and are usually allowed to be appealed to intermediate (nontrial) appellate courts. The highest state courts also pick their cases by and large (i.e., they don't have to hear all appeals). Most, though not all, have the appellation Supreme Court of the State of ____. New York's highest court, however, is known as the New York Court of Appeals.

It should be pointed out here that state supreme courts all have their own constitutions to interpret, just as the U.S. Supreme Court has its own. And federal/state constitutional interplay is becoming ever-more important in American law—and life. This is because no state will be allowed by the U.S. Supreme Court to restrict the rights of any citizen granted to him or her by the United States Constitution; but states are, in fact, free to expand those rights. They may do so when the state constitution can be read to provide adequate and independent state grounds for the expansion.[6]

Increasingly, perhaps because of the conservative bent of the current Supreme Court, state courts are expanding the scope of civil liberties, striking down state public school funding laws as denying children from poor districts a substantially equal opportunity to have access to education funds, and knocking out the results of searches and seizures that the U.S. Supreme Court has held *not* prohibited under the U.S. Constitution.[7]

---

[5] Certain cases under the Civil and Voting Rights Acts are still subject to mandatory jurisdiction, but there have been very few such appeals in recent years.

[6] *Michigan* v. *Long*, 463 U.S. 1032 (1983).

The broad issues of determining the balance of power between the federal and state courts and the proper boundaries of the separation of powers among the three branches of the federal government are too complicated to be discussed here. Generally, however, we will address these issues in such specific areas as regulation, antitrust, and the like as they arise. Clearly, the initial 1787-1788 concerns of the citizens of the newly united states about just how much power the President should have vis-à-vis the Congress, and how much power the federal government should have vis-à-vis the individual states, have not, and never will be, fully settled. Not any more than rights such as "due process" or "equal protection of the laws" can be settled solely by reference to the intent of men (not women) who argued about them in 1787 and 1868. That is *not* a weakness in our system. It is, in fact, a primary factor in our unique, democratic growth.[8]

3. The Decision Structure: Where to Find the Law

Many nations employ legal systems that depend almost entirely on written laws or codes initially instituted many centuries ago. Lawyers tend to refer to such jurisdictions as operating under "a Civil Code." This is different from our American (and from the British) system, which is referred to as a system of "common law."

That term "common law" is really quite ambiguous. Basically, however, it refers to a legal system that does not depend for its authority on a set of written statutes (laws, or a Code). Rather, it is a legal system based upon rules deduced (mainly by judges), over time, from the basic customs and institutions of the people and related to their sociopolitical/economic conditions. These deduced rules *do* change and expand as society does; however, once rules are laid down (i.e., decided) they are venerated as precedent and are changed very cautiously and deliberately, and the changes explained very carefully, and *in writing*, for all to see. This common-law principle of following precedent is referred to as *stare decisis*.

Now we do have statutes in America, of course. And regulations, mountains of regulations. This does not, however, change the fact that our *basic* jurisprudence, or body of law, is passed down, over time, carefully,

---

[7] See cases described in S. Wermiel, "State Supreme Courts Are Feeling Their Oats about Civil Liberties," *Wall Street Journal*, June 15, 1988; W. Green and A.D. Marcus, "Texas School Funding Is Unconstitutional," *Wall Street Journal*, October 3, 1989; J.S. Kaye, "Celebrating Our Other Constitution," *New York State Bar Journal* (April 1988).

[8] The case of *Morrison* v. *Olson*, 108 S.Ct. 2597 (1988) involving the constitutionality of independent counsel (regarding investigation/prosecution of high-level executive branch misconduct) is discussed clearly in a professional journal article highlighting the general *separation of powers* issue: Steward and Nelson, "Separation of Powers, Cont.", *American Bar Association Journal* (September 1988).

in written decisions, for all to see and to follow in the general interest of preserving law and order.

It should be obvious then that written case law is crucial to our common-law system. That leads inexorably to the question: Exactly where and how is it to be found?

American case law is found in volumes of case *Reports* in law libraries. Law students take weeks, if not months, to master their library systems, and it would be both cruel and futile to try to be thorough here. Let it be said that, basically, written case decisions *on the federal level* are found in various Reports contained in three basic categories:

1. Those containing cases decided in district courts are in volumes labeled Federal Supplements and cited, for example, as 25 F.Supp. 139 (1929): 25 being the volume number, 139 being the page, 1929 the year of the decision. F.Supp. 2d refers to later decisions in the series.

2. U.S. Court of Appeals decisions (and some district court decisions) appear in a second series of volumes labeled *Federal Reporter* and cited—Fed.—(year), or—Fed. 2d—(year) etc.

3. U.S. Supreme Court decisions appear in several different sets of volumes, the major ones being (a) the United States Reports, cited as U.S.; (b) Supreme Court Reports, cited as S.Ct., and (c) Lawyers Edition, United States Supreme Court Reports, cited as L.Ed. The Lawyers Edition doesn't carry all the U.S. Supreme Court cases as U.S. and S.Ct. both do, only those deemed particularly significant. You will sometimes find a particular Supreme Court case cited by the U.S. volume, sometimes by the S.Ct. volume, but never by L.Ed alone.

State court decisions are found in too many books to list here, but there are two *main* sources: regional Reports such as Atlantic, North East, South East, Southern, South West, North West and Pacific Reports concerning several states each, and cited, for example, *Kilroy* v. *Kilroy*, 19 N.E. 2d 433 (1950)—for Vermont. And state court decisions are also found in State Reports; for example, Ill.-(1951), which would mean reports of the Illinois Supreme Court, at least from 1819 on when this set of Reports began.

One might ask, How would I know if one of the decided cases to be found in one of these thousands of volumes has, in fact, been overruled? That is, the case is no longer valid? Well, there are volumes called Shepherd's Citations, covering *all* U.S. law cases, believe it or not, which list not only the case but all other cases that *mention* it, as well as overrule it. One might well see the value of computerized searches here!

4. Reading the Cases: How to Go about It

In 1966 some residents sued the Commonwealth of Virginia to have that state's $1.50 annual poll tax declared unconstitutional. The case is substantially reprinted below:

HARPER V. VIRGINIA STATE BOARD
OF ELECTIONS
383 U.S. 663, 16 L. Ed. 2d 169, 86 S. Ct. 1079 (1966)

Justice Douglas delivered the opinion of the Court.

These are suits by Virginia residents to have declared unconstitutional Virginia's poll tax [$1.50 annual tax]. The three-judge District court dismissed the complaint.

While the right to vote in federal elections is conferred by Art. I, S2, of the Constitution, the right to vote is nowhere expressly mentioned. It is argued that the right to vote in state elections is implicit, particularly by reason of the First Amendment and that it may not constitutionally be conditioned upon the payment of a tax or fee. We do not stop to canvass the relation between voting and political expression. For it is enough to say that once the franchise is granted to the electorate, lines may not be drawn which are inconsistent with the Equal Protection Clause of the Fourteenth Amendment.

We conclude that a State violates the Equal Protection Clause of the Fourteenth Amendment whenever it makes the affluence of the voter or payment of any fee an electoral standard. Voter qualifications have no relation to wealth nor to paying or not paying this or any other tax. Our cases demonstrate that the Equal Protection Clause of the Fourteenth Amendment restrains the States from fixing voter qualifications which invidiously discriminate.

Long ago in *Yick Wo* v. *Hopkins*, the Court referred to "the political franchise of voting" as a "fundamental political right, because it is preservative of all rights." Recently in Reynolds v. Sims, 377 U.S. 533 (1964), we said, "Undoubtedly, the right of suffrage is a fundamental matter in a free and democratic society. Especially since the right to exercise the franchise in a free and unimpaired manner is preservative of other basic civil and political rights, any alleged infringement of the right of citizens to vote must be carefully and meticulously scrutinized."

We say the same whether the citizen, otherwise qualified to vote, has $1.50 in his pocket or nothing at all, pays the fee or fails to pay it. The principle that denies the State the right to dilute a citizen's vote on account of his economic status or other such factors by analogy bars a system which excludes those unable to pay a fee to vote or who fail to pay.

It is argued that a State may exact fees from citizens for many different kinds of licenses; that if it can demand from all an equal fee for a driver's license, it can demand from all an equal poll tax for voting. But we must remember that the interest of the State, when it comes to voting, is limited to the power to fix qualifications. Wealth, like race, creed, or color, is not germane to one's ability to participate intelligently in the electoral process. Lines drawn on the basis of wealth or property, like those of race, are traditionally disfavored. See *Edwards v. California* (Jackson, J., concurring); *Grivvin v. Illinois; Douglas v. California.* To introduce wealth or payment of a fee as a measure of a voter's qualifications is to introduce a capricious or irrelevant factor. The degree of the discrimination is irrelevant. In this context—that is, as a condition of obtaining a ballot—the requirement of fee paying causes an "invidious" discrimination (*Skinner* v. *Oklahoma*) that runs afoul of the Equal Protection Clause.

We agree, of course, with Mr. Justice Holmes that the Due Process Clause of the Fourteenth Amendment "does not enact Mr. Herbert Spencer's Social Statics" (*Lochner* v. *New York*). Likewise, the Equal Protection Clause is not shackled to the political theory of a particular era. In determining what lines are unconstitutionally discriminatory, we have never been confined to historic notions of equality, any more than we have restricted due process to a fixed catalogue of what was at a given time deemed to be the limits of fundamental rights. Notions of what constitutes equal treatment for purposes of the Equal Protection Clause *do* change (*Brown* v. *Board of Education*).

In a recent searching re-examination of the Equal Protection Clause, we held, as already noted, that "the opportunity for equal participation by all voters in the election of state legislators" is required. *Reynolds* v. *Sims.* We decline to qualify that principle by sustaining this poll tax.

Our conclusion, like that in *Reynolds* v. *Sims*, is founded not on what we think governmental policy should be, but on what the Equal Protection Clause requires.

We have long been mindful that where fundamental rights and liberties are asserted under the Equal Protection Clause, classifications which might invade or restrain them must be closely scrutinized and carefully confined. See, e.g., Skinner v. Oklahoma.

Those principles apply here. For to repeat, wealth or fee paying has, in our view, no relation to voting qualifications; the right to vote is too precious, too fundamental to be so burdened or conditioned.

Reversed.

Justice Black, dissenting.

State poll tax legislation can "reasonably," "rationally" and without an "invidious" or evil purpose to injure anyone be found to rest on a number of state policies including (1) the State's desire to collect its revenue, and (2) its belief that voters who pay a poll tax will be interested in furthering the State's welfare when they vote. Certainly it is rational to believe that people may be more likely to pay taxes if payment is a prerequisite to voting. And if history can be a factor in determining the "rationality" of discrimination in a state law, then whatever may be our personal opinion, history is on the side of "rationality" of the State's poll tax policy. Property qualifications existed in the Colonies and were continued by many States after the Constitution was adopted.

The Court denies that it is using the "natural-law-due-process formula." I find no statement in the Court's opinion, however, which advances even a plausible argument as to why the alleged discriminations which might possibly be effected by Virginia's poll tax law are "irrational," "unreasonable," "arbitrary," or "invidious" or have no relevance to a legitimate policy which the State wishes to adopt. I can only conclude that the primary, controlling, predominate, if not the exclusive reason for declaring the Virginia law unconstitutional is the Court's deep-seated hostility and antagonism, which I share, to making payment of a tax a prerequisite to voting.

Justice Harlan, whom Justice Stewart joins, dissenting.

The Equal Protection Clause prevents States from arbitrarily treating people differently under their laws. The test evolved by this Court for determining whether an asserted justifying classification exists is whether such a classification can be deemed to be founded on some rational and otherwise constitutionally permissible state policy. This standard reduces to a minimum the likelihood that the federal judiciary will judge state policies in terms of the individual notions and predilections of its own members, and until recently it has been followed in all kinds of "equal protection" cases.

Reynolds v. *Sims*, among its other breaks with the past, also marked a departure from these traditional and wise principles. Unless its "one man, one vote" thesis of the legislative apportionment is to be attributed to the insupportable proposition that "Equal Protection" simply means indiscriminate equality, it seems inescapable that what

Reynolds really reflected was but this Court's own views of how modern American representative government should be run. For it can hardly be thought that no other method of apportionment may be considered rational.

In substance the Court's analysis of the equal protection issue goes no further than to say that the electoral franchise is "precious" and "fundamental," and to conclude that "to introduce wealth or payment of a fee as a measure of a voter's qualifications is to introduce a capricious or irrelevant factor." These are of course captivating phrases, but they are wholly inadequate to satisfy the standard governing adjudication of the equal protection issue: Is there a rational basis for Virginia's poll tax as a voting qualification? I think the answer to that question is undoubtedly "yes."

Property and poll-tax qualifications, very simply, are not in accord with current egalitarian notions of how a modern democracy should be organized. It is of course entirely fitting that legislatures should modify the law to reflect such changes in popular attitudes. However, it is all wrong, in my view, for the court to adopt the political doctrines popularly accepted at a particular moment of our history and to declare all others to be irrational and invidious, barring them from the range of choice by reasonably minded people acting through the political process. It was not too long ago that Mr. Justice Holmes felt impelled to remind the Court that the Due Process Clause of the Fourteenth Amendment does not enact the laissez-faire theory of society. *Lochner.* The times have changed, and perhaps it is appropriate to observe that neither does the Equal Protection Clause of the Amendment rigidly impose upon America an ideology of unrestrained egalitarianism. . . .

When reading the case above, or any other case, certain basic elements are to be considered:

a. What is the name of the case?

b. What court considered it?

c. Where can the full case be found (assuming it to be abridged if it is not in the original report)?

All that is clear enough here. Next, you will want to consider the following:

d. *What are the facts here?* Not allegations or suppositions or guesses. Those things belong in a trial court. By the time the case reaches an appellate court, the facts will be settled (except in the rare case where there was no evidence to support the facts). Often facts are complicated, but in this case they are not. The facts are that the

Commonwealth of Virginia did charge a poll tax of $1.50 a year, that some Virginia residents did not want to pay it, and still wanted to vote.

e. What's the main issue? It isn't who should "win" since that is always a general issue. Judges sometimes talk too much—though not here—and, one must often work hard to locate the issue. In this case, the issue is simply stated (though not necessarily simply resolved): Is the Virginia poll tax law unconstitutional?

f. *What did the court decide?* Here it decided *yes*, the law is unconstitutional.

g. *Why did the court so decide?* Here things can get more complicated. Some of the things a court says in coming to its conclusion are directly relevant to the decision. But some others are tangential to the decision, peripheral to it. Those statements, and the reasoning behind them, that *do* contribute directly to the decision are part of it and can be used by other lawyers, in later cases, to influence the court to find for their clients for the same reasons (i.e., they come under the rubric of *stare decisis*). The tangential statements are merely *dicta* (i.e., interesting, maybe even fun, but not reasoning leading directly to the result, namely the decision). You will note here that Justices Harlan and Stewart, who disagreed with the decision of the majority of six judges, represented by Justice Douglas, got sassy. They said, in effect, that Douglas's reasoning was not really relevant to his decision, that it was really only *dicta*, and not true Constitution-related reasoning. Of course, Harlan and Stewart did not put it *that* way! "Captivating phrases" were the words they used. But to get back to *why* the Supreme Court decided as it did: The majority found that the Fourteenth Amendment to the Constitution (the Equal Protection clause) was violated by the charging of a poll tax because such a tax invades and restrains citizens' right to vote on account of their economic status. Go back to the decision and look for the words. Remember, you do not read a case originally to see if you agree with it, but to see just what it says and why it says it, and how.

h. *Is there a dissent?* If so, you should go with the same procedure; that is, what was the main issue *for the dissenters?* How did *they* decide the case? And why? In the end, of course, it may not matter what dissenters say. But if the dissent is powerful enough, or the dissenters become powerful enough, it surely might matter, and it could be important to understand exactly the position of the dissenters. Recall that in *Roe* v. *Wade* (the original 1973 abortion case) the main dissenter was William Rehnquist.

5. Alternative Dispute Resolution

Not all legal disputes go through the lengthy and expensive process of trials, appeals, and cases in the Reports.

Trials can be avoided by settlement. The overwhelming majority of cases *are* settled, both civil (usually for money) and criminal (by copping a plea). Sometimes settlements are brought about by the competent use of *discovery procedures* which eliminate surprises and hidden traps before any in-court action starts. The four basic procedures in discovery are written interrogatories, production of documents, depositions, and requests for admissions—all done before trial.

Then, too, there are specific options for resolving disputes. Lawyers often refer to them, collectively, as ADR—alternative dispute resolution.

Negotiation, mediation, and arbitration are basic tools in ADR, and some specific structures include private judging, ombudsmen as investigators and reporters, the use of minitrials and summary jury trials, and settlements moderated by impartial third parties.[9]

6. Civil and Criminal Law Generally: The Substance

Throughout this text we will be studying many specific areas of American law, and what we intend here is to suggest some general, overall structure into which the rules and reasoning we will encounter can be placed.

Law arises out of the Constitution, out of the case-law decisions of courts, and out of legislation on both the local and the federal level. Regulations promulgated by administrative agencies arise out of legislatively delegated authority, and we shall deal substantively with these later on.

Law is basically civil or criminal. Civil law can be very costly to litigants in the end, in terms of actions one might have to take, and money that might have to be paid out. But criminal law goes beyond money (e.g., fines and confiscations); here, defendants can lose their freedom and even their lives.

In civil cases, the parties are generally private persons or organizations, although government can, indeed, be party to a civil lawsuit. In criminal cases, government is *always* a party. It represents the people. Because losing a criminal case is such a serious matter for a defendant, the burden of proving guilt is much higher than the civil burden of proving the other party committed a wrong (i.e., caused a personal injury or violated a contract). The criminal burden of proof is generally charac-

---

[9] A useful article here is L. Ray, "Emerging Options in Dispute Resolution," *American Bar Association Journal*, (June 1989). It is also useful to remember that ADR, like discovery procedures, can also be expensive, and may not provide the best results. There are pros and cons to using both procedures (or not using), particularly ADRs. See C. Killefer, "Some Disputes Still Deserve Their Day in Court," *The Wall Street Journal*, October 12, 1992.

terized as requiring proof of guilt *beyond a reasonable doubt*; the civil law as proving *by a preponderance of the evidence* (i.e., that it is more likely than not) that the alleged wrong has been committed against you.

Civil law is basically either tort or contract law. *Tort law* comes into play when harm is caused to one or more parties by another party or set of parties. That harm can be to one's physical person, to one's psyche, or reputation, to one's privacy, and certainly to one's property. And that harm can be caused deliberately or negligently.

Contract law comes into play through a breach of provisions in some contract, whether it be express or implied.

Now let us get specific. It is time to deal with product liability law. We shall begin with a general reference table, and then examine some cases.

II. PRODUCT LIABILITY

A. Grounds for Recovery

Negligence:
Fault/failure to use due care in manufacture, design, and/or distribution of the product. The failure to use due care must be the proximate cause of the consumer's injury, and the consumer must be a person to whom a duty of care is owed. Defenses apply.

Warranty:
(Part tort law, part contract law.) Must be a sale or lease of a product—*not* a service—and the warranty may be express (specifically made) or implied. What is ordinarily implied is that the product is fit for the use for which it is intended (i.e., merchantable). Negligence is irrelevant, but the breach of warranty must be proved, as well as the proximately caused damage.

Intentional misconduct:
Manufacturer, designer, distributor, etc., at the time of manufacture, design, distribution, etc., *knew*, or was *reckless* in its failure to discover, that the product, as manufactured, designed, distributed, etc., was defective and would likely cause injury in normal use.

Strict liability:
If a product contains a proven defect in design or manufacture, and if the consumer is injured as the result of that defect while using the product in the way it was intended to be used, and the consumer was not aware of that defect, there is a liability. Some jurisdictions further require that the defect render the product "unreasonably" dangerous. Generally speaking, a product is

"defective" if it is not fit for its intended use, or is in a condition not within the reasonable contemplation of the ultimate consumer.

Absolute   Does not exist in product liability law.B. Some Law
liability: Cases

B. Some Law Cases

- *MacPherson* v. *Buick Motor Co.* (1916)
- *Henningsen* v. *Bloomfield Motors Inc.* (1960)
- *Greenman* v. *Yuba Power Products, Inc.* (1963)
- *Grimshaw* v. *Ford Motor Co.* (1981)

Ordinary negligence is not highlighted in these cases (although legal *duty* is) except that in *Greenman* there was actual negligence in the design and construction of the power tool at issue; however, chronologically and substantively, the first three cases do run the duty, broad warranty/strict liability gamut. The final case involves serious misconduct on the part of the manufacturer, and it sheds a very special light on the one great socioeconomic issue that goes to the heart of the product liability debate: *Who should bear the risk of the costs to the individual and to society that result from the manufacture and distribution of products that cause harm?* And, of course, how, exactly, should those costs be measured?

There is a third issue as well: Should product liability be taken out of the "common law" court track, at least in great measure, by state or local legislatures? By the United States Congress? If so, to rectify what "common law" wrong?

In examining the cases try to relate to the questions posed in the earlier section titled "Reading the Cases."

MACPHERSON V. BUICK MOTOR CO.
217 N.Y. 382, 111 N.E. 1050 (1916)
(N.Y. Court of Appeals)

Cardozo, J.

The defendant is a manufacturer of automobiles. It sold an automobile to a retail dealer. The retail dealer resold to the plaintiff. While the plaintiff was in the car it suddenly collapsed. He was thrown out and injured. One of the wheels was made of defective wood, and its spokes crumbled into fragments. The wheel was not made by the defendant; it was bought from another manufacturer. There is evidence, however, that its defects could have been discovered by reasonable inspection, and that inspection was omitted. There is no claim that the defendant knew of the defect and willfully concealed it. . . . The charge is one, not of fraud, but of negligence. The question to be determined is whether the defendant owed a duty of care and vigilance to any one but the immediate purchaser.

The foundations of this branch of law, at least in this state, were laid in *Thomas* v. *Winchester*. A poison was falsely labeled. The sale was made to a druggist, who in turn sold to a customer. The customer recovered damages from the seller who affixed the label. "The defendant's negligence," it was said, "put human life in imminent danger." A poison, falsely labeled is likely to injure any one who gets it. Because the danger is to be foreseen, there is a duty to avoid the injury.

. . . .

. . . Early cases suggest a narrow construction of the rule. Later cases, however, evince a more liberal spirit. . . . [We] turn to the latest case in this court in which *Thomas* v. *Winchester* was followed. That case is *Statler* v. *Ray Mfg. Co.* The defendant manufactured a large coffee urn. It was installed in a restaurant. When heated, the urn exploded and injured the plaintiff. We held that the manufacturer was liable. We said that the urn "was of such a character inherently that, when applied to the purposes for which it was designed, it was liable to become a source of great danger to many people if not carefully and properly constructed."

. . . The defendant argues that things imminently dangerous to life are poisons, explosives, deadly weapons—things whose normal function it is to injure or destroy. But whatever the rule in *Thomas* v. *Winchester* may once have been, it has no longer that restricted meaning. . . . A large coffee urn (*Statler* v. *Ray Mfg. Co.*, supra) may have within itself, if negligently made, the potency of danger, yet no one thinks of it as an implement whose normal function is destruction. . . .

We hold, then, that the principle of *Thomas* v. *Winchester* is not limited to poisons, explosives, and things of like nature, to things which in their normal operation are implements of destruction. If the nature of a thing is such that it is reasonably certain to place life and limb in peril when negligently made, it is then a thing of danger. Its nature gives warning of the consequences to be expected. If to the element of danger there is added knowledge that the thing will be used by persons other than the purchaser, and used without new tests, then, irrespective of contract, the manufacturer of this thing of danger is under a duty to make it carefully. That is as far as we are required to go for the decision of this case. There must be knowledge of a danger, not merely possible, but probable. . . . The proximity or remoteness of the relation is a factor to be considered. We are dealing now with the liability of the manufacturer of the finished product, who puts it on the market to be used without inspection by his customers. If he is negligent, where danger is foreseen, a liability will follow. . . .

. . . Beyond all question, the nature of an automobile gives warning of probable danger if its construction is defective. This automobile was designed to go 50 miles an hour. Unless its wheels were sound and strong, injury was almost certain. It was as much a thing of danger as a defective engine for a railroad. The defendant knew the danger. It knew also that the car would be used by persons other than the buyer. This was apparent from its size; there were seats for three persons. It was apparent also from the fact that the buyer was a dealer in cars, who bought to resell. . . . The dealer was indeed the one person of whom it might be said with some approach to certainty that by him the car would not be used. Yet the defendant would have us say that he was the one person whom it was under a legal duty to protect. The law does not lead us to so inconsequent a conclusion. Precedents drawn from the days of travel by stagecoach do not fit the conditions of travel today. The principle that the danger must be imminent does not change, but the things subject to the principle do change. They are whatever the needs of life in a developing civilization require them to be.

. . . .

In this view of the defendant's liability there is nothing inconsistent with the theory of liability on which the case was tried. It is true that the court told the jury that "an automobile is not an inherently dangerous vehicle." The meaning, however, is made plain by the context. The meaning is that danger is not to be expected when the vehicle is well constructed. The court left it to the jury to say whether the defendant ought to have foreseen that the car, if negligently constructed, would become "imminently dangerous." Subtle distinctions are drawn by the defendant between things inherently dangerous and things imminently dangerous, but the case does not turn upon these verbal niceties. If danger was to be expected as reasonably certain, there was a duty of vigilance, and this whether you call the danger inherent or imminent. In varying forms that thought was put before the jury. We do not say that the court would not have been justified in ruling as a matter of law that the car was a dangerous thing. If there was any error, it was none of which the defendant can complain.

We think the defendant was not absolved from a duty of inspection because it bought the wheels from a reputable manufacturer. It was not merely a dealer in automobiles. It was a manufacturer of automobiles. It was responsible for the finished product. It was not at liberty to put the finished product on the market without subjecting the component parts to ordinary and simple tests. Under the charge of the trial judge nothing more was required of it. The obligation to inspect must vary with the nature of the thing to be inspected. The more probable the danger the greater the need of caution.

. . . .

The judgement should be affirmed, with costs.

HENNINGSEN V. BLOOMFIELD MOTORS, INC.
Supreme Court of New Jersey
161 A. 2d 69 (1960)

[A Mr. Henningsen of New Jersey bought a Plymouth car for his wife from Bloomfield Motors, Inc. Mrs. Henningsen suffered injuries when the car ran off the road due to a defective steering mechanism. The couple sued Chrysler Corp. and Bloomfield Motors, Inc. No negligence was proved. The contract of sale from Bloomfield Motors to Mr. Henningsen provided that there were no warranties express or implied on the car except one providing for replacement of defective parts. The trial court judge sent the case to the jury on the claim of breach of warranty. The jury found for the couple, against both of the defendants. An excerpt from the decision on appeal, follows.]

Francis, J.

The Claim of Implied Warranty Against the Manufacturer

In the ordinary case of sale of goods by description an implied warranty of merchantability is an integral part of the transaction. . . . The former type of warranty simply means that the thing sold is reasonably fit for the general purpose for which it is manufactured and sold. . . .

. . . With these considerations in mind, we come to a study of the express warranty on the reverse side of the purchase order signed by Claus Henningsen. At the outset we take notice that it was made only by the manufacturer and that by its terms it runs directly to Claus Henningsen. . . .

The terms of the warranty are a sad commentary upon the automobile manufacturers' marketing practices. Warranties developed in the law in the interest of and to protect the ordinary consumer who cannot be expected to have the knowledge or capacity or even the opportunity to make adequate inspection of mechanical instrumentalities, like automobiles, and to decide for himself whether they are reasonably fit for the designed purpose. But the ingenuity of the Automobile Manufacturers Association, by means of its standardized form, has metamorphosed the warranty into a device to limit the maker's liability. . . .

The manufacturer agrees to replace defective parts for 90 days after the sale or until the car has been driven 4,000 miles, whichever is first to occur, if the part is sent to the factory, transportation charges prepaid, and if examination discloses to its satisfaction that the part is defective. It is difficult to imagine a greater burden on the consumer, or a less satisfactory remedy. . . . Moreover, the guaranty is against defective workmanship. That condition may arise from good parts improperly assembled. There being no defective parts to return to the maker, is all remedy to be denied?. . .

The matters referred to represent only a small part of the illusory character of the security presented by the warranty. Thus far the analysis has dealt only with the remedy provided in the case of a defective part. What relief is provided when the breach of the warranty results in personal injury to the buyer?. . . But in this instance, after reciting that defective parts will be replaced at the factory, the alleged agreement relied upon by Chrysler provides that the manufacturer's "obligation under this warranty" is limited to that undertaking: further, that such remedy is "in lieu of all other warranties, express or implied, and all other obligations or liabilities on its part." The contention has been raised that such language bars any claim for personal injuries which may emanate from a breach of the warranty. . . .

. . . Chrysler urges that since it was not a party to the sale by the dealer to Henningsen, there is no privity of contract between it and the plaintiffs, and the absence of this privity eliminates any such implied warranty. . . .

Under modern conditions the ordinary layman, on responding to the importuning of colorful advertising, has neither the opportunity nor the capacity to inspect or to determine the fitness of an automobile for use; he must rely on the manufacturer who has control of its construction, and to some degree on the dealer who, to the limited extent called for by the manufacturer's instructions, inspects and services it before delivery. In such a marketing milieu his remedies and those of persons who properly claim through him should not depend "upon the intricacies of the law of sales. The obligation of the manufacturer should not be based alone on privity of contract. It should rest, as was once said, upon 'the demands of social justice.'" [citation omitted]

Accordingly, we hold that under modern marketing conditions, when a manufacturer puts a new automobile in the stream of trade and promotes its purchase by the public, an implied warranty that it is reasonably suitable for use as such accompanies it into the hands of the ultimate purchaser. Absence of agency between the manufacturer and the dealer who makes the ultimate sale is immaterial.

The Effect of the Disclaimer and Limitation of Liability Clauses on the Implied Warranty of Merchantability

. . . What effect should be given to the express warranty in question which seeks to limit the manufacturer's liability to replacement of defective parts, and which disclaims all other warranties, express or implied?. . .

The warranty before us is a standardized form designed for mass use. He [the buyer] takes it or leaves it, and he must take it to buy an automobile. No bargaining is engaged in with respect to it. In fact, the dealer through whom it comes to the buyer is without authority to alter it; his function is ministerial—simply to deliver it. . . .

The gross inequality of bargaining position occupied by the consumer in the automobile industry is thus apparent. There is no competition among the car makers in the area of the express warranty. . . .

. . . Under the law, breach of warranty against defective parts or workmanship which caused personal injuries would entitle a buyer to damages even if due care were used in the manufacturing process. Because of the great potential for harm if the vehicle was defective, that right is the most important and fundamental one arising from the relationship. Difficulties so frequently encountered in establishing negligence in manufacture in the ordinary case make this manifest. In the context of this warranty, only the abandonment of all sense of justice would permit us to hold that, as a matter of law, the phrase "its obligation under this warranty being limited to making good at its factory any part or parts thereof" signifies to an ordinary reasonable person that he is relinquishing any personal injury claim that might flow from the use of a defective automobile. . . .

. . . The verdict in favor of the plaintiffs and against Chrysler Corporation establishes that the jury found that the disclaimer was not fairly obtained. . . .

The Defense of Lack of Privity Against Mrs. Henningsen

Both defendants contend that since there was no privity of contract between them and Mrs. Henningsen, she cannot recover for breach of any warranty made by either of them. On the facts, as they were developed, we agree that she was not a party to the purchase agreement. Her right to maintain the action, therefore, depends upon whether she occupies such legal status thereunder as to permit her to take advantage of a breach of defendants' implied warranties. . . . We are convinced that the cause of justice in this area of the law can be serviced only by recognizing that she is a such a person who, in the reasonable contemplation of the parties to the warranty, might be expected to become a user of the automobile. . . .

It is important to express the right of Mrs. Henningsen to maintain her action in terms of a general principle. To what extent may lack of privity be disregarded in suits on such warranties?. . . It is our opinion that an implied warranty of merchantability chargeable to either an automobile manufacturer or a dealer extends to the purchaser of the car, members of his family, and to other persons occupying or using it with his consent. It would be wholly opposed to reality to say that use by such persons is not within the anticipation of parties to such a warranty of reasonable suitability of an automobile for ordinary highway operation. Those persons must be considered within the distributive chain. . . .

Under all of the circumstances outlined above, the judgements in favor of the plaintiffs and against the defendants are affirmed.

GREENMAN V. YUBA POWER PRODUCTS, INC.
Supreme Court of California
59 Cal. 2d 57 377 P. 2d 897 (1963)

[In this case, the California plaintiff bought a power tool manufactured by the defendant, Yuba. A piece of wood the plaintiff had in the tool, using the tool as it was meant to be used, flew out of the tool and hit him on his forehead, injuring him severely.

There were several issues here, including one involving notice of injury from plaintiff to maker and retailer. The major issue, however, deals with *warranty*. The evidence presented by the plaintiff at the trial was sufficient to show that the tool was defectively designed and constructed. There were also express warranties in the manufacturer's brochure that the jury could have found (and did find) were breached. Yuba appealed and lost. Our interest here is in Judge Traynor's exposition of the *strict* liability concept in product liability law.]

Traynor, J.

Moreover, to impose strict liability on the manufacturer under the circumstances of this case, it was not necessary for plaintiff to establish an express warranty as defined in section 1732 of the Civil Code. A manufacturer is strictly liable in tort when an article he places on the market, knowing that it is to be used without inspection for defects, proves to have a defect that causes injury to a human being. Recognized first in the case of unwholesome food products, such liability has now been extended to a variety of other products that create as great or greater hazards if defective.

Although in these cases strict liability has usually been based on the theory of an express or implied warranty running from the manufacturer to the plaintiff, the abandonment of the requirement of a contract between them, the recognition that the liability is not assumed by agreement but imposed by law [citations], and the refusal to permit the manufacturer to define the scope of its own responsibility for defective products [citations] make clear that the liability is not one governed by the law of contract warranties but by the law of strict liability in tort. Accordingly, rules defining and governing warranties that were developed to meet the needs of commercial transactions cannot properly be invoked to govern the manufacturer's liability to those injured by their defective products unless those rules also serve the purposes for which such liability is imposed.

We need not recanvass the reasons for imposing strict liability on the manufacturer. They have been fully articulated in the cases cited above. (See also 2 Harper and James, Torts SS 28.15-28.16, pp. 1569-1574; Prosser, Strict Liability to the Consumer, 69 Yale L.J. 1099; *Escola* v. *Coca Cola Bottling Co.*, 24 Cal. 2d 453, 461, 150 P. 2d 436, concurring opinion.) The purpose of such liability is to insure that the costs of injuries resulting from defective products are borne by the manufacturers that put such products on the market rather than by the injured persons who are powerless to protect themselves. Sales warranties service this purpose fitfully at best. (See Prosser, Strict Liability to the Consumer, 69 Yale L.J. 1099, 1124-1134.) In the present case, for example, plaintiff was able to plead and prove an express warranty only because he read and relied on the representations of the Shopsmith's ruggedness contained in the manufacturer's brochure. Implicit in the machine's presence on the market, however, was the representation that it would safely do the jobs for which it was built.

Under these circumstances, it should not be controlling whether plaintiff selected the machine because of the statements in the brochure, or because of the machine's own appearance of excellence that belied the defect lurking beneath the surface, or because he merely assumed that it would safely do the jobs it was built to do. It should not be controlling whether the details of the sales from manufacturer to retailer and from retailer to plaintiff's wife were such that one or more of the implied warranties of the sales act arose. (Civ. Code S 1735.) "The remedies of injured consumers ought not to be made to depend upon the intricacies of the law of sales." (*Ketterer* v. *Armour & Co.*, D.C., 200 F. 322, 323; *Klein* v. *Duchess Sandwich Co.*, 14 Cal. 2d 272, 282, 93 P. 2d 799.) To establish the manufacturer's liability it was sufficient that plaintiff proved that he was injured while using the Shopsmith in a way it was intended to be used as a result of a defect in design and manufacture of which plaintiff was not aware that made the Shopsmith unsafe for its intended use.

The judgement is affirmed.

GRIMSHAW V. *FORD MOTOR CO.*
119 Cal. App. 3d 757 (1981)

Tamura, Acting Presiding Justice.

A 1972 Ford Pinto hatchback automobile unexpectedly stalled on a freeway, erupting into flames when it was rear ended by a car proceeding in the same direction. Mrs. Lilly Gray, the driver of the Pinto, suffered fatal burns and 13-year-old Richard Grimshaw, a passenger in the Pinto, suffered severe and permanently disfiguring burns on his face and entire body. Grimshaw and the heirs of Mrs. Gray sued Ford Motor Company and others. Following a six-month jury trial, verdicts were returned in favor of plaintiffs against Ford Motor Company. Grimshaw was awarded $2,516,000 compensatory damages and $125 million punitive damages; the Grays were awarded $559,680 in compensatory damages. On Ford's motion for a new trial, Grimshaw was required to remit all but $3 1/2 million of the punitive award as a condition of denial of the motion.

Ford appeals from the judgement and from an order denying its motion for a judgement notwithstanding the verdict as to punitive damages. . . .

. . . .

The Accident:

In November 1971, the Grays purchased a new 1972 Pinto hatchback manufactured by Ford in October 1971. The Grays had trouble with the car from the outset. . . .

On May 28, 1972, Mrs. Gray, accompanied by 13-year-old Richard Grimshaw, set out in the Pinto from Anaheim for Barstow to meet Mr. Gray. . . . [T]he Pinto suddenly stalled and coasted to a halt in the middle lane [of the freeway]. It was later established that the carburetor float had become so saturated with gasoline that it suddenly sank, opening the float chamber and causing the engine to flood and stall. . . . [T]he driver of a 1962 Ford Galaxie was unable to avoid colliding with the Pinto. . . .

At the moment of impact, the Pinto caught fire and its interior was engulfed in flames. . . . By the time the Pinto came to rest after the collision, both occupants had sustained serious burns. When they emerged from the vehicle, their clothing was almost completely burned off. Mrs. Gray died a few days later of congestive heart failure as a result of the burns. Grimshaw managed to survive but only through heroic medical measures. . . .

Design of the Pinto Fuel System:

In 1968, Ford began designing a new subcompact automobile which ultimately became the Pinto. . . . Ford's objective was to build a car at or below 2,000 pounds to sell for no more than $2,000.

Ordinarily marketing surveys and preliminary engineering studies precede the styling of a new automobile line. Pinto, however, was a rush project, so that styling preceded engineering and dictated engineering design to a greater degree than usual. Among the engineering decisions dictated by styling was the placement of the fuel tank. It was then the preferred practice in Europe and Japan to locate the gas tank over the rear axle in subcompacts because a small vehicle has less "crush space" between the rear axle and the bumper than larger cars. The Pinto's styling, however, required the tank to be placed behind the rear axle leaving only 9 or 10 inches of "crush space"—far less than in any other American automobile or Ford overseas subcompact. In addition, the Pinto was designed so that its bumper was little more than a chrome strip, less substantial than the bumper of any other American car produced then or later. . . . Finally, the differential housing selected for the Pinto had an exposed flange and a line of exposed bolt heads. These protrusions were sufficient to puncture a gas tank driven forward against the differential upon rear impact.

Crash Tests:

During the development of the Pinto, prototypes were built and tested. . . .

The crash tests revealed that the Pinto's fuel system as designed could not meet the 20-mile-per-hour proposed standard. Mechanical prototypes struck from the rear with a moving barrier at 21-miles-per-hour caused the fuel tank to be driven forward and to be punctured, causing fuel leakage in excess of the standard prescribed by the proposed regulation. A production Pinto crash tested at 21-miles-per-hour into a fixed barrier caused the fuel neck to be torn from the gas tank and the tank to be punctured by a bolt head on the differential housing. . . .

The Cost to Remedy Design Deficiencies:

When a prototype failed the fuel system integrity test, the standard of care for engineers in the industry was to redesign and retest it. The vulnerability of the production Pinto's fuel tank at speeds of 20- and 30-miles-per-hour fixed barrier tests could have been remedied by inexpensive "fixes," but Ford produced and sold the Pinto to the public without doing anything to remedy the defects. . . . Equipping the car with a reinforced rear structure, smooth axle, improved bumper and additional crush space at a total cost of $14.30 would have made the fuel tank safe in a 34- to 38-mile-per-hour rear end collision by a vehicle the size of the Ford Galaxie. If, in addition to the foregoing, a bladder or tank within a tank were used or if the tank were protected with a shield, it would have been safe in a 40- to 45-mile-per-hour rear impact. If the tank had been located over the rear axle, it would have been safe in a rear impact at 50 miles per hour or more.

Management's Decision to Go Forward With Knowledge of Defects:

. . . Harley Copp, a former Ford engineer and executive in charge of the crash testing program, testified that the highest level of Ford's management made the decision to go forward with the production of the Pinto, knowing that the gas tank was vulnerable to puncture and rupture at low rear impact speeds creating a significant risk of death or injury from fire and knowing that "fixes" were feasible at nominal cost. He testified that management's decision was based on the cost savings which would inure from omitting or delaying the "fixes."

. . . .

Ford contends that the court erroneously admitted irrelevant documentary evidence highly prejudicial to Ford. We find the contention to be without merit.

(1) Exhibit No. 125:

Exhibit No. 125 was a report presented at a Ford production review meeting in April 1971, recommending action to be taken in anticipation of the promulgation of federal standards on fuel system integrity. The report recommended, inter alia, deferral from 1974 to 1976 of the adoption of "flak suits" or "bladders" in all Ford cars, including the Pinto, in order to realize a savings of $20.9 million. The report stated that the cost of the flak suit or bladder would be $4 to $8 per car. . . . A reasonable inference may be drawn from the evidence that despite management's knowledge that the Pinto's fuel system could be made safe at a cost of but $4 to $8 per car, it decided to defer corrective measures to save money and enhance profits. The evidence was thus highly relevant and properly received.

Ford contends that its motion for judgement notwithstanding the verdict should have been granted because the evidence was insufficient to support a finding of malice or corporate responsibility for such malice. The record fails to support the contention. . . .

Through the results of the crash tests Ford knew that the Pinto's fuel tank and rear structure would expose consumers to serious injury or death in a 20- to 30 mile-per-hour collision. There was evidence that Ford could have corrected the hazardous design defects at minimal cost but decided to defer correction of the shortcomings by engaging in a cost-benefit analysis balancing human lives and limbs against corporate profits. Ford's institutional mentality was shown to be one of callous indifference to public safety. There was substantial evidence that Ford's conduct constituted "conscious disregard" of the probability of injury to members of the consuming public.

Ford's argument that there can be no liability for punitive damages because there was no evidence of corporate ratification of malicious misconduct is equally without merit. . . .

There is substantial evidence that management was aware of the crash tests showing the vulnerability of the Pinto's fuel tank to rupture at low speed rear impacts with consequent significant risk of injury or death of the occupants by fire. There was testimony from several sources that the test results were forwarded up the chain of command. . . .

While most of the evidence was necessarily circumstantial, there was substantial evidence from which the jury could reasonably find that Ford's management decided to proceed with the production of the Pinto with knowledge of test results revealing design defects which rendered the fuel tank extremely vulnerable on rear impact at low speeds and endangered the safety and lives of the occupants. Such conduct constitutes corporate malice. . . .

In *Richard Grimshaw* v. *Ford Motor Company*, the judgement, the conditional new trial order, and the order denying Ford's motion for judgement notwithstanding the verdict on the issue of punitive damages are affirmed.

C. Is Product Liability Antimarket?

Please note that although Grimshaw was awarded $125 million in punitive damages by the jury, the judge took away $121,500,000 or 97.2 percent of the total. If Grimshaw refused to accept the reduced total, he would be forced to undertake another trial. The reduction of a jury's damage award by the judge is referred to in law as a *remittitur*. We will examine this concept further—together with the issue of punitive awards—in our discussion of "Damages" in Chapter 4.

As a result of this case and other lawsuits, Ford recalled 1.7 million Pintos (and Mercury Bobcats) in 1978. In the fall of 1987, Ford recalled

4.1 million cars and light trucks for engine fire–fuel line problems. Clearly, product liability cases can help to move the cause of consumer protection forward.

It has been argued, on the other hand, that product liability law couple with the fear of litigation and damage awards, has moved innovation and product development backwards in the United States. A 1989 study by the Rand Corporation was inconclusive on the point. It found that while 85,000 product liability suits had been brought in 1986 (a four-fold jump from 1976), only a small portion of the nation's 360,000 manufacturers were ever involved. Half of the cases targeted only 80 companies, and some of those companies were involved in thousands of suits (e.g., asbestos litigation). The study concluded that "the data does not support either the notion that product liability is crippling American business or that it isn't."[10]

The total number of businesses sued would not seem to be conclusive on the point of producer concern about the *likelihood* of being sued under product liability laws. A decision not to continue developing a product line out of fear of litigation would not be reflected in the data.

Still, no foreign producer who has developed a new product, or who sells any product, has any competitive product liability edge in the United States. The laws apply equally to everyone selling here. And the contention that domestic product liability costs are so high as to affect substantially American international business competitiveness is one that would be very hard to prove.

Using the automobile industry as an example, one might note that GM, Ford, and Chrysler have invested some $170 billion to improve productivity and quality over the last decade. That expenditure has substantially improved the 1981 figure of 400 percent more defects per U.S. vehicle than the Japanese average. But we are still slightly higher on defects per car than the Japanese are (1.6 per vehicle to 1.2). It would be hard merely to fault product liability law for the current problems afflicting the U.S. automobile industry—leaving out, say, American management and labor practices and the productivity issue, and Japanese dumping, vertical price fixing and tax avoidance through transfer pricing.[11]

A focal market question regarding product liability law in America is: Who ought to bear the burden for harm caused by manufactured products in the marketplace, and to what degree? And if we cannot be certain about the answer, we *can* be certain about the fact that the answer

---

[10] Terence Dungworth, author of the study, quoted in K. Klages, "Faulty Products," *American Bar Association Journal* (September 1989), p.32.

[11] See K.L. Kearns, "Is Japan About to Do in the Big Three?" *The Washington Post National Weekly Edition*, June 24-30, 1991, p. 23. See also White, Patterson, and Ingrassia, "Long Road Ahead: American Auto Makers Need Major Overhaul to Match the Japanese," *The Wall Street Journal*, January 10, 1992.

is, at least in part, beyond economics and law alone. There is a serious ethical issue involved as well. Note the issue (and the ambivalence) as expressed by a well-known American writer on economic matters:

> One of the saboteurs of U.S. competitiveness is our system of tort liability. Under that system, judges declare bad luck to be illegal, and lawyers share in the catch like the crew of a fishing vessel.

> But every once in a while there is reason to appreciate what is almost the only institution in U.S. life that holds people responsible for the consequences of their actions.[12]

III. PRODUCT LIABILITY, MASS TORTS, AND THE CHAPTER 11 (BANKRUPTCY) INTERSECTION

A. Mass Torts, Class Actions, and Chapter 11

In 1972 the first Dalkon Shield lawsuit was filed. The Dalkon Shield was an intrauterine device (IUD) manufactured by the A.H. Robins Company. Tiny and crabshaped, the IUD was touted as an extraordinarily effective birth control mechanism. Several million women purchased and used the Dalkon Shield. In fact, the device was soon alleged to be a substantial causative factor in consumer pelvic inflammatory disease, ectopic (displaced) pregnancies, septic abortions, infertility, and even death. And there were substantial allegations that the manufacturer knew (and kept from the consumer the fact) that its product could be harmful to the health and well-being of its users.

The Dalkon Shield cases[13] are excellent examples of the serious legal/economic/market problems raised by massive claims that have their origin in one particular product.

The problem is too complex to be fully delineated here in all of its legal ramifications. However, there are two major factors that are worth pursuing in some detail: the consolidation of numerous lawsuits, often into what are termed "class actions," and the use of Chapter 11 bankruptcy proceedings to avoid the problems caused to the company by overwhelming damage claims.

---

[12] M. Mayer, "Another Nonstarter," *The American Banker* (October 9, 1987), p. 1. Mr. Mayer's article focused on the S&L situation (as of 1987) and was remarkably prescient on the issue of lack of responsibility and its consequences. There has been much political activity directed toward federal government intervention in the product liability area. A bill to regulate product liability suits (limit the common law) was narrowly defeated, on procedural grounds, in the U.S. Senate, in September 1992.

[13] See, for an interesting history, E. Couric, "The A.H. Robins' Saga," *The American Bar Association Journal* (July 1986).

Class-action lawsuits are those undertaken on behalf of *all* persons of a similar class whose claims arise out of the same alleged wrongful action. While many individuals may band together to sue as a group, they are not involved in a legal class action if other individuals with similar status are also able to sue separately on their own behalf. Some plaintiffs may, of course, object to being lumped into one class, and may insist on pursuing their cases individually.

The major issue in a proposed class action relates to whether there is, in fact, an identifiable class of persons with "standing" (the legal right) to sue, and, if there is, whether there is a legally sufficient administrative (social) economic basis upon which to justify the *certification* by a court of this specific group's right to have all actions for harm from this product limited to those who join them to form a single combined, coordinated *class*.

In the Dalkon Shield cases, there had been many court verdicts against A.H. Robins by 1984. In October, Robins requested that the court certify all Dalkon Shield claimants seeking punitive damages as a class, thereby consolidating all such claims into one single action. The court denied the request. In the following year, four plaintiff attorneys in Minnesota who represented 2,000 claimants failed in their bid to have *all* Dalkon Shield claimants certified as a class and limited to one joint action. By this time, Robins had settled 10,000 claims at a cost of more than $100 million, and several thousand claims were still pending.

At this point, Robins filed for Chapter 11 bankruptcy protection.

Chapter 11 of the United States Bankruptcy Code sets out a voluntary bankruptcy petition process that is unlike the one under Chapter 7, which results in straight liquidation of the company. When a judge grants a Chapter 11 petition, which is focused on allowing the company to undergo a period of reorganization, all creditors are barred from pursuing claims against the company during the reorganization period. A creditor's committee (or more than one if there are several classes of creditors) is formed to negotiate and oversee the conditions under which the petitioner company can remain a going concern. The in-place management of the Chapter 11 firm usually remains in control of day-to-day operations; however, the creditor's committee oversees, and has the power to affect, those operations. The bankruptcy judge acts as an official mediator/arbitrator, and even decision-maker, when necessary. The actual reorganization plan is usually drafted by the firm, but it must be ratified by the creditor committee(s).

When a class action or an enormous number of separate claims are pending against a company filing a Chapter 11 petition, many issues arise. Not the least involves the question of fairness. The firm has caused widespread harm. Should plaintiffs be allowed to continue pursuing the claims in the normal course (e.g., to recover for outstanding medical bills)?

Or is it more equitable under the circumstances to allow the company to be protected for an indeterminate period in order to reorganize while continuing its usual operations?

In November 1985, all Dalkon Shield claims in the United States were ordered transferred to the Richmond, Virginia, bankruptcy court where Robins's Chapter 11 petition had been filed. At this point, the combined plaintiffs (not yet certified as one class) formed a 38-member (creditors) committee. The committee was later dissolved by the judge, who himself faced motions from plaintiff attorneys to disqualify himself on conflict of interest grounds, and then a court of appeals hearing when he refused to do so. Robins fired its own lawyers and replaced them, and the plaintiffs' committee attempted to fire its special counsel. The judge forced Robins to recoup almost $2 million in "improper" payments to its executives during the reorganization period, and Aetna, Robins's insurer, sued the firm separately for $57 million seeking to recover payments made in excess of policy limits. And plaintiffs' lawyers failed to agree on whether to have all plaintiffs certified as one class, or to continue to undertake thousands of separate lawsuits (which latter option terrified the weary judge).

One begins to understand here the complexities involved in a commingling of product liability claims, massive numbers of plaintiffs, and a Chapter 11 filing. One suspects that even Charles Dickens's *Jarndyce v. Jarndyce, Bleak House* protagonists would be awed by it all!

In the end, a Dalkon Shield Claimant's Trust was established to deal with some 85,000 pending claims. The Trust process was initiated in December 1987, when Robins was ordered by the judge to set aside $2.48 billion to pay all claims. This apparent outside-the-market resolution of Robins's defective-product-based problem led to an in-the-market bidding war for the firm, and to a lawsuit challenging the judge's authority to set up such a settlement plan. The U.S. Supreme Court refused to entertain the objection in November 1989; American Home Products acquired Robins; the Trust was affirmed—and the legal morass lingers on.

It lingers in the form of complaints that the Claimant's Trust is administered in a hostile, secretive fashion and that the money is, in any case, clearly insufficient. The end result appears to be that the mass tort problem in product liability law (and, as we shall see in Chapter 4, in "toxic torts") has not yet come to be an eminently satisfactory outside solution to this particular form of market inefficiency.

In that connection, we must take note of the very *first* massive tort litigation to be commingled with a Chapter 11 bankruptcy proceeding: The 1982 Johns Manville Company filing, which allowed that firm to continue normal business operations protected from tens of thousands of pending asbestos damage claims.

The Manville Personal Injury Settlement Trust, originally valued at $1.7 billion, was all but depleted by mid-1991. A panel of judges set up to review the enormous economic/legal problems raised by asbestos litigation came to some bleak conclusions:

> Thousands are dying before their asbestos cases come close to being decided. More and more major [asbestos] manufacturers. . . are seeking refuge from such proceedings behind the protection of bankruptcy law. And lawyers from all sides and the insurance companies are walking away with fees that consume two-thirds of the available resources. . . . [We] conclude that all available industry funds will be depleted within a few years.
>
> For every case that is settled or tried, nearly two are being filed, in large part because often-fatal diseases caused by exposure to asbestos, like mesothelioma, a malignant tumor of the lungs, can take decades to become apparent. [We] predict that the numbers of court cases, at last count 30,401, will grow by 50 percent in the next three years.[14]

B. Chapter 11: Some Ethical Concerns

There is an economic "exit from the market" process that occurs when an insufficiently competitive firm can no longer compete. The process is called "bankruptcy"—a mechanism for allocating resources. Chapter 11 clearly allows for some deviation from this exit process, particularly in the case where a firm that otherwise qualifies for liquidation is allowed to continue to operate.

The combined legal/economic/ethical issue that must be kept firmly in mind in any Chapter 11 filing is this: Is the discipline of the marketplace, upon which our economic system is based, actually being thwarted? Put another way, the question is whether a specific filing was really made in good faith (i.e., to support the legal focus of Chapter 11 to allow for reorganization and continued existence *when no other course is possible*). Although the bankruptcy code does not require that a company actually be insolvent before filing a Chapter 11 proceeding, good faith would seem to require the presence of very special considerations before protection is even sought as well as granted.[15]

---

[14] Quote from S. Labaton, "Judges Struggle to Control a Caseload Crisis," *The New York Times*, March 10, 1991. It is interesting to note here that ten U.S. district court judges around the country approved an order by two of them, in August 1990, to create a national class action of all federal and state asbestos lawsuits. However, the class certification was overturned within three weeks by the U.S. Court of Appeals for the 6th Circuit.

Although recent law has sought to make certain unilateral corporate actions more difficult, Chapter 11 filings can still result in the unilateral abrogation by the petitioner of existing collective bargaining agreements. Chapter 11 filings may result as well in limiting liability for cleaning up some toxic waste sites and, as we have seen, can hold off massive tort claims.

And yet, other firms operating in the normal way, *in competitive markets*, are facing the same labor, environmental, and product liability concerns as Chapter 11 firms. The question therefore

> for defenders of the notions of a free market and of market discipline in American enterprise is that actions currently taken under Chapter 11, while perfectly legal. . . may be moving inexorably in the direction of a race to the courthouse to enable solvent, albeit troubled, corporations to gain positive advantages over competitors. Such a race. . . eventually undermines the free market system, as well as other laws. . . such as environmental protection or labor laws.

> Yet competitors. . . "have the wolf by the ears" in that they cannot safely renounce the use of Chapter 11 filings as a means of reducing operating costs unless *all* significant competitors in that line of business refrain from filing as long as they are solvent. . . [fair play] demands that all solvent competitors refrain from filing, but self-preservation demands that all competitors retain the capacity to file. . . .[16]

Chapter 11, in other words, may be seen by some firms as more "efficient" for them than open competition in a free market.

A final nod in the direction of bankruptcy and ethics in the free market system would have to be aimed at what has been called "vulture

---

[15] It has been suggested that the Johns Manville filing was not made in good faith. See M.J. Roe, "Bankruptcy and Mass Tort," *84 Columbia Law Review* (1984).

[16] The quotation is from the seminal article on Chapter 11 looked at as sword and shield: W.F. Todd, "Aggressive Uses of Chapter 11 of the Federal Bankruptcy Code," *Economic Review*, FRB of Cleveland, Quarter 3, 1986. See also K. Helliker, "Prepackaged Bankruptcies Become Weapons for Firms," *The Wall Street Journal*, October 2, 1990, and B. O'Brian, "Chapter 11 Airlines, Struggling to Survive, May Depress Prices, Profits at Strong Carriers," *The Wall Street Journal*, July 9, 1991. The ultimate in cynicism about the bankruptcy process in America may be the thought expressed in the Business Section of *The New York Times*, March 17, 1991, p. 2. under the title "The Great Bankruptcy Shield": "France had the Theatre du Grand Guignol, presenting murder, rape, torture and suicide. The United States has the bankruptcy courts. . . ." Finally, the U.S. Supreme Court ruled, in June 1991, in the case of *Toibb* v. *Radloff*, that *individuals* may now file to reorganize *their* finances under Chapter 11. John and Mary Doe may now join R.H. Macy and Co., L.J. Hooker Corp., Allied Stores, Federated Department Stores, Carter Hawley Hale Stores, and a gaggle of U.S. airlines, steel companies, and others, in the Chapter 11 line.

investing," or the bankruptcy "endgame": dealing in the equity and debt paper of distressed (often Chapter 11) firms. This process has been referred to as playing the game of inefficient markets, wherein the players make less than completely informed bets on whether companies progress from deep trouble to profitability, or from poverty to utter ruin.

There is little humor in the potential conflict-of-interest problem, for example, created by a vulture investor (perhaps even an investment banking firm using its own and its investor's money) who buys a Chapter 11 firm's debt paper and becomes a creditor committee member. What is that person (or firm's) primary obligation? Is it to obtain a short-term profit on one's (or one's client's) investment in the fastest (legal) way possible? Or is it to promote the long-term best interests of the struggling firm, its employees, its clients, its community and perhaps the economy in general?

The distinguished American economist Charles P. Kindelberger, in a strong letter to the editor of *The Wall Street Journal*, took a jaundiced view of Wall Street's role here:

> The story, "Wall Street Prepares for a Failure Boom" conveys an obscene quality of vultures hovering over a dying animal, especially the remark about Campeau attracting attention because of its valuable assets "which can be sold for a restructuring and to help pay the lawyers' and bankers' bills."
>
> I was reminded of the third world debt problem. . . [which] attracted a slew of merchant banks and investment houses who offered their services to indebted countries on retainers of several million dollars a year. So far as I have been able to observe, the payoff on these fees have been virtually nil. . . .
>
> It was of great interest that your story nowhere mentioned any return to creditors or equity holders from the anticipated bankruptcies over which Wall Street seems to be salivating.[17]

---

[17] Letter to the Editor, "Wall Street Salivating Over Bankruptcies," *The Wall Street Journal*, January 21, 1990. See also Pauley, Friday, and Adams, "Sifting Ashes on Wall Street: Turnaround Artists Prosper Rescuing Failed LBOs, *Newsweek*, September 4, 1989. For a review of European legislation in this area, see M. Abbott, "Insolvency, the Best Solution: Everything You Always Wanted to Know About Something You Do Not Even Want to Think About," *Corporate Finance* (February 1991). *The New York Times* has devoted a good deal of critical space to the serious question of whether Chapter 11 is basically an unethical law. See D.B. Enrriquez, "The Vulture Game," *New York Times Magazine*, July 19, 1992; A.R. Rogerson, "Rethinking the Law That Gives Golden Eggs After the Goose Is Dead," *The New York Times*, April 5, 1992, and Bradley and Resenzweig, "Time to Scuttle Chapter 11," *The New York Times*, March 8, 1992.

In Lieu of the Philosopher's Stone

We might want to think about parties at interest and value-weighing with regard to issues like these:

    1. Congressperson Bumble has legislation in the hopper that would limit product liability lawsuits to cases of provable negligence (would eliminate warranty) except where the manufacturer or seller has made a specific warranty in writing. Also, damages in any one case would be limited to $100,000. Punitive damages are not allowed. This is to be a federal law pre-empting all state law and the common law.

    With regard to each of the provisions above:

    (a) Whose interests would you consider to be at stake?

    (b) Given the groups or persons who would be affected by the passage of such a law, exactly what are the values to be weighed on behalf of each of them? That is, just which shareholder values? Which consumer values? Which social values (for the social system)? Are there others? How do you decide how much each value weighs? Do you bring personal values with you to tip the scales? How has the whole process been affected, for you, by the materials you read in this chapter?

    2. The *Yale Law Journal* published an article in 1992 that argued, in effect, that it was time to scuttle Chapter 11, meaning that Chapter 11 should be repealed, and all companies put on a pay-your-bills-when-they're-due-or-otherwise-go-out-of-business basis.

    If the authors of the article reasoned correctly (i.e., as you would), would such a conclusion really be acceptable? Exactly which interests are at stake in such a decision? Are they the interest of companies in financial trouble (i.e., their shareholders?). All U.S. companies? Troubled company employees? Unions? The U.S. economic system? Vulture investors?

    You have to know *what happens* under Chapter 11 to get to your decision, correct? What is *ethical* about Chapter 11? Unethical? *Does* re-organization enhance the social welfare? Is *that* a relevant issue to be weighed? What is *the* relevant issue? What is the "social welfare" (in the case of Chapter 11, that is)?

    Decide: Get rid of Chapter 11 or not—and on what *ethical* basis, or are ethics in no way an issue?

    3. A final "values" issue and product liability question: If Ford's "money crunchers" were correct in the *Pinto* case (that is was cheaper to risk the maiming and killing of owners than to change the car design), wasn't the choice *not* to change an excellent example of the "wealth maximization" principle? Why punish Ford (and its shareholders) for deciding to do what is ordained by the one inviolable capitalist value: *wealth maximization*?

Or is it perhaps true that it is always best to begin the process of weighing *all* affected interests—where managerial decisions are concerned—by assuming that no value is so sacred that it cannot be outweighed in any given case? And where have you heard *that* before?

On whether or not one has a duty to maximize wealth in a competitive free market society, you might enjoy reading Ronald Dworkin's discussion in *Law's Empire*, cited in Chapter 1, note 1 of this text. Especially see Dworkin's "The Question of Justice," pp. 285-288.

4

Environmental Issues and the Law of Damages

COMING UP IN THIS CHAPTER

This chapter has seven major headings, and that is a lot, but the materials do fit together. Here's how:

To deal with *any* environmental issue, be it economic, scientific, legal, or ethical, one must begin with basic information about environmental concerns, both domestic and international. The function of Sections I and especially II and III is to provide that information. Section II is international in its focus—that is, it covers such concerns as ozone layer depletion—while Section III focuses on the United States.

Section IV, the largest of the seven sections, is also related to domestic concerns. It is large because it examines the What-to-Do and How-to-Do-It aspects of the problem (i.e., What are the considerations *for taking action*, and what approaches are available?). Here, we are moving toward outside-the-market interference with free market operations (in the presence of market failure); thus, we are headed for "The Law." Section IV then discusses key laws with which market participants must deal. And because the law provides sanctions, we are required to read some law cases to see how (and why) the law does this in specific important instances. The first case (*Fleet Factors*) says to business managers: "Watch out. The extent to which environmental laws affect *your* market may (unpleasantly) surprise you!" The second case (*Frezzo Bros.*) explains clearly, and firmly, how and why environmentally flawed managers can end up doing jail time.

Of course, if the government doesn't come down on you for perceived "wrongful" environmental activity, *consumers* might, as Section IV also demonstrates. Finally, the section focuses on serious, overall, economic considerations related to environment, market failure, and consequent ethical issues. It also touches upon some of the positive economic aspects for free marketeers arising out of environmental concerns.

Having discussed product liability and class-action lawsuits in Chapter 3, and the environment thus far in Chapter 4, we put them together in Section V by zeroing in on "toxic torts." We chose to use the *Cryovac* case here, despite its relating to only one plaintiff, because almost all aspects of the complex problem raised by toxic materials damage to human beings are clearly set forth in this case. And we follow *Cryovac* with a focus on the issue of massive toxic torts (e.g., several industries contributing to the chemical poisoning of public drinking water in a large city).

The most important factor with toxic tort cases (as with product liability cases in general) is the cost (i.e., *damages*). Thus, Section VI offers a brief review of the elements of damages in law, and the related economic concept of the present value of money (the *Ursini* case). Related to the damages issue is the specific entity known as *punitive* damages. Such damages could come close to rendering a business terminal, so they are discussed here too.

Finally, concern, anger, and fear on the part of market managers involved with the market-meddling legal system have led to a public outcry (orchestrated by the insurance industry) that the U.S. tort system must be changed because it is inefficient—and maybe even unethical in its picking of the market's deep pockets. Section VII deals briefly with that issue.

Free competitive markets, the environment, and the law (of torts and damages and penal sanctions) make up a social amalgam bound to heat up ethical debate. Some specific ethical issues are raised in this chapter. Others bob about the surface in many places. You will want to test your analytical perceptions with the materials that conclude the chapter.

I. INTRODUCTION

In Chapter 2, we referred to externalities as side effects arising out of economic activity that may be beneficial or damaging. For example, a beneficial externality occurs when householders who beautify their own property help raise the value of all homes in the neighborhood. On the other hand, externalities can be truly disadvantageous. For example, iron and steel plants may produce particulates, sulfides and acid mist, which pollute the air as they produce the product.

Environmental degradation is a prime example of what is meant by the term "negative externality."

A major problem here would seem to be that there are no markets for the constituent elements of a nontoxic habitat for living things. This is largely for two reasons. First, defining and enforcing property rights is impossible in the case of such "commodities" as air and water. In the main they belong to everybody and to nobody. Second, negotiating mutually beneficial "environmental" trades presents insuperable market development problems.

In the face of *environmental* negative externalities, the issue then becomes how best to use outside-the-market forces to deal with market failure. In the ecological market sphere, the key question is how to utilize these forces in such a way as to encourage, rather than discourage, the healthy development of free markets *simultaneously with* the healthy development of the overall environment, upon which producers, consumers, and natural resources all depend.

II. WHAT PROBLEMS WITH THE ENVIRONMENT? AN INTERNATIONAL FOCUS

A. Environmental Indicators: What and Where?

A good illustration of worldwide economic and social concern with threats to the environment can be seen in the focus of the Organization for Economic Cooperation and Development (OECD). The OECD is composed of the following member nations: Australia, Austria, Belgium, Canada, Denmark, Finland, France, Germany, Greece, Iceland, Ireland, Italy, Japan, Luxembourg, the Netherlands, New Zealand, Norway, Portugal, Spain, Sweden, Switzerland, Turkey, the United Kingdom, and the United States.

> In May, 1989, the OECD Council, meeting at Ministerial level, called, *inter alia*, for a next generation work program on environmental economics that would integrate environment and economic decision making more systematically and effectively as a means of contributing to sustainable development. In July, 1989, the Paris Economic Summit reinforced this; in July, 1990, the Houston Economic Summit, in its declaration, reiterated its call upon the OECD to carry forward work on environmental indicators.[1]

"Environmental indicators," as the OECD uses that term, means *data used to* (1) measure environmental performance with respect to the

---

[1] *Environmental Indicators* (OECD: Paris, 1991), p. 8. The excerpt from the July 1990 G-7 Economic Summit quoted in the Paris text reads: "We encourage the OECD to accelerate its useful work on the environment and the economy. Of particular importance are the early development of environmental indicators and the design of market-oriented approaches that can be used to achieve environmental objectives."

level, and changes in the level, of environmental quality and related objectives defined by national policies and international agreements (this data would be gathered partly to respond to the public's right to know about basic trends in air and water quality and other aspects of the environment affecting their health and well-being); (2) integrate environmental concerns in sectoral policies (e.g., agriculture, energy, and transportation); and (3) integrate environmental concerns in economic policies more generally through *environmental accounting* at the macrolevel (for example, through the development of satellite accounts to the system of national accounts, and through work on national resource accounts).[2]

As of 1991, the OECD had developed 18 environmental indicators such as carbon dioxide emissions, greenhouse gas emissions, wastewater treatment, land use changes, waste generation, use of forest resources, threatened species, public opinion, and the like.[3]

What is the state of the environment that has precipitated such widespread concern? We might turn first to Eastern Europe:

> Comecon is an ecological disaster zone. A third of Bulgaria's forests are damaged by acid rain; the Black Sea is polluted by sewage oil and industrial waste; and heavy metals are destroying its farmlands. Czechoslovakia is no better: 70 percent of its rivers are heavily polluted; 40 percent of sewage is untreated; half its forests are dying or damaged, and pollution-related cancers and infant mortality are soaring. In Poland 95 percent of rivers are heavily polluted—the Vistula rendered biologically dead by mine wastewater; over half its farmland is polluted by acid and heavy metals. The World Bank estimates that 10 percent of Poland's GDP is lost through illness and industry's inability to cope with corrosive, contaminated water. In Hungary and Romania, air pollution is out of control as a result of the burning of arsenic- and sulphur dioxide-rich brown coal; sewage treatment is inadequate and there are high levels of pollution-related heart disease and infant mortality. If cleaning up East Germany will cost Dm100 billion ($58.6 billion), then cleaning up the rest of Eastern Europe could cost as much as Dm500 billion ($293 billion). . . . [4]

---

[2] A later section of this chapter contains further discussion of the system of national accounts and the issue of "environmental accounting."

[3] It should be pointed out here that a private, independent U.S. organization, The Worldwatch Institute, began, in 1992, to publish an annual of environmental indicators. The first issue, *Vital Signs 1992: The Trends That Are Shaping Our Future* (Worldwatch Institute: Washington, D.C., 1992), is designed to fill perceived official gaps in the gathering, analyzing, and disseminating of global environmental data.

[4] S. Brady, "Here Comes the Credit Crunch," *Euromoney* (cover story) April, 1990, p. 6. See also M. Simons, "Europeans Begin to Calculate the Price of Pollution," *The New York*

Environmental concerns in Europe are hardly restricted to the eastern portion. Some examples of concerns being voiced as the world moves into the last decade of the twentieth century are set forth here.

In Sweden, 16,000 lakes have been acidified to the extent that sensitive organisms have disappeared; high concentrations of chlorinated hydrocarbons in North Sea coastal areas (together with land-based pollutant discharges) are of major concern because they are in potential conflict with the North Sea's role as Europe's most important fishing area. Some 14 percent of *all* the forests in Europe (including the Black and Sieberg forests in Germany) were, by the mid-1980s, damaged seriously. The main culprit: acid precipitation, caused mainly by emissions of sulfur and nitrogen into the air, which return to earth either dry in the form of gases and particles, or wet as acid rain or snow, or, in the form of fog and cloud droplets, as condensation. Soil erosion and consequent desertification have both become matters of great concern in Spain. Overgrazing and drainage practices in Denmark have damaged heaths, fens, and bogs resulting in serious harm to some bird species (e.g., a reduction in black grouse from 2,400 in 1943 to 40 in 1980).[5]

No area of the world is exempt from environmental concerns such as air pollution. In China and India industrial timber cutting is also producing a (timber supply) crisis. Annual cutting in China exceeds growth by some 100 million cubic meters. India's forests have been shrinking by 1 million to 5 million hectares (2.5 million to 5 million acres) per year. In Brazil, India, and the Philippines, governments hoping to encourage economic development "seem to end up subsidizing wholesale forest destruction."[6]

Many ecological concerns must be classified as *transnational*. Toxicity, like trade, crosses and crisscrosses national boundaries but, unlike trade, it comes always in the form of undesired negative externalities. Two of the most serious (and interrelated) global environmental degradation concerns are stratospheric ozone depletion and the "greenhouse effect."

Times, December 9, 1990, and *Green Revolutions: Environmental Reconstruction in Eastern Europe and the Soviet Union* (Worldwatch Paper 99, November 1990).

[5] Data from *The State of the Environment* (OECD: Paris, 1991) pp. 63, 81, 100, 137).

[6] Brown, et al., *State of the World, 1991* (Worldwatch Institute/W.W., Washington, D.C.: Norton, 1991), pp. 76-77. Economic recovery in Eastern Europe will be slower for at least a decade in the face of environmental problems. See B. Hagerty, "For Eastern Europe, Pollution Becomes an Issue Amid Economic Restructuring," *The Wall Street Journal*, April 24, 1992, M. Simons, "Pollution Blights Investment, Too, in Eastern Europe," *The New York Times*, May 13, 1992, See also C.Bogert, "Get Out the Geiger Counters," *Newsweek*, November 2, 1992.

Ozone is the gas in the atmosphere (the ozone layer) that prevents the most harmful solar ultraviolet radiation from reaching the earth in intolerable quantities. Ozone *loss*, therefore, is dangerous—to human skin and eyes, animal life, and the productivity of aquatic and terrestrial ecosystems.

The ozone depletion process results from a series of chemical reactions—catalytic chain reactions—in which one substance destroys another one. The initial destruction substances here are synthetic chemicals called *chlorofluorocarbons* (CFCs). These CFCs originate in industrial processes related to the manufacture of solvents, flexible foam products, refrigerators, air conditioners, and spray can propellants. The CFCs float up several miles into the troposphere where they appear to be immune to destruction. They eventually float farther upward into the stratosphere, are broken down by sunlight, and produce chlorine. Chlorine destroys ozone (i.e., makes "holes" in the ozone layer). Considering that 1985 data demonstrate a worldwide industrial use of approximately 2-1/4 billion pounds of CFCs—and that a single atom of chlorine can, over time, destroy 10,000 ozone molecules—the ongoing ozone depletion process is, to say the least, unsettling.[7]

Carbon dioxide (CO_2), which originates in significant measure from emissions from fossil fuel combustion, and from deforestation/land use changes, plus methane and nitrogen, which are, in the main, naturally occurring, together with CFCs, make up the four main constituents responsible for the so-called greenhouse effect. But the most important culprits are CO_2 and CFCs, since they contribute most (approximately 70 percent) to the process.

The greenhouse effect is probably best understood as a "trap" phenomenon. The sun provides a lot of heat to the earth. If there were no way for the planet to give back excess heat, we would all reach a boiling point, literally. In fact, our planet utilizes some of the heat for warmth and does radiate the rest back into the atmosphere. A variety of gases have *always* existed on earth, in essence to regulate what heat stays and what radiates back out and beyond us. That is why our planet has not been scorched fatally by the sun.

The problem today, according to many climatologists, is that we are accumulating (trapping) *too much* warmth here on earth. Their theory is that so much burning of fossil fuels—added to emissions from other transportation, industrial, and chemical activities—has led to vastly increased levels of such gases as CO_2, carbon monoxide, methane, nitrous oxide, and CFCs, and that these gases—and particulates—trap too much

---

[7] See for data and general description, Brennan, *Levitating Trains and Kamikaze Genes* (New York: John Wiley, 1990), pp. 104-105.

heat here in our atmosphere. It is feared this could result eventually in raising the temperature on earth, melting polar ice caps, raising ocean levels, and producing drought and other, mainly destructive, agricultural patterns.

On the other hand, some experts argue that on all the scientific evidence available, the greenhouse effect is a tempest in an environmental teapot.

Actually, the most balanced, and we believe, persuasive argument for taking this phenomenon seriously is the one made by 52 Nobel laureates and 725 members of the United States Academy of Sciences, in writing, in 1990, to the President of the United States:

> Global warming has emerged as the most serious environmental threat of the 21st century. There is broad agreement within the scientific community that amplification of the earth's natural greenhouse effect by the buildup of various gases introduced by human activity has the potential to produce dramatic changes in climate. The severity and rate of climate change cannot yet be confidently predicted, but the impacts of changes in surface temperature, sea level, precipitation, and other components of climate could be substantial and irreversible on a time scale of centuries. Such changes could result in severe disruption of natural and economic systems throughout the world. More research on global warming is necessary to provide a steadily improving data base and better predictive capabilities. But uncertainty is no excuse for complacency. In view of the potential consequences, actions to curb the introduction of greenhouse gases, including carbon dioxide, CFCs, methane, nitrogen oxides, and tropospheric ozone, must be initiated immediately. Only by taking action now can we insure that future generations will not be put at risk.[8]

Two other transnational environmental issues should be mentioned here since they raise economic, ethical, and legal environmental issues. They are discussed below.

B. Hazardous Waste Disposal

Hazardous waste is a domestically produced product. However, figures from OECD nations indicate that more than 1.7 million tons were exported from them in the five-year period between 1983 and 1988, and that there are now 100,000 hazardous waste border crossings actually recorded

---

[8] "Appeal by American Scientists to Prevent Global Warming," *Nucleus Magazine* (Spring 1990).

annually. "Seeking safe sites" is one explanation, but another has to be that those who are financially able to do so pay those who are in financial distress to accept exported hazardous waste, with and without safe storage sites available, so as to satisfy hard-currency needs. Such exporters are often evading strict country-of-origin production and disposal standards and putting poorer populations at risk.[9]

C. The Producer-User Chain

Some manufactured products become dangerous sources of pollution only *after* they are actually used by the downstream consumer. The United States is a mercury polluter, Canada a lead polluter, the Netherlands a cadmium polluter. In each of these cases, however, the major source of the pollution is from consumed products that originated beyond the consuming nation's borders. Says the OECD:

> . . . downstream displacement of environmental problems in the production-consumption-residue process considerably broadens the responsibility of industry, which can no longer remain oblivious to the fate of the products which it makes (in terms of their transport, storage and destruction).[10]

Transnational pollution can result from accident, as in the April 1986 Chernobyl nuclear reactor explosion, and in the Basel chemical warehouse fire of November 1986, which released 33 tons of toxic chemicals into the Rhine River. But such sudden accidents—horrible though they may be—are not more dangerous over the long term than more insidious, continuous, and less publicized damage to the environment: damage that may be caused by the increasing complexity of risk management in the face of new technological development, and by a less than adequate corporate concern for the long-term well-being of all living things. Thirty-three tons of chemicals blown into the Rhine from one accident site does raise management issues; however, 10,000 tons of toxic substances discharged annually into the Rhine from nonaccidental sources poses a good many more.

Fortunately, there is a developing awareness at the international level that the transnational character of threats to the environment gives

---

[9] See also N.C. Nash, "Latin Nations Getting Others' Waste," *The New York Times*, December 16, 1991, and for broader study, *The International Traffic in Hazardous Waste*, (Center for Investigative Reporting/Swan Lake Press, New York: 1990). See for an example of problems within the new European Community; B. Hagerty, "Jarred by Toxic Discovery, France Acts to Restrict Imports of German Garbage," *The Wall Street Journal*, August 21, 1992.

[10] Note 5, *supra*, at p. 191.

a new dimension to the term "national security"—one going well beyond the scope of the more familiar military aggressions. The *Montreal Protocol on Substances That Deplete the Ozone Layer*, signed by 24 countries in September 1987, is one example of this awareness. The Protocol, which went into effect on January 1, 1989, was further strengthened at a June 1990 meeting in London attended by some 100 countries. At that meeting, five CFCs earmarked for reduction in the 1987 Protocol were outlawed completely in all signatory nations as of the year 2000: 20 percent to be eliminated by January 1, 1992; 50 percent by January 1, 1995; and 85 percent by January 1, 1997.[11]

In June 1992, the United Nations Environment Program (UNEP) sponsored a large gathering of world leaders (12 days, 178 participant nations) to promote international environmental awareness and action. The "Earth Summit" did not produce solid working agreements with solid sanctions. However, it *did* produce a U.N. Commission on Sustainable Development, which, like the fairly successful U.N. Commission on Human Rights, could, even without sharp, legal teeth, move nations to action (or to forbearance) through observation, analysis, and publicity! The Earth Summit also produced an 800-page blueprint on "sustainable development" and a "Rio Declaration" consisting of 27 basic principles. Finally, two major treaties were signed (by 150 nations) that dealt with global warming and the loss of biological diversity.

III. WHAT PROBLEMS WITH THE ENVIRONMENT? A DOMESTIC FOCUS

It could be argued that the United States of America, annually, services an environmental debt greater than its national debt.

The Environmental Protection Agency (EPA) has identified 30,000 toxic waste sites—mainly industrial in origin—that need some sort of remediation. More than 1,000 of them are very high priority (i.e., in horrible condition) and could cost an average of $21 million each to clean up. Then there is the separate hazardous waste damage to be rectified, which has arisen out of the operations of many nuclear arms facilities, such

---

[11] For a full exposition of the political process that produced this remarkable exercise in international environmental diplomacy, see Richard E. Benedick, *Ozone Diplomacy: New Directions for Safeguarding the Planet* (Cambridge, Mass.: Harvard University Press, 1991). See also H.French, "Strengthening Global Environmental Governance," in Brown and others *State of the World, 1992*. In light of recent data confirming ozone depletion as advancing rapidly (e.g., "Ozone Depletion Over South Pole Accelerates," *The New York Times* (National Section) September 29, 1992), negotiators at an international conference in Copenhagen, in November 1992, amended the Protocol to require a total (100%) phaseout of CFCs by 1996!

as the one in Rocky Flats, Colorado, which produced plutonium triggers for nuclear weapons.

> Equally impressive are the costs of correcting and making safe existing damage related to utility-generated acid rain, air pollution from automobiles, nontoxic municipal trash disposal, agricultural pesticide runoff and scores of other vastly destructive types of contamination. With very little effort. . . it is possible to reach a grand total cost larger than the federal debt of $2.8 trillion. . . .
>
> [As to] the annual costs of servicing our environmental debt. . . just complying with federal regulations aimed at checking further deterioration (in 1988) cost businesses, utilities and local government $85 billion. Municipal trash collections cost $24 billion. Keeping drinking water free of environmental contaminants costs about the same.[12]

According to an EPA draft report that was being circulated within the government at the end of 1990, the United States spent 2 percent of its gross national product (GNP) on controlling pollution and cleaning up the environment in 1987, and can expect to spend close to 3 percent by the year 2000, with almost 1 percent of GNP being spent on waste alone. Costs to municipalities and to states will be very high in addition to expenditures by the federal government. The same draft report did estimate, however, that costly U.S. pollution controls had already vastly lowered sulfur dioxide, nitrogen oxide, airborne particles, carbon monoxide, and lead emissions into the air.[13]

IV. CONDITIONS FOR MARKET INTERFERENCE

A. Overview

Action to deal with environmental dangers demands dollars. But whether the money comes from the public or the private sector, both inside *and* outside-the-market good sense would seem to require effective and efficient policy decisions in three major areas:

- *The Scientific*. Which situations/conditions are in fact hazardous to the environment and require market intervention?

---

[12] M. Silverstein, "Facing a Huge Environmental Debt," *The Chicago Tribune*, November 25, 1989.

[13] Report cited at length in W.K. Stevens, "2% of GNP Spent by U.S. on Cleanup," *The New York Times*, December 23, 1990.

- *The Politico-Social-Legal.* To what extent, and in what manner, may citizens be coerced into changing their personal consumption/disposal habits? To what extent should businesses be coerced into changing their practices and policies? How can government avoid taking conflicting environmental positions?
- *The Economic.* Must politico-social-legal decision making be affected by *cost* at the levels of
  whether or not to legislate/litigate at all? and
  how best to legislate/litigate cost effectively?

B. Scientific Considerations

Scientific considerations should be paramount at the level of whether there is sufficient data upon which to base a decision to take action. Global warming, or the greenhouse effect, presents a good example of scientific conflict (i.e., some scientists do disagree on the extent of environmental danger here and thus on the need for action and expenditures). In dealing with physical science, as in dealing with medical issues, policymakers cannot afford to wait for *certainty* before moving ahead. But surely, scientific opinion must be weighed carefully before market coercion is undertaken.

> History is littered with the refuse of over-enthusiasms; necessary caution is a mark of vibrant and compassionate professionalism, not a conceit of effete disengagement. We [environmentalists] will only be effective if we speak with the authority of genuine intellectual integrity.[14]

C. Politico-Social-Legal Considerations

In terms of the individual consumer, politico-social-legal considerations have to take account of the reality that citizens (read voters) are far more easily persuaded to exercise their rights than they are their obligations. For example, trash/solid waste problems (and costs) are, to an appreciable degree, related to consumer activity in four major areas: discarded waste paper, paper plates and paper napkins, food scraps, and yard waste. Individual lifestyles, then, ought to be subject to change here. The question is, how far will (elected) policymakers go to make that understood?[15]

---

[14] S.J. Gould, "It's Not Too Late If We're Not Too Crazy," *The New York Times*, April 22, 1990 (Book Review).

[15] While this chapter concentrates upon business, rather than individual, activity, the reader wishing to pursue the matter of individual environmental behavior might well begin with J.E. Young, *Discarding the Throwaway Society* (Worldwatch Paper 101, January 1991), and Alan Durning, *How Much Is Enough? The Consumer Society and the Future of the Earth* (Washington, D.C.: Worldwatch Institute, 1992).

1. Policy Approaches

In terms of outside-the-market intervention into environmentally related *business conduct*, there are four major policy approaches to be considered (either alone, or in some sort of combination):

- *Prevention*, in the sense of utterly prohibiting particular practices (e.g., forbidding the release of specific chemicals into a waterway in any quantity).
- *Control*, in the sense of circumscribing particular practices (e.g., requiring the use of "scrubbers" [cleaning devices] in factories in order to reduce the toxic content of certain emissions).
- *Remediation*, in the sense of providing redress for harm already caused by particular business practices (e.g., allowing recovery of money damages in court, or the payment of all costs incurred [or to be incurred] for cleaning up a toxic waste site).
- *Direct Consumer Action*, in the sense of self-starting actions such as financial support for environmental organization agendas, or litigation based on alleged common-law rights and/or specific enabling legislation.

2. Legal Statutes

Statutes are the primary tool for prevention, control, and remediation. Environmental laws are ubiquitous. However, there are eight major federal environmental statutes apart from laws aimed at land stewardship, or fish and wildlife protection (i.e., conservation-oriented laws).[16] These eight major statutes are published in the series of numbered volumes entitled *The United States Code* (U.S.C.):

- *The Clean Air Act* (42 U.S.C. as amended by Pub. L. 101-549, 11/15/1990). This statute provides the standard for ambient air quality related to such problem areas as smog, toxic emissions, acid rain, and the like. It sets compliance-with-standards deadlines, and provides penalties for violations.
- *The Clean Water Act* (33 U.S.C. Sections 1251-1387). This act covers federal water pollution control generally, and is known

---

[16] For an economic-social overview of the conservationist-oriented environmental area (National Parks, rivers, trails and wilderness, fish and wildlife protection), a good overview publication is J.V. Krutilla and A.C. Fisher, *The Economics of Natural Environments: Studies in the Valuation of commodity and Amenity Resources* (Washington, D.C.: Resources for the Future, 1985).

also as the Federal Water Pollution Control Act., as amended in 1987 by the Water Quality Act.

- *The Safe Drinking Water Act* (42 U.S.C. Sections 300f to 300j-11) focuses on groundwater protection programs.
- *The Rivers and Harbors ("Refuse") Act* (33 U.S.C. Sections 401-407) controls, along with the Safe Drinking Water Act above, the sanctions applied to water polluters.
- *The Resources Conservation and Recovery Act* (42 U.S.C. Sections 6901-6987). This statute regulates generation, transportation, and disposal of certain hazardous wastes.
- *The Comprehensive Environmental Response Compensation and Liability Act*, referred to as "CERCLA" (42 U.S.C. Sections 9601-9657). This key statute contains the *Superfund Law* of 1986, which set up a $1.6 billion fund to locate and clean up hazardous waste sites. The Superfund Law is also known as SARA—The Superfund Amendments and Re-Authorization Act.
- *The Toxic Substances Control Act* (15 U.S.C. Sections 2601-2629). This act relates to the manufacture, processing, distribution, and disposal of chemicals presenting unreasonable risk of injury to people or to the environment.
- *The Federal Environmental Pesticide Control Act of 1972* (7 U.S.C. Section 136) This statute, which amended the previous Insecticide, Fungicide and Rodenticide Act, covers all aspects of the toxic pesticide market, from manufacture through sale and use.

Another closely related federal statute is the *Federal Food, Drug and Cosmetic Act*, insofar as that act relates to the storage and sale of adulterated foods (21 U.S.C. Section 331K).

It must be emphasized here that in addition to more than 20 federal statutes dealing in one way or another with environmental matters, there are also many individual state laws. Some examples are California's strict toxic emission laws and North Carolina's basically prevention-oriented antipollution program. As reflected in 1988 data, 36 states employed a total of some 27,000 people in various environmental departments. While state commitments (and capabilities) in the environmental area vary greatly, no business can afford not to be aware of the compliance requirements under both state and federal laws.[17]

---

[17] For an overview of state efforts, see J.P. Lester, "A New Federalism? Environmental Policy in the States," in N.J. Vig and M.E. Kraft, eds., *Environmental Policy in the 1990s* (Congressional Quarterly Press, 1990). Nonsmokers might enjoy reading E. Gold, "New York State's Clean Indoor Air Act," *New York State Bar Journal* (April 1991). And on the (sometimes severe) problems of corporations having to deal with many different states and their varying laws, see J. Holusha, "Some Corporations Plead for the Firm Hand of Uncle

It is difficult to imagine that any business manager in the final decade of the twentieth century could be considered fully qualified in his or her job in the absence of any familiarity with federal and state environmental laws related to the manager's business. That relationship may be there even where the outward form and content of the business would *seem* to put it beyond the reach of any environmental statute *and* associated mountains of regulations. Some examples follow.

3.The *U.S.* v. *Fleet* Case

An excellent illustration of the pervasiveness of environmental laws can be seen in the following case, brought by the federal government against a secured financial creditor for the costs of a toxic waste cleanup under CERCLA.

U.S. v. *FLEET FACTORS CORP.*
901 F. 2d 1550 (11th Cir.1990)

[In this case, the Environmental Protection Agency incurred costs of $400,000 to dispose properly of 700 fifty-five gallon drums of toxic chemicals and 44 truckloads of asbestos material—all found on the property of the SPW Company. SPW was bankrupt. Fleet Factors Corp. held a large interest in SPW facilities primarily to protect its security interest (i.e., Fleet Factors Corp. was a secured creditor). The EPA sued Fleet for the cleanup costs as an "owner or operator" of SPW. The lawsuit was brought under the CERCLA statute already discussed in this chapter. A portion of the court's decision in this case follows. All footnotes referred to in the decision are omitted.]

B. Fleet's Liability Under Section 9607(a)(2)

[5] CERCLA also imposes liability on "any person who at the time of disposal of any hazardous substance owned or operated any. . . facility at which such hazardous substances were disposed of. . . ." 42 U.S.C. S9607(a)(2). CERCLA excludes from the definition of "owner or operator" any "person, who, without participating in the management of a. . . facility, holds indicia of ownership primarily to protect his security interest in the. . . facility." 42 U.S.C. S 9601(20)(A). Fleet has the burden of establishing its entitlement to this exemption. There is no dispute that Fleet held an "indicia of ownership" in the facility through

---

Sam," *The New York Times*, February 24, 1991.

its deed of trust to SPW, and that this interest was held primarily to protect its security interest in the facility. The critical issue is whether Fleet participated in management sufficiently to incur liability under the statute.

[6] The construction of the secured creditor exemption is an issue of first impression in the federal appellate courts. The government urges us to adopt a narrow and strictly literal interpretation of the exemption that excludes from its protection any secured creditor that participates in any manner in the management of a facility. We decline the government's suggestion because it would largely eviscerate the exemption Congress intended to afford to secured creditors. Secured lenders frequently have some involvement in the financial affairs of their debtors in order to insure that their interests are being adequately protected. To adopt the government's interpretation of the secured creditor exemption could expose all such lenders to CERCLA liability for engaging in their normal course of business.

Fleet, in turn, suggests that we adopt the distinction delineated by some district courts between permissible participation in the financial management of the facility and impermissible participation in the day-to-day or operational management of a facility. In *United States v. Mirabile*, the first case to suggest this interpretation, the district court granted summary judgement to the defendant creditors because their participation in the affairs of the facility was "limited to participation in financial decisions." No. 84-2280, slip op. at 3 (E.D.Pa. Sept. 6, 1985 WL 97). The court explained "that the participation which is critical is participation in operational, production, or waste disposal activities. Mere financial ability to control waste disposal practices. . . is not. . . sufficient for the imposition of liability." Mirabile, No. 84-2280, slip op. at 4. . . .

The court below, relying on *Mirabile*, similarly interpreted the statutory language to permit secured creditors to

> provide financial assistance and general, and even isolated instances of specific, management advice to its debtors without risking CERCLA liability if the secured creditor does not participate in the day-to-day management of the business or facility either before or after the business ceases operation.

Fleet Factors Corp., 724 F.Supp. at 960 (S.D.Ga. 1988); accord Guidice, at 561-62; Nicolet, 712 F.Supp. at 1205. Applying this standard, the trial judge concluded that from the inception of Fleet's relationship with SPW in 1976 to June 22, 1982, when Baldwin entered the facility, Fleet's activity did not rise to the level of participation in management sufficient to impose CERCLA liability. The court, however, determined that the facts alleged by the government with respect to Fleet's involvement after Baldwin entered the facility were sufficient to preclude the granting of summary judgement in favor of Fleet on this issue.

Although we agree with the district court's resolution of the summary judgement motion, we find its construction of the statutory exemption too permissive towards secured creditors who are involved with toxic waste facilities. In order to achieve the "overwhelmingly remedial" goal of the CERCLA statutory scheme, ambiguous statutory terms should be construed to favor liability for the costs incurred by the government in responding to the hazards at such facilities. The district court's broad interpretation of the exemption would essentially require a secured creditor to be involved in the operations of a facility in order to incur liability. This construction ignores the plain language of the exemption and essentially renders it meaningless. Individuals and entities involved in the operations of a facility are already liable as operators under the express language of section 9607(a)(2). Had Congress intended to absolve secured creditors from ownership liability, it would have done so. Instead, the statutory language chosen by Congress explicitly holds secured creditors liable if they participate in the management of a facility.

Although similar, the phrase "participating in the management" and the term "operator" are not congruent. Under the standard we adopt today, a secured creditor may incur section 9607(a)(2) liability, without being an operator, by participating in the financial management of a facility to a degree indicating a capacity to influence the corporation's treatment of hazardous wastes. It is not necessary for the secured creditor actually to involve itself in the day-to-day operations of the facility in order to be liable. . . .

This case resulted in a flurry of action by lenders aimed at the EPA and Congress. They wanted a new law, or at least a new rule, that would, in effect, exempt them from Fleet Factor-like liability. Environmental groups protested, arguing that the purpose of the law was to provide an incentive for lenders to underwrite loans carefully and for borrowing businesses to have an incentive to be clean.[18] Whether or not some different legislative, judicial, or administrative rule ever makes clear a different liability for lenders in the future, one thing *is* clear right now:

---

[18] See Marcus and Pollock, "EPA Plans Rule to Curb Liability on Loans to Owners of Waste Sites," *The Wall Street Journal*, February 14, 1991; and Marcus and Stevens, "Banks' Burden in Waste Cleanups Is Overstated, According to Study," *The Wall Street Journal*, April 11, 1991. See generally also B.J. Fedder, "In the Clutches of the Superfund Mess," *The New York Times*, June 16, 1991.

Environmental laws are pervasive, and any business operating in ignorance of such laws is on a dangerous path.

It is important to emphasize here that money damages are not the only consequence of violating environmental laws. In some cases, criminal sanctions may be imposed, even upon corporate officers. All eight of the principal federal environmental statutes previously listed—and many such state statutes—back up enforcement through criminal prosecution as well as providing for financial payments. Congress made sure to include corporations in the definition of "person" in these laws, for the purpose of criminal prosecution. In fact, it appears that any corporation whose policy *knowingly* diverges from the requirements set out in environmental law can be found guilty of specified violations even if the corporation did not have the ability to control or abate those violations.[19]

We will now take a look at a criminal prosecution of a corporate environmental wrongdoer.

4.The *U.S.* v. *Frezzo* Case

The case excerpt below illustrates a typical criminal proceeding under environmental law, and it gives a rather clear example of *what specific laws say, how they are interpreted, and, practically speaking, how they are effectuated at the trial court level.*

UNITED STATES V. FREZZO BROS., INC.
546 F. Supp. 713 (1982)

Defendants were tried before a jury in October 1978, for violations of the Water Pollution Act, specifically 33 U.S.C. S 1311(a) which provides:

> (a) Except as in compliance with this section and sections 1312, 1317, 1328, 1342, and 1344 of this title, the discharge of any pollutant by any person shall be unlawful.

---

[19] *U.S.* v. *Mackin Construction Company*, 388 F. Supp. 478, 480 (1975). And see, D. Stipp, "Toxic Turpitude: Environmental Crime Can Land Executives in Prison These Days," *The Wall Street Journal*, September 10, 1990. In an effort to persuade companies to come forward voluntarily and admit to violations and cooperate with the government in remediation, the Department of Justice issued guidelines in July 1992. They set out official policy on prosecutorial discretion in such cases. On the other hand, various amendments to CERCLA, CWA, and the Clean Air Act have added new criminal penalties or augmented existing ones. Moreover, 42 U.S.C. Sec. 4321 now requires that, by October 1, 1995, there shall be not less than 200 criminal investigators in the employ of the EPA. For legal sanctions against polluters in the European Community, see M. Wright, "The Long Arm of Environmental Law," *Tomorrow* magazine, Vol. 2, No. 3, (1992).

33 U.S.C. S 1319(c) further provides:

> Any person who willfully or negligently violates section 1311.
> . . of this title. . . shall be punished by a fine of not less than
> $2,500 nor more than $25,000 per day of violation, or by
> imprisonment for not more than one year, or by both.

The jury, during the Court's instructions, was read the indictment which alleged that on certain dates in 1977 and 1978, the defendants "did willfully and negligently discharge pollutants, that is, waste-waters from mushroom compost manufacturing operations, into the waters of the East Branch of the White Clay Creek, a navigable water of the United States, without having obtained a permit from the Administrator of the Environmental Protection Agency for said discharge." The Court then instructed the jury as to the elements of the crime and as to the statutory definition of "pollutant," a definition that encompasses "dredged soil, solid waste, incinerator residue, sewage, garbage, sewage sludge, munitions, chemical wastes, biological materials, radioactive materials, heat, wrecked or discarded equipment, rock, sand, cellar dirt and industrial, municipal, and agricultural waste discharged into the water." 33 U.S.C. S 1362(6).

The jury was told "If you find that the substance allegedly discharged by a defendant is any one or more of the items specified in the statute's definition of 'pollutant,' then you may find that the substance is a pollutant." The jury was also instructed as to the statutory definition of a point source (33 U.S.C. S 1362(14)), navigable waters (33 U.S.C. S 1362(7)), the terms "willfully" and "negligently," and the meaning of intent and specific intent under the criminal law. So informed, the jury returned a verdict of guilty, finding that the defendants had willfully or negligently discharged pollutants from a point source into navigable waters without a permit. In fact, the evidence at trial showed that defendants never applied for a permit, a fact not contested by defendants' counsel. Furthermore, counsel for the defendants never suggested at trial, in post-trial motions or argument or on the initial appeal to the Third Circuit, that the defendants were in any way exempt from the permit requirements of 33 U.S.C. S 1311(a) and 33 U.S.C. S 1342.

Section 402 of the Water Pollution Act, 33 U.S.C. S 1342 sets forth the permit system of the Act (known as the National Pollutant Discharge Elimination System or NPDES). The statute provides, in relevant part,

> The Administrator may, after opportunity for public hearing,
> issue a permit for the discharge of any pollutant, or combina-
> tion of pollutants, notwithstanding section 1311(a) of this title,

upon condition that such discharge will meet either all applicable requirements under sections 1311, 1312, 1316, 1317, 1318, and 1343 of this title, or prior to the taking of necessary implementing actions relating to all such requirements, such conditions as the Administrator determines are necessary to carry out the provisions of this chapter.

33 U.S.C. S 1342(a)(1).

The Administrator [of the Environmental Protection Agency] is authorized to prescribe such regulations as are necessary to carry out his functions under this chapter.

Pursuant to these grants of authority, the Administrator and the EPA promulgated regulations governing the issuance of pollutants that would, in the absence of having been issued a permit, violate 33 U.S.C. S 1311(a) and exempting some discharge activities from permit requirements. These regulations, at the time of the trial of the Frezzo Brothers, were codified at 40 C.F.R. S125.1, et seq. The issuance of a permit did not and does not give the permit-holder a "license to pollute." Rather, the permit is issued only after a hearing and is designed to limit the amount of pollution where, for technological reasons, some pollution is deemed unavoidable. . . .

[Defendants' fines and convictions were upheld]

While permits were allowed for "unavoidable" pollution, the provisions of the Water Pollution Act set forth above are basically *prevention* oriented (". . . the discharge of *any* pollutant. . . shall be unlawful"). The *Fleet Factors* case is, of course, one example of the *remediation* approach to environmental law market coercion. The new Clean Air law changes are an excellent example of the *control* approach. The following areas of that law are illustrative:

- *Smog*: Geographic areas (e.g., cities) that are moderately polluted (or worse) must cut smog 15 percent or more within six years.
- *Alternative fuels*: Beginning in 1995, all gasoline sold in the nine most smog-filled U.S. cites must be cleaner burning, reformulated gasoline that cuts emissions of hydrocarbon and toxic pollutants 15 percent. By the year 2000, the reductions must equal 20 percent.
- *Acid rain*: A total of 111 dirtiest power plants in 21 states must cut sulfur dioxide emissions by 1995 for a total cut nationwide of 5 million tons; however, plants using high sulfur coal that com-

mit to buying scrubber (cleansing) devices can get an extension to 1997.[20]

The areas of environmental concern are so vast, and bureaucratic turf protectors/policymakers so numerous, that it remains to be pointed out that conflicting government political/legislative positions are a clear and present danger. One egregious example: Tobacco growers in the United States are granted federal subsidies to produce their product; public health agencies spend tens of millions of dollars to put these same growers out of business. Another: Water shortages in America's Far West are a distinct peril to large populations. However, the U.S. Bureau of Reclamation is underpricing irrigation water by $15 billion a year, with about half of those funds being used to grow crops that are officially in surplus.[21]

Are such conflicting policies mere evidence of bureaucratic bumbling? Or are there ethical issues involved, related, for example, to the uses and abuses of lobbying, and the questionable application of national power to favor local businesses—even at the risk of endangering the public health?[22]

5. Direct Public/Consumer Action

Before leaving the area of political-social-legal activity dealing with environmental degradation posed by market failure, we must take note of the phenomenon of *direct consumer action*.

Two major environmentally related disasters were motivating forces behind two key consumer action areas.

---

[20] The complete 1990 Clean Air Act is, of course, massive and detailed. For those who want to familiarize themselves with the key provisions without the necessity of hiring a legal translator, the October 12, 1990, *The Wall Street Journal* contains a sizable table listing such provisions as they existed (or did not exist) immediately before the new law, the President's proposal for change of the old law, and finally the provisions of the final bill. All are under the heading "The Changing Clean Air Law." See also "23d Environmental Quality Index: The Year of the Deal," *National Wildlife* (February-March 1991), at pp. 33, 35. California went the act one better on smog: D.J. Jefferson, "California Adopts Strictest Smog Laws in the Nation to Reduce Auto Pollution," *The Wall Street Journal*, October 1, 1990, and M.L. Wald, "California's Pied Piper of Clean Air," *The New York Times*, September 13, 1992.

[21] For a fuller explanation of these and other conflict problems, see J.D. Montgomery, "Horror in the Greenhouse and Other Tales of the Environment," *Harvard Magazine* (September-October 1990). Water problems, ranging from ocean pollution (e.g., M. Specter, "The World's Oceans Are Sending an S.O.S.," *The New York Times*, May 3, 1992) to drinking water/farming water scarcities, worldwide (e.g., Sandra Postal, *Last Oasis: Facing Water Scarcity* (New York/London: Norton/Worldwatch, 1992), are looming larger as we approach the twenty-first century.

[22] See G. Lee, "Even in War, Somebody's Got to Read the Legislative Fine Print: The Wheel of Special Interests Keeps on Turning," *The Washington Post National Weekly Edition*, February 4-10, 1991. (See also as an example of special interest costing taxpayers a bundle and promoting erosion of coastal areas in the U.S.: L. Gruson, "D'Amato Shift Dooms a Bill on Insurance," *The New York Times*, October 4, 1992.

On December 3, 1984, methyl isocyanate gas leaks from a Union Carbide plant in Bhopal, India, killed more than 2,500 people and seriously injured thousands more. In February 1989, Union Carbide and its Indian affiliate deposited $465 million with the Reserve Bank of India in full payment of all damages. All criminal charges in the case were dropped.

Within the United States, one result of the Bhopal disaster was *The Emergency Planning and Community Right-to-Know Act* (1986). This law was adopted by Congress over the strong protests of industry and opposition by the White House. Under this act, some 20,000 plants across America are required to disclose their discharge of more than 300 chemicals. Data gathered by the government are released annually in a document entitled *The Toxic Release Inventory*, which first appeared in 1989.

There are problems with the *Inventory*. Some dangerous chemicals are not on the required reporting list (e.g., the insecticide Malathion). Small businesses (nine or fewer employees) are exempt from filing reports. And the published *Inventory* itself is massive, often obscure, makes plant or industry comparisons very difficult, and gives no indication of health risks.

Despite all this, the *Inventory is* a phenomenal achievement. Larger environmental groups can and do decipher it and release clear, understandable information to the public. The data have encouraged citizen action throughout the country against exposed polluters. As the result of *Inventory*-inspired local community controversy and advocate action, many Fortune 500 companies have announced "voluntary" reductions in toxic emissions and the like. One example of many is the northern California environmental group that learned a Chevron refinery was storing and using chlorine in the treatment of cooling water. Chevron was persuaded to stop using the chemical at the plant. American Cyanamid (in Louisiana), the Raytheon Company (in Massachusetts), and IBM (in Silicon Valley) are other examples of *Inventory* exposure followed by remedial action/cessation of activity.[23]

Another example of concerted public action was set in motion by the March 24, 1989, grounding of the oil tanker *Exxon Valdez* in Alaska's Prince William Sound. That accident resulted in the spilling of 11 million gallons of crude oil into pristine, fertile waters.

That ecological disaster gave rise to a new coalition of environmentalists and investors who, in September 1990, made public a new code, under the title *The Valdez Principles*, now known as the *Coalition for Environmentally Responsible Economics (CERES) Principles*. They call

---

[23] See R.B. Smith, "Right to Know: A U.S. Report Spurs Community Action by Revealing Polluters," *The Wall Street Journal*, January 2, 1991. The "Inventory Law" is contained in Title III of the 1986 SARA. The EPA's "Form R," which companies must fill out for the *Inventory*, revised as of July 1, 1992, is 9 pages long and comes with 61 pages of instructions!

upon companies to deal with the impact of products and production on employees, the community, and the environment. The *CERES Principles* also require companies to appoint an environmental expert to their board of directors, and to establish and publicize an annual environmental audit of worldwide operations.

CERES is a public-interest group and can apply no legal sanctions. However, there are other kinds of sanctions, as the following quote illustrates. When asked if his company would pay any heed to *The Valdez Principles*, a General Motors spokesperson replied, "We will obviously take a look at it. These are major investors that we work with regularly."[24]

Another and more direct route the public may take is, of course, the lawsuit. The *Exxon Valdez* affair provided an outstanding example here, not only in terms of financial remediation, but also in terms of introducing new issues in environmental law.

There has been massive civil litigation in the *Exxon Valdez* case. The company was indicted on five criminal counts for violating the 1972 Ports and Waterways Safety Act and the Dangerous Cargo Act, which carry fines of up to $700 million. There were 181 separate civil lawsuits filed in both federal court and Alaska state courts, with thousands of plaintiffs represented by more than 75 law firms.

The *Exxon Valdez* disaster raises such issues as: how to manage complex environmental litigation; how to evaluate and recover natural resource damages; how to apply punitive damages law in environmental torts; how to determine what groups qualify to be certified as class-action plaintiffs; and how to clarify the relationship between federal environmental law and state strict-liability statutes.

As of mid-1991, efforts at settlement of these cases had not been achieved, and the enumerated issues remain to be resolved in both Alaskan and federal courts.[25]

D. Economic Considerations

There are at least four key areas related to the problem of environmental market failure that must be addressed within an economic focus. They all raise ethical considerations, but the following seem more evident in the first area: *professional / corporate considerations versus personal / society considerations.* That is to say, when corporate economic concerns are

---

[24] William Winters, quoted B.J. Fedder, "Who Will Subscribe to the Valdez Principles?" *The New York Times*, September 10, 1989.

[25] These and other issues are well presented and discussed in S. Keeva, "After the Spill," *American Bar Association Journal* (February 1991). It should be noted that settlement of all government/criminal complaints against Exxon in 1991 did *not* dispose of any civil lawsuits by private plaintiffs, nor the issues raised by these lawsuits.

substantial, and in conflict with the environmental public interest, which is to prevail?

Imagine yourself to be the chief financial officer (CFO) of Widget Corporation, married, with three children, ages 2, 5, and 7. One result of your company's production process is the discharge of several thousand tons of Widgicarbons per year into the river that meanders through your home office community. Widgicarbons are not now legally prohibited, nor are they yet on the *Toxic Release Inventory* list. However, recent scientific tests appear to have established a firm link between low-level ingestion of widgicarbons and liver cancer death in laboratory animals. The EPA has introduced legislation to ban emissions of any widgicarbons everywhere on the grounds that young children particularly are at risk of cancer from ingesting them. Your company (together with other powerful companies in the Widget industry) is fighting adoption of the new legislation.

You and other company officials are called to a meeting by your CEO and told: "If this legislation passes, we will be hit with staggering costs to change our manufacturing processes. We could be forced to file Chapter 11 proceedings. I expect all of you to go to Washington to lobby against this pernicious bill. *Actively!* Especially you, CFO, because you are in the best position of all of us to demonstrate the horrendous financial effects that will flow from passage of this bill outlawing widgicarbons, and there are fifteen hundred jobs that could be lost in this town alone. Maybe even yours! I'll be watching you closely and depending on your loyalty to our company."

What action would you, as *CFO of Widget Company*, want Congress to take? As *a parent of three children*? How do you intend to deal with the CEO's request to testify with great vigor in Washington against banning widgicarbons?

A second area relates to *cost-effectiveness* or rather the difficulty of determining it. Even when all parties concerned agree that the market alone cannot resolve the conflict and some sort of intervention is called for, the determination of cost-effectiveness is somewhat elusive. The variables, if not the techniques themselves, that need to be considered to calculate the true "costs" or true "benefits" (realized or forgone) of environmental policies and laws are at the very least controversial. This is particularly true as these policies and laws relate to economic growth and technological development.

Would a cost-benefit analysis, made 15 years ago, of the economic feasibility of instituting expensive, mandatory cleanup procedures in Department of Energy nuclear weapons facilities, have had a more efficient result than the one we face now? Which is to say, a current estimated cleanup cost of $100 billion. Would it have been more "efficient" to have cleaned up facilities 15 years ago in terms of the public health? Was the decision to hide the toxic truth from the public unethical at *any* price?

An argument could be made that the *basic premises* underlying cost-benefit analysis are unclear *in the context of environmental issues.* These basic premises have been stated as being twofold: (1) The purpose of economic activity is to increase the well-being of the individuals who make up the society, and (2) Each individual is the best judge of how well off he or she is in a given situation.[26] The first premise stands on the term "well-being" and seems definitionally shaky. The second premise, when informational deficiencies related to known and knowable ecological risk for each individual are considered, is demonstrably deficient.

A major problem, of course, is that cost-benefit analysis relates, generally, to *economic* well-being, whereas environmental quality is not necessarily definable on just that basis—at least not in the long-term view.

The Office of Management and Budget under President Ronald Reagan made "regulatory impact assessments" (RIAs) required for all environmental regulatory proposals. These RIAs were, in fact, cost-benefit analyses, and they served to shift environmental debate away from health and environmental quality to economics.[27] The RIAs did not prove to be satisfactory in methodology or result.

None of the above justifies eliminating cost-benefit analysis as one tool for application in environmental policy formulation. On the contrary, to the extent that costs and benefits *are* reasonably determinable in a given situation, they must be calculated and factored into the policy/lawmaking decision. It is argued, rather, that the special complexities of environmental policy make standard cost-benefit analysis difficult, and the difficulties must be acknowledged.

An excellent example of such complexity is the Clean Air Act. "Benefits" associated with air pollution prevention provisions are more difficult to assess than the dollar costs resulting from nonmarket policy/law intervention. Does cancer, for example, have any measurable cost (to family, community, nation) beyond medical bills, lost wages and, possibly, welfare system dollars? And what is the actual "value" of a forest? Are biodiversity and the pleasure of family nature walks true elements of "value"?[28]

---

[26] A.M. Freeman III, "Economics, Incentives and Environmental Legislation," Chapter 7 in N.J. Vig and M.E. Kraft, eds., note 17, *supra*, at pp. 147.

[27] See the discussion by R.L. Andrews, "Risk Assessment, Regulation and Beyond," Chapter 8 in N.J. Vig and M.E. Draft, eds., note 17, *supra*, at p. 176-177.

[28] P.R. Portney's "Economics and the Clean Air Act," in *The Journal of Economic Perspectives* (Fall 1990), is a valiant attempt at cost-benefit analysis, and is valuable. Various statements made therein are, nevertheless, a puzzlement. For example: with the bald statement that certain "epidemiological evidence" in some particular instance "is not convincing," the author goes on to say: "Taking all things into account, the benefits

Is cost-benefit analysis in the environmental area solely a question of economics/law/business practice, or does it also involve *ethical judgments* in terms of policy formulation? And if it does, what "value" do we assign to the issues of "right and wrong" in opposition to some truly substantive impediments to the development of specific areas of economic and technological development?

The third area of environmental market failure deals with *the means of intervention with the free market process* in order to prevent environmental degradation. It has been suggested that *incentive rather than coercive* forces be used to preserve the free market process. The prominent example is the tradable discharge permit (TDP) system, incorporated into the Clean Air Act. Companies that make deeper cuts in emissions than are mandated through specific time lines win pollution "credits." These credits can be stockpiled by the recipient for future personal use should it begin to pollute beyond the legal limits. Or, the credits could be marketed freely to other companies that currently pollute beyond the legal limits. These marketable credits-to-pollute (which have been valued as high as $500 per ton of "excess" pollution) are referred to as TDPs. Interestingly, the Clean Air Act gives "grandfather" standing to *existing* polluters, who will be given TDPs *free*. Here, it would seem, politics outdistanced ethics.

Needless to say, environmentalists, industrialists, ethicists, and economists vary greatly in their views about the costs and benefits involved in TDP transactions. The proposition that pollution is a tradable commodity that can be monitored and measured by the market on a national—or even international—basis is, to say the least, debatable.

Tax policy has also been advanced as an incentive-focused approach. The suggestion is that by actually replacing a sizable portion of current income taxes with "green" taxes we could encourage environmentally sound market policies. The major proponents of a green tax approach suggest seven specific areas for targeting: (1) $100 per ton on the carbon

---

associated with the urban air quality provisions should fall into the range of $4-$12 billion per year" (p. 177). The benefits to whom, one might ask, and unto what generation? Anyway, why not $7-$21 billion? Professor K.E.F. Watt argues that science and economics, in fact, provide us with too little guidance in the area of environmental decision making to avoid disaster much less evaluate its actual or probable consequences. See *Science and the Future 1993*, (Encyclopaedia Britannica, Chicago, Ill., pp. 346-352). An equally serious issue is raised by the potential "costs" of conflicting environmental statute/private property rights; e.g., wetlands preservation requirements vs. free use of private property. See Barret and Gutfeld, "Administration to Urge Broader Limits on Health, Safety, Environmental Rules," *The Wall Street Journal*, January 3, 1992. The weighing of public rights (to wetlands) vs. private rights (to use of private property) raises *all* of the issues covered in Section IV of this chapter. And, as of year-end 1992, the U.S. Supreme Court had not completely clarified the situation here: re land use environmental compensation to property owners. See: *Lucas v. South Carolina Coastal Council*, 112 S.Ct. 2886 (1992). And see also: J. Carlton, "Takings Don't Always Favor Takers," *The Wall Street Journal*, November 10, 1992.

content of fossil fuels; (2) $100 per ton of generated hazardous wastes; (3) $64 per ton on paper and paperboard produced from virgin pulp; (4) a tax of 50 percent on all pesticide sales; (5) $150 per ton of sulfur dioxide emissions; (6) $5.83 per kilogram of chlorofluorocarbon sales; and (7) $50 per cubic foot of groundwater depletion. These taxes, it is argued, would raise about $130 billion annually and allow for a personal income tax cut of almost 30 percent.[29]

The green tax argument that ecological taxes are efficient in that they adjust prices to reflect a market activity's *real cost* raises another closely related, serious issue. The subject was alluded to in a critical comment by an economist who faulted economics as being methodologically incapable of confronting environmental matters properly because

> [neoclassical theory] suffers from a total failure to distinguish the problem of optimum allocation of resources from the problem of optimal scale of the entire economy relative to the ecosystem in which the economy is physically embedded as a fully dependent system.[30]

The fourth area related to the problem of environmental market failure deals with the *proper economic measure of wealth*. A good deal of national and international attention has very recently focused on whether the interaction of the environment with the economy is adequately reflected in the national accounts. National accounts, through both a product and an income approach, measure the spending, income, and output of a nation essentially in monetary terms.[31]

> The key issue is whether the national accounts neglect the consumption of environmental resources and thereby overstate the amount of income that can be consumed today without reducing the capacity to produce tomorrow.

> The strikingly different character of relations in the natural world has, until now, kept study of the two realms largely separate. However, as part of the review now taking place of the United Nations System of National Accounts (SNA), last revised in 1968, a number of proposals have been made to revise the portrayal of

---

[29] L.R. Brown and others, note 6 at p. 182-185. See also S. Postel, "The Greening of America's Taxes," *The New York Times*, May 19, 1991.

[30] Herman E. Daley, cited in A.C. Kelley, "Economic Consequences of Population Change in the Third World," *Journal of Economic Literature*, (December 1988) pp. 1719.

[31] For a general discussion of national accounts, see P. Samuelson and W. Nordhaus, *Economics*, 13th ed. (New York: McGraw-Hill, 1989), pp. 107-117, 978).

the relationship between overall economic activity and the natural world within which it takes place.

Companies have found ways to account for their interactions with the environment. . . . At the macro level, however, it has proved difficult to measure the interaction of economic activity and the environment and to integrate these measurements into the national accounts.[32]

Certainly, adjusting national accounts for environmentally related interactions will be difficult; however, as the supranational financial institutions, OECD, the European Community and others have seen, there needs to be developed, whether in the national accounts or perhaps in a separate "satellite" account, some substantive, meaningful way to reflect, nationally, the environmental import of economic activity.[33]

Arguments pro and con on behalf of either side of the issue in *each* of the four aforementioned areas can be found in recent press as well as academic journal articles.[34]

E. Some Positive Results

There have been two quite positive results of the serious politico-social-legal focus on environmental concerns in the United States. The first is the development of many excellent individual programs in the areas of clean energy and atmosphere, clean water, land stewardship, fish and wildlife protection, and water and toxic reduction and recycling.[35]

---

[32] International Monetary Fund, "The Economy and the Environment: Revising the National Accounts," *IMF Survey* (June 4, 1990), pp. 161, 168-169; see also Ahmad, El Serafy, and Lutz, *Environmental Accounting for Sustainable Development* (Washington, D.C.: The World Bank, 1990)

[33] See "Environmental Audits Being Considered by EC," *The Wall Street Journal*, February 11, 1991. You might, at this point, wish to review the material on OECD "Environmental indicators" which appears early in this chapter. And see for a recent publication on the theme of the environment as reshaper of the global economy: L.A. Bower and others, *The State of the World 1993* (New York and London: Norton/Worldwatch, 1993).

[34] See, on the one hand, B. Commoner, "Free Markets Can't Control Air Pollution," *The New York Times*, April 15, 1990, and on the other, R. Koenig, "AER*X Wants to Be in the Middle of Pollution Rights: Firm Expects Trading of Credits to Take Off If Clean Air Bill Passes," *The Wall Street Journal*, July 30, 1990. Montgomery makes a case for the effectiveness of tradable permits in the area of removing lead from gasoline in *Harvard Magazine*, note 21, *supra*, at p. 37. But see, *re* ethical complexity: S. Rose-Ackerman, "Selling Pollution 'Rights' (a review)," *International Economic Insights* (May-June 1991). A recent article on specific trades/sales and issues involved is J. Taylor, "Smog Swapping: New Rules Harness Power of Free Markets to Curb Air Pollution," *The Wall Street Journal*, May 14, 1992.

[35] An excellent beginning descriptive list may be found in Piltz and Machado, *Searching for Success* (Washington, D.C.: Renew America, 1990).

The second is a clear recognition by a large segment of American industry that environmental awareness is a precondition to market success. Some of that awareness may indeed provoke mere public relations responses, and thereby hangs an ethical issue. However, there is no doubt but that Conoco's decision to build double-hulled tankers designed to reduce oil spills, and the Heinz Company's decision to cease fishing for tuna on dolphin sightings or to use drift nets, are but two examples of actual action steps taken to deal with ecological concerns. Such steps do not equal a new corporate ethic, but they are environmentally positive.

Perhaps most important, major American corporations, such as the Minnesota Mining and Manufacturing Company (3M), have found not only that there is public appreciation (and thus, indirectly, consumer-related profits) for their acting environmentally responsible, but that there are also direct operational savings. The 3M Company showed steady revenue and earnings growth over the five-years of 1986 to 1990 while reducing air emissions over the same period by 2 million pounds annually. Its target by 1993 is to eliminate almost 40 million pounds per year more, so that total emissions in 1993 will be less than a third of what they were in 1987. The 3M Company will do so by building environmentally sound processes into product design and manufacturing, by investing in pollution-control equipment for older plants, and by forfeiting, rather than selling, its tradable discharge permits. The foundation of the TDP decision by 3M was its belief that it should reduce pollution, not help other companies to pollute.[36] The lesson here is that 3M expects its actions will actually result in lower costs and higher profits.

But 3M is not alone. AT&T, Carrier, Clairol, W.R. Grace, Polaroid, Reynolds Metals, Union Carbide, and Whyco Chromium are other examples of corporations that have seen net savings result from environmental compliance.[37]

---

[36] See J. Holusha, "Hutchinson No Longer Holds Its Nose," *The New York Times*, February 3, 1991.

[37] A.K. Naj, "Industrial Switch: Some Companies Cut Pollution by Altering Production Methods," *The Wall Street Journal*, December 24, 1990; S. McMurray, "Cleaning Up: Chemical Firms Find That It Pays to Reduce Pollution at Its Source: Altering Processes Makes Production More Efficient," *The Wall Street Journal*, June 11, 1991. See also A. Zich "Keeping Tabs on Risky Business (U.S. Environmental Auditing)" Vol. 1, No. 2 *Tomorrow* magazine (1991), pp. 24-29, and H.E. Davis, "The Environment: Take the Initiative or Face the Consequences," *A.N.A. / The Advertiser* (Fall 1991). See also P. Oster, "Cleaning Up on Cleaning Up in the European Community," *The Washington Post National Weekly Edition,* (June 22-28, 1992). International, national, and regional business alliances to deal with economic and environmental challenges are springing up (e.g., The Council of Great Lakes Industries). See Allerdice, Mattoon, and Tests, "Alternative Approaches to Meeting Economic and Environmental Challenges," *Chicago Fed Letter* (November 1992).

V. THE TOXICITY OF TORTS

A. The *Cryovac* Case

Earl v. Cryovac, A Div. of W. R. Grace
722 P 2d. 725 (1989)

Burnett, Judge

This is a toxic tort case. James Earl has alleged that his lungs were injured when he was exposed at work to vapors emitted from a plastic film manufactured by the Cryovac division of W.R. Grace Company. He filed a worker's compensation claim against his employer and filed this tort action against Cryovac. The worker's compensation claim was settled. In this case, the district court entered summary judgement against Earl, holding that he had failed to establish any causal connection between his injury and Cryovac's product. . . .

In Part I of our opinion, we discuss the elements of toxic tort action, the requirement of proximate cause, and the use of expert testimony to establish causation. In Part II, we focus on the issue of causation in the present case, summarizing the evidentiary facts and the opinions of expert witnesses. In Part III, we enunciate the standards governing summary judgements. . . .

I

[i,2] When a plaintiff brings an action against the manufacturer of a product, seeking damages for negligence or for strict liability in tort, he carries the burden of showing (1) that he has suffered an injury, (2) that the product was defective or unsafe when it left the control of the manufacturer, and (3) that the plaintiff's injury was proximately caused by the product. If the product is alleged to be unsafe because it is toxic, the causation issue turns upon two subsidiary questions: (a) Did the product, or a substance in the product, have the capacity to cause the type of harm claimed by the plaintiff? (b) Was the plaintiff's exposure sufficient to produce a toxic effect? Farber, *Toxic Causation* 71 MINN.L.REV. 1219 (1987).

[3] Because toxic torts typically involve a period of latency between exposure and manifestation of injury, the outcome of the litigation often will turn upon the issue of causation. This issue may be addressed by general or particular evidence. General evidence, derived from research in medicine, chemistry or other disciplines of science, may establish the toxic potential of a substance under certain condi-

tions of exposure. Particular evidence, arising from diagnosis and treatment of the plaintiff's ailment, may prove that an exposure has occurred and may demonstrate a manifestation of the product's toxic potential.

A

Both types of evidence, general and particular, are probative as to the legal requirement of proximate cause. . . . Proximate cause, in the sense of cause in fact, embraces two closely related elements:

> First, an event is the cause in fact of a succeeding event only if the succeeding event would not have occurred "but for" the prior event. Thus, an act or omission is not the cause in fact of ensuing damage if the damage likely would have occurred anyway. The second element is a requirement that the first event be a "substantial factor" in producing the succeeding event. [Citation omitted.] Thus, a defendant's conduct is the cause in fact of an event only if it was a material element and a substantial factor in bringing it about.

When a case goes to trial, the existence of proximate cause, like any other required element of the plaintiff's case, must be established by a preponderance of the evidence. The trier of fact must be persuaded that the plaintiff's claim of causation "is more probably true than not true." By employing a probability standard, the law strikes a balance between plaintiffs' and defendants' rights. It avoids compelling a plaintiff to meet the virtually impossible burden of proving causation with certainty in order to obtain compensation for an injury. It also avoids compelling a defendant to pay damages when his connection with the plaintiff's injury is nothing more than a mere possibility. This balance reflects a value judgement based on our society's intuitive sense of civil justice. See generally *Calabresi,* Concerning Cause and the Law of Torts, 43 U.CHI.L.REV. 69 (1975).[38]

---

[38] Some scholars have questioned the applicability of the probability standard to mass toxic tort cases. See, e.g., Wright, *Causation in Tort Law,* 73 Cal.L.Rev. 1735; Note, *Trans-Science in Torts,* 96 Yale L.J. 428 (1986). Mass toxic tort cases present unique problems such as indeterminate plaintiffs, e.g., *Allen v. United States,* 588 F.Supp.247 (D. Utah 1984) or indeterminate defendants, e.g., *Sindell v. Abbott Laboratories,* 26 Cal.3d 588, 163 Cal. Rptr. 132, 607 P.2d 924 (1980). See generally M. Peterson and M. Selvin, *Resolution of Mass Torts: Toward a Framework for Evaluation of Aggregative Procedures* (Institute for Civil Justice, 1988). Because the instant case does not present these unique problems, we have no occasion to depart from our customary formulation of the proximate cause requirement or of the plaintiff's burden of proof [Court footnote].

When doctors and scientists evaluate causation, however, they do not strike a value-based balance. In their work, they apply standards of greater or lesser rigor than probability. See generally Nesson, *Agent Orange Meets the Blue Bus: Fact-Finding at the Frontier of Knowledge*, 66 B.U.L.REV. 521 (1986) (Hereafter cited as *Fact-Finding at the Frontier of Knowledge*). In scientific research, where the replication of an observed event is the ultimate test of truth, the usual standard of causation is a high degree of certainty. Conversely, in diagnosis and treatment of a specific patient, where the objective is to find a cure or to prevent further harm, a doctor may ascribe causal significance to a possibility that falls short of a probability.

Accordingly, when the courts apply medical and scientific evidence to a question of causation, they must interpret the evidence carefully in light of the applicable standard. They may not assume that a causal relationship is probable merely because a physician deems it significant in his diagnosis and treatment of a patient's condition. Neither may they assume that a causal relationship is improbable merely because it has not been documented in a body of research literature where a high degree of certainty is demanded. These distinctions are particularly important in a toxic tort case where, as here, the issue of causation is framed by the expert opinions of scientists and treating physicians.

B

Causation is a question of fact for the jury to resolve. However, the admissibility of expert testimony on that subject is a question for the trial judge to decide. The judge's decision rests on three criteria. First, the witness must be qualified as an expert who possesses "scientific, technical, or other specialized knowledge [that] will assist the trier of fact to understand the evidence or to determine a fact in issue. . . ." Second, if the qualified witness intends to give testimony containing an opinion or inference, and such testimony will be based on facts not otherwise in evidence or within the expert's personal knowledge, then the facts must be "of a type reasonably relied upon by experts in the particular field. . . ." Third, if the testimony is relevant and admissible under the foregoing criteria, it may nevertheless be excluded if its probative value would be "substantially outweighed by the danger of unfair prejudice, confusion of the issues, or misleading the jury, or by considerations of undue delay, waste of time or needless presentation of cumulative evidence."

[4] In many toxic tort cases (including, as we shall see, the present case), the controversy over expert testimony arises from the second of these criteria. The question is whether the experts' opinions are based

upon facts known to them or otherwise admitted in evidence—and, if not, whether the facts are "of a type reasonably relied upon by experts in the particular field". . . . In addressing these questions, a trial judge must take care not to allow his decision on the admissibility of expert testimony to be influenced by this perception of whether the testimony would be persuasive to a jury at trial. The weight given to expert testimony is to be determined by the jury. In evaluating the facts upon which an expert bases an opinion, the judge must not "infringe upon the fact-finder's role in assessing the weight of the expert testimony."

[5] It is particularly important in toxic tort cases, and in other litigation where highly technical issues are presented, that the judge not exclude expert testimony by second-guessing the facts upon which the experts choose to rely. "Judges, after all, are lay persons, no matter how well-read they are in science." *Fact-Finding at the Frontier of Knowledge, supra*, at 531. If an expert is qualified to render an opinion, based on his expertise in the subject, then he must be accorded substantial deference in the selection of data upon which he chooses to base his opinion. With this constraint in mind, we now turn to the evidence adduced during the summary judgement proceedings in the present case.

II

On the causation issue, the plaintiff's case rested largely upon the testimony of three qualified expert witnesses. The first to be deposed was Charles E. Reed, M.D., the plaintiff's primary treating physician. Dr. Reed was, and is, board-certified in internal medicine and in the subspecialty of pulmonary disease. He examined the plaintiff on many occasions, ran numerous laboratory and clinical tests, and devised a treatment program that ultimately alleviated many of the plaintiff's symptoms.

Dr. Reed obtained a patient history which paralleled the deposition testimony of the plaintiff himself. The plaintiff worked in the meat-packing industry for approximately twenty-five years, of which twenty years had been spent in "slaughter" rooms and the most recent five years had been spent in a "packing" room. Until moving to the packing room, the plaintiff had not suffered any severe breathing disorders. At one time, he had been a smoker of cigarettes, but he had discontinued this habit ten years before seeing Dr. Reed. Approximately seven years before he saw Dr. Reed, the plaintiff was hospitalized briefly for shortness of breath; however, no diagnosis was made, and he suffered no severe symptoms until he began work in the packing room. In Dr. Reed's opinion, this prior history was unremarkable.

The plaintiff consulted Dr. Reed, upon reference from another physician, when he experienced a worsening problem of chest tightness and shortness of breath. He noticed that his symptoms would temporarily subside during weekends and vacations, but would resume when he returned to work in the packing room. Dr. Reed learned that the packing room contained a machine that wrapped meat in plastic bags and then heated the plastic in water at or near the boiling temperature. The hot water caused the plastic to shrink tightly around the meat; accordingly, the machine was known as a "shrink tunnel." Because the packing room was kept at a low temperature, the boiling water in the shrink tunnel produced a heavy fog. Some employees, who later submitted affidavits in this case, reported that they could smell plastic, and occasionally burning plastic, in the air.

Dr. Reed also learned that the plastic material used in the packing room was a shrinkable thermoplastic "barrier bag" manufactured by Cryovac. Dr. Reed found medical literature documenting the existence of "meat-wrapper's asthma" or "meat-wrapper's syndrome," a chronic lung disease observed in employees of meatpacking plants and butcher shops where plastic bags were cut by a thermal process known as a "hot wire." The disease, which produces symptoms similar to those experienced by the plaintiff in this case, has been attributed in the literature to the release of vapors during the heating of the plastic material. As noted by Dr. Reed, the researchers are satisfied that a causal connection exists between the heated plastic and the disease, although the precise chemical (or group of chemicals) responsible for the etiology of the disease has not been identified.

In consultation with Dr. Reed, the plaintiff quit his job in the packing room at the meatpacking plant. During the course of treatment prescribed by Dr. Reed, his symptoms gradually receded. When asked to characterize the plaintiff's condition at the time depositions were taken in this case, Dr. Reed stated that the plaintiff suffered from chronic obstructive pulmonary disease. He observed that "some of the reversible component of his disease [has] completely cleared leaving a residual component of chronic obstruction."

Upon these facts, Dr. Reed formed an opinion, expressed in his deposition, that the plaintiff's disease was caused or exacerbated by exposure in the workplace to vapors emitted from the plastic bags as they were heated in the shrink tunnel. Dr. Reed described this causal connection not merely as a possibility but as a "high probability." . . .

[The remainder of this case deals with the legal issues related to summary judgement. The decision of the court here was that James Earl, the plaintiff, *did* have a legal right to have his case heard and decided by a jury. The case was sent back for a trial on its merits.]

B. The Meaning of Torts and Toxic Tort

We began this portion of the chapter with the *Cryovac* case because it is a good illustration of the basic problems involved in dealing with a special kind of tort case.

A "tort," as we observed in Chapter 3, is a *harm* caused to one or more parties by another party or parties. That harm can be to one's physical person, to one's psyche, or reputation, to one's privacy, and, of course, to one's property. And that harm can be caused deliberately or *negligently* (i.e., through a failure to use proper care under the particular circumstances surrounding the harm).

Environmental, or "toxic" torts (i.e., harm caused primarily by toxic substances) present new complexities in otherwise well-developed common-law areas—most of them covered in *Cryovac*.

Let us review these complexities by assuming another case that raises *Cryovac* (toxic tort) issues to a higher, and even more complex level.

Assume that 30 plaintiffs from the town of Wolfield bring suit against Winburn Company in 1991, alleging that Winburn dumped chemical waste during the years 1973 to 1988 that poisoned their town well water. That as a result of drinking that water, members of ten families were poisoned, including seven young boys and girls who died of leukemia, and several babies allegedly sustained birth defects.

Examine the numerous issues: *Did* Winburn actually dump all those chemical wastes? Was the groundwater pollution of some Wolfield wells the consequence of Winburn chemical wastes? Were the injuries of these plaintiffs the result of drinking water befouled by toxic waste? If so, what are the injuries and deaths "worth"?

We are involved here with the *Cryovac* issues of *causation* and *proximate cause* in an area where some scientific aspects of cause and effect are mired in uncertainty.

Imagine now, in our Winburn/Wolfield case, that Winburn Company was not the only toxic waste dumper, but rather that three corporations all dumped different dangerous wastes at the same time. If someone *is* liable for damages, which one(s)? Which chemicals poisoned the groundwater? Which injuries were caused by which chemicals? Does it matter? Do all three companies pay? How much and to whom?

Let us go a step further. Let us assume that Wolfield is a large city of 3 million residents, some 1 million of them users of contaminated drinking wells. Given the same causation/proximate cause basic issues, how do we deal with the next level of issues, namely nine offending corporations and 3,000 plaintiffs, with some of the cancer deaths occurring in families with long histories of cancer and other past family ills not too dissimilar from those "caused" by the offending chemicals? And finally, how long a period of time should be allowed for future lawsuits that could arise amongst the remaining exposed residents? This is the "latency period" problem in toxic torts. Cancer (e.g., as a developmental medical phenomenon) is very far from the simplicity of a broken bone.

That these hypotheticals are hardly unrealistic is attested to by the tens of thousands of asbestos cases still pending in U.S. courts, with two new (longer latency period) cases still being filed for every one disposed of! Then there are the *Exxon Valdez* suits, and the DES cases, (DES was a pregnancy drug that produced fetal injuries into the next generation, not always seen before puberty). To compound matters, DES was manufactured by several companies. This adds to the latency problems, the horrendous problem of proving *which* manufacturer was the source of the DES that produced, for example, a daughter's vaginal cancer manifested at age 19, a cancer occurring almost 20 years after her mother stopped buying and using the drug.

The law, of necessity, has developed some rules to deal with these issues. In DES-like cases, many courts use the "market share" theory of liability. Every manufacturer of a harmful product is liable for a plaintiff's damages sustained as the result of a proven, causally related toxic injury, but only to the extent of its market share in the offending product.[39]

The law is still struggling with latency-period problems (how long before all claims are buried?), as well as with proximate cause and burden-of-proof issues.

Insurance companies are particularly concerned with long latency periods. For how long must their coverage persist on particular policies? How do insurance company statisticians take account of this toxic tort phenomenon?

Hovering over the serious *medico-legal issues* (does toxic chemical X cause cancer?), are *policy issues* (What term of years should be put into a statute of limitations?) and *common law tort issues* of proximate cause and the like. One must surely feel the presence of the pervasive ethical question: What is *fair* here? And how do we determine what result *is* fair (just, equitable, ethical) and to whom? And then, of course, how do we best go about making the determination?[40]

---

[39] A discussion of market-share theory in a recent case may be found in "DES Liability Resolved," *New York State Bar Association Digest*, 352 (April 1989).

[40] An excellent overview article dealing with all of the fundamental issues in toxic torts is J.M. Strock, "Coming to Terms with the Compensation Conundrum," *The American Bar Association Journal* (September 1985). A separate insurance company issue is raised by the "clean up" (remediation) cases; for example, under CERCLA: When is an offender's insurance company liable (even many years after the "dirtying" took place) for expensive clean-up costs? Does it matter that the policyholder/polluter was an unknowing offender?

VI. THE ELEMENTS OF DAMAGES: A BRIEF LOOK

We have dealt generally with damages here and in earlier chapters. Let us look very briefly now at the *elements,* or *categories of damages in law.* Basically, there are four categories of damages to which dollar figures are assigned when harm is claimed (and proved):

I.   General compensatory
    A. Pain and suffering, past and future
        1. Pain
        2. Embarrassment from disfigurement
        3. Loss of life's pleasure
    B. Emotional distress

II. Special compensatory
    A. Medical expenses, past and future
        1. Doctor's bills
        2. Hospital bills
        3. Medicine
        4. Equipment
        5. Physical therapy
        6. Psychological therapy
        7. In-house nursing care
        8. Modification of living environment
    B. Earnings, past and future
        1. Diminished or lost capacity

III. Punitive or exemplary

IV. Derivative actions
    A. Loss of consortium or lost services
        1. Spouse
        2. Child
    B. Death actions (wrongful death or survivor)
        1. Burial expenses
        2. Consider all the above items[41]

A knowing one? Some courts, and juries, seem to make that distinction, holding insurance companies *not* liable when the policyholder was a deliberate polluter. The language of the policy, of course, is relevant in such cases. See also for specific insurer liability cases S. Goldberg, "CGL Wars," *American Bar Association Journal* (November 1992) (is the real issue whether the pollution is "sudden" or accidental?). *The other side* of the toxic damage/insurance issue is set forth in G. Steinmetz, "Insurers Discover Pollution Can Bolster Bottom Line," *The Wall Street Journal*, August 19, 1992.

[41] I-IV excerpted from Charfoos and Christensen, "Measuring Damages," *American Bar Association Journal* (September 1986).

A. General Compensatory

General compensatory damages, though sometimes difficult to put an exact price on, do not cause much consternation in the legal system. On appeal, appellate courts generally hold that a jury's determination of money damages in this area should not be reduced or overturned unless it is shown to be the result of passion or prejudice or it clearly appears from uncontroverted evidence that the amount awarded bears no reasonable relationship to the loss suffered by the plaintiff.[42]

B. Special Compensatory and Derivative Actions

Special compensatory damages are directly calculable in terms of the past, and, without too much difficulty, in terms of the future as well. Both general and compensatory damages, however, as well as damages in derivative actions, must face particular *economic considerations*, as exemplified by the following case:

C. Present value of Damages:
The *Ursini* v. *Sussman* Case

Ursini v. *Sussman*
541 N.Y.S. 2d 916 (Sup. 1989)

Ira Gammerman, Justice:
In this medical malpractice action the plaintiff's attorney was retained and the action instituted after July 1, 1985. Thus, when on January 17, 1989, the jury returned a verdict in favor of the plaintiff for $500,000 past and $5,000,000 future damages, it became necessary for the court to apply the provisions of CPLR 5031.
The jury's $5,000,000 award for future damages was itemized as follows: $2,000,000 for loss of earnings for a period of 44 years; $500,000 for therapy for a period of 14 years; $500,000 for attendant care for a period of 50 years; $2,000,000 for pain and suffering for a period of 58 years.
Pursuant to CPLR 5031 subdivision (b), the court is to enter a lump-sum judgement for the past damages awarded (here $500,000) and for future damages not in excess of $250,000. The statute further provides that ". . . any lump-sum payment of a portion of future damages shall be deemed to include the elements of future damages

---

[42] See, for example, *Boden* v. *Crawford*, 552 N.E. 2d 1287 (1990).

in the same proportion as such elements comprised of the total award for future damages as determined by the trier of fact."

Thus, a portion of the $250,000 lump-sum must be deducted from each of the awards for future losses in appropriate proportion. . . .

Allocating those percentages to the $250,000 lump-sum award reduces the awards for future damages as follows: loss of earnings—$1,900,000 (reduced by $100,000 or 40% of $250,000); therapy—$475,000 (reduced by $24,000 or 10% of $250,000); attendant care—$475,000 (reduced by $25,000 or 10% of $250,000); pain and suffering—$1,900,000 (reduced by $100,000 or 40% of $250,000). . . .

It next becomes necessary to determine the present value of the now reduced future payments to be made to the plaintiff. The first step is to divide the reduced payments by the number of years determined by the jury (with the exception of the award for pain and suffering which is divided by ten). That produces the following result: Loss of earnings—$43,181.82 in the first year increased at 4% per year compounded annually for 44 years; therapy—$33,928.57 in the first year increased at 4% per year compounded annually for 14 years; attendant care—$9,500 in the first year increased at 4% per year compounded annually for 50 years; pain and suffering—$190,000 in the first year increased at 4% per year compounded annually for 10 years.

Pursuant to 5031 subdivision (e) the attorney's fee is to be based on the present value of an annuity contract that will provide for the above payments. The statue requires that such present value be ". . . determined in accordance with generally accepted actuarial practices by applying the discount rate in effect at the time of the award. . . ."

[1] Leaving aside the question of what discount rate is to be used, it must be determined whether in computing present value in accordance with generally accepted actuarial practices the fact that a substantial portion of the annuity is non-guaranteed, that is, terminates with the death of the plaintiff, should be considered. It can be argued that the possible premature demise of the plaintiff is a factor that would be considered by an actuary in determining present value. The statute, however, provides that present value determination shall be made by applying the discount rate to the full amount of the remaining future damages and further that the period of time used to calculate the present value of the annuity contract shall be the period of years determined by the trier of fact, except that the period of time applicable to the pain and suffering award should be no more than 10 years. If the possible early death of the plaintiff is considered in calculating present value then such calculation would be on less than the full amount of the remaining future damages and would be based upon a period of years less than that determined by the jury. Thus, in

computing present value, the court will not consider the possibility of infant plaintiff's early death.

[2] Over the past several years at least nine economists have testified (for both plaintiff and defendant) in cases involving claims for future losses. In discussing the appropriate discount rate to be used in reducing future losses to present value, the testimony of all nine fell within the range of six to eight percent. The court, thus, is adopting a discount rate of 7.5%. The use of such a discount rate (at the upper end of the six to eight percent range) is, in my view, in keeping with the intent of the legislature. A higher discount rate reduces the attorney's fee, thus providing greater payment to the client and further serves to reduce the defendant's premium (or cost) for the annuity policy required by the judgement.

Reducing the future payments to present value using the 7.5% discount rate results in the following: present value of award for loss of earnings—$1,000,477; present value of award for therapy—$380,125; present value of award for attendant care—$232,154; present value of award for pain and suffering—$1,617,480, for a total of $3,230,263.

D. Punitive Damages

Punitive damages raise sensitive issues. In a state case that reached the U.S. Supreme Court, an Alabama judge instructed the jury that punitive damages were not intended to compensate the plaintiff for any injury (harm), but were to punish the defendant and protect the public by deterring the defendant and others from doing such wrong in the future—and, that the jury did not have to award this class of damages.

This is a reasonable, basic characterization of punitive damages. But one must add that punitive damages are not awarded to punish conduct arising from a mistake of law or fact, an honest error of judgment, or overzealousness, or even ordinary negligence. Rather, the defendant's conduct must indicate something stronger: malice, gross negligence, deliberate wrongdoing, and the like.

Trial court judges and appeals court judges have the power to review punitive damage awards. The trial judge, after a jury verdict in his or her court, may order the plaintiff to accept a reduction (called a *remittitur*) or face a new trial. We saw a good example of this in the Ford Pinto case, set out in Chapter 3. It is up to a reviewing judge to determine, generally speaking, if the award is so great that it indicates prejudice, partiality, corruption, or some other improper motive.

The Supreme Court was asked to decide whether punitive damages were unconstitutional, either because they constituted an "excessive fine" under the Eighth Amendment, or because standards for assessing them were so vague that they violated due process. In both instances the Supreme Court refused to find the assessment of punitive damages to be unconstitutional. The Court felt "objective criteria" were essential, but that that issue was really for the trial and appellate courts. More Supreme Court reviews of individual cases could come, but the basic constitutionality of punitive damages is established.[43]

Are punitive damages to some degree based upon ethical considerations? If so, how does one really assign an "economic value" to particular "social value" transgressions in cases of reprehensible, noncriminal harm?

VII. DAMAGES AND THE INSURANCE CRISIS

According to insurance companies, Americans are outrageously litigious, juries are utterly shocking in their cavalier disregard of both law and human decency as they gleefully rob insurance companies of their money, and plaintiff lawyers are a disreputable band of larcenists.

According to plaintiff lawyers, insurance companies are rapacious, incompetent, immoral, and conspiratorial, and never pay enough.

This overall situation is often referred to as an "insurance crisis." During times of such crises, insurance rates rise precipitously, and certain categories of liability insurance become unavailable at any price.

Arguments about the quality and quantity of jury verdicts, high insurance rates, and policy shortages ought to be susceptible to rational debate, and ethical issues should clearly be part of the discussion.

It is true that a very large amount of jury awards are paid out (cumulatively) by insurance companies every year—even after deducting *remittiturs* from insurance company figures. The real issue is, why? Ornery general litigiousness is one factor. So is a *general* societal focus on "big bucks" both inside and outside the courtroom. And high tort awards are a reality. However, a reasonable case can be made that a sizable portion of jury-based monetary awards in fact result from contract disputes engaged in by and between business concerns.[44]

---

[43] Punitive damages do not violate the Eighth Amendment: *Browning-Ferris Industries of Vermont, Inc.* v. *Kelco Disposal, Inc.*, 109 S. Ct. 2909 (1989). Nor are they violative of due process: *Pacific Mutual Life Insurance Company* v. *Haslip* 111 S. Ct. 1032 (1991). Then again, they might be subject to *some* specific requirements. In the case of *TXO Production Corp.* v. *Alliance Resources Corp.*, No. 92-479, the U.S. Supreme Court agreed to hear argument again on both procedural and proportional issues (November 30, 1992).

[44] See P.M. Barrett, "Litigation Boom? Professor Turns Up New Culprit," *The Wall Street Journal*, October 17, 1988. Cf. M. Geyelin, "Product Suits Yield Few Punitive Awards," *The Wall Street Journal*, January 6, 1992. Also, "Judges, More Than Jurors, Side with Personal Injury Plaintiffs," *The Wall Street Journal*, July 23, 1992.

It is probably true that at certain times and in certain jurisdictions, juries do act cavalierly in terms of gliding over facts to arrive at insurance company "deep pockets," and that consequent expenditures indeed hurt insurers' profits. However, it is also true that insurance companies have suffered severe losses as a result of engaging in price-cutting wars in order to bring money in as quickly as possible to invest for high return. Deliberately underpricing known risks so as to make (often bad) investments is not the kind of misbehavior public juries should be blamed for.[45]

It is also true that plaintiffs' lawyers have their special organizations and meetings where they exchange experiences and sharpen each other's professional skill knives (as most professional groups do). But charges have been made, backed up by formal lawsuits filed by attorneys-general representing 19 states, that many large insurance companies engaged in a massive, illegal conspiracy. Alleged company actions to control the insurance market included conspiracy to limit liability coverage, and to drive up rates for businesses and governments amounting to an illegal boycott under antitrust laws.[46]

The insurance situation in the United States needs strengthening in *many* particulars, not limited to tort law. However, *all* parties involved in the damages dilemma bear responsibility for its current state and thus for its repair.

Meanwhile, one might profitably consider *all* the value issues involved in this debate, and heed the following advice with regard to the American tort system:

> . . . virtually any serious discussion of possible revision of the tort system will excite a reiteration and reexamination of fundamental value preferences: personal, institutional, cultural. Not surprisingly, those preferences differ widely and may conflict. They must be acknowledged and addressed before the public policy debate on this topic may proceed to a conclusion in an intelligent, informed, and sensitive manner.[47]

---

[45] See R.T. McGee, "The Cycle in Property/Casualty Insurance," *F.R.B. New York, Quarterly Review* (Autumn, 1986). It would surely be unfair to characterize insurance company investment expertise in general as lacking in merit. However, the Equitable Life Assurance Society failure—among others—in 1991 does indicate a distressing lack of investment acumen, at least upon occasion. And see, on the issue of insurance company fraud, M. Brannigan, "Castle in the Sand: A Florida Insurer's Fall. . . ," *The Wall Street Journal*, December 23, 1991. See also H.R. Riske, "Was There a Liability Crisis? *The American Bar Association Journal* (January 1989).

[46] R.B. Schmitt, "Court Revives Anti-Trust Suit Against Insurers," *The Wall Street Journal*, June 19, 1991, and P.M. Barrett, "Justices to Hear Insurer Collusion Case," *The Wall Street Journal*, October 6, 1992.

[47] "Final Report of the Seventy-Eighth American Assembly: Tort Law and the Public Interest" (pamphlet), *American Assembly of Columbia University*, May 31, 1990, p. 5. See

IN LIEU OF THE PHILOSOPHER'S STONE

We might want to think about parties at interest and value-weighting with regard to issues such as the ones that follow.

Professor Richard N. Gardener's recent book analyzes events that took place in Rio de Janeiro, Brazil, from June 3 to June 14, 1992. That book (published by the Council on Foreign Relations Press) focuses not only on what happened at the UNCED conference (Earth Summit), but, also on what the decisions made there mean for the future. It is a good, brief work and we recommend it. But it is the title we wish to call your attention to here: *Negotiating Survival.*

Survival is a very strong word. Keeping it in mind, let us also call to your attention the following:

In the Postscript to his book *An Inquiry into the Human Prospect* (New York: W.W. Norton & Co., Inc., 1980), economist Robert L. Hielbroner cites this quotation from a British economist, taken from *Business and Society Review*:

> Suppose that, as a result of using up all the world's resources, human life did come to an end. So what? What is so desirable about an indefinite continuation of the human species, religious convictions apart? It may well be that nearly everybody who is already here on earth would be reluctant to die, and that everybody has an instinctive fear of death. But one must not confuse this with the notion that, in any meaningful sense, generations who are yet unborn can be said to be better off if they are born than if they are not.

Professor Heilbroner then quotes from a book by another economist teaching at the Massachusetts Institute of Technology. That young economist made it clear in his book that in terms of geologic time (4.5 billion years) being thought of as one trip around the world on a Concorde-like jet, humans got on eight miles before the end, and industrial man just six feet before the end. Moreover, the sun will swallow up the earth in 12 billion years, so only three more round trips are left to be made. Says our MIT economist:

> That led me to think: Do I care about what happens a thousand years from now. . . . Do I care when man gets off the airplane? I

---

also M.F. Grady, "Torts: The Best Defense Against Regulations," *The Wall Street Journal*, September 3, 1992.

think I basically [have come] to the conclusion that I don't care whether man is on the airplane for another eight feet, or if man is on the airplane another three times around the world.

Our two economist friends share a "rational" ethical position. Professor Heilbroner is outraged by it, as are we, but, we wonder, how do *you* feel? Would the Adam Smith of *The Wealth of Nations* be in agreement with our two "rationalist" professors? How about the Adam Smith of *A Theory of Moral Sentiments*? Did you catch, in this chapter, the way we reconcile the two seemingly conflicting Smith positions?

Dr. Garrett Hardin published an article in *Science* magazine in 1968 that has since become a classic. Titled "The Tragedy of the Commons," it is about scarcity and reality and pleads for a fundamental extension in morality in order to ensure human survival.

Vice-president Albert Gore, in his book *Earth in the Balance* (Boston: Houghton Mifflin, 1992) also takes the survivalist ethic as a given. He claims that we humans have lost our sense of spiritual connection with nature—with the natural world, that we must restore the "inner ecology of human experience," which, for him, is highlighted by

the balance between respect for the past and faith in the future, between a belief in the individual and a commitment to the community, between our love for the world and our fear of losing it.

We have presented several points of view and two clear-cut, basic ethical values here. Whatever the environmental/economic issue, whichever might be the parties affected by a managerial or governmental decision, and whatever other "values" are being weighed in the face of whatever data (financial, scientific, or social)—would these basic values *predetermine the decision*? If so, what does *that* mean when we debate the "rightness" and "wrongness" of a difficult environmental/economic/social decision on any particular issue?

What basic value(s) do *you* bring to environment/economic issues? Do your values much affect your perception of just which groups have a legitimate interest affected by your decision? Do your basic values predetermine your weighting process as well?

We are talking here about environmental issues. However, you might want to ponder—*as an economist*, or *as a lawyer*, or *a broker*, or whatever—some of the basic values you bring to other of the subject areas contained in this book.

And perhaps also ponder the notion of why there can never be any such thing as a philosopher's stone.

5

Fraud, Legal and Financial Agency, Ethics, and the Fiduciary Relationship

COMING UP IN THIS CHAPTER

We are going to examine some legal concepts here that bring the common law about as close as it ever gets to dealing directly with *ethically* unacceptable market behavior.

These legal concepts are *fraud* and *fiduciary relationships*. The concept of *agency* is the first step on the road to examination of fiduciaries.

There is, of course, a difference between being "negligent" or "careless" or "mistaken" and being fraudulent/dishonest. We shall keep the differences in mind.

We first examine in this chapter the general notion of fraud at common law and then in legislation. Consumer fraud and deceptive business practices are defined by statute in most states. The fairly straightforward law case of *Duhl* v. *Nash Realty* is typical of such legislation. You might want to keep in mind as you read the case just how far law has come since the old days of "buyer beware" (*caveat emptor*). You might want to ask yourself why the progression from you're-on-your-own to "little FTC laws."

The rather lengthy *Manufacturers Hanover Trust* case follows *Nash* because it is a good illustration of two things: First, it is a case that contains material on three types of fraud—at common law, by legislation, and specific to *one* area, in this case *securities fraud*. Second, this is a case involving the liability of a large accounting firm, and we are witnessing very large liability issues develop in this area. You might want to ask yourself in this case: Just how many parties should an accountant firm be liable to when it issues a misleading report on a client? And why.

The brief *Dean Witter* case is a simple introduction to the legal concept of *agency*. We are using law cases in this chapter because they seem apt here where the major issues *are* legal relationships.

We move from legal agency (which relates to general agency relationships among agents, principals, *and the parties affected by them*) to *fiduciary* relationships (more the personal duties and obligations between agent and principal alone). We use narrative material to bring you into the agency/fiduciary circle, and then proceed to a recent series of Delaware fiduciary cases centered around mergers and acquisitions, and leveraged buyouts. These Delaware cases are used because they eventually face up to one of the hardest problems markets and law must face at one of their key linkage points: *Exactly* what is the nature of fiduciary relationships in the case of managers and the corporation? *Who* must do *what* and for *whom*?

We pause a moment, after the fourth (*Paramount/Time*) case, to examine a different "agency" theory: the one pertaining to finance. And it is different from *legal* agency, the latter being the only one by which managers are judged in a court of law. We note the differences between legal and finance agency theory, and we conclude from our examination of both, that there *is* a definable ethical construct that can explain the nature of the legal fiduciary relationship. And if we are correct, managers actually have a duty in law to consider the best interests, when they act, of broad groups in society, going well beyond the direct and immediate interests of their shareholders.

I. FRAUD

A. Common Law

At *common law* in order to recover damages from another party for fraud, the plaintiff must prove (as to acts of the defendant) the following:

- a conscious misrepresentation or concealment of the truth, and
- an intent to benefit by causing the plaintiff to rely on the untruth to his or her detriment (i.e., by parting with money or property, or by entering into a contract) and that
- the misrepresentation was *material* (i.e., directly related to the harm caused) and that
- there was an *intent* to cause the plaintiff to rely on the misrepresentation to his or her detriment, and of course

- that the plaintiff actually did *believe, rely,* and *suffer* provable *harm.*[1]

It must be added here that, at common law, *intent* on the part of one sued for fraud *can be presumed* in the presence of a reckless disregard of the truth.

There is also a common-law concept of *constructive fraud,* which involves

- a breach of duty by someone in a confidential relationship with another, with
- reliance on the misused relationship causing harm.

We shall be looking at "breach of duty" more specifically later on, especially in connection with corporate officers and directors.

Fraud can result from a conscious misrepresentation or concealment made in a writing, in an oral statement, or in connection with specific conduct, or even from silence in a situation that calls for speaking the truth.

And if the fraud is tinged with legal *malice* (i.e., perpetrated with personal ill will beyond a mere design to materially benefit) the injured party can sue for punitive damages.[2]

Common-law fraud clearly deals with unethical behavior, but what if the "misrepresentation or concealment" is the result of stupidity or negligence on the part of the defendant, rather than a deliberate intent to deceive, and thereby profit from, another? There is a remedy at common law for that action, too. Though sometimes referred to loosely as a form of fraud, the proper name is *negligent misrepresentation.* In negligent misrepresentation, a defendant is responsible at law if, in the course of his or her business or profession, the defendant supplies misinformation for the guidance of others in their business transactions that they rely on to their detriment. The defendant is responsible, that is, if he or she "fails to exercise that care and competence in obtaining and communicating the information which its recipient is justified in expecting."[3]

With respect to *contracts,* specifically, here are some common-law fraud considerations:

One can avoid a contract entered into, in whole or in part, in reliance on a *fraudulent misrepresentation.*

---

[1] The general common-law rules on fraud actions may be found in many state cases. See, e.g., *Rogers* v. *Hickerson,* 716 S.W. 2d 439 (Missouri 1986) and *Wagner* v. *Castell,* 663 P.2d 1020 (Arizona 1983).

[2] *Rogers* v. *Hickerson, supra.*

[3] *Duhl* v. *Nash Realty,* 429 N.E. 2d 1267, 1276 (Illinois 1982).

One can avoid a contract entered into through *duress* or *menace*, where free will is overcome by the threat of a wrongful act (e.g., "If you don't sign this contract your store will most likely burn down!").

One can avoid a contract entered into through *undue influence*, which generally means coercion beyond ordinary persuasion (e.g., "If you don't sign this contract, Grandma, we don't know where the money will come from to keep you here with us!"). Not an illegal act, to be sure, but calculated to destroy the capacity to enter freely into a willing, perceived-to-be-fair bargain.

B. Legislation

Legislation can, of course, take fraud beyond the common law. Basically, there are two observable types of statutory fraud: *general*, in the sense of being applied to a wide range of business dealings, and *specific*, in the sense of being applied to one key area of market endeavor.

"Little FTC laws" are a good example of the former.

An example of the latter are frauds defined by securities laws.

Unfair and deceptive trade practices in general (and this includes some types of unfair competition perhaps not actionable under formal antitrust laws) are covered by special legislation in almost every U.S. state. Such legislation has been around since the late 1960s and is patterned after the Federal Trade Commission Act, 15 U.S.C. § 45 et seq. The problem with the FTC law was that it gave the government the right to pursue "unfair and deceptive trade practices" but it gave no such right to private parties. Here is where, and why, the states stepped in.

Some state "little FTC laws" prohibit "unfair" acts, while others prohibit "unconscionable" acts. All are meant to provide consumers (and in some cases, competing businesses) with a means of redressing essentially unethical behavior. These consumer-protection-oriented laws allow recovery, in many cases, for behavior that would not be actionable in a suit for fraud at common law.

The following law case from Illinois illustrates just how far most of these state laws go.

Duhl v. *Nash Realty*
429 N.E. 2d 1267 (Illinois 1982)

[In this case, a broker was sued both for common law fraud and for violation of the Illinois Consumer Fraud and Deceptive Business Practices Act. Footnotes are omitted in the case excerpt printed below, as are all of the court's citations to other Illinois cases].

IV

Section 2 of the Consumer Fraud and Deceptive Businesses Practices Act (Ill. Rev. Stat.1979, ch. 121 1/2, par. 262), provides in part:

> §2. Unfair methods of competition and unfair or deceptive acts or practices, including but not limited to the use or employment of any deception, fraud, false pretense, false promise, misrepresentation or the concealment, suppression or omission of any material fact, with intent that others rely upon the concealment, suppression or omission of such material fact, or the use or employment of any practice described in Section 2 of the "Uniform Deceptive Trade Practices Act," approved August 5, 1965, in the conduct of any trade or commerce are hereby declared unlawful whether any person has in fact been misled, deceived or damaged thereby. In construing this section consideration shall be given to the interpretations of the Federal Trade Commission and the federal courts relating to Section 5(a) of the Federal Trade Commission Act.

The defendants moved to dismiss plaintiffs' claim under the Act contending that the plaintiffs failed to show that there was any misrepresentation made of a statement of fact. . . and that there was an intent to deceive. These are the identical objections raised as to the fraud count (except that here defendants contended plaintiff failed to "show"; a contention which, as already pointed out, is clearly improper and insufficient in a motion to dismiss). This court has already ruled, in the discussion of the fraud count, that the complaint did allege an intentional misrepresentation of a present fact. More importantly, however, none of these elements are required by the Act.

Section 2 of the Act (which was held to apply to misrepresentations by real estate brokers to prospective purchasers in *Beard* v. *Gress* (1980), indicates a decisive move on the part of the Illinois legislature to enact broad protective coverage of consumers from the many types of deceptive or unfair selling and advertising techniques used by businesses. . . . The sections clearly expand the consumers' rights beyond those of the common law, and provide broader consumer protection than does the common law action of fraud. . . . There is a clear mandate from the Illinois legislature that the courts of this State utilize the Act to the utmost degree in eradicating all forms of deceptive and unfair business practices and grant appropriate remedies to injured parties [numerous citations omitted]. . . .

A Plaintiff suing under the Act need not establish all of the elements of fraud as the Act prohibits any deception or false promise.

. . . And it is clear from the language of the Act, particularly its reference to false promises, that liability is not limited to existing material facts. Furthermore, it is well established that under the Act the intention of the seller (his good or bad faith) is not important and a plaintiff can recover under the Act for innocent misrepresentations [numerous citations omitted].

For the foregoing reasons, the judgement of the trial court dismissing the claim in contract is affirmed. However, the dismissal of the other counts is reversed and the case remanded for further proceedings. . . .

Please note that, in addition to recovery for "deception," "false promises," "unfair techniques," and the like, the plaintiff could recover here for harm caused by "innocent misrepresentations."

Hasn't the court here gone beyond holding people responsible for reprehensible business behavior? Why would it do that? Or put properly, why did the Illinois legislature do that?

Are we in a situation somewhat similar to that brought about in the product liability cases? The issue seems to be this: In a case in which the consumer is harmed by some "innocent" (clearly not deliberate or intended) act or product defect, which party should be required to bear the resulting losses?

Nash Realty is hardly a value-free legal or socio-econo-legal decision.

Market participants would do well to ponder the reasons for (or read another way, the attitudes which determined) the rapid development of little FTC laws throughout the nation.[4]

We turn now to federal fraud legislation covering fraud in specific market areas. Securities fraud is a good example. The following case, basically a lawsuit by Manufacturer's Hanover Bank against Arthur Andersen & Co., illustrates the broad thrust of congressional and regulatory agency fraud legislation.

Manufacturers Hanover Trust Company, **Plaintiff-Appellee and Cross- Appellant v.** *Drysdale Securities Corporation; Drysdale Government Securities, Inc.; BMC Acquisition Corp.,* **doing business under the name Buttonwood Management;** *Arthur Andersen & Co.;*

---

[4] An excellent overview article here is Gilleran and Stadfeld, "Little FTC Acts Emerge in Business Litigation," *ABA Journal* (May 1, 1986). One might profitably ponder the clearly ethical (and other) implications of the Massachusetts case discussed at page 60 of the cited *ABA Journal*: "A business suing a business may have to show greater unfairness than a consumer suing a business. [Massachusetts] has held that the defendant's conduct 'must attain a level of rascality that would raise an eyebrow of someone inured to the rough and tumble world of commerce'."

David J. Heuwetter; Joseph V. Ossorio; and Peter J. Wasserman, Defendants, *Arthur Anderson & Co.*, Defendant-Appellant and Cross-Appellee

Nos. 794, 858, 795
United States Court of Appeals for the Second Circuit
Slip Opinion
Argued March 17, 1986
September 8, 1986, Decided

Appeal-Statement:
Appeal from a judgement entered in the United States District Court for the Southern District of New York, Richard Owen, Judge, in favor of plaintiff for $17 million plus interest and costs after a jury trial in an action seeking to recover damages claimed as a result of alleged false representations by an accounting firm made on behalf of a government securities dealer.

Judgement affirmed in part. Award of pre-judgement interest vacated and remanded.

Docket Nos. 85-7827, 85-7865, 85-7929. . .

Opinion:
Before: Pierce, Miner and Altimari, Circuit Judges

Pierce, Circuit Judge:

The defendant accounting firm appeals from a judgement entered in the United States District Court for the Southern District of New York, Richard Owen, Judge, after a jury returned a verdict against it. The jury awarded plaintiff $17 million, to which the district judge added pre-judgement interest, post-judgement interest and costs, in a civil action seeking damages for losses that Manufacturers Hanover Trust Company ("Manufacturers" or "MHT") claimed to have suffered as a result of certain alleged misrepresentations that Arthur Andersen & Co. ("Andersen") made on behalf of Andersen's client, Drysdale Securities Corporation ("DSC") and its successor, Drysdale Government Securities, Inc. ("DGSI"). The district judge submitted seven separate theories of liability to the jury: misrepresentation or material omission "in connection with" the purchase or sale of securities, in violation of section 10(b) of the Securities Exchange Act of 1934, 15 U.S.C. § 78j(b), and Rule 10b-5, 17 C.F.R. 240.10b-5, promulgated thereunder; misrepresentation or material omission "in" the purchase or sale of securities, in violation of section 17(a) of the Securities Act of 1933, 15 U.S.C. § 77q(a) (2); misrepresentation or material omission in a "prospectus" or "oral communication," in violation of section 12(2) of the Securities Act of 1933, 15 U.S.C. § 771(2); conspiracy to violate the above federal securities laws; aiding and abetting in the violation of the above federal securities laws; common law negligence; and common law fraud. The jury returned a general verdict, following which the judge requested that the jury state the cause or causes of action on which the verdict was premised, which it did.

On appeal, Andersen argues principally that the district court lacked federal subject matter jurisdiction; that the requisite loss causation standard for liability for securities fraud was not met; that plaintiff MHT caused its loss by its own recklessness; that it was error for the district judge to submit a negligence theory to the jury; that in selecting and instructing the jury the district judge deprived Andersen of a fundamentally fair trial; and that reversal of any of MHT's claims requires reversal of the entire verdict. MHT cross-appeals for a mini-trial exclusively on the issue of punitive damages. We affirm the judgement in favor of plaintiff in the amount of $17 million and deny the relief requested on cross-appeal. We also remand for further proceedings on the issue of pre-judgement interest only.

BACKGROUND

In this civil action MHT sought damages against the Andersen accounting firm, which it asserts made misrepresentations as to the financial status of DGSI, a company created by DSC to transact business through trading in repurchase agreements ("repos") or resale agreements ("reverse repos") *n1* involving government securities. DSC, a brokerage house since 1889, engaged in a scheme to purchase and sell government securities through repos and reverse repos beginning in May 1980 and ending in May 1982, just three months after DSC had transferred the repo business to a separate, newly capitalized, corporation called DGSI. The appellees presented evidence to the jury that Warren Essner, a senior Andersen audit partner, misrepresented DGSI's net worth as $20.8 million when it actually was negative $190 million.

[*n1* In a reverse repo transaction, which in economic terms is the identical transaction from the seller's perspective, DGSI would promise to resell government securities on a certain date, and the party dealing with DGSI would rely thereon.]

DSC had transferred the repo business to DGSI in February 1982 for two related reasons. First, it wanted to satisfy banks that had been serving as DSC agents (acting for an undisclosed principal) and that had begun to demand that DSC provide adequate assurances of sufficient capital to absorb the risk of insolvency in the repo market. Evidence was introduced showing that beginning in December 1981, DSC received requests for an audited financial statement from Chase Manhattan Bank, Chemical Bank, U.S. Trust Co., and MHT. Second, DSC wanted to avoid a New York Stock Exchange audit of DSC repo capitalization. The concerns for DSC's financial stability developed as DSC began to lose money because of financial losses in its securities trading and alleged misappropriation of monies by DSC Chairman Joseph Ossorio and DSC trader David Heuwetter. *n2*

[*n2* Ossorio and Heuwetter ultimately pleaded guilty to crimes relating to securities fraud.]

The mechanics of DGSI's repo business are not disputed. Ossorio and Heuwetter created a so-called "Ponzi" scheme that profited from the use of coupon interest on securities sold. The essence of the scheme was DGSI's exploitation of an important difference between government securities transactions in (1) the "securities" of "cash" market, in which securities are straightforwardly purchased and sold at market prices, and (2) the "repo market," in which government securities are purchased and sold pursuant to repo or reverse repo transactions. In the securities market, the price of a government security, such as a United States Treasury note, includes the market price of a particular issue and the accrued "coupon interest" on the security (i.e., the value of government payments due on the security at the time of the sale). In the repo market, the accrued coupon interest is paid only on the repurchase (or resale) transaction; the initial "loan" of the security is made at a price that includes only the market value of the security. Before the security is repurchased, its price will be "marked to market" periodically to reflect changed value. By borrowing increasing volumes of government bonds through reverse repos, selling them in the cash market and utilizing the cash and temporarily obtained accrued coupon interest to meet obligations on previously borrowed bonds and to conduct other trades, DGSI managed to stay solvent between February 1, 1982 (when DGSI was created, with the liabilities it had inherited from DSC) and May 17, 1982, when DGSI's ultimate collapse occurred and investors lost some $300 million.

Unlike Ossorio and Heuwetter, Warren Essner, a partner at Andersen, and Andersen itself, were not principals in this scheme. There is no evidence that they profited from it, or that they stood to gain anything from DGSI's precarious situation. Rather, Essner and Andersen had a limited role relating to the creation of DGSI. The fundamental issue in this case involves the scope of liability that flowed from this limited role.

Andersen had audited DSC in 1977 and 1978, but had no business relationship with it again until January 8, 1982. On that date, Ossorio contacted Essner at the Andersen firm regarding tax and accounting concerns in the contemplated creation of DGSI. Essner and Ossorio drafted a January 31, 1982 letter announcing DGSI's information and discussing its capitalization. The letter was intended for the benefit of potential DGSI clients and indicated that DSC would transfer $5 million net assets and liabilities to DGSI. (These assets and liabilities constituted repo and reverse repo positions in DSC's portfolio.) In addition, it stated that Heuwetter would invest $12.8 million and Ossorio $2.7 million, bringing the total capitalization to almost $21 million.

There was evidence that during a meeting on January 31, Heuwetter had cautioned Essner about an $11 billion "matched book" *n3* of repos and reverse repos that DSC controller Dennis Ruppert (who later pleaded guilty to state securities fraud charges) had fictitiously manufactured to create in part the purported $5 million transfer of DSC positions to DGSI. The true positions concealed by this false "matched book," *n3* Heuwetter testified, could not be disclosed, for fear that "if the dealer community found out the size of the positions that I was playing with. . . we would be out of business the next day. . .".

[*n3* In a "matched book," a government securities dealer maintains approximately equivalent positions in repos and reverse repos.]

On the evening of January 31, 1982, Essner prepared a "Statement of Subordinated Debt and Equity" to support the January 31 letter. This document did not disclose the size of the government securities positions transferred from DSC to DGSI. It reflected a purported capitalization of $20.8 million ($5 million net assets and liabilities transferred from DSC plus $15.8 million cash). There was evidence that Essner prepared the statement without consulting DSC's books and records, which, in any event, allegedly had been in incomprehensible disarray.

On and after February 1, Heuwetter delivered copies of the letter and statement to financial institutions including MHT. However, Chase and MHT pressed for an audited financial statement prepared by an independent accounting firm, even though both had been doing business with DGSI since its inception on February 1.

The parties dispute whether Ossorio asked Essner to prepare an audited statement by January 31 or during the week of February 8.

In either event, on behalf of Arthur Andersen, Essner prepared a "report on specified elements of a financial statement," which purported to constitute an unqualified opinion prepared in accordance with Generally Accepted Auditing Standards ("GAAS"). There is disputed evidence, however, that Essner never had conducted an audit, and that Essner later manufactured work papers in an apparent effort to legitimize his previous reports. MHT presented evidence at trial that Essner's and Andersen's work violated several procedures required by GAAS n4 as well as many of Andersen's own Audit Objectives and Procedures ("AOP"). n5 For preparing the letter, statement and report, Andersen billed and received from DSC $14,400. There is no evidence of any other payment from Essner to Andersen.

[n4 For example, MHT adduced evidence that Andersen: Failed to examine DGSI books or records even though Essner knew that $11 billion of securities positions were being transferred from DSC to DGSI; failed to audit the assets and liabilities transferred from DSC to DGSI even though Essner assigned to them a new value of $5 million; failed to investigate the adequacy of the internal controls of DSC and DGSI; failed to verify either that the $15.8 million in deposits in the Chemical account had cleared or that the amounts deposited were free from off-sets; failed to comply with GAAS related party disclosure procedures; failed to check for the existence of any material transactions between the date of the audit report and the date that field work was completed; and dated the audit report prior to the completion of audit field work.]

[n5 For example, MHT adduced evidence that Andersen: Never arranged for a second partner review; failed to have an audit team work on the audit; failed to complete a job arrangement letter; failed to have the audit referenced by an Andersen auditor not connected with the audit; failed to complete a related party checklist or investigate whether the transaction was done at arm's length; added to Essner's audit work papers, long after the purported audit, materials that were unrelated to that audit; and failed to satisfy Andersen's requirements that a report on a special element of a financial statement be, in the words of Andersen's own accounting expert, "more extensive" than the report that Essner produced.]

Andersen introduced evidence that at no time did MHT request a DGSI balance sheet as of February 1, 1982, or a DGSI balance sheet or income statement as of any later date. Andersen also introduced evidence that MHT inadequately monitored DGSI's creditworthiness and MHT's own risk exposure, in contrast to other financial institutions, several of which extricated themselves from business dealings with DGSI in time to avoid the kind of loss that MHT ultimately suffered. MHT countered with evidence that its internal control over relevant economic risks associated with its business with DGSI was reasonable when viewed in light of prevailing industry practice.

DISCUSSION

This case requires us to consider the role of the accountant, and the scope of his liability, in presenting to the financial community information about a financial institution seeking to attract or maintain business in transactions involving agreements to repurchase (or resell) government securities. In an SEC enforcement action arising from many of the same facts herein, we earlier held that the allegation that DSC and three of its officers, and Andersen and Essner, violated section 10(b) of the 1934 Act, and Rule 10b-5 thereunder and section 17(a) of the 1933 Act stated a valid federal cause of action. SEC v. Drysdale Securities Corp., 785 F.2d 38 (2d Cir.), cert. denied, 106 S. Ct. 2894 (1986). In this case we are called upon to review jurisdictional, substantive and procedural issues arising from MHT's private action against Andersen for allegedly misrepresenting DGSI's financial status. . . .

II. Section 10(b)

. . . It is clear that on the record evidence a fact-finder could conclude that Andersen's misrepresentations as to DGSI's solvency induced MHT (and other financial institutions) to do business with the newly-formed DGSI. There was evidence that the financial community, including MHT, sought assurance of adequate capitalization of DSC amidst growing concerns of insufficient funding; that Andersen materially misstated DGSI's capitalization in its audited financial statement; and that copies of the Andersen statement were distributed in Andersen envelopes with Andersen's knowledge to various financial institutions including MHT. There was evidence that MHT Senior Vice President Stephen Goodhue, head of MHT's Wall Street Department, relied primarily, though not exclusively, on the Andersen statement in approving DGSI for its government securities business. In light of this evidence, Andersen challenges the adequacy of the charge and the sufficiency of the evidence not as to "transaction causation" but only as to "loss causation."

The requirement of "loss causation" derives from the common law tort concept of "proximate causation." See *Marbury Management,* 629 F.2d at 708 (citing Restatement (Second) of Torts § 548A (1977)). In addition to this requirement as to the significance of the misrepresentation in the chain of causation, "loss causation in effect requires that the damage complained of be one of the foreseeable consequences of the misrepresentation." Id. (citing *Olek v. Fischer,* [1979 Transfer Binder] Fed. Sec. L. Rep. (CCH) P96,898, at 95,702-03 (S.D.N.Y. 1979), aff'd, 623 F.2d 791 (2d Cir. 1980). . . .

When it comes to evaluating the evidence of "loss causation," we cannot accept Andersen's argument. . . that "there is simply no direct or proximate relationship between the loss and the misrepresentation.". . . Id. at 313-314. There was certainly evidence upon which a rational trier of fact could find, as the jury apparently found, that Andersen, by its misrepresentations, induced MHT to enter into repurchase agreements with DGSI involving the particular underlying government securities. The financial community had come to mistrust DSC's solvency before the Andersen report was issued. In this context, the Andersen report portrayed a new, highly capitalized company on whose promises to repurchase and resell particular government securities, an institution such as MHT could reasonably rely. Andersen was aware that its report was intended to be and actually was circulated to institutions including MHT for the purpose of inducing them to participate in government securities repurchase agreements. . . .

Thus Andersen was held liable, here, beyond the boundaries of the provider-client relationship.[5]

By now, some of you may have thought about this question: On what ground are "innocent" principals to be held responsible for the unethical, harmful behavior of their subordinates? The following case is instructive.

Harrison v. *Dean Witter Reynolds, Inc.*
695 F. Supp. 959 (Illinois 1988)

Memorandum Opinion

Brian Barnett Duff, District Judge

Plaintiffs Hudson T. Harrison and Harrison Construction, Inc., have sued Dean Witter Reynolds, Inc. ("Dean Witter") and two of its broker-dealers, John M. Carpenter and John G. Kenning ("the brokers"), in a twelve-count First Amended Complaint arising out of an alleged scheme to defraud over one hundred investors in municipal bonds. The complaint alleges violations of the Securities Exchange Act of 1934 ("the Securities Exchange Act"), 15 U.S.C. § 78j, the Racketeer Influenced and Corrupt Organizations Act ("RICO"), 18 U.S.C. § 1961 *et seq.*, and a number of state laws. Eight of the counts—the Securities Exchange Act, RICO and various state law claims—involve allegations of fraud. Dean Witter has moved to dismiss these eight ("the fraud

---

[5] In the wake of the S&L scandals (see Chapter 7), accounting firms have been shown to have lacked candor at the very least, and have taken some serious losses, although given insurance coverage and tax relief, not as serious as they might have been. See S.Labaton, "$400 Million Bargain for Ernst," *The New York Times*, November 25, 1992. Accountants are not alone. See D.B. Henriques, "Falsifying Corporate Data Becomes Fraud of the 90s," *The New York Times*, September 21, 1992.

counts") pursuant to Rules 12(b)(6) and 9(b) of the Federal Rules of Civil Procedure.

DISCUSSION

The Fraud Counts

Dean Witter attacks all of the fraud counts on the grounds that they allege fraud but fail to state with particularity the fraudulent acts of which Dean Witter as an entity, as opposed to the brokers individually, is accused. Yet, Dean Witter does not clearly articulate the basis for this argument.

On the one hand, it suggests that such specificity is mandatory because, absent proof of Dean Witter's fraudulent conduct, Dean Witter cannot be held liable; an agency theory, it seems to argue, would not suffice. On the other hand, it includes Count II in this attack despite the fact that Count II alleges violations of § 20(a) of the Securities Exchange Act, 15 U.S.C. § 78t(a), and thus would not require proof that Dean Witter engaged in wrongdoing distinct from its employees before it could be held accountable. This suggests that Dean Witter's real problem with the fraud claims is that plaintiffs do not allege with sufficient clarity whether they rely solely on "vicarious" liability theories, or also on the specific wrongdoing of other Dean Witter officials.

[1,2] In any case, the general attack on the fraud counts cannot prevail. Although Dean Witter cites *Henricksen* v. *Henricksen,* 640 F.2d 880 (7th Cir. 1981), for the proposition that its "vicarious" liability is limited to that provided by § 20(a), *Henricksen* actually held just the opposite: a broker-dealer firm is accountable under traditional common law agency theories for the wrongdoing of its broker-dealers, including violations of statutory and regulatory securities laws. *See generally* Jacobs, *Litigation and Practice Under Rule 10b-5* § 40.06. Thus, each of the fraud claims against the brokers state a claim against Dean Witter as well.

Furthermore, while the complaint is not a model of pleading clarity, it does provide Dean Witter with sufficient notice of the claims against which it must defend. At this stage of the litigation, plaintiffs need not state with specificity the other Dean Witter officials involved in the (alleged) fraudulent scheme. See generally Note, "Pleading Securities Fraud With Particularity Under rule 9(b)," 97 Harv. L.R. 1432 (1984). Accordingly, Dean Witter's motion to dismiss all eight fraud counts will be denied. . . .

Dean Witter could be held liable here, as a company, for acts of its broker-dealers, both on specific security law fraud grounds, and on *legal agency theory* as well.

Let us examine this "agency" business.

II. LEGAL AGENCY AND THE FIDUCIARY RELATIONSHIP

A prestigious, nonpartisan, basically advisory body, the American Law Institute defines the agency relationship as follows:

> The fiduciary relation which results from the manifestation of consent by one person to another that the other shall act on his behalf and subject to his control, and consent by the other to so act.

The key phrase in *legal* agency is "subject to his control." Given the consensual nature of the basic agency relationship (i.e., that principal and agent agree to engage in it), the continuing control factor is crucial to the determination of a whole host of rights and obligations in law and society arising out of the operations resulting from the agency relationship.

The law views the agency relationship in terms of *the rights and obligations* not only of the principal and agents but, additionally, of third parties involved with them (e.g., a supplier of goods to the principal through the agent's contract, or a pedestrian suing the principal personally for damages caused by the principal's truck driven, on official business, by the agent). The major question the law addresses in terms of the agency relationship is therefore: Exactly what *are* the rights and obligations of principals and agents—to each other and to third parties, which is to say, society at large?

If the principal is obliged to accept responsibility for the agent's actions, it is clear that the principal must always maintain control over the agent. But in addition to control, there is the issue of *authority,* more specifically, the authority of the agent, as conferred upon him or her by the principal.

An agent's authority can be *express* (i.e., delegated by the principal to the agent by means of specific oral or written instructions) or *implied* (i.e., the agent can bind the principal regarding everything normally thought of as connected to the principal's job). A furniture salesperson, for example, can bind (make legally responsible) the store that employs her, by signing a contract of sale with a customer in the usual course of business. Put another way, the customer can rely on the salesperson's implied delegated authority to sell what she shows. A salesperson in the bedroom furnishings department is not likely to have been delegated the authority to sell the store owner's car off the company parking lot. Any customer who comes in for a bed and buys a Cadillac is undoubtedly stuck with a lemonlike deal—that is, no car at all.

An agent's authority can also be *apparent*. For example, even if the same salesperson had in fact been fired an hour before entering into a contract for a bedroom set with a customer, if the customer could not reasonably be expected to know that, the store is bound. Of course, the store might sue the salesperson for any losses attributable to the sale.

What we have been discussing here is the basic nature of the agency relationship, in law, with a larger focus on its broad aspects, not only as between the principal and agent but also in relation to the *outside world*. Now let us return to the American Law Institute definition again, and note the word "fiduciary."

Basically, the term *fiduciary* pertains to the very special nature of the relationship between the principal and the agent—to the very special behavior demanded of the agent in his or her dealings with the principal.

The core of the fiduciary relationship is *loyalty,* specifically the loyalty owed by the agent-fiduciary *to the principal*. We need to examine specific sets of behavior arising out of that *loyalty* concept.

To begin with, the law (at least the corps of judges that espouse it) has had a love affair with the fiduciary concept for a very long time. This has produced two results: (1) a body of definitional prose ranging from the inspirational to the banal, and (2) a focus on the ethical nature of human behavior in a special relational circumstance that has, thus far, defied entirely accurate legal definition.[6]

Many (perhaps most) lawyers might deny that the basis of the fiduciary concept is the demand for ethical behavior. That is, a demand that principal-agent relationships—*given their substantial effect upon the society in which they operate*—have to be trustworthy and productive *over the long term* (i.e., of the highest moral caliber) if they are to be socially and economically efficient. But we argue that the purpose of law is not simply to resolve disputes or to mandate structures but, rather, to protect and preserve the values by which men and women living in a free republic choose to live their lives. In this view, it would be hard to deny that "fiduciary" is in fact an ethical construct.

The overall nature of the fiduciary relationship was expressed by Judge Benjamin Cardozo in a famous case[7] as "the duty of the finest loyalty." Specifically, he said:

---

[6] "Perhaps because the subject matter is so sprawling and elusive, there has been little legal analysis of the fiduciary concept that is simultaneously general, sustained and astute." R.C. Clark, "Agency Costs Versus Fiduciary Duties," Chapter 3 in Pratt and Zeckhauser, eds., *Principals and Agents: The Structure of Business* (Cambridge, Mass.: Harvard Business School Press, 1985), p. 71. This insightful work will be cited hereafter as Clark, *Agency*.

[7] *Meinhard* v. *Salmon*, 164 N.E. 545 (1928).

Many forms of conduct permissible in a workaday world for those working at arm's length are forbidden to those bound by fiduciary ties. A trustee is held to something stricter than the morals of the marketplace. Not honesty alone, but the punctilio of an honor the most sensitive is then the standard of behavior. As to this there has developed a tradition that is unbending and inveterate. . . . Only thus has the level of conduct for fiduciaries been kept at a level higher than that trodden by the crowd. It will not consciously be lowered by a judgement of this court.

In a more recent New York case, the court referred to the fiduciary relationship this way:

A fiduciary relationship is one founded on trust or confidence reposed by one person in the integrity and fidelity of another. The term is a very broad one. It is said that the relation exists, and that relief is granted in all cases in which influence has been acquired and abused, in which confidence has been reposed and betrayed. The origin of the confidence and the source of the influence are immaterial. The rule embraces both technical fiduciary relations and those informal relations which exist whenever one man trusts in and relies upon another. Out of such a relation, the law raises the rule that neither party may exert influence or pressure upon the other, take selfish advantage of his trust or deal with the subject-matter of the trust in such a way as to benefit himself or prejudice the other except in the exercise of the utmost good faith and with the full knowledge and consent of that other, business shrewdness and hard bargaining being totally prohibited as between persons standing in such relation to each other. A fiduciary relation exists when confidence is reposed on one side and there is resulting superiority and influence on the other.[8]

The major obligations of a fiduciary have been said to arise out of *an affirmative duty to disclose* to the principal any and all information in his or her possession that bears upon any decision the principal is about to make; *a special duty of care* in the exercise of *any* and *all* delegated authority, the said duty being generally defined as that degree of care, skill and diligence which an ordinary, prudent person would exercise in the management of one's own affairs; and *a specific obligation to avoid taking*

---

[8] *Mobil Oil Corp.* v. *Rubenfeld*, 339 N.Y.S. 2d 623 (1972) at p. 632 (reversed on unrelated grounds, 370 N.Y.S. 2d 943 (1975) and again at 390 N.Y.S. 2d 59 (1976).

any personal advantage from one's position, especially (though not only) when to do so would result in any detriment whatsoever to the principal. The only exception to this obligation would be specific authority spelled out in a legal contract. This obligation is sometimes referred to as the fiduciary ban on self-dealing, or on appropriating corporate opportunities to oneself. This would, of course, include the phenomenon known as "insider trading."[9]

Before focusing in on fiduciary relationships and corporate directors and managers specifically, it must be pointed out that we have thus far concentrated on the fiduciary concept and on fiduciary obligations in a general way. The specific obligations of a specific fiduciary to his or her specific principal must always, of course, be examined in the light of specific circumstances. Trouble is always bound to come when, for example, the general and all-pervasive *duty of care* is applied to particular complained-of director and other manager actions.

The duty-of-care notion often presents the rock-and-a-hard-place problem. If corporate managers, especially directors, are held to too high a standard of behavior and effort, they might well avoid ever taking on the job. If, however, they are held to too low a standard, insufferable problems arise relating to progress, performance, and trust. The law (and litigants) have a hard time here, and each case requires a close examination as to whether "sound" or "prudent" business judgment was exercised by the manager in a given situation.

In a well-known New York case[10] the highest court of the state gave expression to an already famous common-law doctrine, referred to as *The Business Judgment Rule:*

> [T]he doctrine bars judicial inquiry into actions of corporate directors taken in good faith and in the exercise of honest judgment in the lawful and legitimate furtherance of corporate purpose.

That seems to be a fairly specific prescription. If the director acts *in good faith,* and *in the exercise of honest judgment,* and *in the lawful and legitimate furtherance of corporate purpose,* the court will not enter into any judicial inquiry concerning the director's actions (i.e., will not allow complainants such as shareholders, the opportunity to present in court any detailed course of dealing leading to the complained-of action). Why? Because if all the criteria are met, the court will apply "The Business Judgment Rule"; it will not attempt to second-guess the director.

Clear enough?

---

[9] See, generally, Clark, *Agency,* note 6, *supra,* at p. 71-75.

[10] *Auerbach v. Burnett,* 343 N.E. 2d 994 (1979).

Let us look at the Delaware case of *Smith* v. *Van Gorkom*.[11] Delaware cases are very important in American corporation law because Delaware is the legal home of so many major American companies. In *Van Gorkom*, shareholders of the Trans Union Corporation sued the company's directors in a class action for being negligent (violating their duty of care) in recommending a particular merger. The directors argued that they had, in good faith and in the exercise of honest judgment, made a business judgment that the court need not examine through full inquiry. Answered the court:

> Under the business judgement rule there is no protection for directors who have made an unintelligent or unadvised judgement. A director's duty to inform himself in preparation for a decision derives from the fiduciary capacity in which he serves. . . . In the specific context of a proposed merger of domestic corporations, a director has a duty. . . to act in an informed and deliberate manner in determining whether to approve an agreement of merger before submitting the proposal to the stockholders. . . .

The court went on to hold that the directors here did not adequately inform themselves and, in fact, "were uninformed as to the intrinsic value of the company." The shareholders won a lot of money!

The following quote from Robert Clark's preface to his fine text, *Corporate Law* (Boston: Little, Brown, 1986), seems apt here:

> . . . the law displays a constant tension, and a constant striving for a good balance, between the fiduciary duties of care and loyalty on the one hand and the business judgement rule on the other. The central problem of corporate law—the optimal control of managerial discretion—is a thoroughly pervasive one in all modern societies. . . .

Mergers and acquisitions and leveraged buyouts (LBOs) have served to highlight another fiduciary-related tension producer in this business judgment/duty-of-care game. In such market endeavors, management is moving headlong into areas involving its personal interests (e.g., golden parachutes, maintaining positions of power—even buying the company itself). In such cases, the balance between giving directors/managers deference and giving them, as fiduciaries, a very difficult time is very hard to maintain.

---

[11] 488 A.2d 858 (1985).

In such cases, the law has another test that it often sees fit to apply, one often referred to as the *Intrinsic Fairness Doctrine.* This doctrine *requires* that the court apply a stringent test to determine (measure) whether the fiduciary has met high standards of good faith, loyalty, and avoidance of conflict of interest.

So here, for example, in an LBO, where the challenged situation does contain what appears to be a built-in potential for self-dealing, the court *will* allow the detailed course of dealings to be examined.

What this means, to lawyers, is that the directors being sued cannot rely on the Business Judgment Rule to help them escape from lawsuits unscathed.

In a period of furious and hostile mergers and acquisitions, and an avalanche of LBOs, the Delaware court was bound to leave its mark in the corporate law constant-striving-for-a-good-balance area.

Five cases in the period between 1985 and 1990 are illustrative.

The first, *Smith* v. *Van Gorkom,* we have already encountered. Here evidence that there had never been done a proper valuation study that the directors could rely on prior to agreeing to sell the company was sufficient to deny the directors the benefit of the Business Judgment Rule. It is reasonable to assume, however, that this decision was, at bottom, the result of the court's appraisal of the directors' honesty and fairness, not of their intelligence or stupidity. The court referred quite candidly to the directors' breach of "their fiduciary duty of candor by their failure to make true and correct disclosures of all the information they had. . . ."[12]

In the case of *Unocal* v. *Mesa Petroleum,*[13] the directors turned down a two-tier, front-loaded, hostile bid for Unocal, which is to say, a bid that offered cash to those shareholders who sold their stock before a certain percentage of outstanding stock had been purchased, with every later shareholder getting only buyer-evaluated junk bonds for being foolish enough to hesitate. The directors, in fact, put in place a defense to hostile takeovers that would have involved the purchase, by Unocal, of all the second-tier stock at full price. The unsuccessful bidder, in its challenge to the Unocal defense, was certainly hampered in its suit by the obvious coercive nature of its two-tier, front-loaded bid. And the directors were saddled with the obvious fact that their jobs and the value of their own stock were on the line. The court was faced with the problem of deciding whether the hostile takeover "defense" was to be judged, in effect, under the Business Judgment Rule. Examine, carefully, the following excerpts from the court's opinion (footnotes and citations omitted).

---

[12] Ibid., at p. 893.
[13] 493 A.2d 946 (1985).

In connection with the board's exercise of corporate power to forestall a takeover bid our analysis begins with the basic principle that corporate directors have a fiduciary duty to act in the best interests of the corporation's stockholders. . . . As we have noted, their duty of care extends to protecting the corporation and its owners from perceived harm whether a threat originates from third parties or other shareholders. But such powers are not absolute. A corporation does not have unbridled discretion to defeat any perceived threat by any Draconian means available.

The restriction placed upon a selective stock repurchase is that the directors may not have acted solely or primarily out of a desire to perpetuate themselves in office. Of course, to this is added the further caveat that inequitable action may not be taken under the guise of law. The standard of proof. . . is designed to ensure that a defensive measure to thwart or impede a takeover is indeed motivated by a good faith concern for the welfare of the corporation and its stockholders, which in all circumstances must be free of any fraud or other misconduct. . . . However, this does not end the inquiry.

B

A further aspect is the element of balance. If a defensive measure is to come within the ambit of the business judgement rule, it must be reasonable in relation to the threat posed. This entails an analysis by the directors of the nature of the takeover bid and its effect on the corporate enterprise. Examples of such concerns may include: inadequacy of the price offered, nature and timing of the offer, questions of illegality, the impact on "constituencies" other than shareholders (i.e., creditors, customers, employees, and perhaps even the community generally), the risk of nonconsummation, and the quality of securities being offered in the exchange. . . .[14]

The court went on to hold that the Business Judgment Rule was applicable here. Therefore, the directors had nothing more to prove. Their defense was upheld.

Please notice something potentially confusing here from the point of view of what the directors' fiduciary duties to a stockholder really are. The court recited the truism that "corporate directors have a fiduciary duty to act in the best interests of the corporation's stockholders." Most stockholders, and others, have taken this to mean a duty to see to it that they are able to obtain the highest possible price for their stock currently available in the market. It is, of course, quite possible that this particular stockholder interest (i.e., let me sell *now* to whoever is paying the best

---

[14] Ibid., at p. 955.

possible price, so as to maximize my immediate shareholder value) would not be consistent with the best interests of creditors, or employees, or certainly the community generally. And yet the court also says that, in putting defensive measures in place against a high dollar offer, the directors' fiduciary duty to enhance the immediate value of a stockholder's holdings does not preclude taking into account the fiduciary's concern with "other than shareholders."

Exactly what this actually meant came up for debate again in an extraordinary case in 1990.

But first came *Shamrock Holdings* v. *Polaroid*[15] and *Mills Acquisition* v. *Macmillan, Inc.*,[16] in 1989.

In the *Polaroid* case, management set up an employee stock option plan (ESOP) and placed enough Polaroid shares into it to put control of the company out of the grasp of the hostile bidder. The bidder took Polaroid to court. We excerpt here a portion of the *Polaroid* decision:

[1-5] It is settled law that directors are responsible for managing the business and affairs of a Delaware corporation and, in exercising that responsibility, they are "charged with an unyielding fiduciary duty to the corporation and its shareholders." *Smith* v. *Van Gorkom,* Del.Supr., 488 A.2d 858, 872 (1985). Ordinarily, where the directors are disinterested, their decisions will be protected by the business judgement rule, "a presumption that in making a business decision the directors. . . acted on an informed basis, in good faith and in the honest belief that the action taken was in the best interests of the company." *Aronson* v. *Lewis,* Del.Supr., 473 A.2d 805, 812 (1984). Where the business judgement rule is properly invoked, the directors' decision will be upheld absent an abuse of discretion. However, the protections of the business judgement rule will not be afforded to directors who fail "to inform themselves, prior to making a business decision, of all material information reasonably available to them." *Ibid.* Directors have "an affirmative duty" to protect the financial interests of the stockholders and must "proceed with a critical eye" in acting on their behalf. *Smith* v. *Van Gorkom,* 488 A.2d at 872.

[6] The business judgement rule is available to directors even where they are responding to a takeover threat. In those circumstances, however, there is an omnipresent specter that a board may be acting primarily in its own interests. . ." *Unocal Corp.* v. *Mesa Petroleum Co.,* Del.Supr., 493 A.2d 946, 954 (1985). As a result, before the business judgement rule will be applied in this context, the directors must establish "reasonable grounds for believing that a danger to corporate

---

[15] 559 A.2d 1261 (1989).
[16] 559 A.2d 257 (1989).

policy and effectiveness existed" and the defensive measure chosen by the board must be "reasonable in relation to the threat posed. . . .[17]

The court went on here to hold that the establishment of the ESOP did come under the protective mantle of *Unocal stare decisis;* that is, there were "reasonable grounds for believing that a danger existed." What the court in fact did was to invoke an intrinsic fairness-like doctrine, make a factual judgment that it was not breached, and then applied the Business Judgment Rule!

In the *Macmillan* case, a corporate auction bidding process was involved. To defeat a hostile bid, Macmillan directors gave an option to another (friendly) bidder to purchase four key corporate divisions, thus rendering the corporation an unworthwhile corporate target; that is, the directors put into effect a "lock-up" or "poison pill" by arranging a sell-off of their company's "crown jewels." A complicating factor here was that the "friendly" bidder's offer involved some leveraged buy-out processes that certainly could have inured to the benefit of Macmillan's own directors. In the face of this fact, particularly, the Delaware court moved quickly to the moral high-ground.

The following excerpt from the *Macmillan* case is focused on the balance issue *re:* Business Judgment and Intrinsic Fairness (the latter not always named as such by the courts). But we must also keep in mind the issue of whether, despite the systemic avoidance of words like "unethical", this court *is* engaged in an ethical inquiry regarding corporate finance practices.

Mills Acquisition v. *Macmillan, Inc.*
559 A. 2nd 1261 (1989)
(excerpted with citations omitted)

B

[6] It is basic to our law that the board of directors has the ultimate responsibility for managing the business and affairs of a corporation. 8 *Del.C.* § 141(a). In discharging this function, the directors owe fiduciary duties of care and loyalty to the corporation and its shareholders [citations omitted]. This unremitting obligation extends equally to board conduct in a sale of corporate control. *Smith* v. *Van Gorkom,* Del.Supr., 488 A.2d 858, 872-73 (1985).

[7] The fiduciary nature of a corporate office is immutable. As this Court stated long ago:

---

[17] 559 A.2d 257, 269.

Corporate officers and directors are not permitted to use their position of trust and confidence to further their private interests. While technically not trustees, they stand in a fiduciary relation to the corporation and its shareholders. . . . This rule, inveterate and uncompromising in its rigidity, does not rest upon the narrow ground of injury or damage to the corporation resulting from a betrayal of confidence, but upon a broader foundation of a wise public policy that, for the purpose of removing all temptation, extinguishes all possibility of profit flowing from a breach of the confidence imposed by fiduciary relation.

[Citation omitted] Not only do these principles demand that corporate fiduciaries absolutely refrain from any act which breaches the trust reposed in them, but also to affirmatively protect and defend those interests entrusted to them. Officers and directors must exert all reasonable and lawful efforts to ensure that the corporation is not deprived of any advantage to which it is entitled.

[8] Thus, directors are required to demonstrate both their utmost good faith and the most scrupulous inherent fairness of transactions in which they possess a financial, business or other personal interest which does not devolve upon the corporation or all stockholders generally. When faced with such divided loyalties, directors have the burden of establishing the entire fairness of the transaction to survive careful scrutiny by the courts.

[9, 10] Under Delaware law this concept of fairness has two aspects: fair dealing and fair price. . . . "Fair dealing" focuses upon the actual conduct of corporate fiduciaries in effecting a transaction, such as its initiation, structure, and negotiation. This element also embraces the duty of candor owed by corporate fiduciaries to disclose all material information relevant to corporate decisions from which they may derive a personal benefit. *See* 8 *Del.C.* § 144. "Fair price," in the context of an auction for corporate control, mandates that directors commit themselves, inexorably, to obtaining the highest value reasonably available to the shareholders under all the circumstances. . . .

III

[11] The voluminous record in this case discloses conduct that fails all basic standards of fairness. . . .[18]

---

[18] 559 A.2d 1261, 1280.

The court refused, of course, to apply the Business Judgment Rule, and the poison-pill defense failed. Then came the year 1990.

Paramount Communications, Inc. v. *Time, Inc.*
571 A.2d 1140 (1989)

[This decision was actually released on March 9, 1990. The following is a brief statement of the main facts in the case:

As early as 1983-84, the Executive Board of *Time* began to consider expansion into the entertainment industry. In 1987, a special Executive Committee recommended expansion specifically in order to complement *Time*'s existing HBO and cable networks and to better enable it to compete on a global basis. *Time* and Warner Brothers began discussing a joint venture in 1987, with formal approval, in 1988, from *Time*'s Board of Directors to negotiate an actual merger. Two sticking points developed— the exact nature of the fiscal transaction (i.e., all cash, or share swaps, etc.) and the shape of postmerger governance. In the fall of 1988, *Time* discussed its interest in expanding with others on an informal basis. However, the deal with Warner was in fact worked out in March, 1989, and approved by both the *Time* and Warner boards. On May 24, 1989, *Time* sent out proxy statements to its shareholders relative to a vote on the merger, which was to be accomplished through a stock swap specifically. By the end of May, the merger appeared to be a "done deal," *Time-Warner* appeared to be a media colossus with international scope, and there was *no* consequential merger debt at all.

However, on June 7, 1989, with Time stock selling at $126 per share, Paramount made a $175 per share, all cash offer for all outstanding Time stock. Although Paramount declared at the time that the deal could be consummated by July 5, legal impediments would have held up the deal for up to a full year, even if Time accepted it. Time did not. Time's board refused the offer, estimating that the value of Time, in a control premium situation, was higher than the $175, and further, that dropping its deal with Warner and being taken over by Paramount was a threat to the best interests of the corporation. More M&A (merger and acquisition) machinations followed; Time and Warner changed the framework of their deal to a Time immediate cash purchase of 51 percent of Warner's stock, with the other 49 percent to be purchased at a later date, and Paramount went to court. At a hearing before a chancellor, Paramount asked to have the Time-Warner deal enjoined (legally stopped in its tracks before finalization). The chancellor refused to issue the requisite injunction. Paramount appealed.]

HORSEY, Justice:

Paramount Communications, Inc. ("Paramount") and two other groups of plaintiffs ("Shareholder Plaintiffs"), shareholders of Time Incorporated ("Time"), a Delaware corporation, separately filed suits in the Delaware Court of Chancery seeking a preliminary injunction to halt Time's tender offer for 51% of Warner Communication Inc.'s ("Warner") outstanding shares at $70 cash per share. The court below consolidated the cases and, following the development of an extensive record, after discovery and an evidentiary hearing, denied plaintiffs' motion. In a 50-page unreported opinion and order entered July 14, 1989, the Chancellor refused to enjoin Time's consummation of its tender offer, concluding that the plaintiffs were unlikely to prevail on the merits. In re Time Incorporated Shareholder Litigation, Del.Ch., C.A. No. 10670, Allen, C., 1989 WL 79880 (July 14, 1989).

On the same day, plaintiffs filed in this Court an interlocutory appeal, which we accepted on an expedited basis. Pending the appeal, a stay of execution of Time's tender offer was entered for ten days, or until July 24, 1989, at 5:00 p.m. Following briefing and oral argument, on July 24 we concluded that the decision below should be affirmed. We so held in a brief ruling from the bench and a separate order entered on that date. The effect of our decision was to permit Time to proceed with its tender offer for Warner's outstanding shares. This is the written opinion articulating the reasons for our July 24 bench ruling. 565 A.2d 280, 281.

The principal ground for reversal, asserted by all plaintiffs, is that Paramount's June 7, 1989 uninvited all-cash, all-shares, "fully negotiable" (though conditional) tender offer for Time triggered duties under Unocal Corp. v. Mesa Petroleum Co., Del.Supr., 493 A.2d 946 (1985), and that Time's board of directors, in responding to Paramount's offer, breached those duties. As a consequence, plaintiffs argue that in our review of Time board's decision of June 16, 1989 to enter into a revised merger agreement with Warner, Time is not entitled to the benefit and protection of the business judgement rule.

Shareholder Plaintiffs also assert a claim based on *Revlon* v. *MacAndrews & Forbes Holding, Inc.,* Del.Supr., 506 A.2d 173 (1986). They argue that the original Time-Warner merger agreement of March 4, 1989 resulted in a change of control which effectively put Time up for sale, thereby triggering Revlon duties. Those plaintiffs argue that Time's board breached its Revlon duties by failing, in the face of the change of control, to maximize shareholder value in the immediate term.

Applying our standard of review, we affirm the Chancellor's ultimate finding and conclusion under Unocal. We find that Paramount's tender offer was reasonably perceived by Time's board to pose a threat to Time and that the Time board's "response" to that threat was, under the circumstances, reasonable and proportionate.

Applying Unocal, we reject the argument that the only corporate threat posed by an all-shares, all-cash tender offer is the possibility of inadequate value.

We also find that Time's board did not, by entering into its initial merger agreement with Warner, come under a Revlon duty either to auction the company or to maximize short-term shareholder value, notwithstanding the unequal share exchange. Therefore, the Time board's original plan of merger with Warner was subject only to a business judgement rule analysis. See *Smith v. Van Gorkom*, Del.Supr., 488 A.2d 858, 873-74 (1985).

[The Court here examines, at length, the facts in the Time-Warner-Paramount struggle, from 1983-84 to 1989. It then goes on.]

II

[1] The Shareholder Plaintiffs. . . contend that the March 4 Time-Warner agreement effectively put Time up for sale. . . requiring Time's board to enhance short-term shareholder value and to treat all other interested acquirors on an equal basis. The Shareholder Plaintiffs base this argument on two facts: (i) the ultimate Time-Warner exchange ratio of .465 favoring Warner, resulting in Warner shareholders' receipt of 62 percent of the combined company; and (ii) the subjective intent of Time's directors as evidenced in their statements that the market might perceive the Time-Warner merger as putting Time up "for sale" and their adoption of various defensive measures.

The Shareholder Plaintiffs further contend that Time's directors, in structuring the original merger transaction to be "takeover-proof," triggered. . . duties by foreclosing their shareholders from any prospect of obtaining a control premium. In short, plaintiffs argue that Time's board's decision to merge with Warner imposed a fiduciary duty to maximize immediate share value and not erect unreasonable barriers to further bids. Therefore, they argue, the Chancellor erred in finding: that Paramount's bid for Time did not place Time "for sale"; that Time's transaction with Warner did not result in any transfer of control; and that the combined Time-Warner was not so large as to preclude the possibility of the stockholders of Time-Warner receiving a future control premium.

Paramount asserts only a *Unocal* claim in which the shareholder plaintiffs join. Paramount contends that the chancellor, in applying the first part of the *Unocal* test, erred in finding that Time's board had reasonable grounds to believe that Paramount posed both a legally cognizable threat to Time shareholders and a danger to Time's corporate policy and effectiveness. Paramount also contests the court's finding that Time's board made a reasonable and objective investigation of Paramount's offer so as to be informed before rejecting it. Paramount further claims that the court erred in applying *Unocal's* second part in finding Time's response to be "reasonable." Paramount points primarily to the preclusive effect of the revised agreement which denied Time shareholders the opportunity both to vote on the agreement and to respond to Paramount's tender offer. Paramount argues that the underlying motivation of Time's board in adopting these defensive measures was management's desire to perpetuate itself in office.

The Court of Chancery posed the pivotal question by this case to be: Under what circumstances must a board of directors abandon an in-place plan of corporate development in order to provide its shareholders with the option to elect and realize an immediate control premium? As applied to this case, the question becomes: Did Time's board, having developed a strategic plan of global expansion to be launched through a business combination with Warner, come under a fiduciary duty to jettison its plan and put the corporation's future in the hands of its shareholders?

[2-4] While we affirm the result reached by the Chancellor, we think it unwise to place undue emphasis upon long-term versus short-term corporate strategy. Two key predicates underpin our analysis. First, Delaware law imposes on a board of directors the duty to manage the business and affairs of the corporation. 8 Del.C. § 141(a). This board mandate includes a conferred authority to set a corporate course of action, including time frame, designed to enhance corporate profitability. Thus, the question of "long-term" versus "short-term" values is largely irrelevant because directors, generally, are obliged to chart a course for a corporation which is in its best interests without regard to a fixed investment horizon. Second, absent a limited set of circumstances as defined under Revlon, a board of directors, while always required to act in an informed manner, is not under any per se duty to maximize shareholder value in the short term, even in the context of a takeover. . . .

Paramount and the individual plaintiffs extrapolate a rule of law that an all-cash, all-shares offer with values reasonably in the range of acceptable price cannot pose any objective threat to a corporation or its shareholders. Thus, Paramount would have us hold that only if the value of Paramount's offer were determined to be clearly inferior to the value created by management's plan to merge with Warner could the offer be viewed—objectively—as a threat.

Implicit in the plaintiff's argument is the view that a hostile tender offer can pose only two types of threats: the threat of coercion that results from a two-tier offer promising unequal treatment for nontendering shareholders; and the threat of inadequate value from an all-shares, all-cash offer at a price below what a target board in good faith deems to be the present value of its shares [citations omitted]. Since Paramount's offer was all-cash, the only conceivable "threat," plaintiffs argue, was inadequate value. We disapprove of such a narrow and rigid construction of *Unocal,* for the reasons which follow.

Plaintiffs' position represents a fundamental misconception of our standard of review under *Unocal* principally because it would involve the court in substituting its judgement as to what is a "better" deal for that of a corporation's board of directors. To the extent that the Court of Chancery has recently done so in certain of its opinions, we hereby reject such approach as not in keeping with a proper *Unocal* analysis. *See, e.g., Interco,* 551 A.2d 787, and its progeny; *but see TW Services, Inc.* v. *SWT Acquisition Corp.,* Del.Ch., C.A. No. 1047, Allen, C. 1989 WL 20290 (March 2, 1989).

The usefulness of *Unocal* as an analytical tool is precisely its flexibility in the face of a variety of fact scenarios. *Unocal* is not intended as an abstract standard; neither is it a structured and mechanistic procedure of appraisal. Thus, we have said that directors may consider, when evaluating the threat posed by a takeover bid, the "inadequacy of the price offered, nature and timing of the offer, questions of illegality, the impact on 'constituencies' other than shareholders. . .the risk of nonconsummation, and the quality of securities being offered in the exchange." 493 A.2d at 955. The open-ended analysis mandated by *Unocal* is not intended to lead to a simple mathematical exercise: that is, of comparing the discounted value of Time-Warner's expected trading price at some future date with Paramount's offer and determining which is the higher. Indeed, in our view, precepts underlying the business judgement rule militate against a court's engaging in the process of attempting to appraise and evaluate the relative merits of a long-term versus a short-term investment goal for shareholders. To engage in such an exercise is a distortion of the *Unocal* process and, in particular, the application of the second part of *Unocal*'s test, discussed below.

In this case, the Time board reasonably determined that inadequate value was not the only legally cognizable threat that Paramount's all-cash, all-shares offer could present. Time's board concluded that Paramount's eleventh hour offer posed other threats. One concern was that Time shareholders might elect to tender into Paramount's cash offer in ignorance or a mistaken belief of the strategic benefit which a business combination with Warner might produce. Moreover, Time viewed the conditions attached to Paramount's offer as introducing a degree of uncertainty that skewed a comparative analysis. Further, the timing of Paramount's offer to follow issuance of Time's proxy notice was viewed as arguably designed to upset, if not confuse, the Time stockholders' vote. Given this record evidence, we cannot conclude that the Time board's decision of June 6 that Paramount's offer posed a threat to corporate policy and effectiveness was lacking in good faith or dominated by motives of either entrenchment or self-interest. . . .

Finally, we note that although Time was required, as a result of Paramount's hostile offer, to incur a heavy debt to finance its acquisition of Warner, that fact alone does not render the board's decision unreasonable so long as the directors could reasonably perceive the debt load not to be so injurious to the corporation as to jeopardize its well being. . . .

This case, which approved the Time, Inc., purchase of Warner, seems clearly to hold that maximizing immediate shareholder value is *not* an inviolate fiduciary duty. This raises several issues of rather keen econo-legal-social significance:

- If not the promotion of immediate maximum share value, what is the exact nature of the director/manager fiduciary duty to the stockholder?

- Is it possible, consistent with director/manager corporate fiduciary duties, that there could be duties (other than specific contractual ones) owing to creditors, customers, employees "and perhaps even the community generally?" Would they outweigh fiduciary duties to stockholders? Would it be consistent with economic "efficiency" for the law to hold that? Would it be consistent with wealth maximization?

- If it were perceived to be in the corporation's best interests to honor (even *noncontractual*) obligations to creditors, customers, employees and perhaps even the community generally, in whatever temporal frame, would it then be legitimate to argue that in honoring these obligations (performing specific duties) the directors/managers *would be* fulfilling a fiduciary duty to the corporation? If so, what noncontractual obligations might be involved here? And how might they relate to the survival and profit of the corporation?

- What about the stockholders? Could their "best interests" be at odds with those of the corporation (in *any* temporal frame)? And if such a thing were possible, to which of the two would the director/manager-fiduciary duty extend?

- Is one actually involved here with economic and/or legal and/or ethical concerns? Are they in conflict? What seems to be the correct approach to director/manager-stockholder fiduciary relationships?

III. THE AGENCY THEORY IN CORPORATE FINANCE AND THE ISSUE OF ETHICAL CONSTRUCTS

We will close this chapter with a reference to an economics/finance approach to agency and then will return to the issues just mentioned.

Finance, like law, has its agency construct, but the two are not the same. It is important to understand how they differ.

"Financial agency," as one component part of a theory of the firm, has a legitimate role to play. It seems to be quite useful in helping to delineate an overall theory of corporate finance. But it is not legal reality, and that should be remembered. Courts deal less with outside system theoretical constructs than with day-to-day human behavior as measured by *legal standards*.

In any event, whereas the key focus of legal agency is *control* (of the agent by the principal), the key focus of financial agency is *costs*.[19]

> We define an agency relationship as a contract under which one or more persons (the principal(s)) engage another person (the agent) to perform some service on their behalf which involves delegating some decision making authority to the agent. If both parties. . . are utility maximizers. . . the agent will not always act in the best interests of the principal. The *principal* can limit divergencies from his interest by establishing appropriate incentives for the agent and by incurring monitoring costs designed to limit the aberrant activities of the agent. . . . We define *agency costs* as the sum of:
>
> (1) the monitoring expenditures by the principal
> (2) the bonding expenditures by the agent
> (3) the residual loss.[20]

This theory does not deal with how to structure the "contractual" agency relationships; rather, it investigates the "incentives faced by each

---

[19] M. Jensen and W. Meckling, "Theory of the Firm: Managerial Behavior, Agency Costs and Ownership Structure," *Journal of Financial Economics* 3 (1976). Reprinted in *The Modern Theory of Corporate Finance*, M. Jensen and C. Smith, eds. (New York: McGraw Hill, 1984), pp. 78-133, cited hereafter as *Jensen and Smith.*

[20] *Jensen and Smith*, p. 81.

of the parties and the elements entering into the determination of the equilibrium contractual form characterizing the relationship between the manager (i.e., agent) of the firm and the outside equity and debt holders (i.e., principals)."[21]

In this economist view, the "firm" itself—which could be *any organization,* from a small private club to a multinational corporation—is nothing more (or less) than "a set of contracting relationships among individuals."[22]

To begin with, manager/directors are not, legally, agents of stockholders.[23] Stockholders (and or debtholders) do not have legal power to direct and control the activities of the "agent." And this reality is not changed by the fiction of the principal's "delegating some decision making activity to the agent." Certainly real-life principals do delegate to controlled agents sufficient authority to perform assigned tasks. However, the spectacle of many thousands of "principals" (stockholders), often spread out over several continents, truly "delegating" authority "by contract" to one board of directors and a few executives, is a fiction that severely challenges any willing suspension of disbelief.

In fact, setting the ultimate goal of a corporation, choosing the corporation's line of business, hiring and firing the full-time managers who will, in fact, run the company, and exercising supervisory power over the corporation's day-to-day business—all clearly principal powers—are *not* stockholder powers.

> Stockholders of a large publicly held corporation *do not* do these things; as a matter of efficient operation of a large firm with numerous residual claimants they *should not* do them; and under the typical corporate statute and case law they *cannot* do them.[24]

What this means is that while there may indeed be justification for a financial agency construct as a tool for designing a theory of corporate finance, it should be kept in mind that such a construct could—and in this

---

[21] Ibid. at pp. 82-83.

[22] Ibid. at p. 83.

[23] The following comparison between legal and economic agency derives much from Clark, *Agency,* note 6, *supra.* Any such comparison would have to!

[24] Clark, *Agency* at p. 57. The authors point out that shareholders do have the right to sue directors of a corporation (derivative lawsuit); however, such a right carries no complementary right to control directly or to specify the acts directors take on behalf of the corporation. In fact, under usual circumstances, stockholders don't even have the right to have a court examine for them all the details and circumstances related to such director acts (the Business Judgment Rule). And if such an examination is allowed, it is based on a fiduciary theory, *which is nowhere to be found clearly delineated in the economic agency literature.*

case, does—at the same time, tend to obscure a real understanding, *in economic terms,* of the true *legal* relationship between stockholders and managers. For example, what *is* the nature of their legal relationship if, in fact, they do not actually bargain over and contract about its terms (or even "implicitly" or "virtually" do so)?

Characterization of "the firm" as merely a nexus of contracts is, by extension, an equally troublesome economic fiction. Are we actually to assume that all of corporation law, as laid down in statutes and common-law cases at the level of every state and in the federal (and sometimes even foreign) realm as well, and by which stockholders, debtholders, managers and many other parties are legally bound, is nothing more than a "code" of some sort? That is, a "code" originating in numberless contracts between stockholder principals and manager-agents defining rights and duties?

We are not aware of any satisfactory working concept that currently serves to bridge the gap between legal and economic agency, yet this is a gap that ought to be bridged to have a more economically and legally effective, mutualistic theory of agency. We do suggest, however, that one might profitably begin to bridge the gap by means of the *fiduciary concept*.

The argument here is simply this: that while some elements of the fiduciary concept might well be what parties to a corporate endeavor might reduce to a written contract (if they could negotiate without transaction costs), much is not. And what is not is rooted in the law's insistence that very special moral behaviors are expected in particular circumstances that are beyond the scope of all usual specific, contractual terms.

Let us, in this connection, reexamine the puzzle posed a few pages back.

In the *Unocal* and *Paramount Communications* cases, the court referred to the duty of corporate directors to act in the best interests of the corporation's shareholders, yet both cases also emphasized the necessity for directors to be concerned about "constituencies other than shareholders," including "perhaps even the community generally." Moreover, the *Paramount* case specifically held that maximizing shareholders' immediate profit is *not* the essential element in a director's fiduciary duty.

Whether one feels that *Unocal* and *Paramount* were rightly or wrongly decided is irrelevant to a serious consideration of the major issues these cases raise:

- To whom, exactly, is a corporate manager's fiduciary duty owed, and why?
- Why does such a fiduciary duty exist in law at all?

The first major perplexity here is how a fiduciary duty can ever exist in the absence of a basic agency relationship. If the stockholder-manager link does not come up to a principal-agent relationship, how can there be *any* fiduciary duty extant? Similarly, if a manager/director owes some consideration to employees, suppliers, perhaps even to the public at large, what fiduciary basis may be found for all that?

We would argue that the sole manager fiduciary duty is to the development, enrichment, and continued healthy existence of the corporation *in the society within which it functions.*

When the law sanctioned the creation of the entity "corporation," it did not do so for the primary purpose of enriching individual shareholders. Rather, it did so for the purpose of utilizing this (corporate) entity to help forward the growth and general welfare of the body politic. Now, to accomplish this purpose efficiently certainly required investor protection, and the opportunity for investor enrichment. However, stockholder protection and enrichment are merely appropriate *means* to a justifiable *end*. We Americans, who are so incredibly proficient at knowing *how* to do things, and so much less proficient at determining *why* we do them, would profit much here by keeping the ends/means distinction foremost in our minds.

The manager/director is, then, the agent of the corporation (principal), bound by his and her fiduciary duty to further the principal's ends. It seems reasonable to assume that this fiduciary duty to the principal includes undertaking to forward the means to accomplish these ends in a responsible (putting the principal's interests first) and efficient fashion. Thus are shareholders, and constituencies other than shareholders (i.e., creditors, customers, employees, and "perhaps even the community generally") brought within the ambit of the agent's fiduciary duty to the principal (corporation). Specifically, the agent's ancillary fiduciary duty to these *nonprincipals* arises out of the basic fiduciary duty to support *all* groups mutualistically linked to the development, enrichment, and continued healthy existence, over time, of the principal (i.e., the "corporate enterprise").[25]

Such an interpretation of the nature of this agent's fiduciary duty is consistent with the notion that the primary purpose of corporate activity is wealth maximization. In fact, we would argue that the only effective, efficient *end* of the legal animal, "the corporation," is maximization of the wealth of the body politic within which it functions, on a mutualistic growth basis. Even more, that one key *means* of achieving that end is the forwarding and protection of investor profit. Any act of the agent serving to defeat that means would be a violation of the agent's fiduciary duty *to the principal.*

---

[25] See portion of *Mesa Petroleum Case* cited at note 14, *supra*.

Why, it remains to be asked, does the fiduciary duty exist at all? We submit that the terribly demanding duty exists because of the extraordinary importance of business enterprises, such as corporations, to the growth and development of the body politic (society). And that the duty is tied, specifically, to the inability of these enterprises (and, by extension, society) to survive *in a democratic republic* in the absence of a *legally enforceable* duty of all agents, charged with serving the enterprise's best interests, to do so *honorably* and with *integrity*.

Economists and lawyers, as professionals, are *embarrassed* by the use of such words as "honor" and "integrity" in connection with their formal economic and legal processes. We would suggest that such professionals engage in an honest review of the last decade's financial system (and other business) behaviors, together with the behavior of businesses' legal accessories. They would find their professional *embarrassment* to be very much misplaced.

We do not deny the reality of the assertion that many (though hardly all) managers can and do act in their own self-interest to the detriment of the best interests of the corporation. We also accept that resultant costs can be high (though certainly not only to stockholders). We therefore feel that it is useful to have *market* and *legal contract* and *statutory* controls on managerial activity. What we assert is that it is impossible to conceive of any combination of these three controls that would be sufficient to provide fully for the optimal welfare of the business enterprise, and thus for the body politic.

Once market and legal contract and statutory controls have done all they can, society is still left, on occasion, with one less-than-fully-addressed and major impediment to trustworthy, healthy, efficient business enterprise function: unethical human behavior. Only an *ethical construct*, *incorporated into law and carrying legal sanction*, can deal effectively with this serious, residual threat both to free market business enterprises and, by extension, to the health of the *free democratic republic* in which they are imbedded, and upon which they are utterly dependent.

We would label that ethical construct *fiduciary duty*.

IN LIEU OF THE PHILOSOPHER'S STONE

We might want to think about parties at interest and value weighting with regard to issues like these:

1. We placed a heavy focus in this chapter on the true nature of *the fiduciary relationship*. Is there any doubt in your mind, regardless of how it is interpreted, that the fiduciary relationship is an ethical construct? Is this really a case where "you shall" and "you ought" are the same thing in law? If one were to disagree with the *Time-Warner*

case, and with the entire concept of a corporate (and thus a manager) duty to weigh other than shareholder profit maximization in decision making, what then? Would an insistence on a fiduciary duty to shareholder profit maximization solely be an insistence on a certifiably "scientific" economic right, rather than a moral one? Or isn't the shareholders-alone "ought" the same as the all-affected-parties "ought" in terms of *each* proceeding from *some* ethical base?

Which "ought" do you really favor and, exactly, why? And which one on ethical grounds, without reverting to mathematical "proofs" and such, or invisible hands, or assumed market perfection?

2. Here is an interesting aside on Time-Warner—the corporation, not the case: Within a brief period in 1992, the company released a rap record by Ice-T called "Cop Killer," which caused police and many others much consternation. The corporation defended the record as constitutionally protected freedom of expression. Then the company published Madonna's book Sex, described by one magazine as a "Sodom High Yearbook." Time Warner, now the world's biggest media and entertainment company, has been criticized for promoting, selling, and profiting hugely on sex and violence.

Do you find the criticism valid? What interest do you weigh here? Is there any ethical reason to hold this corporation to a higher standard of corporate behavior than any other (e.g., a maker of household appliances)? Is the fact that it is a media giant appealing directly, and on a very broad geographical scale, to minds and emotions (young and old) of any relevance? Can we talk about (ethical) standards here without running the risk of censorship of corporate expression? And if there are to be no standards at all, what risk is our society running?

If you were a Time-Warner executive—with power and authority—would you consider drawing any lines short of what is legally allowable, in terms of sex and violence? Or anything else?

3. *The New York Times*, in 1992, focused on the issue of corporate fraud (F.Norris, "Fraud Among the Buds This Spring," May 10, 1992, and a major front-page story by D.B. Enriques, "Falsifying Corporate Data Becomes Fraud of the 90s," September 21, 1992). Which parties at interest, and just which ethical values, are at issue for you in terms of the role of accounting firms in this difficult business? The U.S. General Accounting Office, through its corporate financial audits division, severely criticized several leading accounting and financial-management groups for issuing toothless guidelines relating to corporate financial fraud (L.Berton, "U.S. Criticizes Plan for Business to Fight Fraud," *The Wall Street Journal*, December 2, 1992). The voluntary guidelines issued were called "a weak approach" entailing "a retreat from the public interest."

Is it right to force accountants to become tough watchdogs of business? If so, why? Aren't there a lot of (both business and societal) interests here? How would you define them? And weigh them? As the chief financial officer of a corporation? As an accounting firm CFO? As an S&L depositor? As a government regulator? Why should the interests be different in each case? Or the weighting of them?

6

Regulation

With an Emphasis on Financial Markets

COMING UP IN THIS CHAPTER

When one examines the interplay of law and the free market system in terms of the resultant effect on competition, innovation, and consumer welfare, no single area commands more attention (or generates more disputes) than the one called *regulation*. Moreover, policy-making here often requires the formulation of judgments involving both ethical and economic/financial market considerations. Health care and environmental legislation, and consequent rule-making, are two apt examples.

It would be unusual to find an active business person or consumer who did not have an opinion on the subject of government regulation. It would be more unusual to find one who had a truly *informed* understanding of its fundamental structure, and where and how it fits within our American constitutional "Rule of Law" system. It may be easier to argue that regulation is the oppressor of free markets, on the one hand, or the salvation of the consumer on the other, than to attempt to understand the basic structure and function of the regulatory system. However, intelligent, mutually beneficial compromise in the face of disagreement can never be based on biased perceptions.

Therefore, we will begin this chapter with an examination of the roots of our regulatory process and its (sometimes uneasy) place in our constitutional system. And we will illustrate some key structure and function issues through the example of the Federal Reserve, America's central banking system.

We begin by examining both U.S. constitutional law and administrative law in terms of our separation of powers/checks-and-balances system. Then, having in mind, in overview fashion, how the general regulatory structure works, we turn to regulators in action.

We utilize the Federal Reserve Board and discuss several of that particular regulator's "orders"—which banks must obey. Our first formal administrative "case" involves the *Industrial Bank of Japan, Ltd.* We follow the reported materials with a basic guide on how to read a regulatory body order.

At this point, the reader would have to wonder: If judges write decisions and Fed board members, and Securities Exchange Commissioners and other regulators issue "orders," just which power prevails here and what are the limits of regulator authority?

The *Dimension Financial* law case explains with a fair degree of clarity what the limits of federal agency rule-making are (i.e., just how the judicial system polices the regulator's power). The next case, *Blinder, Robinson*, does the same; however, it relates far more to rather personal kinds of regulatory behavior (partiality) and makes interesting reading on that account.

By the time we leave this chapter, we should be in a good position to pursue with a sharper insight the serious and complex issues of commercial and investment banking, and also securities markets and money-manager regulation. Certainly we can pursue with greater understanding the relationship between ethics and regulations on both the domestic and international levels.

It should be noted that, through the good graces of the publisher of *Congressional Quarterly*, we have provided the reader with a graphic illustration showing how legislation (often leading to regulations) is proposed and either enacted into law or defeated, either through floor vote or presidential veto (Figure 6.1).

We will then proceed to broaden our perspective with specific examples of regulation—and deregulation and reregulation—from finance areas of great importance to our economy in the last decade of the twentieth century: commercial banking, investment banking, securities markets, and money management.

I. ARE REGULATORY BODIES REALLY CONSTITUTIONAL?

Law schools teach a course that is usually titled "Administrative Law." That course, like the operations of many federal and state government administrative agencies it surveys, is usually a complex, and sometimes arcane, enterprise. We will not fully enter its precincts here, for fear that

FIGURE 6.1   How a Bill Becomes a Law

This graphic shows the most typical way in which proposed legislation is enacted into law. There are more complicated, as well as simpler, routes, and most bills never become law. The process is illustrated with two hypothetical bills, House bill No. 1(HR 1) and Senate bill No. 2 (S 2). Bills must be passed by both houses in identical form before they can be sent to the president. The path of HR 1 is traced by a solid line, that of S 2 by a broken line. In practice most bills begin as similar proposals in both houses.

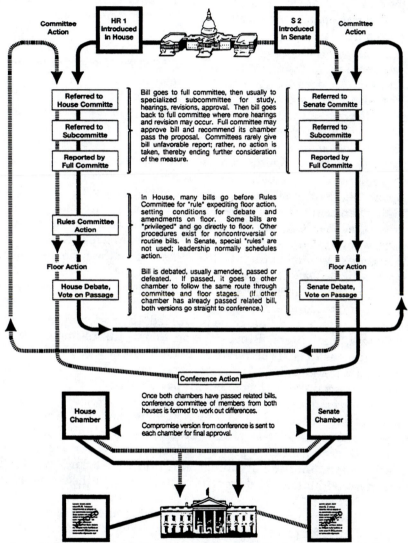

Committee Action

HR 1 Introduced In House

S 2 Introduced In Senate

Committee Action

Referred to House Committe

Referred to Subcommitte

Reported by Full Committe

Bill goes to full committee, then usually to specialized subcommittee for study, hearings, revisions, approval. Then bill goes back to full committee where more hearings and revision may occur. Full committee may approve bill and recommend its chamber pass the proposal. Committees rarely give bill unfavorable report; rather, no action is taken, thereby ending further consideration of the measure.

Referred to Senate Committe

Referred to Subcommitte

Reported by Full Committe

Rules Committee Action

In House, many bills go before Rules Committee for "rule" expediting floor action, setting conditions for debate and amendments on floor. Some bills are "privileged" and go directly to floor. Other procedures exist for noncontroversial or routine bills. In Senate, special "rules" are not used; leadership normally schedules action.

Floor Action

House Debate, Vote on Passage

Bill is debated, usually amended, passed or defeated. If passed, it goes to other chamber to follow the same route through committee and floor stages. (If other chamber has already passed related bill, both versions go straight to conference.)

Floor Action

Senate Debate, Vote on Passage

Conference Action

House Chamber

Once both chambers have passed related bills, conference committee of members from both houses is formed to work out differences.

Compromise version from conference is sent to each chamber for final approval.

Senate Chamber

Compromise bill approved by both houses is sent to the president, who can sign it into law or veto it and return it to Congress. Congress may override veto by a two-thirds majority vote in both houses; bill then becomes law without president's signature.

the reader would abandon all hope of comprehension. What we shall do instead is attempt to simplify a situation whose complexities, in terms of operating an efficient democratic government, are best illustrated by Figure 6.2, which shows clearly that the present government of the United States contains more entities (such as departments, agencies, administrations, commissions, boards, authorities and systems) than could have been dreamt of in the philosophies of Franklin, Jefferson, and Adams.

Administrative law is a broad term referring basically to *legislation* creating and empowering administrative agencies, to *agency practices and procedures*, and to *court review of agency actions*. It also refers to the exercise of agency power including the enforcement of rules and regulations, as well as to the *rights of businesses and individuals* affected by agency operations.

In federal government parlance, the very term for entities that, in one form or another, administrate is confusing. As Figure 6.2 illustrates, there are entities within the Executive Branch itself with agency-like functions (e.g., Office of National Drug Control Policy, the "Drug Czar's" Office). Then there are the governmental departments with cabinet secretaries (e.g., the Department of Defense). Then come the so-called independent regulatory entities (e.g., the Securities and Exchange Commission). Where do they all fit? Where does the ultimate authority for each reside? Does it matter?

Under the American constitutional system, it matters a whole lot. The United States is a representative democracy. In the eyes of the Founding Fathers (and, it is to be presumed, the Founding Wives, Mothers, Sisters, Daughters, Brothers, and Sons), the ultimate test of all governance was to be its *accountability to the governed*. North American colonists had had a bellyful of being responsible to, without having substantial accountability from, an all-powerful and distant government.

The result was a written constitution establishing a basic governmental structure aimed at thwarting tyranny at every turn: the *checks and balances system*. This system is based solidly on a *separation of powers* that guarantees that no single branch of government can wield a despot's club, and, equally important, that each branch will be given as much individual power as merits protection from the depredations of any other.

The many rewards of power possession and the seemingly basic animal instinct for protecting it against loss have served, on the whole, to discourage collusion among the three branches of American government. It has always been argued by many citizens, in fact, that intolerable governmental indecision, delay, and strife have resulted from the constant interbranch head-banging brought about by the constitutional separation of powers, checks-and-balances process. While that may on

FIGURE 6.2 Government of the United States

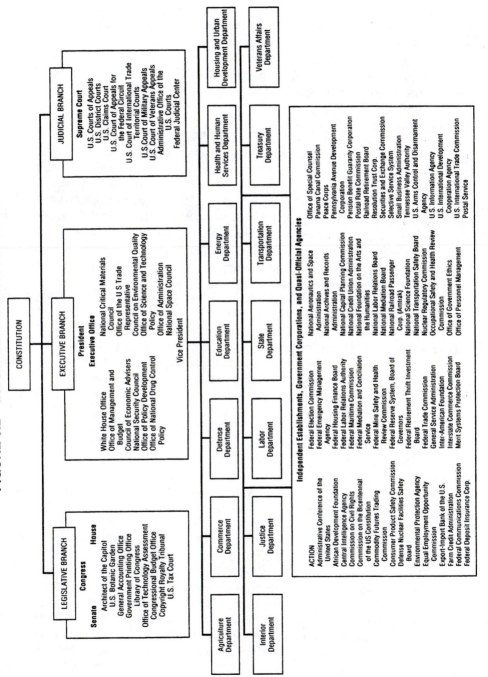

CONSTITUTION

LEGISLATIVE BRANCH

Congress

Senate

Architect of the Capitol
U.S. Botanic Garden
General Accounting Office
Government Printing Office
Library of Congress
Office of Technology Assessment
Congressional Budget Office
Copyright Royalty Tribunal
U.S. Tax Court

House

EXECUTIVE BRANCH

President

Executive Office

White House Office
Office of Management and Budget
Council of Economic Advisers
National Security Council
Office of Policy Development
Office of National Drug Control Policy
National Critical Materials Council
Office of the U S Trade Representative
Council on Environmental Quality
Office of Science and Technology Policy
Office of Administration
National Space Council

Vice President

JUDICIAL BRANCH

Supreme Court

U.S. Courts of Appeals
U.S. District Courts
U.S. Claims Court
U.S. Court of Appeals for the Federal Circuit
U.S. Court of International Trade
Territorial Courts
U.S. Court of Military Appeals
U.S. Court of Veterans Appeals
Administrative Office of the U.S. Courts
Federal Judicial Center

Agriculture Department

Commerce Department

Defense Department

Education Department

Energy Department

Health and Human Services Department

Housing and Urban Development Department

Interior Department

Justice Department

Labor Department

State Department

Transportation Department

Treasury Department

Veterans Affairs Department

Independent Establishments, Government Corporations, and Quasi-Official Agencies

ACTION
Administrative Conference of the United States
African Development Foundation
Central Intelligence Agency
Commission on Civil Rights
Commission on the Bicentennial of the US Constitution
Commodity Futures Trading Commission
Consumer Product Safety Commission
Defense Nuclear Facilities Safety Board
Environmental Protection Agency
Equal Employment Opportunity Commission
Export-Import Bank of the U.S.
Farm Credit Administration
Federal Communications Commission
Federal Deposit Insurance Corp.

Federal Election Commission
Federal Emergency Management Agency
Federal Housing Finance Board
Federal Labor Relations Authority
Federal Maritime Commission
Federal Mediation and Conciliation Service
Federal Mine Safety and Health Review Commission
Federal Reserve System, Board of Governors
Federal Retirement Thrift Investment Board
Federal Trade Commission
General Service Administration
Inter-American Foundation
Interstate Commerce Commission
Merit Systems Protection Board

National Aeronautics and Space Administration
National Archives and Records Administration
National Capital Planning Commission
National Credit Union Administration
National Foundation on the Arts and the Humanities
National Labor Relations Board
National Mediation Board
National Railroad Passenger Corp. (Amtrak)
National Science Foundation
Nuclear Regulatory Commission
National Transportation Safety Board
Occupational Safety and Health Review Commission
Office of Government Ethics
Office of Personnel Management

Office of Special Counsel
Panama Canal Commission
Peace Corps
Pennsylvania Avenue Development Corporation
Pension Benefit Guaranty Corporation
Postal Rate Commission
Railroad Retirement Board
Resolution Trust Corp.
Securities and Exchange Commission
Selective Service System
Small Business Administration
Tennessee Valley Authority
U.S. Arms Control and Disarmament Agency
U.S. Information Agency
U.S. International Development Cooperation Agency
U.S. International Trade Commission
Postal Service

occasion be frustratingly true, it is likewise the case that no tyrant has ever succeeded in seizing the reins of central government, and that the United States of America has had the longest run as a free democratic republic in the history of the world.

The real problem has been, and still is, squaring the accountability concern with the necessity of dealing with an ever-growing, increasingly complex economic and social system where governing requirements stretch well beyond the human capacities of a Congress and a President.

The dilemma is not difficult to describe.

There was a time when snake-oil salesmen sold colored water from covered wagons as a curative for most human diseases; when a few individuals gathered on sidewalks or in parks to sell a few stocks, face-to-face, to a few other people who actually understood the process; where radio did not exist, or television; when bankers simply undertook to accept and to lend money very carefully; and pollution had mostly to do with horse droppings along the public way. In such times, the danger of human deception and loss was ever-present, of course, but not on such a scale as to threaten the overall public welfare.

Now there are a plethora of new "miracle" drugs and related products, widely distributed, astonishingly effective, and potentially deadly; stock markets all over the world at least partially linked technologically, hawking diverse straight and derivative products of such a nature as to merit admiration, confusion, and terror; communication links so massive in number, scope, and importance as to provoke national and international considerations of availability and need; bank activities of such breadth, complexity, daring, and risk as might have frozen the blood of Alexander Hamilton; and surely chemicals of such intricate design and effectiveness as to presage the dawn of a new, more bounteous, and enriching world—if they don't destroy this one first.

How does one Congress (charged by the Constitution with making all laws) agree upon, and promulgate, enough specific laws to cover every disturbing situation, every conflict, and every concern that might arise from the activities and operations of all the individuals and entities involved in the magnificent maze of twentieth-century (not to mention upcoming twenty-first century) economic and social activity? And how does an Executive Branch (charged by the Constitution with *executing* the laws) adequately govern such an incredibly complex state of affairs? And finally, how does a Judiciary (charged by the Constitution with *interpreting* the laws; i.e., granted "the judicial power") go about deciding, in every single contested circumstance, upon which branch ultimate authority and responsibility devolves, and when and if that responsibility has been constitutionally exercised?

What has happened as life and the systems that both sustain and complicate it have grown more complex is that those charged with governance have had to establish and maintain new entities to assist them.

There are now 14 cabinet-level Executive Branch departments, plus councils and various agencies and offices to help the President govern. And both the Legislative and Judicial branches have many entities supporting their central functions directly. However, it is to the "Independent Establishments, Government Corporations and Quasi-Official Agencies" to which we would direct our attention now (see Figure 6-2). Those among them referred to often as "Independent Regulatory Commissions" are the ones generally focused upon in arguments about "the regulators" and their "regulations." The names are familiar: The Federal Communications Commission (the FCC), and the Securities and Exchange Commission (the SEC), for example, are two of the prominent ones.

Who are the "regulators"? What is the source of their power? What are their limits? And if our Constitution has established only three branches of government, just where do these entities fit?

We must assume, since making national law is the function of Congress, and since regulations have power similar to law, that these entities must have their origin in legislation. And so they do.

It is for the Congress to determine which national needs and concerns merit legislation, to identify the major purposes of the legislation (the laws) relating to such needs and, where necessary, to delegate the power to a body of experts to make the necessary rules to effectuate, and to oversee the forwarding of, those purposes.[1] It is not difficult to understand why Congress would focus on the safety and soundness of the national banking system as a major object of legislative concern, for example. It is also not difficult to understand why it would be utterly impossible for Congress to have attempted, by itself, to undertake to examine each application for a new bank holding company, to grant or deny each application to form or to purchase a new subsidiary, and to determine whether banks are being fair to all the communities in which they function. Congress instead passed the Bank Holding Company Act (12 U.S.C. § 1841 *et seq.*), which gives the Federal Reserve Board (also created by Congress) authority to undertake these, and many other, tasks.

Laws of Congress establishing regulatory bodies and the key issues upon which they are to focus are often referred to as "enabling" legislation. It is the sole authority by and through which the regulatory body functions (i.e., is *enabled* to function).

---

[1] See, generally, Kurland, "The Rise and Fall of the 'Doctrine of Separation of Powers,'" 85 *MichiganLaw Review 592 (1986).*

Why, then, are all congressionally created regulatory bodies not shown in Figure 6-2 as being directly under the "Legislative Branch"? For one thing, the leadership of the body is appointed by the President of the United States (the Executive) and is expected to reflect presidential philosophy vis-à-vis agency functions. For another, the determination of whether a regulatory body has exceeded its granted authority is undertaken by the courts (the Judiciary).

Are these regulatory bodies, then, a fourth branch of government, beyond the constitutional pale? Are they truly not locatable in terms of accountability? Insofar as each is not totally limited to one of the three constitutional branches, perhaps the term "fourth branch" could be used loosely. But in point of fact, they are not an independent, stand-alone branch of government at all.

One might postulate a President who issues an Executive Order abolishing the Congress, or a Judicial Decree from the Supreme Court abolishing the Presidency, or a Law of Congress abolishing the Supreme Court. The result of each of these actions would be a flurry of psychiatric activity, or perhaps criminal trials, but certainly no branch of constitutional government would go out of business. One might then postulate a Law of Congress abolishing the Securities and Exchange Commission. The result of this action would be that the SEC staff would pack up their belongings and say goodbye. Whether Congress would then have to bring into being another body to deal with the regulation of financial markets in some other way is irrelevant. What is relevant is that the "fourth branch" is made up of entities totally dependent on the authority and power of the "Constitutional Big Three" branches.

This is not to say that the rule-making and adjudicatory functions of a regulatory agency are not substantial, or that they are exercised efficiently in all cases, or that they are not subject to abuse. We shall examine some problems in these areas shortly. But it must be noted that Congress did respond, in 1946, to criticism of regulatory bodies that, as the result of their being given legislative authority to issue *rules, regulations, and orders* (administrative directions with the force of law), were becoming very powerful in some key economic and social areas.

Congress, in its exercise of constitutional authority, passed the Administrative Procedure Act (5 U.S.C. § 500-576), which defines (i.e., sets the boundaries for) "rules," "orders," and "sanctions"; covers all aspects of the "rule-making" function (in terms of publication of materials, advance notice of proposed rules, and the like); and guarantees the rights of persons to testify and to be accompanied by a lawyer and to appeal agency decisions. The sum total of the act's many provisions is to provide for monitoring, for citizen participatory rights, and for standards for judicial review in connection with the operations of all "independent" regulatory bodies.

II. REGULATORY BODY FUNCTIONS AND JUDICIAL REVIEW

A. The Federal Reserve

Herewith, an order of the Federal Reserve Board:

The Industrial Bank of Japan, Ltd. Tokyo, Japan
Order Approving the Acquisition
of a Bank Holding Company

The Industrial Bank of Japan, Ltd. ("IBJ"), Tokyo, Japan, a registered bank holding company, has applied for Board approval under section 3 of the Bank Holding Company Act (the "Act") (12 U.S.C. § 1842) to acquire up to 75.1 percent of the voting shares of J. Henry Schroder Bank & Trust Company, New York, New York ("Bank"). IBJ has also applied under section 4(c)(8) of the Act (12 U.S.C. § 1843 (c)(8)) to acquire up to 75.1 percent of the voting shares of J. Henry Schroder Banking Corporation ("JHSBC"), New York, New York, an investment company chartered under Article XII of the New York Banking Law (New York Investment Company), and through JHSBC to engage in the following activities: commercial lending; issuing letters of credit; purchasing and discounting acceptances; buying and selling foreign exchange; receiving and maintaining credit balances in connection with international trade; purchasing, acquiring, investing in and holding stock of any corporation and selling and disposing of such stock, provided that (unless otherwise authorized by the Board) no such investment shall exceed 5 percent of the voting securities of any corporation; and operating a foreign branch at Grand Cayman, Cayman Islands, and engaging at that office in transactions of the type that it can engage in at its home office. In addition, IBJ has applied to acquire indirectly shares of J. Henry Schroder International Bank, Miami, Florida, a corporation chartered pursuant to section 25(a) of the Federal Reserve Act (the "Edge Act") (12 U.S.C. § 611 *et seq.*) and owned by Bank.

Notice of the applications, affording interested persons opportunity to submit comments, has been given in accordance with sections 3 and 4 of the Act. The time for filing comments has expired, and the Board has considered the applications and all comments received in light of the factors set forth in section 3(c) of the Act, the considerations specified in section 4(c)(8) of the Act, and the purposes of the Edge Act.

IBJ, with total assets equivalent to approximately $85.7 billion, is the largest of three long-term credit banks in Japan and the fifteenth largest banking organization in the world. IBJ operates 23 branches in Japan and operates five branches, twenty-three representative offices, eight subsidiaries and one agency internationally. In the United States, IBJ operates a branch in New York with total assets of approximately $4.5 billion and an agency in Los Angeles with total assets of approximately $2.1 billion. In addition, IBJ owns all of the outstanding voting shares of Industrial Bank of Japan Trust Company, New York, New York, with total assets of approximately $2.6 billion. Applicant has selected New York as its home state under the Board's Regulation K(12 C.F.R. § 211.22(b)).

Bank, with total assets of approximately $1.9 billion, is the 24th largest commercial bank in New York State. Currently, over 95 percent of the outstanding voting shares of Bank are owned by Schroders plc, London, England, a registered bank holding company. IBJ proposes to acquire immediately 51 percent of the voting shares from Schroders plc, and to acquire approximately an additional 24 percent of Bank within 18 months of the initial purchase of shares.

Section 3(c) of the Act requires in every case that the Board consider the financial resources of the applicant organization and the bank or bank holding company to be acquired. As the Board has previously stated, review of the financial resources of foreign banking organizations raises a number of complex issues that the Board believes require careful consideration and that the Board continues to have under review. In this regard, the Board has initiated consultations with appropriate foreign bank supervisors and notes that work is currently in progress among foreign and domestic bank supervisory officials to develop more fully the concept of functional equivalency of capital ratios for banks of different countries. Pending the outcome of these consultations and deliberations, the Board has determined to consider the issues raised by applications by foreign banks to acquire domestic banks on a case-by-case basis.

In this case, the Board notes that the primary capital ratio of Applicant as publicly reported is below the minimum capital guidelines established by the Board for U.S. bank holding companies. While the Board regards this as a negative factor, the Board notes that Applicant is in compliance with the capital and other financial requirements of the appropriate supervisory authorities in Japan and that Applicant's resources and prospects are viewed as satisfactory by those authorities. Applicant also has historically experienced relatively low loan losses and a strong liquidity position. In addition, Applicant has a substantial and relatively stable funding base of government and corporate deposits and medium- and long-term debentures that, as a long-term credit bank, Applicant is permitted to issue under Japanese law. The Board has also considered other information regarding the financial condition of Applicant, including its substantial portfolio of securities of publicly held Japanese companies carried on Applicant's books at cost, which is substantially below their current market value. Finally, the Board notes that Applicant's current U.S. operations are satisfactory.

The Board expects that Applicant will maintain Bank as among the more strongly capitalized banking organizations of comparable size in the United States. Based on these and all of the other facts of record, the Board concludes that the financial and managerial factors are consistent with approval of this application.

Applicant's subsidiary bank in New York and Bank are both wholesale banks that operate in the Metropolitan New York banking market. Both institutions control a relatively small share of the market for commercial banking services in Metropolitan New York. Upon consummation of the proposed acquisition, Applicant would control approximately 1.18 percent of the deposits held by commercial banks in the Metropolitan New York banking market. Accordingly, the Board has determined that consummation of this proposal would not have significant adverse effects on existing or potential competition in New York or in any relevant banking market. The Board has also determined that considerations regarding the convenience and needs of the communities to be served are consistent with approval of this application.

In acting on IBJ's application to acquire JHSBC, the Board must first determine that these activities are closely related to banking or managing or controlling banks. The Board has previously determined by order that ownership and operation of a New York Investment company is closely related to banking. In making that determination, the Board considered the unique statutory powers of New York Investment Companies and the fact that the lending and banking activities involved were generally offered by commercial banks. In this case, the activities proposed by Applicant are substantially similar to those authorized by order in previous Board decisions: In light of this and other facts or record, the Board believes that the proposed activities of JHSBC are closely related to banking for purposes of section 4 of the Act.

In acting on applications under section 4 of the Act, the Board is required to determine whether the performance of proposed activities by an applicant "can reasonably be expected to produce benefits to the public, such as greater convenience, increased competition, or gains in efficiency that outweigh possible adverse effects, such as undue concentration of resources, decreased or unfair competition, conflicts of interests, or unsound banking practices." (12 U.S.C. § 1843(c)(8)).

Applicant's proposed acquisition would maintain an existing source of banking services in New York and add an additional source of strength to JHSBC. There is no evidence in the record that indicates that Applicant's proposal would result in any undue concentration of resources, decreased or unfair competition, conflicts of interest or unsound banking practices.

Accordingly, the Board has determined that the benefits to the public, subject to the conditions described above and commitments made by Applicant, would outweigh any potentially adverse effects.

The financial and managerial resources of Applicant are also consistent with its acquisition of J. Henry Schroder International Bank. This acquisition would result in the continuation of the international services currently provided, and is consistent with the purposes of the Edge Act. Accordingly, the board finds that the indirect acquisition of J. Henry Schroder International Bank by Applicant would be in the public interest.

Based on all of the facts of record, the Board has determined that the applications under sections 3 and 4 of the Act and under the Edge Act should be, and hereby are, approved. The acquisition of shares of Bank shall not be made before the thirtieth calendar day following the date of this Order, and none of the proposed acquisitions shall be consummated later than three months after the date of this Order, unless such time is extended for good cause by the Board or by the Federal Reserve Bank of New York, pursuant to delegated authority. The determination with respect to Applicant's acquisition of shares of the nonbanking companies discussed herein is subject to all of the conditions set forth in Regulation Y, including sections 225.4(d) and 225.23(b) (12 C.F.R. 6 §§ 225.4(d) and 225.23(b)), and to the Board's authority to require such modifications or termination of activities of a bank holding company or any of its subsidiaries as the Board finds necessary to assure compliance with, and prevent evasions of, the provisions and purposes of the Act and the Board's regulations and orders issued thereunder.

By order of the Board of Governors, effective November 29, 1985.

Voting for this action: Vice Chairman Martin and Governors Partee and Rice. Voting against this action: Governor Seger. Absent and not voting: Chairman Volcker and Governor Wallich.

James McAfee
Associate Secretary of the Board

Additional Views of Vice Chairman Martin and Governor Rice

We join in the opinion and Order issued by the Board finding that, under the specific facts and circumstances of this case, the financial condition of Applicant, after making appropriate adjustments for differences between foreign and domestic regulatory and banking practices and requirements, is consistent with approval. We would, however, like to note our continuing concern, expressed in previous cases, regarding acquisitions by foreign banking organizations whose publicly reported capital is well below the Board's capital guidelines for U.S. banking organizations and the unfair competitive advantage that foreign banking organizations with low capital may thus have over comparable sized domestic banking organizations. A regulatory standard that would permit acquisitions by a foreign banking organization with low capital even after appropriate adjustments are made would allow such foreign banking organizations a clear advantage in many aspects of their competition with domestic banking organizations including pricing of services and bidding for domestic bank acquisitions. We believe that, consistent with the principles of competitive equality and national treatment, foreign banking organizations that have applied to acquire a domestic bank should be judged against financial and managerial standards, including capital adequacy guidelines, that are similar to those applicable to domestic banking organizations. In this regard, we are following carefully the progress of discussions currently underway among foreign and domestic bank supervisory officials to develop more fully the concept of the functional equivalency of capital ratios for banks of different countries.

November 29, 1985
(all footnotes omitted)

Dissenting Statement by Governor Seger

I dissent from the Board's action in this case. I share the concerns expressed by Vice Chairman Martin and Governor Rice that foreign banking organizations whose publicly reported capital is well below the Board's capital guidelines for U.S. banking organizations have an unfair competitive advantage in the United States over domestic banking organizations and should, I therefore believe, be judged against the same financial and managerial standards, including the Board's capital adequacy guidelines, as are applied to domestic banking organizations.

In addition, I am concerned that, while this application would permit a large Japanese banking organization to acquire a bank in the U.S., U.S. banking organizations are not permitted to make comparable acquisitions in Japan. While some progress is being made in opening Japanese markets to U.S. banking organizations, U.S. banking organizations and other financial institutions, in my opinion, are still far from being afforded the full opportunity to compete in Japan.

November 25, 1985

(Printed in: 72 Federal Reserve *Bulletin* 71 (1986).)

The basic questions one should ask when reading this (or some other) regulatory body order are:

- Exactly what job is the regulator engaging in here?
- By what authority, exactly, is it doing so?
- What specifically authorized, *and directed,* review areas does the regulatory body highlight here?
- What, if any, special circumstances appear in this matter?
- What rationale(s) is given for the conclusion(s) reached by the body?
- What is the nature of the conclusion reached by the dissenter(s)?

In connection with the dissent in this *Industrial Bank* matter, let it be noted that Governor Seger held her ground, dissenting every time the Fed saw fit to allow Japanese holding companies to expand here in the United States (e.g., *In the Matter of Long Term Credit Bank of Japan, Ltd., Federal Reserve Bulletin* [October 1989], p. 721). Is Governor's Seger's strictly a business/market concern, or is she proceeding as well from ethical premises?

The following case delves deeply into the *limits of regulatory agency authority.*

BOARD OF GOVERNORS OF THE FEDERAL RESERVE SYSTEM V. DIMENSION FINANCIAL CORPORATION ET AL.
474 U.S. 361, 106 S. Ct. 681, 88L.Ed. 2d 691 (1986)

CHIEF JUSTICE BURGER delivered the opinion of the Court.
We granted certiorari to decide whether the Federal Reserve Board acted within its statutory authority in defining "banks" under S 2(c) of the Bank Holding Company Act of 1956, 12 U.S.C. § 1841 *et seq.,* as

any institution that (1) accepts deposits that "as a matter of practice" are payable on demand and (2) engages in the business of making "any loan other than a loan to an individual for personal, family, household, or charitable purposes 'including' the purchase of retail installment loans or commercial paper, certificates of deposit, bankers' acceptances, and similar money market instruments." 12 CFR § 225.2(a)(1)(1985).

I

A

Section 2(c) of the Bank Holding Company Act defines "bank" as any institution "which (1) accepts deposits that the depositor has a legal right to withdraw on demand, and (2) engages in the business of making commercial loans." 70 Stat. 133, as amended, 12 U.S.C. § 1841(c).

This case is about so-called "nonbank banks"—institutions that offer services similar to those of banks but which until recently were not under Board regulation because they conducted their business so as to place themselves arguably outside the narrow definition of "bank" found in § 2(c) of the Act. Many nonbank banks, for example, offer customer NOW (negotiable order of withdrawal) accounts which function like conventional checking accounts but because of prior notice provisions do not technically give the depositor a "legal right to withdraw on demand." 12 U.S.C. § 1841(c)(1). Others offer conventional checking accounts, but avoid classification as "banks" by limiting their extension of commercial credit to the purchase of money market instruments such as certificates of deposit and commercial paper.

In 1984, the Board promulgated rules providing that nonbank banks offering the functional equivalent of traditional banking services would thereafter be regulated as banks. 49 Fed. Reg. 794. The Board accomplished this by amending its definition of a bank, found in "Regulation Y," in two significant respects. First, the Board defined "demand deposit" to include deposits, like NOW accounts, which are "as a matter of practice" payable on demand. 12 CFR § 225.2(a)(1)(A)(1985). Second, the Board defined the "making of a commercial loan" as "any loan other than a loan to an individual for personal, family, household, or charitable purposes," including "the purchase of retail installment loans or commercial paper, certificates of deposit, bankers' acceptances, and similar money market instruments." 12 CFR § 225.2(a)(1)(B)(1985).

B

Cases challenging the amended Regulation Y were commenced in three Circuits and were consolidated in the United States Court of Appeals for the Tenth Circuit. The Court of Appeals set aside both the demand deposit and commercial loan aspects of the Board's regulation. 744 F. 2d 1402 (1984). The court did not discuss the demand deposit regulations in detail, relying instead on the holding of an earlier Tenth Circuit case, *First Bancorporation* v. *Board of Governors* 728 F. 2d 434 (1984). In *First Bancorporation,* the court noted that the statutory definition of demand deposit is a deposit giving the depositor "a *legal right* to withdraw on demand." The court recognized that "withdrawals from NOW accounts are in actual practice permitted on demand." But, since the depositary institution retains a technical prior notice requirement it does not, for the purposes of Congress' definition of "bank," accept "deposits that the depositor has a legal right to withdraw on demand."

The Court of Appeals also concluded that the Board's new definition of "commercial loan" was at odds with the Act. The legislative history revealed that in passing § 2(c) Congress intended to exempt from Board regulation institutions whose only commercial credit activity was the purchase of money market instruments. Although agencies must be "able to change to meet new conditions arising within their sphere of authority," any expansion of agency jurisdiction must come from Congress and not the agency itself. 744 F. 2d, at 1409. Accordingly, the Court of Appeals invalidated the amended regulations.

We granted certiorari. 471 U.S. - (1985). We affirm.

II

The Bank Holding Company Act of 1956, 12 U.S.C. § 1841 *et seq.,* vests broad regulatory authority in the Board over bank holding companies "to restrain the undue concentration of commercial banking resources and to prevent possible abuses related to the control of commercial credit." S. Rep. No. 91-1084, p. 24 (1970). The Act authorizes the Board to regulate "any company which has control over any bank." 12 U.S.C. § 1841(a)(1).

The breadth of that regulatory power rests on the Act's definition of the word "bank." The 1956 Act gave a simple and broad definition of bank: "any national banking association or any State bank, savings bank, or trust company." 12 U.S.C. § 1841(c) (1964 ed.). Experience soon proved that literal application of the statute had the unintended consequence of including within regulation industrial banks offering limited checking account services to their customers. These institutions accepted "'funds from the public that are, in actual practice, repaid on demand.'" Amend the Bank Holding Company Act of 1956: Hearings on S. 2253, S. 2418, and H.R. 7371 before a Subcommittee of the Senate Committee on Banking and Currency, 89th Cong., 2d Sess., 447 (1966)(letter to the Committee from J. L. Robertson, Member, Federal Reserve Board). Although including these institutions within the bank definition was the "correct legal interpretation" of the 1956 statute, the Board saw "no reason in policy to cover such institutions under this act." Congress agreed, and accordingly amended the statutory definition of a bank in 1966, limiting its application to institutions that accept "deposits that the depositor has a legal right to withdraw on demand.

The 1966 definition proved unsatisfactory because it too included within the definition of "bank" institutions that did not pose significant dangers to the banking system. Because one of the primary purposes of the Act was to "restrain undue concentration of. . . commercial credit," it made little sense to regulate institutions that did not, in fact, engage in the business of making commercial loans. S. Rep. No. 91-1084, p. 24 (1970). Congress accordingly amended the definition, excluding all institutions that did not "engag[e] in the business of making commercial loans." Since 1970 the statute has provided that a bank is any institution that:

> (1) accepts deposits that the depositor has a legal right to withdraw on demand, and (2) engages in the business of making commercial loans. [12 U.S.C. § 1841(c).]

III

In 1984, the Board initiated rulemaking to respond to the increase in the number of nonbank banks.*n3* After hearing views of interested parties, the Board found that nonbank banks pose three dangers to the national banking system. *First*, by remaining outside the reach of banking regulations, nonbank banks have a significant competitive advantage over regulated banks despite the functional equivalence of the services offered. *Second,* the proliferation of nonbank banks threatens the structure established by Congress for limiting the association of banking and commercial enterprises. See 12 U.S.C. § 11843(c)(8) (bank holding company can purchase nonbanking affiliate only if entity "closely related to banking"). *Third*, the interstate acquisition of nonbank banks undermines the statutory proscription on interstate banking without prior state approval. 49 Fed. Reg. 794, 835-836 (1984). Since the narrowed statutory definition required that both the demand deposit and the commercial loan elements be present to constitute the institution as a bank, the Board proceeded to amend Regulation Y redefining both elements of the test. We turn now to the two elements of this definition.

n3 The Board explained that since 1980 a large number of insurance, securities, industrial and commercial organizations have acquired FDIC insured financial institutions that are the functional equivalent of banks. The Board also noted that the powers of previously unregulated industrial banks "have substantially expanded. . . making them for all intents and purposes banks" for the purposes of the Bank Holding Company Act. 49 Fed. Reg., at 834.A

A

The Board amended its definition of "demand deposit" primarily to include within its regulatory authority institutions offering NOW accounts. A NOW account functions like a traditional checking account—the depositor can write checks that are payable on demand at the depository institution. The depository institution, however, retains a seldom exercised but nevertheless absolute right to require prior notice of withdrawal. Under literal reading of the statute, the institution—even if it engages in full-scale commercial lending—is not a "bank" for the purposes of the Holding Company Act because the prior notice provision withholds from the depositor any "legal right" to withdraw on demand. The Board in its amended definition closes this loophole by defining demand deposits as a deposit, not that the depositor has a "legal right to withdraw on demand," but a deposit that "as a matter of practice is payable on demand."

In determining whether the Board was empowered to make such a change, we begin, of course, with the language of the statute. If the statute is clear and unambiguous "that is the end of the matter, for the court, as well as the agency, must give effect to the unambiguously expressed intent of Congress." The traditional deference courts pay to agency interpretation is not to be applied to alter the clearly expressed intent of Congress.

Application of this standard to the Board's interpretation of the "demand deposit" element of § 2(c) does not require extended analysis. By the 1966 amendments to § 2(c), Congress expressly limited the Act to regulation of institutions that accept deposits that "the depositor has a legal right to withdraw on demand." 12 U.S.C. § 1841(c). The Board would now define "legal right" as meaning the same as "a matter of practice." But no amount of agency expertise—however sound may be the result—can make the words *"legal right"* mean a right to do something "as a matter of practice." A legal right to withdraw on demand means just that: a right to withdraw deposits without prior notice or limitation. Institutions offering NOW accounts do not give the depositor a legal right to withdraw on demand; rather, the institution itself retains the ultimate legal right to require advance notice of withdrawal. The Board's definition of "demand deposit," therefore, is not an accurate or reasonable interpretation of § 2(c).

B

Section 2(c) of the Act provides that, even if an institution accepts deposits that the depositor has a legal right to withdraw on demand, the institution is not a bank unless it "engages in the business of making commercial loans." Under Regulation Y, "commercial loan" means "any loan other than a loan to an individual for personal, family, household, or charitable purposes," including "the purchase of retail installment loans or commercial paper, certificates of deposit, bankers' acceptances, and similar money market instruments."

The purpose of the amended regulation is to regulate as banks institutions offering "commercial loan substitutes," that is, extensions of credit to commercial enterprises through transactions other than the conventional commercial loan. In its implementing order, the Board explained that "it is proper to include these instruments within the scope of the term commercial loan as used in the Act in order to carry out the Act's basic purposes: to maintain the impartiality of banks in providing credit to business, to prevent conflict of interest, and to avoid concentration of control of credit." 49 Fed. Reg., at 841.

As the Board's characterization of these transactions as "commercial loan substitutes" suggests, however, money market transactions do not fall within the commonly accepted definition of "commercial loans." The term "commercial loan" is used in the financial community to describe the direct loan from a bank to a business customer for the purpose of providing funds needed by the customer in its business. The term does not apply to, indeed is used to distinguish, extensions of credit in the open market that do not involve close borrower-lender relationships. Cf. G. Munn & F. Garcia, *Encyclopedia of Banking and Finance* 607 (1983). These later money market transactions undoubtedly involve the indirect extension of credit to commercial entities but, because they do not entail the face-to-face negotiation of credit between borrower and lender, are not "commercial loans."

This common understanding of the term "commercial loan" is reflected in the Board's own decisions. Throughout the 1970's the Board applied the term "commercial loan" to exclude from regulation institutions engaging in money market transactions. For example, in

D.H. Baldwin Co., 63 Fed. Res. Bull. 280 (1977), the Board noted that although savings and loans participated in the Federal funds market and issued certificates of deposit, they were not "technically 'banks' for the purposes of the Act" because they did not make commercial loans. The Board recognized that savings and loans resembled banks but concluded that "the decision should be left to Congress whether, in light of the policies underlying the Bank Holding Company Act, such 'near-banks' should be treated as 'banks' or 'nonbanks.'" See also *American Fletcher Corp.,* Fed. Res. Bull. 868, 869 and n. 8 (1974) (savings and loans participate in the federal funds market and offer certificates of deposit but may not be deemed "banks" within the meaning of the Act). In 1976, the Board's Legal Division found that the broker call loans "do not appear to have the close lender-borrower relationship that is one of the characteristics of commercial loans." Letter to Michael A. Greenspan, from Baldwin P. Tuttle, Deputy General Counsel, pp. 2-3 (Jan. 26, 1976) (App. 100A-101A). A 1981 internal memorandum summarized the Board's longstanding interpretation of the commercial loan definition:

> The Board also has concluded that, although commercial in nature, the purchase of federal funds, money market instruments (certificates of deposit, commercial paper and bankers acceptances) are not considered commercial loans for the purposes of section 2(c) of the Act, despite the fact that for other statutory and regulatory purposes these instruments may be considered commercial loans. [Federal Reserve System, Office Correspondence (Feb. 10, 1981) (App. 97A)(emphasis in original).]

The Board now contends that the new definition conforms with the original intent of Congress in enacting the "commercial loan" provision. The provision, the Board argues, was a "technical amendment to the Act designed to create a narrowly circumscribed exclusion from the Act's coverage." Brief for Petitioner 41. The Board supports this revisionist view of the purpose of the "commercial loan" provision by citing a comment in the "legislative history" indicating that at the time the provision was enacted, it operated to exclude only one institution, the Boston Safe Deposit & Trust Co. The Board does not go so far as to claim that the commercial loan amendment was a private bill, designed only to exempt Boston Safe. It suggests, however, that because the amendment was prompted by the circumstances of one particular institution, the language "commercial loan" should be given something other than its commonly accepted meaning.

The statute by its terms, however, exempts from regulations *all* institutions that do not engage in the business of making commercial loans. The choice of this general language demonstrates that, although legislation may have been prompted by the needs of one institution, Congress intended to exempt the class of institutions not making commercial loans. Furthermore, the legislative history supports this plain reading of the statute. The Senate Report explained:

> The definition of "bank" adopted by Congress in 1966 was designed to include commercial banks and exclude those institutions not engaged in commercial banking, since the purpose of the act was to restrain undue concentration of commercial banking resources and to prevent possible abuses related to the control of commercial credit. However, the Federal Reserve Board has noted that this definition may be too broad and may include institutions which are not in fact engaged in the business of commercial banking in that they do not make commercial loans. The committee, accordingly, adopted a provision which would exclude institutions that are not engaged in the business of making commercial loans from the definition of "bank." [S. Rep. No. 91-1084, p. 24 (1970).]

The only reference to Boston Safe is in a lengthy banking journal article that Representative Gonzalez entered into the *Congressional Record*. See 116 Cong. Rec. 25846, 25848 (1970) (indicating that Boston Safe was "[v]irtually the only bank that does no commercial lending"). Such a passage is not "legislative history" in any meaningful sense of the term and cannot defeat the plain application of the words actually chosen by Congress to effectuate its will. Finally, even if the legislative history evidenced a congressional intent to exclude only Boston Safe, which it does not, the Board's expansive definition of "commercial loan" would be an unreasonable interpretation of the statute. At the time the commercial loan provision was enacted, Boston Safe did not "make commercial loans," but did purchase money market instruments such as certificates of deposit and commercial paper. Recognizing the common usage of the term "commercial loan" and the purpose of the 1970 amendment, the Board in 1972 advised Boston Safe that it was not, in fact, a bank for the purposes of the Bank Holding Company Act:

> The Board understands that Boston Safe purchases "money market instruments," such as certificates of deposit, commercial paper, and bank acceptances. In the circumstances of this

case, such transactions are not regarded as commercial loans for the purposes of the Act. [Letter to Lee J. Aubrey, Vice President, Federal reserve Bank of Boston, from Michael A. Greenspan, Assistant Secretary, Board of Governors, p. 2 (May 18, 1972) (App. 94A).]

Nothing in the statutory language or the legislative history, therefore, indicates that the term "commercial loan" meant anything different from its accepted ordinary commercial usage. The Board's definition of "commercial loan," therefore, is not a reasonable interpretation of § 2(c).

C

Unable to support its new definitions on the plain language of § 2(c), the Board contends that its new definitions fall within the "plain purpose" of the Bank Holding Company Act. Nonbank banks must be subject to regulation, the Board insists, because "a statute must be read with a view to the 'policy of the legislation as a whole' and cannot be read to negate the plain purpose of the legislation." The plain purpose of the legislation, the Board contends, is to regulate institutions "functionally equivalent" to banks. Since NOW accounts are the functional equivalent of a deposit in which the depositor has a legal right to withdraw on demand and money market transactions involve the extension of credit to commercial entities, institutions offering such services should be regulated as banks.[n6]

n6 In a related argument, the Board contends that it has the power to regulate these institutions under § 5(b), which provides that the Board is issuing regulations "necessary to enable it to administer and carry out the purposes of this chapter and prevent evasions thereof." 12 U.S.C. § 1844 (b). But § 5 only permits the Board to police within the boundaries of the Act; it does not permit the Board to expand its jurisdiction beyond the boundaries established by Congress in § 2(c).

The "plain purpose" of legislation, however, is determined in the first instance with reference to the plain language of the statute itself. *Richards* v. *United States* 369 U.S. 1, 9 (1962). Application of "broad purposes" of legislation at the expense of specific provisions ignores the complexity of the problems Congress is called upon to address and the dynamics of legislative action. Congress may be unanimous in its intent to stamp out some vague social or economic evil; however, because its Members may differ sharply on the means for effectuating that intent, the final language of the legislation may reflect hard-fought compromises. Invocation of the "plain purpose" of legislation at the expense of the terms of the statute itself takes no account of the processes of compromise and, in the end, prevents the effectuation of congressional intent.

Without doubt there is much to be said for regulating financial institutions that are the functional equivalent of banks. NOW accounts have much in common with traditional payment-on-demand checking accounts; indeed we recognize that they generally serve the same purposes. Rather than defining "bank" as an institution that offers the functional equivalent of banking services, however, Congress defined with specificity certain transactions that constitute banking subject to regulation. The statute may be imperfect, but the Board has no power to correct flaws that it perceives in the statute it is empowered to administer. Its rulemaking power is limited to adopting regulations to carry into effect the will of Congress as expressed in the statute.[n7]

> [n7] The process of effectuating Congressional intent at times may yield anomalies. In TVA v. Hill, 437 U.S. 153 (1978), for example, we were confronted with the explicit language of a statute that in application produced a curious result. Noting that nothing prohibited Congress from passing unwise legislation, we upheld the enforcement of the statute as Congress had written it. Congress swiftly granted relief to the petitioner in Hill; but did so in a fashion that could not have been tailored by the courts. See Pub. L. 95-632, § 5, 92 Stat. 3760.

If the Bank Holding Company falls short of providing safeguards desirable or necessary to protect the public interest, that is a problem for Congress, and not the Board or the courts, to address. Numerous proposals for legislative reform have been advanced to streamline the tremendously complex area of financial institution regulation. See, e.g., Blueprint for Reform: Report of the Task Group on Regulation of Financial Services (July 1984). Our present inquiry, however, must come to rest with the conclusion that the action of the Board in this case is inconsistent with the language of the statute for here, as in *TVA* v. *Hill*, 437 U.S. 153, 194 (1978), "[o]nce the meaning of an enactment is discerned. . . the judicial process comes to an end."

Affirmed.

JUSTICE WHITE took no part in the consideration or decision of this case.

The *Dimension Financial* case should be subject to the same considerations applied to all judicial decisions as set forth in Chapter 3. Here, specifically, we might amplify by including the following:

- What market failure is being addressed by the Fed and Court here?
- Why are they addressing it differently?
- We edited out most of the footnotes in this case. Why then, do you think, is footnote 3 still included? Does the answer relate importantly to the previous two questions? In that connection, are not footnotes 6 and 7 included for the same reason footnote 3 is?
- Do you think the Supreme Court was or was not sympathetic to the purposes of the contested Fed action in this case? Where in the decision, is the answer found?
- If the Supreme Court understood (and perhaps even agreed with) the Fed's motivation, why did they reverse the Fed here? Is footnote 7 relevant to your answer? Is not the constitutional basis of regulatory power the focal issue here? What fact(s) in sum defeated the Fed here?

The Federal Reserve, of course, is but one of the regulatory bodies that exercises authority over U.S. financial markets.

B. The Securities and Exchange Commission

Congress has passed laws that govern securities transactions in the United States. The Securities and Exchange Act of 1933 covers the issuance of new stock; the Securities and Exchange Act of 1934 covers trading in issued securities. Much has been added to the acts since the mid-1930s, of course. The regulating agency set up to administer and enforce the national securities laws, by this legislation, is the SEC—the Securities and Exchange Commission. We will deal with the SEC in more detail later.

It should be noted here that securities activities are basically interstate in nature, and thus fall within the powerful federal ambit. However, the individual states each have an interest in protecting citizens of the state in the securities area. All 50 states, the District of Columbia, and Puerto Rico have securities laws pertaining to the issuing and sale of securities within their borders. These state statutes are referred to, collectively, as "blue sky laws."

While securities laws could be characterized broadly as an attempt to protect investors against fraud, one might best consider these laws as focused upon getting out the facts. Which is to say that the laws are aimed at ensuring as full a disclosure of all relevant details as possible regarding stock issuance and trade, so that the investor is able to make fully informed, rational decisions with regard to the investors' securities transactions.

Because the 1933 act covers issuance of stock, the basic regulator task involves *registration procedures* aimed at truth-in-offering. The 1934 act requires registration also when new classes of securities are issued, but basically it focuses on reporting. This means getting out to (disclosing to) the general investing public all the facts about the condition of a company and its stock that will make for fair, trustworthy markets and market transactions.

The major reporting documents required of all companies within SEC jurisdiction are: the 10K (their securities, who owns them, their directors and officers, their holdings, and changes in the company's business likely to affect its financial condition); the 10Q (quarterly report on gross sales and income); and the 8K (new acquisition and changes in company control).

In recent times, the 1934 Securities Act has become prominent for its Section 10, which covers "Manipulative and Deceptive Devices"—a broad enough term to cover insider trading. Later in this text we shall pursue the Section 10 rules (and related Section 16 rules, as well as the Insider Trading Sanctions Act of 1984, and Section 13's takeover/tender offer rules).

For now, we shall be content to point out that, as powerful as the SEC may be perceived to be, it too is not immune to severe criticism from the courts.

BLINDER, ROBINSON AND COMPANY V. SECURITIES AND EXCHANGE COMMISSION
837 F. 2d 1099 (1988)

[In this case, Blinder, Robinson, a leading broker-dealer in penny stocks, and its president were found guilty of securities fraud under both the 1933 and 1934 Securities and Exchange Act provisions. The case went before an Administrative Law Judge and the courts. An ALJ is an official appointed to conduct hearings for a regulatory agency and to make recommendations to the agency head regarding orders to be issued. The ALJ is appointed under civil service rules and is therefore protected against arbitrary dismissal by an agency. Over 1,000 ALJs serve in many federal departments and agencies. The fraud findings were upheld at all levels of appeal, and the SEC then applied sanctions against the company and its president, suspending the firm's registration for 45 days and its right to engage in underwriting activity for two years. The federal appeals court in this case affirmed the fraud findings and the sanctions against the firm. The issue here was the sanction imposed on the president, which was permanent disbarment from association with any broker-dealer. The president had

*sought to ameliorate the harsh penalty on himself by introducing evidence
before the SEC to the effect that some of his censured behavior had actually
been undertaken on the advice of his counsel. The SEC refused to hear that
evidence. The opinion in this case was by Circuit Judge Starr.]*

. . . 2. Administrative Procedure Act Challenge. Both petitioners
(Blinder & Co. and its president) devote considerable energy to attacking the sanctions imposed by the SEC as arbitrarily severe. We have
been provided with the following arguments in particular: (1) the SEC
subjects over-the-counter firms to disproportionately unfavorable
treatment in comparison to the Big Board-member firms that similarly
run afoul of statutory or regulatory rules and requirements; (2) the
SEC, in violation of fundamental requirements of administrative law,
failed sufficiently to justify the harsh sanctions visited on petitioners;
and (3) the two-year suspension of the firm from all underwriting and
private placement activities exceeds the maximum period of suspension authorized under section 15(b)(4) of the 1934 Act. Impressive
decisional authority is summoned to buttress the first two points,
including an opinion by late Judge Friendly in *Arthur Lipper Corp.* v.
SEC, 647 F. 2d 171 (2d Cir. 1976), cert. denied, 434 U.S. 1009 (1978),
where the Second Circuit set forth a variety of factors to employ in
evaluating sanctions imposed by the SEC, and an opinion by our
colleagues in the Fifth Circuit in *Steadman* v. *SEC,* 603 F. 2d 1126 (5th
Cir. 1979), aff'd 450 U.S. 91 (1981), where the court erected a daunting
standard to justify permanent exclusion from the securities industry.
[P]ermanent exclusion from the industry is "without justification in
fact" unless the Commission specifically articulates compelling reasons for such a sanction. . . .

The SEC invokes, in response, similarly impressive authority
supporting the unquestioned proposition that the crafting of an appropriate remedy is peculiarly within the province of an expert agency,
and can appropriately be judicially disturbed only where the remedy
is "unwarranted in law or. . . without justification in fact. . . . SEC Brief
at 11, quoting *Butz* v. *Glover Livestock Comm'n Co.,* 411 U.S. 182,
185-86 (1973). Commission counsel points to the detailed reasons
articulated by the SEC in visiting such substantial sanctions on
petitioners. The SEC summarizes its position this way:

> Given the district court's findings that petitioners engaged in
> an ongoing series of deliberately fraudulent transactions that
> included a deceptive sales campaign, arranging non bona fide
> transactions to give the appearance that the [American Lei-
> sure] offering was sold out, misleading their own counsel and

then ignoring counsel's advice, violating the escrow agreement, failing to return investors' money as required, and engaging in prohibited trading in the putative aftermarket, this conclusion [as to sanctions] should need no further explanation. . . .

In the course of recounting petitioners' manifold sins, Commission counsel suggests that the factors on which the *Lipper* court relied are not present here. Among those are the following:

Unlike Mr. Lipper, petitioners [in this case] did not seek counsel's advice as to the totality of the conduct held to violate the securities laws; and, on the only issue that they did seek advice, their purchase of [American Leisure] securities, they rejected the advice they received. . . .

By their own words, then, Commission counsel have indicated the relevance of petitioners' relationship with counsel. Petitioners have been weighed in the balance and found wanting, in part because of their disdain for (or failure to secure) counsel's advice. That failure, as the Commission sees it, plainly related to the conclusion that the American Leisure offering was permeated with deliberate fraud. . . . But the obvious problem with the SEC's conclusions relating to Mr. Blinder's relationship with counsel is that they assume the Commission had before it the full record germane to determining whether factors such as those emphasized by the Lipper court were present. That assumption, for reasons already stated, is ill-founded by virtue of the refusal even to consider potentially relevant evidence.

In brief, we are persuaded that the fundamental principle of administrative law that an agency act in a non-arbitrary, non-capricious fashion is necessarily implicated by the SEC's refusal to permit evidence with respect to a salient factor. That is, in meting out sanctions, the Commission cannot adequately weigh the factors that it concedes should be considered without having before it the full set of facts necessary for reasoned consideration.

Thus, our analysis in this section of the opinion is inevitably affected by the Commission's error, discussed in the preceding section, in refusing to consider evidence relating to the relationship with counsel on grounds of issue preclusion. We will therefore not extend further the length of this opinion, which is obviously but another (albeit important) chapter in this long-lived litigation. Instead, we will put down our pen and remand the case to the Commission for further action consistent with this opinion. On remand, the SEC will, of course, be obliged to satisfy the strictures of the APA by articulating an adequate rationale for whatever decision it may reach.

In this regard, we would be less than candid if we did not flag for the Commission our concern that petitioners have mounted a non-frivolous claim that they have been singled out for disproportionately harsh treatment. Petitioners list a series of instances which, they contend, demonstrate that the SEC's hand comes down more heavily on smaller, newer firms than it does on old-line, or a least more established, houses with the right sort of exchange memberships. The allegation is thus not simply that penalties have differed from case to case. As the colloquies at oral argument suggested, each case in securities regulation, as elsewhere, is different. Those inevitable differences and gradations in fact can best be discerned and articulated by the Commissioners whose job it is to come to just these sorts of judgements. But it does not exceed our appropriate function to indicate that we have seen warning signs. What is alleged here are not mere disparities, see *Butz* v. *Glover Livestock Comm'n Co.*, 411 U.S. 182, 187 (1973), but rather an asserted SYSTEMIC PATTERN OF DISPARATE TREATMENT, resulting in predictably, disproportionately harsh sanctions being visited upon firms such as *Blinder, Robinson*. If the Commission believes that the alarms are false, then it should say so and explain why what might appear to be troubling systemic variances are in fact not such variances at all, or, alternatively, variances justified by the circumstances of this case. Finally, we emphasize in this respect that the Commission's broad discretion in fashioning sanctions in the public interest cannot be strictly cabined according to some mechanical formula. Nothing that we say suggests in the slightest that the Commission does not enjoy wide latitude in fashioning appropriate sanctions; such latitude is inherent in the Commission's broad grant of power from Congress, and is confirmed by such teachings as the Supreme Court's decision in *Butz*.

A closing observation is in order: Nothing that we have said today should suggest any intent on our part to intrude into the domain of the previous litigation between these parties in the Tenth Circuit. Petitioners stand condemned for serious violations of the securities laws, and we have held today that it is entirely appropriate and lawful for the SEC to carry out is statutory responsibilities in crafting a suitable and appropriate sanction in response to those violations.

But the Commission must do more than say, in effect, petitioners are bad and must be punished. Petitioners do not stand alone; they are, alas, only two in a long line of enterprises and individuals who have seen fit to conduct themselves in violation of the law of the land. It is because of the SEC's experience in dealing with such unhappy matters that it has the sensitive function, ordained by Congress, of deciding petitioners' fate. In this setting the commission is not simply rendering a policy judgement; nor is it simply regulating the securities markets; it is, rather, singling out and directly affecting the livelihood of one commercial enterprise and terminating (possibly forever) the professional career of the firm's founder. Faced with a task of such gravity, the Commission must craft with care.

For the foregoing reasons, the order of the Commission is vacated and the case is remanded for further proceedings consistent with this opinion.

IT IS SO ORDERED.

The main thrust of both *Dimension* and *Blinder* is that regulating agencies are to be held accountable under basic constitutional principles. It would, of course, be naive to expect that all regulatory agency overreaching could be both recognized and rectified; nevertheless, the argument that regulatory agencies in the United States are "fourth branch" constitutional outlaws is simply not supportable.[2]

---

[2] One of the best (brief) pieces on regulatory agency authority, accountability, and the Constitution can be found in 103 *Harvard Law Review* pp. 279-90 (1989). The discussion there arises out of the case of *Mistretta* v. *U.S.*, 109 S. Ct. 647 (1989), involving the U.S. Sentencing Commission. The issue in *Mistretta* came down to whether any commingling of the three central branch powers must be unconstitutional (the "formalist" approach), or whether constitutionality is determined on the basis of whether or not, on balance, an agency authority's infringements on the core functions of one branch are outweighed by the gains from the challenged delegation (the "functional" approach). The Supreme Court has used both approaches on different occasions. The first Gramm-Rudman law case, *Bowshar* v. *Synar*, 478 U.S. 714 (1986), is an example of the formalist approach. The White House tapes case, *The United States* v. *Nixon*, 94 S.Ct. 3090 (1974), is an example of the functionalist approach. And on the issue of impartial administrative agency judging, see *1616 Second Avenue Restaurant* v. *New York State Liquor Authority*, 551 N.Y.S. 2d 461 (1990). This case held that even the mere appearance of having prejudged a case disqualifies an administrative official from participating in an administrative decision.

A major constitutional issue has apparently avoided court scrutiny. It involved the authority of the Executive Branch to revise regulations issued by administrative agencies under congressional enabling legislation. *The White House Council on Competitiveness*, headed by then Vice President Quayle, had been accused of secretly deciding which regulation would be changed in what way as it determined "efficiency." See P.G. Hilts, "At Heart of Debate on Quayle Council: Who Controls Federal Regulation?" *The New York Times* (December 16, 1991). The 1992 elections rendered such issues moot.

Finally, in the wake of airline failures in the United States in the 1990s, one might want to look further into the regulatory history of the airline industry (deregulation). See L. Uchitelle, "Off Course," *The New York Times Magazine* (September 1, 1991) and E. R. Beauvais, "For Competition in the Air, Bring Back Anti-Trust," *The Wall Street Journal* (February 4, 1992).

IN LIEU OF THE PHILOSOPHER'S STONE

We might want to think about parties at interest and value-weighting with regard to an issue like this:

In March 1992, the Bush administration decided that high regulatory cost reduced disposable income and that this had adverse health consequences. The White House regulatory chief, in fact, blocked a Department of Labor (DOL) proposal to expand regulations limiting workplace exposure to a group of toxic chemicals. His argument: Each $7.5 million of regulatory expenses could result in one additional death from lowered incomes. And since the DOL-proposed regulations could cost $163 million, between 8 and 14 more people would die than would be saved by reducing worker exposure to the regulated toxic substances.

This executive decision raises the issue of "risk analysis" in connection with issuing regulations. The world of risk analysis and regulation has been referred to as "bizarre" and described by one journalist thusly: "Risk analysis begins with scientific studies, usually performed by academics or government agencies, and sometimes are incomplete or disputed. The data from the studies are then run through computer models of bewildering complexity, which produce results of implausible precision."

If, as is very often the case, risk analysis carries more risk than acceptable analysis, what should ethically conscious regulators do in order to come to a right decision (i.e., promulgate a good regulation)?

Please do not try to argue that there is no such thing as a good regulation in the first place. That puts you in the position of having to argue with other people who want to defend the equally senseless position that there is no such thing as a bad one.

Congress, for better or worse, decides policy (passes enabling legislation), but that still leaves room for a lot of filling in.

Try to reduce to writing, if you can, a few general rules for promulgating good regulations. Whose interests should be considered, and how are they to be weighted when they are competing? Naturally there will be times when the clearly measurable costs of the regulation will be so high (or low) that you have a sensible answer staring you in the face. But when science and math just don't do it (for a really conscientious person), then what?

Government administrators face that issue all the time. Most business managers (and lawyers and accountants and lots of others) have to live with the results. Do you have some clear ideas on how to make things better?

7

Regulating
Financial Markets

Commercial Banking

COMING UP IN THIS CHAPTER

This chapter and the one following it, are the two longest in this book. They concentrate specifically on the U.S. domestic financial system, and on its relationship with the international financial system as a whole.

Commercial banking (as set apart, for the moment, from investment banking) is the cornerstone of America's financial system. How it is set up and how it operates are matters not only of enormous economic significance but also of legal, political, social, and ethical significance. How American banking fares determines in some consequential degree how *every* American citizen fares—as well as a sizable number of people living in other nations.

What we will attempt to do here is examine the structure and function of commercial banking with an eye to fulfilling the mandate we set up for ourselves in the Foreword: to determine in a real-world context whether there are weaknesses or failures in the banking system that result from its operations; to focus clearly upon key ethical, legal, and public-policy perspectives pertaining to such weaknesses and failures; and to suggest some creative, just, and productive possible steps in the direction of adding strength and fairness to the commercial banking system in the United States.

Section I provides general background on the development of U.S. banking, with an emphasis on banking and bank legislation from the 1920s to the 1980s. We look particularly at the tools for regulation, and at how well they do or don't work in practice. We examine and discuss market activity and regulation in the context of several key issues: deposit insurance, S&Ls, and the scope of commercial banking with a particular emphasis on competition and the related *Glass-Steagall* and interstate banking areas. Since the commercial/investment bank nexus has been assiduously avoided by the Congress, the Federal Reserve Board has had to face up to existing restrictive law. The board's very important Citibank/J.P. Morgan/Banker's Trust Order is included for you to read—carefully—and to ponder, not only for what it says about the allowable commercial/investment banking mix (economics and finance), but also for what it says about legislature/policy responsibility (ethics). The dissent is most instructive.

Section II provides general background on mid-twentieth-century to present-day developments in international commercial banking. We look at Euromarkets, international banking myopia, less-developed country debt, and at Europe 92 and what it might mean to the United States and the world financial markets. We examine, as well, the issue of regional versus international free trade.

Section III examines possible regulatory changes in the areas of deposit insurance, the resolution of bank failures, and the overarching issue of expanding competition and level playing fields.

Throughout the chapter, keep your eye on the ever-present question: What is, and what *ought* to be, the relationship between all this banking market activity and banking market players—and the body politic within which they operate?

I. COMMERCIAL BANKING: DOMESTIC

A. A General Regulatory (and Deregulatory) Overview

The United States of America is unique in the banking area in several ways. With more than 11,500 commercial banks, some 2,500 savings institutions, and approximately 14,000 credit unions, we have more existing depository units than any other nation in the world. With numbers like that, bank failures might well be expected. And, at least since 1890, we have always had our share of these. Two big questions are: What is the point at which such failures can no longer be tolerated by the system? And what exactly do we do then, and why?

No one can fully explain why our banking system has come to contain so many players. Populism (limit the power of each of those greedy people), rugged individualism, the entrepreneurial spirit, and, certainly, geographical size have each contributed to the phenomenon.

But whatever the reasons, the results are clear. Entry into the market has been relatively easy, and the number of institutions U.S. regulators must oversee has become truly awesome.

We begin our review of banking regulation with the 1920s, the Stock Market disaster, and the desperate days of the 1930s. Following the great crash of 1929, a good deal was made (politically) of the fact that banks had, in the previous decade, exercised their power to deal in stocks, bonds, and customer deposits all at the same time. The charge was that banks had done that in a pernicious fashion, thus contributing to financial collapse. Pundits are still debating the factual accuracy of charges against the banks; however, there is no arguing about the national mood at the time and the resultant legislation and regulation.

The Banking Acts of 1933 and 1935 contained at least six important features. They:

- Prohibited paying interest on checking accounts.
- Gave the Federal Reserve (established in 1913 by the Federal Reserve Act, 12 U.S.C.; ch. 6) power to impose interest-rate ceilings on time deposits. The Federal Reserve (Fed) implemented this enabling law (controlled bank interest rates) by means of its Regulation Q.
- Established the Federal Deposit Insurance Corporation (FDIC).
- Gave the Fed Board of Governors power to set reserve requirements for banks and to set stock margin requirements.
- Prohibited interstate banking except by consent of the state or states involved (this was in accordance with a 1927 law, The McFadden Act).
- Banned commercial bank participation in the investment banking business, and banned investment banks from the commercial banking business: The Glass-Steagall Act provisions.

It should be noted that when Federal Deposit Insurance went into effect in 1934, the per account per bank limit was $2,500. There was no denying the need to avoid, in the future, the kind of agony suffered by tens of thousands of families whose life savings had disappeared in the massive bank failures of the previous several years. Nevertheless, on the third day of the "bank holiday" of March 1933, a prescient President Franklin Roosevelt, stated:

> [as to] guaranteeing bank deposits. . . the general underlying thought behind the use of the word "guarantee". . . is that you guarantee bad banks as well as good banks. The minute the government starts to do that the government runs into a probable

loss. . . . We do not wish to make the United States Government liable for the mistakes and errors of individual banks, and put a premium on unsound banking in the future.[1]

Following the legislation of, and gradual recovery from, the 1930s, to well up into the 1960s, the economic environment for depository institutions was relatively stable. The regulatory mandate to assure a safe, sound, and dependable banking system, coupled with the value accruing to banks from protection of the industry and from government guarantees, encouraged *reasonable* risk-taking by intermediaries, public confidence, and economic growth.

Nevertheless, regulatory structures and functions, prior to emergency banking legislation adopted in 1989, were, to put it charitably, a tangled web. Figure 7-1 lists ten regulatory functions and five regulators, and does not include individual state-based regulation. While federally chartered (national) banks are, by and large, the biggest U.S. banks, a more numerous portion (more than 60 percent) of all U.S. banks are, in fact, state chartered and subject to state regulation in addition to Federal Reserve and FDIC oversight when indicated.

Now a special word on savings and loan institutions (S&Ls). Prior to 1932, thrift institutions were strictly under state control. But with the Great Depression, in order to help a rapidly shrinking home mortgage lending industry, the Congress passed the Federal Home Loan Bank Act of 1932. The act created a dozen Federal Home Loan Banks with a Federal Home Loan Bank Board to act as their supervisory agent. Then, in 1933, the Home Owners Loan Act provided for the chartering and regulation of federal S&Ls. And following naturally, in 1934, the National Housing Act created a deposit insurance fund for S&Ls, namely the Federal Savings and Loan Insurance Corporation (FSLIC, now deceased).

It is interesting to contemplate that the National Housing Act set a primary reserve fund goal of 5 percent of insured deposits for the FSLIC, which was never met. Its primary reserve fund never exceeded 2 percent. And, given deposit insurance ascending levels of per account coverage, from $2,500 up to $15,000, then $20,000, $40,000 and the present $100,000, together with the fact of enormous deposit growth, and borrowing access to the U.S. Treasury, plus legislated reductions in deposit insurance rates—it seems fair to say that the FSLIC (and the FDIC) faced an unreasonable risk of insolvency for a good many years.[2]

---

[1] Quote from FDR's first presidential news conference. Cited in B. Ely, "Federal Deposit Insurance Is Beyond Any Fix or Reform," *American Banker*, August 27-28, 1990.

[2] Interesting historical information on S&Ls is contained in M. Dotsey and A. Kuprianov, "Reforming Deposit Insurance: Lessons from the Savings and Loan Crisis," *Economic Review*, FRB of Richmond (March/April 1990), pp. 10-19.

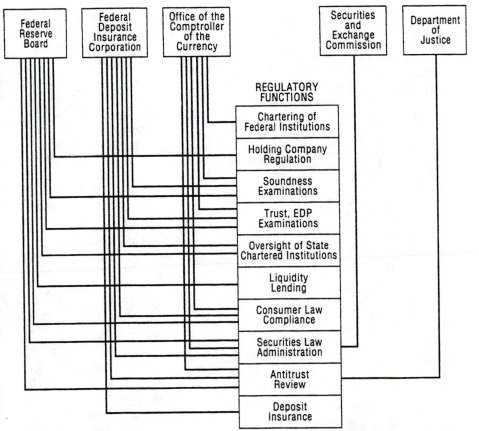

FIGURE 7.1 The Tangled Web of U.S. Bank Regulation ("The Time Bomb Ticks Away," *Financial Times*, April 6, 1988).

Rising inflation and high interest rates in the late 1960s and the 1970s found the S&Ls with nondiversified, basically long-term, fixed-rate, mortgage portfolios. As rates they had to pay depositors shot past their mortgage rates of return, the S&Ls floundered, and by the beginning of the decade of the 1980s, S&Ls were beginning to sink. FSLIC-insured S&Ls lost almost $9 billion in 1981 and 1982 alone, years in which their net operating income totalled $16 billion.[3]

Would-be home owners, builders, and various related supporting groups did exactly what American interest groups angered at regulations generally do: They took their complaints to Washington. The word they carried this time was: *deregulation.* The result was the Depository Insti-

---

[3] Ibid., p. 11.

tutions Deregulation and Monetary Control Act of 1980 (DIDMCA), and the Depository Institutions Act of 1982 (the Garn-St. Germaine Act).

These laws focused on S&Ls but, in several key particulars, they also affected commercial banks. Some examples of the provisions of the two laws were that they:

- permitted federal thrifts (S&Ls) to offer trust services and credit cards and, more important, to diversify their portfolios by offering nonmortgage consumer loans and commercial real estate loans, and allowed the thrifts to invest in corporate debt securities
- permitted *all* depository institutions to offer personal NOW accounts and money market deposit accounts without a ceiling rate
- established a federal committee to set deposit ceilings while, at the same time, supervising an orderly six-year phaseout (1980–1986) for them. Regulation Q depository interest rate ceilings were on their way out.

It should be obvious by now that the operation of financial markets in the United States has been, is, and will forever be linked to the operation of law. In this sense, financial markets are not "free," nor are they, like some marvelous new kitchen oven, self-cleansing at all times. This is not to say that "the law," with which markets continually cohabit, is always insightful, sensible, or efficient. All of which seems to suggest that markets and law, like other cohabitants, would do well to listen to, understand, be sympathetic to, and compromise constructively with one another.

Unfortunately (we say authoritatively with hindsight), neither market-oriented banker petitioners and their friends (read lobbyists and pressure groups) nor congressional lawmakers (read politicians) seemed able to come to terms with a few key realities existing in the early 1980s:

- *The economic environment was demonstrably unstable.* Inflation jumped from 6 percent to 14 percent between 1970 and 1980. During that time, the Regulation Q ceiling rate for bank interest rose from 4 percent to just under 6 percent. Market interest rates ballooned from 4 percent to 15 percent.
- *Competition and technology were eroding the protected position of banks.* By 1980, technology was promoting large-scale, fast-track financial transactions while at the same time computer processing costs were falling. Although banks could access this technology, so could other intermediaries. Investment bank cash management accounts, for example, absorbed billions of depository dollars. Additionally, larger corporations used investment banks to issue their own paper rather than borrow from

commercial banks. S&Ls, meanwhile, saw their market challenged by a security-backed secondary mortgage market.

- *The value of the bank franchise was diminishing.* In the face of competition (disintermediation), bankers could conclude that they had less of an asset to protect. This fact, coupled with the continued existence of deposit insurance guarantees, could point some bankers down the path of excessive risk-taking.

- *The regulator load was increasing.* Bank regulators who relied on stable environments, protected positions, and franchise value to encourage compliance were now in danger of losing an implicit asset of their own, and thus of having to assume a far heavier oversight burden.

This was not exactly the time, one might surmise, to do what the banking community and lawmakers actually did: Deregulate to a tremendous extent without adding in any way to the oversight function.[4]

B. The Tools of Banking Regulation

Ultimately, the test of any set of tools is whether they are complementary, and whether they are being used to accomplish clearly thought-out (nonconflicting) goals. Certainly one must be sure that each tool is sound and fit to undertake and perform the tasks it is assigned. Banking regulation failed all the tests in the case of the S&Ls, and regulation also failed to obtain sufficiently high grades in the commercial banking area. Before we look at just how they worked we might list the four major tools of bank regulation:

- *Bank capital requirements;*
- *On site examination and inspections;*
- Both of the above at the bank holding company, as well as the individual bank level;
- (as an ancillary tool) market force monitoring; i.e., depositor and securities market-corrective actions.

1. Capital Requirements

Three basic levels of bank capital are to be considered here: The first is *Tier 1 capital*, which consists mainly of common equity and perpetual preferred stock. Regulator capital ratios here are based upon Tier 1

---

[4] For a full exposition of these phenomena, the reader can refer to two fine sources from the same author: L.J. White, *The S&L Debacle: Public Policy Lessons for Bank and Thrift Regulation* (New York: Oxford University Press, 1991, chap. 5), and "On the Measurement of Bank Capital," *Journal of Retail Banking* (Summer 1991).

capital as a percentage of risk-weighted assets. *Tier 2 capital* consists of supplementary capital elements, limited-life preferred stock and subordinated debt, and loan loss reserves up to certain limits. Regulator capital ratios here are based upon Tier 2 capital as a percentage of unweighted assets. *Total capital*, (Tier 1 plus Tier 2) as a percentage of risk- weighted assets is the third and final regulator capital ratio. The regulator's ability to require specific numerical ratios (e.g., Tier 1 capital must amount to at least 4 percent of risk-weighted assets) is the heart of the capital requirement tool.[5]

Risk-weighting refers to regulator (examiner) assessment of assets and off-balance sheet items on the basis of broad judgments of relative credit risk. Each item is multiplied by the appropriate regulator-set risk-weight to arrive at the credit-equivalent amount. Cash as an asset, for example, would carry a risk-weight of zero (and result in no diminution of the face amount of the asset). Commercial real estate loans, on the other hand, would be assigned a very high percent (much diminishing the face amount of the asset). Before being risk-weighted, *off-balance sheet items* are also multiplied by a credit conversion factor, and only then by the designated risk factor. For example, an outstanding long-term loan commitment to a private corporation would have a regulator-set conversion factor—say 50 percent—applied *before* the risk-weighted assessment percent is called into play.[6]

2. On-site Examination and Inspection

There is little doubt but that "on-site examinations remain the cornerstone of [the Fed] supervisory program."[7] They assist the regulators to assess bank management effectiveness, risk-control systems, internal operating practices, and capital adequacy. The standard procedure for on-site examination of individual banks is referred to as the CAMEL ratings system. CAMEL refers to capital adequacy, asset quality, management, earnings, and liquidity. Similar ratings, when applied to bank holding companies, are referred to, collectively, as BOPEC: bank subsidiaries, other subsidiaries, parent, earnings, and capital adequacy. A composite rating number is arrived at when the examination is fully completed,

---

[5] See, generally A.D. Brenner, J.V. Duca, and M.M. McLaughlin, "Recent Developments Affecting the Profitability and Practices of Commercial Banks," *Federal Reserve Bulletin* (July 1991).

[6] See M.C. Alfriend, "International Risk Based Capital Standard: History and Explanation," *Economic Review* of the FRB of Richmond (November/December 1988) pp. 30-31. See also: "Box 1: Selected Asset Categories and Risk Weights under the Risk-Based Capital Standards," *Economic Review* of the FRB of San Francisco, Number 3, 1992 at page 56.

[7] M. Johnson, September 19, 1989, statement before a congressional committee, *Federal Reserve Bulletin* (November 1989), p. 743.

and it determines whether the bank is then placed on the endangered list, issued orders to shape up in certain areas, or maybe, even congratulated.

Bank holding company (BHC) examinations are crucial in light of the growth of this particular phenomenon. A BHC has the capacity to control a good many subsidiaries, not all of them in the commercial banking business. Some BHC nonbanking operations are financial in nature (e.g., insurance). But many subsidiaries conduct a variety of nonfinancial businesses, some 275 or so in number by published account, in such areas as animal husbandry and water supply.[8] *As of 1988, there were more than 1,400 BHCs operating in the United States, some of them owning one or two banking organizations. A total of 284 of them, however, controlled $2.36 trillion of assets, or 87 percent of the total of $2.72 trillion under BHC control.*[9] *Thorough, careful on-site examination and inspection of the BHC itself—apart from its individual banks—would appear to be a matter of great importance.*

3. Bank Monitoring by the Market

It would seem to make good sense (theoretically) to assume that risk-averse depositors and investors—as well as the securities markets—would single out the weak and faltering banks and take (or recommend that others take) their business elsewhere. That is the way competitive markets assure efficiency. Thus the market should serve as an ancillary regulator.

C. Some Observations of the Tools at Work

1. Capital Requirements

The Federal Reserve has always required some sort of capital adequacy measure. It has, however, changed its determinants many times since 1945. But the United States, Belgium, Canada, France, Germany, Italy, Japan, the Netherlands, Sweden, the United Kingdom, Switzerland, and Luxembourg have been working together for some time on acceptable international capital adequacy measures. Such measures were set down as *the Basle Accord,* and were adopted by all these nations in December 1988. This agreement takes full cognizance of two basic world banking needs in an era of almost borderless capital mobility and competition. First, it aims at assuring a safe and sound international banking system

---

[8] J.N. Lian and D.T. Savage, "The Nonbank Activities of Bank Holding Corporations," *Federal Reserve Bulletin (May 1990),* p. 280.

[9] Ibid., p. 283. See, also, for more specific information on the 100 or so major BHCs that belong to the Association of Bank Holding Companies: Bank Holding Company Facts (Spring 1990), Washington D.C. The Spring 1989 edition states that all BHCs in the United States held 90.79 percent of all domestic banking deposits in the nation at that time.

and, second, at assuring a level playing field for all banks in the highly competitive international banking market. Led by the Bank of England and the U.S. Federal Reserve, representatives of the dozen nations cited above hammered out the agreement, by committee, and under the auspices of the Swiss-based Basle Bank for International Settlements (BIS).

The central bank of the United States (the Federal Reserve, or simply the Fed) has, of course, adopted the Basle Accord. It has made the Basle risk-based capital standards applicable to *all* U.S. banks, not just international banks, which is all the accord requires. Moreover, the Fed has determined that it will apply a similar risk-based ratio framework to BHCs on a consolidated basis.

Under the Basle Accord (sometimes loosely referred to as the BIS Accord), there exist definitions for Tier 1, Tier 2 and combined capital, and four risk weights for assets and off-balance sheet items (0, 20, 50, and 100 percent). The following percentages are mandated for all international banks (to be enforced by each nation's central bank): An 8 percent overall risk-based capital ratio, of which at least 4 percent must come from Tier 1, by year-end 1992.[10]

An argument to the effect that the Basle Accord represents a step forward in international banking cooperation and is a laudable contribution to international financial system safety can and should be made. This is quite different, however, from an argument that the Basle Accord has established a fully reliable, fail-safe, capital-standard framework. *That* argument would be impossible to support. Consider these three matters:

- The Basle Accord focuses on minimum capital requirements related to credit risk embodied in the bank's assets and off-balance sheet instruments. The accord does *not* deal with other key risks in international banking (e.g., interest rate risk, a serious and complex matter, for which no adequate, broadly accepted formula yet exists).[11] Among other things, this situation could motivate banks to substitute interest rate risk for credit risk in

---

[10] A good basic review of the Basle Accord can be found in M.C. Alfriend, note 6, *supra*. Three updates on the results of the Basle Accord are: D. Fairlamb, "How the Capital Quest Is Reshaping Banking," *Institutional Investor* (March 1991); C. Gewirtz, "The Great BIS Capital Standard Stretchout?" *The International Economy* (March/April 1991); M.W. Brauchlin, "Japan's Big Banks Slash Assets in Rush to Comply with New Capital-Ratio Rule," *The Wall Street Journal* (May 5, 1991). A recent broad-view perspective, including the political, is E.B. Kapsstein, *Supervising International Banks: Origins and Implications of the Basle Accord: Essays in International Finance* No. 185, December 1991 (Department of Economics, Princeton University, Princeton, N.J.).

[11] See J.V. Haupt and J.A. Embersit, "A Method for Evaluating Interest Rate Risk in Commercial Banks," *Federal Reserve Bulletin* (August 1991). The Basle Committee is now working on this area. Some other uncovered areas: liquidity, position, mismatch, and netting risks. See also J.A. Neuberger, "Risk-Based Capital Standards and Bank Portfolios," FRB San Francisco, *Weekly Letter* Number 92-02 (January 10, 1992).

structuring their balance sheets. When one considers that mortgage-backed securities made up 17 percent of the aggregate securities portfolio of U.S. commercial banks at year-end 1988, and 35 percent by early 1991 (6.5 percent of total banking assets) one might suspect that this is already happening.[12]

- Most international banks headquartered outside the United States and Japan are empowered now to engage fully in securities activities at home and abroad (and U.S. and Japanese banks abroad). There are no accepted, international capital or other regulatory standards in the securities area. We shall return to this subject again.

- There are serious domestic (and, subsequently, international) questions to be pursued in the area of *asset evaluation*. Risk-weighting loses its true value if the asset to be weighted is inefficiently—or even dishonestly—priced to begin with. This has proven to be a matter of serious consequence in the United States. Some would argue that the entire issue involves nothing more than coming to an agreement on "realistic accounting procedures." Others might argue that "realistic accounting" has all too often proved to be a euphemism for "hiding the truth," with the result being to empty taxpayers' pockets.

How to value real estate is an important item here. The major issue is whether regulations should require banks to be subject to market value accounting (MVA). Bankers argue that short-term problems in real estate cannot be evaluated on a moment-in-time basis, that the proper evaluation is what their property will be worth when the market recovers. *Now* is never the time to set lower values (take large write-offs) if now is in hard times. Regulators argue that riding out problems on the wings of an accountant has not proven beneficial to the health of the banking system (or the public).

There appears to be a difference between "marking-to-market" and MVA. The former represents today's going price; the latter, a realistic reflection of what the median term value of the loan (collateral) is likely to be. Bankers argue that MVA is imprecise and leads to overly tight lending practices and illiquidity. Regulators argue that unrealistic lender asset valuations will continue to result in disastrous credit evaluation practices and a host of other banking ills that threaten the entire system.[13]

---

[12] Haupt and Embersit, *supra*, pp. 625-26.

[13] See D.B. Hilder, "Property Problem: As Loans Sour, Banks and Regulators Argue How to Value Realty," *The Wall Street Journal (December 13, 1990)*. Accounting rules that allow banks to report loans at original value, particularly real estate loans, make a big bank bailout "almost inevitable" according to P.J. Vaughan and E.W. Hill, *Banking on the Brink: The Troubled Future of American Finance* (Washington, D.C.: Washington Post Co. Briefing Books, 1992).

Certainly there are honest financial market participant differences of opinion that need to be resolved. However, there is evidence that, all too often, less-than-ethical banking behavior has played a consequential part in asset *mis*calculation and resultant banking woes.

And the asset evaluation problem, in its economic complexity and in its ethical perspective, is not confined by any means to the United States of America.

Risk-based capital requirement considerations have not been moved up to the "resolved" level simply because the Basle Accord exists.

2. On-site Examination and Inspection

Here we seem to be involved with both the quantitative and qualitative aspects of these key tools.

The argument has long been advanced that both federal and state bank examiners are too few in number, and that they are sometimes not up to the difficult task of evaluation and analysis in a time of exploding technology and proliferation of banking activity under the direction and control of skilled (and, from time to time, devious) banking personnel.[14] Former Fed Vice Chairman Manuel H. Johnson, when he indicated quite clearly the immense importance of on-site examinations to the Fed's supervisory program, also stated that:

> Conditions of the past several years, in both the banking and thrift industries, have imposed significant pressures on our field examination resources.[15]

E. Gerald Corrigan, president of the Federal Reserve Bank of New York, told the Senate Committee on Banking, Housing and Urban Affairs that

> examinations can only be as good as the examiners. I am proud of [mine] and I know that they are damn good. . . . But let's be realistic. The Federal Reserve Bank of New York employs 206 bank examiners whose average tenure is eight years and whose average salary is about $50,000. But these 200 individuals [and their staffs] are directly responsible for inspections of seven of the fifteen largest bank holding companies in the country with aggregate assets of more than $650 billion; federal examinations of five of the ten largest banks in the United States. . . as well as standby

---

[14] See J. Bussey and C. Ansberry, "Ailing Watchdogs: State Bank Examiners Often Lack Numbers and Skills to Do Work," *The Wall Street Journal* (July 16, 1985); M. Langley, "Federal Examiners Are Drawing Fire," *The Wall Street Journal* (July 16, 1985).

[15] See note 7, *supra*.

or back-up examination authority for about 250 foreign banking institutions operating in New York. . . .

What I am suggesting, of course, is that the demands on the bank examination process, regionally and nationally—a power that I regard as the bedrock of the overall supervisory process—are enormous. . . . [T]he Congress must recognize that to get it right will entail added resources of not inconsequential dimensions. . . .[16]

Mr. Corrigan is referring, with justifiable pride, to perhaps the most sophisticated core of bank examiners in the nation. Problems of expertise, salary, tenure, and the like take on even more significance when one considers, beyond the federal level, the very real problems facing the 50 *state* bank supervisory authorities.

There is, quite clearly, a rather disturbing international flavor to the bank supervisory process that includes, a least to some degree, the site-examination process. Until very recently, fundamental regulatory responsibility for the offices of foreign banks was placed upon state bank examiners. And as one journalist, writing in connection with the mid-1991 Bank of Credit Commerce International scandal (BCCI), put it rather wryly, their "abilities and resources vary widely."[17]

BCCI was able to avoid detection before its meltdown—and the loss of billions of dollars—by conveniently avoiding home-country regulation. The method used was to avoid having any home country at all, and thus never having to explain its bizarre and scandalous lending and borrowing procedures.[18] The authority for, and the tools to conduct, on-site examinations *in the hands of the central authority* is bound to be key to any resolution of the problems of adequate control of foreign banks, in any country.

In the United States one might ask: Given seemingly threadbare purses, where on the priority scale should added funds for capable bank examiners be placed on the state and federal levels? Apart from obvious financial market-focused decisions, is there a "fairness" (ethical) dimen-

---

[16] Corrigan statement of May 15, 1991, contained in the *Federal Reserve Bulletin (July 1991), p. 559.* An interesting issue regarding bank examinations is whether "independent" commercial auditors have any role to play. L. Berton, *"Give Independent Bank Auditors Some Real Independence," The Wall Street Journal* (June 6, 1991). It is encouraging to note that on September 14, 1992, the Fed announced the adoption of a joint agreement with the Conference of State Bank Supervisors to encourage joint efforts: *Federal Reserve Bulletin* (November 1992), p. 834.

[17] J. Gerth, "Scandal Reveals Holes in Rules for Foreign Banks," *The New York Times* (July 7, 1991).

[18] For a reader-friendly, if simplistic, account of the BCCI fiasco, see J. Beaty and S.C. Gwynne, "The Dirtiest Bank of Them All," *Time Magazine* (cover story, July 29, 1991). For recent regulatory response to BCCI and corresponding updated material, see Section III, *infra* on the new Federal Deposit Insurance Corporation Improvement Act of 1991.

sion involved here? Should the nature, and reach, of the banking system influence your answer?

3. Bank Monitoring by the Market

Here there would seem to be clear market failure in two respects:

- *Securities markets,* when stock prices over a substantial period of time are coordinated with contemporaneous, real-world banking problems, demonstrate a lack of capacity to evaluate ongoing banking exposure and risk.[19] Like the calvary in a western movie, the market will surely arrive at the proper place, but by the time it does will the pioneers not only have bet, but already lost, their lives?

- *Bank depositors* are hardly likely to be of much help in monitoring the financial health of their banks. For one thing, they lack motivation (they are insured). For another, they lack sophistication. As a Fed governor put it once, the monitoring task doesn't belong with depositors in the first place:

  Let me illustrate an analogue. I would not want the transportation department, instead of hiring engineers to conduct inspections, to put up signs at every bridge saying "cross at your own risk."[20]

A good deal of the material we have examined in banking thus far would seem to indicate that one reason for market failure in the field, generally, has to be the deposit insurance system. We shall give that matter some space of its own.

D. The Deposit Insurance Issue: An Overview

Deposit insurance was introduced in the Great Depression years of 1932–1933, which were characterized, in terms of the financial system, by a national banking panic. By the end of 1933, one-half of all the U.S. banks that had been in existence in 1920 were gone (but not forgotten). The federal solution for preventing massive runs of dollars into mattresses and gold was to make the government of the United States a guarantor, within certain quantitative limits, of the liabilities of private bankers. The medium for this transaction was the Federal Deposit Insurance Corpora-

---

[19] R.E. Randell, "Can the Market Evaluate Asset Quality Exposure in Banks?" *New England Economic Review* (July/August 1989). The author's researched answer was a resounding "no!"

[20] From an address by Wayne Angell to the Banking Conference of the Federal Reserve Bank of Atlanta, March 19, 1991. "Rules, Risk and Reform: A Proposal for the Next Decade," p. 5.

tion (FDIC), which came into being on January 1, 1934, with coverage set at $2,500 per depositor per bank.

President Franklin Roosevelt was not the only one convinced at the time that the federal insurance plan placed the nation firmly between the rock and a very hard place. The American Bankers Association felt that

> the plan is inherently fallacious. . . one of these plausible, but deceptive, human plans that in actual application only serve to render worse the very evils they seek to cure.[21]

FDIC coverage rose to $5,000 in 1934, to $10,000 in 1950, $20,000 in 1969, $40,000 in 1974, and $100,000 in 1980. The U.S. Treasury and Federal Reserve banks put up $289 million as the original capital of the FDIC. Banks ever since have paid premiums on their insured deposits into the FDIC (and the FSLIC).

Bank premiums prior to 1992 had always been flat and not risk inclusive (i.e., annual premiums paid into the federal insurer were the same for all banks across the board—a flat rate per dollar of insured deposits). The rate was not adjusted for bank size (assets), risk, or any other factor. These premiums cover insurance on some $2 trillion of deposits in U.S. commercial banks alone (and they are still but lightly risk-weighted).

Such a system was the very antithesis of the commercial insurance business, where the failure to account for varying risk levels and to assess varying related premiums can lead to insolvency—and seems to have done so in America in the early 1990s.

An interesting question is why, if the federal deposit insurance system was a disaster waiting to happen, did the disaster not occur during the first half century of the insurance coverage? Perhaps ethical behavior wasn't fully put to the test in the financial system during that time, and when it was the system failed. And there is no doubt that a similar failure can be ascribed to the political and legal systems.

To put an argument to that effect in context, we need to consider seriously the *moral link* between deposit insurance and banking. What banks obtained with the coming of the FDIC—and later the Federal Savings and Loan Insurance Corporation, or FSLIC—was the priceless ingredient of *public trust*. It seems fair to say that from the late 1930s to the 1980s, the public's trust, first in the FDIC-FSLIC, came to connect with the banks themselves, as well as the government. And that trust, together

---

[21] "The Guaranty of Bank Deposits," Economic Policy Commission, American Bankers Association, 1933, p. 43. FDR's concern is cited at note 1, *supra*. An excellent historical analysis of the development of Federal Deposit Insurance is M.D. Flood, "The Great Deposit Insurance Debate," *Federal Reserve Bank of St. Louis* (July/August 1992), pp. 51-72.

with an exclusive intermediation franchise in clearly important areas, amounted to a major implicit asset for the banks.

The issue now raised is: What was the consideration (the *quid pro quo*) banks were expected to give in return? And to whom, in fact, was this "consideration" owed?

We think it clear that the *quid pro quo* owed by each and every insured and protected bank was a very high duty of care and responsibility to assure the safety and soundness of the system that sustained it. And this duty of care ran, ultimately, to the taxpaying public, which not only relied upon the integrity of the system but which, in actuality, stood behind it as its ultimate "deep pocket."

To carry the full import of this bank duty a necessary step further, we refer the reader back to Chapter 5 and the fiduciary relationship. The key fiduciary duty of each bank director and officer to the bank would be to carry out all of his or her agent functions in such a way as to guarantee the inviolability of this basic duty. While forwarding the best interest of the bank's shareholders would be an important part of assuring bank strength, there can be no doubt that shareholders had to come second to a bank officer and director fiduciary duty to the bank itself—to assure that it honored its primary obligation (and, thus, assured its survival).

We would put a name to this very high duty of care and responsibility. We would call it: *public stewardship*.

Banks (and bankers) were now to engage in risk-taking, not in the usual entrepreneurial sense, but as *caretakers of the public interest*. This is not to say that they had no duty to their shareholders arising out of their fiduciary duty to the bank (shareholders, by the way, who also benefitted from government/taxpayer largesse), nor an obligation never to undertake risk. No business could survive such strictures, and public stewardship in a democratic market society does not impose them. The requirement of public stewardship is that the steward bank's agent must conduct business while keeping in mind that his or her actions must always relate, in part, to the safety and soundness of the system. For the system is one upon which the entire citizenry relies for its financial security, and it is the citizenry upon which the steward relies for both consumer and insurer support.

A banker's propensity to take undue risks in the search for personal and shareholder profit (to some appreciable degree in reliance upon the existence of deposit insurance to bail him or her out) is described in the economic literature as "moral hazard." We hold that term in some disfavor, because it has an odd mechanical ring to it, almost as if it were, in fact, a professional's ethical escape clause. What we are actually relating to is human behavior below an acceptable ethical level, demanding scrutiny, and not to be eased off by the use of economic models or the lack of legislation.

Public stewardship seems to have been accepted by the overwhelming majority of American bankers through the 1970s, influenced no doubt by the value of the franchise. As we discussed earlier, volatile economic conditions produced many changes that led to serious competition in the financial intermediation business from investment banking and other groups as disparate as auto manufacturers, retail sales organizations, and even travel agencies. Fed in no small measure by computer-related technology as well as by oil shocks and other troubling economic conditions, the value of the banking franchise fell.[22]

Without doubt, bankers were required to be public stewards while many of those around them acted more like robber barons. That is a matter to be considered; however, it surely does not make the case for abolition of the public stewardship standard, and certainly not as long as the public bill for bailing bankers out continues to be due and payable.

We can now examine some specific examples of interplay among deposit insurance, banker, politician, regulation, and ethics.

E. The Matter of the S&Ls

Material on the S&L problem in America in the 1980s and 1990s is ubiquitous. There is no arguing the fact that America underwent a financial debacle of enormous proportions—probably a present value loss of at least 200 billion dollars.[23]

The disaster was not an unforseen occurrence. Published works of merit warned of impending crisis.[24] What, then, actually happened?

It should be noted at the outset that unlike the FDIC, the S&L insurer, FSLIC, was not set up as a separate operating entity. It was made a ward of the Federal Home Loan Bank Board (FHLBB), already charged with being the supervisory agent of a dozen Federal Home Loan banks. By 1950 the FSLIC/FHLBB had cut deposit insurance assessments for the

---

[22] An excellent review of the 1970s and early 1980s forces underlying financial innovation in the United States and their quantitative impact on the structure of depository markets and the like may be found in A. Broaddus, "Financial Innovation in the United States: Background, Current Status and Prospects," *Economic Review*, FRB of Richmond (January/February 1985). See also M.M. Lind, "The Impact of Deregulation and Environmental Forces Competition," in Friars and Gogel, eds. *The Financial Services Handbook* (New York: Wiley Interscience, 1987).

[23] Some 194 billion as of early 1993, given the request of the Clinton administration of March 1993 for 45 billion more. A. R. Karr, "Administration Raises Request for S&L Bailout," *The Wall Street Journal*, March 17, 1993.

[24] Edward J. Kane, *The Gathering Crisis in Federal Deposit Insurance*, (Cambridge, Mass.: MIT Press, 1985). See also, S.I. Greenbaum, "Deregulation of the Thrift Industry: A Prologue to International Problems and Risks," Reprint No. 84, Kellogg Graduate School of Management, Northwestern University, 1986.

S&Ls from 1/4 of 1 percent of total deposits to 1/12 of 1 percent, even though the insurance fund was well below the enabling legislation's called-for 5 percent coverage for all insured accounts. The argument for lowering the rates was that enhanced regulation and supervision would be enough to keep losses below the historical average.[25]

By 1980, Congress finally came to the conclusion that the interest rate squeeze on S&Ls, which were being forced to lend long (on fixed-rate mortgages) and borrow short (on fixed passbook liabilities), necessitated a broader view of the scope of the activities of S&Ls. It passed DIDMCA and Garn–St. Germaine. Now S&Ls were able to move ahead. By 1982, they could make commercial real estate loans, consumer loans, commercial loans, and even take equity positions in investment projects.

At the same time, regulators jettisoned the entire concept of enhanced regulation and supervision. Minimum capital requirements for thrifts were lowered in 1980 and 1982. Accounting rules were twisted and bent to avoid the reality of net-worth provisions. The number of supervisors and field examiners also fell.[26]

What happened here was that Congress and the S&L regulators took some accomplished riders off their horses, put them in 120-mile-an-hour sports cars, and pulled all the troopers off the highways. Then Congress began giving these vehicles away to some people who were unfit even to ride children's tricycles.

Public stewardship in too many cases gave way to excessive risk-taking, gross negligence, even outright felonious behavior. Some bankers could now see a possibly wondrous upside, and a downside that did not include disaster.

While many S&Ls were placing their bets, the politicians and regulators were hard at work, practicing *forbearance.* It does not do to refer to their activities under some general "moral hazard" heading. One must examine and judge specific behaviors.

Apart from the example of previously cited works,[27] several key articles by society's message bearers, the media, carried tidings of misbehavior. In January 1987, *The Wall Street Journal* began an article titled

---

[25] Dotsey and Kuprianov, note 2, *supra,* pp. 10–11.

[26] L.J. White, "Banking Deregulation and Consolidation: An Industrial Organization Perspective," paper presented at the Western Economic Association International Conference, Revised Draft, August 1991 (Stern School of Business of New York University) pp. 13-14. Professor White argues rather persuasively that a confusion of economic regulation and health-safety-environment legislation was at fault here. See also on this key point L.J. White, "A Cautionary Tale of Deregulation Gone Awry: The S&L Debacle," Leonard N. Stern School of Business, Department of Economics Paper (Mimeo) No. EC-92-1, January 1992.

[27] See note 24, *Supra.*

"Tricky Ledgers," with the lead sentence: "Accounting flim-flam and wishful thinking are pervading the financial system." The *Journal* went on:

> From the troubled Southwest to the nation's capital, government and banking officials are resorting to new extremes of. . . gimmickry to avoid facing up to huge losses on loans made by banks, thrifts and federal farm lenders. . . . [T]he Farm Credit System plans to keep two sets of books—one a rose-tinted version. . . and the U.S. government keeps open more than 100 insolvent savings and loan associations at the cost of $5 million a day. . . .
>
> Nonetheless, only the most bearish observers talk of a full-scale crisis. . . .
>
> George T. Gould, undersecretary of the Treasury, says the administration has [to] buy time with accounting gimmicks and other forms of loss deferral. . . . He concedes, however, that a government check "at the front end" could. . . be cheaper in the long run. And if agricultural and oil prices remain weak, he says, "None of this is going to work". . . .
>
> [Another government official] now says he sought. . . accounting changes because, without them, "it was clear that sooner or later we would need taxpayer money." Other officials characterize his [orders] to them as "Let us try some phoney-baloney accounting, or we can cause chaos."[28]

Of course, chaos came after the "phoney-baloney." And it could surely be argued that what happened with the S&Ls could be characterized not just as shoddy decision making, but as clearly unethical behavior. It led, among other things, to a savings and loan industry divided into two convergent parts,

> the living and the dead. This terminology portrays firms where enterprise-contributed capital has been lost, as soulless "zombie" institutions. Debt and equity claims against a zombie firm lose their natural link to the riskiness of the assets they support because [they] trade principally not on the [negative] earning power of the [zombies'] own resources but on the comfort given by FSLIC guarantees. . . .

---

[28] J. Bailey and C.F. McCoy, "Tricky Ledgers: To Hide Huge Losses, Financial Officials Use Accounting Gimmicks. . . But Few Expect Real Crisis," *The Wall Street Journal* (January 27, 1987).

. . . capital forbearance (by regulators) brings dead firms back to a malefic form of quasi-life in which they attack the living, turning the prey they feed on to zombies, too. . . [they] do this by sucking deposits away from their competitors by offering high interest rates and bidding down loan rates on high risk projects. This squeezes profit margins, and the proliferation of weak competitors and risky positions ultimately raises deposit insurance premiums for everyone.[29]

There seems to be little doubt that several key factors helped precipitate the S&L crisis:

- S&Ls were forced for too long to remain in an interest rate straitjacket.
- Exogenous economic factors (e.g., skyrocketing interest rates) contributed to S&L stresses.
- Lawmakers, regulators, and industry lobbyists indulged in unwise and unethical behavior, often to promote their own self-interest or to avoid personal blame for a fiasco.[30]
- Many S&L executives were overzealous in their pursuit of funds, careless in their credit evaluations, and ignorant of the consequences of many of their actions. A shocking number thought only of their own enrichment and power, or were actually felons who simply looted their banks and the public treasury. Sadly, there were also others who would never personally steal a pin, but seemed unconcerned enough to give their vote of confidence to colleagues actively engaged in robbing their depositors. All of these participants were emboldened to transgress their public stewardship, in great measure because of government deposit insurance guarantees.

The President of a national TV news network expressed his moral outrage this way:

. . . It's hard to find anything in this country—or in history—as costly as the savings and loan scandal. No war, no defense program, no social program, no other scandal has ever cost what this will cost. . . .

---

[29] E.J. Kane, "The High Cost of Incompletely Funding the FSLIC Shortage of Explicit Capital," *Journal of Economic Perspectives* (Fall 1989), pp. 36, 37.
[30] See Edward J. Kane, *The S&L Insurance Mess: How Did It Happen?* (Chicago, Ill: The Urban Institute Press, 1989), esp. chap. 4.

You wonder: If just a piece of [the] money could be directed else-where, how many murders could be prevented, how many homeless could be helped, how many diseases could be conquered, how many police could be hired, how may parks could be built? . . . It just isn't right. . . .[31]

The legislative response to this crisis when it no longer could be contained was: The Financial Institutions Reform, Recovery and Enforcement Act (FIRREA) of August 1989, often referred to as "the S&L Bailout Law."[32] FIRREA did the following:

- Abolished the FHLBB and transferred S&L regulatory functions to a new Office of Thrift Supervision (OTS) in the Treasury Department.
- Set up a new Federal Housing Finance Board (FHFB) under Department of Housing and Urban Development jurisdiction to oversee the 12 district Federal Home Loan banks.
- Set up a new Resolution Trust Corporation (RTC) to liquidate, or in some manner dispose of, failed S&Ls and their assets. The RTC was given $50 billion to begin this job. By common agreement much, much more is needed, and will continue to be needed for some time.
- Expanded the governing board of the FDIC and gave it responsibility for overseeing a new Savings Association Insurance Fund (SAIF) and Bank Insurance Fund (BIF). FSLIC, of course, is gone.
- Raised S&L capital requirements.
- Required high S&L insurance premiums but still not the risk-weighting of individual banks.
- Restricted amounts of commercial real estate loans an S&L may make to no more than 400 percent of capital.
- Required S&Ls to raise the proportion of housing and housing-related assets in their portfolios.

Figure 7-2 is an attempt to portray the functional interrelationships of the new S&L regulatory team. Some who have viewed it have offered the opinion that it is less to insure a safe and sound system than to provide assurance that no single government entity can ever be singled out as responsible for any particular system failure.

---

[31] Michael Garner, "Biggest Robbery in History—You're the Victim," *The Wall Street Journal* (August 9, 1990).

[32] P.L. 101-73 (1989).

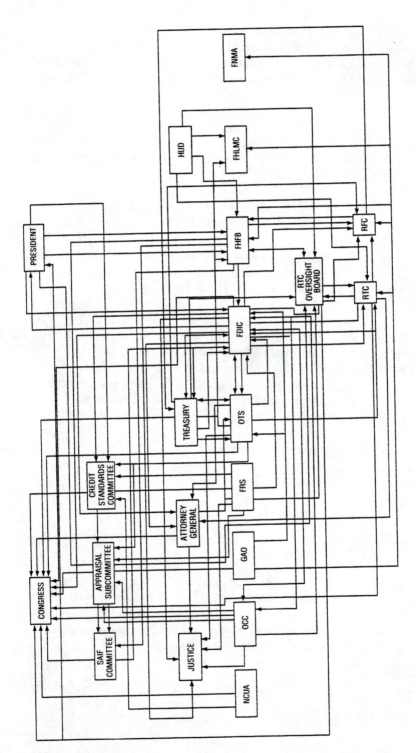

FIGURE 7.2 The Government's S&L Mop-Up Team: Functional Interrelationships. (*Harvard Magazine*, January/February 1991)

Perhaps that isn't true.[33]

Before attempting an analysis of just what form substantive deposit insurance reform might take and, on a broader scale, what might be the optimum in S&L *de-* and *re-*regulation, let us turn our attention to commercial banking. The concerns in that area overlap those that have just been discussed, and supported solutions should, in any event, encompass the banking system as a whole.

F. Focusing on Some Specific Commercial Banking Concerns: An Overview

When dealing with commercial bank regulation issues, the reader should recall that the Federal Reserve has primary responsibility in some cases (bank holding companies, national banks, and all other U.S. banks that are Fed members with access to Fed borrowing privileges and the like); the FDIC in others (all banks covered by FDIC insurance), and the Comptroller of the Treasury also has some responsibility (all national banks). Some 40 percent of American banks are members of the Federal Reserve, and approximately one-third of all banks hold national charters. The many banks that are *state* chartered also come under the supervision of the *state banking authority* as well as, where relevant, the Fed and the FDIC. Our dual (federal-state) system is unique in the world, although whether it is logical and defensible is a subject for a different text.[34]

Commercial banks do seem to have been the subject of more regulatory effort over a longer period of time than was applied to the S&Ls. Nevertheless, the state of the Federal Deposit Insurance Corporation in the early 1990s is one indication that the effort has not been enough.

> The net cost of [commercial] bank failures has escalated from $2.8 billion in 1989 to $6.5 billion in 1990, and an estimated $15.9 billion (for 1991), virtually depleting the Federal Deposit Insurance Corporation's insurance fund to a point where taxpayer money may be needed to finance future failures. . . . FDIC Chairman L. William Siedman was forced to admit that as many as 440 banks would fail this year and the next [1990–1992]. . . . That would boost the drain on what was a $20 billion FDIC insurance fund. . . to $23 billion—wiping it out and leaving it in debt. . . .
>
> Siedman maintains a public posture of some optimism. "The good news is that the government stands behind the banks," [he] says.

---

[33] See also E. Brewer III, "Full Blown Crisis, Half Measure Cure," *Economic Perspectives* of the FRB of Chicago (November/December 1989).

[34] A good text is L. Ritter and W. Silber, *Principles of Money, Banking and Financial Markets* (New York: Harper Collins, 1991), pp. 75-78.

"The bad news is that you [the taxpayers] stand behind the government."[35]

As of May 1992, FDIC insurance premiums advanced from 23 cents to an average of 28 cents per $100 of domestic deposits in order to provide some cushion for anticipated Treasury borrowings by the agency.[36]

The question: "How did the commercial banking business come to this pass?" does not lend itself to any easy answer. However, the following comment by a respected chief executive officer of a bank is certainly a good beginning:

> By nature, commercial banking operates on thin margins and modest capital which afford little cushion for asset risk. The fortunes of banks are determined largely by public policy, economic conditions and management capabilities. The convergence of shortcomings in all of these areas has created unusual institutional problems and failures and systemic stress.[37]

According to this CEO, and many others inside and outside the banking system:

> Prostitution of deposit insurance over time permitted and encouraged the gradual deterioration of credit quality, risk pricing and capital cushions of the financial system. The result was an expansion of debt and business activity which surpassed economic fundamentals and realism. . . .[38]

We begin our examination of commercial banking by highlighting a few key activities related to both domestic and world financial markets.

---

[35] H. Rowen, "Bailing Out the Banks," *The Washington Post National Weekly Edition* (June 24-30, 1991). The U.S. Office of Management and Budget has predicted an FDIC/BIF shortfall of $22.5 billion by the end of FY 1995. See M. Levonian, "Deposit Insurance: Recapitalize or Reform?" *FRB of San Francisco Weekly Letter*, No. 91-36 (October 18, 1991).

[36] While banks are not assessed any premiums on foreign deposits, they are assessed on total domestic deposits. This evens up somewhat the obvious advantage the foreign deposit exemption gives to America's largest banks. Actually, under the new FDIC bank laws, to be discussed in Section III Infra, the premiums that took effect January 1, 1993, range from 23 to 31 cents per $100 of domestic deposits.

[37] Opening remarks of J.G. Medlin, Jr., CEO, First Wachovia Corporation, at the panel discussion of the Rule, Risk and Reform Banking conference of the Federal Reserve Bank of Atlanta, March 19, 1991.

[38] *Ibid.*

1. Past Data, Future Understanding

Unlike the situation with the S&Ls, the commercial banking indus-try as a whole earned almost $15 billion in profits in the first nine months of 1990, even taking into account set-asides for loan losses. Moreover, total banking capital was in the vicinity of $218 billion (the highest in U.S. history). Commercial banks further held $52.3 billion in other reserves.[39]

For far too many commercial banks, however, losses during the same period were the worst in 50 years, and some of the bad performers were U.S. money center banks.

A total of 166 banks in 28 states, Puerto Rico, and Washington, D.C., had capital ratios ranging from 0.06 to 2.94 (i.e., below the 3.0 *minimum* desired by regulators; raised to 4.0 in early 1991). Banks whose nonperforming loans exceeded 8 percent of total assets (a serious signal of impending trouble) numbered 120 in 29 states, Puerto Rico, and Washington, D.C. These were only the worst.

The FDIC's year-end 1990 list of banks it considered vulnerable to failure, or requiring close supervision—a list not "publicly available"—indicated 1,046 banks with $408.8 billion in assets, just about one-eighth of the commercial banking industry total.[40]

Finally, four of America's top ten bank holding companies were, arguably, in the position of having total capital-to-asset ratios of less than the minimum of 3 percent.[41]

---

[39] The data in this section, unless otherwise noted, appears in the lengthy front-page article by M. Quint (with J.C. Freed), "Banks Under Stress: The Legacy of Excess," *The New York Times* (February 19, 1991), pp. 1, 34, 35. *The New York Times* sources, from which its analyses were drawn, were balance sheets and income reports from 12,926 FDIC-insured banks as of September 30, 1990; a computer-assisted search of these reports; and data compiled by Shearson, Lehman Brothers from company filings with the SEC.

[40] *Ibid.* p. 34. The FDIC list changes every quarter. According to R.J. Vaughan and E.W. Hill, "Banks on the Brink: Pay Now or Pay Later," *The Washington Post National Weekly Edition* (November 2-8, 1992), the list still had over 1000 banks on it—exactly 1,044 as of March 1992, representing likely-to-fail bank assets of $570 billion (more than was at risk at the end of 1990). See K.H. Bacon, "Commercial Bank Profits Set Records," *The Wall Street Journal* (September 10, 1992).

[41] According to *The New York Times* analysis, the four banks were Citicorp (2.3%), Chase Manhattan (2.47%), Security Pacific (2.08%) and NCNB (2.57%). *The Times* referred to these ratios as "adjusted." As *reported,* all were above 4%. According to Salomon Brothers data, cited in *The Wall Street Journal,* May 30, 1991, two of these banks had a total of $2.25 billion in nonperforming real estate loans outstanding in the fourth quarter of 1990, while eight other leading New York City banks had some $2.6 billion more of such nonperforming loans outstanding in the same period. See also M. Pacelle, "Quick Home Loans Have Quickly Become Another Banking Mess," *The Wall Street Journal* (July 5, 1991). Real estate loans, at year-end 1991, had gone from 14.5% of U.S. bank assets in 1980, to nearly 25%; moreover, at $850 billion, real estate loans accounted for more than one-half of total bank industry loan growth in the 1980-91 period. The fastest-growing segment was commercial real estate loans. These, of course, have "presented the [main] problem to the banking industry." See statement of John LaWare to a U.S. House Committee in *Federal Reserve Bulletin* (September 1992), p. 679.

One of the banks with a year-end 1990 less-than-3.0-percent-capital ratio was the Bank of New England (BNE), with $13.2 billion in assets. BNE was taken over by the FDIC in January 1991. The failure of BNE, the third largest bank in the New England region, followed hard upon the closing by Rhode Island's governor of 45 banks and credit unions in that state when their private insurer failed and left 300,000 accounts uninsured!

The real issue for us here does not lie in specific banking system figures for the third quarter of the year 1990, or for any other quarter in any other single year. By year-end 1992, in fact, surviving S&L's were doing somewhat better. And the lowest (short-term) interest rates in decades, engineered by the Fed to help strengthen a weak banking system, were boosting commercial bank earnings. But loans were still at very low levels, and questions were being asked about the long-term efficacy of banks being into the Treasury Bond business, and not in traditional banking.[42] What happened only in 1992 is not *the* issue any more than was the third quarter of 1990.

The real issue is: What happened in the financial market area of commercial banking in the previous decade that left the system in such a sorry state as of 1990? If we cannot learn from our experience in dealing with rapid financial market changes in the 1980s, we will surely deal poorly with continuing—perhaps even more rapid—change throughout all of the 1990s and into the year 2000!

2. Interstate Banking

American banks have been prevented by law from operating subsidiary banks in another state without that state's permission (the Douglas Amendment). Further, banks have been denied the right to operate *branches* of their banks in all states other than their own (the McFadden Act). America underwent much liberalization in the decade of the 1980s with regard to the bank subsidiary issue.

The major impetus for expansion of interstate banking was the U.S. Supreme Court case of *Northeast Bancorp, Inc. v. Board of Governors of the Federal Reserve System*.[43] The Court decided that it was legal (constitutional) for states within a region (in this case, New England) to band together to allow unlimited interstate banking within the region, but restricted to the banks already in the region. *Northeast Bancorp* said that the Fourteenth Amendment to the Constitution, which guarantees equal

---

[42] "Earnings to the Rescue," *Euromoney* (November 1992), pp. 42-44; S. Lipin and K.H. Bacon, "Bank Earnings Surge. . . Wide Interest Rate Spreads Keep the Bankers Happy. . . Worrying About Next Year," *The Wall Street Journal* (October 30, 1992). See also M. Mayer, "Why Lend? Banks Have the Fed," *The Wall Street Journal* (September 9, 1992).

[43] 105 S. Ct. 2545 (1985).

protection of the law to all, was not violated by regional compacts that, in effect, shut New York, California, and other money-center banks out completely. The Supreme Court ruled that banking is a "profound" local (state) concern, and states therefore have the right to protect their local banking institutions. So it is safe, apparently, to let regionals get as big as they like, but outsiders present a danger. The argument was not terribly persuasive,[44] but it was certainly the law, and regional interstate banking took off, particularly in the Northeast and Southeast. As of mid-1992, only Hawaii and Montana did not have legislation on the books permitting—or scheduled to permit—some form of interstate banking. The overwhelming majority of states also permitted interstate branching for banks headquartered within the state, some three-fourths allowing that on an unlimited statewide basis.[45]

It must be kept in mind that there are two interstate banking issues that must be considered when contemplating the structure and function of domestic banking in the twenty-first century:

- Should *all* banks be permitted to operate subsidiary banks in all states (i.e., should the Douglas Amendment be repealed)?
- The inability to branch freely across state lines requires the setting up of separate subsidiaries, which necessitates such expenditures as are required by separate boards of directors, extra management layers, and additional capital. Should full interstate branching be allowed (i.e., should the McFadden Act be amended)?

We will return to these issues in Section III of this chapter dealing with financial markets and regulation.

3. Risky Loans, Exotic Products, and "Ethical" Regulations.

The following banner headlines appeared in the same newspaper in the same year, and were written by the same reporter:

---

[44] In fact, in a case that looked similar, but involved insurance companies rather than banks, the Supreme Court decided, in the very same year, that states did *not* have a profound local concern. *Metropolitan Life Insurance Company* v. *Ward*, 105 S.Ct. 1676 (1985). Justice O'Connor made fairly good sense when she commented that the only major difference between *Northeast Bancorp* and *Ward* were the Court's contrary decisions!

[45] For a deeper historical prospective and specific state-by-state detail, see R.T. Clair and P.K. Tucker, "Interstate Banking and the Federal Reserve: A Historical Perspective," *Economic Review* of the FRB of Dallas (November 1989); J.W. Gunther, "The Movement Toward Nationwide Banking," *Financial Industry Studies* of the FRB of Dallas, December, 1992. Year-end 1991 federal banking legislation avoided interstate banking issues. See Section III, *infra*.

"LBO Loans Made by Banks Appear to Perform Well, Comptroller Reports" (January 31, 1989).

"U.S. Comptroller Fears Bank's Risk in Buy-Out Loans" (November 16, 1989).[46]

How did everything change for the worse so fast? The answer, "deteriorating economic conditions," all by itself is less than satisfactory. Even if there were some truth in it, it should be obvious to the reader, as it became to the Comptroller of the Currency's examiners, that many of the healthy loans of January 1989 must have been suffering from "overly optimistic economic assumptions."[47]

The response to bank loan exposure to highly leveraged transactions (HLTs), which amounted to $100 billion by mid-1989, was, of course, more stringent government regulation. The Comptroller of the Currency put into effect a system to monitor HLTs at all national banks where such loans made up more than 2 percent of total assets. The Fed required each and every bank loan made for buy-outs, acquisitions, recapitalizations, and the like to be reported. This, remarked one journalist, was the equivalent of "setting a cat among the pigeons."[48]

With such LBO loans exceeding a quarter trillion dollars between 1986 and 1989, it is hardly a wonder that so many loan losses were suffered in this area.[49]

The data presented here would seem to indicate that the state of credit and risk evaluations and bank management, in a substantial portion (though hardly all) of America's banks, left something to be desired.

There are certainly exogenous, often regional, economic factors that affect the health of lending institutions (e.g., falling land prices). Still, the Midwest suffered a serious downturn in the late 1970s and early 1980s with no large rise in bank failures. And even in Texas, the majority of banks in the 1980s simply did *not* fail. It is difficult to believe that temporary adversity would prove fatal to a bank in the presence of a high capital adequacy ratio, efficient liquidity risk management, a cost-effective

---

[46] Both stories were by Paul Duke, Jr., and appeared in *The Wall Street Journal*.

[47] Quoted from the November 16, 1989, Paul Duke story.

[48] L. Sandler, "Bank Stocks Face Headache from Loan List," *The Wall Street Journal* (November 30, 1989).

[49] An LBO loan is one made to the purchasers of a company who do the deal largely with debt. Repayment requires either a very healthy operating cash flow, or the profitable sale of the purchased company's assets. The relationship between the nature of the deal and the highly visible presence of commercial banks has something to do with the fact that substantial fees are involved. According to the Sandler story, note 48 *supra*, Citibank's exposure only represented 148 percent of its common equity. A $6.1 billion exposure represented 225% of Chemical Bank's common equity at that time.

overall management operation, and a responsibly conservative management focus.[50]

There is one other factor equally crucial to bank performance: the integrity of top management. Outright fraud and actual theft are easy to condemn, but there is another area that requires our attention. Apart from incompetence and even negligence lies the failure to honor the high degree of responsibility required by bank management public stewardship. Risk-taking motivated by a degree of personal ambition and greed not dreamt of in Adam Smith's philosophy,[51] and intricately linked to deposit insurance protection from risk's full downside consequences, has no place in any safe, sound, and trustworthy bank or banking system.

Asset securitization may well be a boon to banks and, to some degree, to the public as well. However, one could question how heavy a role such assets (as securities backed up by pools of car loans, credit card loans, and the like) should play in an already swollen and perhaps not yet fully understood credit market.[52]

Mortgage-backed securities, government guaranteed and unguaranteed, held by domestic banks at the close of 1990 came to about $200 billion. A legitimate question is: Are bank managers being sufficiently prudent to analyze risk and return for these securities at a level sufficient to encourage public trust?[53] The question is particularly relevant in the area of mortgage "strips" or "tranches"—not even the original, full mortgage-backed securities themselves, but rather a tail-end derivative purchased in substantial quantities by commercial banks. Such derivatives carry high rates of return, but they also carry risk serious enough to cause them to be labeled, in some Wall Street circles, as no more than "toxic waste."[54]

---

[50] Cf. J.W. Gunther, "Texas Banking Conditions: Managerial Versus Economic Factors," *Financial Industry Studies*, FRB of Dallas, October 1989. L.E. Browne and E.R. Rosengren, "Real Estate and the Credit Crunch," *New England Economic Review*, November/December, 1992.

[51] Those whose ad nauseam citation of Adam Smith's "pro-greed" stance is used to excuse all self-serving behavior that is not provably illegal ought to read Smith's *Theory of Moral Sentiments* now and then, esp. chap. 2 on "Justice and Beneficence," and chap. 3 "Of the Utility of This Constitution of Nature." See Chapter 1 of this text for the direct references made there to Smith's *Theory*.

[52] See, e.g., C. Mitchell, "Banks Pour Money Into Banks Backed by Credit Card Loans," *The Wall Street Journal* (March 23, 1990). On the need for regulators to watch securitization carefully, see C.T. Carlstrom and K.A. Samolyk, "Securitization: More Than Just a Regulatory Artifact," *Economic Commentary*, FRB of Cleveland (May 1, 1992); and Kavanaugh and Edwards, Jr.; "Asset-Backed Commercial Paper Programs," *Federal Reserve Bulletin* (February 1992).

[53] C.D. Smith, "Analyzing Risk and Return for Mortgage Backed Securities," *Economic Review* of the FRB of Atlanta (January/February 1991).

[54] The quote is from M. Mayer and appears in his very disturbing article, "The Commercial Bank Bailout of 1995," *The Wall Street Journal* (May 7, 1990). There is also some serious

Creative accounting did not much help the S&L industry in the last quarter of the twentieth century, and is not likely to do the commercial banking sector much good as it approaches the dawn of the twenty-first. One example of a possible problem is the "restructured loan." This is an otherwise non-(interest) accruing loan that is turned into an accruing loan by the simple expedient of renegotiating it at lower interest, often *below* current market rates. It is thus removed from the non-performing to performing category in a sort of alchemistic sleight of hand.

The Bank of Boston Corp., in 1990, publicly announced a $100 million decline in nonperforming assets. But a later filing with the Securities and Exchange Commission showed that $76 million of those loans were renegotiated at some 1.5 percent under the banks's own cost of funds. A bank could argue that if it writes off a percentage of a loan, renegotiates the rest, and obtains its interest on the renegotiated amount, the remaining amount is "performing." Perhaps the answer is that a renegotiation at below market rates does not write off negative consequences with regard to the bank's future earnings.

In such a case, is redesignation of the new loan as "performing" unethical? Or are banks simply, one more time, "on the leading edge of bank accounting?"[55]

Finally, we want to record here an interesting characterization by the business press of the nature of certain bank regulations. The FDIC, in light of the connection between overly generous loans to insiders and the failure of some banks and thrifts, discussed prohibiting their regulated banks from investing in real estate in which bank insiders had an equity interest. The title of the business press story read: "FDIC Prepares to Tighten Rules on Ethics for Banks."[56]

How many bank regulations, one wonders, ought now to be retitled to make clear that they are "Rules on Ethics"? And how many more regulations ought now to be issued in light of the very existence of such a formal categorization?

Or is it perhaps more important to ask: Will *any* combination of "Rules and Regulations" ever render a financial system trustworthy in the presence of large numbers of managers who refuse to internalize their essential responsibility to act as agents with a fiduciary responsibility *to honor their principal's duty* to be a steward of the public interest?

---

concern that individual investors could become dangerously enmeshed in this mortgage-security derivatives business. See B. Donnelly, "Small Investors' Hunger for CMOs Scares the Pros," *The Wall Street Journal* (November 11, 1991).

[55] See R. Suskind, "Some Banks Use Accounting Techniques That Conceal Loan Woes, Regulators Say," *The Wall Street Journal* (November 29, 1990).

[56] *The Wall Street Journal* (August 9, 1991), p. A-10.

4. The U.S. Payment (Clearing) System

Payment systems are a set of contractual arrangements through which particular operating units function to transfer value between parties. Some units may function so as to bring about an immediate, irrevocable value transfer. Others may perform their functions in a provisional manner. There are two major systems in the United States. One is the Clearing House Interbank Payments System (CHIPS), a private credit transfer mechanism operated by the New York Clearing House. CHIPS averaged some 150,000 transfers a day in 1990, those having a daily average value of some $890 billion. The other is the Federal Reserve operated Fedwire. Fedwire involves transfers across the books of Federal Reserve banks, of commercial bank-to-bank reserve balances, and of commercial bank-to-bank book entries involving U.S. Government and constituent agency securities, in a delivery versus payment environment. In 1990, the average daily number of Fedwire fund transfers was 225,000, with a daily average of some $790 billion. The average daily securities transfers and value amounted to 45,000 and $400 billion per day, respectively.[57]

At 420,000 transfers a day, with a total daily value in excess of $2 trillion, we need not belabor the point that payment systems are key to the efficient functioning of the country's financial markets. And while a full exposition of the structure and function of such systems are beyond the scope of this book, it is necessary to point out the financial/ethical importance of the phenomenon of "daylight overdrafts" within the system.

Whenever there is an intraday extension of credit in connection with a CHIPS or Fedwire transaction—that is, when payment transfer instructions are given by an account holder and honored, even though that (bank) account holder does not have sufficient balances immediately available—then there is a daylight overdraft. If the (bank's) account balance is not sufficient to cover an inevitable transfer at the end of the day, the daylight overdraft becomes an overnight loan! If the overdraft (or loan) can be depended upon by the instructing bank to be covered, particularly on Fedwire, at no cost intraday and/or on a low rate overnight basis, is there not a risk of "moral hazard?" Which is to say, is there not a risk that errant public stewards will allow the Fed to carry the risks and costs?[58]

The high level of daylight overdrafts and the exposure of the Fed to credit risk finally resulted in the necessity of the central bank's moving

---

[57] See B.J. Summers, "Clearing and Payments Systems: The Role of the Central Bank," *Federal Reserve Bulletin, (February 1991), esp. p. 82.*

[58] The response—"But what can you expect when a regulator issues a license to steal?"—seems to us to be self-incriminating. Banks have to decide to put that spin on the rules and then play the twisting game.

in the direction of closely monitoring overdrafts and setting up some sort of fee structure for the use of intraday credit.[59]

The need for an efficient, trustworthy payments system is obvious. What is not so obvious is the extent to which the central bank should act as a guarantor (insurer) for so many payment transactions. Private enterprise plays a greater role here in both Canada and Great Britain. The issues seem to be: how best to control risk, and, how to bring home the message to all participants that ultimately the honor (and solvency) of the system depends, to a great degree, upon participants.

Payment system issues get stickier in the presence of international considerations. Twenty-four-hour, around-the-world financial markets will compel regulators to examine liquidity, credit, market, delivery, and systemic risks ever more carefully as they evaluate their outstanding payments systems. In the face of cross-border or multicurrency transactions, several payment systems could be involved, and the "reliance on position netting and the lack of delivery vs. payment, leaves market participants with temporary exposures which are large relative to their capital."[60] Clearly, the participation of central banks in the international payments systems process should be carefully worked out so as to avoid the creation of excessive (and unethical) risk-taking behavior.

5. On Levelling Playing Fields: The Glass-Steagall Issue

Competition has surely been pressing hard on commercial banks. Technological developments and investment banking and other group innovations have taken away commercial bank customers, reduced profit margins, and moved banks into some activities in which the distinction between opportunity on the one hand, and unmanageable risk on the other, has been blurred. We have examined some relevant financial areas here, but one sizable, and very important one remains: the corporate debt and equity paper markets. Here we must examine Glass-Steagall legislation.

---

[59] On October 7, 1992, the Fed issued formal revisions to its program for payment system risk reduction. A fee of 25 basis points for average daily total daylight overdrafts will begin to be phased in as of April 14, 1994. See: D.L. Mengle, "Behind the Money Market: Changing and Settling Money Market Investments," *Economic Review* of the FRB of Richmond, September/October 1992.

[60] The quote is from an article by H. Baer and D.P. Evanhoff, "Payments System Issues in Financial Markets That Never Sleep," *Economic Perspectives*, FRB Chicago (November/December 1990). The authors estimate that the value of transfers taking place each night (in government securities, derivative products, and foreign exchange) could be as high as $110 billion (see pp. 6, 13). See also E.J. Stevens, "Comparing Central Banks' Rulebooks," FRB of Cleveland, *Economic Review* (Quarter 3, 1992); "Staff Study: Clearance and Settlement in U.S. Securities Markets," *Federal Reserve Bulletin* (March 1992) and generally G.R. Juncker, B.J. Summers, and F.M. Young, "A Primer on Settlement of Payments in the United States," *Federal Reserve Bulletin* (November 1991).

In its attempt to separate commercial from investment banking in 1933 (on the theory that the commercial bank co-mingling of functions helped contribute to the "Crash/Depression"), Congress enacted two principal prohibitions that took on the title of the *Glass-Steagall law*.

Section 16 (of the Banking Act of 1933) limits commercial bank dealings in "securities and stock" to "purchasing and selling such securities and stock without recourse, solely upon the order, and for the account of, customers, and in no case for its own account. . . ."

Section 21 makes it unlawful for any investment banking-type operation to conduct ordinary, usual commercial bank functions. A third key section in this highly visible arena is Section 20, which makes it unlawful for a commercial bank to "affiliate" itself in any manner with "any corporation, association, business trust, or similar organization *engaged principally* in the stock, bonds, debentures, notes or other securities business" (italics added).

By 1987, commercial banks were feeling the pinch of disintermediation. They saw investment banks competing with them to satisfy corporate funding needs on a level heretofore not contemplated. But Section 16 of the law was an absolute prohibition against any commercial bank direct competition with investment banking.

However, *bank holding companies* had grown in size and power and were by that time engaged, as we have seen, in a variety of businesses *through subsidiaries*. What did the 1933 banking law say about them? Merely that commercial banking couldn't affiliate with any entity *engaged principally* in investment banking. What did that word "principally" mean? Its very presence seemed to suggest something less than an *absolute* prohibition. Citicorp, J.P. Morgan & Co, and Bankers Trust decided to set up subsidiaries to do some "limited" investment banking and thereby test the Section 20 waters. On April 30, 1987, the Federal Reserve Board, in a 3-2 decision, issued the following order (covering a total of 35 pages).[61]

Orders Issued Under Section 4
of the Bank Holding Company Act

Citicorp, New York, New York,
J.P. Morgan & Co., Incorporated, New York, New York
Bankers Trust New York Corporation, New York, New York

---

[61] Citicorp/Morgan/Bankers Trust Order, *Federal Reserve Bulletin* (June 1987), pp. 473-508.

Order Approving Applications to Engage in Limited Underwriting and Dealing in Certain Securities

Citicorp, J.P. Morgan & Co., Incorporated, and Bankers Trust New York Corporation, New York, New York (collectively "Applicants"), bank holding companies within the meaning of the Bank Holding Company Act ("BHC Act"), have each applied for the Board's approval under section 4(c)(8) of the BHC Act and section 224.21 (a) of the Board's Regulation Y, 12 C.F.R. § 225.21(a), to engage through wholly owned subsidiaries, Citicorp Securities, Inc. ("CSI"), J.P. Morgan Securities Inc. ("JPMS"), J.P. Morgan Municipal Finance Inc. ("JPMMF") and BT Securities Corporation ("BTSC"), respectively, in underwriting and dealing in, on a limited basis, certain securities that member banks may not underwrite and deal in, specifically:

(1) municipal revenue bonds, including so-called "public ownership" industrial development bonds;

(2) mortgage-related securities (obligations secured by or representing an interest in residential real estate);

(3) consumer-receivable-related securities ("CRRs") (obligations secured by or representing an interest in loans or receivables of a type generally made to or due from consumers); and

(4) commercial paper.

These securities (hereinafter "ineligible securities") may be held by member banks for investment purposes under section 16 of the Banking Act of 1933 (the "Glass-Steagall Act") (12 U.S.C. § 24, Seventh), but may not under that section be underwritten or dealt in by member banks. (directly)

Applicants have previously received Board approval under section 4(c)(8) of the BHC Act for the above mentioned subsidiaries (collectively the "underwriting subsidiaries") to underwrite and deal in U.S. government and agency and state municipal securities that state member banks are authorized to underwrite and deal in under section 16 of the Glass-Steagall Act (hereinafter "eligible securities"). These eligible securities include certain municipal revenue bonds (issued for certain housing, university or dormitory purposes) as well as mortgage-related securities issued or sold by certain agencies of the federal government. The proposed new underwriting and dealing activities would be provided in addition to the previously approved activities, with the subsidiaries serving customers through offices in New York and, in the case of Citicorp, in several other cities in the United States. [n4]

[n4] (notes 1-3 omitted) For purposes of the Order, in accordance with common industry usage, the term dealing refers to the business activity of holding oneself to the public as being willing to buy and sell securities as principal in the secondary market.

Part I. Introduction and Summary of Findings

These applicants raise fundamental questions concerning the scope of the Glass-Steagall Act's restrictions on the securities activities of member bank affiliates. Their resolution requires application of a statute adopted over 50 years ago in very different circumstances to a financial services marketplace that technology and other competitive forces have altered in a manner and to an extent never envisioned by the enacting Congress. Applicants' member bank affiliates seek to activate until now dormant provisions in section 20 of the Glass-Steagall Act to participate in underwriting and dealing in certain securities, so long as they are not engaged principally in this activity.

In its evaluation of the issues raised by the applications, the Board has been guided, as it must, by the terms of the statute and the underlying Congressional intent and purposes of the Act as evident in its structure and legislative history. Thus, the Board fully recognizes that Congress, through the Glass-Steagall Act, intended to separate commercial banks from general securities underwriting firms. Both the Board and the federal courts have often articulated the potential dangers to commercial banks from general underwriting activities that motivated the Congress in enacting the Glass-Steagall Act. The Board remains fully sensitive to these concerns.

Nevertheless, despite these dangers, the Congress drew a clear distinction between member banks and their affiliates in the Glass-Steagall Act. Except for certain specifically enumerated securities, including government securities, member banks were prohibited under the Glass-Steagall Act from engaging in any underwriting whatsoever. Member bank affiliates, on the other hand, were given a different statutory treatment under section 20 of the Act.

Member bank affiliates are permitted to participate in otherwise impermissible securities underwriting so long as they are not "engaged principally" in this activity. While prior to this time, there apparently has been no incentive to test the meaning of this authorization, the Board is now asked to apply it to specific proposals to engage in certain underwriting activities. Thus, the Board's task is to apply this explicit Congressional authorization to the proposed activities, but in a manner that gives effect to the Congressional intent in adopting the Glass-Steagall Act. Because of the precedent-setting nature of these applications, the Board has given them careful attention, extending over a period in excess of a year, during which time the statutory language, the legislative history, and the implications of these proposals for banking organizations and the financial markets generally have been carefully analyzed by the Board on a number of occasions. In addition, the Board conducted a hearing before the Board members on these important issues.

For the reasons set out in its decisions in the *Bankers Trust* and *Chase* cases, the Board believes it is bound by the statutory language of section 20 to conclude that a member bank affiliate may underwrite and deal in the ineligible securities proposed in the applications, provided that this line of business does not constitute a principal or substantial activity for the affiliate. The Board reaffirms its conclusions in those cases that Congress intended that the "engaged principally" standard permit a level of otherwise impermissible underwriting activity in an affiliate that would not be quantitatively so substantial as to present a danger to affiliated banks. The Board believes that it is only on this basis—that the activity would be insubstantial—that Congress concluded that, despite the hazards from underwriting that caused it to ban banks from engaging in underwriting, this activity would be permissible for the affiliates of member banks.

The Board devoted a considerable effort to evaluation of the factors that should be used to determine the level of ineligible underwriting and dealing activity that would not exceed the substantiality threshold. Taking into account its precedent in the administration of the Glass-Steagall Act and the comments at the hearing on this issue, the Board again concluded that the principal factors that should be included in this judgement are gross revenue and market share. As explained in the detail below, the Board believes that these factors are not susceptible to manipulation to increase artificially levels of activity and fairly reflect the amount of involvement of a bank affiliate in securities underwriting.

With respect to the appropriate quantitative level of ineligible activity permitted under section 20, the Board concludes that a member bank affiliate would not be substantially engaged in underwriting or dealing in ineligible securities if its gross revenue from that activity does not exceed a range of between five to ten percent of its total gross revenues. The Board also believes that a similar range should apply to the market share test it believes is established under section 20. This range was established by reference to the Board's interpretations of the "primarily engaged" standard in section 32 of the Glass-Steagall Act.

As discussed below, under these interpretations, a company could not generally be considered engaged substantially in ineligible securities activity if its gross revenues from that activity did not exceed 5 percent of its total gross revenues. Where underwriting volume was not large in absolute terms, however, somewhat higher levels of revenue were permitted, but generally not greater than 10 percent of total gross revenues.

Applying this framework to the current applications, the Board came to the conclusion that, in view of the fact that the volume of ineligible securities activity projected by Applicants would be very large in absolute terms, the lower end of the permissible range, 5 percent, should determine whether Applicants' gross income or market share from ineligible activity would be substantial. The Board recognizes that this 5 percent threshold for measuring the concept of "engaged principally" is a conservative interpretation of the level of activity permitted by section 20. The Board believes that a conservative step-by-step approach is merited in applying the provision of a statute that was intended to deal with a crisis in our banking system and that has not been extensively interpreted by the courts as applied to the applications now before the Board.

In light of experience, the Board will consider, not later than one year from the date of this Order, whether, under the framework established by the Board in this Order, somewhat higher levels of activity would be consistent with the Board's finding that underwriting and dealing in ineligible securities in an affiliate of a member bank is permissible so long as the level of this activity measured by gross revenue and market share is not substantial. . . .

Unlike the United States Congress, the Federal Reserve demonstrated the courage necessary to face the overriding economic/political/social issue here: Did substantial changes in domestic financial markets (not to mention elements of overseas competition) now require elimination of Glass-Steagall? What, in fact, did the "safety and soundness" of the American banking system require—that is, where did the most risk lie: in levelling the new playing field, or perhaps even in further constricting it? The Fed majority here saw the danger: The Order addressed capital investment, capital adequacy, and credit extension by lending affiliates to customers of the underwriting subsidiary; it addressed limitations to maintain the separateness of an underwriting affiliate's activity, disclosure, a range of specific conflicts of interest, and the like. Whether these issues were resolved satisfactorily by the Fed majority is a subject for debate. The necessity for the Fed to act decisively is not.

The *dissent* from the Order was by Fed Governor Angell, and the powerful Chairman, Paul Volcker:

We regret we are unable to join the majority in approving the pending applications.

The regret reflects the fact that, as a matter of policy, we support the idea that affiliates of bank holding companies underwrite and deal in commercial paper, municipal revenue bonds, and 1–4 family mortgage-related securities, the activities involved in the Board's decision. Moreover, we agree generally with the nature of the limitations placed upon the activities in the Board decision, assuming the threshold question of their legality in the *particular form proposed* can be answered affirmatively.

Our point of difference involves precisely that question of law. Section 20 of the Glass-Steagall Act provides that no member bank may be affiliated with any corporation engaged principally in the underwriting of stocks, bonds, debentures, notes or other securities. We believe the plain words of the statute, read together with earlier Supreme Court and circuit court opinions, as we understand them, indicate that government securities are indeed "securities" within the meaning of section 20. Consequently, it appears to us that the applications approved today, as a matter of law, involve affiliations of member banks with corporations that are in fact not only "principally engaged" in dealing and underwriting in securities, but in fact would be wholly engaged in such activities, thereby exceeding the authority of law.

Our point is not merely one of legal formalisms. The interpretation adopted by the majority would appear to make feasible, as a matter of law if not Board policy, the affiliations of banks with some of the principal underwriting firms or investment houses of the country. Such a legal result, we feel, is inconsistent with the intent of Congress in passing the Glass-Steagall Act.

As the Board as a whole has repeatedly urged, the plain and desirable remedy to this legal and substantive morass is a fresh Congressional mandate. We urge the Congress to provide straightforwardly the authority for bank holding companies to conduct, with appropriate safeguards, the kinds of activities permitted by the Board in its decision, the practical import of which is confined to a relative handful of large bank holding companies with substantial government securities operations.

(notes omitted)

The dissenters, it seems to us, made some solid points, the most important one being contained in their final paragraph. As of early 1993, after several years of growing banking industry woes, Congress had yet to act on the matter covered in this administrative order.

This Order was challenged by the securities industry, of course, but the challenge was defeated when the U.S. Supreme Court refused, on June 13, 1988, to disturb a federal court of appeals ruling upholding the Fed action as being within their (enabled) ambit.

The Fed later increased the allowable gross revenue limit from 5 percent to 10 percent, and the Fed sanctified affiliate dealing in asset-backed securities, futures, options, and foreign exchange. The Fed also approved affiliate subsidiary investment advisory operations and underwriting and dealing in corporate debt—all subject to the 10 percent limitation. It may be said that, as of 1992, bank holding company affiliates could act, for all intents and purposes, like any other investment bank, subject to the ten percent limit (or to a limit, some have ventured to suggest, subject to ten percent and creative accounting principles).[62]

II. COMMERCIAL BANKING: INTERNATIONAL

A. The Eurodollar and Interbank Markets: An Overview

The Eurodollar market over the last half century or so has helped foster rapid growth in international banking. It actually developed after World War II ended. The Soviet Union and its satellites did not want to chance putting dollar holdings into U.S. banks where they could be subject to attack—and attachment—by American litigators. Eastern Europe dollar holdings went mainly into Soviet banks in London and Paris. These banks redeposited into other European banks, particularly those in London. Higher (than U.S.) yields attracted a good many more dollar deposits, and

---

[62] In their Order issued on November 22, 1989 (J.P. Morgan & Company Incorporated, *Federal Reserve Bulletin*, January 1990), the Fed approved of a process whereby a bank holding company's affiliated banks can extend credit to an issuer whose debt securities have been placed by a section 20 subsidiary "where the proceeds would be used to pay the principal amount of the securities at maturity" (p. 39). No one dissented with regard to this implicit guarantee process. See also *Banc One Corporation, Columbus, Ohio:* (Order permitting interlock between a banking organization and its Sec. 20 affiliate.) 75 FRB 756 (1990). See also what Congress *did not* do vis-à-vis Glass-Steagall in year-end 1991 legislation at Section III, *infra*. We would call attention to the Fed's year-end 1992 Rule promulgated (as an amendment to Regulation Y) "to augment the permissible nonbanking activities for bankholding companies to include the provision of full service securities brokerage under certain condition. . . " and more. See *Federal Reserve Bulletin* (October 1992), pp. 774-75. Finally, on January 26, 1993, the Fed modified its rules to allow a new process for measuring compliance with the 10 percent limit. This did not satisfy Governors Mullins and Bengall. They dissented, saying that the proper procedure for the Federal Reserve Board would be to *increase* the 10 percent level! See *Federal Reserve Bulletin*, March 1993, pp. 226-32. Congress has yet to act.

the market grew tremendously. Today, the Euromarket stands on its own for yield, liquidity, and convenience reasons, not as a place to avoid litigation.

The prefix "Euro" in our time, however, actually is misleading. A Japanese yen is "Eurocurrency" if it is on deposit *outside* of Japan—in which case it is a "Euroyen." A Eurodollar is simply a dollar on deposit in a bank that "resides" outside the United States. Although London is the central Eurocurrency market, *Eurobanks* need not even be located in Europe. A Eurobank is simply a financial intermediary that bids for time deposits and makes loans in a currency other than that of the country in which it is located.[63]

Eurocurrencies are held as specified time deposits or as CDs, but they are not deemed deposits on which checks are drawn in the regular course of business. Balances may be transferred by wire or cable between banks.

The *interbank market* itself has at least four interrelated functions:[64]

Distribution (efficiently allocating international funds from non-bank surplus units to nonbank deficit units);

Liquidity (providing an efficient avenue to cover temporary short-falls of funds);

Hedging (providing an efficient market mechanism through which banks can hedge foreign interest rates and foreign exchange exposures) and;

Regulatory avoidance (providing a mechanism to avoid certain costs of domestic regulation and taxes).

According to the International Monetary Fund (IMF), cross-border industrial nation interbank liabilities and claims amounted, in 1990, to some $4.165 trillion.[65]

B. Specific International Banking Market Activities

1. The Technology Explosion

International banking activity has grown tremendously in the decade of the 1980s, aided in great measure by the *technology explosion*.

---

[63] See G. Dufey and I. Giddy, *The International Money Market* (Englewood Cliffs, N.J.: Prentice Hall, 1978).

[64] See A. Saunders, "The Interbank Market, Contagion Effects and International Financial Crisis," Salomon Brothers Working Paper Series No. 385, June 1986.

[65] *IMF International Financial Statistics Yearbook*, 1991. It should be noted here that the rapid growth and increasing complexity of international financial transactions have produced a significant deterioration in international capital flow statistics. *Report on the Measurement of International Capital Flows* (IMF, Washington, D.C. 1992).

Electronic bank balance and transaction reporting systems exist that provide *worldwide* system access to balances, value date, balance history, data from other banks in summary detail, autodial facilities, funds transmittal, with new items available for access every month. Treasury workstations of international bank clients can utilize bank and transaction reports, funds transfer, cost position worksheets, general ledger interface, "what if" modeling capabilities, networking capabilities, links to bank reporting systems, internal systems, and the like.

Rapid growth and expansion of international capital flows carry with them the opportunity for dazzling economic and social progress. They also carry the risk of serious systemic problems, and we will address that issue further in specific contexts.

2. Some examples of product areas

- *Loan arrangements* include multi option facilities (MOFs) that can offer the borrower a revolving line of credit that can be drawn upon in the form of cash, acceptances, or Euronotes. The bidding structure here (e.g., for large international corporation accounts) is such that competitive, syndicated loan margins on MOFs (and other international lines of credit) have often been razor-thin (34 basis points) and facility fees no better (5 to 10 basis points only).[66]

- *Swaps* (straight exchanges of fixed rate debt for floating debt and vice-versa) interest rate generally fixed to floating, and cross-currency.

- *Options and Futures*

- *Guarantees*, Acceptances, Transactions with Recourse, Standby Letters of Credit, Documentary Letters of Credit (Commercial Letters of Credit), Warranties and Indemnities, and Endorsements. These constitute the area of *guarantees and contingent liabilities, generally*.[67]

- A whole host of *derivative products* beyond the so-called *plain vanilla* (standard) options and futures.[68] The generic term "deriva-

---

[66] See "Lend the Money, Then Sell the Debt," *Euromoney* (August 1989), p. 99. A follow-up article stated that the loan market had moved into "an era of lending for 'general corporate purposes,' a euphemism for banks providing un-needed funds at bargain rates for the sake of a continuing relationship with a client. . . ." See "Euroloans: LBOs Are Where the Markets Are at," *Euromoney* (September 1989), p. 191.

[67] See *Report of Basle Committee on Banking Regulations and Supervisory Practices*, Appendix, "Glossary of Terms, Guarantees and Similar Contingent Liabilities," Basle, Switzerland, April 1986.

[68] For a descriptive list of more complex forward, futures, and options products such as Interest Rate Caps, Floors, Collars and Scouts, Participating Forward Contracts, Range Forward Contracts, etc., see Coopers and Lybrand, *A Guide to Financial Instruments* (Euromoney Publications, 1987), at "Hedging Instruments, pp. 113-20. Those with a taste

tives" relates to hybrid instruments customized to reflect price movements of underlying currencies, commodities, stocks or bonds. These bets on the future performance of the underlying basic instrument are all recorded *off* bank balance sheets. The fundamental concern for the players here is the financial reliability of the party on the other side. And if international unreliability leads to default (partial or total), just which laws apply to whom, and where? Geographically, what law applies to a four-nation deal, for example?

Those questions are not academic. The British High Court, that of the House of Lords, actually ruled that all swap-related deals entered into by certain municipalities in England and Wales were *ultra vires*—lawyer talk for "beyond the legal capacity of the party to enter into such contracts in the first place." The result of the ruling was that the swaps here (exchanges of interest payments) failed, leaving counterparties with some £400 million in losses. The costs involved in a defaulted swap replacement go beyond the assumption of higher rates. Regulatory, legal, and accounting costs will be reflected in the full replacement damage.[69]

Foreign exchange trading has become an important revenue source for large international commercial banks in a time of hard-pressed profits. In foreign exchange (FX) markets, governments attempt to keep the value

---

for the esoteric in bonds might enjoy reading about such derivatives as Bunny Bonds, Flip Flop Notes, Dutch Auction Notes, and Debt with Forward Commitment; *ibid.*, pp. 24-32. Derivatives are often birthed and buried quite rapidly, so one should not rely too heavily on the staying power (and relative safety) of each and every new one that comes along. For an insightful look at the $3 trillion world interest rate and currency market in Swaps (mid-1992), see: R.H. Litzenberger, "Swaps: Plain and Fanciful," *The Journal of Finance*, July, 1992.

[69] See R. Aggarwall, "True Cost of Default," *Corporate Finance* (February 1991), and N. Bray, "U.K. Row Over Swaps Debate Stirs Doubts About London as a Banking Center," *The Wall Street Journal* (June 3, 1991). The collapse of the Bank of New England (BNE) in 1991 required the bank's traders, the Fed, and the Comptroller of the Currency to unwind some $30 billion in BNE currency and interest rate contracts around the world in the face of international banks scrambling to close the door on them. BNE escaped disaster, but not without being "raped" on occasion (in the words of a BNE official). The entire process of getting out while going down caused a senior branch examiner in the comptroller's office to remark that "for certain banks there is a lot of exposure" in the market for derivative securities. C. Torres, "Dangerous Deals: How Financial Squeeze Was Narrowly Averted in Derivatives Trade," *The Wall Street Journal* (June 18, 1991). The swap market has come in for serious criticism from the New York Fed, whose president has commented: "Some of the specific purposes for which swaps are now being used may be quite at odds with an appropriately conservative view of the purpose of a swap, thereby introducing new elements of risk or distortion into the marketplace." F. Norris, "Swapping Woes: A Fed Official Sees Problems," *The New York Times* (Market Watch, February 9, 1992). See also: S. Lipen, "Many Banks Change Strategies to Manage Rate Risk: Swaps Are Increasingly Used," *The Wall Street Journal*, February 10, 1993.

of their money stable by buying and selling currencies, and corporations whose international operations involve multiple currencies attempt to hedge against the ups and downs of the several currencies with which they have to deal. The size of this FX market is enormous. According to a survey in April 1989, which was released simultaneously by the central banks of several major countries (including the United States, England, and Japan), FX worldwide daily turnover exceeded $500 billion per day.[70]

The hallmark of the FX market is volatility. One example is the journey of the U.S. dollar over the first six months of 1991. During that period, the dollar rose 27 percent against the German mark. And then, in one month (July), it fell a full 5 percent.[71] During the first quarter of 1991, the 15 largest U.S. commercial banks that trade actively in the FX market for corporate customers and for their own accounts showed profits of $701 million—up 27 percent over the previous quarter. At Bankers Trust, FX profits constituted 53 percent of net income.[72]

The obvious affection of these commercial banks and other FX traders for instability in the market has been the subject of criticism:

> Apparently, banks consider the taking of long term positions based on fundamentals, or of any sort of position in the forward exchange market as too "speculative and risky". . . but the banks are willing to trust their spot exchange traders to take large, open positions, provided they close most of them out by the end of the day, because these operations are profitable in the aggregate. (It is almost as if the banks do not realize that a strategy of making a series of repeated one day bets in foreign currency is just as risky as a strategy of buying a portfolio of foreign securities and holding them). . . . A typical spot trader does not buy and sell on the basis of any fundamental model, but rather. . . on the basis of knowledge as to which other traders are offering what deals at any given time, and a feel for what their behavior is likely to be later in the day.[73]

From the point of view of regulation, the focal question has been put well by another commentator:

---

[70] Data cited in M.R. Sesit, "Japan Playing a Bigger Role in Global Currency Market," *The Wall Street Journal* (September 14, 1989). More recent secondary source estimates put the daily FX market (1992) at more than $600 billion per day.

[71] Data cited in J. Feurbringer, "A Profitable Niche in Today's Grim World of Banking," *The New York Times* (August 4, 1991).

[72] The data source was Shearson, Lehman Brothers, cited in Feurbringer, *supra*.

[73] J.A. Frankel, "International Capital Mobility and Exchange Rate Volatility," in *International Payments in the 1980s*, Conference Series No. 32, Federal Reserve Bank of Boston, 1988, p. 183.

Does the foreign exchange market set the exchange rate on a path that minimizes excess volatility and misallocation of resources over time? Or are asset markets shortsighted, extrapolating current trends without much concern about cumulative misalignments? . . . [T]he very operation of the foreign exchange market is discouraging in this respect. . . [and] we argue that markets that trade on noise may well cause cumulative departures from a path supported by fundamentals. . . .

The growing body of evidence supporting the lack of rational expectations in foreign exchange markets has dramatic implications. . . . If [they] do not work efficiently, then there is definitely the potential (and the need) for policy intervention to improve the allocation of resources. . . .[74]

C. International Banking, Capital Market Integration and the Question of Disaster Myopia

The preceding discussion is not an argument for placing heavy and unnecessary regulatory brakes on international banking. Banks have been major players in stimulating competition and in bringing about a growing integration of domestic and offshore markets, thus improving portfolio liquidity and diversifying risk (i.e., clearly increasing efficiency). However, the ability of borrowers to locate alternative sources of credit, and of lenders to place funds in global markets, has also rendered less predictable the relationships among monetary instruments, money stock, and nominal income. And certainly the path to capital flight has been made much more open and accessible.[75]

In their seminal article, "Disaster Myopia in International Banking,"[76] Professors Guttentag and Herring address a crucial issue here: Do international banks tend to assume excessive exposure to insolvency?

---

[74] R. Dornbush, "The Adjustment Mechanism: Theory and Problem," in *International Payments. . .* , note 73, *supra*, pp. 213, 214, 216. The speculative attacks on European currencies by foreign exchange traders in September 1992 (especially the British pound) did more than simply unsettle markets on a temporary basis. It is estimated that 30 billion markka was spent by the Finnish central bank to prop up its currency; 24 billion Deutsche marks to prop up the Italian lira, and 10 billion pounds to prop up British sterling. How many taxpayers were in *that* game? See R. Smith, "The Big Casino," *The Wall Street Journal* (September 18, 1992), J. Jaffee, "After the Geldkrieg," *The New York Times* (September 20, 1992), and B. Hagerty, G. Whitney and T. Roth, "EC Faces New Round of Currency Turmoil," *The Wall Street Journal*, February 2, 1993.

[75] See *Determinants and Systemic Consequences of International Capital Flows* (International Monetary Fund Occasional Paper No. 73, 1991).

[76] *Essays in International Finance*, No. 64, Princeton University Department of Economics, September 1986.

These authors argue that financial institutions engage in many activities that expose them to credit and funding shocks, and the authors accuse these institutions of susceptibility to "disaster myopia" (i.e., a systemic tendency to underestimate shock probabilities). The authors assert that there is a perceptual bias in international banking generally, leading to excessive insolvency exposure.

The authors discuss *transfer shock* (involving an unwillingness or inability to convert local currency into the currency of the creditor); *foreign exchange shock* (an abrupt rate change that could reduce the creditor's capital and income); *interest rate shock;* and *funding shock* (sudden credit restriction jeopardizing an institution's ability to refinance maturing liabilities).

Professors Guttentag and Herring express particular concern for—and discuss thoroughly—the special dangers posed to international banking by transfer and funding shocks. Among the reasons they advance for the existence of disaster myopia are: poor information, the profit potential in activities that expose to these shocks, and the perception that government assistance would be forthcoming if, in fact, a major shock was suffered.

It must be said that the two academics do not demonstrate the high probability of a major shock actually occurring; rather, they do demonstrate "that exposure to such shocks has increased markedly over the last two decades."

We should note the reappearance here, on an international basis, of a key American domestic banking ethics issue: promiscuous risk-taking based upon the existence of a back-up government/taxpayer bailout. In the domestic case we have non-risk-adjusted, government deposit insurance. In the international area, deposit insurance is but one element. The other (larger) one is the "deep pockets" of central banks and their access to public treasuries. How many governments—in the industrialized nations, at least—would sit by and allow one of their major international banks to collapse, even under the weight of management's own unethical behavior?

Aside from the obvious concern with a worldwide financial system subject to "moral hazard," international banking presents a related, perplexing problem that is legal, economic, and ethical in its ramifications. Assume, for the sake of argument, that an international bank is going under. If question 1 is: Must a bailout occur? then question 2 might very well be: Whose deep pocket is to be picked?

Once more, Professors Guttentag and Herring have highlighted a serious issue:

> The internationalization of banking extended deposit and loan relationships across national boundaries. Deposits at a bank

located in one country may be denominated in the currency of another. Banks headquartered in the home country may be controlled by foreign banks or by foreign residents who are nonbanks.

A bank's residential jurisdiction may not correspond to the jurisdiction in which its owners reside or the jurisdiction of the currency in which most of its transactions are denominated.

With the internationalization of banking, it is no longer obvious that the central bank where a bank resides will or can be effective (Lender of Last Resort) for that bank.[77]

Central banks might well be expected to work together to stand behind individual banks with temporary problems caused by exogenous economic/business factors. However, the concept of public stewardship ought to be factored in appropriately in the international as well as the national context, when a bank's crumbling foundations are substantially the result of moral rot.

D. The Problem of Less-Developed-Country (LDC) Debt

This is an outstanding example of myopic international banking behavior, and it presents an opportunity to examine regulatory responses to such myopia. Innumerable books and articles focus on the origins and consequences of the disaster faced by so many banks that participated in the growth of LDC debt through private borrowing,[78] and we will not examine the problem in detail here. We must be satisfied to point out the following:

---

[77] Guttentag and Herring, "Emergency Liquidity Assistance for International Banks," Mimeo (September 22, 1986), pp. 32-33. It is only fair to point out that the authors note the "early and insightful analysis" of this problem in A. Frankel, "The Lender of Last Resort in the Context of International Banking," *Columbia Journal of World Business* (Winter 1975). The liquidation in 1992 of EFIM, a state-owned conglomerate of the Italian government, accompanied by a refusal to honor the EFIM debt, left foreign banks in quite a quandary. See P. Gumbel, "Italian State Firm's Breakup Angers Banks," *The Wall Street Journal* (August 20, 1992). And see, generally, E.G. Corrigan, "Challenges Facing the International Community of Bank Supervisors," *Quarterly Review* FRB of New York, Autumn 1992, and R. C. Effroo, ed., *Current Legal Issues Affecting Central Banks* (IMF, Washington, D.C., 1993).

[78] A brief listing includes: H. Lever and C. Huhne, *Debt and Danger* (Boston: Atlantic Monthly Press, 1986); Benjamin Cohen, *In Whose Interest? International Banking and American Foreign Policy* (New Haven: Yale University Press, 1986); Jeffrey D. Sachs, *New Approaches to the Latin American Debt Crisis: Essays in International Finance*, No. 174 (Princeton, N.J.: Princeton University Department of Economics, July 1989); B. Boehmer and W.L. Meggison, "Development of Secondary Market Prices for Developing Country Syndicated Loans," *Journal of Finance* (December 1990); B. Eichengreen, "Historical Research on International Lending and Debt," *Journal of Economic Perspectives* (Spring 1991).

- While many LDC borrowers had some solid assets as borrowing collateral (e.g., Mexico and Brazil) they relied too heavily on private rather than government or supranational equity lenders. This exposed them to the vagaries of interest rate fluctuations and a host of economic ills that private borrowers from profit-making institutions are always heir to.

- Lenders too often relied on demonstrably defective concepts ("Sovereign Borrowers Never Fail"/"Everybody's Making Money, So Why Shouldn't We"?) rather than on solid information and credit analysis. Banks, including such supranationals as the Worldbank and the IMF, even failed often to ask such basic, non-trivial questions as: How much do you already owe, and to whom? And, are our debtors utilizing our money in such a way as to promote (rather than destroy) their credit-worthiness?

- There is, in fact, evidence indicating that sovereign borrowers themselves did not know how much they owed and to whom. Nor how much their private sector was borrowing, or their sources.

- Much borrowed money disappeared into the maw of government enterprises unresponsive to any market demands or pressures, or went to individual, politically motivated subsidies, to armaments, to bloated government payrolls—and into private pockets.

- As private loan money flowed in without changing rigid, nonmarket, government-controlled economies, private citizen wealth flowed out (capital flight). Thus, domestic governments were deprived of essential savings and investment capital. Much of this was their own fault, of course; however, it is only fair to point out that these various currencies often ended up in the more than willing hands of the very banks whose borrowers were thereby rendered even greater credit risks. One can easily discern that beyond economics and "good" business, ethical issues are lurking here.

- The bad side of the LDC debt mess includes the fact that the face value of LDC debt bears little relationship to its going market value. For example, as of November 1988, the face value of 12 heavily indebted nations (Argentina, Brazil, Chile, Colombia, Ecuador, Mexico, Peru, Philippines, Poland, Romania, Venezuela and Yugoslavia) was $283.1 billion. The actual market value was $118.1 billion. Moreover, the face amount of debt was *up* by $8 billion over 1986, while the market value over the same period had gone down by $83.5 billion.[79] Further, by the

---

[79] Table II, "Developing Country Debt Index," Boehmer and Megginson, "Development of Secondary Market Prices," note 78, *supra*, p. 1522 (1990).

first quarter of 1991, interest payment arrears of debtor countries had quadrupled since 1989, to about $28.6 billion.[80]

- The question of "debt relief" is thereby raised, and it is fraught with the danger of "moral hazard." If, for example, Poland doesn't have to pay its interest, why should Brazil? Equally bad is the fact that debt relief could prove to be a transitory benefit. Those nations that take advantage of it could find themselves frozen out of foreign lending and investment. For example, in May 1991, the Japanese informed Poland that it could have debt relief, but that taking it would mean no more Japanese government credits.[81] What, then, are banks to do about making the hard-headed determination of the worth of the LDC debt they still hold, and then acting on that determination when reality and existing loss reserves do not yet stand on an equal footing? And what the banks cannot forget to factor in is that in the wake of persistent poverty and dreadful individual and family suffering come social unrest, political instability, and environmental degradation. And, in the case of Eastern Europe, the specter of economic refugee outmigration could prove damaging to all European progress.

- The good side of the LDC debt mess is that there has been real progress in the economic reform area in Latin America, to an extent not fully recognized, including more restoration of fiscal discipline, reordering of public expenditure priorities, tax reform, financial liberalization, privatization, and deregulation.[82]

- Information gathering on individual debtors and creditors has become quite sophisticated, both on the individual bank level and with the establishment of such umbrella groups as the Institute of International Finance (IIF), which gathers data, under-

---

[80] "Debtor Nations Slip Behind in Their Interest Payments," *The Wall Street Journal* (April 24, 1991). The World Bank published an excellent guide to the external debt of 114 nations, which is up dated periodically. See *World Debt Tables*, 1991-92 edition (Philadelphia: World Bank Publication 1992).

[81] "Debt Relief Endangers Third World Prospects," "The Outlook" *The Wall Street Journal* (May 6, 1991).

[82] See John Williamson, *The Progress of Policy in Latin America* (Washington, D.C.: Institute for International Economics, 1990). One might nevertheless question whether private investors are jumping the gun somewhat by buying so much new Argentinean and Brazilian government paper being issued in the billions. Much of it is already being labeled "junk." See T. Kamm, "Latin America Escapes the Jaws of Debt," *The Wall Street Journal* (August 29, 1991). Swapping bank debt, at a discount, for new long-term bonds (known as "Brady Bonds" after the U.S.Treasury Secretary's 1989 initiative) has thus far proven lucrative; P. Truell, "Latin America Debt Holders Scored Big Gains, Index Shows," *The Wall Street Journal* (October 2, 1991). For an excellent overview, see Leipold and others, *Private Market Financing for Developing Countries* (Washington, D.C.: IMF, 1992). And trading LDC debt—a $600 million per year market—is not free from ethical problems. See P. Truell, "Trading of Debt of Third World Is Investigated," *The Wall Street Journal*, March 19, 1993.

takes on-site missions, and issues reports to its international membership.[83]

In the United States, the Federal Reserve, the Office of the Comptroller of the Currency (CC), and the FDIC have developed a supervisory system to evaluate certain international transactions. The focus is upon country exposure (the amount of lending to any one country) and country risk (the economic, political and social developments to be considered relative to the country's ability to make timely payments of interest and principal as a borrower—and of its businesses to do the same). Within the area of country risk lies transfer risk (the ability, here of LDCs, to obtain the proper currency with which to pay their debt). "Country Exposure Report" forms must now be filed quarterly with the government under the provisions of the International Lending Supervision Act of 1983—one more example of the mutualistic dependency of markets and law (read: regulation).

The active FED/CC/FDIC group in this area is the Interagency Country Exposure Review Committee (ICERC), which assesses transfer risk and attempts to ensure uniform treatment of risks. ICERC meets three times a year to review conditions in countries where transfer risk to U.S. banks is significant.[84] An example of ICERC action was their order to U.S. bankers to write off 20 percent of $2.9 billion in loans to Argentina in July 1990.[85]

Perhaps most important of all, the LDC debt mess has done more than expose less-than-commendable bank lending practices in the West's international financial system. *It has also exposed the serious systemic weaknesses and failures of nonmarket, planned, and controlled economies.* The inability of nonmarket-economy debtors to pay their obligations has cast the spotlight upon those market processes that less developed nations must undertake in order to assure economic growth and national prosperity.

---

[83] Located in Washington D.C., the IIF has a membership of some 170 major banks worldwide.

[84] For material on the supervisory system, its structures, and its functions, see M.G. Martinsen and J.V. Haupt, "Transfer Risk in U.S. Banks," *Federal Reserve Bulletin* (April 1989).

[85] See R. Guenther, "Federal Regulators Order Banks to Take Write-Offs on Loans to Brazil, Argentina," *The Wall Street Journal* (July 2, 1990). A new agreement with Brazil in July 1992 (just before its president was driven out of office in disgrace) to restructure $44 billion in bank debt was hailed as the end of the LCD crisis. Just $26 billion or so lost, and a bit of opportunity cost. Actually, "no catastrophe." S. Lipin, "Bankers Escape Latin Debt with Little Damage: Losses in Region Will Look Tiny Next to Real Estate Collapse, Analysts Say," *The Wall Street Journal* (July 16, 1992). And see: R.M. Kubarych, "Ten More Lessons of the Debt Crisis," *International Economic Insights*, September/October 1992, pp. 62-63.

Those nations that help finance and support the supranational banks (such as the World Bank and the IMF) now properly insist that further loan support to LDCs must be tied to basic economic system changes (e.g., establishing secure property rights, privatization, deregulation, fewer government subsidies, and so forth).

Fidel Castro, the last of the Caudillo Communists, was ideologically correct to insist that LDCs should repudiate their debts. Despite his outward insistence that to repay these debts would be immoral (a twist that would have brought a wry smile to George Orwell), Castro's eye was likely fastened on the real concern: LDC economic systems were not capable of growing sufficiently to meet their obligations. Thus, direct challenge to the underlying systems themselves was bound to come, the systems would fail, and a Pandora's box would thereby be opened: Systemic economic change in the Communist world had to loose the fierce desire for freedom and human dignity so long repressed, and that would mark the end of communism.

Open, competitive markets have triumphed, even in the midst of evidence of some shortcomings. However, it would be a dreadful mistake to attribute the world-shaking events that have occurred in Eastern Europe and the former Soviet Union solely to economic factors. Unarmed citizens standing in the path of advancing tanks in the Kremlin were not making an economic statement. Their desperate yearning for freedom, democracy, human dignity, and self-determination was the power that sustained them and the "army" of citizens rallying to their support. We can be proud of the capacity of free markets to provide for the public good, but we cannot forget the reality of their interdependence with the Rule of Law that is the basic support of any democratic system.

And that, of course, in one way or another is the overall focus of this book.

In the meantime, consider these questions: As borrower nations struggle to do their part to remedy a lending/debt catastrophe they certainly helped to create, who is to pay for the misjudgments and ethical lapses for which the lenders themselves were responsible? Is that solely an objective business issue? If not, what meaning does that have in dollars and cents? Is the West (and are its banks) under some moral obligation to contribute rationally and productively to LDC national development, particularly in areas concerning the very poor, as these nations struggle to secure democratic rights and economic progress?[86]

---

[86] Cf. *World Development Report 1990: Poverty* (Washington, D.C.: World Bank Publications, 1990), esp. pp. 2, 3, "Policies for Attacking Poverty."

E. Europe 1992

This is a two-word catch phrase that seems to characterize some cataclysmic event that should have taken place at the end of 1992. As such, "Europe 1992" is a phrase that has been oversold, certainly in the perspective of 1993!

Europe 1992 came into being, initially, as the result of a white paper calling for the elimination of all internal trade barriers in Europe by the end of 1992. One might characterize this proposal to set up a single, united, open marketplace for some 340 million consumers as a "single market initiative."[87] The four basic objectives to accomplish this plan are: the elimination of border controls; the opening up of public procurement; harmonization of technical standards and regulations, and liberalization of capital movements and related financial services.[88]

A second initiative in this European Community (EC) unity thrust relates to a single-monetary-policy initiative, focused on contributing to the benefits of a single market. The shorthand for this thrust is European Monetary Union (EMU). The focus here is on the irrevocable fixing of European exchange rates and the establishment of a total irrevocable convertability of currencies and complete freedom of capital movements in fully integrated financial markets. The eventual introduction of a common currency, the EC Executive Commission insists, will create, all by itself, $130 billion in EC efficiencies.[89]

The vision encompasses, ultimately, a fully operational European System of Central Banks (ESCB), which would assume the decision-making process from national authorities and the complete control of exchange market intermediations in third currencies. The ESCB would be operated by the EC. At this point, the EC would complete the transition to a single EC currency.

Problems with this theoretical construct were apparent in 1992. The treaty signed at Maastricht, Holland, in December 1991, related to the creation of EMU; it was defeated by Danish voters in a referendum; barely passed by the French electorate; and was in trouble at year's end in Britain

---

[87] The white paper was issued by Jacques Delors in his capacity as president of the European Commission. Entitled "Completing the Internal Market," it sets forth some 300 directives to achieve a unified European market. It is often referred to as the "Delors Commission White Paper."

[88] For a recent analysis of the Europe 1992 phenomenon, see L.C. Hunter, "Europe 1992: An Overview," *Economic Review* of the FRB of Dallas (January 1991). An extraordinary reference work on the entire European Community, which contains huge amounts of economic and social data, is *The Economist Atlas of the New Europe* (New York: Henry Holt & Co. 1992).

[89] The formal report on this second thrust was presented to the European Council in 1989. Again a product of the Delors Committee, it is entitled, "Economic and Monetary Union in the European Community." See also "Delors Report Sets Out Steps to European Economic and Monetary Union," IMF *Survey* (July 2, 1990), p. 203.

and in Germany. The single European currency concept appears to be becoming, rather, a two-tiered system with a small core group of currencies, led by the mark, in one, and the weak ones (like the pound) in another.[90]

There are two major issues raised by Europe 1992 plans, one general and one specific to the United States.

The general issue is whether the grand design can be fully implemented. And if not, what progress toward it might be achieved by 1993—or by 1999 for that matter? Some problems are apparent:

- Europe clearly suffers from an inability to mesh political and military gears. The EC's constituent members could not agree, for example, on a unified position during the 1990–1991 Persian Gulf crisis,[91] nor on the 1992, and continuing, crisis in Bosnia (the former Yugoslavia). One complication here is that these gears must often work in tandem with economic matters. For example, the meeting of the General Agreement on Tariffs and Trade (GATT), which began the decade of the 1990s, was unable to reach a major international (free) trade agreement, largely because EC members France and Germany would not abandon *agricultural subsidies,* which resulted in dumping their surplus grains on world markets below production costs, and which have caused serious internal EC problems vis-à-vis the United States.

- The failure of GATT to reach an agreement highlights a larger concern regarding world trade arrangements: To what degree should we be concerned about the economic-social-political ramifications of an international turn to regional and bilateral arrangements, rather than world free trade; for example, the EC and the U.S.-Canada-Mexico process? What happens to nations left out of all of the regional/bilateral restricted loops?[92]

---

[90] A full presentation of the structure and functions of key EC entities and legislation may be found in *The Economist Atlas,* note 88, *supra,* pp. 130-135. EC legislation and cooperation procedures are also set forth in S. Key, "Mutual Recognition: Integration of the Financial Sector in the European Community," *Federal Reserve Bulletin* (September 1989). An EC paper titled "The Transition to Monetary Union" has been published by the *Centre for Economic Policy Research* (London, 1990). The more recent developments may be seen in "Report on ERM (two articles on solidifying monetary union)," *International Economic Insights* (November/December 1992), pp. 35-39; M.R. Sessit, "Europe's ERM Is Becoming a 2-Tiered System," *The Wall Street Journal* (November 24, 1992).

[91] A fact that occasioned this remark from Belgian Foreign Minister Mark Eyskens: "Europe is an economic giant, a political dwarf, and a military worm."

[92] N.S. Fieleke, "One Trading World or Many: The Issue of Regional Trading Blocs," *New England Economic Review* (May/June 1992); L. Aguilar, "The North American Free Trade Agreement: The Ties That Bind," *Chicago Fed Letter,* No. 61 (September 1992); R.W. Apple, Jr., "Trade New World: As It comes Together, It's Pulling Apart," *The New York Times* (November 29, 1992). See also Richard Pomprit, *International Trade Policy with Imperfect Competition* (Special Papers on International Economics, Princeton University, August

- There is little doubt that socio-political events further complicate matters for the European Community: The reunification of Germany and consequent West German commitments and concerns, along with the desire of newly independent Eastern European nations to be admitted to the EC, are examples. There is also the question of just how the nations of the European Free Trade Association, which includes the Scandinavian countries, should relate to the EC in the (perhaps insulting) absence of a promised complete integration. Then there is the overarching issue of how much power and authority can really (with political safety) be transferred from sovereign nations into EC bodies, particularly in terms of a single currency and one all-powerful central bank.

- Most of the legislation needed to create the single market, if not the single monetary policy, had been adopted in advance of the 1992 deadline. Nevertheless, reality suggests that the complex issue of central versus constituent state power has never been fully resolved in a satisfactory manner by any confederation of states ever known. That includes the United States of America, which has had over 200 years experience trying to work out the issue—and with the enormous (and singular) advantage of operating under one central (federal) Constitution accepted and revered by every single constituent state.

- Finally, the legislation in place makes specific reference to the free flow of people as well as goods. In light of the possibility of mass migration from less developed nations into the EC's twelve member nations, how "open" can borders actually be? The immigration problem is bound to be a complicating political-social-economic factor in total European unity. And it probably will prove to be so well beyond 1992 and 1993. The most chilling factor in 1992 was the rise of the neo-Nazis in Germany and the violence unleashed there upon immigrants.[93]

A second focus on Europe 1992 would have to be on its specific meaning to the United States in general, and to the American financial system in particular. Two items will be considered here, one micro and one macro in nature.

1992), p. 17. And J.J. Schott, "North America Integrates," *International Economic Insight*, September/October 1992.

[93] See, Post, Breslau, and others, "A Fortress Mentality," *Newsweek* (December 9, 1991) pp. 36-38 and C.R. Whitney, "The Germans' New Perception: Disorder," *The New York Times* (November 22, 1992). See also "Labor and Immigration," *The Economist Atlas*, note 88, *supra*, pp. 138-139.

- The *micro* question is, Just how will reciprocity work, in terms of American banks, in the European Community? Under EC reciprocity provisions, a non-EC bank (financial firm) would be prohibited from establishing or acquiring a subsidiary in any EC member state unless the bank's home country granted "reciprocal treatment" to banks from all member states. For example, if the United States retains some form of commercial bank/investment bank separation of functions, and EC banks don't, will that make it impossible for American banks to establish or acquire subsidiaries in the EC? Or does reciprocal or equal treatment mean, in effect, "the same treatment all home country banks are accorded?"[94] Is there a "fairness" issue involved in the answer here, or just a business or "political" decision?

- The *macro* question is many-faceted: What would be the result of a single European currency on the powerful international role now played by the dollar? Specifically, what decrease would there be in the vulnerability of that currency to exchange rate changes? And if the ECU (the current "European currency" pegged to all the others) becomes the accepted *single* EC currency, will there in fact come into being a true multiple reserve currency system worldwide?[95]

Finally, what will a new single European market and financial order mean in the general area of international economic policy coordination? Should the group of 7 become the group of 3 (the EC, the U.S. and Japan)? Would that make it easier or more difficult to integrate exchange rate and macroeconomic considerations more effectively and then undertake other substantial tasks?[96]

- Most of the questions centering around Europe 1992 are economic and financial in nature.

---

[94] Direct branches of U.S. banks would not be subject to reciprocity, but would not benefit from an EC directive permitting EC-wide expansion. Rather, they would be subject to separate regulation by each home state. Cf. also S. Kumiharu, "The External Dimensions of Europe 1992: Its Effects on Relations Between Europe, the United States and Japan," in Padea-Schioppa, ed., "Europe 1992: Three Essays" *Essays in International Finance*, No. 182 (May 1991), Princeton University Department of Economics, International Finance Section.

[95] These and other interesting issues are discussed in C.R. Henning, "Wake Up America!" *The International Economy* (March/April 1991). For an excellent review of the history of EMU, see M.J. Chriszt, "European Monetary Union: How Close Is It? *Economic Review*, FRB of Atlanta (September/October 1991). See also "European Leaders Agree to Treaty on Monetary Union (Maastricht)" IMF *Survey* (January 6, 1992), pp. 2-4.

[96] Cf. Wendy Dobson, *Economic Policy Coordination: Requiem or Prologue? (Washington, D.C.:* Institute of International Economics, 1991). Cf. also, "G-7 Summit Process Must Change, Says Group of Thirty Study," *IMF Survey* (August 12, 1991), and H. Rowen, "The G-7: Making It Work Again," *The Washington Post National Weekly Edition*, March 15-21, 1993.

- Most of the questions centering around Europe 1992 are political in nature.
- Most of the questions centering around Europe 1992 are legal in nature.
- Some of the questions centering around Europe 1992 are ethical in nature, for they involve not just profit and loss, sovereign power, and the operation of laws and regulations, but they also involve decision making that will affect the dignity, freedom, and well-being not just of nations but of people, who must certainly be the primary object of governmental and economic system concern.[97]

At the conclusion of Chapter 8 we will involve ourselves in an International Financial Market Exercise aimed at encouraging some thought about, some discussion of, and perhaps even some possible resolutions to broad issues raised in part by our international banking discussion.

But first we will attempt to highlight some directions specific regulatory issues might take in dealing with the key domestic banking problem of deposit insurance/bank failure/and a level playing field—and how this problem relates to the future shape of banking in the United States.

III. FINANCIAL MARKETS AND REGULATING TOWARD THE YEAR 2000: WHERE DOES AMERICAN DOMESTIC BANKING GO FROM HERE?

A. General Overview

In this concluding section of the chapter, we will examine the shape U.S. commercial banking might take over the final decade of the twentieth century in terms of what seem to be the most serious concerns of the system: *deposit insurance, resolving bank failures,* and *competition / level playing fields*.

But first, an observation: Whatever that shape may be *will* be determined as much by law as by untrammeled market forces. And if and when law (and consequent regulation) does more harm than good, the market's bad behavior is sure to be one of the major contributing factors,

---

[97] Jacques Delors has been quoted as saying that he believes that only a free market can generate wealth, but that states and companies then have a moral duty to share this wealth fairly: "Our union," he says, "must be as efficient as the United States, but without falling into its errors. It must be deeply rooted in social justice. . ." Quoted in J. Ardagh, "Will the New Europe Please Sit Down," *The New York Times* (November 10, 1991). See also on the social dimensions of economic restructuring in general: "The Gains from Latin America's Adjustment Must Be Consolidated," *IMF Survey*, December 14, 1992, pp. 376-77.

meaning that while policymakers—elected or academically anointed—are quite capable of falling into harmful error by tripping over their own political feet, they are all too often pushed over the edge by demonstrable market failures. This is particularly so when market failures are tainted with immorality, which erodes public trust, produces public anger, and often results in excessive, unproductive policies and regulations.

And, in the case of our "free" market system, if bad behavior can produce bad law, so can negligent definition. Reasonable men and women, commanding good pay for their skills, ought to be expected at the very least to understand well, and to define clearly, the market problems they are about to take steps to correct.

One might begin, for example, with the oft-expressed opinion that new policy in the U.S. domestic banking market ought to proceed from these "facts": that the market is presently overcompetitive, overstuffed (with excess capacity), and, generally speaking, sick or dying. Steps must therefore be taken to promote consolidation, and to allow for commercial bank participation in wider and wider markets (e.g., insurance and investment banking).

Data seem to indicate that between 1984 and 1992 the number of U.S. commercial banks in operation fell from 14,500 to 11,500. Despite that diminution, two other pieces of information would seem to indicate that there is less than meets the eye in those figures. New banks over the same period of time entered the industry at a 1.6 percent annual rate. Though slightly lower than during 1980–1985, this rate is higher than it was in either the 1960s or the 1970s. Banks certainly have failed and exited the market, but others have failed and been absorbed by other banks or bank holding companies. Even banks in healthy operating condition have been absorbed. So, while the absolute number of banks are going down, new entities and bank consolidation processes do challenge the bold conclusion that these numbers clearly define a dying industry.[98]

There is also evidence available to demonstrate that, while competition by nonbank entities surely has been increasing rapidly, the market has not contracted so much as to warrant wringing out "excess capacity" by transferring resources to other industries.

Commercial banks do profit from nonbank intermediary activities: Corporate issuers of commercial paper, for example, do pay banks for essential backup credit lines, and all checks written against money market mutual funds must be cleared, for a fee, through commercial banks as well.

---

[98] J.H. Boyd and S.L. Graham, "Investigating the Banking Consolidation Trend," *Quarterly Review, FRB of Minneapolis (Spring 1991).* This well-documented and somewhat startling article will be cited further as Boyd and Graham.

Furthermore, off-balance-sheet products of commercial banks do not show up in the asset totals used to measure market share. An example would be such loan guarantees and letters of credit.[99] Another example is the billions of dollars of loans sold in secondary markets, with the bank as originator or servicer.[100]

And there are "truisms" around that require more thoughtful analysis. There seems to be data, for example, demonstrating that "consolidation produces economies of scale" is one truism that doesn't hold in the domestic banking market. That, in fact, in this market, the greater the size, the more that efficiency *decreases*.[101] It can also be argued that consolidation in the commercial banking industry is not always motivated by economies of scale, but rather by wrongheaded government—and free marketeer—policies. Merger *within the same geographical market* seems to be encouraged by regulators and eagerly undertaken by bankers anxious to increase monopoly rents.[102] And then there is the clear and present propensity of regulators to protect large banks from the full consequences of inefficient (and, perhaps, unethical) management on the grounds that "clearly there are some institutions whose collapse the financial markets would find intolerable."[103]

The focus of this overview is not on the actual specifics of the future shape of banking; rather, it is simply to suggest that the basis for decision making must be very carefully examined (i.e., what our *ends* ought to be, and why) *before* we begin wrestling with the *means* to achieve them.

To conclude this overview we would like to suggest that in every discussion of ends and means, we keep in mind this overarching issue: whether in any specific case we are unwittingly (or worse, wittingly)

---

[99] See note 67, *supra*.

[100] Boyd and Graham, p. 9. See also E.G. Corrigan, "Rebuilding the Financial Strength of the U.S. Banking System," FRBNY *Quarterly Review* (Summer 1992).

[101] J.A. Clark, "Economies of Scale and Scope at Depository Financial Institutions: A Review of the Literature," *Economic Review*, FRB of Kansas City (September/October 1988). See also A. Srinivasan, "Are There Savings from Bank Mergers?" FRB of Atlanta *Economic Review* (March/April 1992).

[102] See, for example, *First Hawaiian Inc.* Order Approving the Acquisition of a Bank Holding Company 77 *Federal Reserve Bulletin* 52 (1991) (Governor Mullins dissenting); *Fleet/Norstar Financial Group Inc.* Order Approving the Acquisition of a Bank Holding company and Banks, 77 *Federal Reserve Bulletin* 750 (1991) (Governors Angell and Kelly dissenting). See also the Boyd and Graham (note 98, *supra*) discussion of the U.S. Justice Department loosening of its bank merger (anticompetition) guideline in 1982, and another example of the resultant merger activity, e.g., in the Minneapolis-St. Paul area. See: *First Bank System, Inc.*, Minneapolis, Minnesota, Order Approving Merger of Bank Holding Companies with 3 governors dissenting on the effect on competition issue. *Federal Reserve Bulletin*, January 1993, pp. 50-54. And on the statistical measure of concentration used by the Fed and the Justice Department, see: S.A. Rhodes, "The Herfindahl-Hirschman Index," *Federal Reserve Bulletin*, March 1993, p. 188.

[103] We refer here to the misleadingly titled "too-big-to-fail" doctrine, which will be discussed *infra*.

working at cross-purposes in our commercial banking-law-and-economics interdisciplinary endeavor. That is, we should determine whether market forces may be working toward moving the inefficient out of the banking market, while lawmakers and regulators (and even some marketeers) are hard at work keeping them in.[104]

B. Deposit Insurance and Resolving Bank Failures

These two issues seem to us to be so closely linked as to require consideration jointly.

There are two major issues in bank closures: *when* to close them down, and *how* to close them down. And deposit insurance is linked to both, together with allied ethical issues.

It is not difficult to articulate a general "when-to" standard. Banks can, legally, be closed when they are "insolvent," that is, when their liabilities exceed their assets. The problem here is twofold: First, *when* a bank is actually insolvent is not always easy to determine, and second, waiting for insolvency might not be the most constructive way to handle a severely distressed bank situation.

If, for example, in the determining-insolvency scenario, a bank holds fixed-rate assets, and market interest rates go way up, are the "assets" (e.g., fixed-rate mortgages) still worth the same amount? Under generally accepted accounting principles, until the mortgages are sold they are listed at original book value. We have already examined the market value accounting concept as it applies to real estate assets, so we are now able to see, whether the issue is proper capital asset ratios or solvency evaluation, that both technical and ethical issues are involved.

Waiting for insolvency, in any event, could prove to be as frustrating as waiting for Godot. Not because insolvency might never arrive, but rather that by the time it does, the costs will have overwhelmed the event. As long as a terminal but not yet expired bank remains in operation it can, by the grace of deposit insurance, continue to lose money without losing customers.

Actually, the failing bank may be a *more* attractive place to deposit funds, because it pays higher interest rates to attract them. Investment banking houses, for example, have generated a good deal of fee income from breaking large amounts of investment money into $100,000 pieces, and then placing the pieces in high-interest paying, failing or borderline banks. This is the "brokered deposit" phenomenon that clearly played some role in the overall S&L debacle. Of course, a viable market for

---

[104] Cf. Boyd and Graham, *supra*, at p. 13. See also Dotsey and Kuprianov, note 2, *supra*, at p. 22.

brokered funds can fill an important niche in the financial market system. That market fails, however, when it is utilized to seek out high returns offered by underperforming banks *on the basis of all underlying risk being absorbed by the nonparticipating general public.* "Moral hazard" seems a more or less innocuous description for this particular kind of behavior.

Still, it could be argued, even technical insolvency should not necessarily force the closure of a bank. Perhaps it is simply in a temporary bind. And exogenous disruption today can fracture values that may be healed tomorrow. Moreover, if the cost of closure is high today, who knows what tomorrow will bring? We might, for example, wait out a real estate storm, and by doing so avoid insurance fund insolvency and local bank market dislocation entirely, somewhere down the line.

This process of waiting, of allowing time to see insolvency reversed and resolved, is referred to as "forbearance." Forbearance may be prompted by technical considerations (this is really a well-managed bank with resolvable problems), by political considerations (you *will not* close down my constituents' bank), by self-serving considerations (as a regulator, I do not want to look bad), or by corruption pure and simple (I take money to keep them in business).

Forbearance, in light of the S&L horror, has fallen into disfavor as we shall see when we examine the new FDICIA law *infra.* There is clearly some advantage of hindsight in some loudly articulated antiforbearance positions. It is nevertheless true that reality is worth one's attention even when encountered late.

With regard then to the *when-to-close the bank,* certain directives seem to be worth considering:

- Regulators could be given authority to close down banks *before* they are technically insolvent. Such authority would have to be clear, would require guidelines, and action could be effective only after being detailed clearly, in writing.

- Forbearance in any form could be indulged in only after the reasons therefore were reduced to writing, filed with the regulator, signed, approved, and available for public inspection under the Freedom of Information Act.

- All assets could be subjected to market value accounting (MVA).

- Brokered deposits could be made uninsurable.

We turn now to the area of *how-to-close,* and there are three major options (once the decision has been made that a bank cannot be allowed to remain in operation):

Option 1 is simply to padlock the doors, pay off depositors up to the $100,000 limit, and leave the over-$100,000 depositor and the noninsured (e.g., offshore accounts) to absorb their particular losses.[105]

Option 2 is simply to padlock the doors, and to pay off *all* depositors, onshore or offshore, one hundred cents on the dollar, without regard to insurance limits.

Option 3 is to allow the bank to operate, probably with regulator supervision, only until its sale to another banking entity can be arranged. If such sale were arranged, Option 2 would, in effect, be accomplished in a roundabout way, since no one would lose any money, except, of course, for the insurance fund, which must put together a package acceptable to a profit-seeking buyer. Such a package would usually include the insurance fund's swallowing all bad loans and other "adversely classified" assets so that the buyer never purchases the trouble that brought the bank down in the first place. In fact, the insurance fund can even guarantee the buyer that if any bad assets turn up later, the fund will purchase them so as to the leave the buyer whole. The chief charge of the Resolution Trust Fund, set up under FIRREA, is to sell and recoup for us taxpayers billions of such "adversely classified" assets.

The problem with Option 1 is that it is a bullet, and many regulators and most politicians are disinclined to bite it. The new FDICIA law, discussed *infra*, does not bite, although it snaps a little. The argument that Option 1 simply costs too much money is, in the light of the S&L losses, demonstrably deficient. A more effective argument against Option 1 is that utilizing it would greatly upset all depositors having more than $100,000 as well as offshore depositors. Those folks would not appreciate being asked the obvious question: As a large investor and as one familiar with insurance contract limits, why should you not bear the loss of your own defective monitoring? That question itself seems reasonable enough in the context of a competitive free market system. However, the reality seems to be that abandoning over $100,000 and offshore free market depositors would create a crisis of confidence and trigger a run—especially by nondomestic depositors—on all large American banks.

When we recall the complex, interlocking, national, and international payments system structure and function, it is not difficult to imagine the possible adverse effect on America's (and possibly the world's) banking system stability, should a run ever to occur.

The concern that such a bank run might have occurred in 1984 prompted the FDIC to put together a $4.5 billion package to save the Continental Illinois Bank & Trust Company from the consequences of its

---

[105] Under the U.S. deposit insurance system, nondomestic deposits are not included in figuring premiums. They are therefore not covered by deposit insurance funds unless the FDIC chooses to cover them!

several follies. At the time, Option 1 would clearly have been cheaper in dollars and cents. At that time, U.S. regulators stated publicly that the U.S. banking system would never allow large, including foreign, depositors to be hit with losses. This position came to be known as the "too-big-to-fail" doctrine. In almost all cases, this is a misnomer, of course, even when technical insolvency is still a run away. It really is the "too-big-to-be-allowed-to-suffer-the-consequences-of-having-failed" doctrine. The euphemism is illuminating.

This doctrine, which would be totally unacceptable to anyone in the direct form of Option 2, has been adhered to openly since 1984. It is clearly productive of "moral hazard"; that is, it is a way for profit-seeking supporters of "free competitive markets" to protect themselves from risk at the expense of the general taxpaying public.

Many have questioned both the practicality (would the closure of Continental Illinois and resultant losses truly have been unbearable?) and the ethics of the "too-big-to" doctrine.

The ethical issue highlighted by this doctrine came to the fore with a vengeance in 1990, with the closing of the Freedom National Bank (FNB) in New York. FNB, an African-American bank in Harlem, had deposits of about $91 million, some $15 million of which fell in the over-$100,000 deposit category. Many meritorious depositors, such as the United Negro College Fund and the National Urban League, as well as respected churches conducting antidrug and other community programs, fell into that $15 million category. The FDIC closed FNB in November 1990 and announced that the $100,000 limit would be scrupulously observed in every case (in other words, Option 1).

In August 1990, the FDIC had accepted Option 3 (and by extension, Option 2) in the case of the failed National Bank of Washington (NBW). In the NBW case, the FDIC assumed more than $500 million in bad loans and questionable "assets" so that NBW could then be acquired by Riggs National Corporation, another Washington, D.C., banking entity. This deal not only fully protected many over-$100,000 domestic deposits but also $37 million in offshore deposits in NBW's Bahamas branch as well.[106]

Federal regulators later claimed that they had tried to arrange for FNB to be acquired, but couldn't find a buyer. No figure appeared to be given for any FDIC package offered to sweeten the deal. The FDIC, after pressure, did agree to pay some $7.5 million in uninsured claims out of the sale of FNB's assets. Racism was not necessarily the issue here. The $1.1 billion domestic and foreign deposit size status of NBW versus the $91

---

[106] See K.H. Bacon, "Failures of a Big Bank and a Little Bank Bring Fairness of Deposit Security Policy into Question," *The Wall Street Journal* (December 5, 1990).

million domestic deposit size status of FNB is sufficient explanation and raises clearly the fair dealing issue.

The first session of the 102d Congress, at year's end 1991, produced P.L. 102-407(1991): *The Comprehensive Deposit Insurance Reform and Taxpayer Protection Act of 1991*. The short title of this new law is the *Federal Deposit Insurance Corporation Improvement Act of 1991* (FDICIA). The full legislation is 170 pages long, and we will emphasize three of its major provisions here, those regarding PCA (prompt corrective action): bank closures; too-big-to-fail etc.; and risk-based deposit insurance. Other matters we must relegate to a footnote.[107]

---

[107] Subtitle B (Secs. 111-115) covers *Supervisory Reform*. It mandates *annual* on-site inspections for all insured depository institutions with assets over $100 million, and 18-month inspections for those with under $100 million. A weakness: Federal regulators can allow a state-regulated bank examination to substitute for its own (Sec. 111d(3)). Subtitle B carries other bank reporting requirements. Subtitle C (Secs.121-123) relates to *Accounting Reforms*. It requires only that a bank follow "generally accepted accounting principles." However, federal regulators are authorized to require something tougher if accuracy of financial position, effective supervision, or the ability to take prompt, corrective action so requires. And federal supervisors may also develop a "method for insured depositor institutions to provide supplemental disclosure of fair market value of assets and liabilities, to the extent feasible and practicable, in any balance sheet, financial statement, report of condition or other report."

In this connection, the Financial Accounting Standards Board (FASB), in its Statement 107, December 1991, required banks (and all other companies) to disclose the fair market value (FMV) of all financial instruments—on and off-balance sheet—for which it is practical to do so. *But the disclosure is to be footnoted only.* This has disturbed the banks, which think it is too much to ask, and the new chief accountant of the SEC, who thinks it is too little. He wants FMV data *on the balance sheet itself.* See K.G. Salwen, "SEC Seeking Updated Rules for Accounting," *The Wall Street Journal* (January 9, 1992). A thorough recent article on MVA and banks, which also reflects upon the "moral hazard" inherent in historical cost accounting in the presence of deposit insurance, is T. Mondochean, "Market Value Accounting for Commercial Banks," *Economic Perspective*, FRB of Chicago (January/February 1991). See also R.G. Blumenthal, "FASB Moves Closer to Forcing Banks to Value Securities Near Market Prices," *The Wall Street Journal* (September 11, 1992).

The new law *is* much tougher on foreign banks. It gives federal regulators real power to oversee and to deal with all foreign banking operations within the United States (Secs.201-210). Further, revised Basle Group standards now require that international banking regulatory authority be divided between the bank's home country and the host countries where it operates. But the new international rules are weak although the Fed's will in the United States is strong. On this BCCI-inspired matter, see G.N. Kleiman, "Global Banking's Myopic Regulators," *The New York Times* (October 11, 1992), "Federal Reserve Enforcement Actions and BCCI," statement of J.V. Mattingly, Jr., General Counsel of the FRB to a Senate Committee, May 14, 1992, *Federal Reserve Bulletin* (July 1992) pp. 509-511 (relating to all Fed efforts re the BCCI failure, under the provisions of the law referred to as The Foreign Bank Supervisor and Enhancement Act of 1991). Effective January 28, 1993 are all new Fed regulations pertaining to Fed supervision and regulation of foreign banking organizations. They do tighten up substantially on all foreign banks. See *Federal Reserve Bulletin*, March 1993, pp. 206–214.

What the new law does *not* do is deal head on with the overall issue of whether efficiency, fair play, and/or competitiveness concerns require *substantive* changes in our current *overall* financial system. It makes no substantive changes, for example, in Glass-Steagall, McFadden, or Douglas. It could be argued that by doing *nothing* in this area, Congress *did* deal head on. But one cannot escape the judgment that P.L. 102–407 is a short-term sidestep.

Section D of the FDICIA requires federal regulators to take "prompt regulatory action" regarding weak banks. The Federal Reserve, the Comptroller of the Currency, the FDIC, and the Office of Thrift Supervision jointly adopted and released the final rules for "Prompt Corrective Action" (PCA) required within section D, by its section 38.[108]

The rule sets up five categories for banks. Each category carries "capital measures" that are guides to regulator mandatory actions and discretionary actions to be applied to banks within the category. As of December 19, 1992, all banks are denominated (1) Well capitalized, (2) Adequately capitalized, (3) Undercapitalized, (4) Significantly undercapitalized, (5) Critically undercapitalized. The capital measures determining the denomination (category) are: The total risk-based capital ratio of the bank, its Tier 1 risk-based capital ratio, and the leverage ratio. For the (1) bank (the best), the ratios are 10.0, 6.0, and 5.0 or greater, respectively. For the terminal bank (5), only one ratio matters: a ratio of tangible equity to total assets that is 2.0 percent or less.[109]

Category 5 banks must be placed in receivership within 90 days "unless the appropriate agency and the FDIC concur" that other action would better achieve the purposes of the PCA.

The key to section 38 is that, by and large, regulators still determine which banks get closed up and which don't. Regulator discretion, like infantry foot soldier slogging, has yet to be eliminated by technological development. Issues still remain, such as: Will regulators act tardily or too hastily (except perhaps for category [5]); will they lower a bank's credit rating at the most efficient time and in the most efficient way? And, of course, one cannot be certain that PCA will save a substantial amount of money; however, it is probably true that PCA *is* a reasonable first step in the attack on regulatory forbearance.

Forbearance raises a second issue, which is the "too-big-to-fail" doctrine. There is nothing in the new law that mandates *no more* too-big-to-fail etc. There is language making it more difficult to protect deposits over $100,000, but the end result is still regulator discretion.

As of June 30, 1992, more than $1 billion in insured deposits was sitting in category (5) banks, (to be closed on December 19, 1992), which is a small number of banks relative to the U.S. total in that worst of all

---

See, e.g., M. Jacobs, "A Failure of Nerve on Banking Reform," *The New York Times* (December 8, 1991).

[108] Effective December 19, 1992, as 12 CFR, Part 208: *Federal Reserve Bulletin, (November 1992), pp. 835-44.*

[109] Illustrative tables and lists of actions that regulators must and/or may take can be found in R.A. Gilbert, "The Effects of Legislating Prompt Corrective Action on the Bank Insurance Fund," *FRB of St. Louis* (July/August 1992).

possible categories. On the question of just who will be protected above $100,000, one can only say that, as of October 1992, regulators allowed over $100,000 depositors to take losses in 58 percent of 85 banks closed, up from just 17 percent in 1991. However, two big problems remain: First, it is the depositors in the big banks who seem to remain protected, and *more* of these depositors in the smaller ones who seem to take the hit. Second, although more depositors are being allowed to lose above $100,000 since FDICIA went into effect, there is no way for any depositors to know whether *their* bank is too small to be saved. There doesn't seem to be reasonable fairness here, and in its absence how can market discipline really be expected to work?[110]

Finally, with regard to FDICIA, Title III, Section 302, mandates the establishment of a risk-based assessment system for insured depository institutions by January 1, 1994. The details are complex and may or may not survive, intact, that long. Some movement in that direction was made in 1992, with new premiums taking effect in January 1993 ranging from 23 cents for each $100 of domestic deposits for the healthiest banks to 31 cents per $100 for the weakest, with re-evaluations (currently) planned every six months.

The new law, then, does not take definitive steps to deal with overall deposit insurance changes.

Let us examine that issue through these alternative considerations:

1. Abolish deposit insurance.
2. Lower deposit insurance limits.
3. Privatize deposit insurance.
4. Require risk-adjusted insurance premiums throughout the entire system.
5. Restrict deposit insurance to "narrow bank" deposits.
6. Make deposit insurance coverage unlimited.
7. Beef up regulatory powers and processes to provide more adequate backup for *any* chosen deposit insurance system.

---

[110] See (for the data contained in the paragraph,) K.H. Bacon and S. Lipin, "Stiffer Standard: Under New Bank Law, More Large Depositors Face Losses in Failures," *The Wall Street Journal* (October 22, 1992). Specific examples of disparity in treatment, by size, are contained in the article. See also M. Quint, "A Tough Call: What to Reveal on Sick Banks," *The New York Times* (August 27, 1992). See, in connection with FDICIA and restrictions on Federal Reserve Bank authority to undercapitalized banks, W.F. Todd, "FDICIA's Discount Window Provisions," *Economic Commentary* of the FRB of Cleveland, December 15, 1992.

There is little support for consideration 1 above. It is generally agreed that there should be a safe, dependable, and convenient medium for basic transactions and savings for the general public at some reasonable level.

The major problem with consideration 2, although it is an attractive political cosmetic, is that below-the-limit depositors could go from bank to bank (or account to account) with *all* their money, and thus little relief would be applied to the overall system. Moreover, it does nothing at all to deal with the inequitable "too-big-to-fail" doctrine. Over-the-limit depositors would go to the same safe big banks to guarantee themselves full coverage.

Consideration 3 is an excellent free market theoretical construct, but it requires the avoidance of several realities that give cause for reflection:

- If the deposit insurance market is one that appeals to private insurers, why have they thus far avoided insuring all deposits over $100,000 in non-too-big-to-fail banks?
- As private insurers, would they be subject to government supervision? Assuming that they would be, would state governments be able to pay for adequate supervision, and be willing to, if the primary deep pocket wasn't in *their* pants? They did not do a good job in Rhode Island. There, the private Rhode Island Share and Deposit Indemnity Corporation (RISDIC) proved to be unsafe and unsound, despite state oversight. RISDIC collapsed, causing some 350,000 accounts to be frozen and unreachable—and this in a state with a total population of little over a million people. Then, too, there were the failures of private deposit insurance companies in Ohio and Maryland in 1985.[111] And if private insurers do fail, how far behind will the Federal Reserve be? Then, there is the cost: The range between unconscionable giveaway and predatory pricing is very broad. And upon just what risk-based data will private premiums be based?
- And, of course, there are insurance company "crises." Where is the guarantee that there will be no deliberate underpricing in order to obtain the best business (or *any* business), that could result later in withdrawal of coverage; or in no available coverage at all at any price? And would private insurers be emboldened to withdraw coverage in the belief that government would have to step in anyway where the banking system is involved?

---

[111] For a full account of the RISDIC debacle, see the statement of Richard Syron, president of the Federal Reserve Bank of Boston, to a congressional committee on April 17, 1991, in the *Federal Reserve Bulletin* (June 1991) at p. 429.

Recent experience in the insurance area is not particularly encouraging.

Partial privatization would seem to have one advantage: while not eliminating the "moral hazard" problem, it could bolster oversight/examination standards. If one assumes more vigilance on the part of private insurers, they could serve as an early warning system to supposedly less risk-adverse government regulators—that is, the government could tie its premiums to those of the private insurer. But would a regulator-dependent private insurer be tempted to add cost-savings to good relations behavior and rely a bit too heavily on the governmental regulators, who, after all, represent free staff to them?

We realize that we are assuming the probable presence here of private insurer "moral hazard." To any argument that this is not a reasonable consideration, we would answer, with Dr. Johnson, that a contrary position represents the triumph of hope over experience.[112]

Risk-based premium assessments—in this case as determined by government (consideration 4)—would seem to be fairer than nonrisk-based, and could even serve as a warning flag to potential investors by linking rising cost to risk. It would not be easy, however, to develop the essentials of an examination system that would measure all risks adequately (for government or for a private insurer), at least not under circumstances where market value accounting is shunned. Moreover, Fed Chairman Alan Greenspan has pointed out that deposit insurance premiums are already high and that "the range of premiums necessary to reflect risk difference adequately and to induce genuine behavioral changes might be wider than feasible."[113]

No less a personage than Nobel Laureate James Tobin has suggested the consideration 5, "narrow bank" concept: In this narrow bank scenario, all *insured* demand, savings, and time deposits would have to be invested by the receiving bank solely in safe assets, mainly Treasury or federally guaranteed government securities. There would be no ceiling on insurance coverage. The narrow bank could be a totally separate entity, or an entity within a larger bank holding company structure. It could even be a department in a large bank. Its assets, however, would have to be completely segregated. Any other (non-narrow) bank could conduct

---

[112] Moreover, the early 1990s are surely a difficult time period in which to assert that U.S. private insurance companies do not, like government entities, fall into serious financial difficulties. See, for example, R.W. Kopcke, "The Capitalization and Portfolio Risk of Insurance Companies," *New England Economic Review*, July/August, 1992.

[113] Statement by Alan Greenspan before a U.S. Senate committee, the *Federal Reserve Bulletin (July 1991), at p. 433. See also: Y.S. Chan, S.I. Greenbaum and A.Y. Thakar "Is Fairly Priced Deposit Insurance Possible?" Journal of Finance*, March 1992. ("It is impossible." p. 243).

any business it liked within normal regulatory practice, but none of its depositors would be insured in any amount. This would guarantee these depositors nothing more than a higher rate of return than narrow banks would pay.

There are unanswered questions here, of course. If we assume, as Professor Tobin seems to, that all banks will be subject to some government regulation in order to assure a meaningful, functioning, overall interme-diary system,[114] who serves as the lender of last resort in the face of runs on the *uninsured* banks? And would there be runs of consequence in terms of the overall intermediary system? What might be the effect upon the domestic and international payment system? In sum, will the economy and the public still be at risk in one way or another? Finally, would such a dual system be competitive internationally with large all-service foreign banks that are backed by central banking authorities?

The interesting aspect of unlimited insurance (consideration 6), which at first blush seems to be preposterous, is that it is the only proposal on our list that guarantees the demise of the outrageous "too-big-to-fail" doctrine. In the absence of unlimited coverage for all, the doctrine, while it could perhaps be exercised with greater circumspection than it has been in the past, could not safely be abolished. It appears to be a necessary evil. It is difficult to see how responsible government officials could be denied utterly the right to exercise judgment on the probable danger to the system of some particular big bank failure (and the new FDICIA law does not disallow the exercise of that judgment).[115]

Left standing alone, however, consideration 6 could prove to be as dangerous as it looks. In fact, it already has proven to be—though we tend to adopt it, in the case of the biggest banks, in a more circuitous fashion.

However, if solidly linked with consideration 7 (beef up regulatory powers), we would argue that consideration 6 would be the fairest and most efficient deposit insurance system of them all. The real issue here is safety and soundness at *any* coverage size. We could begin to envision keeping deposit insurance costs within reasonable bounds, even without a cap, if we instituted a truly responsible regulatory regime. Some essential com-ponents of the regime would be:

- Acceptance by the public and by national and local government that such a regime is high priority, even though it will cost a good deal of money up front, and call for ongoing commitment. It will still be inexpensive in the end.

---

[114] James Tobin, "Keep Deposit Insurance but Protect Taxpayers," *The Wall Street Journal* (May 29, 1991).

[115] See statement by Fed Board member John B. LaWare before a congressional committee on May 9, 1991, the *Federal Reserve Bulletin* (July 1991) pp. 549-54.

- Acceptance by national and local government of the fact that banks are their *charge,* not their *constituency.* Their constituency is the public that supports the banks. Any argument that this is not true has been rendered worthless by the S&L horror, the subsequent transfer of public funds into the bank bailout process, and the resultant damage to public services that taxpayers will be forced to suffer unto succeeding generations. "Constituency training" for all bank examiners should be required. And this is clearly an ethical as well as a financial issue.

Any government plan to "solve" the "banking problem" that does not make a total commitment to full funding for a tough, highly structured, fully supported, public-safety-oriented regulatory system would be, at best, a palliative, at worst a fraud and, in either case, a prelude to eventual problems of desperate magnitude.

If it can be argued convincingly that any such plan requires a political commitment beyond the capacity of legislators at any governmental level, then it must be accepted as well that both the competence and the trustworthiness of bankers and legislators are simply not insurable risks.

The central elements of a "tough, highly structured, fully supported public-safety-oriented regulatory system" would certainly include:

- Market value accounting (MVA).
- Risk-level capital requirements based upon MVA information, and utilizing the Basle Accord as a minimum base for all banks. Minimums would vary with particular activity risks assumed.[116]
- Long-term subordinated debt as a mandated minimum percentage of the required capital level of every bank.
- Actuarially determined, risk-based deposit insurance premiums utilizing MVA information.
- Early intervention authority for regulators (from dealing with dividend distribution to closing and locking the doors).
- Adequate national and local funding for a trained corps of regulator/examiners charged with time-specific, *full-scope,* on-site inspections.[117]

---

[116] It is worth recalling that, prior to the institution of deposit insurance, the typical bank capital ratio in the United States was approximately 15%. *These* days cannot be the *old days* to be sure, but putting a reasonable amount of one's own capital at risk is an old-time capitalist process that deserves to be treated with *some* respect.

[117] Limited rather than full-scope bank examinations, and a concomitant low level of supervision on the part of the Office of the Comptroller of the Currency, have both been blamed for the CC's comparatively poor record regarding failures of banks under its supervision. S. Schmidt, "Who Was Watching While the Banks Were Going Bust?" *The Washington Post National Weekly Edition* (September 16-22, 1991).

- Adequate initial and ongoing examiner skills training and upgrading, with some emphasis on clarity with regard to who their proper constituency is (and is not). Attitude is never irrelevant to the regulator task at hand.[118]

The result of a tough, highly structured, fully supported, public-safety-oriented regulatory process need not be an uncreative, strait-jacketed, noncompetitive banking system. On the contrary, aside from allowing for full insurance coverage for all banks, and for substantially decreasing the risk of a second intolerable banking fiasco, such a beefed-up regulatory process should be the foundation for a highly competitive system with *no* legal restrictions on bank participation in any kind of financial business.

C. Interstate Banking and Glass-Steagall

The two major thrusts in the direction of expanded commercial banking powers are: (1) full and free interstate banking, including branching, and (2) full participation in all debt and equity markets.

There is no doubt that present restrictions in interstate banking are "inefficient" in terms of dollar costs to those banking units that look to expand domestically. However, eliminating and/or amending the Douglas Amendment and the McFadden Act requires resolution of two types of interests:

- *Those of the banking community* who argue that unrestricted national banking would enable banks to so diversify their portfolios as to avoid dependency on the (mis)fortunes of just one region. Moreover, as the full-access process proceeds, consolidation of banks would occur, also making for increased banking efficiency.

- *Those of communities at large* who argue that serious issues of concentration, credit access, and conflict of interest would arise out of unrestricted national banking. Specifically, that many regional, and even local, bank mergers would occur as part of an overall, developing bank merger pattern[119]; that these mergers

---

[118] A succinct overview of the various alternatives to the current unsatisfactory banking structures is L.J. White's "What Should Banks Really Do?" Revised draft of a paper presented at the Contemporary Policy Issues Session of the Western Economic Association International Conference of June 30, 1991 (Stern School of Business of New York University, July 1991). It is interesting to note that the Chemical/Manny Hanny merger order from the Fed contains a dissent by Governor Angell, who expressed concern about too little capital being available to support this merger. Chemical Banking Corporation Order, 78, *Federal Reserve Bulletin* 74, 88 (1992).

[119] As of the third quarter of 1991, five mergers (Bank America and Security Pacific; NCB Corp. and C&S Sovran; Chemical Bank and Manufacturer's Trust; National City and

would restrict and/or overprice bank credit with relation to small- and medium-sized local businesses, and that large, full-service banking units could press for customer acceptance of linking or tying arrangements regarding discrete financial—and even nonfinancial—services offered by the lender.[120]

It can be argued that the number of U.S. banks simply has to fall, perhaps to as low as 5,000 nationwide, in order to have an efficient market; that the market itself will fairly resolve short-term dislocations in credit supply, which probably will occur with unrestricted national banking; and finally, that banks and/or banking markets can be trusted, in any event, not to squeeze borrowers unfairly through tying arrangements.

Two immediate concerns come to mind in response. First, with regard to those several thousand banks that could be either absorbed or made extinct: Might they not, in defense, attempt to utilize the deposit insurance franchise in a manner inconsistent with the public interest? That is, won't we be in for a time of serious "moral hazard" as they all fight for their individual existence? Second, regarding the element of public trust: Banks cannot expect to enjoy too much of that in the face of a decade's worth of experiential data.

The end result, regarding complete freedom for interstate banking, may be that the Federal Reserve will have to utilize an expanded and toughened version of the Community Reinvestment Act (CRA) to regulate community fairness in bank operations relative to credit access and related matters. The CRA (12 U.S.C. § 2901 *et seq.*) is legislation aimed primarily at ensuring that the convenience and (credit) needs of the community, particularly low-income neighborhoods, are fairly met by banking institutions. It would be important, in the face of total interstate operating freedom, for the Fed to keep clearly in mind that communities, not bankers, are its constituency here.[121]

Ameritrust; Wachovia and South Carolina National) were announced involving some $12.5 billion in M&A "deals." See R. Smith, "Big Bank Mergers Come as Boon to a Wall Street Thirsty for Deals," *The Wall Street Journal* (August 16, 1991). And, of course, the Bank of America-Security Pacific merger in April 1992 resulted in a $192 billion bank—number 2 in size in the United States.

[120] Cf. K.H. Bacon, "U.S. Worried Bank Mergers May Hurt Firms," *The Wall Street Journal* (September 25, 1991), citing concerns of James Rill, assistant U.S. Attorney General in charge of the Justice Department's Antitrust Division. In public testimony before the House Banking Committee, Mr. Rill cited a Federal Reserve Board study finding that commercial loan rates to small businesses are "substantially higher in cases where such businesses have only a small number of local commercial banks to which they can turn for their important credit needs." See also: F.W. Martin and G. Nih, "Thrifts' Push Into Interstate Operations May Corrupt Review of Policy for Banks," *The Wall Street Journal*, March 9, 1993.

[121] For a recent Fed order involving a Community Reinvestment Act (CRA) challenge to a requested bank acquisition, see Appleton City Bankshares, Inc. (Order Denying Acquisition of a Bank 77 *Federal Reserve Bulletin*, 1003 (1991). See also A.J. Fishbein, "Satisfying Your

The question of full bank participation in all debt and equity markets (i.e., repeal of Glass-Steagall) is also a subject for serious debate.

Clearly, American (and Japanese) banks are the only major-nation banks *not* allowed to deal fully in domestic investment banking activities. Certainly the reality of domestic nonbank financial market competition argues for the creation of a level playing field in this area.

The contrary argument is, of course, the one that has sustained Glass-Steagall for so long: System safety and soundness demands a wall between commercial and investment banking.

It seems to us apt, in the case of Glass-Steagall particularly, to point out that *freedom to compete* and *strict regulation* are actually quite compatible concepts.[122] To argue otherwise is to confuse, yet again, the distinction between *ends* and *means*. If one key *end* (goal) of a free market society is to foster a healthy, *fully competitive* commercial banking system *operating in the best interests of society*, then there are surely a number of *means* available to achieve such an end. Two of these are:

- Laws aimed at giving system participants the right to compete fully in all areas relevant to system growth (and repeal of laws inconsistent with that expressed end), and

- Laws (and regulations) aimed at promoting the safety and soundness of commercial banking in order to help ensure its continuing good health and competitiveness in all such areas.

An example of the first proposal would be the repeal of Glass-Steagall. An example of the second would be a strong regulatory system focused on such financial and ethical areas as equity capital level and capital adequacy and on conflicts of interest.

In this investment banking area, both financial and related ethical risks are, to a substantial degree, amenable to both inside-the-market and outside-the-market forces. Eventually, the market will probably punish

---

Examiner and Satisfying Your Community Are *Not* Always the Same," *ABA Bank Compliance* (Autumn 1990), pp. 2-5. The importance of CRA (among other things) gives one reason for deep concern that the U.S. Treasury Department would even consider diminishing the Fed role in banking regulation over the next decade. See K.H. Bacon, "Treasury's Plan to Overhaul Banking Could Diminish Fed's Regulatory Role," *The Wall Street Journal* (February 8, 1991). And for the shocking data on racial bias in American mortgage lending, see P.Thomas, "Behind the Figures: Federal Data Detail Pervasive Racial Gap in Mortgage Lending," *The Wall Street Journal* (March 31, 1992); and J.R. Wilke, "Some Banks' Money Flows Into Poor Areas—and Causes Anguish: Even As They Stint on Credit, They Finance Lenders Who Get Sky-High Rates," *The Wall Street Journal* (October 21, 1992). See also, E.T. Lowe, "Clinton To Push Community Development Banks," *U.S. Mayor*, February 15, 1993.

[122] See L.J. White, note 26, *supra*.

the incompetent and the wicked, but in the interim there must be legal sanctions (and consequent regulation).

One essential element of the regulatory system, with regard to freedom of entry into various new markets, would be the requirement for regulators, working with MVA-based information, to set particular and higher, capital standards for individual bank and bank holding company entry into new markets with higher levels of risk. These higher capital ratios could be required, specifically (triggered), by an entry into a new market category or, generally, by bank and/or bank holding company risk profile.[123]

Giving freedom to compete to all commercial banking institutions healthy enough to do so raises additional issues. One of them pertains to other systems affected that continue to compete with commercial banks. Investment banks come to mind. It is sufficient to observe that simple repeal of Glass-Steagall would allow investment banks to operate commercial banks too (i.e., *insured* depositories).

But how about basically *nonfinancial* commercial organizations? Should they also be allowed to combine with commercial banking? The arguments for and against allowing such a combination would seem to turn on the following issues (each of them related to risk).

- Would combining commerce and banking lead to serious conflicts of interest and unfair competition?[124]
- Would contagion be a concern? That is, if the auto industry, for example, owned and insured commercial banks and weakened badly, would the banking system (or at least the taxpaying public) be put in jeopardy?
- How far might the federal safety net be stretched in the case of specific commerce/banking problems?

Reasonable people might differ in their perception of the ultimate consequences of the preservation, or repeal, of Glass-Steagall, but they should not disagree on this: What the proper policy and (goal) should be can only be determined after all the opportunities and risks are clearly stated and, as clearly, weighed.

---

[123] See "Legal Developments: Final Rule—Amendment to Regulations H and Y, Appendix A—[Amended], *Federal Reserve Bulletin* (October 1990), pp. 847-49.

[124] See statement by E. Gerald Corrigan before a congressional committee, April 11, 1991, *Federal Reserve Bulletin (June 1991)*, pp. 415-21. The president of the New York Federal Reserve Bank argues strongly against the combination. See also L.J. Master, "Banking and Commerce: A Dangerous Liaison?" *FRB of Philadelphia Business Review* (May/June 1992).

One final comment on the domestic commercial banking regulation area: Martin Luther King, Jr. stated, in connection with the role of law in human affairs, that

> Morality cannot be legislated, but behavior can be regulated. Judicial decrees may not change the heart, but can restrain the heartless.[125]

We would agree, but would append the caveat to read: *to a degree.* There will always be a limit to what markets or law can do, separately or in cooperative combinations, to assure a healthy, competitive, and profitable economy *in the face of determined unethical behavior.* Maximum efficiency in the face of minimum morality, we are convinced, is an impossibility. What is necessary for the healthy existence of any inside-*and* outside-the-market structure for the future is not the presence of the millennium. Rather, it is the conscious recognition of the need for, and the consequent striving toward, a *public stewardship* paradigm worthy of the world's first truly great capitalist Republic.[126]

We have postponed our examination of the international-banking-related portion of *Regulating Financial Markets Toward the Year 2000,* because we want to include there investment banking, securities markets, and money management.

Let us turn to those areas next.

IN LIEU OF THE PHILOSOPHER'S STONE

We might want to think about parties at interest and value-weighting with regard to issues like this one:

> While a great many ethical issues are raised in connection with commercial banking market activity, one might reasonably conclude that the concept of "public stewardship" stands out as overshadowing all the others.

1. Do you feel that commercial banks, and therefore bankers, do have some special public responsibility beyond that of other market managers generally in product and service areas? If so, why? If not, why not?

---

[125] From a speech in Nashville, Tennessee, December 27, 1962.

[126] "It cannot be urged too strongly [that] the answer to lower risk [is] better bankers. When they are good, they are very, very good. When they are bad, the American public can't afford them." D.C. Colen (former vice-president, Citicorp), "Save Bankers from Themselves by Regulation," *The New York Times* (August 4, 1991), p. 14 ("Letters").

2. Do you feel that even if the answer is yes that the responsibility is fulfilled as long as regulations are obeyed? And that the bank's lawyers always have the right, of course, to find (legal) ways to get past the regulations?

3. Assuming for the moment the existence of "public stewardship." How should it be defined or characterized? That is, what public interests can be identified and weighed along with shareholder interests, and on what basis (regarding which goals/values) would you assign these weights?

Let us look at one simple example: Given $1 million for your bank to place, and a choice between investing in Treasury securities at 7 1/4 percent (no risk), or loans to small business owners in the community—with *good* borrower records but in slow economic times (clearly some risk)—how do you go about making choices? Of course you would want more data than you have here, but this really is the question: Would you assume the existence of some special "public ought," a value, that you would weigh in coming to an investments decision?

4. If there is some "public stewardship" requirement for banks, is it conceivable that the requirement could operate against the best interests of the bank's shareholders? Or could an argument be made that what is good or right for the bank is always consistent with acting with a view to the public interest—even if the act is inconsistent with immediate horizon shareholder enrichment?

5. If potential investors were to be convinced that banks and bank managers *are* public stewards, would they be likely to keep their money out of bank stocks on that account?

8

Regulating
Financial Markets

*Investment Banking, Securities
Markets, and Money Management*

COMING UP IN THIS CHAPTER

The three financial market areas to be discussed in this chapter merit, at the very least, one entire volume each. That is, they would require that kind of coverage were an attempt being made here to describe and detail their substantive functions fully. We are aiming at something different.

We intend to give an overview of the structure and function of investment banking, securities markets, and money management sufficient to allow us to identify market strengths and weaknesses. We will then be able to focus clearly on ethical, legal, and public policy perspectives in this chapter as we did in the previous one. There are a large number of issues here for us to deal with from an ethical perspective.

We begin (in Section I.A) with investment banking: what these entities are and, with some examples, what they do. We discuss several activities that highlight Wall Street accomplishment and Wall Street risk, risk we feel is also being borne by those who are not the customers of investment bankers. These activities include junk bond dealing, mergers and acquisitions, leveraged buyouts and restructuring, for example. We look at the Treasury market and at derivative products as well. We also look at insider trading, an area where weighing competing values is surely important (e.g., efficiency versus the public trust.)

We close section I.A with a serious ethical issue, not unlike one we examined in Chapter 7: Ought there be a fiduciary relationship assumed by (investment) bankers that is owed to the body politic within which the bankers perform their functions and earn their money?

An examination of the securities markets (Section I.B) follows the same pattern as the previous section: We describe the structure of the markets involved, their accomplishments and the risks imposed upon players and nonplayers alike. The role of technology is examined, as are the structures of some key international markets and the issues of market linkage and market integration—two rather different matters. Program trading and the questions of securities market openness and secrecy are followed by materials on the major matter of domestic and international security market regulation. Regulation here quite clearly involves interdisciplinary issues we have worked on before: economic efficiency, legality, technology, and fairness.

Section I.C (money management) deserves a bit more exposition. Any *complete* view of the field of money management would have to include substantial materials on investment companies, including a perusal of open-end funds, closed-end funds, mutual funds, and the like. And certainly if substantive management methodology was our focus, we would also need to look closely at functions, policies, securities analysis and portfolio construction, and performance evaluation. We have a different money-management purpose in mind, and others far better qualified than we have published superb materials in the field overall, which the reader would be well advised to consult.[1]

We focus in Section I.C on pension funds and pension fund management. We do so for one important reason: We believe that all financial managers (plus other executives) in U.S. corporations will be involved in some way in a company pension fund. Moreover, pension funds involve tens of millions of workers, and roughly $2.5 trillion in the United States. Finally, this subject is important because pension funds are an excellent paradigm for the enormous institutional investor phenomenon in this country: institutional investors exercise control over more than 50 percent of total investor assets in American securities markets.

We begin by looking at the issue of "prudence" in money management generally, a mixed financial/legal/ethical issue if ever there was one. We examine the Employment Retirement Income Security Act of 1974 (ERISA), and one of its offspring: the Pension Benefit Guarantee Corporation (PBGC). This brings us to issues such as valuing pension plans and funded and unfunded liabilities. And unfunded liabilities in the face of government guarantees brings us back to an old issue: "moral hazard." We discuss pension plan termination, and the singular phenomenon of

---

[1] For example, W. Sharpe and G. Alexander, *Investments*, 4th ed. (Englewood Cliffs, N.J.: Prentice Hall, 1990, esp. chaps. 20 and 22); Frederick Amling, *Investments: An Introduction to Analysis and Management*, 6th ed., (Englewood Cliffs, N.J.: Prentice Hall, 1989, esp. chap. 22).

public pension plans. We end this entire section with a close look at the power—and obligations—of pension funds.

Section II concludes the chapter. It is an Exercise.

We have tried to bring together in the Exercise *all* of our financial market issues *from Chapters 7 and 8.*

Simply stated, the Exercise is the chance for you to put your data and your thoughts together, to weigh competing economic and ethical concerns, and to make some decisions, specifically decisions about what law/regulations, if any, would make good sense, *to you*, in your assignment, and to decide what structure(s) and what function(s) would result in the most efficient *and* the fairest international financial market system.

I. EXAMINING MARKET STRUCTURE

A. Investment Banking

1. An Overview

As we observed in Chapter 7, the decade of the 1990s began with the distinctions between commercial and investment banking beginning to blur. Nevertheless, it is still possible to delineate specific functions that do categorize particular financial sector firms involved in the saving/investing and borrowing/lending processes.

First of all, not all firms that deal in stocks, bonds, and the like are in fact "investment banks." Many firms act solely as investment advisors; others are brokers who deal only as American (and regional) stock exchange members, or as over-the-counter securities traders or brokers, or perhaps as New York Stock Exchange specialists, traders and market makers.[2] There are full-line brokerage houses that do more than buy and sell (and offer specific information and recommendations concerning) stocks and bonds. They may also provide asset management, work with real estate syndications, do acquisitions and the like, and deal in other areas such as commodities, foreign currency, and hedging.

Investment banks, on the other hand, while doing *all* of the above, further engage in activities specific to their "banker" role. These include underwriting/market making through debt issues (straight and convertible mortgage-related and asset-backed), and through equity issues (common stock, preferred stock and initial public offerings). Herewith, are five areas of investment banking:

---

[2] Section I.B provides specific information on the structure and function of the various stock exchanges.

- Underwriting involves the investment banking firm in three major functions: *designing the issue* (i.e., determining type, quantity, pricing, and timing), *distributing the issue* (i.e., finding buyers), and, most important, *purchasing the issue* (i.e., the specific underwriting function), wherein the purchasing investment bank buys the new securities and undertakes the risk of not being able to sell them all for more than it paid for them.

- Mergers and acquisitions (M&A) and leveraged buyouts (LBOs).

- Venture capital (new business startups/ventures).

- Corporate finance (e.g., profit evaluations/recommendations, and/or restructurings).

- Merchant banking (taking actual equity positions in deals, including providing bridge loans to clients involved in, for example, LBOs or mergers and acquisitions).

2. How Money Is Made: The Changing Face of Investment Banking

There was a time when the largest percentage of investment bank income came from the sale of stocks and bonds. In fact, in 1970, when fully one-half of all income arose out of this source, "securities firm" was the often used general term for *all* Wall Street businesses. However, as the final decade of the twentieth century dawned, the 50 percent figure had dropped to approximately 17 percent. Investment banker income came far more from various types of "fees," most of them involving M&A, LBOs, corporate finance, and merchant banking activities.[3] While much of what propels Wall Street profits is cyclical in nature,[4] there seems little doubt but that the divergence between "brokerage firms" and "investment banks"

---

[3] Relevant data from the Securities Industry Association is cited to illustrate these figures in W. Power, "A Bumpy Road between '80-'89 Wall Street," *The Wall Street Journal* (December 28, 1989). It must be pointed out, however, that trading stock for their own accounts fattens investment banking profits enormously (e.g., $357 million in one quarter alone for Morgan Stanley). See M. Siconolfi, "Morgan Stanley and Alex Brown Report Much Stronger Results for Third Quarter," *The Wall Street Journal* (October 23, 1991).

[4] Late 1991, for example, saw a sharp rise in stock and bond sales and profits, and underwriting of equity and debt rose in concert. The third quarter of 1991 was the second best in Wall Street underwriting history. The top ten firms wrote more than 86 percent of the $408.3 billion in business in the first three quarters of the year; W. Power, "Merrill Strengthens Underwriting Lead as Salomon Stumbles in the Rankings," *The Wall Street Journal* (October 1, 1990) (citing as its source Securities Data Company). See also R. Smith, "As Merger Fees Dry Up, Wall Street Thrives Selling Mountains of New Stock," *The Wall Street Journal* (November 15, 1991). Full 1991 data contained in "Year End Review of Underwriting," *The Wall Street Journal* (January 2, 1992), p. R-32. In the first three quarters of 1992, underwriting fees broke all records. See data at p. 12, *The Wall Street Journal*, October 1, 1992). However, sizzling markets come and go, and it seems to be, per M. Siconolfi, that "As Diversified Firms Prosper on Wall Street, Others Falter," *The Wall Street Journal* (October 9, 1992).

will continue to grow, not because the larger, more highly capitalized houses will be out of the securities sales and commission business—that is, selling securities in the secondary (stock exchange) markets—but because they will be far more involved in other fee-focused profit centers.[5]

One issue we might raise and then return to later is this: In just what way is the public interest affected by the many new risk-reward activities large and powerful investment banks have become involved in? This assumes, of course, that what investment bankers do in fact *has,* or ought to have, a relationship to the public interest. Let us examine a few of these activities.

3. Dealing Seriously With Junk

Bonds offered publicly with a Standard and Poor's rating of less than BBB- , or a Moody's rating of less than Baaa3—or, with no rating at all—have earned the title of "junk bonds." According to the Federal Reserve Board's Capital Markets Section, junk bond issues, which amounted to some $8 billion in 1982, rose to a high of $40 billion in 1986, and totalled some $135 billion in the peak years of 1986-1989.[6]

While Drexel Burnham Lambert was clearly the junk bond king of the 1980s, other investment banking houses played substantial roles in the issuance of this paper.[7] Some facts to be kept in mind in connection with this less-than-investment-grade-paper phenomenon are:

- Junk bonds began to take off in the early 1980s. *Providing a high-yield market for companies that cannot issue investment-grade debt, yet have sufficient substance to justify investor risk, makes perfect market sense.* However, two wrong turns were taken in the mid-1980s. The first had to do simply with quality and quantity: Too much of this paper began to be issued by too many companies whose management, assets, and market pros-

---

[5] According to the Securities Industry Association the ten largest investment banking houses' $18 billion in total equity capital (at year's end 1989) represented more than 61 percent of all the equity capital in the entire securities industry. See W. Power, note 3, *supra.* Of course, since 1989, one of the top ten has disappeared (Drexel Burnham Lambert), and number two (Salomon Brothers) appeared—as of late 1991—to be substantially downsizing. Moreover, the Shearson/Smith Barney, Harris Upham merger of March, 1993, resulting in the new firm, Smith Barney Shearson, may well be a portent of yet more change in the investment banking arena. One of every four stockbrokers in America will be working either for Smith Barney Shearson or Merrill Lynch, and more consolidation of firms and regimentation of products could be on the way. See W. Power and M. Siconolfi, "New Colossus; Smith Barney Shearson Emerges, Reflecting a Shifting Wall Street," *The Wall Street Journal*, March 15, 1993.

[6] See M.H. Pickering, "A Review of Corporate Restructuring Activity, 1980-1990," Federal Reserve System Staff Study, No. 161, May 1991, chart 2, p. 5.

[7] With some, like Morgan Stanley, actually promoting and supporting studies focusing on the more positive aspects of junk bonds.

pects were, to put it bluntly, "junky." The second had to do with the fact that too much of the paper was issued not for purposes such as internal growth or general firm refinancing, but rather for mergers and acquisitions, and stock repurchases.

In 1989, Drexel Burnham Lambert issued its own report indicating that 71 percent of junk bonds floated in 1988 were either to finance or refinance acquisitions or leveraged buyouts. In 1989, more than half of all junk bond proceeds were intended to complete current acquisitions, to repurchase stock, or to refinance previously completed transactions that had resulted in the retirement of stock. As one observer noted:

> Junk bond financing was also used extensively to complete divestitures and other restructurings that did not involve equity retirements. Indeed, many of the junk bonds now in financial difficulty were issued in connection with the purchase of assets of previous leveraged buyouts.[8]

Moreover, in what had to be one of the more reprehensible acts in the S&L tragedy, junk bond issuers, utilizing the essential services of investment bank underwriters, sold billions of dollars in junk bonds to savings and loan institutions whose strong suit was government (taxpayer) insurance, not investment acumen or skilled credit analysis. When S&L junk "investments" collapsed, along with the junk bond market in general,[9] the cost of the failures were passed on to the taxpayers who never knew they'd been exposed to such a risk, having played no part whatsoever in assuming it.[10]

The refrain "the returns from owning junk bonds are more than sufficient to compensate for the risk of default" as applied to this situation is, at best, a shrill obscenity.

---

[8] Pickering, note 6, *supra*, at p. 4.

[9] See, e.g., M. Winkler and C. Mitchell, "Trading in Junk Bonds Collapses, Touching Off Big Treasury Rally," *The Wall Street Journal* (October 16, 1989). The junk bond market collapsed in 1990, was very weak in 1991, and prospered fabulously in most of 1992 in the face of collapsing interest rates. However, as the junk grew junkier, we see, according to R. McGough and T. Vogel, "Cracks Appear in Red Hot Junk Bond Market," *The Wall Street Journal* (October 19, 1992).

[10] The Resolution Trust Corporation (RTC) sold off some $1.75 billion in failed S&L junk bonds in a three-month period in early 1991. The face-value losses on these sales are a public responsibility. The remaining portfolio of S&L junk bonds, estimated in April 1991 to be close to $6 billion even after the years of sell-offs (and losses), will also cost the taxpayers money. See G. Anders, "RTC Is Unloading Its Junk Bonds at Furious Pace in A Seller's Market," *The Wall Street Journal* (April 15, 1991). For a listing of the 20 S&Ls with the greatest junkbond exposure, see R.B. Schmitt, "Drexel Collapse Exacerbates S&L Woes," *The Wall Street Journal* (February 16, 1990).

Given the scale of the investment-bank-aided junk bond disaster, how is one to characterize this *commercial* banking-related headline: "Banks See Golden Opportunity in Junk"? Or consider this statement within the story by the head of the "high yield" group at a money center bank: "Credit is something we feel we know a little bit about." Banks can thrive in the "minefield of junk" by using "the skills we have developed in our banking practice."[11]

Finally, while it would be hard to deny that Michael Milken of Drexel Burnham Lambert was the chief villain of the junk bond debacle,[12] there were others around to share in the shame. A senior executive at Morgan Stanley illustrated this fact back in 1985 when he told a reporter:

> We really are laying the groundwork for one hell of a market bust. [There is] too much use of [highly leveraged financial arrangements]. We're doing this stuff, too. . . . You ought to see the sort of deals going on in [the Morgan Stanley securities trading room] there. Everybody's gonna get carried out when the junk bond market goes.[13]

4. Mergers and Acquisitions, LBOs, Restructurings, and the Issue of High Leverage and Debt

A well-respected American investment banker summed up his concerns about "the leveraging explosion" at the end of the decade of the 1980s by stating that:

> . . . it is the prolonged, and highly undesirable, shift away from equity towards debt financing by many business corporations that is especially worrisome now. This shift has accelerated. . . as a result of the corporate merger, acquisition and leveraged buyout mania which. . . has heightened the disregard for capital. I believe that unless something is done to forestall excesses that are almost inevitable in this area, the health of the free enterprise system in the United States will be endangered. . . .

---

[11] R. Smith, "Banks See Golden Opportunity in Junk," *The Wall Street Journal* (May 15, 1990). Do you see any ethical issues in this "business skills" decision?

[12] The most detailed story of the Milken outrages is to be found in James B. Stewart, *Den of Thieves* (New York: Simon & Schuster, 1991).

[13] Cited in an article by A.L. Malabre, Jr., "Heard in the Suite: Boom, Bust and Bewilderment," *The Wall Street Journal* (December 5, 1985). It seems that, for the very first time, a system will be established for the public reporting of prices and trading volume in the junk bond market. The National Association of Securities Dealers expects to have the system in operation by 1994. See C. Harlem, "SEC Clears Way for System to Report Prices and Volume in Junk Bond Market," *The Wall Street Journal*, (March 19, 1993).

Over the past five years, the debt of U.S. nonfinancial corporations has gone up by an estimated $840 billion and the equity position has contracted by nearly $300 billion. . . nonfinancial corporate debt has grown by 15.4% annually. . . . In the process, interest payments by [these] corporations now amount to about 26% of internal cash flow. . . . To put these numbers in perspective, these payments now preempt more internal cash flow than during the recessions of 1982 and 1974 when this ratio was 22% and 19% respectively. . . .[14]

Soon after that summing up, a new recession was publicly acknowledged. That long recession has raised yet again the issue of the direct relationship between high *debt* and the *depth and duration* (if not the initiation) of economic recessions.

There are economists who insist that "high debt ratios that factor in leveraged buyouts, recapitalizations, highly leveraged mergers and stock repurchases. . . can be a virtue because they provide strong incentives for efficiency, even where the specter of bankruptcy is concerned."[15]

Still, the various economic problems faced by the nation in its most recent recession would not appear to be a good example of financial market efficiency. And many economists would argue that, to a substantial degree, such problems are in fact related to the huge growth of debt in the 1980s. A year-end 1991 paper, estimating the amount of debt that corporations added to their balance sheets between 1984 and 1990 as $1.1 trillion, and stock buyouts during that period as more than a half-trillion dollars, stated:

Essentially, corporations were just crossing the word "stock" off their stock certificates and penciling in the word "debt." Very little growth-related economic activity was involved in this process, just a lot of very expensive financial transactions. Nevertheless, it caused debt aggregates to soar relative to economic growth and destroyed what up until then had been a solid statistical relationship between nonfinancial debt and real growth.[16]

---

[14] From H. Kaufman, "The Decapitalization of American Corporations." Speech presented at the National Press Club, Washington, D.C., January 10, 1989. By 1990, according to the Federal Reserve, interest payments were closer to 35%. *Federal Reserve Bulletin* (August 1990), p. 593 *et seq.*

[15] M.C. Jensen in congressional testimony delivered on February 1, 1989, and printed as "Is Leverage an Invitation to Bankruptcy?" *The Wall Street Journal* (February 1, 1989). Professor Jensen pointed out at the time that the "success of LBOs" was probably not due simply to a bull market economy, and that though a less positive economy might pose problems, the "indications are that organizations such as Drexel Burnham Lambert. . . has [sic] anticipated these problems. . . [and] could work them out if government regulatory authorities just didn't interfere."

[16] S. Strongin, "Credit Flows and the Credit Crunch," Chicago Federal Reserve Bank Letter No. 51, November 1991.

The author of the above quote then went on to argue that such activities have obscured the exact nature of the credit flow/credit crunch dilemma of the 1990–1991 recession—a case of "the explosion in purely financial transactions" making it difficult to determine exactly what credit policies should be undertaken to deal with the problem.

It would be fruitless here to attempt any final, definitive resolution of the issue: Did the M&A/LBO/recapitalization boom truly result in a lean/mean, well-managed corporate sector, or simply in a debt-ridden private (as well as public) sector? How can one determine at present whether all this financial activity was, overall, "good" or "bad" for the economy? Professional journal articles demonstrating fiercely, with mathematical formulas and creative hypotheses that it was good/bad (take your pick) are ubiquitous.[17]

What we would like to examine, briefly, is the actual nature and extent of the activity, and the roles played in it by investment bankers (and their lawyers). As one authority noted:

> From the beginning of 1984 through 1989, mergers and acquisitions, including leveraged buyouts (LBOs) totaled $535 billion. . . . Corporations' repurchases of their own shares amount[ed] to nearly $230 billion [more] over the same period. . . .
>
> In the late 1980s, leveraged buyouts. . . were structured so that most of the purchase price, sometimes as much as 90 percent, was borrowed.[18]

---

[17] An interesting example of the debate, early on, is a work recording the opinions of economists on every conceivable side of the issue: L.E. Browne and E.S. Rosengren, eds., *The Merger Boom* (Federal Reserve Bank of Boston, 1988). A rather interesting article, which discusses the issue of whether takeover premia in fact represents efficiency gains, is R. Morck, A. Shleifer, and R.W. Vishny, "Do Managerial Objectives Drive Bad Acquisitions?" *The Journal of Finance* (March 1990). Society's message-bearers view the situation from different angles. Compare F.R. Bleakley, "A Decade of Debt Is Now Giving Way to the Age of Equity," *The Wall Street Journal* (December 16, 1991), with J.M. Berry, "Paying the Piper: The Bill Comes Due for a Decade of Debt," *The Washington Post National Weekly Edition* (January 20-26, 1992). Clearly, the Federal government participated to the fullest in the debt enhancement game. In addition to an all time record annual deficit of $290.2 billion set in fiscal 1992, it has outstanding unfunded government liabilities (beyond the $3.5 trillion gross federal debt outstanding) in the amount of $4 trillion. See D. Altig, "Federal Credit and Insurance Programs: Beyond the Deficit Diversion," *Economic Commentary*, FRB of Cleveland, November 15, 1992; A.B. Abel "Can the Government Roll Over Its Debt Forever?" *Business Review*, FRB of Philadelphia, November/December 1992.

[18] Pickering, note 6, *supra,* at p. 2. Note the discrepancies in the Kaufman, Strongin, and Pickering debt and buyout figures, all of which range from very high to astronomical. We may have to go beyond the twentieth century before we can be sure of the exact extent of the financial activity that took place during 1980s. However, according to Pickering, the 1984-1989 period produced 115 M&A transactions of $1 billion or more involving U.S. nonfinancial corporations. In 1990 there were an additional 12. Of the group of 127, nine were either in default or exceedingly close thereto by December 1990. *Id* at Tables A.4-8. During the same 1984-1989 period, there were more than 1,800 LBOs of companies

There was, then, even acknowledging some discrepancy in actual figures, a lot of activity and leveraging of debt in what was often referred to as "the market for corporate control." Proponents of this particular free market cited the major justification for its existence as manager shortcomings. Some of the management faults cited were enormous salaries, outrageous perks, misfeasance, malfeasance, nonfeasance, and outright felonious behavior.[19]

It cannot be denied that anti-manager arguments were buttressed with a host of distasteful examples. Still, many honorable and competent CEOs were unfairly tarred with this broad brush. Much more importantly, even if American management was actually as horrendous as the "executive-phobes" claim, it does not follow at all that the answer to the problem is to allow corporate raiders, insider officers, and venture capitalists (who once focused on investing in new and exciting product-producing businesses) to leverage the economy to the hilt for their own personal gain.

The slothful manager argument is rescued from being a nonsequitur only if it is assumed that the legitimate purpose of managers of American corporations is to make individual shareholders as rich as possible as quickly as possible, consistent with legality. If that assumption is questioned, the argument falls that instituting a controlled-panic-in-the-face-of-bankruptcy management process is productive of capitalist efficiency.

Without desiring to repeat material already set forth in Chapter 5, we would simply comment briefly here that the notion of the corporation as a manager/shareholder private preserve, with the rest of the body politic being no more than poachers, is, demonstrably, *not the law* and, arguably, not ethical.

Moreover, other concerns arise out of the high-leverage activity under discussion, no matter what one's opinion might be about the true nature of the American corporation.

---

involving transactions in excess of a million dollars. While individual transaction prices are not necessarily available, the total value of these transactions appeared to be approximately $230 billion. Pickering Table.

[19] Harvey Segal's *The Reshaping of the American Economy* is an example of this particular focus (New York: Viking Press, 1989). Quite clearly, the enormous salaries of CEOs were, with justification, a target for attack on many levels, including the ethical. The sight of CEOs of American auto companies traveling to Japan late in 1992 to complain to the Japanese was ludicrous (U.S. auto exec average compensation being $2 million annually versus $400,000 for a Japanese exec). Selfishness at the top of U.S. corporations *is* subject to criticism; however, there is something troubling about Wall Street practitioners using it to justify hostile M&A or LBOs in the light of some of *their* compensation behavior! See R.J. McCartney, "Let's See, $23 Million a Year Comes Out to About $11,000 an Hour," *The Washington Post National Weekly Edition* (September 30-October 6, 1991).

- America did enter the 1990s (and recession) overloaded with debt, a substantial portion of which is traceable to M&A, LBOs and corporate restructuring activity (and the allied use of junk bonds).

- All this action seems to have done very little to affect the much criticized enormous salaries of many CEOs, some of whom are where they are, and collecting the fortunes they do, as the direct result of M&A and LBOs (as are the fortune-collecting Wall Street managers who put them there).

- A lot more evidence remains to be adduced that massive employee layoffs and community disruption and dislocation following shareholder M&A and LBO enrichment is economically and morally justifiable on efficiency or any other grounds. There is just too much evidence to the contrary that needs to be dealt with far more seriously than it has been in the 1980s.[20]

- There are simply too many examples extant of the damage to the economy resulting from highly leveraged transactions, to accept "efficiency" arguments uncritically. And some such arguments have about them a faint taste of disgrace that should trouble any concerned society. Two examples follow.

First, consider a major lumber company forced to sell off its assets fast in order to pay down a choking LBO debt. The assets here were not corporate divisions that could be spun off without harming the total parent firm's operations (and one wonders how many of them there *truly* are). The assets were old-growth redwood trees, turned into lumber so fast as to make neither conservationist nor *business* sense.[21]

Second, some U.S. corporations became so overloaded with debt that they could no longer make the investments needed to compete, and they ended up being sold to foreign concerns, which captured sizable U.S.

---

[20] It is much to the credit of the financial press that the press has examined this concern smack in the middle of their front pages. See particularly the effort of Susan Faludi, "The Reckoning: Gateway LBO Yields Vast Profits but Exacts Heavy Human Toll. The '80s Strife Buy-Out Left Some Employees Jobless, Stress-Ridden, Distraught. Owner KKR Hails Efficiency," *The Wall Street Journal* (May 16, 1990). A book that examines the "perversion" of classic venture capital into LBO seeking "merchant capital" for faster payoffs (without as much risk as is involved in starting up new business) is W.D. Bygrave and J.A. Timmons, *Venture Capital at the Crossroads* (Cambridge, Mass.: Harvard Business School Press, 1992).

[21] See "Wall Street Goes Wild," *Worldwatch* Magazine (November/December 1989), p.32. To make things even worse, some lumber companies not ladened by debt have depleted their forests in order not to appear asset rich and therefore a takeover target: "Let's face it," a lumber company supervisor is quoted as saying in the *Worldwatch* article. "The market forces and the threat of stock market takeovers won't let us do otherwise." Compare D.G. McNeil, Jr., "How Most of the Public Forests Are Sold to Loggers at a Loss," *The New York Times* (November 3, 1991).

market share. A prime example is the Uniroyal/Goodrich tire company. In Uniroyal's case, an argument was publicly made, in August 1989, by a partner in a private investment firm specializing in LBOs, that his 1988 leveraged buyout of Uniroyal was proof of the "spirit of entrepreneurship," which would carry this U.S. firm to victory.[22] Yet two months after this individual's statement appeared in the press, Uniroyal was sold to the French group Michelin. The chairman of the buyout firm, who was subjected to criticism for selling off yet another basic U.S. business to foreign competition (and too quickly), responded to *The Wall Street Journal* thusly:

> We were leveraged. It would have been difficult to spend the kind of money we needed to spend over a long period in order to be in the forefront.[23]

The general public may in fact be unsophisticated about the world of finance and may lack the expertise necessary to appreciate the efficiencies involved in enormous, individually profitable M&A and LBO maneuvers. However, the public *attitude* toward such "deals" is real enough: mistrust, distrust, anger, and fear. And that critical attitude will have to be dealt with, since society's message-bearers are not about to allow it simply to fade away.[24]

One cannot help but wonder how Uniroyal had, in fact, been "valued" at the time of an LBO that so quickly necessitated sale. This leads us into an examination of the role played by investment banks in the high debt leverage business.

We might begin by examining three major functions of investment banks in M&A and LBO corporate restructuring:

- *Searching for and identifying target companies:*
    for takeover/LBO action.

    to be protected against takeover/LBO action.

---

[22] B.C. Ames, "Taking the Risk Out of Leveraged Buyouts," *The Wall Street Journal* (August 7, 1989).

[23] Holland, "Who's Bankrolling the Buyout Artist?" The New York Times (October 8, 1989).

[24] It is not out of place to suggest that the nagging persistence of public concern and fear about the economy, and jobs in it, which helped prolong the recession of 1991, had its genesis in business behavior described in our text. See, for example, A. Murray and D. Wessel, "Swept Away: Torrent of Layoffs Shows Human Toll of Recession Goes On," *The Wall Street Journal* (December 12, 1991) and A.R. Karr, "Data Mask Slump's Injury to Work Force: 'Mild' Downturn Cuts a Broad and Diverse Swath," *The Wall Street Journal* (December 26, 1991). There is good reason to believe that heavy debt and fear for job safety contributed to the November 1992 election results. Certainly as late as August 1992 one headline stated: "New Debt Phobia Is Slowing the Economy," *Wall Street Journal* (August 8, 1992), "The Outlook." See also S. Murfson, "A Problem Too Big to Ignore, Too Awful to Face," *The Washington Post National Weekly Edition* (October 5-11, 1992).

- *Estimating relevant variables for measuring economic costs and gains on the deals (corporate valuation and deal costs):*

  valuing the firm relative to such variables as cash flow, earnings, assets-liabilities, and stock price: present and past. And, equally important, determining the corporation's "break-up" value[25]

  determining (estimating) planning and transactions costs, including legal and financial

  determining (estimating) types and amounts of additional financing remaining to get the job done

- *Doing the deal:*

  giving hour-by-hour advice

  underwriting and disposing of the debt paper, rated and junk, that underpins the deal

  (perhaps) acting as a guarantor source—that is, providing actual financing (through bridge loans or equity participation), i.e., acting as a *merchant banker.*

And, of course, investment banks can and do act, on their own behalf, as arbitrageurs in connection with other M&A and LBO deals. Which is to say, they bet on the spread between a takeover stock's present price and the higher price it will command when the deal is done. By buying and selling a stock simultaneously, the arbitrageur takes no risk in terms of just how high the stock will go. The real risk is, of course, that no merger or takeover will actually take place, and the stock will drop back down to a pre-deal level—or below.

It should be noted here that some of the valuation and doing-the-deal endeavors often find the investment bank working with another equally expensive partner—*the law firm.* Lawyers advise on

- compliance with laws and regulations regarding such issues as filings, tender offers and the like;
- tax ramifications of deals;
- the validity of defenses in place;
- antitrust considerations;
- development of new defenses and delaying tactics.

---

[25] See D. LeBaron and L.S. Speidell, "Why Are the Parts Worth More Than the Sum? Chop Shop, a Corporate Valuation Model," in Browne and Rosengren, eds., *Merger Boom*, note 17, at pp. 78-95.

And lawyers, of course, participate in ongoing litigation arising out of a deal in progress (e.g., depositions and production of documents by way of "discovery.")[26]

A serious issue raised by the enormous fees paid out in M&A, LBOs, and restructuring activity focuses on where the hundreds of millions of dollars expended for advice, loans, litigation, and the like actually comes from. "Efficiency" gains, perhaps: businesses divested, work forces thinned, enormous interest payments to be faced, and a controlled panic management methodology.

And yet (most often with regard to the junk-bond underpinning of deals), the argument can be made that the personal greed and inclination to private profit on the part of investment bankers, corporate raiders, lawyers and accountants actually fed the M&A and LBO boom, and it did so to the detriment of many investors large and small and to innocent noncombatants now without work or contracts; it did it also to the detriment of the American taxpayer.

The long-term answer to whether the massive American M&A and LBO boom of the 1980s was, in fact, positive and efficient must be left to economic (and other) historians. At the moment, however, we do know this:

- That the powerful financial incentives involved in doing these deals (M&A revenues totalled as much as 25 percent of an investment bank's total annual revenues of a billion dollars as far back as 1986), *plus* arbitrage department profits from speculating in one's own merger department deals, inclines a dispassionate observer at least to question seriously whether economic forces alone accounted for the M&A/LBO phenomenon.[27]

- Just as S&L and commercial bankers in many cases produced serious eventual losses by initially overvaluing assets, so it is al-

---

[26] Costs in these proceedings can be massive. In the Allied Stores/Campeau affair, in 1986, just one "notice of deposition" filing, in a single four-day period, required depositions from scores of employees of Allied Stores, ASC Acquisition Corp., Shearson Lehman Brothers, Goldman Sachs & Co., Manufacturers Hanover Trust Co., Citibank, N.A., Prudential Bache Securities, Inc., Salomon Brothers Inc., and Bear, Sterns & Co., together with the production of enough documents to threaten the stability of a massed formation of steel wheelbarrows. There were many billable lawyer hours in all that! See *Allied Stores Corporation and ASC Acquisition Corp., Plaintiffs; against Campeau Acquisition Corp. et al, Defendants, U.S. District Court, District of New York, 86 Civ. 8207 (PWL) "Notice of Depositions" and attached "Schedule of Documents," October 26, 1986.*

[27] The frightful Campeau/Federated Department Stores deal alone produced some $600 million in professional fees. See John Rothchild, *Going for Broke* (New York: Simon & Schuster, 1991). See also J.B. Stewart and D. Hertzberg, "The Deal Makers: Investment Bankers Feed a Merger Boom and Pick Up Fat Fees," *The Wall Street Journal* (April 2, 1986), and G. Anders, "LBO Odyssey: Playtex Goes Through 4 Buy-Outs Since 1985, Enriching Top Officer," *The Wall Street Journal* (December 17, 1991).

leged did investment bankers. Interco, the large St. Louis shoe and furniture conglomerate, is one example of where "optimistic forecasts were cooked up and then replaced by one with even less to support them, in which 'worst case' scenarios assumed every future year would produce higher operating profits than any previous year, and in which one forecast took a possible recession into account by assuming it would cause profits to increase." The result: Interco went broke because it borrowed too much money on these projections. The investment bankers involved claimed that the problems occurred only because management deceived them.[28]

Perhaps the same was true for the Campeau/Federated Department Stores deal. Here the Campeau holding company drained Allied Stores so as to finance the acquisition of Federated Department Stores. But here, Allied Stores bondholders, big losers in that M&A deal, sued the Campeau holding company and its bankers for damages. They alleged that when the Campeau company took Allied's money, they knew Allied would thereby be rendered insolvent by the transaction—that is, they unfairly denuded and destroyed it without conferring any real benefit upon it. At common law, this is a "fraudulent conveyance," and those directly damaged can receive compensation from all those responsible for the complained-of action. As of late 1991, the Allied investors appear to have settled their claim in bankruptcy court for $192 million. There were similar *fraudulent conveyance* claims pending in bankruptcy proceedings of drugstore chain Revco, and of Interco, Circle K Corp., and dress designer McCall Pattern.[29]

None of the material presented in Sections 3 and 4 of this chapter proves beyond a reasonable doubt that inordinate investment banker (and lawyer, accountant, and others) greed produced a 1980s M&A and LBO boom harmful to American society. It would, however, be disingenuous to assert that such inordinate greed and allied unethical behaviors did not exist, or that they did not produce at least one clear negative effect on American society: a lack of public trust.

Before discussing loss of trust further, let us examine a few more investment-bank risk-reward activities.

---

[28] States the author of the Interco account, "It's not the first time Wall Street has used that explanation when investors lost money." F. Norris, "If the Numbers Don't Work, Find New Ones," *The New York Times* (October 27, 1991).

[29] R.J. McCartney, "The Might of the Living Buyout Victims," *Washington Post National Weekly Edition* (August 26-September 1, 1991). Interestingly enough, the profit possibilities in depressed bonds represented by possible fraudulent conveyance claims made them into hot investment items. Ibid.

5. Risk-Controlled Arbitrage, Brokered Certificates of Deposit, and Derivatives in General

"Risk-controlled arbitrage" was promoted by investment bankers to S&Ls as a foolproof hedge in the mid-1980s. A favorite guaranteed profit-maker would involve, for example, the purchase of several hundred million dollars worth of mortgage backed securities, paying a fixed rate of 11.5 percent. The S&L would fund the purchase with deposits and/or debt at a variable rate of, say, 9 percent. Then the S&L would also purchase a variety of hedges to cover itself against a rise in its own borrowing rates—for example, interest rate swaps, caps, and even some very exotic instruments like interest-only strips of cash flows. The outcome was supposed to be that these investment-bank instruments, and associated mathematical constructs ("Your pool of long-term securities will not be paid off for seven years"), guaranteed a fully protected profit spread between investment yield and deposit costs *no matter which way short- and long-term interest rates went.*

The problem was that the investment banker's math was wrong and the hedges didn't work in practice the way theory said they would. Long-term rates went down, existing mortgages were refinanced, short-term rates stayed up, and S&Ls were now on the wrong side, with lower-yielding assets mismatched with expensive debt and hedging instruments. Hundreds of S&Ls together had borrowed a total amount of tens of billions of dollars to enter these foolproof deals and eventual losses came to more than a billion dollars and helped bring about the collapse of several sizable S&Ls. As one observer noted:

> . . . investment bankers [had] fanned out across the country to sell thrifts on arbitrage systems. For them the idea was a bonanza, with fees for advice, for arranging purchase of mortgage securities, for building hedges, for executing trades to maintain hedges—and for unwinding a thrift's positions when the system fell apart. . . .[30]

The whole idea was later characterized by one regulator as "a siren song that found many gullible listeners, and it proved terribly damaging"[31] to taxpayers, in the end.

Then there were the enormous brokered funds broken up into $100,000 lots and placed in Federal Deposit Insurance-guaranteed certificates of deposit. Investment banks placed large chunks of these funds in deteriorating S&Ls because the S&Ls paid the highest interest rates in

---

[30] C. McCoy, "Many Big S&L Losses Turn Out to Be Due to a Financial Gamble," *The Wall Street Journal* (August 9, 1991).

[31] Ibid.

order to maintain at least an upright zombie status. Investment-banking fees for putting these funds into banks, which could do the economy as a whole little good and lots of harm, ranged from 3/5 of 1 percent to as high as 4 percent. Even at 3/5 of 1 percent, an investment bank's commission on each $100,000 certificate of deposit (CD) was almost twice what a broker made on the average order to buy or sell stocks.[32]

Derivatives are hybrid instruments. Neither stocks nor bonds, they derive their existence from the underlying stocks, bonds, currencies, or commodities upon which they are based. Derivatives are, in effect, bets on which way the underlying asset will go in the future. Commercial and investment banks are deeply involved in both creating and dealing in them. As the S&L risk-controlled arbitrage fiasco demonstrated, these instruments do not always perform properly. They do, however, bring bankers lots of money. The market in stock and stock index warrants alone in 1990, for example, saw its top ten world participants—among them Salomon Brothers, Merrill Lynch, Morgan Stanley, Bankers Trust, and Citicorp—participate in a volume level of some $6 billion.[33]

The *total* "derivatives market" is estimated to be in the vicinity of $3 trillion to $10 trillion,[34] with large investors, both domestic and international, able to get an investment bank to tailor derivatives to their needs. The major problem these derivatives present is their capacity to operate beyond the reach of any government regulation.

The major problem in the United States is how to characterize these hybrids. Are they securities? Futures? Commodities? We do regulate each of these, only differently. Some hybrids have elements of all three. One attorney familiar with the field has been quoted as saying:

> The law is in a confused state, and products are being tinkered with to be pigeonholed in the law. The public isn't getting more protection, and the product isn't getting sounder.[35]

---

[32] See M. Mayer, "Banking on the Government," *Modern Maturity* (October/November 1991) at p. 67, and R.R. Moore, "Brokered Deposits: Determinants and Implications for Thrift Institutions," *Financial Industry* Studies, FRB of Dallas (December 1991).

[33] Comprising, roughly, 80 percent of that market: C. Torres and B. Donnelly, "Rivals Challenge Banker's Trust in Derivative Securities Business," *The Wall Street Journal* (December 15, 1990) citing as its source IFR BondBase.

[34] C. Torres, "Bull Market for Derivatives Outruns Rules," *The Wall Street Journal* (July 24, 1991). There is a *Dictionary of Derivatives* (Euromoney Research Guide, June 1992), which spells out 15 major categories and subcategories within them, and which describes the major exchanges where they can be traded. The *Dictionary* provides, among other things, "a detailed examination of the more complex combinations." Eurobonds (bonds issued by a corporation, government, or other borrower outside its area country) took on an interesting derivative configuration in 1993 with "collared floaters," "inverse coupon floaters," and "step-up recovery floaters (SURFS)." See G. Mitchell, "'Funnies' Spark Light-Hearted Reversal in Once-Sedate Market for Eurobonds," *The Wall Street Journal*, March 24, 1993.

Regulatory confusion is never productive of safety. This is particularly true in areas where bankers profit much *from explicit or implicit government guarantees.* Questions have finally been raised regarding the Federal National Mortgage Association, the Federal Home Loan Mortgage Corporation, and the Student Loan Marketing Association (Fannie Mae, Freddie Mac, and Sallie Mae). While not carrying the explicit backing of "the full faith and credit" of the United States Treasury, these Government-Sponsored Enterprises (GSEs) are assumed by all to have an implicit government guarantee. The guarantee is clearly reflected in the fact that Fannie, Freddie, and Sallie debt carry a higher interest rate than comparable Treasury debt, *but* a lower rate than the *safest* corporate debt.

And yet, they are only lightly regulated, hardly supervised, and have outstanding more than one-half trillion dollars in loans (i.e., home mortgages and student loans). Both the packaging and the distribution of home mortgages· are important investment bank endeavors. The U.S. Congress has evidenced concern very recently about potential problems to the taxpayer from this enormous amount of debt,[36] and economists, too, have begun to manifest serious concern about the total $4 trillion in unfunded federal government liabilities.[37] Nevertheless, not much danger is seen here by nongovernment participants. They argue that full privatization of these entities (and thus exposure to free market competition), or increased capital requirements, or the mandatory issuance of subordinated debt—all calculated to relieve taxpayers of the ultimate burden of making good on any failures[38]—are to be shunned here. The reason given is that

---

[35] *Ibid.* According to Mr. Torres' sources, it's just getting more profitable, with "most big players making [profits of] between $100 million and $200 million a year. The enormous profits in derivatives on an international level (e.g., cross-rate notes) have resulted in "enormous winnings" for investment and commercial banks, raising the issue of whether they might not involve "taking some kind of serious risk." C. Torres, "Spanning the Globe to Become No. 1 on Wall Street," *The Wall Street Journal* (November 6, 1991). See also S. Lipin and W. Power, "Derivatives Draw Warnings from Regulators," *The Wall Street Journal* (March 25, 1992).

[36] J. Knight, "Are Those Icebergs or Icecubes Out There: Congress Probes for More Potential Fiscal Disasters," *Washington Post National Weekly Edition* (October 23-29, 1989). Congress probes, but is usually too timid to act responsibly. A bill to regulate Fannie Mae and Freddie Mac died when Fannie Mae opposed it vigorously. K. Bradsher, "Mortgage Industry Bill Withdrawn in House," *The New York Times* (September 29, 1992).

[37] A total of $4 trillion as of December 31, 1989. See R.H. Webb, "The Stealth Budget: Unfunded Liabilities of the Federal Government," *Economic Review*, FRB of Richmond (May/June 1991). See also *Controlling the Risk of Government-Sponsored Enterprises* (U.S. Congressional Budget Office, 1991), and M. Mayer, "Another Favor for Fannie Mae and Freddie Mac," *The Wall Street Journal* (October 22, 1991), and Martin and Pozdena, "Taxpayer Risk in Mortgage Policy," *FRBSF Weekly Letter*, No. 91-44, December 20, 1991.

[38] It should be remembered that the S&L insurer (FSLIC) did not carry the "full faith and credit" backing of the U.S. Treasury. That was clearly not a condition precedent to a massive taxpayer bailout.

these actions would negatively affect liquidity in this essential government-related market.

That litany has been heard before in defense of relative freedom from regulation in essential government-related markets. Let us examine the most important of all those markets now.

6. The Saga of U.S. Treasury Securities

In 1991 the U.S. Treasury bill, bond, and note market was at a level of about $2.3 trillion, with average daily trading volume in excess of $120 billion. Up to the mid-1980s, it was unregulated. *Liquidity* in this crucial market for United States government debt *was all,* it was argued. Regulation would be the death of it.

Then several government securities dealers failed. A kiting scheme in government paper collapsed when bonds on loan and subject to recall ("repos") turned out to be nonexistent and, therefore, nondeliverable. A great sum of money was lost.

The Government Securities Act of 1986 was then put into effect to deal with this heretofore unregulatable market. The new law, and subsequent regulations, set rules for record keeping, capital standards, and financial reporting, (i.e., required some broker accountability). Liquidity survived.

The 1986 law did *not* require the regulator (the U.S. Treasury Department) to have its dealers set up any internal controls for bids on government securities. In fact, it dealt only with the secondary market for government paper. The law said nothing at all about the primary auction process.

The Treasury auction process has been basically three tiered: First, the Treasury announces it will auction off a specific amount of bills or notes or bonds and sets a bidding deadline. Next, securities firms (and some few members of the public) place bids for the offered paper in special boxes at 25 Federal Reserve banks and branches. These boxes are opened by Fed officials as soon as the deadline expires. They collate the bids and send the information to Washington. There, Treasury officials review the bids and take those with the lowest interest rates up to the amount required to sell out that auction's offering.

Then, of course, the dealers and securities firms whose bids "won" at the auction sell their purchased government securities at prices slightly above the Treasury acceptance price, thus making their intermediary profit.

There are 39 so-called primary dealers, chosen by the Fed, and they are obligated to bid regularly for specific amounts at specific prices at Treasury auctions in exchange for their elite positions—elite because the Treasury market they operate in is the world's largest and safest and sets the interest rate standard for America's financial system. Also, because of the Primary Dealers Treasury Borrowing Advisory Committee, these dealers even exercise direct influence over the Treasury's decisions on the size and term (number of years to maturity) of offerings at auction.[39]

Since the SEC supervises securities dealers, they, the Fed, and the Treasury Department make up the government triumvirate overseeing this crucial market system. And yet this system, even after 1986, was known to be one of the most loosely regulated in the nation. One of the reasons for this state of affairs is the overwhelming need of the federal government to continue to place its ever-growing mountain of debt.

There are some rules in the game. A key one is that no single buyer at the primary auction can purchase more than 35 percent of the total offering. The reason for this is obvious. There is usually a great secondary market demand for U.S. Treasuries. Anyone who walks away from a primary auction with all, or almost all, of the paper (i.e., corners the market) is in a position to rule (to profit excessively in) the ready and waiting secondary market.

There is a third market for Treasury securities, which is referred to as "when issued." Some five days before an already announced auction is to take place, securities dealers and their customers begin negotiating for the securities—in effect, making bets on what the price will be and, subsequently the price on the secondary market. Data from the "when issued" market helps the bidder-dealers gauge the demand for the paper they will be bidding on. Deals entered into in the "when issued" market could also prove to be a terrible trap for securities dealers if they have to pay distorted prices to a bidder-dealer who has cornered the auction market.

It would certainly seem that regulators would do everything in their power to see to it that all bids and auctions are completely honest and above board.

But as the summer and fall of 1991 finally showed the world, bidders have often been dishonest and have hit below the belt. "Collusion [and] price fixing have long been rife in [the] Treasury Market."[40] according to one source. Many big bond dealers have been accused of sharing information with rivals in order to avoid having to bid too high.[41] And dealers have long been accused of flouting purchase limit rules as well.

---

[39] See D. Wessel, "The Bond Club: Treasury and the Fed Have Long Caved in to 'Primary Dealers,'" *The Wall Street Journal* (September 25, 1991).

[40] M. Siconolfi, M.R. Sesit, and C. Mitchell, "Hidden Bonds," *The Wall Street Journal* (August 21, 1991), p. 1.

[41] Some of those accused and named in the Siconolfi et al story, note 40, *supra*, are Salomon Brothers, Morgan Stanley & Co., First Boston Corp., Citicorp, Daiwa Securities, and Greenwich Capital Markets, Inc. They all issued strong denials. Still, see M.R. Sesit and L.P. Cohen, "Japanese Brokerage Firms to Settle SEC Charges," *The Wall Street Journal* (February 25, 1993).

In August 1991 one of the dealers was caught. Salomon Brothers publicly admitted to violations of the 35 percent rule. In fact, by September 1991 it was made clear that Salomon Brothers Inc. controlled an incredible 94 percent of two-year Treasury notes supposedly sold to competitive bidders at auction in May 1991. This was done by Salomon through the unauthorized use of customer names and, possibly, with the collusion of other parties.[42]

It is not amusing to recall that, in 1990, the U.S. General Accounting Office (GAO) recommended that Congress authorize rule-making aimed at both selling practices and price information in the Treasury market, since both areas raised the risk of abuses! Nothing came of the recommendation, of course.[43]

However, under new rules announced by the Treasury Department in late October 1991, *all* broker-dealers (not just the elite 39) were to be allowed to bid at auction on behalf of their customers, without putting up a deposit or guarantee.[44] Some skeptics argue that the primary reason for action now is to blunt the seeming desire on the part of Congress to generate new and more far-reaching enabling legislation.

What form future regulation of the Treasury market ultimately takes remains to be seen, but clearly there was a market failure here and the necessity for intervention. We will discuss the issue of outside regulation versus self-regulation, and related matters, further on in this chapter, but one thing is already clear: Unethical behavior here has brought about a situation that ought to be regarded as a national disgrace and acted on accordingly.[45]

---

[42] Salwen, L.P. Cohen, and M. Siconolfi, "Salomon Reveals It Had Control of 94% of Notes at May Auction," *The Wall Street Journal* (September 5, 1991).

[43] Cf. J. Connor, "Agencies Disagree on Need for Congress to Look at Rules on U.S. Securities Sales," *The Wall Street Journal* (April 5, 1991).

[44] P. Thomas and T. Herman, "Treasury Sets Up Bidding Rules Aimed at Cleaning Up Troubled Auctions," *The Wall Street Journal* (October 28, 1991). See also K.G. Salwen, "Primary Dealers Set to Lose More Clout," *The Wall Street Journal* (January 22, 1992). As of late 1992, the Treasury was about to launch a one-year trial of a new method of selling its debt. K.G. Salwen and J. Connor, "Treasury to Try 'Dutch' System at Its Auctions," *The Wall Street Journal* (September 4, 1992). See also V.V. Chari and R.J. Weber, "How the U.S. Treasury Should Auction Its Debt," *Quarterly Review*, FRB of Minneapolis, Fall 1992.

[45] Treasury market manipulation is not a victimless crime. Small bond trading houses, commercial banks, and research firms and their customers suffer losses. See C. Mitchell, "Market Mayhem, Salomon's 'Squeeze' in May Auction Left Many Players Reeling," *The Wall Street Journal* (October 31, 1991). These losses are, more or less, measurable. Loss of public confidence in the integrity of U.S. markets is not, but is no less important for that. As of early 1993, record keeping practices in the government securities markets made it nearly impossible for the SEC and other investigating agencies to examine transactions satisfactorily. SEC chairman Richard Breedon is quoted as saying: "We would like the authority to say you can't keep records on a scroll." *The Wall Street Journal* (March 18, 1993), p. C24.

7. Insider Trading: A Truly Interdisciplinary Confusion

There are really two kinds of "insider" trading. The first refers mainly to persons, (i.e., to *corporate officers and directors*) who trade in the stock of their own companies in the usual course of investing. There are SEC disclosure and timing rules for such managers, and some have been called to account for infractions from time to time. However, this has not been a major area of litigation.

The second type of insider refers less to persons and more to *the information* involved (i.e., the information upon which trades are based).

What is "insider information"? Basically speaking, it is material information, usually related to the value of a corporation's securities, that is *not* available to the general investing public.

The clear intent of securities laws in the United States to "protect the investing public and honest businesses,"[46] is well defined this way:

> [The securities laws were designed to] leave it to market forces to determine the quality of the securities offered and the price and terms at which they trade, but seek to cleanse and perfect the process by which such transactions take place by requiring full and truthful disclosure, from the informed to the ignorant, of all facts and circumstances material to such transactions the concealment of which (unless otherwise justified) would create misleading impressions or permit unfair practices; i.e., fraud.[47]

Actual securities laws are contained in Title (Volume) 15 of the U.S. Code.[48] However, three portions of the law are key to the substantive fraud areas: material omissions and misrepresentations in connection with the purchase and sale of securities; broker-dealer fraud apart from insider trading (e.g., "churning"); and insider trading and stock "parking." These three portions are Sections 10, 13, and 14.[49]

Section 10 covers "Manipulative and Deceptive Devices"; Section 14(e) covers "Untrue statements of material fact or omission of fact with respect to tender offer"; and Section 13 (d) requires "reports by persons

---

[46] Quote from the original congressional statement of intent regarding the 1933 Securities Act: S. Rep. No. 47, 73d Congress, 1st Sess. 1 (1933).

[47] S.S. Arkin and E.C. Dudley, *Business Crime: Criminal Liability of the Business Community*, Sec. 17.01 at 17-6 (1988).

[48] The all-important Securities Exchange Act of 1934 is to be found at 15 U.S.C. § 78c-hh. The act contains 34 sections covering all aspects of the securities business, including margin and registration requirements, reports, proxies, and the like—as well as fraud provisions.

[49] Section 17 of the 1933 Securities Act also relates to fraud, and broker "churning" comes under Section 15(c) as well as under Section 10. However, Sections 10 and 14 are most often used, and Section 13, the "parking" law, has been utilized very often in more recent times.

acquiring more than five percent of certain classes of securities." We will refer to the specific wording of these key sections as we encounter the related cases.

The earliest insider trading cases were pretty much confined to true "insiders"—or managers and directors and large stockholders—who traded on the basis of undisclosed information. A well-known example involved successful results of a company's mining exploration that managers received and profited on before the general public was informed about them. Here, the courts uniformly punished the insider traders on basically fiduciary principles.[50]

Then, as concern about wheeler-dealing began to grow, government prosecutions began to be undertaken against non-"insiders" for trading on "inside information."

The three Supreme Court cases that have thus far defined the law relating to material nonpublic information trades by outsiders—often referred to as "tippees"—are:

- *Chiarella* v. *United States* 445 U.S. 222 (1980)
- *Dirks* v. *SEC* 463 U.S. 646 (1983)
- *Carpenter et al.* v. *United States* 108 S. Ct. 316 (1987).

Each of those cases involved congressional enabling Section 10(b), and the SEC regulation promulgated thereunder: Rule 10b-5.

Section 10(b) prohibits the use "in connection with the purchase or sale of any security. . . of any manipulative or deceptive device or contrivance in contravention of such rules and regulations as the Commission may prescribe."

Rule 10b-5 makes it unlawful "to employ any device, scheme or artifice to defraud" or "to engage in any act. . . which operates. . . as a fraud or deceit upon any person in connection with the purchase or sale of any security."

In *Chiarella*, an employee of a printing establishment that did private, confidential tender-offer announcements, traded on information contained in the announcements in advance of their being made public. The Supreme Court reversed his 10b-5 conviction on the grounds that the statute was simply a general antifraud statute that codified the common law. The High Court held that to find a tippee guilty, there had to be a breach of duty to the corporation involved, or to its stockholders, on the part of the tippee. This was necessary in order to satisfy the common-law fraud requirement of a breach of fiduciary duty, or other similar relation of trust and confidence, between the parties to the fraudulent transaction.

---

[50] *SEC* v. *Texas Gulf Sulphur Co.* 401 R. 2d 833 (2d Cir. 1968).

The Supreme Court did not say that Congress could not promulgate a statutory definition of fraud that would cover tippees even in the absence of such a relationship (i.e., set up a less stringent duty). The Supreme Court merely said that Section 10(b) was not explicit evidence of a congressional intent to do so.[51]

Chief Justice Warren Burger dissented. He argued that information obtained by a trader through "hard work, careful analysis, and astute forecasting" was valuable personal property and always usable, but information obtained through an illegal act was not.[52]

In *Dirks,* a stockbroker was given information by a corporate insider to the effect that the insider's corporation was suffering serious financial difficulties. Acting upon this tip, Dirks sold his brokerage clients out of the stock before the roof fell in. The Supreme Court reversed his Rule 10b-5 conviction. The justices ruled that a tippee who used information from an insider with a corporate fiduciary duty or similar relation of trust and confidence could be a "derivative" taker and be as guilty as the insider. However, here the insider did not personally benefit, so he breached no duty for his own enrichment and Dirks was therefore not a "derivative" insider.

Courts of appeals then began to use the Burger dissent to present a new theory of liability under Rule 10b-5: the theory of "misappropriation." By this theory, if a tippee obtained inside information from his own company about another company, and used it to personal advantage, then even without a duty to the other company, he could be found guilty of violating Rule 10b-5. He was violating his duty to an owner of the information, in this case his own company, by misappropriating (stealing) it.[53]

The Supreme Court faced the misappropriation theory in the *Carpenter et al v. U.S.* case, and failed to resolve it. There, a journalist who compiled information for the *Wall Street Journal,* "Heard on the Street" column used the information to trade on. He and some associates acted on the information before the column appeared in the *Journal* and thereby profited on the public's reaction once it did appear. The High Court upheld convictions based on mail-fraud statutes (using the U.S. mails—through which many copies of the Journal are sent—to defraud). But one seat on the Court was vacant at the time, and the misappropriation theory vote was 4–4, so that focus on Rule 10b-5 is yet to be voted on by the full Supreme Court.

---

[51] Cf. *Chiarella*, 445 U.S. at 233.

[52] *Chiarella*, 445 U.S. at 240.

[53] *United States v. Newman* 664 F.2d 12 (2d Cir. 1981) cert. denied, 464 U.S. 863 (1983). This theory would have done in *Chiarella*, of course.

The SEC, however, had not stood still after the *Chiarella* decision. It turned to Congress's enabling law at Section 14(e), which reads as follows:

> It shall be unlawful for any person to make any untrue statement of a material fact or omit to state any material fact necessary in order to make the statements made, in the light of the circumstances under which they are made, not misleading, or to engage in any fraudulent, deceptive, or manipulative acts or practices, in connection with any tender offer or request or invitation for tenders, or any solicitation of security holders in opposition to or in favor of any such offer, request, or invitation. The Commission shall, for the purposes of this subsection, by rules and regulations define, and prescribe means reasonably designed to prevent, such acts and practices as are fraudulent, deceptive, or manipulative.

Using this enabling law, the SEC, in 1980, promulgated Rule 14e-3(a):

> If any person has taken a substantial step or steps to commence, or has commenced, a tender offer (the "offering person"), it shall constitute a fraudulent, deceptive or manipulative act or practice within the meaning of section 14(e) of the Act for any other person who is in possession of material information relating to such tender offer which information he knows or has reason to know is nonpublic and which he knows or has reason to know has been acquired directly or indirectly from:
>
> (1) The offering person,
>
> (2) The issuer of the securities sought or to be sought by such tender offer, or
>
> (3) Any officer, director, partner or employee or any other person acting on behalf of the offering person or such issuer, to purchase or sell or cause to be purchased or sold any of such securities or any securities convertible into or exchangeable for any such securities or any option or right to obtain or to dispose of any foregoing securities, unless within a reasonable time prior to any purchase or sale such information and its source are publicly disclosed by press release or otherwise.

Then, in 1989, along came Robert Chestman.

Every securities law professor's dream, Mr. Chestman was a stockbroker with a client by the name of Keith Loeb. Mr. Loeb was married to Shirley Witkin. Shirley Witkin's mother's maiden name was Waldbaum. Shirley's mother was, in fact, the sister of Ira Waldbaum, the president and controlling shareholder of Waldbaum supermarkets. So Shirley was Ira's niece. Mr. Chestman was well aware of the Loeb-Witkin-Waldbaum interfamily relationship. From 1982 to 1986, Mr. Chestman traded Waldbaum stock for the Loebs.

On November 21, 1986, Ira Waldbaum agreed to sell his company to the A&P supermarket chain for $50 per share. The stock was then selling for about $25. After the (friendly) tender offer had been made, Ira agreed with his sister and his children to tender their shares along with his, but he cautioned his fellow family members that the sale was confidential and should not be discussed before the public announcement. Ira's sister did tell her daughter Shirley, but was careful to give her the same caution Ira had given her. Shirley told her husband, Keith, but gave him the same family caution, adding that if he told anyone "it could possibly ruin the sale."

There is no record of Keith's response to Shirley. But on November 26, 1986, (the day after he was told of the sale) Keith phoned his broker Robert Chestman, and told Chestman that he had "some definite, some accurate information" that Waldbaum was about to be sold at a "substantially higher" price than its market value. He asked Chestman what he should do. Chestman's response was that he could not advise Loeb "in a situation like this," and that Loeb had to make up his own mind.

Mr. Chestman had no trouble making up his own mind. He bought 3,000 shares of Waldbaum stock for his own account at $24.65 a share. Then, during the same day, he bought 8,000 more from his clients' discretionary accounts at prices ranging from $25.75 to $26.00 per share—including 1,000 shares for Keith Loeb.

That very same day, November 26, after the market closed, the tender offer was publicly announced. The next day, the stock jumped to $49 a share.

Following an SEC investigation, Loeb disgorged his profits and paid a fine. Chestman chose to go to trial, charged with violating Rule 10b-5, mail fraud, and ten counts of fraudulent trading in violation of Section 14e and SEC Rule 14e-3(a).

Mr. Chestman's U.S. district court conviction on all counts was heard on appeal before a three-judge panel of Circuit Court of Appeals judges. The judges threw out all of the convictions in three separate opinions.[54] Because of a conflict in this decision, the 2d Circuit Court of Appeals decided to rehear the case *in banc* (with all 12 judges in attendance). One judge retired from the bench after the hearing on November 9, 1990, and did not participate in the decision.

---

[54] *United States* v. *Chestman*, 903 F.2d 75 (1990).

The 11 remaining judges decided as follows:

- Five voted to reinstate the convictions for fraud connected with a tender offer [14e-3(a)], and to affirm the reversal of the Rule 10b-5 fraud counts.
- Five voted to convict on *all* counts, including mail and wire fraud.
- One voted to affirm the reversal of *all* the convictions on *all* counts.
- The result therefore was: conviction on Rule 14e-3(a), and not guilty on all other counts.

The 2d Circuit Court of Appeals, *in banc*, ruled that the SEC did not exceed its statutory authority under Sec. 14(e) in promulgating Rule 14e-3.[55] The rule can cover transactions on the open market and not only transactions between the tender offerer and a shareholder of the target company. It can create "a duty in *all* traders falling within its ambit to abstain or disclose, without regard to whether the trader owes a pre-existing fiduciary duty to respect the confidentiality of the information."[56] The rule can (and does) go beyond the common-law elements of fraud. Here, the Congress made a broad delegation of rule-making authority to the SEC to deal with a particular problem (fraud related to tender offers) and the appeals court could not say that what the SEC did was arbitrary, capricious, or manifestly contrary to the statute.

Thus, what it takes now to convict a tippee is:

1. the use of insider information connected in some meaningful manner to a tender offer, and
2. evidence from which a jury could infer that the tippee knew, or should have known, that the information was non-public and came from an insider

Six of the eleven judges held that Rule 10b-5 did not apply here because Loeb had no fiduciary or similar relation of trust and confidence with Waldbaum, Inc., that would make Chestman a derivative tippee. The simple existence of a marriage or familial relationship was insufficient!

The powerful 2d Circuit Court of Appeals (in New York) has therefore upheld the right of the SEC, in tender-offer cases, to establish fraud rules going beyond strict common law requirements. Several "insider trading" issues still remain to be resolved, however. These include the following:

---

[55] *United States* v. *Chestman*, (1991) 947 F.2d551.

[56] 947 F.2d at 559.

- Will the U.S. Supreme Court agree with its highly respected 2d Circuit Court on this 14e-3(a) case finding?
- Why shouldn't every provable use of insider information under Rule 10b-5 be subject to a similar Rule 14e-3(a)-like securities fraud standard? Would it not be if Congress saw fit to legislate that way, specifically? The Supreme Court has intimated that Rule 10b-5 could, indeed, be broadened to go beyond fraud at common law.[57]
- Should (could) Congress make this murky area clearer by simply defining "insider trading" specifically, just as it has specifically increased penalties for this wrongful act?[58]
- What is all the fuss really about here? Doesn't the insider trading phenomenon in a real, practical sense connect to one Supreme Court justice's comment on the pornography phenomenon: "I may not be able to define pornography, but I certainly know it when I see it"?

We would suggest that the Congress, in this rare case, is probably right in not attempting a precise definition. To define precisely what insider trading is, is also to define precisely what it is not. Such a definition would likely become another law firm profit center (and a loss to taxpayers who foot the cost of the judiciary).

The real problem here does not lie mainly in legal definition, because the real issue is not the degree of consanguinity between firm/insider/Tippee. *The issue is whether using nonpublic information to gain personal advantage ought to be perceived as economically, legally, and ethically "good" or "bad" for U.S. securities markets, and more, for America's body politic in terms of the overall value system it chooses to live by.*

A purely economic construct could be—in fact, *has been*—designed that "demonstrates" that the free, untrammeled use of *all* information makes the market more "efficient." How information gets into the market is not important. Therefore, unless an insider—and, by extension, a tippee of that insider—has literally "stolen" his inside information—that is, committed a legal crime (which neither Chiarella nor Dirks nor Loeb nor Chestman did)—then that information is freely usable. And its use will make markets more efficient. There is no room for any misappropriation

---

[57] Cf. note 53, *supra.*

[58] The Insider Trading Sanctions Act of 1984 (ITSA), 15 U.S.C. § 78a-i, and the Insider Trading and Securities Fraud Enforcement Act of 1988, P.L. 100-704, raised damages and focused on firms' responsibilities for broker actions, but did *not* precisely define "insider trading."

theory here, and more, no room for such laws as 14e, or SEC Rules like 14e-3(a).

Moreover, it is argued, under this free-flow-of-all-information-efficient-markets theory, there are no losers resulting from insider information use. The insider's gains are not made at anyone else's "expense" in "any relevant sense."[59] By this argument, government regulation of insider information prevents the enhancement of shareholder value.[60]

Still, it is hard to see exactly how Mr. Chestman's insider trades, done less than a full day before the information was made public, made U.S. markets more "efficient." And it is even harder to see why those folks who sold 11,000 shares to him were not hurt "in any relevant sense" when their *former* stock, in less than 24 hours, doubled in value—that is, when all that value went into the pocket of someone who knew, at the time he took their stock, that the value was absolutely going to skyrocket.

While it might be consoling to the buyer to think of the sellers here as faceless and therefore unreal, in truth they *are* as real as the profit made from them.

It surely must seem to the disinterested observer (which, we admit, is not us) that the "efficient market" construct, as used here, truly totters under the weight of real-world "moral hazard." We would agree with the writer who recently stated in strong and persuasive professional terms, that "It is somewhat awkward to reconcile the view" of insider trading as the guarantor of efficient markets and the protector of entrepreneurship in the modern corporation "with the almost universal opprobrium that society directs toward practitioners of inside trading." This economist-writer (who is cited below) commented further on the argument that insider trading is an incentive for corporate managers and directors—that is, that insider trading on nonpublic insider information is an "efficient" compensation device. He argues that this process

> creates a moral hazard problem. An individual who has the ability both to generate and to trade on inside information is given the perverse incentive to generate "bad" news, which is easier to create than "good" news, yet equally profitable to trade on (by selling short instead of buying long).[61]

---

[59] Henry G. Manne, *Insider Trading and the Stock Market* (New York: Free Press, 1966), p. 61.

[60] Carlton and Fischel, "The Regulation of Insider Trading," *Stanford Law Review* (May 1983). The underlying assumption really being, of course, that there is no other reason whatsoever for the existence of securities markets but enhancing shareholder value—and the quicker the better!

[61] Both quotations are from, L.M. Ausubel, "Insider Trading in a Rational Expectations Economy," *The American Economic Review* (December 1990), pp. 1025, 1026.

We are in full agreement with former Chief Justice Burger that information obtained by a trader through hard work, careful analysis, and astute forecasting is valuable personal property. Such information is legitimate stock in trade, and its use may well make the market more efficient. And it could well be that distinguishing such information from prohibited (position-inequality, unearned) insider information would have to be carefully determined by a trier of fact. But none of the above presents a persuasive argument for maintaining *any* econo-legal construct that supports an unfair, unequal market that cannot be trusted by the general investor.

If the general investor remains distrustful, the market will suffer thereby *in the long term* (i.e., capital formation will eventually suffer). Confidence in the market (that one's return will not be diluted by insider trading) promotes investment by outsiders. This helps corporate directors and managers as well. And it helps investment bankers and arbitrageurs, too, since initial public offerings (IPOs) and secondary trades contribute to their livelihoods. An excellent case can be made that *banning insider trading* can effect a Pareto improvement and is, in reality, over the long term, economically efficient.[62]

If the law is determined to utilize *economic* constructs as the basis for establishing *legal* precedent, it should examine those constructs carefully to be sure that, in any responsible long-term view, they are productive of a morally, as well as an economically, sustainable society. Any legal precedent that jettisons honesty and fairness for some supposed economic "efficiency" principle is bound to prove "inefficient" in the long run.[63]

8. Section 13(d): "Parking" Violations

In the pursuit of full disclosure to market participants of all material information about firms and their traded shares, the SEC has set reporting requirements for purchases of 5 percent or more of any company's

---

[62] Ibid. The United States is not alone, of course, in its struggle with insider trading. Japan's "insider trading" law is a farce, and German law a problem. See B. Michener, "Germany Lags on Insider Trading Curbs," *The Wall Street Journal* (August 17, 1992). Two areas now being looked at carefully by the SEC are insider trading in junkbonds and, interestingly enough, at mutual funds. D.B. Henriques, "On Patrol Along the Chinese Wall," *The New York Times* (April 19, 1992).

[63] It could be argued that securities markets are doing well in spite of alleged scandals (i.e., not suffering from any lack of confidence). It must be pointed out that there *has* been some sanction-oriented response to insider trading to help bolster confidence. Moreover, the effects of lack of confidence are not always manifested on a daily or monthly basis. They surface from time to time in a rather observable manner (e.g., October 1987 and November 1991). Reaction to scandal has even been too extreme (e.g., in the market for corporate control). The Supreme Court has gone pretty far in allowing states to set up legal defenses to corporate takeovers. Compare *Edgar* v. *Mite Corp.*, 475 U.S. 624 (1982), with *CTS Corp.* v. *Dynamics Corp. of America*, 481 U.S. 69 (1987). In any event, when the market rises as the Fed pushes short-term interest rates down, what investors then *seem* to be left with is the only game in town. But that alone does not make the game safe for bettors.

stock. The purpose of this Section 13(d) reporting requirement is twofold: First, it allows the public to know that a substantial interest in a particular stock has been acquired, and just who has acquired it. Second, it allows the SEC to ascertain whether or not a broker-dealer is within the limit on the amount of debt it can incur in relation to capital. The SEC allows brokers and dealers to count cash and stock as capital; however, cash is counted at 100 percent, and stocks are heavily discounted.

Therefore, if Broker A, who already owns 4 percent of Widget shares, asks Broker B to buy 4 percent more for him, with the promise to Broker B that he will later purchase those shares at a guaranteed profit to Broker B, then Broker A has a double benefit. He keeps his ownership of 8 percent of Widget hidden (or, say, his ownership of 16 percent if he uses Brokers C and D to do the same), plus, Broker A shows a cash (capital) position larger than reality warrants (since Broker A is in fact already committed to the purchase of Widget stock).

The Widget stock is, of course, "parked" with Broker B (and perhaps Brokers C and D, etc.). "Parking" is a criminal and civil offense, and brokers, arbitrageurs, and investment bankers have paid fines and gone to jail for indulging in the practice in violation of Section 13(d).

Moreover, the "parking" violation of *investment banker minimum capital position requirements* leads us into the final investment bank focus on investment banking safety in general.[64]

---

[64] There are other issues that raise ethical concerns in investment banking: Possible conflict of interest between a firm's brokerage division and its investment banking house is surely one. When the investment bank is underwriting a particular issue, does its brokerage side abstain from pushing that issue? One hears of "Chinese walls" to prevent criss-crossing, but we know of no one who has ever actually seen one. Cf. J. Kristol, "How to Restructure Wall Street," *The Wall Street Journal* (November 1, 1991).

A rather serious issue is also raised by the manner in which disputes between brokers and customers are resolved; e.g., in such areas as "churning," (where brokers buy and sell securities in order to generate commissions, not to fulfill customer investment objectives: See Sec. 15c of the Securities Law and Rule 15c 1-7). The United States Supreme Court has sanctioned arbitration, rather than the courts, as the proper forum for all dispute resolution between brokers and their clients. Since most of the arbitration is done by panels on which securities industry people play a prominent role, serious issues of trust and confidence in the process—and its fairness—are often raised. See, for example, D. Henriques, "When Naivete Meets Wall Street," *The New York Times* (December 3, 1989). Appeal to the courts is possible but court review of arbitration decisions is so bare-bones minimal as to be, in most cases, relatively meaningless. The outcry against industry-loaded panels has been so great that some industry support has been forthcoming for independent arbitration forums such as the American Arbitration Association. See M. Siconolfi, "Brokerage Firms Stop Opposition to Arbitration," *The Wall Street Journal* (March 5, 1991). For some insight into generally respected arbitration processes see B.L. Hines, "Post-Trial Blues—Did I Win?" *New York State Bar Journal* (April 1990). It has even been argued that changes in industry panel rules since 1989, plus growing lawyer sophistication, has begun to even up customer choices between American Arbitration Association and industry-controlled panels. See D.J. De Benedictis, "Arbitration Fair to Stock Buyers," *ABA Journal* (February 1992). See also B.P. Noble, "New Questions about Arbitration," *The New York Times* (June 14, 1992).

9. Investment Banks and Public Responsibility

When Drexel Burnham Lambert was faced with a liquidity crisis, the Drexel parent reached down into its broker subsidiary for cash. When Drexel's condition deteriorated even further, it attempted once more to pick its subsidiary's pocket. The SEC intervened, barred any further transfer of funds, and Drexel filed for bankruptcy protection.[65]

The Drexel Burnham affair put a spotlight upon the extremely serious issue of investment banking (and brokering) house safety and soundness and the industry's relationship to the public interest.

In the United States, the SEC requires securities firms to hold one dollar in assets for each dollar of liabilities, plus a 2 percent cushion, and assets are risk-weighted (cash and Treasury bills at 100 percent of value, 85 percent of value for highly rated stocks, and zero value for real estate). However, there is some question regarding the safety and soundness of investments anyway, because *only* broker-dealers are thus regulated. An affiliate of the same investment banking house (or large independent broker-dealer) that controls the brokerage operation could be set up, say, to issue large bridge loans in big LBO deals. These large loans do not have the effect of dropping capital below regulatory (required) levels. In actual fact:

> Investment banks, which are increasingly active in (truly enormous off-balance sheet commitments) have no explicit capital requirements, since they uniformly conduct these activities outside the regulated broker-dealer in separate, unregulated affiliates. Who is to say how all these off-balance sheet contingencies will behave in some future episode of financial distress when some participants in the system fail to meet their obligations? Who is confident that the capital requirements behind these activities are adequate?[66]

At a time when both complex new instruments and deals are being packaged and undertaken by investment banks, and computers are moving the funds in often mysterious ways, should we not be concerned a bit more than we are about the likelihood, and consequence, of market failures?

---

[65] See S. Black, "Wall Street Objects to Plan to Toughen Net Capital Rules for Brokerage Firms," *The Wall Street Journal* (November 12, 1990).

[66] H. Kaufman, "Credit Crunches: The Deregulators Were Wrong," *The Wall Street Journal* (August 8, 1991). After a full year of debate, the SEC finally voted to require the filing of quarterly reports by some parent companies and affiliates of brokerage houses. But the final rules were well watered down from original posed requirements. See K.G. Salwen, "New SEC Rules Require Disclosure of Parent Firms," *The Wall Street Journal* (July 16, 1992).

There are two arguments in favor of not being concerned: (1) There is a securities firm insurance fund to cover customers of organizations that go "belly up," and (2) investment banks are not direct recipients of tax-payer-backed government insurance guarantees. Nor are they the objects of Federal Reserve perks such as access to the discount window. Therefore, whatever risks these banks take is strictly the business of their owners.

In fact, there is a brokerage insurance fund whose explicit assets come from within the industry. It was set up in 1970 as a nonprofit corporation by the U.S. Congress, and it is called the Securities Investment Protection Corporation (SIPC). It serves most brokerage accounts up to a maximum of $400,000 in securities, plus $100,000 in cash—and only in terms of returning these "on deposit" assets to each customer if the broker goes bankrupt. The SIPC does not cover many margin accounts, does not cover any commodities accounts, and, of course, neither covers any other investments made with or through an investment bank nor guarantees or repays any lost or foregone profits.

Apart from the fact that SIPC protection is limited, it is, more importantly, dependent even in its restricted coverage on the public purse. Its enormous implicit asset is a $600 million line of credit with the U.S. Treasury, which its managers have argued should be increased to $1 billion in order "to promote investor confidence."[67]

The more serious argument—that investment banks do not have access to Federal Reserve perks, or to the Fed's deep pocket—raises a fundamental question for policymakers. Is not the investment banking business relying upon the public purse to cover any real disaster in the industry, just as commercial banks and S&Ls have? And does that reliance not call, as well, for public stewardship behavior on the part of investment banks as the *quid pro quo* in this bargain? And does it not call for a far greater and more substantive effort on the part of regulators to help assure compliance with such stewardship requirements?

We must begin by insisting that financial market discipline is *not* fully operative in the investment banking market. One could counter that Drexel Burnham was allowed to die. But we have to answer: Perhaps so, but taxpayers will have to pay a portion of the cleanup bill for the junk bond mess the company left behind. The Drexel affair has not answered this ever-present concern, namely

> could the collapse of a major securities house cause a general crisis as would the collapse of a major bank? And would the authorities step in to prop [it] up? . . . The official stance of central banks

[67] M. Siconolfi, "SIPC Protection Doesn't Guarantee Investors a Solid Night's Sleep," *The Wall Street Journal* (August 8, 1991).

around the world is that they are concerned only with the stability of the commercial banking system and the failure of a non-bank securities house would be of no more concern than the failure of an individual company. The reality may be different.[68]

In fact, in the stock market crash of October, 1987, the Federal Reserve announced publicly and rapidly that it would provide as much credit as the markets needed to stem the tide (SIPC was, of course, an irrelevancy at the time). And the Fed then proceeded to rescue the markets (and the investment banks and their owners) from disaster by keeping (commercial) lending banks in line. That is, by jawboning, and pumping money into the system and thereby avoiding massive failures in the face of rapidly declining share prices.

This is not to argue that what the Federal Reserve did was wrong. Investment bank insolvency in the face of rapid market decline could surely spread to other parts of the financial system. In addition to massive amounts of failed bank loans being added to an already heavy bad loan load, there could have been enormous (off-balance sheet) swap defaults, and losses, as well as losses in other interlocking investment/commercial banking areas.

Nevertheless, one worries about such arguments as have been advanced by academics and others, that reality, in a time of extreme securities market volatility, requires investment bank bailouts.

> Investment banks have grown so large. . . that the Federal Reserve cannot allow them to fail. . . . The Fed must recognize the declining distinction between commercial and investment banks by providing investment banks limited access to the discount window and becoming lender of last resort to the major investment banks. This will help insulate the financial system from collapse.[69]

Perhaps so, but might such a "recognition" also encourage investment bankers, as it did S&L and commercial bankers, to engage even more freely in excessive risk taking? Would the Fed not be openly dumping one more set of multibillion-dollar entities into the too-big-to-be-allowed-to-suffer-the-consequences-of-failure pot?[70]

---

[68] N. Osborne, "Safety Nets for Securities Houses," *Euromoney* (November 1987).

[69] J.D. Hatfield (Wharton School), "Stock Market Crash Lessons," *The New York Times*, Letters to the Editor (February 26, 1988).

[70] This was a reality not lost on Fed Chairman Greenspan, apparently, as he faced the October 1989 market mini-crash. Mr. Greenspan refused to make any immediate public announcement of his plans concerning the provision of credit to the markets. Another (nameless) Fed official did, in fact, make such an announcement on his own, angering Mr. Greenspan. The Chairman injected only a small amount of reserves into the system. See

Policymakers must carefully consider investment bank behavior in the several aspects of debt leveraging, insider trading, and the like in terms of articulating responsible regulatory mechanisms in this particular financial market. Again, the regulators' constituency here is not the investment banker (or the banker's profit maximizing shareholders). The true constituents are the public and the markets upon which the body politic relies, whether or not they manage or own any banks.

If, for example, Glass-Steagall were to be abolished, how best might regulators oversee investment banking operations so as to help advance successful broad competition—in light of the fact that market failure might well (once more) be put upon taxpayers, whose individual wealth had never been the focus of maximization?

And concerns about the strength and safety of security houses/investment banks are certainly not exclusively domestic. The International Organization of Securities Commissions (IOSCO), headquartered in Canada and comprised of 80 regulatory agencies around the world, is very much concerned. The IOSCO has been dealing for some time with the issue of capital standards.

No accord, such as the commercial bank Basle Accord, has been reached regarding standardized investment bank capital levels that could be considered safe enough for firms conducting businesses in an interdependent global marketplace, a marketplace where central bankers might well have to battle (i.e., pay to combat) contagious market failure, whatever its particular banking source.

Problems exist that hinder the goal of international standards in investment banking. National (domestic) securities regulators are concerned about requiring high capital levels and setting realistic standards for measuring a firm's net worth. Tough standards may equate with safety and soundness; however, they also make it harder to compete with foreign firms whose standards might be lower (and less safe not only for its citizens but also for the rest of us).

Then there is the question of just who should regulate whom if barriers between investment and commercial banking disappear completely throughout the world (i.e., if we have global "universal banking").

"Is Fed's Greenspan Cautious to a Fault?" "The Outlook" section, *The Wall Street Journal* (October 30, 1989). It seems to us that Mr. Greenspan was valiantly attempting to prevent re-affirmation (for the second time in two years) of what we would term "the Chicago Exculpation." That is, "If you're a big enough player in *any* financial market game, the national and international ramifications of allowing you to pay the consequences of your folly are such that you can depend on a Federal Reserve bailout—that is, we encourage 'moral hazard.'"

For those who would argue that Federal Reserve money is *not* public money, we would point out that Fed profits go to the U.S. Treasury, which is backstopped by the taxpayer. The lower the profit, the higher the backstopper risk.

In the meantime, products and technological processes leap ahead in linked world markets, while regulators limp behind. Rewards may be produced for many, yet risk is shared by all.

There is no substitute here for coordinated econo-legal, regulatory mechanisms aimed at establishing and maintaining safe, trustworthy, albeit reasonably risk-taking, world financial markets. But even enlightened regulation is not enough.

Market players must accept personal responsibility along with financial reward, for such dependable, trustworthy markets. They must adopt and internalize a "Code of Conduct," an ethical stance that recognizes their responsibility. There must be no loss of public trust, and there must be a continuous effort to minimize the possibility of serious public financial cost. A highly respected investment banker has stated it well:

> A code of conduct is as essential for financial markets as it is for society as a whole. After all, we in financial markets have a great public trust. We hold the savings and temporary funds for all of society. How well we carry out this responsibility will have a great impact on economic progress and, as history clearly shows, we in the financial markets will never escape public scrutiny and judgment.[71]

B. Securities Markets

1. The National Exchanges and the Traders: A Structural and Functional Overview

(a). The New York Stock Exchange (NYSE). The New York Stock Exchange was incorporated in 1971, some 108 years after it had begun operations under that name.[72] It now has more than 1,300 mem-

---

[71] Henry Kaufman, "Past Blunders and Future Choices," from the *Herman Kroos Memorial Lecture*, Salomon Brothers, Inc., Bond Market Research publication (March 1988), p. 9. It is important to call attention here to the fact that 1992 found the SEC arguing that law firms representing clients backed up by public funds *now have a duty to the public as well!* A major U.S. law firm representing S&Ls was forced to pay $41 million in settlement of an SEC action, and suffer the humiliation of having a senior member banned for life from representing thrifts. See "Kaye Scholer: The Tremors Continue," *The ABA Journal* (July 1992), pp. 51-61. There is absolutely no reason to believe that an investment banker's duty to the public welfare is, or should be, any less than that of his legal counsel. And then there are the books in the *J'accuse* genre, which do much to hurt the public trust in investment banking: Cf. the list reviewed and commented on in "Mean Street," by M.M. Thomas, in the *Wilson Quarterly* (Winter 1992), pp. 90-93, where Thomas comments that Wall Street bankers' "worst depredations. . . depended on access to. . . the Public Capital. . . commitments and subsidies from the American taxpayer. . . ."

[72] Sources utilized for Section B (the national exchanges) were: P.A. Abken, "Globalization of Stock, Futures and Options Markets," *Economic Review*, FRB of Atlanta (July/August 1991); Robert A. Schwartz, *Equity Markets, Structure, Trading and Performance* (NY: Harper and Row, 1988); Frederick Amling, *Investments*, 6th ed. (Englewood Cliffs, N.J.: Prentice Hall, 1989); and Robert A. Schwartz, *Reshaping the Equity Markets* (NY: Harper Business, 1991).

bers, each holding a seat, which seat serves as his or her membership card. Some seats are leased to nonmembers with NYSE permission.

Members are either *commission brokers*—who take orders placed with their brokerage firms by the public and see that they are executed; *floor brokers*—who assist the commission brokers when necessary in executing their orders; or *floor traders*—who do not deal with the public's orders but rather deal for themselves, acting actually as competitive market makers. There are also *specialists*—who are duty-bound to make and maintain a fair and orderly market in those specific stocks for which they are registered as specialists. There are some 400 of these specialists, each handling perhaps four of the roughly 2,000 NYSE-listed stocks. These specialists act as brokers to the floor traders and floor brokers (who are sometimes lumped together under the general term "floor traders") when they deal with "limit orders"—stop orders. However, their main task lies in "making markets" (buying and selling from their own inventory) in the face of an imbalance between buy and sell orders for their assigned stocks. Buying and selling from their own accounts allows specialists the opportunity for profit in return for stepping into the breach to assure orderly price transition (i.e., for intervening in trading to keep the price changes acceptably small and for playing by all the NYSE specialist operation rules). Overall, about 10 percent of share purchases and sales on the NYSE result in specialists staking their own capital in the trade.

The NYSE, as can been seen from the various activities described, is both an agency and an auction market. It is an auction market, however, where the key "auctioneers" are confined to specific stocks and are bound to specific duties in furtherance of the overall system.

While the NYSE is mainly thought of in terms of its *trading floor*, it also operates an automated board system (ABS) primarily used for smaller, electronically handled orders, and, since 1980, a futures exchange—the NYFE. The NYFE handles futures contracts for the NYSE composite index, other market indexes, a commodity price index, and options on the NYSE composite futures. There is "pit trading" at the NYFE—i.e., crowd trading by dealers shouting out buy–sell orders to each other while confined together in a tiered, semicircular pit (see section (f)).

For its stock to be listed on the NYSE, a corporation must meet certain minimum size and quality requirements related to earnings, number of shares publicly held, number of shareholders owning at least 100 shares, net corporate assets, and the like. Basically, the issuing corporation must have at least $18 million in net tangible assets, have 1.1 million publicly held shares, and a pretax income of not less than $2.5 million per annum.

The total number of shares traded in the United States in listed stocks is approximately 85.2 billion annually. Of this amount, just over 46 percent is handled by the NYSE, the remainder by the regional exchanges, and by third, and fourth, and over-the-counter markets (see below). However, in terms of *dollar volume* of shares traded per annum, the NYSE is more dominant, at 63.7 percent of the total. It is, therefore, paramount in the area of big trades—that is, blocks of more than 5,000 shares each.

The first NYSE million-share trading day was December 15, 1886 (1.2 million shares total), and the first 600-million-share trading day was October 19, 1987 (604.3 million total). The only other 600-million-share day was October 20, 1987 (608.1 million total). Average daily NYSE volume is now in the vicinity of 195 million, with peak daily volume at perhaps 290 million shares traded.

(b). The American Stock Exchange (AMEX). Beginning, basically, as an outdoor, curb exchange, the AMEX came in from the cold in 1921. There are some 660 regular members (seats) at the AMEX, plus Associate and Options Principal members as well as Options Trading Permit Holders.

AMEX floor members consist of specialists, commission brokers, and *floor traders*—each of whom trades in both listed and unlisted securities. Companies whose shares are listed on the AMEX—now under 860, down from a high of 892 in 1980—are subject to smaller minimum size and quality requirements than are imposed by the NYSE. The AMEX conducts trading in common stocks, warrants, put-and-call options on stocks, stock indexes, and U.S. Treasury securities. It also provides a market in corporate bonds and trades options on gold bullion through a subsidiary market.

In terms of trading volume in equities, the AMEX ranks well behind the NYSE and NASDAQ (see below), and somewhat behind the combined regional exchanges as well (at 3.9 percent of the per annum total as of 1990). This is also true with regard to dollar volume (at 1.8 percent of the total in 1990).

(c). Regional and Local Exchanges. The Midwest Exchange (Chicago), the Pacific Stock Exchange (Los Angeles and San Francisco), and the Philadelphia Stock Exchange, though small, do the largest portion of a regional/local business that also includes the Boston, Cincinnati, Spokane, Salt Lake City, and Colorado Springs exchanges. All of these are registered with the SEC. There is also a Honolulu Exchange with a total volume so small it is exempt from SEC regulation. All the regional and locals, together, account for some 8.5 percent of the market value of the total securities traded on U.S. exchanges. Actually, by 1989, the big three regionals/locals accounted for more than 22 percent of the individual trades in NYSE-listed stocks, and more than 10 percent of their total volume. This is due in part to the fact that they are part of an Intermarket Trading System (ITS) that exposes orders in any U.S. stock market to the best bid

and offer of market makers anywhere in the system. Thus the regional and local specialist can actually compete with the NYSE specialist by quoting a better price.

(d). The Third and Fourth Markets. These are "off-exchange" markets where trading takes place in stocks that are listed on the exchanges. In 1989, some 5 percent of all NYSE—listed stock trades (and 3.2 percent of their total volume) were made through traders who share prices, and even give rebates to brokers who pass orders to them. These traders then match public buyers with public sellers with no exchange intermediary involved at all. The third market is mainly for small-share trades (under, say, 1,100 shares) made through automated systems.

The fourth market involves large investors (e.g., financial institutions) who trade exchange-listed issues directly with each other, mainly through the Institutional Network computerized communications system (Instinet), discussed below.

(e). Over-the-Counter/NASDAQ. While not an exchange in the usual sense of the word, the over-the-counter market (OTC) is, like the exchanges, a key secondary market. One should think of three OTC markets: the *Debt Market,* made up of federal, state, and municipal bonds and corporate bonds; the *National Quotation Bureau Pink Sheets,* made up of written, published quotations for some 15,000 issues, representing small or unknown companies, companies where one family holds most of the stock, companies in whom there is little or no speculative interest, etc. There is not always a market for these "pink sheet" stocks, of course. Finally, there is the *National Association of Securities Dealers Automated Quotation System* (NASDAQ), which is the key OTC market.

NASDAQ is an automated nationwide communications network providing bid/ask prices to more than 6,000 broker-dealers registered with the NASD. These dealers are such as handle only OTC issues; or, some may be investment banking houses that do new equity and debt issue business; or perhaps commercial banks making a market for government securities; or a municipal bond house, a full-line national firm, a mutual fund distributor, or even an insurance company variable annuity broker.

NASDAQ is known as the house of "small" stocks since the minimum listing requirement, with regard to company asset size, is only $2 million. There are also low minimum requirements regarding the required number of shares of stock outstanding—and stock selling price.

Nevertheless, NASDAQ's share and dollar volume in U.S. equity markets is substantial: more than 33 billion of the total 85 billion shares traded in 1990, with a value of $452.4 billion out of a total value of some $2.1 trillion for all equities traded in the United States in that same year.

Shares traded represented each of the three "tiers" of NASDAQ stock: the small company shares that trade infrequently and are highly volatile: the $50 million to $300 million companies regarded as the traditional OTC issues; and the "blue chips," the NASDAQ National Market System Companies (NMS), such as Apple Computer and MCI Communications—now widely held by large institutional investors (some 43 percent of NMS stocks by mid-1990).

Finally, NASDAQ leads *all* American exchanges in indirect foreign equities trading. Foreign corporations wishing to avoid SEC full-disclosure requirements issue American Depository Receipts (ADRs), which are certificates issued against actual equity shares and purchased and placed into trust accounts by U.S. commercial and investment banks. The 215 ADRs listed on exchanges or with NASDAQ are negotiable and widely traded. Although NASDAQ figures appear to be somewhat inflated by NYSE accounting standards, it would seem that, in 1990, NASDAQ did trade some 2.2 billion ADRs, representing 87 separate ADR issues, and a dollar volume of $21 billion out of a total of some $100 billion in trades.

(f). Futures and Options Exchanges.

If Dante had seen the Treasury bond pit at the Chicago Board of Trade, he would have added another circle to his vision of hell. Imagine a ring of steps around an octagonal floor, about 35 feet in diameter on the step, occupying the northwest corner of a wood-paneled trading room the width of a city block. Some 600 men and women stand jammed together in this pit, shouting and gesticulating, sometimes swaying in unison like tulips in the wind, from 8 o'clock in the morning when trading begins until 2 o'clock in the afternoon. Nobody goes to lunch, and few will risk losing their places by visiting the bathroom. Such abstinence is possible because almost everyone is under 35. ("Don't be confused by those gray heads you see," said the Virgil showing a visitor around. "They're 28 years old, too.")

The Treasury bond pit works by open outcry, which means that each bid and offer is good only for the instant of utterance and must be incessantly repeated. The noise is devastating.

These men and women, with their primitive gestures and raucous calls, are buying and selling contracts to purchase, at a particular price on a particular future date, $100,000-face-value United States Treasury Bonds with an 8 percent yield. On Black Monday, the New York Stock Exchange traded about $21 billion in stocks, and this one pit in Chicago traded more than $50 billion in Treasury bond futures contracts.[73]

The futures and options exchanges, in addition to the Chicago Board of Trade (CBOT), include (in the United States) the Chicago Mercantile Exchange, the Chicago Board Options Exchange (CBOE), and futures and options operations of the NYSE, the AMEX, and the Pacific and Philadelphia regional exchanges—to name just those with allied specific automated trading systems.

Of course, U.S. Treasury Bond futures represent but one of many choices. There are the S&P 500, soybean meal, wheat, cocoa, crude oil, Eurodollars, French T Bonds, Nikkei 225, gold, silver, etc.—i.e., *commodities, currencies, stock indexes, gilts,* and much more by way of tradable *options* and *futures* contracts. Some 387 million such contracts were traded in 1990 in the top 20 options and futures markets alone.[74]

The "open outcry" system, utilized in options and futures pit trading by exchange-member floor traders, using hand signals and whatever else is necessary to attract attention, requires the presence of exchange officials. They record the price and amount of each transaction.

Like the NYSE and the AMEX, futures and options trading has, to now, required a physical site and continuous human interaction.

Automation is in the process of changing all that, though to what degree, exactly, has not yet been determined.

2. Technology and Automated Trading

There are two technology focuses in automated trading. In the first, technology is harnessed to aid person-to-person (floor, pit, or telephone) trading. In the second, the human being to human being process simply disappears.[75]

The NYSE uses an automated routing system to route both small-share (less than 2,099) and large-share orders to floor brokers and specialists. It is called the Super Designated Order Turnaround System (Super-Dot), having progressed from its birth in 1976 as just plain DOT. This electronic wonder, which, as DOT, had an original daily routing capacity of 100 million shares, can handle well over 600 million shares daily now.

---

[73] From M. Mayer, "Suddenly It's Chicago," *New York Times Magazine* (March 27, 1988).

[74] Abken, note 72, *supra,* at Table 3, p. 7.

[75] The *Abken* article is an examination of up-to-date (mid-1991) operating, and proposed automated trading systems and, as such, provided much data for this section, esp. at pp. 6-12 and 15-16. Excellent sources of information have been (and, annually, are) the specific exchange *Fact Books;* e.g., *The New York Stock Exchange Fact Book, 1991,* and the *NASDAQ Fact Book, 1991.* An interesting newspaper update on the Chicago exchanges is B.J. Feder, "Chicago's Exchanges Look Toward an Electronic Salvation," *The New York Times* (November 29, 1992). Feder cites as the total figure for 1991 *world* trade in options and futures: 500 million contracts. And this figure does *not* include the CBOE volume of 500,000 stock/stock indexes contracts each day.

And it is headed for a capacity of 1 billion shares daily early in the decade of the 1990s. Some three-quarters of all NYSE daily orders are processed through SuperDot. This includes the NYSE's after-hours "Crossing Session I" whereby buy and sell orders are matched by SuperDot at 5 P.M.

NASDAQ has three in-house automated systems: The Small Order Execution System (SOES) handles public buy/sell orders of less than 1,000 shares, routing automatically to the dealer offering the best quote. SelectNet handles share orders larger than 1,000 and performs more functions. *Portal* handles privately placed offerings, resales, and automatic linkage trading.

Regional exchanges utilize their own systems in many cases, for order routing and execution (e.g., MAC, SCOREX, PACE, and BEACON).

Futures exchanges have *Globex*, which went into operation in the summer of 1992. Globex is intended to automate and link participating exchanges around the world. It will automatically match and execute orders entered into the system by traders working through their computers. Globex has a good deal more developmental work in store, but it does mark the beginning of a substantive change in the open outcry system.

Reuters Holdings PLC has two electronic trading subsidiaries, *Instinet* and the *Crossing Network*. Instinet is an electronic order execution system utilizing screen trading that allows anonymous trading by subscribers. Spreads are often available to institutional investors on Instinet, which are lower than those offered through NASDAQ dealers and exchange specialists. This results, of course, in spreads being sliced quite thin by involved competitors.

Reuter's Crossing Network allows entire portfolios of stocks to be sold at the closing price on primary markets (e.g., NYSE) or the mean of OTC bid-ask prices. It is, in effect, a low-cost alternative to organized exchange transactions for institutional "passive" portfolio managers. Another Crossing Network-type automated system is *Posit* (Portfolio System for Institutional Trading) operated by Jeffries & Company, a registered broker-dealer. Using Posit, portfolio trades can be executed at market opening or closing prices, or even at prespecified times of day. It also operates off-hours as well.

Volume on Instinet, the Crossing Network, and Posit is formidable. The first two already had some 4.5 percent of all NYSE volume by mid-1991, and Posit does some 3 million shares a day in NYSE and NASDAQ stocks. The absolute numbers may not be huge, but growth is: Reuter's two systems increased their business at an annual average of 45 percent between 1986 and 1991.[76]

---

[76] Cf. G. Anders and C. Torres, "The New Market: Computers Bypass Wall Street Middlemen and Stir Controversy," *The Wall Street Journal* (August 28, 1991).

The NYSE has accommodated the sharp rise in institutional large-block trading (of 10,000 or more shares at once) through the development of an "upstairs" market. Here, block "positioners" match buyers and sellers, and sometimes take positions themselves. They then route the sale through the floor specialist for execution. Naturally, low commission rates are charged. Nevertheless, the NYSE's long-time dominance is facing a very serious challenge.

3. A Brief Overview of the International Exchanges

Individual exchanges around the world have become very active over the last decade in trading their *domestic* securities. Mexico, Hong Kong, Singapore/Maylasia, and the smaller European nations are some examples of steady growth. And more and more equities are going global. By 1989, eleven national exchanges were showing a *foreign* equity turnover, at home, in excess of $600 million per annum.[77]

Nevertheless, even with the rapid growth of many exchanges worldwide, "the important conduits through which international savings are channelled remain in New York, Tokyo, and London".[78] U.S. transactions in all foreign securities in 1990 (aggregate purchases and sales) amounted to more than $253 billion—up from less than $18 billion on 1980. Aggregate purchases and sales of U.S. securities in British and Japanese markets alone amounted to $151 billion in 1990—up from $15 billion in 1980.[79] In the arena of foreign *bonds* having maturities of one year or more, total U.S. transactions came to approximately $650 billion in 1990—up from $35 billion in 1980. Aggregate purchases and sales of all such U.S. bonds in the British and Japanese markets amounted to $2.6 trillion in 1990—up from $123 billion in 1980.[80]

The London International Stock Exchange (ISE) is the single most active world market in foreign stock trading, with an average foreign issue volume (in 1990) of some £1.3 billion daily—slightly more than 50 percent of its *total* daily exchange volume in domestic and foreign stocks. A dealer market very similar to NASDAQ, ISE utilizes a quote-display process

---

[77] "Top Foreign Equities on International Exchanges," *Euromoney (May 1990)*, pp. 63-64. *NASDAQ claimed the figures understated their total foreign-sector turnover, and inserted an advertisement to the effect (giving their "correct" figure) in Euromoney (July 1990), p. 15.*

[78] A.D. Loehnis, "Volatility in Global Securities Markets," *Economic Insights* (November/December 1990), p. 17.

[79] P.A. Abken, *Economic Review*, note 72, *supra*, Table 1, p. 3. Abken's Foreign Transaction tables were derived by the Federal Reserve Bank of Atlanta from the U.S. Department of the Treasury, *U.S. Treasury Bulletin* (Winter 1991), Table CM-V-5 and (Winter 1981), Table CM-VI-10.

[80] Ibid., Table 2, p. 5. A *fully* automated trading system for every single transaction (*Tauras*) was abandoned by the London Stock Exchange early in 1993 after an expenditure of more than one half billion dollars for development.

called the Stock Exchange Automated Quotation System (SEAQ) for large trades. Small orders (of less than 5,000 shares) are executed automatically on ISE's corollary Stock Automated Exchange Facility (SAEF).[81]

The Tokyo Stock Exchange (TSE) does not utilize the NYSE specialist system. Overseers, called *saitori*, use their own computers to monitor floor trader and computer-arranged trades, and to approve prices. Fewer than 200 of the total number of TSE issues are still handled manually. A Computer Assisted Order Routing and Execution System (CORES) handles all other actively traded TSE issues. As monitors, *saitori* have more authority than do American specialists. For example, they can actually suspend trading briefly in the face of extreme volatility.[82]

Automation of overseas futures and options markets—for example, automated pit trading (APT) on the London International Financial Futures Exchange (LIFFE), fully automated, integrated clearing on the Deutsche Terminborse, and the CORES-F fully automated derivatives markets systems on the TSE—has led to very heavy global futures and options trading.[83] The volume is bound to increase enormously when Globex becomes fully active (e.g., involving U.S. markets with even more overseas players, such as the *Marche a Terme des Instruments Financiers* in France).

4. Linkage and Integration in World Securities Markets

There is no doubt that *linkages* between U.S. and foreign stock and bond markets are increasing in terms of trading patterns and processes. What is doubtful is whether there is, in fact, true international market *integration*.

The linkage phenomenon may be illustrated by the example of "exchange-for-physicals" (EFP) transactions.[84] In an EFP, the process could begin with a stock index futures purchase on an American futures exchange, and could end overseas with an unwinding of the position taken.

---

[81] Ibid., p. 12. An interesting brief review of all EC securities exchanges may be found in *The Economist Atlas of the New Europe* (New York: Henry Holt and Co. 1992), pp. 102-105.

[82] Ibid. Serious questions have been raised, of course, about the trustworthiness and reliability of the Japanese stock market in general in the face of astonishing government intervention. See Q. Hardy, "Tokyo Bounce: Japanese Stocks Surge, But Apparent Reasons Make Investors Queasy," *The Wall Street Journal* (March 19, 1993).

[83] Ibid., pp. 15-16. Some examples are the 16.3 million Japanese government bond futures contracts traded on the TSE (1990), and the 9.6 million German bond futures contracts traded on LIFFE (1990). See also T. McAuley, "Europe's Futures Markets Hotly Pursue U.S. Leaders," *The Wall Street Journal* (December 27, 1991). According to Euromoney's *Dictionary*, note 34, *supra*, 1991 contract volume on LIFFE was 83.5 million shares *total* and on TIFFE (Tokyo International Futures Exchange) some 15 million contracts total.

[84] See Robert W. Kolb, *Understanding Futures Markets*, 3rd ed. (Miami, FL: Kolb Publishing Company, 1991), pp. 17-18.

For example, a high-volume (institutional) buyer who wants to purchase an S&P 500 index stock portfolio at low (commission and market impact) cost can purchase its futures on the Chicago Mercantile Exchange (CME). It can then find an over-the-counter trader in London holding the underlying basket of stocks represented by the futures and close out its position with that trader (i.e., do the EFP). The trade has been completed now while bypassing both the NYSE and CME.[85]

After-hours trading (in the U.S.) is involved here, of course. London trades an estimated "10 million to 15 million" shares of such NYSE-listed stock daily while at the same time it "offers big players anonymity by not forcing them to disclose the stocks in their trades or the prices."[86]

Such linkages have helped lead to the establishment of after-hours trading in the United States, a phenomenon that has enormous implications for the future of securities trading both in America and elsewhere. We will pursue that matter further on.

True market *integration* is yet another issue.

It may help to focus on the integration issue by recalling the date October 19, 1987:

- *Record Falls on Wall Street Trigger Worldwide Slides:*
- *Heavy Selling Hits Bourses All Over Europe.*

That was the banner headline of the October 20, 1987, issue of the Financial Times of London. The reason for the market crash as given by the Times was: "Widespread Fears of Recession."

But according to Arthur B. Laffer, monetary policy caused the crash. It was "not tight enough."[87] Paul Craig Roberts felt that the problem was that monetary policy was "too tight already."[88] A Research Fellow at a Center of Statistical Mechanics at a large American University disagreed with Nobelist Kenneth Arrow, who had stated: "I don't think anything can explain a fall of 20 percent in one day." Explained the research fellow: "Physicists know that the events of sudden rise or fall with strong correlations can be well described by bifurcations or relaxation oscillations in nonlinear systems."[89]

Maybe so.

---

[85] Of course, many such overseas-market-linked OTC transactions can involve other than stock index derivatives.

[86] K.G. Salwen and C. Torres, "Big Board After-Hours Trading May Lead to a Two-Tier Market," *The Wall Street Journal (June 13, 1991). See also W. Power, "Big Board Tries to Lure Program Trades from London," *The Wall Street Journal* (November 23, 1990).

[87] *The Wall Street Journal* (October 22, 1987).

[88] Ibid.

[89] P. Chen, Letter to the Editor, *The New York Times (December 6, 1987), p. 5.

Nevertheless, it does not seem out of line to advance the argument that every reason put forth to explain why the market plummeted 508.32 points in one day, must be awarded the old Scotch jury verdict: "Not Proven."

Nicholas Brady, appointed to head a special commission to investigate the crash, did not attempt a definitive answer to the question: exactly what caused this dreadful event to occur?[90] What the report did conclude was that "the financial system approached breakdown," and that massive, computerized program trading (selling "portfolio insurance") helped to intensify the fall. The Brady Commission recommended that, since all financial markets (stocks, option, futures) were really one market, there should be one overall regulator, preferably the Fed; that margin requirements should be consistent between stocks and derivatives; and that "circuit breakers" should be installed, such as trading halts, to cool things down when volatility appeared to be getting totally out of hand.

Some margin hikes for derivatives were later put in place, and circuit breakers were eventually installed to deal with dramatic price moves; for example, halting trading for an hour if the market falls 250 points in one day (NYSE); halting Chicago Mercantile Exchange S&P futures trading for 30 minutes if that market drops 12 points in one day, and diverting all program trading on the NYSE if the CME calls a halt in fact. Also, program trading is blocked for the day after the Dow Jones Industrial Average moves up or down 50 points.[91]

It is important to point out that the Brady Commission study was the major post-October 1987 examination of the market crash to take place in the world and, more importantly, it is a fact that the crash that year did not result in any

> natural constituency of securities markets supervisors to analyze how close the system came to disaster or to devise future safeguards.[92]

The crash did, however, prompt a good deal of discussion on the issue of world financial market *integration*. For example, does volatility

---

[90] The formal citation to the report is: Brady et al, *Report of the Presidential Task Force on Market Mechanisms (January 8, 1988). It was submitted to the President, the Secretary of the Treasury, and the Chairman of the Federal Reserve Board.*

[91] The Brady Commission Report is voluminous. A rather good analysis of its major points may be found in J.B. Stewart and D. Hertzberg, "Market Medicine: Scope of the Proposals by Brady Commission Shows Gravity of Crisis," *The Wall Street Journal* (January 11, 1988).

[92] Loehnis, note 78, *supra*, at p. 16. It should be noted that the Brady Report did not represent the only U.S. effort at understanding what had occurred. The SEC, the GAO, and the Commodity Futures Trading Commission used 440 people to produce 1,650 pages worth of reports.

in one market necessarily spread over to all markets? And are all differences in markets (e.g., the reward-to-risk ratio)[93] equalized around the world? And how highly correlated *are* price measurements across markets and to what extent do they pierce transaction costs?[94]

By and large, academicians seem to agree that world stock markets are *not* integrated, although there is some disagreement, of course.[95] If they are correct, why then do precipitous drops in one large action market sometimes "spread" to other markets?[96]

The answer to that conundrum is not really clear, although it may be that traders in one national market may not have the same information available to them as traders in another national market. Therefore, when massive passive (computerized) trades in one market drive down prices, traders elsewhere can misinterpret the fall as being caused by specific, serious, adverse data and follow the computer "noise" down. In such cases, unobserved hedging programs, for example, can destabilize *linked* but not truly *integrated* markets in a scenario where "rational" expectations (*based not on fundamentals, but simply on what the traders seem to be doing!*) lead to an irrational result.[97]

A foreign-exchange trader has explained rather well the non-fundamentals, "perception"-based trading phenomenon:

> Ninety percent of what we do is based on perception. It doesn't matter if that perception is right or wrong or real. It only matters that other people in the market believe it. I know it's crazy. I may think it's wrong. But I lose my shirt by ignoring it. This business turns on decisions made in seconds. If you wait a minute to reflect on things, you're lost.[98]

---

[93] C.R. Harvey, "The World Price of Covariance Risk," *The Journal of Finance* (March 1991). According to Harvey, the reward-to-risk ratio is twice as large in Japanese stock markets as it is in American markets.

[94] D. Neumark, P.A. Tinsley, and S. Tosini, "After-Hours Stock prices and Post-Crash Hangovers," *The Journal of Finance* (March 1991). These authors hold that "only larger price changes pierce the transaction cost barriers between markets."

[95] See, e.g., "The International Transmission of Stockmarket Fluctuations," Paribas: *CONJECTURE* (October 1988).

[96] Sometimes, but not always. The Nikkei average plunged in July 1987 (to below 23,000), while the Dow Jones and FT-SE 100 in the U.K. were on the rise. The huge declines in New York and London in October 1987 were not matched in Tokyo, which fell back only slightly below its August high of 26,000. Then when a rampaging Tokyo later fell from 39,000 to 16,000, New York (and London) markets certainly did not follow suit. Nor did the NYSE mini-crash of October 1989 prove to be internationally contagious. See also J. Fuerbringer, "Equities March Their Separate Ways," *The New York Times* (November 24, 1991).

[97] G. Gennotte and H. Leland, "Market Liquidity, Hedging, and Crashes," *The American Economic Review* (December 1990).

[98] This quote from a foreign-exchange (Fx) trader at a major money center bank (which profits hugely on Fx trading) appears in W. Mossberg, "Making Book on the Buck," *The Wall*

It is beyond the scope of this chapter to argue the case for or against the assertion that securities markets around the world are inefficient. It would seem to be enough at this juncture to point out the following: International securities markets will continue to *link up* to an even greater degree in trading activity and trading processes; that it is far from certain that they will also become *integrated* in such a way as to promote informational symmetry, overall cost of-doing-business convergence, and the like; and that despite a terrifying market crash and a slew of American follow-up reports and actions, we still

> do not know how institutions and financial instruments and techniques formed and developed in the 1980s will cope under macroeconomic circumstances that promise to be very different.[99]

5. The Program Trading Phenomenon

It is really not possible to discuss modern securities markets processes or problems without some reference to the program trading phenomenon. Thus, before going on to a further examination of related domestic and international securities markets concerns, we are going to describe program trading briefly.[100]

Program trading, in one of its major manifestations, is an outgrowth of advanced technology applied to a tried and true financial market process called "arbitrage" Arbitrage is the simultaneous purchase and sale of an asset (such as a commodity or a currency) in two or more markets that are reflecting price differences or discrepancies. The arbitrage action has two results: (1) The arbitrageur profits from the difference, and (2) the market differential is erased, thus making markets more efficient.

When applied to the stock and stock derivatives markets, and utilized together with sophisticated telecommunications systems and computing facilities, arbitraging reaches the *program trading* level and truly moves markets. Whether it moves them only temporarily or not is arguable, but even temporary movements in a game can be permanently damaging to some of its less sophisticated—or, perhaps, geographically removed—players.

In any event, while the singular purchase of options and futures is risky (and, conversely, very rewarding when one wins), stock index arbi-

---

Street Journal (September 23, 1988).

[99] Loehnis, note 78, *supra*.

[100] With help from Albert S. Neubert, whose "How Program Trading Works," appears in Frederick Amling, *Investments* (Englewood Cliffs, N.J.: Prentice Hall, 1989), 6th ed., pp. 738-40. The emphasis here *is* on program trading and *arbitrage*, not on large "basket" trades, simply, or on program selling as "insurance."

trage carries no risk at all. What it requires is a large amount of capital, so that when a futures contract is not at the same level as the S&P 500 index, for example, arbitraging those markets can produce a guaranteed profit. The market price discrepancies are generally quite small, and they can be caused by market forces (e.g., supply and demand of and for futures contracts), market margin differentials, and the like. When the aforementioned highly sophisticated equipment picks up the discrepancies, it can then set in motion enormous buying and selling (arbitrage) activity. When arbitrageurs (e.g., investment banking houses trading for their own accounts) buy or sell huge baskets of stocks and, at the same time, sell the futures contracts derived from them, the prices of the stocks involved can move sharply.

The brief outline above is a very simplified description of program trading/stock-index arbitrage. In actuality,

> It is a highly sophisticated technique requiring extensive resources, including elaborate telecommunications systems and computing facilities. The participants are professionals. . . . They must be well capitalized, because the amounts of money needed to engage in basis (*program*) trading are enormous—at least $5–$10 million. It has been estimated that the total pool available to conduct stock-index arbitrage is several billion dollars and is growing.[101]

Certainly the individual investor can participate in this big-time game by entrusting his (or her) money to an institutional money manager. But if the investor craves independence and the opportunity to make his or her own decisions, the individual investor must either be prepared to handle risks beyond those normally present when betting on fundamentals, or exit the market. And while the U.S. market rise in the latter half of 1991 saw some small investors coming back into the game,[102] the reality is that, in the face of technological innovation and seeming volatility, the individual investor has been saying his (and her) goodbyes.

Seventy-five percent of all NYSE trading is done by large institutional traders,[103] and the question is: Does it really matter? It has been argued that as long as the individual continues to participate through mutual funds or pension funds it surely doesn't matter. But others identify

---

[101] Ibid., p. 740.
[102] M. Siconolfi, "Little Guys Make Big Moves Into Stock Market," *The Wall Street Journal* (November 8, 1991). Even here the writer admits that small investor participation, while higher than in 1990, still makes up only 25 percent of all trading on the NYSE (as of November 1991).
[103] *Ibid.*

the exodus with a socially debilitating lack of trust and confidence, and with a withdrawal of long-term, fundamentals-oriented support for many companies in need of capital, which cannot be counted on to show quick profits and are therefore labeled "risky." Some Security Industry Association data seems to indicate also that the flow of funds out of direct ownership has not gone, dollar for dollar, back into mutual funds.[104]

All of which presents a situation for the markets that Federal Reserve Board Governor David Mullens has characterized as "not dire news, but it's not good news, either."

Program trading cannot be held solely accountable for driving small investors out of the market. The natural progression of technology-induced innovation has played its part, as have other developments over time.

But program trading has indeed raised several issues which have not helped to persuade investors that stock markets are either honest, fair, or transparent.

> More and more Wall Street executives, corporate officials, money managers and traders have come to believe that some investment firms are using [computerized] trading tactics to take advantage of their inside knowledge of customers' trading plans, to the detriment of the customers. . . [and] using their financial power in jittery trading environments to make the markets even more volatile for their own benefit.[105]

"Frontrunning" is the term applied to several program trading tactics that certainly seem to qualify as dishonest and unfair. *Self-frontrunning* occurs when traders use the first step of index arbitrage to make large transactions; for example, to begin rapid buying of stock index futures contracts to push up corresponding stock prices on the NYSE. As others move to buy contracts, the originator sells out at his own manufactured profit.[106]

Self-frontrunning, it is argued, is harmless, and even somewhat risky to the originator. It is, nevertheless, manipulation and certainly has

---

[104] M. Siconolfi, "Individual Investors' Holdings of U.S. Stocks Fall Below 50% of Total Market for the First Time," *The Wall Street Journal* (November 13, 1992). When all mutual fund assets are added in, however, individuals own 55.9% of all stock. Their ownership in 1965 was 84.1%. *Ibid.* Mutual fund assets, *including* all money market as well as stock and bond funds totalled $1.6 trillion at year-end 1992. See C. Gould, "The Economy's $1.6 Trillion Gorilla," *The New York Times* (January 17, 1993).

[105] K. Eichenwald, "Program Trading's Other Ills," *The New York Times* (November 5, 1989).

[106] J. Crudele, "Stock Market Manipulation—Games Brokers Play," The (Bergen, N.J.) *Record* (May 26, 1991). See also: S. Antilla, "The Murky World of Frontrunning," *The New York Times* (February 7, 1993).

nothing whatsoever to do with market fundamentals—but rather more to do with casino gambling. *Intermarket frontrunning* occurs when a broker uses information about an impending transaction for a customer; for example, to sell 500,000 shares of stock so as to trade ahead of that (certain) sale in the related futures market. While self-frontrunning is admitted to exist, intermarket frontrunning is not (publicly), and in any event was not necessarily considered to be wrong by some Securities and Exchange Commission members, the SEC argument being that we ought not to be quick to condemn the performance by a firm of "a limited agency function" for a sophisticated customer that "does not entail any categorically predetermined relationship or any broad set of inherent obligations."

This is not an argument calculated to promote a positive attitude toward, and a healthy respect for, technology and the modern securities marketplace.[107]

6. Linkage, Competition, and the Gradual Erosion of Openness in U.S. Securities Markets

(a). Rule 144 A. Section 4(2) of the Securities Act of 1933 provided an exemption from registration requirements; i.e., allowed an issuer of shares to sell them without registering all pertinent corporate information with the SEC, and to make the issue available to prospective purchasers. But the exemption was confined to "transactions by an issuer not involving any public offering." And further, the law prohibited the *resale* of Section 4(2) securities until the securities were registered (or fell under some other exemption).

However, in April 1990, the SEC promulgated Rule 144A, which provides a "safe harbor" exemption for such *resales*. Under Rule 144A, 4(2), unregistered securities *can* be resold like all other securities, if they are sold to a "qualified institution buyer." Such a buyer is defined as one who invests $100 million or more in securities of issuers not affiliated with it, or is a registered broker-dealer who invests $10 million or more in like manner.

Rule 144A was promulgated to allow foreign companies to raise private capital in the United States without having to comply with this country's high disclosure standards. Allowing for resale was the key, of

---

[107] See T.E. Ricks, "SEC Splits in 3-2 Vote Over the Nature of a Brokerage Firm's Duties to Client," *The Wall Street Journal* (July 11, 1988). In addition to front-running, there is "Gunning" (engineering price movements in futures markets to trigger stops and computer-generated signals to buy and sell_ and "Tape-Shooting," a sophisticated form of frontrunning where short-term traders watch NYSE electronic tape for footprints of a big buyer or seller and then go into action by buying or selling in advance of the big guy's move. See S. Pulliam and Dorfman, "Tape-Shooting Irks and Hurts Major Investors, Who Respond by Shipping Big Trades Overseas," *The Wall Street Journal* (September 11, 1992).

course. Competition, it was thought, required the move. Our disclosure standards, compared with competitor nations (i.e., our *Regulations*), were choking our market, the argument ran.

The contrary argument, of course, is that American securities laws were promulgated to protect investors by promoting complete disclosure (i.e., open markets) and that such disclosure encouraged both liquidity and efficiency.

Another concern about Rule 144A is that once *a private market* is promoted, there is erosion of the central market (The National Market System, or NMS) mandated by Congress in 1975. The NMS was mandated to link the NYSE and the regional exchanges so as to guarantee *all* investors access to the most competitive pricing.

Broker-dealers who could previously operate solely as an intermediary between issuers and purchasers of privately placed securities may now purchase the issues as principals and resell to any qualified buyer.[108]

(b). *After-Hours Trading and Further Secrecy Concerns.*

As the NYSE watched its market being eroded by foreign competition, it developed a plan, and in May 1991 the NYSE received approval of the SEC for after-hours trading on the Big Board. Specifically, to recapture some or all of the approximately 15.2 million shares being traded elsewhere after its close, the NYSE undertook, in June 1991, to operate two *after-hours* trading sessions—one 45-minute order matching session, and one 75-minute session for crossing baskets of stocks.[109]

A key concern with the after-hours trading session is this: Neither the size of the trades nor the names of the brokerage firms participating after hours are publicly disclosed. Only an overall volume figure and an overall dollar figure for the entire crossing session will be made public. Therefore, the *only* possessors of good information on *who* traded *what* with *whom* will be the parties privy to the actual trades.

London, of course, is a "dark" market. Since January 1991, the London Stock Exchange ended "real time" disclosure. Trades are reported 1 ½ hours *after* they have occurred.

---

[108] The remaining issue here is whether any American purchasers, even huge institutions who are used to full disclosure, will become heavy buyers without such disclosure. See D.B. Henriques, "A Shortcut for Foreign Firms: Investors Say No," *The New York Times* (September 15, 1991).

[109] See Salwen and Torres, note 86, *supra*. The Philadelphia Stock Exchange trades currency options and futures 20.5 hours a day. Amex will undertake a 45-minute after-hours session as well, and it hopes to arrange with Reuters, the CBOE, and the Cincinnati Stock Exchange to ply the after-hours trade, globally, in stock, stock options, and other derivatives. At the end of one year of after-hours trading, results were disappointing, at least with regard to the matching session. According to the NYSE, however, the crossing session had recaptured a third of the market that had been lost. See C. Torres, "Much Ballyhooed 'After Hours' Trading So Far Fails to Live Up to Expectations," *The Wall Street Journal* (May 28, 1992).

Moreover, the NYSE waives all exchange fees with regard to basket trades (computer-assisted program trading), and buyers and sellers are exempted from the "short-sale" rule that prevents all other market participants from selling individual stock aggressively into a falling market.

In October 1991, the SEC approved *Nasdaq International*, which allows 3:30 A.M. (the London stock market opening time) to 9:00 A.M., electronic trading of large OTC stocks (and some shares of NYSE and AMEX listed shares as well). That system, through which American and European brokerage firms can conduct their after-hours trading, began in early 1992.

Here, too, secrecy is paramount. At 9 A.M., at the end of the session, NASDAQ provides the high and low bids for any stock with two or more market makers, along with the aggregate trading volume for the overnight session. Who purchased what from whom, and for how much, is the business of individual participants only.

The 200th anniversary of the NYSE was celebrated in mid-1992, but the secrecy issue cast a bit of a pall over the festivities. Not in terms of after-hours trading secrecy, but rather in terms of less than complete disclosure of corporate data to market participants.

At issue are the strict rules on financial disclosure required of all companies listed on U.S. exchanges. The NYSE would like to see these rules waived for large foreign companies that are subject to far less demanding accounting and disclosure rules, at home, than the SEC requires here. Argues the NYSE: The SEC's "technical rules" here are causing a large loss of business to U.S. exchanges. The SEC in fact would require foreign companies to keep two sets of books, and if the SEC continues to refuse to waive these "technical rules" the NYSE could eventually become merely a regional marketplace.

The SEC argues that differing accounting and disclosure rules abroad would subject the U.S. investor to undue risk. Germany is the major case in point. Under the German accounting system, a corporation decides just what earnings it cares to report. There is no requirement whatsoever that earnings reported to the public have to be accurate. This leaves a small group of insiders privy to the *entire* situation within the company, and they are free to trade against the public. This would make things unequal—for example, for Chrysler stock to trade against Daimler-Benz, which could list its liability for postretirement benefits as zero, something Chrysler could not. This issue is another in the two-tier stock market debate.[110]

---

[110] See M. Siconolfi and K.G. Salwen, "Big Board, SEC Fight Over Foreign Stocks," *The Wall Street Journal* (May 13, 1992).

Surely competition in securities markets is a matter to be considered, and to be responded to, seriously, and yet one must worry, too, that the losers in this gradual erosion of the fairness-and-openness focus of the original U.S. securities laws are all the smaller market makers in the nation, whose ability to compete will be lessened. And as investors lose needed information, the structure and function of the primary marketplace, the central information source, could be whittled away. It is odd, one commentator remarked, that the SEC should choose the time of the U.S. government bond market scandal to encourage some measure of secrecy through after hours trading. Then he added:

> It is conceivable that the SEC's efforts will bring in a bit more business for American brokers and trading systems, even as investors lose needed information. Some trading will be siphoned from other, more open American markets, and perhaps they will demand to be allowed to keep secrets to stay competitive. In the current SEC atmosphere, a meek assent is likely.
>
> Eventually, the SEC may regret the steps it is now taking. It is to be hoped that the markets will not have been irreparably harmed in the meantime.[111]

Secrecy may or may not have helped boost the British stock exchange profits, but it surely has not eliminated competition problems or unethical responses to them.

In October 1991, officials at London's Futures and Options Exchange admitted to paying selected traders to carry out dummy trades so as to inflate volume and bring in business. The payments made appear to be in the vicinity of £200,000.[112]

The third member of the big three securities marketers, Japan, ended 1991 mired in scandal. The big secret there was that the nation's four major investment banking houses had paid out more than 65 billion yen (some $500 million) to large customers who had lost money with them

---

[111] F. Norris, "At the SEC, Another Move for Secrecy," *The New York Times* (October 22, 1991). And compare: W. Power and K.G. Salwen, "Big Board's Donaldson Says SEC Rules Could Cost Exchange Its Global Standing," *The Wall Street Journal* (December 12, 1991) with F. Norris, "Maxwell Saga: Bad Accounting Aided fraud," *The New York Times* (December 18, 1991). In October 1992, the SEC approved an NYSE amendment to its Rule 72. The new "clean cross" rule will allow brokers to arrange (or "cross") trades of 25,000 shares or more between two customers while ignoring customers on the NYSE floor unless floor orders are at a better price. Up to that time, "upstairs" block trades had to take pending floor orders into account. See C. Torres, "Big Board Set to Allow Bypass of Floor Trades," *The Wall Street Journal* (October 26, 1992).

[112] N. Bray, "Scandal Spotlights U.K. Exchange's Ills," *The Wall Street Journal* (October 22, 1991).

in the market.[113] Despite the fact that in Japan large corporations hold some 70 percent of all equities and usually do not trade them actively, there *are* many small investors, and they subsidized, to some degree, the payoff to the large and wealthy investors.

While the events in New York, London, and Tokyo described herein are not at all similar, the fundamental concern is: Do markets that are not transparent present long-term dangers both to their players and to the societies which support them and which they are "serving"? And transparency (openness) is but one concern to which securities markets regulators need to turn their attention. Let us examine some others.

7. Key Regulatory Issues

(a). Domestic Considerations. Apart from considerations of openness and fairness, which are crucial to any market, there is the fundamental issue in the United States of who should regulate whom?

To some degree, the various exchanges regulate their own players directly. For example, the NYSE has forbidden brokerage firms trading on the Big Board from purchasing large blocks of stock and afterwards issuing "buy" recommendations on that same stock to customers.[114] Exchanges may also be regulated by their own associated watchdogs, referred to as self-regulatory organizations (SROs). The National Futures Association (NFA), for example, is an SRO for the commodities industry and has come in for much criticism for being a terribly sleepy watchdog.[115] Then, of course, there are the federal agency overseers. The government regulator for the commodities industry is the Commodity Futures Trading Commission (CFTC). It, too, has been criticized. For one thing, it has asked Congress *not* to give it legal power to pursue insider trading on the commodities exchanges.[116] The Commodity Exchange itself (COMEX) has come in for some probing (by the U.S. Attorney in

---

[113] By August 1991, the payback figure appears to have risen to "nearly a billion dollars." M.R. Sesit and K.G. Salwen, "SEC Sends Queries to Japanese Firms Involved in Refunding Scandal," *The Wall Street Journal* (August 1, 1991). For a full account of the scandal-ridden Japanese stock market, and the astonishingly casual attitude of Japanese politicians toward partnerships with organized crime, see J. Sterngold, "Japan's Rigged Casino," *The New York Times Magazine* (April 26, 1992), and J. Sterngold, "Scandal's Details Tainting Japan Party," *The New York Times* (November 29, 1992). See also the reference to the Japanese government market prop-up scandal at note 82, *infra*.

[114] W. Power, "Firms Told: Issue 'Buy,' Then Load Up," *The Wall Street Journal* (April 9, 1991). For an example of NASD activity in the self-regulatory area, see "NASD Disciplines Firms, Individuals Over Infractions," *The Wall Street Journal* (October 18, 1991) p. A 9E.

[115] J. Bailey, "Commodities Abuses Have Long Continued Despite NFA Scrutiny," *The Wall Street Journal* (October 16, 1990).

[116] Cf. K.G. Salwen and S. Block, "CFTC Gets in Habit of Rejecting Advice of Its Own Judges in Disciplinary Cases," *The Wall Street Journal* (May 12, 1992).

Manhattan) in connection with the cheating of customers in its pits through various illegal trading practices.[117]

Serious regulatory questions are raised in connection with hybrid instruments (derivatives), and the major one involves regulator jurisdiction.

The CFTC, through the federal Commodities Exchange Act, has exclusive jurisdiction over futures exchanges and their clearing organizations. The act can be read, and has been read by the CFTC, as granting the CFTC jurisdiction not just over "commodity" products but all products with regard to futures, and also over goods, services, rights, and interests. This is a matter of some concern to the Fed (e.g., do bank swaps have a "futures" element in them?)[118] and to the SEC (since it is responsible for options instruments, for broker-dealers who trade *everything*, and for securities markets).

American markets are not served well by regulatory jurisdiction turf battles, either in or out of court. And the exclusivity provisions of the Commodities Exchange Act have cast a pall over many markets—the swaps market particularly. The Federal Reserve has taken the lead in pushing for limits on CFTC jurisdiction,[119] and several attempts have been made at congressional legislation to define more clearly just who has what jurisdiction over whom with regard to burgeoning derivatives.[120]

Clearly, consideration of market (and public) safety and soundness—along with innovative competitiveness—cries out for congressional clarity here.[121]

---

[117] L.P. Cohen, S.W. Angrist, and K.G. Salwen, "U.S. Probes Comex Aides Over Uncovering of FBI Sting," *The Wall Street Journal* (April 19, 1991). While there were many acquittals in the fraud-in-the-pits, three-year sting operation, there were also 30 convictions and guilty pleas for illegal trading practices as of early 1991. None of this lack of market integrity seemed to bother investors at risk; futures volume continued to rise anyway: Cf. "Rolling with the Punches," *Corporate Finance* (December 1990; Special Supplement, III-IV).

[118] Three-year and 5-year interest rate swaps "futures" trade on the CBOT, along with corn and soybean futures, and new hybrids are being developed constantly, raising the jurisdictional (and market safety) stakes all the time. Cf. S.W. Angrist, "In Search of the Hot Futures Contract," *The Wall Street Journal* (April 8, 1991).

[119] See Alan Greenspan's Statement to the Congress of April 16, 1991, in the *Federal Reserve Bulletin* (June 1991), pp. 423-25.

[120] One example is H.R. 965, 102d Congress, 1st Session, February 19, 1991: "A Bill to establish a Markets and Trading Commission in order to combine the function of the Commodity Futures Trading Commission and the Securities Exchange Commission in a single independent regulatory commission, and for other purposes." This is a concept worth pursuing, assuming one can get beyond systemic turf and power issues.

[121] It must be noted that another area where some confusion reigns regarding U.S. securities has to do with federal vs. state regulatory jurisdiction. The SEC wants to see state power slashed on the ground that the states are stifling U.S. international security market competitiveness. State regulators answer that they are the last bastion of safety for their citizens, and they point to the fact that they file ten times as many enforcement actions as the SEC. See "War Erupts Between SEC Chief Breeden and State Securities Regulators," *The Wall Street Journal* (December 7, 1990), p. 1. The record of the 102d Congress in dealing with important securities legislation was not a very good one. See K.G. Salwen, "Several

And just as clearly, the safety and soundness of *non*- U.S. markets (and populations) would seem to require the sensible resolution of similar regulatory concerns, particularly because very few, if any, foreign jurisdictions have come as far as Americans have in dealing with the exponential growth in derivative products. All of which leads us to our final "Securities Markets" concern.

(b). International Considerations. In our discussion of investment banking, we have already alluded to the fact that there are no international financial market agreements extant regarding securities transactions.

It is surely high time to come to grips, *on a global basis*, with the issue of systemic risk *in worldwide securities markets*. Lacking the equivalent of central bankers such as the Fed and the Bank of England, and an allied sponsor such as the Bank for International Settlements, how is one to begin? Perhaps we should begin with the key issues to be faced and later with the parties best able first to organize and then begin to resolve them.

All exchanges without exception, should be required to establish *minimal* standards regarding each of the following:

- Capital adequacy requirements must exist for all broker-dealers doing business with the exchange if no SEC equivalent within their jurisdiction exists that has already assumed the responsibility for establishing and overseeing them.

- Uniform criteria for accounting and disclosure of information must be put in place regarding all corporations whose equities or debt paper trade on the exchange.

- Uniform rules on disclosure of trades and traders must be devised. While some degree of secrecy will always exist, the existence of "dark" exchanges should not be tolerated. When the common denominator for openness goes so low as to reach the early twentieth century level of the most secretive Swiss banks, corruption and loss are inevitable, and the uninformed public will end up paying the bill.

- Uniform clearing and settlement procedures should be implemented to deal with inefficiency and risk regarding time-scales for matching and settlement of trades; and a delivery-against-payment system for settling transactions should be immediately effected.

- There must be clear delineation of regulatory responsibility for all aspects of securities and derivatives trading. The depth of regulator commitment to decency cannot be legislated, but, at the very least, one has to know that enforcement responsibility

Major Securities Bills Will Die When Congress Reaches Adjournment," *The Wall Street Journal* (October 7, 1992).

does exist, and *where* and *what* it is. Minimum legislation must close all gaps.

- Entry requirements for doing business on the exchange, and all rules of conduct, should be uniform, without regard to local citizenship.

- International agreements relative to the investigation and enforcement of national securities laws across all nations must be in place so as to frustrate securities border jumpers.

- Participation with commercial central bankers in constructive talks should be required, leading to some general accord on issues related to the "lender of last resort." Securities markets, like investment banks, must, insofar as is possible, be denied access to the trough of "moral hazard."

International action in the stock exchange arena must be focused on safety, soundness, and efficiency. Such action is then directed as well at the prevention of regulator arbitrage, a process that ill serves all who depend on the good health and productive growth of financial markets everywhere.

The most efficient securities market cannot be expected to guarantee either total safety or profits. Risk and some degree of volatility are essential ingredients for market growth. However, what exchange officials must be expected to do is to encourage responsibility and public stewardship, ensure honesty and openness, and guarantee fair competition.

It is easy enough to shrug off these mandates on the ground that they are, in the *real* world, impossible. But in light of rapidly expanding markets, volume, speed-related technology, and products it must be emphasized that, to the extent that such mandates go by the board, there may be a very high price all of us will pay not too far down the line.

C. Money Management

1. Money Management, Law, and the Prudent Man Rule (and ERISA)

The key case in the development of the prudent man rule in law is Harvard College v. Amory, 26 Mass. (Pick) 446 (1830). The trust involved here provided for income to living beneficiaries, with the corpus (remainder) to Harvard College and the Massachusetts General Hospital, equally. This testamentary trust was made up of $50,000 cash. The instructions to the trustee were to "loan the same upon ample and sufficient security, or to invest the same in safe and productive stock, either in the public funds or bank shares or other stock, according to their best judgement and discretion." The trustees invested in insurance and manufacturing stocks, whose value dropped from $41,000 to $29,000. Harvard College sued the trustees on the ground that the rule of law in England was, and always had been, that the only presumptively proper instruments of investment were government securities, so the trustees were liable to them for this loss.

The Massachusetts Supreme Court held that there were no utterly safe investments, that "do what you will, the capital is at hazard." The English rule, said the court, is not applicable in the United States. Here, they held,

> All that can be required of a trustee to invest is, that he shall conduct himself faithfully, and exercise a sound discretion. He is to observe how men of prudence, discretion and intelligence manage their own affairs, not in regard to speculation, but in regard to the permanent disposition of their funds, considering the probable income, as well as the probable safety of the capital invested.

There, then, is the original "prudent man" rule, and it was long considered too daring and dangerous (to beneficiaries) by most state courts to be adopted. Many state legislatures actually passed "list" laws—that is, laws listing the few investments a fiduciary was allowed to make—all others thus being imprudent!

The *Harvard College* case rule was restated in more or less similar fashion in the 1940s by the Trust Division of the American Bankers Association in their Model Prudent Man Investment Act. Included in the act was a broader list of approved investments than state legislatures had ever considered.

The Massachusetts case and the Model Act, plus a famous treatise on trusts by Professor Austin Wakeman Scott of Harvard Law School, and a Restatement of Trusts (based on Scott), complete the picture of our legally defined prudent man (fiduciary/trustee). However, to the basic *Harvard College* definition, Scott added something. He felt the Massachusetts Supreme Court prudent man rule to be applicable to general trust management (administration), but not to specific investments where prudent men, managing *their own* assets, could take risks that a prudent fiduciary managing *your* assets should not. So Scott insisted that fiduciary investments be subject to a rule of prudence measured by the standard of conduct of men who are prudently safeguarding assets *for others*.

Now, what is "speculative" and thus imprudent? Does a fiduciary have a legal duty to concern himself (or herself) with inflation risk and to act to protect the real value of a portfolio? Ought the fiduciary, for example, sell municipal bonds (good interest-bearing securities) and get into growth-common stocks? Hedging instruments? The law *does* consider real value protection a prudent consideration. Moreover, the general rule of law seems to be that if an investment vehicle is widely held by other trust funds and institutional investors, that is *evidence* that such an investment is prudent (but not a *guarantee* that it is).

In fact, in the absence of clear stupidity, cupidity, conflict of interest, or plain bad faith, the courts have, in the past, gone along with trustee decisions. This trend has developed in somewhat the same way as the one in which courts have gone along with corporate director decisions, utilizing the Business Judgment Rule.

But we are now in "modern times." Professor Scott and the 1830 Massachusetts Supreme Court never dreamed of our many puts, calls, straddles, strips, spreads, index options, and 57 varieties of securitized debt, not to mention junk bonds.

The law in fact varies (in the severity of its application of the prudent man rule) in terms of the type of beneficiary for whom the fiduciary is acting—that is, a charitable hospital, university, pension fund, or family member. In terms of the tax exempt institution, the IRS has some controlling guidelines.

(a). The Employee Retirement Income Security Act of 1974 (ERISA) is a special case. It is a modern statute whose prudence standard was not legislatively spelled out until 1979. This federal legislation was set up to establish minimal federal standards for private pension plans. More than 60 million workers and retirees are covered by private retirement programs, and ERISA's attempt to safeguard retirement funds includes some insurance guarantees, of which more will be said later on in this chapter.

The assets covered by ERISA amount to more than $1,800,000,000,000. Given the size of the beneficiary pool, the assets encompassed, and the potential taxpayer insurance liability, one might agree that ERISA should be administered with the public interest very much in mind. ERISA is in fact administered by the U.S. Department of Labor, which issues advisory opinions, from time to time, to provide guidance to pension fund administrators. Investment prudence is only one issue relevant to ERISA. Others include general pension fund administration, and pension plan terminations. The ethical dimension of the latter issue is one we will examine more closely later.

The ERISA definition of "fiduciary" (29 U.S.C. § 1002 (21) (A) 1985) includes administrators as well as investment managers and advisors as well. Fiduciaries who cause fund losses are personally liable for the losses if they are found to be legally at fault, and they cannot contract that liability away (29 U.S.C. § 1109 and 1110 (a)).

However, the definition of a prudent man (fiduciary investor-manager) in ERISA is quite flexible. First, the law does allow the *delegation* of responsibility for investing corpus assets, generally forbidden by U.S. trust law: ". . . a person (who is a fiduciary under ERISA) may appoint an investment manager or managers to manage (including the power to acquire and dispose of any assets of a plan." (29 U.S.C. § 1102 (c) (3) 1985). However, such delegated investment managers must be registered as such under the Investment Advisor Act of 1940 (under which some 9,000 investment advisors are registered with the SEC), or must be a *bank* as defined in that act, or an insurance company qualified as a money manager under the laws of more than one state. Of course, once hired, an investment manager becomes an ERISA fiduciary.

Bevis Longstreth sets forth the following as ERISA's definition of the "prudent man":

> the regulation provides that the statutory duty to act will be satisfied with respect to a particular investment if the fiduciary has thoroughly considered the investment's place in the whole portfolio, the risk of loss and the opportunity for gain, and the diversification, liquidity, cash flow, and overall return requirements of the pension plan. . . (citing 29 C.F.R. § 2550.404 a-1 (b) 1985).[122]

This is certainly a far broader definition than ever conceived of by Professor Scott. In fact, the Labor Department has stated it believes "that the universe of investments permissible under the prudent man rule is not necessarily limited to those permitted at common law" (44 Fed. Reg. 37,225–June 26, 1979).[123]

Case law under ERISA is skimpy. There are few pure prudent man issues in the law books. Most ERISA investment manager suits relate to conflicts of interest, bad faith and the like. A few prudence cases are noted in Longstreth.[124] We might add *Donovon* v. *Damon* (Civil Action No. 84-056, Aug. 2, 1984, U.S. Dist. Ct., Western District of Missouri). Here trustees invested a large portion of pension fund assets in a Mexican bank at high interest at a time of economic crisis in Mexico. The plan suffered losses. The court, emphasizing lack of investment diversity, required the

---

[122] Bevis Longstreth, ed., *Modern Investment Management and the Prudent Man Rule* ((New York: Oxford University Press, 1986). As of 1988, according to the Federal Reserve System, the financial asset mix of private pension funds was: demand deposits and currency 1%; time deposits, 8.1%; U.S. Government Securities, 12.3%; corporate stock, 47.5%; corporate bonds, 15.8%; mortgages, 0.5%; and miscellaneous 14.8%. See Martin, Petty, Keown, and Scott, *Basic Financial Management*, 5th ed.(Englewood Cliffs, N.J.: Prentice Hall, 1991), Table 17-5, p. 662. Private and public pension funds, subsequent to 1988, show a shift from domestic to foreign stocks to some extent (up from 4.5% to 5.6% of total portfolio assets). J.A. White, "Pension Funds Speak: Foreign Stocks in, Property Out," *The Wall Street Journal* (January 3, 1991).

[123] Ibid.

[124] Longstreth, *Modern Investment*, p. 35.

trustees to reimburse all losses personally, barred them permanently from ever serving as a fiduciary of this pension plan again, and barred them as ERISA fiduciaries *en toto* for five years.

As "modern" and flexible as ERISA's prudent man rule might be, the Labor Department does *not* sanction specific investments, by list or whatever, and ERISA money managers do seek safety in numbers. And there is *no* rule of law that would entitle any money manager to assume that, given good faith and considered judgment, *any* and *all* financial market investments are ERISA prudent.

(b). Conclusion. Two questions are of excruciating importance should portfolios deflate and lawsuits pop up at multimillion dollar levels:

- What *is* the modern paradigm of prudence?
- What *should* it be?

The key concern of those who favor a free, full use of any and all available investment techniques and instruments—in the presence of good faith and (documented) informed deliberation by the fiduciary—is this: the *law* could come down against a fiduciary investor who suffers a loss, even though modern *economic* theory would support the risk the fiduciary took.

What *should* the paradigm be? According to the Longstreth text, it should be one that somehow bridges "the gap between law and economics."[125] It should be one that sets out some common economic-theory-prudent-man ground for fiduciaries. From insured (insurance company) plans (the most narrowly defined, legally) to ERISA pension plans (the most broadly defined, legally) fiduciaries should be able to stand on economic, not legal, theory Longstreth argues.

What "economic theory" are we talking about? That is, which one is it that defines the real economic world of investment, rather than an artificial legal one? While Longstreth's conclusions and recommendations take up an entire chapter, his "bottom line" is that the modern interpretation of prudence "should recognize the important and established principle of economics that nothing useful can be said about an investment in the abstract; it can only be judged in terms of its impact on the whole portfolio and the purposes for which the portfolio is held. . . . the modern paradigm for prudence, then, would shift the focus from the disembodied investment [only], to the fiduciary, the portfolio and its purpose. . . ."[126]

Let us examine what we perceive to be problems here:

---

[125] Note 122, *supra*.
[126] Longstreth, p. 156.

1. With so much more of citizen wealth under fiduciary control of one sort or another in our time, do we conclude that (a) "economic efficiency" is paramount, and the law must be eased up greatly, or (b) that some policy of substantive legal fiduciary oversight is more important now than ever before?

2. Assuming for argument sake that the law ought to bow to economic theory in our time, what is the solid, substantive, agreed-upon economic theory to which it, in fact, should bow? Modern portfolio theory? Just how reliable is *it*?

The problem here is well stated by Professor Gregory Udell of New York University.[127] Professor Udell suggests that there are three reasons why the incorporation of modern financial theory into the rule of law may be more difficult than Longstreth suggests.

In order (first) for the courts to accept that no investment is imprudent per se, but must be judged on a case-by-case portfolio basis, the courts not only have to have "an understanding of modern financial theory, but also a *belief* in modern financial theory." But (second) modern financial theory is not a static set of beliefs uniformly accepted by all financial economists, much less lawyers and courts; and even more (third): There is a wide gap that isolates financial economics from the financial community itself. Says Udell:

> If Wall Street practitioners, investors, and financial journalists are uniformly skeptical of modern financial theory, it seems unlikely that a legal approach that embraces its principles will emerge intact. Unfortunately I cannot even substantiate the conjecture that this gap exists with any empirical evidence— much less establish its magnitude. Nevertheless. . . I will offer circumstantial and hypothetical evidence to demonstrate the gap's existence and the difficulties it poses to implementing an unconstrained prudent man rule.[128]

The salient point here seems to be that:

1. Regardless of what prudent man rule is to be applied, lawyers and judges have a lot of learning to do about modern market investments and processes. Even "imprudent" choices must be understood.

---

[127] G.F. Udell, "Modern Financial Theory and Modern Conventional Wisdom" (Mimeo, N.Y.U. Graduate School of Business Administration, November 14, 1986).

[128] Ibid., p. 2.

2. While investor risk will never be abolished by law, nor any fiduciary ever held to the position of an insurer of profit or principal, the law is not likely to abandon judicial oversight to any economic theory.

3. There will always be tension between legal fiduciary duty and economic/financial portfolio theory (here as elsewhere, since each often has distinct and differing policy goals), and thus there will always be fiduciary risk. Also an argument could be made that (a) public financial safety and trust is assisted by such tension, albeit at some efficiency costs, and (b) that risk is what fiduciaries get (well) paid for taking. Those who would want to shoulder less risk might consider confining themselves to trades for their own accounts.

The question of whether, how, and why money managers are driven to trade heavily by the short-term need to outperform other money managers—and whether that, if true, is a "good" or a "bad" thing for beneficiaries, business, and the nation—is a separate (and in some way, surely an ethical) issue—though prudence is clearly involved. We shall return to that issue later.

What is clear, of course, is that in our time, deregulation, innovation, and technological advance hold out the enormous promise of growth, profit—and risk. Therefore, fiduciaries and lawyers, never too far from the courthouse door, had better work together to measure the meaning of both promise and risk very, very carefully.

2. Some Essential Pension Fund Details

(a). Types of Pension Plans and ERISA Coverage. There are two types of pension plans: *defined benefit* and *defined contribution.*

Defined benefit plans pay the worker a specified benefit at retirement. The benefit may be a set number of dollars per month, or some set percentage formula related to the worker's final-year salary.

In a defined contribution plan, a company agrees to make a specific monthly or annual payment to the pension plan. Usually the worker can do the same. There are no guaranteed amounts on retirement here. The pension is worth the total of all monies paid in plus investment earnings.

Contributions to pension plans are tax deductible, and no taxes are levied on the corpus of the funds until, and as, they are distributed to retirees.

According to U.S. Labor Department figures through 1987 (published in mid-1991), there are numerically more defined contribution than defined benefit plans in existence. However, the defined benefit plans are, on the whole, far larger, containing more than 2-1/2 times as much in assets as the defined contribution plans.[129]

ERISA coverage is confined to pension plans provided by private employers with 100 employees or more. Public employee plans (state and federal workers) and private plans with fewer than 100 employees are *not* subject to ERISA jurisdiction.

Because ERISA was created to redress such evils as company malfeasance, bankruptcy, induced termination, and withholding of benefits from employees leaving the company, the law contains certain provisions that:

- Require vesting of pension rights. Workers' pension rights (and benefits) are vested (nonremovable) after 5 years of employment with one employer, after 10 years in a multiemployer contribution plan (usually put together by a union)—or earlier if the employer so provides. In the alternative, the worker can choose 20 percent vesting after 3 years, with 20 percent more for each future 4-year period, or 50 percent vesting when age and service add up to 45 years, increasing to 100 percent 5 years later.
- Require all pension funds covered by ERISA to file an annual report with the Department of Labor. Entitled the 5500 Report, this document contains all data pertinent to ERISA compliance.
- Require a minimum contribution annually to the pension fund sufficient to cover the present value of benefits accruing in the current year. In addition, the company (the plan *sponsor*) is required to amortize over a period of years any supplemental liabilities arising from plan liberalization (e.g., by union contract) or by the retroactive granting of retirement benefits for past service.
- Relate to the tax deductibility of sponsor contributions to the pension fund. Because contributions are tax deductible, maximum as well as minimum limits are set.

ERISA has other provisions as well. Perhaps the most important one not mentioned above is the one that created the *Pension Benefit Guaranty Corporation* (PBGC). The PBGC was meant to be a self-supporting, government operated insurance system that would collect premiums from corporations with defined benefit pension plans. Those premiums would be used by the PBGC to pay pensions when and if corporations

---

[129] See K. Slater, "Retirement Plans That Quietly Melt Away," *The Wall Street Journal* (June 6, 1991). A very substantial article on pension plans states that, while the number of defined benefit plans is falling, the number of workers *covered* by these plans is not. P.B. Abken, "Corporate Pensions and Government Insurance: Deja Vue All Over Again?" FRB of Atlanta, *Economic Review* (March/April 1992).

defaulted on their pension plan obligations. This is reminiscent of both the FSLIC and FDIC, of course, in terms of organizational structure and function. Unfortunately, the PBGC is somewhat like them in terms of defects and failures as well. We shall return to the PBGC shortly.

(b). *Valuing the Defined Benefit Plan:* Funded and Unfunded Liabilities. The key finance (and ethical) area for companies with pension plans to relate to—and for regulators to relate to as well—is that of valuing the defined benefit plan and determining the plan's state of health in terms of its funded and unfunded liabilities.

Pension plans involve two kinds of liability: The first is the obligation to currently retired employees, the second to employees who have not yet retired.

In the case of the first (current retiree) group, the present value of the obligation depends, basically, on two factors: retiree average life expectancy and the discount rate used for the determined time periods. In the case of the second (still earning) group, these two obligations must be added: the benefits these employees have already earned, and the benefits they are likely to earn by the time they actually retire and begin drawing upon fund assets.

The present value of pension fund liabilities must be calculated by discounting future benefits to be paid to present value.

Clearly, both the discount rate chosen for use with regard to current and future pensioners, and the forecasting process utilized to determine future earned benefits in the case of current employees, are, to a large degree, matters subject to human discretion.[130]

The valuation of *assets* required to meet the determined *liabilities* is also, in part, a discretionary matter. First, there is an actual portfolio on hand to be evaluated (past corporate contributions). But, second, there is also the present value of expected future contributions by the company— for future employee services—to be determined. This is an estimate that is sensitive to the discount rate employed.

The present value of pension *liabilities* minus the present value of pension *assets* equals a company's *unfunded liability*. And in the real world, a great many companies do have an unfunded pension liability. A 1980 Financial Accounting Standards Board (FASB) Statement (Statement 36) requires that the assets and liabilities of the company pension plan appear in a footnote to financial statements. Suppliers of capital to

---

[130] Not totally subject to individual discretion, of course. The Financial Accounting Standards Board (FASB) Statement 87 (1985) imposed a standard market discount rate on certain calculations; and ERISA, in 1987, imposed some restrictions as well in terms of allowable valuation interest rates. However, much individual company actuarial discretion remains in those areas referred to in the text, and actuarial assumptions are surely subject to human error of one sort or another.

the company ought to pay careful heed to such footnotes. The wise investor, moreover, would do well to examine carefully all the assumptions behind the actuarial estimates that culminated in the footnote figures. Unfunded pension liability could be the largest liability the company actually has.[131]

There is, unfortunately, a demonstrable connection between the size of some unfunded pension liabilities and the existence of a federally backed *Pension Benefit Guaranty Corporation (PBGC)*.

3. Looking at the Pension Benefit Guaranty Corporation

Established in 1974 under ERISA, the PBGC was meant to insure employees of *defined benefit plans* that they would, within maximum limits, receive their promised benefits. By its rules, the PBGC becomes the trustee of a failed pension plan and assumes both its assets and liabilities. The PBGC insures some 40 million workers in approximately 85,000 defined benefit plans. As with S&L and commercial bank deposit insurance entities, PBGC levies flat, nonrisk-adjusted premiums on companies (unless they are clearly underfunded, in which case the company is assigned a variable-capped rate). As the flat premium is raised in the face of possible catastrophe, many well-funded pension plan companies pay higher premiums than are justifiable, while many underfunded companies are handed a partially free ride.

The PBGC guaranty actually encompasses all guaranteed benefits minus the sum of the assets of the plan and 30 percent of the sponsoring company's equity.[132]

Pension plan failure, followed by a PBGC assumption of liabilities, is not necessarily evidence of bad faith on the part of the sponsor company. There are business failures due to adverse economic conditions, to human error such as misjudgment, and even to negligence, which often explain both the underfunded condition of the pension plan and the collapse of the sponsor. However, there is much evidence extant to the effect that some companies (plan sponsors) have been, and still are, "gaming" (taking unfair

---

[131] Our discussion of pension plan evaluation owes much to James C. Van Horne, *Financial Management and Policy*, 8th ed. (Englewood Cliffs, N.J.: Prentice Hall, 1989), pp. 602-605. We have been somewhat puzzled by the paucity of pension plan materials in the majority of finance texts, given the increasing importance of this area to corporate financial management. It should be pointed out here that under a new FASB rule, all companies, beginning in 1993, must accrue the projected costs of retiree benefits over the working lives of the eligible employees. The rule *has been* that companies may choose to take these costs at the time that benefits are actually paid out to retirees. AT&T, for example, announced at year-end 1991 that it expected to take a charge in the billions to cover this change.

[132] See, generally, A.R. Karr, "Imperiled Promises: Risks to Retirees Rise As Firms Fail to Fund Pensions They Offer," *The Wall Street Journal* (February 4, 1993). The year-end 1992 maximum annual PBGC coverage to any one retiree was $29,250.

advantage of) the PBGC. They are *deliberately* underfunding their plans; boosting estimates of how much they will earn on their investments over the coming years[133]; engaging in risky investments in the (insurance backstopped) attempt to narrow their unfunded liability through risky investment for very high returns; and even engaging in schemes with their employees to minimize joint losses when their pension plan is terminated.[134]

The results of bad business conditions, bad judgment, and too much "moral hazard" behavior on the condition of the PBGC are appalling. In 1987, articles in professional publications, pointed out that at year's end 1986, the PBGC's accumulated deficit, plus impending terminations, approached $4 billion,[135] and that even if Congress were to provide the approximately $4 billion "the burden of future plan terminations could undo the effect" of the infusion.[136] By 1989, the Inspector General of the U.S. Department of Labor was warning that poor regulations and inept enforcement of pension fund laws in the face of existing pension fund conditions were creating a possible "nightmare" dwarfing the S&L crisis. He urged Congress to investigate sponsor abuses and federal pension law shortfalls.[137]

The House Budget Committee unearthed, among other things, the following information: That while the number of pension funds doubled between 1978 and 1988, at the same time

> the number of federal audits of private pension plans dropped from more than 8,000 to about 2,000. In fact, less than 1% of the private

---

[133] General Motors, e.g., at year-end 1990, added $75 million to first-quarter earnings and narrowed its unfunded liability gap by the simple expedient of raising its pension fund portfolio earning estimates. GM decided that its $35 billion portfolio would earn 11 percent per year in coming decades, even though it had been using a 10 percent figure in the high-return years of the 1980s. J.A. White, "Pension Funds Boost Projected Returns Even Though Experts Take a Dim View," *The Wall Street Journal* (October 23, 1990). After reading this article one should see J. White and N. Templin, "GM to Disclose More Details on Pension Gap," *The Wall Street Journal* (November 16, 1992). GM admits its pension gap—unfunded liability—rose from $8.6 billion at the end of '91 to $11 billion in 1992.

[134] Richard Ippolito, *The Economics of Pension Insurance* (Homewood, IL: Irwin for the University of Pennsylvania, Wharton School, 1989). This book was written while its author was chief economist for the PBGC and is, by and large, critical of his own agency. The book is far broader than a list of individual company abuses of the PBGC and is well worth reading. Some argue that moral hazard in the pension area is not as bad as with S&Ls. That may be true, but it hardly eliminates the problem.

[135] For example, T.M. Buynak, "Is the U.S. Pension System Going Broke?" *Economic Commentary*, FRB of Cleveland (January 15, 1987).

[136] Estrella and Hirtle,"Estimating the Fundimg Gap of the PBGC," *Quarterly Review*, FRB of NY, Autumn, 1988.

[137] Quoted by J. King of the Associated Press in "Warning Is Sounded on Pensions," *The (Bergen, N.J.) Record* (June 4, 1989).

plans covered by. . . ERISA, which authorized federal audits of plans affecting 100 employees or more, are audited each year.[138]

By year-end 1991, the PBGC itself, despite premium boosts over the past several years, estimated that while it was only $2 billion short of its current established liabilities, it had a potential exposure of some $40 billion from current underfunded company retirement plans.[139]

Bankrupt steelmaker LTV Corp., all by itself, could cost the PBGC $3 billion—the size of the shortfall in LTV's three pension plans. It was LTV's growing pension plan unfunded liability that led it to seek Chapter 11 bankruptcy protection in 1986. At that time, LTV's three plans were underfunded by $2.3 billion, of which $2.1 billion were PBGC insured. But LTV continued to operate and, under union pressure, set up a new pension plan, leaving the PBGC to absorb the old three it took into Chapter 11 originally. The PBGC balked at what it considered a naked abuse of insurance guarantees, and it ordered LTV to re-assume all responsibility for the three original plans. LTV appealed the order in federal district court. It won there and on appeal. However, the U.S. Supreme Court reversed in June 1990, holding that PBGC, in the face of establishment by a Chapter 11 sponsor of a "follow-on" plan, had the authority to force that sponsor to retake the responsibility for the original plans as well.[140]

As a result of the Supreme Court decision, LTV agreed, with some expected investment help from a Japanese partner, to pump $950 million into the three pension plans. However, LTV creditors in bankruptcy objected to this move on the ground that pension fund liabilities ought not to be favored over other creditor claims. In September 1991, a federal district judge agreed and threw out the $950 million compromise.[141] If that decision holds up to the Supreme Court level—that bankruptcy law negates any pension fund primacy—the *possibility* that the U.S. taxpayer will be facing another insurance guaranty bailout will ascend quickly to the *probability* stage.

---

[138] Representative Richard Armey of the House Budget Committee, citing Labor Department and OMB figures, in "First the S&Ls—Is Pension Insurance Next?" *The Wall Street Journal* (January 31, 1990).

[139] Chart contained in M. Levinson, "Retire or Bust," *Newsweek* (November 25, 1991), p. 50. Among the problem pension plans mentioned in the story was that of Pan American World Airways, which collapsed at year's end with an unfunded liability of $914 million. By year end 1992, James Lockhart former PBGC director told Congress, PBGC faced underfunding of $51 billion, and responsible, conservative economists were sounding alarms. See R.J. Samuelson, "Pension Time Bomb," *The Washington Post National Weekly Edition* (March 15-21, 1993).

[140] The reader might wish at this point to reconsider some of the themes set out in the Chapter 11 bankruptcy materials at Chapter 3, *infra*.

[141] C. Harlan, "LTV's Pension Liabilities Aren't Favored, Judge Says," *The Wall Street Journal* (September 16, 1991).

It has been suggested that the order of claimants in bankruptcy cases should be changed to give pension claims the same primacy as wage claims

> since legal liability should be placed on the party best able to minimize transaction costs. . . . Private credit markets are better candidates for monitoring and evaluating the possibility of bankruptcy than the PBGC or individual workers. . . . Also. . . such a change is much more likely to stop the gaming [of the PBGC].[142]

4. Terminating Pension Plans

Throughout the latter half of the 1980s, in the face of solid market gains, many companies insisted that their pension plans were "overfunded," and then proceeded to terminate them and recapture the "excess." While overall figures are not certain, it would appear that some 2,000 companies recouped somewhere in the vicinity of $20 billion in such "surpluses."[143]

Employers argued that as long as they could meet their defined benefit obligations, the surpluses over that obligated amount belonged to them, since their investment acumen earned the excess. Employees argued that they had, in some cases, foregone salary increases in lieu of pension benefit guarantees and that the surpluses would help protect these benefits in harder times. Moreover, the argument went, the extent of any "surplus" depended on estimates and assumptions that might not be entirely accurate.[144]

The PBGC, seemingly without regard to its own best interests, did nothing to discourage plan terminations, and ERISA law allowed such terminations as long as existing pension obligations appeared to be met.

Without attempting to judge either the efficiency or the fairness of pension plan reversions, certain realities must be recognized:

---

[142] R.V. Burkhauser, book review of Ippolito, note 134, *supra*, in *The Journal of Economic Literature* (December 1990), pp. 1765-66. The "gaming" of the public, in terms of its having to foot the bill for an ultimate costly breakdown, appeared, in early 1992, to be proceeding apace. The Executive branch, in order to justify tax cuts, proceeded to make the PBGC look good by allowing it to use *accrual*, rather than *cash*, accounting. Then using a statistical system called a Monte Carlo Simulation out comes PBGC "savings." See R.J. Samuelson, "Budget Hokus-Pokus," *The Washington Post National Weekly Edition* (February 10-16, 1992).

[143] W.E. Green, "Employees Battle Firms for Pension Plan Surpluses," *The Wall Street Journal* (June 4, 1990).

[144] Compare J.A. Klein, "Without Reversions, Business Won't Play," *The Wall Street Journal* (September 28, 1986), with H.M. Metzenbaum, "Employees Deserve Their Money," *The New York Times* (October 30, 1988).

- Many such reversions were done by corporate raiders, part of whose takeover motivation was the excess funds sitting in the target company's pension plan. Indeed, it would seem that pension plan reversions did result in windfall gains to stockholders, and losses to employees.[145]
- Many companies, following reversions, terminated the defined benefit plans, substituting for them defined contribution plans (thus terminating all guarantees to employees); some companies went bust and dropped consequent underfunded plans onto the PBGC; and many others replaced their pension plans completely with "guaranteed" annuities or guaranteed investment contracts (GICs) calculated to cover what would have been provided by the pension plan.
- In the face of employee uproar, Congress in late 1990, set limits on pension plan reversions: raising the excise tax on assets recovered through reversion to as high as 50 percent in the case of companies not setting up successor pension plans, for example.[146]

Employee and congressional concern seems to have had some justification. In April 1991, the junk bond pall settled over the pension plan system with the largest failure ever of an American insurance company, First Executive Corporation.[147] When First Executive's huge junk bond portfolio dragged it down, those pensioners who now had no fund corpus and had to depend upon the annuities substituted by employers for the obligations of the reverted and now defunct pension plan fund, learned the difference between market and default risk.

Many thousands of such pensioners may lose all or a portion of the retirement benefits they had earned and/or were in the process of earning.[148]

---

[145] "The predominant LBO-related termination . . . is a straightforward termination of a defined benefit plan replaced with a defined contribution plan. These transactions impose large capital losses on workers." R. Ippolito and W.H. James, "LBOs, Reversions, and Implicit Contracts," *Journal of Finance* (March 1992), p. 165.

[146] "Pension Managers Win Some, Lose Some in New Federal Budget," *The Wall Street Journal (October 30, 1990), p. 1.*

[147] It is interesting to observe that less than a year before First Executive's collapse, while it was still bidding on and writing GICs, the company's chairman said, "We have a very strong capital position and a very, very strong cash position and high liquidity." Quoted in D. Rankin, "Junk Bonds' Anxiety Shakes the GIC," The New York Times (May 27, 1990).

[148] As of mid-1991, according to Greenwich Associates: Employee Benefits Research Group, a private company, 38.2% of all defined-contribution plan assets were in guaranteed investment contracts. Charts appear in I. White and E. Schultz, "Insurance Woes Force Employers to Treat GICs Gingerly, Substitute Alternatives," The Wall Street Journal (August 14, 1991). Executive Life alone had "$3.1 billion in more than 30 (GICs) outstanding at the end of 1990, much of that retirement related." A. Hagedorn and S. Hwang, "Unisys Sued for Investing in Executive Life," *The Wall Street Journal* (June 17, 1991). Three other large insurance companies failed at more or less the same time: First Capital Life, Fidelity Bankers Life, and Mutual Benefit Life of New Jersey.

However, angry employee losers in this particular market failure are heading for the courts, alleging a lack of corporate prudence in making the annuity investments they did. The U.S. Department of Labor is following suit, also alleging that some companies made unwise (not prudent) purchases of annuities for pensions.[149] Once more, it appears, the law will be left to determine whether particular problems resulting from large-scale financial activity in the 1980s were the result of bad luck, bad judgment, bad faith, or some combination thereof.

5. Public Pension Plans

A good many public pension funds—those covering federal, state, and local government employees—are quite large, and together make up more than 3/4 of a trillion dollars of capital.[150] They are not covered by ERISA nor, consequently, by the PBGC.

However, these public pension funds are hardly without recourse should they prove financially inadequate to the task of meeting their obligations. They are *public* funds after all, and although not carrying an explicit taxpayer guarantee, they would certainly be subject in one way or another to a call on taxpayer dollars.

A sizable number of public pension funds are active in futures markets, both for hedging and speculative purposes,[151] leaving the issue of prudence lurking on the horizon, perhaps to be called into play in case of big losses and a funding emergency.[152] Another public pension fund activity would seem to be investing in high-stakes, high-risk takeover deals, in some cases at a level well above the ceiling most states have set for investments in high-risk, illiquid securities. Professor Scott's blood would have frozen at the very thought of it.[153]

---

[149] Hagedorn and Hwang, note 148, *supra*. It remains to be pointed out that when an employee's defined benefit plan was first subject to reversion and then changed to defined contribution or closed out in favor of purchased annuities, that employee lost all recourse to the PBGC. *The PBGC covers only defined benefit plans*, and certainly *not* annuities.

[150] Some examples are CALPERS, the California Public Employees fund (the nation's largest public fund) at some $58 billion in assets; the New York State and Local Retirement System (The Common Retirement Fund), at $45 billion; the Virginia State Retirement System at some $12.5 billion, and the Iowa State System at approximately $4 billion.

[151] J. Taylor's "State Pension Funds Try Futures Markets," *The Wall Street Journal* (November 5, 1991) names the Colorado, Wisconsin, Virginia, and Pennsylvania state plans as particular investors.

[152] At least one survey seems to show that private pension funds are also players in the futures markets. See "Pension Forum: Dipping Into Derivatives," *Institutional Investor* (December 1990), p. 173.

[153] Sarah Bartlett, "Gambling With the Big Boys," *The New York Times Magazine* (May 5, 1991) (from her book *The Money Machine: How KKR Manufactured Power and Profits* (New York: Warner Books, 1991). Writes Ms. Bartlett: "To date no public employee fund has suffered calamitous losses from failed LBOs. But a lack of supervision, combined with the financial naivete of many funds and the taxpayer's responsibility for guaranteeing benefits.

While some of the investment strategies of some public funds might well be regarded with suspicion by the taxpaying public, so might be the actions of financially hard-pressed government officials who appear to be eyeing the funds as a source of assistance in difficult times. State and local governments can ease their financial problems in the short term by reducing the amount of money contributed to the public pension pot.

> The most common method is to simply change what is known as "the interest rate assumption," or the rate of return that a state supposes a retirement fund will earn on its investments.[154]

New York State officials, who have done this on occasion, claim that the state pension system has no unfunded liabilities (on its projections), while others feel that reductions do threaten the long-term stability of the pension funds—though perhaps not for a decade or so. New York City forecasted 1990 retirement fund earnings at 8.25 percent, and actually came in at approximately 1 percent. Nevertheless, it raised its 1991 earnings prediction to 9 percent, thus saving a good deal of money and causing one journalist to remark: "At this rate, Yankee management, come April, is bound to predict a pennant."[155]

> *The New York Times* (January 6, 1991), (Business Section).

Apart from the issue of whether the power of government officials to vary pension fund earnings estimates is being misused, or even consciously abused, to the future detriment of the taxpayer purse, one thing is surely clear: The power of both public and private pension funds in financial markets is growing apace.

6. The Power—and Obligations—of Pension Funds

There are many areas where the growing power of pension funds is apparent. Some of them already utilize space-age (computer) technology to do direct deals and to execute very large basket (program) trades—in sum, to undertake faster, cheaper trading.[156] Wall Street investment banks, in an attempt to retain some portion of the pension fund business, are even making available to the funds their own highly sophisticated,

---

. . make the potential for losses and a bailout along the lines of the savings and loan industry all too obvious." *The New York Times Magazine, supra,* at p. 57.

[154] S.H. Verhovek, "States Are Finding Pension Funds Can Be a Bonanza Hard to Resist," *The New York Times* (April 22, 1990).

[155] "Dinkins, the Optimist," The New York Times (January 6, 1991), (Business Section).

[156] S. Bartlett, "A California Pension Fund Cuts the New York Umbilical Cord: From a PC Base, Better Prices, Fewer Money Managers and Lower Fees," *The New York Times* (August 26, 1990).

computerized, stock-trading technology.[157]   Clearly, the role of pension funds in financial markets will continue to expand.

It is even to be expected that as M&A and LBO deals decline as a method for gaining corporate control, proxy-rule changes will assume a greater role. As holders of enormous blocks of corporate shares, pension plans—particularly through their several associations such as; e.g., the Committee on Investment of Employee Benefits, representing $350 billion in private pension funds—will be bigger players in the game. These associations, if not the individual multibillion dollar funds, can of course direct pressure onto both the SEC and corporate management.[158]

Given their enormous buying/trading power, and their consequent influence on management and on financial markets, do pension funds, like corporations, have some sort of public duty to which they should be faithful?

It is simple enough to maintain that pension fund money managers are fiduciaries solely to their (employee) investors. If that were true, their only duty would be to maximize fund participant wealth, within the law, in every single way—that is, as fast as possible, generally.

We believe the argument must be made that pension funds have become exercisers of financial market power to such a degree within our free market system that the duty of fund managers to protect and preserve, as well as to enrich that system, is clear.[159]

Beyond a pension fund *power parallel* with public corporations lies the *insurance guarantee parallel* with banks.

Government has determined (presumably with the consent of the governed) that "private" pension funds are so important to the socioeconomic fabric of our nation as to warrant public protection (pension fund insurance). And the public is both the establisher of, and the lender of last resort to, every "public" pension plan. These facts certainly form the basis for a pension fund money manager duty to the body politic, a duty that, at

---

[157] J.A. White, "Wall Street Is Giving Big Clients Its Program-Trading Firepower," *The Wall Street Journal* (May 1, 1991).

[158] See J.A. White, "Pension Officers Back Proxy-Rule Shifts," *The Wall Street Journal* (April 1, 1991). The writer points out the interesting conflict potential in pension fund power. If GM management, for example, is against a particular proxy rule, and GM pension plan money managers are for it, what is the result? In any case, 1992 saw an enormous shift in SEC policy in terms of giving shareholders a first-class seat at the corporate table. In terms of proxy rules, executive salaries, and like matters, the battle for corporate control looks about to pass from M&A and LBOs to shareholder power. That could take some time, of course, but when the time comes, it will be the big institutional players who will matter. Many corporate boards, seeing this coming, are beginning to flex their muscles. See S. Lohr, "Pulling Down the Corporate Clubhouse," *The New York Times* (April 12, 1992), O.S. Hilzenrath, "A Shareholder's Rebellion," *The Washington Post National Weekly Edition* (October 26-November 1, 1992), and S. Pulliam, "Proxy Battle Against A&P Is Unveiled," *The Wall Street Journal* (February 2, 1993).

[159] Cf. Chapter 5 (Fiduciary Relationships) *supra*, particularly the *Paramount Communications* case.

the very least, both empowers and requires the pension fund money manager to make investment decisions based upon their impact—*measured over an adequate time horizon*—on the public, and which protects and nourishes the manager's immediate constituency.

Nothing in this view of things derogates from the key goal of enrichment of the pension fund participant. On the contrary, serious questions can be raised regarding any pension fund's ability to guarantee *long-term plan stability* by seeking out *short-term profit* or engaging in high-risk speculation.

The salient point, we believe, with regard to the determination of pension fund money manager duty, is

> political and moral rather than financial or economic. Can a modern democratic society tolerate the subordination of all other goals and priorities in a major institution. . . to short-term gain? And can it subordinate all other stakeholders to one constituency. . . ?[160]

We insist that, at the very least, the growing power of pension funds in American financial markets requires more serious consideration than has heretofore been given them in the formulation of public policy aimed at securing the nation's economic future.

II. EXERCISE: SAFETY, PROGRESS, AND FAIRNESS IN INTERNATIONAL FINANCIAL MARKETS

(One work-saver aspect to this exercise: It eliminates the need for an "In Lieu of the Philosopher's Stone" for this chapter, and its consequent irritations.)

Please assume the following: The new World League of Central, Commercial, and Investment Bankers (CCIB) will hold its first meeting ten months from today in Basle, Switzerland. As a member of the Advisory Committee to the International Meetings unit of the Federal Reserve Board of the United States (FRB), you are the recipient of the following directive:

In connection with the CCIB meeting, at which the Central Bankers of the 24 nations comprising the OECD will make up the core unit, you are requested to prepare yourself for an initial brainstorming session at FRB headquarters. The focus of the session will be twofold: *First,* what top-priority issues in the area of international financial markets should our Fed chairman insist be placed on the CCIB agenda? *Second, why* top

---

[160] The quotation is from Peter F. Drucker's "A Crisis of Capitalism," *The Wall Street Journal* (September 30, 1986). We highly recommend a full reading of this piece, which brilliantly captures corporate governance and long-term/short-term horizon issues.

priority for these specific issues? The announced purpose of the CCIB meeting was deliberately left general. The OECD central bankers must particularize it now (i.e., from "Safety, Progress, and Fairness" to specific agenda items).

Please remember that participants will also include 24 heads of commercial and private banks of OECD nations selected by their respective domestic umbrella organizations (e.g., the American Bankers Association and the Securities Industry Association in the United States). Other participants will include the heads of the World Bank and the IMF, and 24 ministers selected by the (nonindustrialized nations) Intergovernmental Group of 24 on International Monetary Affairs to represent them. These ministers will be observers for the first three days and discussants on the final (fourth) day.

You realize, of course, that we hope to be near closure on the issues to be debated on days 1–3 *before* we actually meet in Basle. To *begin* substantive discussions there would be utter folly.

The FRB is aware that leaders of the European Community (EC) in Brussels have expressed their concern to individual leaders of Western European nations that nothing be done at the CCIB meeting to affect negatively their EC programs. The EC realizes that constituent members may, indeed, use this forum to exploit outstanding differences. We Americans do not want to end up as the ham in anyone's sandwich.

There is Eastern Europe to be considered (socially as well as financially), and we are aware of the fact that the Group of 24 representatives—on discussant day—will be pressing hard (before world media folk) on a list of grievances and demands aimed at the industrialized nations.

Given these realities, together with all the international financial market concerns presented by the staggering potential for both world economic progress *and* disaster, we have four big days to plan for! You should be ready to discuss the three top items you recommend that we (the United States) press for agenda inclusion. And be ready also to defend the reasons why you insist on these particular three items.

By the way, you better be prepared, in connection with your choices, to deal with the implications of this statement just received by our Advisory Committee *from the Fed chairman's office:* "Ladies and Gentlemen: I trust you realize that the national financial and governmental leaders who attend the CCIB meeting will bring their *value systems* with them. *Ours* must be clearly articulated and defended wherever necessary during the course of the meeting, whatever the specific subject under discussion. Be clear in *your* minds about *this*."

See you at the brainstorming session.

9

Corporate Power and Social Responsibility and the Issue of Antitrust

COMING UP IN THIS CHAPTER

Americans seem to share a sense of pride in the strength and bigness of major U.S. corporations, particularly in terms of their ability to contend successfully with foreign competition.

On the other hand, there has always been at the very same time a fear of, and anger directed at, certain manifestations of corporate power. This fear and anger have resulted in specific legislative actions designed to curb—and often to punish—what is perceived as being the "wrongful" exercise of that power.

The two quotations that follow should serve to focus upon the concentrated economic power/democratic body politic dichotomy. This dichotomy is surely one key element in the overall *economic efficiency* vs. *individual rights* phenomenon that we examined in Chapter 1:

> Possessory private property in [the U.S.] has been metamorphosed. In its place is a power pyramid. . . . None of this has come about as a result of the villainy of conspiring men. That might have been true in the freewheeling corporation days of a hundred years ago, but it would be [a] ridiculous assumption today. . . . Actually, there has been a kind of continual biological progression over the years. . . . Bigger enterprise was needed to satisfy the desires of the population. . . techniques which made it possible to satisfy certain necessities made it *impossible* to rely only on the individual. Consequently, organization and power, not ownership,

had to meet the resulting problems. The progression has been natural.

[Large U.S. corporations today] represent a concentration of power over economics which makes the medieval feudal system look like a Sunday school party. . . .

We can talk about the various alleged legal controls which somehow or other, when the chips are down, neither control nor even seek to control. We can point out the fear of "monopoly" and "restraint of trade" and say that from time to time this fear has checked the process. True, our law has prevented any one of these power groups from becoming a monopoly, but it has not seriously prevented the concentration of power as power, though it has prevented certain ultimate results. . . .

[A]ll this is not the product of evil-minded men. I believe we must try to work with the system. . . . This does not mean, however, that I am not afraid. I am. I believe it is the content of these systems rather than their form that matters. Their power can enslave us. . . or perhaps set us free beyond present imagination. . . .

We have to accept this power situation as, let us call it, a natural mechanism subject to the control of the body politic as long as we *keep* it subject to that control. The control, I believe, will be essentially intellectual and philosophical, capable of being translated into legal rules when necessity arises. . . .[1]

Given the vital role which corporations currently play and. . . will continue to play in American society, it is imperative that experts, activists and citizens alike comprehend realistically the multi-faceted and complex nature of, corporate. . . power. Such realistic comprehension is essential to the preservation and advancement of social democracy in the United States.[2]

Given the continual populist-type concern with corporate power in America, we begin this chapter, formally, with two views of a distinctly related matter: corporate social responsibility in general.

We then proceed (in Section II) to an examination of three major socio-political-legal areas where legislative action and public attitudes move—as outside-the-market-forces—to counter what is perceived to be the "wrongful" exercise of corporate power: These include legislation such as the Racketeer Influenced and Corrupt Organization Act (RICO); false

---

[1] Adolph A. Berle, Jr., *Economic Power and the Free Society: A Preliminary Discussion of the Corporation* (Fund for the Republic, pamphlet, December 1957, pp. 13-16.

[2] E.M. Epstein, "Dimensions of Corporate Power, Pt. 2," *California Management Review* (Summer 1974), p. 46.

claims against the government (and consequent "whistle-blowing"); and new corporate sentencing rules and guidelines.

We complete our focus on societal responses to perceived abuses of corporate power and other forms of business behavior that threaten free, competitive markets in Section III on *antitrust*.

Given the breadth of "corporate power" coverage here, we chose to limit the number of law cases the reader will be called upon to read.

The RICO issue is so controversial (can we continue to treat some "legitimate" corporations like gangsters, and is government power as bad as that of "big business" when ill-used?), that we included the U.S. Supreme Court case that faced squarely, though not fully, the corporate "gangster" issue (*Northwestern Bell*).

The most recent developments under the False Claims Act are also still in process, and we felt narrative would suffice here.

Case law *is* an integral part of antitrust law and legislation. Nevertheless, we felt that the only way to give the reader a decently well-rounded picture of the legal status of antitrust was to tell about the cases. Actually putting several key cases in the chapter to read comes close (at this final stage of the chapter and the book) to cruel and unusual punishment.

Those of you who feel that you would rather decide for yourself what the cases we discuss actually say are encouraged to go to them directly.

After all, if you have come this far, you *do* have expertise.

I. CORPORATE SOCIAL RESPONSIBILITY

We begin with a quote:

The political principle that underlines the market mechanism is unanimity. In an ideal free market resting on private property, no individual can coerce any other, all cooperation is voluntary, all parties to such cooperation benefit or they need not participate. There are no values, no "social" responsibilities in any sense other than the shared values and responsibilities of individuals. . . .

Unfortunately, unanimity is not always feasible. There are some respects in which conformity appears unavoidable, so I do not see how one can avoid the use of the political mechanism altogether. But the doctrine of "social responsibility" taken seriously would extend the scope of the political mechanism to every human activity. It does not differ in philosophy from the most explicitly collectivist doctrine. . . . That is why, in my book *Capitalism and Freedom*, I have called it a "fundamentally subversive doctrine" in a free society, and have said that in such a society, "there is one and only one social responsibility of business—to use its resources and engage in activities designed to increase its profits so long as it stays within the rules of the game. . . .[3]

We do not agree with Professor Friedman, and would make this argument:[4]

Corporate social responsibility is not merely the equivalent of corporate philanthropy. It is important that corporations with sufficient profit growth give money to public broadcasting efforts, to local symphony orchestras, to local substance-abuse rehabilitation programs and the like. However, social responsibility has to have a broader meaning than is conveyed by mere dollars and cents.[5]

Ethical behavior is an integral part of the responsibility every corporation, like every individual, owes toward that society in which it exists and continuously interrelates in the process of taking and giving. Such behavior, such social responsibility, is independent of the size of this year's profit margin. Moreover, to the extent that any corporation abuses that responsibility, it abuses that society, and establishes its own personal threat, however small, to that society's continued healthy existence.

Philosophers, in and out of economists' garb, raise the issue of whether a body corporate can be thought of as having any moral responsibility at all. Others argue that even if corporations do have some sort of moral responsibility, it is no more than the equivalent of not breaking the prevailing law. Many more manifest their concern with the impossibility of drawing *any* substantive meaning from the terms "ethical behavior" and "social responsibility."

Undoubtedly, the subject of corporate ethics and overall corporate social responsibility is today on America's front burner. The num-

---

[3] Milton Friedman, "The Social Responsibility of Business Is to Increase Its Profits," *The New York Times Magazine* (September 13, 1970).

[4] The following brief essay on corporate social responsibility is from Larry Alan Bear, *The Glass House Revolution: Inner-City War for Interdependence* (Seattle and London: University of Washington Press, 1990), pp. 115-18, 131-32, and is reprinted here with the permission of the publisher.

[5] Equating corporate social responsibility with philanthropic dollars makes it easy to trivialize the entire social responsibility issue; it might seem that all that is really involved here is whether corporate giving to the local opera company is a product of the entertainment preferences of the CEO's wife. Cf. T. Boone Pickens, quoted in the "Verbatim" section of *The Wall Street Journal* (July 19, 1987).

ber of books on the subject alone is proof that concern about it sells.[6] Articles reprinted in anthologies carry titles such as "Can a Corporation Have a Conscience?" together with "Why Corporations Are Not Morally Responsible for Anything They Do."[7]

Can a corporation as an entity be held to ethical standards in society? Or is that impossible because a corporation is an inanimate thing incapable of having any measurable intent? It is difficult to conceive of an American public being concerned with the legal niceties of *actus non facit reum, nisi mens sit rea*.[8] The public has been far more likely to judge a corporation as a real entity, even to the point of characterizing collective corporate ethical and moral standards as at a lower level than those of people in the federal government.[9] What comes out of Widget Corporation is Widget Corporation's doing. When a Widget executive is sentenced to a prison term, that might be a personal tragedy or a law enforcement triumph or both, but one thing is surely clear: When the remaining executives and board members ask, after the felonious fact: "Now what do we do about our image?" they are referring to Widget's distinct, publicly determined persona as a *company*.

There is no denying that men run corporations (more than women as yet, for better or for worse) and that corporations cannot "act" apart from the people they are composed of. But there is also no denying that the people who make up a corporation benefit enormously, and in many ways, from the corporation's distinct legal persona; moreover, it is only through the existence of that discrete persona that they are collectively able to affect the society as a whole, as well as individuals in it. There is no room in the public mind, nor should there be, for some rule of corporate ethical

---

[6] An abbreviated list would include: G. Cavanaugh and A. McGovern, *Ethical Dilemmas in the Modern Corporation* (Englewood Cliffs, N.J.: Prentice Hall, 1988); T. Tuleja, *Beyond the Bottom Line* (New York: Facts on File, 1985); C.S. McCoy, *Management of Values: The Ethical Difference in Corporate Policy and Performance* (Pitman, 1985); Framer and Hogue, *Corporate Social Responsibility*, 2d ed., (Lexington Books, 1985).

[7] R.T. DeGeorge, "Can Corporations Have Moral Responsibility?" *University of Dayton Review* 5 (Winter 1981-1982); K. Goodpaster and J.B. Matthews, "Can a Corporation Have a Conscience?" *Harvard Business Review* (January/February 1982); M.G. Velasquez, "Why Corporations Are Not Morally Responsible for Anything They Do," *Business and Professional Ethics Journal* 2 (Spring 1983). All these articles are reprinted in Chapter 2 of T. Beauchamp and N. Bowie, eds., *Ethical Theory and Business*, 3d ed., (Englewood Cliffs, N.J.: Prentice Hall, 1988).

[8] "An act does not make one guilty, unless one is so in intention."

[9] A. Clymer, "How Americans Rate Big Business," *New York Times Magazine* (June 8, 1986).

immunity, no matter what theoretical argument such a rule is grounded in, including a Kantian metaphysics of morals.[10]

Economist Milton Friedman has argued that a corporation's only social responsibility is to increase its profits while obeying the law and the rules of ethical custom.[11] *Ethical custom* is the joker in Friedman's deck, and he never makes its meaning clear. It would seem to mean a moral level of behavior beyond that required by law which could affect profit priorities. In sum, the conservative Nobel laureate would appear to have opened his own door a bit to the entrance of some social responsibility requirements for the corporation after all. Elsewhere, in the same article in which he refers to a need to follow the rules of ethical custom, Friedman seems to indicate that only existing law needs to be followed in such areas as corporate pollution of the environment.

The argument that adhering to the letter of the law satisfies social responsibility was confronted best by an admonition of Sir Thomas Browne some three hundred years ago: "Let not the law of thy country be the non ultra of thy honesty; nor think that always good enough which the law will make good."[12] More recently, a famous legal philosopher, H.L.A. Hart wrote:

In all communities there is a partial overlap in content between legal and moral obligation. . . . Characteristically, moral obligation and duty, like many legal rules, concern what is to be done, or not to be done, in circumstances constantly recurring in the life of the group. . . . The social morality of societies. . . always includes certain obligations and duties requiring the sacrifice of private inclination or interest which is essential to the survival of any society so long as men and the world in which they live retain some of their most familiar and obvious characteristics.[13]

There is little power in the argument that, as corporations or individuals, we benefit ourselves, our institutions, and our society as much as we can or ought to so long as we simply do unto others within enforceable legal restrictions. One of the complications is that there are too many interrelationships affecting us all that do not have to do with the law. One of these is trust between people,

---

[10] Anyone who truly believes that a corporation has no substantial identity of its own has never been a buyer forced to kick the corporation's "good will" rock at the time of signing the contract of sale.

[11] Friedman, "The Social Responsibility of Business."

[12] Sir Thomas Browne, *Christian Morals*, I.ii (published posthumously in 1716).

[13] H.L.A. Hart, *The Concept of Law* (Oxford University Press, 1961), pp. 166-67.

better left to society and its institutions to sustain than for the law courts to put a price on.[14]

The simplest argument against the existence of corporate social responsibility—even if one concedes some sort of corporate persona—is that a corporation comprises its owners and their agents and nothing more, and therefore, whatever it does within the law is nobody else's business. This argument views the corporation as a private preserve, and the rest of us as poachers. If such *were* the case, it would be hard to see where corporate social responsibility *could* lie outside of that restricted relationship.[15] There are, however, at least two serious problems with this value-free, pseudo-scientific, economist's theoretical construct of the corporation.

First, these "self-contained" corporate entities make enormous use of the very society toward which they claim no responsibility (beyond not bending and twisting the existing law past the courtroom breaking point). For example, they use its tax-supported courts and legislatures to deal with their market failures and internecine warfare. Far more important, they function completely within an entire socioeconomic system of rights and obligations, or cultural values and beliefs, whose continued existence is the only guarantor of theirs. The idea that such a system can continue to support corporations in a healthy state without the corporate exercise of social responsibility toward it is surely problematical.

---

[14] *Trust*, despite being what economists would call "an externality," has a "very important pragmatic value if nothing else. . . . [It] is an important lubricant of a social system." This is true even if, absent a legally imposed fiduciary duty, one cannot sue because one's trust was corporately breached: K.Arrow, *The Limits of Organization* (New York: W.W. Norton and Co., 1957), pp. 22-23. *Loyalty* is a concept much the same. Individual human and corporate teamwork and productivity are surely undermined when bonds of loyalty are destroyed and replaced with anger and resentment over disloyal actions—even if no recovery for them is available in a court of law. See also A. Shleifer and L. Summers, *Breach of Trust for Hostile Takeovers* (NBER Working Paper Series No. 2342, National Bureau of Economic Research, August 1987); and W. Norris, "Ethics of Organizational Transformation in Takeovers, Plant Closings and Cooperative Ventures," Remarks, 7th National Conference on Business Ethics, Bentley College, Waltham, Mass., October 15, 1987.

[15] Former Supreme Court Justice Arthur Goldberg was stunned by this attitude as member of the Advisory Committee on Tender Offers, set up in 1983 as the result of a Senate Banking Committee request. In his separate statement to the Committee Report, Goldberg commented on the total intracorporate tenor of the Report this way: "The Report of [this] Committee makes no significant reference to the public [as well as the corporate] interest. This arises from the misconception that only shareholders are involved and not the public at large. . . [and this] is inadequate. . . . The stock market crash which contributed to the Depression in the 1930s. . . is proof enough of the public interest involved [in securities transactions]." Fox and Fox, *Corporate Management Acquisitions*, Vol. 4 (Matthew Bender & Company, 1985), Appendix IX, letter, pp. 122ff.

The proponents of this limited view of corporate existence and social responsibility claim, however, that the corporations in our economic system are, in fact, the protectors and guarantors of our political system. They argue that corporations provide the financial wherewithal that keeps our democratic way of life alive.

Herein lies the second serious problem. Our relatively free-market capitalist system has been and is the world's finest engine of economic growth; it has thus contributed to the support of our political system. But to argue that U.S. corporations have created, or continue to create, the conditions for liberty and equality is to misread the Declaration of Independence, the Constitution, the Bill of Rights, and our nation's history since 1776, at least.[16] The notion that corporate power and production are democracy's basic protectors, our bulwark against totalitarianism, misses the major point about every system of production. A renowned economist who was a determined free marketeer and anti-collectivist put it this way more than thirty years ago:

It is by no means enough to invoke the laws of the market in appealing to people's enlightened self-interest and their economic reason . . . [since these often lead to attempts] to get more than genuine and fair competition would give. . . . There must be high ethical values which we can invoke successfully; justice, public spirit, kindness, and good will. . . [and] respect for human dignity. These have to come from outside the market and no textbook in economics can replace them. . . . These are the indispensable supports which preserve the market and competition from degeneration.[17]

---

[16] The constitutional issues involved in property rights, civil rights, and social welfare demand more space than this text can give them. Some proponents of the narrow view of corporate responsibility insist that property rights are constitutionally sacrosanct, that they hold an exalted position in our constitutional jurisprudence equal to that of any other "human right." Cf. Jensen and Meckling, "Theory of the Firm: Managerial Behavior, Agency Costs and Ownership Structure," *Journal of Financial Economics* 3 (1976), cited in Jensen and Smith, eds., *The Modern Theory of Corporate Finance* (New York: McGraw-Hill, 1984) p. 80 n. 6. Jensen and Meckling are simply wrong. Of course, we Americans have property rights. But the ultimate "right" is to get a fair price for our property if the government decides to take it away for its own legitimate purposes. That's called "due process." The government has no way to deprive us of our right to religious freedom, or of our right not to have a state religion foisted upon us. There is no "due process" by which such nonnegotiable human rights can ever be paid away. See also the last sentence of Justice Stone's famous dissent in *Morehead, Warden v. New York ex rel Tipaldo*, 298 U.S. 587 (1937), in which he was joined by justices Brandeis and Cardozo.

[17] W. Ropke, *A Humane Economy—the Social Framework of the Free Market* (University Press of America, 1986), pp. 124-25. Originally published as *Jenseits von Angebor und Nachfrage*, 1958.

These indispensable supports, not material goods, must be the very basics of democracy's victory over totalitarianism.

Totalitarianism gains ground exactly to the extent that. . . human[s] suffer from frustration and non-fulfillment of their lives as a whole because they have lost the true, pre-eminently non-material conditions of human happiness. For this reason, it is certain that the decisive battle between Communism and the free world will have to be fought, not so much on the field of material living conditions, where the victory of the West would be beyond doubt, but on the field of spiritual and moral values. Communism prospers more on empty souls than on empty standards. The free world will prevail only if it succeeds in filling the emptiness of its own soul in its own manner and with its own values, but not with electric razors. . . . The material prosperity of the masses is not an absolute standard and a warning against regarding it as the West's principal weapon in the cold war is. . . justified.[18]

Every corporation is morally accountable to the society from which it extracts the essentials of its continued existence. And the term "corporate social responsibility" is one expression of that overall accountability.[19] A more difficult question asks what the exact parameters of that social responsibility might be. Certainly, corporate social responsibility is something more than giving away company money, and something less than a requirement to sacrifice corporate economic viability for the purpose of righting general societal wrongs. Beyond that, like so may other crucial social and ethical issues of our time related to power, wealth, economic growth, and the proper, positive roles of men, women, and institutions in society, there is no escape from the need to draw these parameters by means of individual judgments made in individual circumstances. The task is never easy, and we cannot afford to shirk it for some easy, faulty answers.[20]

---

[18] Ibid., p. 111. (Time seems to have proven Ropke correct, at léast in Eastern Europe and the former Soviet Union.)

[19] For a rather unusual expression about the need for enhanced corporate social responsibility on the part of the United States and Great Britain, see J. Lloyd, "U.S. and U.K. Appeal to the Corporate Conscience," and the editorial, "The Caring Corporation," both in *Financial Times*, May 4, 1988. A report distributed by the White House in 1988 details this concern: "Special Supplement: The British-American Conference on Private Sector Initiatives, London, England, May 2-4, 1988" (White House Office of Private Sector Initiatives, Washington, D.C., 1988).

[20] A famous American economist has cast the general issue of "responsibility" in terms of the ever-present tension between our economic institutions on the one hand and our political and social institutions on the other. His extended discussion is well worth reading: A.M. Okun, *Equality and Efficiency: The Big Tradeoff* (Washington, D.C.: The Brookings Institution, 1975).

Corporate executives are not unaware of the fact that American consumers have begun at least to talk about the need for corporations to behave toward them in a socially responsible fashion.[21] But beyond some media blitz response, how, in your opinion, might social responsibility parameters for business be defined? Must the answer, of necessity, be formulated in terms of an ethical construct? If so, what is yours?

Does corporate America, for you, have some particular responsibility to help deal in a meaningful way with clearly serious problems plaguing the body politic? Poor public education processes, and dangerous drug and alcohol abuse in and outside the workplace, come to mind. If the answer is yes, just what form(s) should this exercise of corporate social responsibility take? Are corporations which do participate in forwarding solutions to such problems simply being "charitable?" Or are they, in any long-term view, actually improving their own future competitiveness and profitability?

Is there any linkage at all, that you can see, between the two corporation-related concepts "social responsibility" and "fiduciary duty"?

II. RESPONDING TO POWER: RICO, FALSE CLAIMS, AND CORPORATE SENTENCING

A. The Racketeer Influenced and Corrupt Organizations Act (RICO)

The RICO statute was passed by Congress in 1970 as part of the Organized Crime Control Act,[22] and it was assumed by many to be, basically, an attempt to keep organized crime out of the ambit of legitimate business. As focused on organized "criminal" activity, certain powerful RICO sanctions seemed to make sense. For example, RICO authorized courts to forfeit any interest a defendant might have (in money, property etc.) acquired through a RICO violation, and to "freeze" (issue restraining orders to prevent transfer of) all assets of the defendant that are potentially forfeitable, pending case resolution.

---

[21] See "Doing the Right Thing: Faced With Increased Public Scrutiny, Businesses Are Scrambling to Become Socially Responsible," Newsweek (January 7, 1991), pp. 42-43, and J. McCormack and M. Levinson "The Supply Police, The Demand for Social Responsibility Forces Business to Look Far Beyond Its Own Front Door," *Newsweek* (February 15, 1993), pp. 48-49. See also: R.H. Frank, "Melding Sociology and Economics: James Coleman's *Foundations of Social Theory*," *Journal of Economic Literature* (March 1992), pp. 147-170, esp. at pp. 168-169 ("Corporate Responsibility").

[22] RICO is Pub. Law 91-452 and can be found at 18 U.S.C. Sections 1961-68 (1988 and Supp. II 1990). Thirty-one states also have RICO-type statutes, two of them being related solely to illicit drugs.

RICO provides criminal punishments, of course, but it also allows the government *and private parties*[23] to seek damages in either state or federal courts (i.e., to bring civil actions).

The major elements requiring a *criminal* finding of guilty under RICO (beyond a reasonable doubt), or a *civil* finding under RICO (by a preponderance of the evidence) are the following: the defendant must have committed two or more acts, constituting a "pattern" of "racketeering" activity involving direct or indirect investment in, or the maintenance of an interest in, or participation in, an "enterprise" affecting interstate or foreign commerce.[24]

The two major concerns here, even if RICO were confined to organized crime activity, would be: What makes up a "pattern" of racketeering activity, and what is an "enterprise"? It would certainly seem that two acts alone do not make a "pattern." Some other evidence of continuity of action is necessary in addition to the minimum two acts.[25] Just what, exactly, *is* necessary is not that clear.

How about "racketeering" activity? The RICO definitions are broad. If the activity is criminally punishable under state law with imprisonment for more than a year, or indictable under certain other federal criminal statutes, or under bankruptcy, securities fraud or drug laws—and this is only a partial list—the activity is "racketeering."

Now for the "enterprise." Prostitution, car theft rings, illegal gambling operations, loan sharking, drug distribution—these are easy. What is harder to take, given the possible range of sanctions, is that commercial and investment banking, securities markets, and even telephone companies are "enterprises" as well. And what has happened with RICO is that it has, over time, been more and more applied to "legitimate" business enterprises in ways that have disturbed those businesses mightily.[26]

H.J. Inc. v. Northwestern Bell Telephone
492 U.S. 229 (1989)

[In this case, customers of Northwestern Bell Telephone filed a class action against the company under RICO. They alleged that for six

---

[23] Defined as "any person injured in his business or property by reason of a violation," of RICO. 18 U.S.C. §1964(c).

[24] *Moss* v. *Morgan Stanley, Inc.*, 719 F. 2d 5, 17 (1983), cert. denied, 465 U.S. 1025 (1984). See also the full discussion of RICO in the *American Criminal Law Review*, Vol. 28, No..3, 1991, pp. 637-67.

[25] *Sedima, S.P.R.L.* v. *Imrex Co.*, 473 U.S. 479 (1985).

[26] "A substantial portion of crimes prosecuted under RICO have been 'white collar' crimes." *American Criminal Law Review*, note 24, *supra*, at p. 639. And see the many cases cited in the article for specifics.

years the company had sought to influence members of the Public Utilities Commission (PUC) by making cash payments to them, by promising them future jobs, and by paying for their parties, for meals, and for tickets to sporting events. And that one result was that the PUC in fact approved rates for the company in excess of a fair and reasonable amount. The plaintiffs sought an injunction against enforcing certain rates, and triple damages under the civil liability provisions of RICO. The U.S. Court of Appeals threw out the customers' case, as a RICO case, on the ground that the telephone company's acts made up a "single fraudulent effort or scheme," and thus was not an established "pattern of racketeering activity."]

Justice Brennan delivered the opinion of the U.S. Supreme Court:

I

RICO renders criminally and civilly liable "any person" who uses or invests income derived "from a pattern of racketeering activity" to acquire interest in or to operate an enterprise engaged in interstate commerce, § 1962(a); who acquires or maintains an interest in or control of such an enterprise "through a pattern of racketeering activity," § 1962(b); who, being employed by or associated with such an enterprise, conducts or participates in the conduct of its affairs "through a pattern of racketeering activity," § 1962(c); or, finally, who conspires to violate the first three subsections of § 1962, § 1962(d). RICO provides for drastic remedies: conviction for a violation of RICO carries severe criminal penalties and forfeiture of illegal proceeds, 18 U.S.C. § 1963 (1982 ed., Supp. V); and a person found in a private civil action to have violated RICO is liable for treble damages, costs and attorney's fees, § 1964(c). . . .

We acknowledge concern in some quarters over civil RICO's use against "legitimate businesses" as well as "mobsters and organized criminals". . . .

But the definition of a "pattern of criminal conduct" in Title X of [the Organized Crime Control Act]. . . shows that Congress was quite capable of conceiving of "pattern" as a flexible concept. . . [and] should thus create a good deal of skepticism about any claim that, despite the capacious language it used, Congress must have intended the RICO pattern element to pick out only racketeering activities with an organized crime nexus. And, indeed, the legislative history shows that Congress knew what it was doing when it adopted commodious language capable of extending beyond organized crime.

Opponents criticized OCCA precisely because it failed to limit the statute's reach to organized crime. See, *e.g.*, S.Rep. No. 91–617, at 215

(Sens. Hart and Kennedy complaining that the Organized Crime Control bill "goes beyond organized crime activity"). In response, the statute's sponsors made evident that the omission of this limit was no accident, but a reflection of OCCA's intended breadth. . . .

The occasion for Congress' action was the perceived need to combat organized crime. But Congress for cogent reasons chose to enact a more general statute, one which, although it had organized crime as its focus, was not limited in application to organized crime. In Title IX, Congress picked out as key to RICO's application broad concepts that might fairly indicate an organized crime connection, but that it fully realized do not either individually or together provide anything approaching a perfect fit with "organized crime." See, e.g., id., at 18940 (Sen. McClellan) ("It is impossible to draw an effective statute which reaches most of the commercial activities of organized crime, yet does not include offenses commonly committed by persons outside organized crime as well").

It seems, moreover, highly unlikely that Congress would have intended the pattern requirement to be interpreted by reference to a concept that it had itself rejected for inclusion in the text of RICO at least in part because "it is probably impossible precisely and definitively to define." Id., at 35204 (Rep. Poff). Congress realized that the stereotypical view of organized crime as consisting in a circumscribed set of illegal activities, such as gambling and prostitution—a view expressed in the definition included in the Omnibus Crime Control and Safe Streets Act, and repeated in the OCCA preamble—was no longer satisfactory because criminal activity had expanded into legitimate enterprises. See United States v. Turkette, 452 U.S., at 590–591, 101 S. Ct., at 2532–2533. Section 1961(1) of RICO, with its very generous definition of "racketeering activity," acknowledges the breakdown of the traditional conception of organized crime, and responds to a new situation in which persons engaged in long-term criminal activity often operate wholly within legitimate enterprises. Congress drafted RICO broadly enough to encompass a wide range of criminal activity, taking many different forms and likely to attract a broad array of perpetrators operating in many different ways. It would be counterproductive and a mismeasure of congressional intent now to adopt a narrow construction of the statute's pattern element that would require proof of an organized crime nexus.

At this Court stressed in *Sedima,* in rejecting a pinched construction of RICO's provision for a private civil action, adopted by a lower court because it perceived that RICO's use against non-organized-crime defendants was an "abuse" of the Act, "Congress wanted to reach both 'legitimate' and 'illegitimate' enterprises." 473 U.S., at 499, 105

S. Ct., at 3286. Legitimate businesses "enjoy neither an inherent incapacity for criminal activity nor immunity from its consequences"; and, as a result, § 1964(c)'s use "against respected businesses allegedly engaged in a pattern of specifically identified criminal conduct is hardly a sufficient reason for assuming that the provision is being misconstrued." *Ibid.* If plaintiffs' ability to use RICO against businesses engaged in a pattern of criminal acts is a defect, we said it is one "inherent in the statute as written," and hence beyond our power to correct. *Ibid.* RICO may be a poorly drafted statute; but rewriting it is a job for Congress, if it is so inclined, and not for this Court. There is no more room in RICO's "self-consciously expansive language and overall approach" for the imposition of an organized crime limitation than for the "amorphous 'racketeering injury' requirement" we rejected in *Sedima,* see *id.,* at 495, 498, 105 S. Ct., at 3284, 3286. We thus decline the invitation to invent a rule that RICO's pattern of racketeering concept requires an allegation and proof of an organized crime nexus. . . .

IV

[12] We turn now to the application of our analysis of RICO's pattern requirement. . . .

Petitioners' complaint alleges that at different times over the course of at least a 6-year period the noncommissioner respondents gave five members of the MPUC numerous bribes, in several different forms, with the objective—in which they were allegedly successful—of causing these Commissioners to approve unfair and unreasonable rates for Northwestern Bell. RICO defines bribery as a "racketeering activity," 18 U.S.C. § 1961(1), so petitioners have alleged multiple predicate acts.

Under the analysis we have set forth above, and consistent with the allegations in their complaint, petitioners may be able to prove that the multiple predicates alleged constitute "a pattern of racketeering activity," in that they satisfy the requirements of relationship continuity. The acts of bribery alleged are said to be related by common purpose, to influence Commissioners in carrying out their duties in order to win approval of unfairly and unreasonably high rates for Northwestern Bell. Furthermore, petitioners claim that the racketeering predicates occurred with some frequency over at least a 6-year period, which may be sufficient to satisfy the continuity requirement. Alternatively, a threat of continuity of racketeering activity might be established at trial by showing that the alleged bribes were a regular way of conducting Northwestern Bell's ongoing business, or a regular way of conducting or participating in the conduct of the alleged and ongoing RICO enterprise, the MPUC.

The Court of Appeals thus erred in affirming the District Court's dismissal of petitioners' complaint for failure to plead "a pattern of racketeering activity." The judgement is reversed and the case is remanded for further proceedings consistent with this opinion.

It is so ordered.

It seems to be clear that RICO, absent new language to the contrary from Congress, will continue to be applied to "legitimate" businesses. However, as Justice Scalia showed in his concurring opinion in *Northwestern Bell*, the definition of a "pattern of racketeering activity" is still unclear. Congress had perhaps better "provide clearer guidance" as to RICO's intended scope or RICO could be in for some constitutional problems revolving around the issue of vagueness.[27]

What is clear, in any event, is that some lawyers and some courts are much bothered by what they see as overzealousness in the application of RICO to legitimate business by prosecutors and by civil plaintiffs seeking triple damages.[28]   And while Congress seems predisposed to review the scope of RICO, the depredations of flawed fiduciaries in S&Ls, and other financial institutions have gone far toward holding up any "reform."[29]

We suggest that if one issue with RICO is: What do we do now to "reform" the statute? an equally important second issue is: How did we get to this point in terms of RICO's focus on so much white collar activity?

The easy answer is "overzealous prosecution," "public greed," and "too-liberal courts." The last of these is demonstrably false at the level of the United States Supreme Court, and the second, if true, *is a shared condition that includes far more members of the American public than RICO plaintiffs, and far more than any one particular statute. It is lamentable but irrelevant.* Overzealous prosecutors there surely are, but we must assume that in the face of public outrage over persecution of the

---

[27] 492 U.S. 229 at 243.

[28] In October 1989, the U.S. Justice Department distributed new guidelines to U.S. Attorneys prosecuting RICO cases that, in effect, urged caution in the use of such weapons as temporary restraining orders (TROs), which amount to pretrial freezing of the defendant's assets (alleging that in fact this is "tantamount to a seizure of property without due process").

[29] Cf. R. McMillan, "ABA Seeks End of Civil RICO Abuses," *The ABA Journal* (October 1991). Cases still appear before the Supreme Court, and a RICO suit against Arthur Young & Co. (now Ernst & Young) is pending before the Supreme Court in its 1992-93 calendar (Number 91-886). Another case, decided early in 1992,(*Holmes* v. *Securities Investor Protection Corp.*), did not do much to settle major issues.

innocent, they (and the Congress) might well have been persuaded to take a different tack. Apparently there is no general outrage against RICO because there is much suspicion within the body politic that indeed economic power *is* wielded from time to time by legitimate institutions in ways utterly incompatible with the public welfare. Moreover, the body politic views RICO as one legitimate tool by which members of the public (e.g. rate payers) can eventually recoup their losses—and see reprehensible activity stopped.

B. The False Claims Act (and *Qui Tam* Whistle-Blowers)

Egregious examples of government procurement fraud, bribery, and illegal exchange of information in the late 1980s[30] served to call attention to an old law adopted to combat fraud in procurement during the Civil War: The False Claims Act.[31] However, while it would be false to refer to such despicable acts as were uncovered by *Operation Ill Wind* as entirely new, it is surely true that, quantitatively, such acts have reached a very dangerous level in our time: In 1988, Department of Justice officials testified that fraud drains up to ten percent of the entire federal procurement budget.[32]

There is little doubt but that large defense contractors are perceived as being extraordinarily powerful in terms of their importance to, and relationships with, government and in terms of their call upon public funds. And there is little doubt either about their power, and the exercise of that power, being perceived with suspicion and distaste by the American public.

Laws attempting to levy sanctions on defense (and other government) contractor fraud are legion: The Major Fraud Act of 1988[33] created a new offense of "procurement fraud," which focuses on all government contract fraud in excess of $1 million. In addition to augmented fines that could mount to $10 million or more, and prison terms up to 10 years, the

---

[30] *Operation Ill Wind* is the name given to one long-term (Naval Investigative Service/FBI) probe into widespread fraud and collusion involving government contractors, middlemen, and the Pentagon. Many millions of dollars in fines have been levied against a number of major defense contractors, and criminal indictments have been forthcoming as well. See 49 Federal Contract Reports (Bureau of National Affairs) 1209 (June 20, 1980); A. Pasztor, "Prosecutors Close in on Unisys, Other Contractors As Arms Procurement Inquiry Gains Momentum," *The Wall Street Journal* (January 8, 1990).

[31] The original False Claims Act (sometimes referred to as "the Abe Lincoln law") was Act of March 2, 1863, C.67, 12 State.696. The first major amendments were made in 1943, the second in 1986. See, for an excellent brief history, *U.S. Ex Rel La Valley* v. *First National Bank of Boston*, 707 F. Supp. 1351 (1988) at 1354-1356. The current (civil) False Claims Act is at 31 U.S.C., Sections 3729-3733.

[32] 49 Fed. Cont. Rep. (BNA) 8,9 (January 4, 1988), cited in *American Criminal Law Review*, note 24, *supra*, at p. 560.

[33] 18 U.S.C. § 1031.

act allows "whistle-blowers" who testify for the government to bring civil suits for damages against their companies if they are punished by the companies for their cooperation.

Moreover, separate laws guard against defective pricing,[34] mischarging,[35] bid collusion,[36] product substitution,[37] and bribes, gratuities, and conflict of interest.[38] And while one defendant could be (and often is) charged with violations of several criminal statutes in connection with one major attack on the public treasury, the False Claims statute—and especially the civil False Claims Act—is the most commonly used law to deal with contractor fraud.[39]

The 1986 amendments to the False Claims Act raised penalties, made proof of violation a bit easier, and, most importantly, strengthened the false Claims Act *qui tam* provisions.[40]

Qui tam means, in Latin, "who as well," and the expression is applied, in law, to suits by private citizens suing for the state and for themselves at the same time.

> With regard to the *qui tam* provisions, the (1986) amendments were designed to "encourage more private enforcement suits." Sen. Rep. 345, at 23–24. The legislative history in both houses of Congress reveals a sense that fraud against the Government was apparently so rampant and difficult to identify that the Government could use all the help it would get from private citizens with knowledge of fraud.[41]

The *qui tam* provisions clearly link public concern over abusive (and unethical) corporate behavior rather directly to specific sanctions aimed at punishing that behavior. Briefly stated, the incentive supplied by the laws to the individual citizen is a percentage of the damages recovered from the fraudulent contractor. Any citizen with knowledge of the commission of a fraud (who was not himself or herself involved in committing it) can bring a lawsuit against the defrauding party, *qui tam.*

---

[34] The Truth in Negotiations Act, 10 U.S.C § 2306(a) (1988).

[35] Criminal False Claims Act, 18 U.S.C. § 287 (1988) and Criminal False Statements Act, 18 U.S.C. § 1001.

[36] The False Claims Act note 31, *supra*, and antitrust laws that will be discussed *infra*.

[37] Usually prosecuted as a false statement or false claim.

[38] There are separate bribery laws that are very broad: 18 U.S.C. § 201 (1988). There is even an Anti-Kickback Act at 41 U.S.C. § 51-58 (1987).

[39] See *American Criminal Law Review*, note 24, *supra*, at pp. 575, 577-78.

[40] 31 U.S.C. § 3730.

[41] *U.S. Ex Rel La Valley*, note 31 *supra*, at p. 1355.

The government has to decide whether to join in the lawsuit. If it does, it takes over the lawsuit completely.

However, citizens who began the lawsuit are entitled to receive between 15 and 25 percent of the amount recovered in the lawsuit, as determined by the judge. If the government chooses not to join in, the citizen receives 25 to 30 percent plus costs, again by the judge's determination. Further, if the government does take over the case, any settlement agreement between it and the defendant is subject to review by the court, which may, in fact, reject it as insufficient.[42]

It has been argued that, despite its enormous potential, *qui tam* has not been as effective as might have been expected.[43] There is no doubt, however, that the existence of *qui tam* has encouraged government prosecution of lawsuits that were not undertaken through the government's own initiative.[44] Finally, there have been cases where the government was, in fact, aware of cost overruns and other problems perhaps involving fraud and still did not sue. Then whistle-blowers did, and at least one federal appeals court has ruled that previous government knowledge of (or complicity in) fraud is no bar to a whistle-blower's lawsuit.[45]

Heightened public scrutiny of corporate behavior has its problematic side. First, it joins together with a plethora of congressional committees and sub-committees—and their thousands of staff people—to make up a less than efficient conglomeration of overseers.[46] Second, the Defense Department has sought to encourage self-regulation by its contractors through a voluntary Defense Industry Initiative. The DII requires those contractors who do sign on to follow a written code of ethics—among other requirements.[47] And such contractors argue that the presence of so many

---

[42] Cf. *Gravitt v. General Electric Co.*, 680 F. Supp, 1162 (1988), appeal dismissed and *cert denied*, 488 U.S. 901 (1988).

[43] *American Criminal Law Review*, note 4, *supra*, at p. 587. By mid-1990, it had produced some $70 million in dollars recovered.

[44] For example, against Teledyne, Inc., alleging overcharges of tens of millions *per year* for nearly a decade on defense contracts: Staff Reporter, "Justice Agency Joins Whistle-Blower Suit Against Teledyne," *The Wall Street Journal* (November 29, 1990). Northrup Corp., in June 1991, paid several millions to settle a *qui tam* suit in which the government joined *after* it was initiated by private citizens. And the Justice Department, in August 1991, joined in another such suit for fraud brought by a nonprofit taxpayer group against General Electric Company. G.E. ended up paying $69 million in fines and damages. The government, which had to be pushed with the lawsuit, moved quickly to cut down the *qui tam* whistle-blower's reward. See A.K. Naj, "Justice Department Seeking to Reduce Reward for Whistle Blower at G.E. Unit,: *The Wall Street Journal* (November 4, 1992). To no avail. The whistle-blower was awarded some $13 million by the court.

[45] See A. Stevens and M. Geyelin, "Defendants in Fraud Cases Are Dealt Blow," *The Wall Street Journal* (May 30, 1991).

[46] There is a Defense Contract Audit Agency (DCAA) and Inspector General (IG) offices in 19 federal agencies, and a Defense Procurement Fraud Unit in the Justice Department!

[47] The "DII" is described in the *American Criminal Law Review*, note 4, *supra*, at p. 585.

investigators and whistle-blowers puts a damper on internal investigations that could produce evidence of potential fraud.

The fundamental problem in the area of corporate procurement fraud is market failure caused by reprehensible corporate behavior. And in the defense industry at least, this behavior is part and parcel of a power position vis-à-vis the taxpayer, which has thus far proven impervious to all existing sanctions.[48] It would seem, in the face of reality, that there is a justifiable burden on the part of contractors to undertake to internalize, organizationally, a higher standard of ethical behavior—as well as more efficient internal auditing and compliance processes. As long as they fail to do so, they will remain the objects of public distrust, and they will have to suffer the consequences—along with all the rest of us—of a seeming inability on the part of government to overcome with fully efficient sanctions basic, systemic contractor moral deficiencies.

C. Sentencing Organizations (to Fines and to Probation)

The Sentencing Reform Act of 1984[49] was passed by Congress for the purposes of promoting certainty in sentencing, of reducing disparities in sentences, and of establishing a Sentencing Commission charged with developing guidelines to guide the discretion of (federal district court) judges who impose sentences. The new Sentencing Commission submitted guidelines to Congress in April 1987, and they went into effect on November 1, 1987.

The very constitutionality of the Sentencing Commission was challenged early on. The grounds for the challenge were that the commission represented an excessive delegation of power by Congress and was a judicial body exercising legislative authority in violation of the separation of powers doctrine.[50] The U.S. Supreme Court held that the Commission was constitutional.[51]

The *Law Review* points out that, as of July 1988, a total of 34 of the then 46 signatures to the DII were, at the time, under investigation for various charges of procurement fraud.

[48] At least with regard to the major defense companies, whose contracts run to billions of dollars annually. See, e.g., E. White, "Pentagon Dodge: Suspended Contractors Often Continue to Get More Defense Business," *The Wall Street Journal* (May 6, 1986).

[49] Pub. Law 98-473 (codified at 18 U.S.C. Secs. 3551-3625, 3673, 3742, and 28 U.S.C. Secs. 991-998 [1988]).

[50] See Chapter 6. The Commission has seven voting members appointed by the President with the advice and consent of the Senate. It is "an independent commission in the judicial branch of the United States," and at least three of its members must be U.S. federal court judges.

[51] *Mistretta* v. *U.S.*, 109 S. Ct. 647 (1989). *Mistretta* is cited in Chapter 6, *supra*, at note 2. Justice Scalia dissented, arguing that the commission, considering the substantive policy exercise it was involved in, was really a "sort of junior varsity Congress." 109 S. Ct. 647 at p. 683.

It must be pointed out that, except for specific antitrust offenses, the 1987 guidelines did not deal with organizations, only natural persons. But subsequent to public hearings held late in 1988 (which hearings generated much political controversy), the Sentencing Commission issued new guidelines in 1989, which provided specifically for the sentencing of organizations.[52]

The guidelines received their share of general criticism on several grounds, including the charge that they reduced guilty pleas, and were thus (time and expense) inefficient in general[53]; moreover it was argued that the organizational sentencing provisions, specifically, were a "fairly explicit rejection of the objective of efficiency in punishment."[54]

The criminal justice system, until 1989, never really took official cognizance of the fact that, beyond the illegal acts of individual organization *persons,* lay an entire *corporate structure and culture* that could themselves be linked both morally and legally to the commission of white-collar crime.[55] This does not mean that corporations were never indicted or convicted as such prior to the 1989 (draft) guidelines. However, there was great disparity in the sentencing of organizations for federal crimes, not only for similar offenses, but even for those committed in the same geographical areas. Moreover, relatively few cases were actively pursued against corporate defendants, and even fewer against sizable publicly held companies.[56] Moreover, a Sentencing Commission Study found that close to one-half of the corporations that were prosecuted and convicted were fined $5,000 or less, probation was imposed in no more than 20 percent of the cases, and any other form of sentencing was rare.[57]

---

[52] *United States Sentencing Commission,* Preliminary Draft: Sentencing Guideline for Organizational Defendants (November 1, 1989).

[53] See G.W. Heaney, "The Reality of Guidelines Sentencing: No End to Disparity," *American Criminal Law Review,* Vol. 28, No. 2, 1991.

[54] J.S. Parker and M.K. Block, "The Sentencing Commission, P.M. (Post Mistretta): Sunshine or Sunset?" *The American Criminal Law Review,* Vol. 27, No. 2, 1989, p. 321. The admittedly important issue of the overarching rationale for *any* specific set of sentencing guidelines is too broad for discussion here; however, on the question of the relationship between the guidelines and crime-control theories, for example, see Parker and Block at pp. 315-18; see also A. von Hirsch, "Federal Sentencing Guidelines: Do They Provide Principled Guidance?" *The American Criminal Law Review,* Vol. 27, No. 2, 1989, esp. pp. 370-73: "Rationales."

[55] Cf. on the general issue of corporate structure and culture: Robert Jackall, *Moral Mazes: The World of Corporate Managers* (New York: Oxford University Press, 1988).

[56] Actually only some 100 or so corporations with $1 million or more in sales and 50 or more employees were convicted of federal crime in the years 1984-1987 (out of a total of some 1,200 corporations convicted during those years). M. Cohen, C.C. Ho, and others, "Organizations as Defendants in Federal Court: A Preliminary Analysis of Prosecutions, Convictions and Sanctions, 1984-1987." *Whittier Law Review,* Vol. 10, 1988, p. 112. Fewer than 40 of the convicted corporations had *any* publicly traded stock.

[57] P. Shenon, "The Case of the Criminal Corporation," *The New York Times* (January 15, 1989).

Subsequent to the promulgation of the 1989 Draft Guidelines—and much debate for months thereafter—the Sentencing Commission sent formal amendments on the guidelines to Congress on May 1, 1991.[58] The newly amended guidelines became (legally) effective on November 1, 1991. They include a new Chapter 8, entitled "Sentencing of Organizations."[59] Under its provisions, *every* organization, corporate or otherwise, is liable to fines and probation for violation of *any* federal prohibitory statutes, such as those relating to antitrust, securities laws, bribery, commercial fraud, money-laundering, criminal enterprises and racketeering, conspiracies, the environment, and a good many more.

The guidelines are complex and will not be detailed here. The reader interested in a thorough understanding of the nation's new sentencing process is referred to the original source: the Commission's *Guidelines Manual* and accompanying *Appendix C*.[60]

We would emphasize here the general structure, merely, with particular reference to two overall areas: determining punishments and factoring in mitigating circumstances.

Punishments are determined by classifying the specific conduct engaged in (e.g., "Offenses Involving the Environment");[61] then by adjusting within the offense category for such elements as, for example, the victim being a law enforcement officer or other "official" victim[62]; then by factoring in the criminal history and livelihood of the defendant.[63] One then proceeds to determine the sentence itself.

Sentences begin with the Sentencing Table[64] with months of imprisonment (depending upon the level assigned to the category of offense and as adjusted) ranging from 0-6 months, to 30 years to life imprisonment. These are referred to as "Guideline Ranges." Judges have discretion, of course, within a sentencing level. Moreover, a judge may sentence outside of the guidelines; however, he or she must specify the reasons for the departure. Moreover, while sentences made within the guidelines may be

---

[58] Pursuant to its authority under 28 U.S.C. § 994 (p).

[59] *United States Sentencing Commission Guidelines Manual*, U.S. Government Printing Offices, ISBN 0-16-035884-1 and 0-16-035894-9 at pp. 347-83, Secs. 8A1.1-8E1.3. (November 1, 1991). See also separate volume *Appendix C Amendments*, U.S. Government Printing Office ISBN 0-16-035893-0 (November 1, 1991), esp. Amendment 422, pp. 245-49.

[60] Ibid. See esp. Chapter 1: "Introduction and General Application Principles," pp. 1-27.

[61] *Guidelines Manual*, note 59 at Chapter Two: Offense Conduct (19 categories of offense), pp. 29-233. For detailed information on the new law and environmental crimes, see G. Lincenberg, "Sentencing in Environmental Crimes," *American Criminal Law Review*, Vol. 24, No. 4 (Summer 1992), pp. 1235-60. See also: H.J. Reske, "Record EPA Prosecutions," *ABA Journal* (March 1992), p. 25.

[62] Ibid., Chapter Three: Adjustments, pp. 235-60.

[63] Ibid., Chapter Four: Criminal History and Criminal Livelihood, pp. 261-77.

[64] Ibid., Chapter Five: Determining the Sentence, pp. 279-325.

appealed only to review whether the guidelines were correctly applied, sentences departing from them are subject to full review by a higher (appellate) court. Probation for individuals is not authorized by the guidelines in any case where the sentence on the Sentencing Table is more than 6 months.

Sentencing might include the imposition of restitution and/or fines, and/or special assessment and/or forfeitures, rather than—or, in addition to—"time" (prison term).

The sentence of an individual may be reduced for specific reasons; that is, mitigated or, perhaps, made tougher, under Sections 5K1.1.–5K2.16,[65] and plea agreements are provided for as well.[66]

The chapter in the Guidelines Manual on the sentencing of organizations[67] states in its "Introductory Commentary" that organizations act only through agents, are vicariously liable for offenses committed by their agents, and that agents are, of course, individually responsible for their own conduct as well. Sentencing of the organization itself, in the *Guidelines Manual*, "is designed so that the sanctions imposed upon organizations and their agents, taken together, will provide just punishment, adequate deterrence, and incentives for organizations to maintain internal mechanisms for preventing, detecting, and reporting criminal conduct."[68]

How is this to be accomplished? By having the organization remedy harm it causes (make victims whole) and by basing the fine levied on two specific elements: the seriousness of the offense *and* the degree of the culpability of the organization; for example, the role of management in the offense:

> Culpability generally will be determined by the steps taken by the organization prior to the offense to prevent and detect criminal conduct, the level and extent of involvement in or tolerance of the offense by certain personnel, and the organization's actions after an offense has been committed.[69]

Probation is specifically authorized for an organizational defendant "when needed to ensure that another sanction will be fully implemented, or to ensure that steps will be taken within the organization to reduce the likelihood of future criminal conduct."[70]

---

[65] Ibid., pp. 320-25.

[66] Ibid., Chapter Six: Sentencing Procedures and Plea Agreements.

[67] Chapter Eight of the *Guidelines*. See note 59, *supra*.

[68] *Guidelines*, p. 347.

[69] Ibid. And see: J.M. Moses, "Firms Pressured Not to Support Accused Aides," *The Wall Street Journal* (March 19, 1993).

[70] Ibid.

The three matters remaining to be discussed with regard to corporate sentencing are: How severe are the sanctions in fact? Precisely what does it take to ameliorate them? And why is so much business conduct once subjected to civil and administrative repercussions only, now the object of particular, substantive criminal actions?

The answer to the question of how severe organizational sentencing might be is: very severe indeed. The top category offense carries a base fine of $72,500,000 but aggravating circumstances could conceivably run the fine as high as $290 million.[71]

Then there is additional probation, which could mandate as part of its terms that the offender organization report its financial condition and the disposition of all of its funds at set intervals; that the offender submit to unannounced examinations of its books and records; that the offender make payments into court regularly, and that the offender be required to develop and then operate a substantive program to prevent and detect violations of law.[72]

That the sentencing guidelines focus on promoting noncriminal behavior (prevention) is made clear by the fact that the same basic organization act which could ultimately produce a $290 million fine, could conceivably produce instead a fine of under $5 million, if the factors present to incur the base fine are *mitigating* rather than *augmenting*. The key mitigating factor in any case is the existence within the organization, *before the fact*, of "an effective program to prevent and detect violations of the law."

It clearly behooves *any* organization to study carefully the ten steps it can take to put together what can be defined broadly as a "due diligence" *compliance program* that qualifies as "effective" under the *Guidelines Manual*, and thus serves to mitigate a criminal sentence.

These steps are contained in the manual at Section 8A1.2., "Commentary" and "Application Notes," 3(K)1-7(iii).[73] Clearly, just as a competent police force cannot be expected to eradicate crime totally, neither will an "effective" compliance program necessarily eliminate crime in the organization totally. However, public relations flackery is not crime prevention in any case, and an organization must, at the very least, have instituted substantive compliance standards and procedures, must have assigned high-level responsibility for the conduct of the in-house program, must have undertaken effective communication of the program throughout the work force; and must have instituted meaningful auditing and enforce-

---

[71] Chapter Eight, Secs. 8C2.4 and 8C2.6, of the *Guidelines*.

[72] Ibid, Sections 8D1.1-8D1.5.

[73] *Guidelines Manual*, note 59, *supra*, at pp. 352-53.

ment procedures. And quite clearly, a serious code of ethical conduct would be of inestimable value to the organization as well.

Finally, one must ask in connection with the sentencing Guidelines—and RICO and the False Claims Act as well as other contractor-fraud statutes—why it is undoubtedly true that "there is a growing trend in the United States toward treating lapses in business conduct as criminal matters"? And that, in addition to federal law, "moves toward broader criminal enforcement are also proceeding apace at the state level [where] prosecutors with enlarged staffs are pursuing companies more vigorously. . . ."[74]

While the growing trend is beyond dispute, the reasons for it are not as clear. To some degree, the recognition of new harms plays a part, as does their severity in terms of effect upon the body politic. Such considerations go a long way toward explaining, for example, criminalization of organizational acts that degrade the environment. Then, too, there is the American populist tradition, which has always required of elected officials that they bash the big fellow now and again. Still, that populism had never before succeeded, in any substantial, or broad measure, in applying severe criminal sanctions to organizations.

It is difficult not to believe that the exercise of corporate power is more and more being perceived by Americans, at the close of the twentieth century, as "a natural mechanism" as capable of "harming the advancement of social democracy" as forwarding it—and doing so to a degree that warrants the restraining use of the criminal law.[75]

At first blush, such an attitude seems to reflect an anticapitalist, anti-free- market bias. Moreover, it could be argued that the United States is being put at a competitive disadvantage through the adoption of such a punitive view of the exercise of corporate power.

We would argue to the contrary. And we would do so on the basis that *in a democracy* the same considerations that require restraints on the exercise of power by the people's representatives and the various branches of their government require similar constraints on the exercise of corporate power. For the former, the basis for the restraints is the language of the Constitution. For the latter, the basis is the goal of liberty and justice *for all*, which is the very spirit of the Constitution. Corporate power misused can contribute to commercial, political and social harm—and thus harm to liberty and justice—whether the result of such misuse is the failure of an

---

[74] Both quotes are from J. Flom, "U.S. Prosecutors Take a Tougher Line," *Financial Times* (October 31, 1991), p. 21.

[75] See Berle Economic Power, and Epstein "Dimensions of Corporate Power," notes 1 and 2, *supra*. And see also: J.M. Holcomb and P. Sethi, "Corporate and Executive Criminal Liability: Appropriate Standards, Remedies and Managerial Responses," and M.T. Tucker, "Corporate Crime and Punishment," both in "Corporate Crime" section of Vol. IV, No. 1, *Business and the Contemporary World* (Summer 1992) pp. 81-167.

inordinate number of depository institutions; the rape by fraudulent contractors of an already despoiled public treasury; out-and-out racketeering activity; or the wholesale disappearance of worker jobs in the wake of a leveraged buyout that enriches these same workers' management by tens of millions of dollars.

Thoughtful outside-the-market control of corporate power strengthens freedom *and* the free market system. The overwhelming majority of Americans already believe, quite sensibly, that free markets encourage commercial growth and personal material well-being. But they must also continue to believe that free markets encourage liberty and democracy too, or we will be in danger of damaging our greatest competitive edge: our *political and social stability*.

That competitive markets alone do not necessarily encourage social stability has been amply demonstrated in the twentieth century.[76] But when free markets work in productive mutuality with social democracy, they certainly do help produce political and social stability and, thus, investor confidence. That, too, has been amply demonstrated in our time: The United States of America, which has long had such stability, has been able to attract essential foreign investment even in the face of interest rates far lower than those offered in the rest of the industrialized world. Given continuing social and political, as well as economic, unrest in most geographical areas of the world, working *democratic* free markets, despite some bumps along the way, will continue to be an outstanding commercial success over the long term.

Democracy is highly competitive, and it is entitled to the protection, if necessary, of the democratic justice system.

None of the above, however, is dispositive of the issue: *How much reining in (and sanction) of corporate power can there be before the corner is turned toward market inefficiency through excess interference?* And that is a very important issue indeed, as has been pointed out before in this book in other outside-the-market-activity contexts.

Still, the Free Market, like Freedom overall, requires constant protective vigilance and oversight in order to survive and grow in a world where individual and organizational power seekers do tend to gnaw, from time to time, at its very vitals. We cannot avoid the reality that choices must be carefully thought out, and made constantly, if one is to maintain the proper balance between *the demands of free markets* on the one hand and *the demands of the democratic social welfare* on the other.

---

[76] China was the very first major Communist nation to encourage the growth of private markets.

The crux of efficient choice regarding proper exercise of corporate power would seem to lie in the acceptance, by *all* of the players in the game, of their moral responsibility for preserving *both* demands.

III. RESPONDING TO POWER; AN OVERVIEW OF ANTITRUST (WITH CASE EXCERPTS)

As we have noted previously, published laws of the United States are listed in many volumes collectively titled *The United States Code* (U.S.C.). The volumes *containing court decisions illustrating the listed laws* are thus "annotated" and the corresponding citation is *U.S.C.A.* Basic antitrust legislation is found at Title 15 U.S.C.A.

The basic laws are *the Sherman Act, the Clayton Act*, and *the Federal Trade Commission Act,* as amended over the years since 1890, by such other legislation as, for example, the *Robinson-Patman* Act of 1936. Table 9.1 is a succinct presentation of the basic antitrust legislative rubric. Please keep in mind, however, that anti-trust law is complex in terms of its focus, its coverage, and its actual application, as well as in the shifting political dynamics that play a part in determining its direction. We can do no more here than attempt a brief overview.

Please note, as an addition to Table 9.1 reprinted above, the existence of Section 4 of the Clayton Act, which states that "any person who shall be injured in his business or property by reason of anything forbidden in the anti-trust laws may sue therefore. . . and shall recover threefold the damages by him sustained. . . ." (*the treble damages provision*—15 U.S.C. Sec. 15, 1988).

It should be noted at the outset that one of the basic tenets of a free market system is that it should be competitive. Competition is the focus of antitrust, which is to say, protection of the right to compete fairly for market share. Totally free competition, however, is like totally free markets: neither of the two exists, nor are they expected to exist. Short of the unattainable then, how does one define and enforce a workable goal?

It should be remembered here that it is hardly enough to say that antitrust protects competitors by prohibiting monopolies and mergers that substantially lessen competition, and by prohibiting restraints of trade and all "unfair methods of competition." To decide specific cases involving these broad areas, courts must define and analyze such complex concepts (and realities) as "monopoly power," "relevant markets," "price fixing," "market concentration," and the like. In an economic system where real success lies in overwhelming the competition, how is *improper,* anticompetitive behavior defined, and *why?*

TABLE 9.1 Important Antitrust* Statutes

Procedurally Oriented	Structurally Oriented	Behaviorally Oriented
ANTITRUST IMPROVEMENT ACT (1976) establishes a *parens patriae* right of action whereby a state can sue for treble damages for the injury suffered by state consumers as a result of antitrust violations FEDERAL TRADE COMMISSION IMPROVEMENT ACT (1980) limits the investigative and rulemaking power of the FTC	SHERMAN ACT (1890) SEC. 2 prohibits monopolies and attempts or conspiracies to monopolize CLAYTON ACT (1914) SEC. 7 prohibits mergers, the effect of which may be substantially to lessen competition or to tend to create a monopoly *Amended (1950), Celler-Kefauver Act.* clarified application of Section 7 to acquisitions of assets	SHERMAN ACT (1890) SEC. 1 condemns contracts, combinations and conspiracies in restraint of trade including vertical and horizontal price fixing, group boycotts, division of markets, etc. CLAYTON ACT (1914) SEC. 2 prohibits price discriminations, substantially lessening sellers' level competition (primary line violations) *Amended (1936), Robinson-Patman Act* prohibits price discriminations, substantially lessening buyer's (and below) level competition (secondary line violations) CLAYTON ACT (1914) SEC. 3 prohibits exclusive dealing and tying arrangements, the effect of which may be to substantially lessen competition FEDERAL TRADE COMMISSION ACT (1914) SEC. 5 prohibits unfair methods of competition; established and defined powers of FTC *Amended (1938), Wheeler-Lea Act* prohibits unfair trade practices, false advertising (STATE) MISCELLANEOUS PRICING STATUTES prohibits sales below cost, predatory pricing, sales insufficiently marked up, price-fixing, etc., generally not successfully enforced

*Note: Statutes are federal unless indicated otherwise.

Source: T.W. Dunfee, J.R. Beliace, and D.B. Cohen, *Business and Its Legal Environment*, 3d ed. Englewood Cliffs, N.J.: (Prentice Hall, 1992), p. 409.

The generally accepted view of U.S. courts is that cases are to be determined by economic analysis in the service of forwarding economic efficiency.

Not everyone agrees that pure economic efficiency should be the singular focus of antitrust laws designed to be pro-competitive. In the famous case of the *United States* v. *Aluminum Company of America*,[77] Judge Learned Hand, referring to the history of antitrust statutes, stated

---

[77] 148 F. 2d 416 (1945).

that "Throughout [their] history it has been constantly assumed that one of their purposes was to perpetuate and preserve, for its own sake and in spite of possible cost, the organization of industry in small units which can effectively compete with each other."

The recent merger boom has highlighted the tension between what might be referred to as the purely economic versus the overall societal view of the proper role of antitrust. Indeed, as put forth recently, some supporters of the economic efficiency focus do not even want the law(s) to be concerned about competition. They "have expressed doubts about the ability of antitrust enforcers to assess correctly the actual effects of marketplace behavior. . . . Indeed, because in their view most markets are naturally competitive or self-correcting, the risk of error lies more with *any* attempt by the government to intervene."[78] In this view, competitively harmful activities are self-correcting anyway, while bad laws and regulations and judges' decisions are not.

This philosophy is countered by those who would argue that beyond efficiency concerns lie distributional concerns that are the proper business of antitrust. In this view, transfers of wealth from consumers to producers and concerns with fairness to competitors must be congressional and judicial concerns.[79]

It is not irrelevant, or irreverent, to point out here that economists disagree about what, exactly, antitrust law (and enforcement) ought, ultimately, to aim at. One should keep that in mind while working one's way through various "objective" economic analyses! Before looking briefly at some key substantive case law, we might look at the issue of how antitrust cases get to court.

Criminal actions for antitrust violations can be brought only by the U.S. Department of Justice. The central focus of almost all criminal prosecutions in the 1980s was horizontal price fixing (e.g., bid-rigging). Successful prosecutions (and prison sentences and fines) have taken place in this area, although some have objected that only particular smaller industries were targeted.

Civil actions can be brought by the Department of Justice, by the Federal Trade Commission, by states under certain circumstances, and by individuals. The Federal Trade Commission's major role in antitrust has to do with merger-related matters, although it has brought civil actions under Section 5 of the FTC Act against such diverse defendants as dentist federations, airlines, auto dealers, and even DuPont. States, as Table 9-1

---

[78] See *Report of the American Bar Association Section of Antitrust Law Task Force on the Antitrust Division of the U.S. Department of Justice* (July 1989), p. 13.

[79] Ibid., p. 14. See also: M. Mayer, "Antitrust the Real Issue in Salomon Scandal," *The Wall Street Journal*, (August 22, 1991).

shows, can bring actions for violations of federal antitrust laws on behalf of its citizen consumers who are injured thereby.

Those who feel that criminal and civil *government*-originated cases are too infrequent to deter sufficiently those violators who stand to profit greatly by their illegal acts argue for *private* enforcement. The treble damages section of the antitrust law certainly imposes risk of financial loss as a very real deterrent to potential violators. Of course, it has also been suggested that such damages might also inhibit economically efficient business conduct that should be encouraged.

On this issue of treble damages and their utility as encouragement of victims to sue despite the tremendously high costs of doing so—and thus as forwarding deterrence and proper governmental purposes—see *Lehrman* v. *Gulf Oil Corp.*[80] And on the issue of how to measure (treble) damages, see *In Re Sugar Industry Anti-trust Legislation.*[81]

While "monopoly" is a key word in the antitrust context, monopoly power is not necessarily violative of the law (Sherman Act, Section 2). The power to exclude some potential competition, and to limit actual competition, if attributable solely to the defendant's ability, economies of scale, research, natural advantages, and adaption to inevitable economic laws, for example, could be nonviolative. Then there are "natural monopolies" like public utilities (which are nevertheless regulated). Basically, a "bad" monopoly is one willfully acquired, or maintained, through exclusionary behavior, rather than through the business acumen described above.[82] A corporation, in the words of one highly regarded United States district court judge, "is denied the right to exercise effective control on the market by business policies that are not the inevitable consequences of its capacities or its natural advantages. . . ."[83]

It was in the *United Shoe* case that Judge Wyzanski passed the ultimate judgment on *intent* in antitrust. The defendant claimed that its pricing and other policies were never intended to monopolize, nor was there any intent even to attempt to monopolize. Answered Judge Wyzanski: "Defendant having willed the means, has willed the ends."

Over the last decade, aggressive behavior by very large companies has been given far more latitude by U.S. courts. A good example is the case of *Berkey Photo, Inc.* v. *Eastman Kodak Co.*[84]

At the time of this lawsuit, Kodak had almost two-thirds of the U.S. consumer camera market, and in excess of 85 percent of the film market.

---

[80] 500 F. 2d 654, cert. denied, 95 S. Ct. 1128 (1974).

[81] 73 F.R.D. (Federal Rules Decision) 322, D.C.PA. (1976).

[82] *United States* v. *Grinnell Corporation*, 384 U.S. (1966).

[83] Wyzanski, J., in *United States* v. *United Shoe Machinery Corp.*, 110 F. Supp. 295 (D. Mass. 1953).

[84] 603 F. 2d 263 (1979).

The basis of the suit was that by creating a new kind of film and withholding from all competitors all the information to process it, Kodak was acting monopolistically. The court disagreed and threw out a verdict for Berkey. How much this result can be attributed to the fact that this was a private treble damages suit and not a suit by the government, and/or how much the court felt it had to allow sizable aggression in the furtherance of economic efficiency, is not entirely clear. What is clear is that the lower court verdict *for* the complaining company and *against* Kodak in that case would probably have been upheld, way back in 1959.

Just as a monopoly, though generally to be avoided, need not be an *illegal* monopoly, not every action contrary to the language of the laws will get a company in antitrust trouble. If the complained-of actions (e.g., combination in restraint of trade) do not in fact have anticompetitive effects, then the combination has not unreasonably restrained competition. Courts refer to the judicial process of examining antitrust cases *beyond the specific acts complained of* so as to determine the actual economic consequences produced by them as "the rule of reason." In rule-of-reason determinations, the plaintiff has the burden of detailing and proving specific adverse impact(s) on competition in the relevant market. Theoretically, a literal violation of antitrust law might, on examination, have *increased* "economic efficiency."

However, and here is where the confusion arises, certain prohibited activities are considered to be so inherently anticompetitive, so market restraining, so "pernicious" that *they are held to be "per se"* illegal and criminally (and civilly) punishable. These "per se" activities, as judicially developed over time, used to be four in number, basically: *dividing up markets; tying arrangements* (e.g., all products you grow on my land must be shipped to market on my rail lines only); *group boycotts*; and *price-fixing*. The state of mind required to be proven in "rule-of-reason" cases, defined by the Supreme Court as "action undertaken with knowledge of its probable consequences,"[85] does not have to be proven in "per se" cases; proof of the acts is sufficient.

The problem is that in *Gypsum* the court *was* involved with a price-fixing prosecution, yet it insisted on distinguishing between basically pernicious (per se) violations of the antitrust laws and what is referred to as the "gray zone of socially acceptable and economically justifiable business conduct" (rule-of-reason). Apparently the court was saying, yes, some actions are per se so pernicious and violative of competitive markets that one does not have to prove *intent or specific negative economic results,* but other actions are not, and then you have to prove both. But the U.S. Gypsum Company was convicted in the trial court of price-fixing, a per se

---

[85] *U.S.* v. *U.S. Gypsum Co.*, 438 U.S. 422 at 424 (1978).

violation. Well, yes, but the proof was not sufficient under a rule-of-reason standard to demonstrate economic inefficiency.

You are not alone in your feeling that this is a bit confusing.

It is also necessary in a Sherman Section 1 prosecution to prove a connection to interstate commerce, rather than a purely local effect (which is state antitrust business, of which, more later on).

Burdens of proof (i.e., who has to prove what and at what level) tend to take on real meaning when one considers that, in criminal antitrust actions, fines levied on a corporation found guilty can be as much as $10 million *per count* and against individuals, $350,000 *per count*.[86] And, of course, civil actions can result in treble damages against a violator.

In the case of *Northwest Wholesale Stationers Inc.* v. *Pacific Stationery and Printing Co.*,[87] the court held that a cooperative buying agency made up of various retailers, when they threw out a member without allowing for any way to challenge their decision, were not engaged in per se violation of Section 1. This despite the fact that such an act clearly smacks of a group boycott. Why was this not a per se violation? Because, said the court:

A plaintiff seeking application of the per se rule must present a threshold case that the challenged activity falls into a category likely to have predominantly anti-competitive effects. The mere allegation of a concerted refusal to deal does not suffice because not all concerted refusals to deal are predominantly anticompetitive. When the plaintiff challenges expulsion from a joint buying cooperative, some showing must be made that the cooperative possesses market power or unique access to a business element necessary for effective competition.[88]

Thus, the court applied the "rule of reason" to determine whether a "per se" action had taken place!

A case grappling with this confusion at the level of the U.S. Supreme Court is *Business Electronics Corp.* v. *Sharp Electronics Corp.*[89]

---

[86] See *U.S. Sentencing Commission*, Guidelines Manual, note 59, *supra*, at pp. 207-208 ("Application note" 7)."Application Note" 3, p. 206, explains how antitrust fines for an organization (under *Guidelines*, Chapter 8) are determined. The Commission *Guidelines* refer specifically to "near universal agreement that restrictive agreements among competitors, such as horizontal price-fixing (including bid rigging) and horizontal market-allocation, can cause serious economic harm," and that the *Guidelines* are particularly concerned about "covert conspiracies." Finally, "the most effective method to deter [the commission of antitrust] crime is through imposing short prison sentences coupled with large fines" p. 207. Absent adjustments, prison sentences run 6 months. However, the courts "have the discretion to impose considerably longer sentences within the guideline ranges," ibid.

[87] 105 S. Ct. 2613 (1985).

[88] 105 S. Ct. at p. 2621.

In this case, the private plaintiff suing Sharp was a dealer in electronic equipment. He was named in 1968 to be the exclusive dealer in Houston, Texas, for Sharp electronic calculators. In 1972, Sharp designated GH as its *second* dealer in Houston. Sharp suggested retail prices for its calculators but left the decisions to its dealers. GH stuck pretty much with the suggested prices. The plaintiff (Business Electronic Corp.) priced below them. GH complained to Sharp that Business Electronics Corp. was a free rider on its promotional efforts and finally, in 1973, GH said to Sharp: Drop Business Electronic Corp. as a dealer within thirty days or I stop carrying Sharp products. GH was large and successful. Sharp dumped Business Electronic Corp. and thus this lawsuit, alleging a conspiracy to terminate a dealer because of its lower pricing, in violation of Section 1 of the Sherman Act.

Business Electronic Corp. won in the trial court on the basis that an agreement between a manufacturer and distributor to terminate another dealer for price cutting is a form of coercion and vertical price-fixing, and per se illegal. Business Electronics Corp. did not have to prove, as it would have to under rule-of-reason analysis, that the conduct complained of in fact *had an adverse impact on competition in the market.* A federal appeals court reversed on the per se issue. The case ultimately ended up in the U.S. Supreme Court.

The Supreme Court held, 6–2, with Justices Stevens and White dissenting, that unless Sharp and GH actually had agreed to set prices between themselves *after* Business Electronics Corp. was gone, this was really a vertical nonprice restraint that had "real potential to stimulate interbrand competition" (Justice Scalia). Why? Because manufacturers use vertical restraints to induce dealers to invest their capital and to provide the kind of services that would attract and keep customers. In sum, if Business Electronics Corp. could *prove* a conspiracy to set prices between Sharp and GH, it had a per se case. If not, it had to *prove* adverse impact (on the *market,* not on *it*). And that would be hard to do in the face of Justice Scalia's reasoning that the purpose of the restraint here was to allow GH to provide better services to its customers (by charging prices that left a margin for service provision).

Thus, despite the fact that there *was* dealer coercion here, applied *for the purpose* of eliminating dealer-level price competition, it would seem that the Supreme Court has informed lower courts that restraints on competition have to be most unreasonable indeed before they can be deemed "per se" in nature—no matter what they look like.[90]

---

[89] 108 S. Ct. 1515 (1988).

[90] Even in the presence of per se violation, a plaintiff in a triple damages suit cannot recover from the violating company for *proven* damages caused *to it* unless that same plaintiff first proves that the per se violation resulted in anticompetitive damage *to the market as a whole.*

While criminal cases, as stated previously, generally fall under Sherman, civil cases are brought not only for Sherman Act violations but also for alleged violations of the provisions of the Clayton Act and its amending statute, the Robinson-Patman Act. Robinson-Patman focuses on price discrimination, with Section 2(b) being the main defense—"Our act wasn't price discrimination, but rather an honest attempt to meet the competition!"

It has been suggested that the goals of the Sherman Act (focused on protecting vigorous price competition) and those of Robinson-Patman (focused on protecting price stability and uniformity) can be conflicting, and that defendants can take advantage of the two seemingly conflicting purposes. However, the *Gypsum* case, cited earlier, did say that a defendant charged with a Sherman Act violation has a duty to show that it possessed information that would cause a reasonable and prudent person to believe that it *had* to set its (allegedly violative) prices in order to fairly meet competition. Now this means that the defendant had better be sure to gather market price information fully and carefully so as to demonstrate its price-setting acts were competitively inspired, not inspired by a desire to use its power unfairly to squeeze out competition. But wait: How can a (potential) defendant honestly set pro-competitive prices without contacting, and exchanging information with, other sellers in the market? Might not *that* kind of activity be construed, in and of itself, as price-fixing? We guess it might. Justice Powell is concerned about that. Try reading what he says in *Gypsum,* 483 U.S., at p. 470.

Let us conclude (having at least left you cognizant of a few complexities in this area of legal action to control market imperfections/inadequacy) with the issue of enforcement of the antitrust laws. If we assume that it *is* U.S. policy to prevent acts in restraint of free markets (whether expressed antimonopoly, price discrimination, facilities discrimination, boycott, or whatever), the question is, How do we best do it—through criminal law, civil law, or both?

Many individual states have beefed up their particular state antitrust enforcement. If the state area interests you, you might want to read a good article on state/federal overlap and history entitled "State Antitrust in the Federal Scheme."[91] It was argued by the Reagan administration—

Atlantic Richfield v. *U.S.A. Petroleum*, 110 S. Ct. 1884 (1990). But watch out! or, as lawyers say: *caveat: Eastman Kodak* v. *Image Technical Services*, 112 S. Ct. 2072 (1992), seems to have toughened the judicial stance against what looks like corporate predatory activity. In this Eastman Kodak case, the Supreme Court decided that even the existence of competition in a primary market (photographic equipment) did *not* preclude a finding of illegal monopoly power in derivative aftermarkets (spare parts and service); i.e., interbrand competition does not bar an antitrust tying arrangements lawsuit.

[91] *Indiana Law Journal*, 375 (1983). Be informed that a very antitrust conservative Supreme Court has nevertheless gone a long way to accommodate *state* antitrust concerns.

and some others—that there are too many (tangible and intangible) costs to criminal prosecution and that the law ought to be changed and enforcement perhaps loosened—that is, that the law promotes inefficiency, impairs competition, and punishes the consumer. Attorney General Meese's comments in this regard can be found in *49 Antitrust & Trade Reg. Rep. (BNA)*, 734, October 31, 1985. The former Attorney General's attitude provides some insight into why antitrust activity during M&As of the 1980s was moribund.

Finally, there is common agreement that would-be despoilers of competitive markets should be deterred; should be deprived of the fruits of their illegality; and should compensate their victims, all because it is in the public interest to do so. The problem, of course, is that one person's power-abusing corporate despoiler could be another person's powerful free marketeer.[92]

It recently allowed California to *undo* a friendly merger by the second and third largest California supermarket chains after that merger had been *approved* by the Federal Trade Commission! *California* v. *American Stores*, 110 S. Ct. 1853 (1990).

[92] It is worth repeating that antitrust law is far more complex than has been hinted at here. The excellent business text cited at Table 9-1 devotes four complete chapters to it! We would conclude our brief overview by pointing out two final areas not referred to in our text:

(a) There are *antitrust exemptions* granted to certain groups, both by express statute; e.g., unions in most cases, and by judicial construction; e.g., organized baseball. There are two other judicial exemptions worth noting: First, the Constitution is read to allow certain Bill of Rights related activities as worthy of upholding over antitrust principles; e.g., group boycotts utilized peacefully to obtain civil rights (protected "free speech/expression"): *NAACP* v. *Claiborne Hardware* 458 U.S. 886 (1982). But whether constitutional rights are being exercised through group power, or just unlawful (antitrust enforceable) acts, is not always easy to determine. See *FTC* v. *Superior Court Trial Lawyers Ass'n.* 110 S. Ct. 768, (1990), discussed and heartily disapproved of at Vol. 4, *Harvard Law Review* (November 1990), pp. 329-339. Second, regarding antitrust exemptions, state anticompetitive action, e.g., price-fixing, has been held lawful as an exercise of proper state power. *Parker* v. *Brown*, 317 U.S. 341 (1943—state prices set for certain California produce). But Supreme Court decisions allowing state immunity from antitrust reached some sort of outer limit in *City of Columbia* v. *Omni Outdoor Advertising Inc.*, 111 S. Ct. 1344 (1991). There, six justices upheld a South Carolina local government's right to engage in an anticompetitive conspiracy with the billboard company, whose majority owner was a personal friend of the mayor and other city council members. The city did it by enacting a billboard ordinance whose effect was to keep out all competition. Justice Stevens, in his dissent, made the telling point that a jury ought to be allowed to determine whether a municipality acted with the sole interest of furthering the anticompetitive interests of a private party (111 S. Ct. at 1362-63).

(b) There are some serious *international* antitrust matters to be considered. For example, Judge Learned Hand in the *Alcoa* case (note 77, *supra*) held that U.S. antitrust laws are applicable to foreign corporations (are "extraterritorial") if the complained-of actions were intended to affect and do affect imports into the United States, *even if those actions were legal in the home country*. How then should U.S. antitrust law deal with Japanese companies whose power-driven *Keiretsu* activities (production, distribution, and finance intercorporate groupings), while legal in Japan, look very much like coercive monopolies and cartels here in the United States? This is a particular concern in the automobile and automotive parts businesses, though hardly confined to them. See M. Yoshitomi, "*Keiretsu*, An Insider's Guide to Japan's Conglomerates," and C. Johnson, "*Keiretsu*, An Outsider's View," both in *Economic Insights* (September/October 1990). See also T.B. Pickens, "Japan's Cartels Hold

IN LIEU OF THE PHILOSOPHER'S STONE

We might want to think about parties at interest and value weighting with regard to issues like these:

1. It is estimated that by year-end 1992, more than 100 large companies in the United States had formally instituted, and were operating, the equivalent of telephone "ethics hot lines." These are special phone numbers for employees to use to call in information about unethical goings on (contract fraud, sexual harassment, whatever) in the company. Your company does not have one, and you are asked to decide whether it should undertake to set one up.

First, for you, which (whose) interests are involved here? The company's interests must include the avoidance of whistle-blower complaints that end up costing a lot of money; e.g., *qui tam* suits that later involve the government. Employees, on the other hand, may well have an interest in sharing in such whistle-blower lawsuit money pots. Are these the only two substantive issues (interests) to be considered here? Is your company concerned about "making right" *all* "bad" company behavior vis-à-vis its employees (harassment, unfairness; e.g., favoritism, racism, chauvinism) even if it might not result in lawsuits? Or, even if all costs (time as well as money) could be shown on a cost benefit analysis to be greater in implementing the hot-line than not implementing it, should management be left, nevertheless, to "carry on" without being subjected to work force complaints? Should employees be more concerned about loyalty to the company and having a "good" place in which to work than in making money by whistle-blowing?

In other words, which values ought employer *and* employee to consider (weigh) to decide whether to set up a hot-line system? Would you want to talk to your work force to get input *for* your decision?

Is there a way to establish an "ethics hotline" that would generate trust and the kind of behavior that would actually be in the best interests of the company and its work force?

Does that not depend upon your ultimate purpose (end/value/"ought to")?

2. Could you conceive of a free-marketeer argument against *all* antitrust laws that would be acceptable to you? Would it not depend on one or both of these propositions:

a. Unregulated free markets are "efficient" and *will* self-correct if left alone, or,

---

a Lot of Hostages, *"The Washington Post National Weekly Edition* (May 6-12, 1991). For some insight into antitrust concerns and "Europe 1992," see "German Official Sees Need for Global Antitrust Work," (staff piece) *The Wall Street Journal* (December 11, 1990).

b. Unregulated free markets are, at very least, *more* efficient than government and, on balance, are preferable to antitrust regulation by government.

If you cannot accept (a) or (b), can you clearly articulate *why* in terms of the values (ought-tos) at issue, and the weights that you assign to them?

INDEX